Internal Structure of the City

Contributors

Janet L. Abu-Lughod

John S. Adams

Roger E. Alcaly

William Alonso

Brian J. L. Berry

Hans Blumenfeld

Fred W. Boal

Larry S. Bourne

Martyn J. Bowden

Lawrence A. Brown

Robert W. Burchell

Martin Cadwallader

Manuel Castells

Lata Chatterjee

William A. V. Clark

Kevin R. Cox

Michael Dear

Donald R. Deskins, Jr.

Ithiel de Sola Pool

Dennis E. Gale

John B. Goddard

Stephen M. Golant

Torsten Hägerstrand

David Harvey

David T. Herbert

John Holmes

Frank E. Horton

James W. Hughes

Franklin J. James

Donald G. Janelle

Ronald J. Johnston

Christopher C. Kissling

Robert L. Knight

Piotr Korcelli

Barry Leighton

Charles Leven

Christopher A. Maher

Doreen B. Massey

Richard A. Meegan

Hugh A. Millward

John R. Miron

Peter A. Morrison

Anthony Mumphrey

Frank Z. Nartowicz

Kevin O'Connor

Risa Palm

Donald N. Parkes

David R. Reynolds

Harold M. Rose

John Seley

John R. Short

James W. Simmons

George Sternlieb

Raymond J. Struyk

Peter J. Taylor

Lisa L. Trygg

Yi-Fu Tuan

Urban Institute

Jon van Til

Karen Walby

Barry Wellman

Forrest B. Williams

Julian Wolpert

Carl E. Youngmann

Internal Structure of the City

READINGS ON URBAN FORM, GROWTH, AND POLICY

SECOND EDITION

EDITED BY

LARRY S. BOURNE

University of Toronto

New York   Oxford
OXFORD UNIVERSITY PRESS
1982

Library of Congress Cataloging in Publication Data
Main entry under title:
Internal structure of the city.
Bibliography: p.
1. Cities and towns—United States—Addresses,
essays, lectures. I. Bourne, Larry S.
HT123.I53 1982 307.7'6'0973 81-18931
ISBN 0-19-503032-X (pbk.) AACR2

Printing (last digit): 9 8 7 6 5 4 3 2 1

Printed in the United States of America

84 005463

Preface

At least since 1975 I have given serious thought to preparing a second edition of *Internal Structure of the City*. That volume, published in 1971 (but compiled in the period 1969–70), has weathered reasonably well, in large part because of the high quality of the individual papers reprinted. Despite this standard of quality, however, that volume is now outdated; the times and the issues have changed, and stimulating new research directions have arisen to replace the old.

Each time that I considered a revision, difficulties arose. Initially, I was diverted by the explosion in the urban literature during the 1970s, by the increasingly wide range of relevant topics, and by the immense diversity of analytical approaches and philosophical perspectives on current urban problems evident in that literature. It became exceedingly difficult to visualize how this rapidly expanding field of study could be adequately represented in one volume, particularly one that incorporated classic papers from the earlier volume. Most of the latter papers still warranted inclusion in a new edition. At the same time, it was equally difficult to fit the new directions and topics of research that characterized the 1970s with those of the first edition. More recently, however, as my own ideas clarified, the rationale for a second edition began to emerge.

For these reasons I decided to compile an entirely new edition, one which roughly followed the organizational format of the first, but one which also had its own internal logic and unique contents. In this way, the first edition also remains intact, standing on its own as a record of its time and place and as a reference source for classic papers on urban structure.

Contents and Editorial Style

In the face of an increasingly diverse and often contradictory and highly specialized literature, no single volume of readings can hope to be comprehensive. The second edition does not pretend to be. It does seek to cover as many as possible of the research topics, policy issues, and alternative approaches that typified urban research in the 1970s and early 1980s— but without sacrificing the standard of quality set by the papers in the first edition.

Among the new topics and policy issues represented by papers in this volume are those concerning urban decline, the inner city, political conflicts, labor markets, energy and urban form, the fiscal squeeze, industrial restructuring, urban crime, women and planning, and the elderly. These topics were selected to provide a mixture of perspectives on sectoral issues, specific problem areas, and those special groups in an urban society with particular unmet needs. The intention was to select papers concerned with analysis rather than description, and with research rather than polemics. Not fully represented, due to a lack of space, are the important papers on such complex topics as urban ecology, the natural environment, and pollution and on urban design, planning, and public administration. These are the subjects of other books.

Editing of papers from many diverse sources inevitably poses problems for an editor. In this volume, an effort has been made to correct errors in the initial printing of the paper and to provide missing or updated references wherever possible and appropriate. To retain the original flavor of the articles, and to avoid editorial errors in cases where information is missing, it was also decided to keep the original style of the paper (e.g., the footnotes and references and U.S. or English spelling).

Intended Audience and Classroom Use

The intended audience of this collection includes all who are interested in the study of urban form and spatial structure, the processes of urban growth and decline, and urban policy. It should be of relevance not only to researchers, but also to practitioners in government, planning, architecture, real estate, and urban development. The interdisciplinary orientation and style of the volume makes it a potentially useful reference for readers in several academic disciplines, particularly geography, planning, economics, sociology, and engineering and in interdisciplinary courses on the city in such programs as urban studies and public policy.

The book is designed for classroom use both as a general reference volume, to be taken off the shelf when necessary, and as a basic textbook. For the latter, it should fit within the scope of a variety of introductory urban courses in the above disciplines as one of several textbooks or as a supplementary readings volume. It is also possible, as the editor has done, to construct more specialized upper division courses and graduate seminars around the themes reflected in the sections and in each of the papers. Instructors in such courses might wish to follow the arrangement of papers as set out here, or alternatively, they might choose to select from or rearrange the papers to suit their preferences or their students' needs. Either way, the organization of the papers itself presents an intellectual challenge to the teacher as well as the student.

Acknowledgments

Any collection of readings depends on the contributions of many individuals and institutions. I am particularly indebted to those authors and publishers who willingly granted permission for me to reprint their papers, often in edited or reduced form to meet space limitations. Without the very high quality of the research undertaken by these contributors, a book of this kind would be impossible. Indeed, one of the principal arguments for the publication of anthologies is precisely the uniformly high quality and varying perspectives on a wide set of issues that only a group of scholars can produce.

I also owe a special thanks to those colleagues and associates who reviewed the initial outline of the volume and provided numerous valuable suggestions on content and organization. Several anonymous referees also provided detailed and constructive comments. They, of course, bear no responsibility for any weakness of the final product.

I am particularly indebted to a number of people at Oxford University Press, notably Joyce Berry, and at the University of Toronto, who guided the compilation and production of this book. Lillian Hesse at the Centre for Urban and Community Studies deserves special thanks for the typing (and retyping) of the manuscript and correspondence, and for seemingly endless photocopying duties.

Finally, I dedicate my portion of this book to my two children, David and Alexandra, who although largely unaware of the details therein, may actually benefit from any resulting improvement in our understanding of cities.

Toronto   L.S.B.
November 1981

Contents

Introduction*

Throughout the 1970s and into the 1980s, cities appeared to move from one crisis state to another. Each of us looking back has a different set of images of what these crises were and are: images perhaps of suburban development sprawling endlessly across prime agricultural land or of massively ugly high-rise redevelopments, overcrowded freeways, deteriorating transit systems, decaying inner city neighborhoods, spreading crime, social unrest, and vandalism. These images in turn are frequently combined with concerns over high land prices, housing shortages, fiscal restraints on the provision of social services, and racial strife. The literature is replete with lists of urban problems, prognoses of impending doom, and prescriptions for survival.

By the mid 1970s, however, some observers were asking what had happened to the urban crisis (Downs, 1975; Tobin, 1979). Have urban problems diminished in severity? Or more likely, have they simply changed their shape and visibility with shifts in public attitudes and political priorities? Some observers have responded by arguing for a retreat from government intervention in urban development and from the strategy of throwing public money at ill-defined problems (Banfield, 1974; Soloman, 1980). Still others have been searching for new definitions and benchmarks against which they could interpret the complex changes and seemingly insolvable problems in the urban reality confronting them (Castells, 1977; Lineberry, 1977; Davies and Hall, 1978; Johnston, 1980).

By the end of the 1970s, other urban issues had risen to replace or to augment the old. In fact, many of the basic parameters of urban structure

---

* A detailed bibliography and suggestions for further reading are provided at the end of the book.

and growth in the 1950s and 1960s had changed, some dramatically. Economic recession, unemployment, and regional shifts in growth accelerated the loss of jobs and population in older central cities, particularly in the larger industrial centers (Sternlieb and Hughes, 1975). Overall population growth rates dropped sharply in most Western countries; indeed some countries registered zero or negative population growth. Migration flows have shifted away from older settled regions toward newer, resource-based and retirement regions, and in the United States the net migration balance has shifted from larger to medium-size and smaller cities (Morrill, 1979).

At the same time the results of a massive demographic transition became apparent with the national trend to lower fertility, fewer children, small household sizes, and an aging population. The contrasts between growing and declining communities have thus increased (Morrison, Part III). The overall result of these trends has been what some authors describe as the new "urban realities" facing developed societies (Sternlieb and Hughes, 1977). Some have argued that the large industrial metropolis itself is now obsolete (Berry, 1975, and Part VIII), and others have described conditions in and options for the metropolis without growth (Alonso, 1978, and Part VII).

Within urban areas these new realities have translated into a rather different set of issues from those prevailing in the preceding decade. Demographic changes have dramatically altered the size and composition of population in most cities, thus altering the face of many neighborhoods and reordering the basic demand for social services, recreation, and housing (Alonso, 1977, and Part VII). Social and environmental problems thought to be typical only of the inner cities have begun to appear— or more appropriately, to be recognized—in many mature suburbs (Leven, 1978; Brown, 1980). Neighborhood decline and environmental decay have become prominent in the literature, contrasting with an interest in the origins and impacts of the return-to-the-city movement on the part of some of the middle class (Laska, 1980; Gale, Part VII). Growing communities, on the other hand, have often attempted to resist the inevitability of *progress* by establishing formal controls to restrict future growth (Scott, 1974). Increased energy costs have also begun to undermine previous projections of continued massive urban sprawl and to call into question the widening separation between home and workplace (van Til, 1979, and Part VIII). Moreover, pollution levels have not diminished, indeed in some instances, the levels of specific pollutants have increased, to become even more dangerous to human health. High crime levels have also persisted (Rose and Deskins, Part VII), and indeed there are disturbing signs of a possible return to the social unrest of the 1960s, although in different forms and for different reasons.

Under these conditions, the 1980s will no doubt produce yet another set of problems and differing interpretations of what should or should not be done. The political and urban planning responses to these problems will also differ (Annals, AAPSS, 1980). In the last two decades, for example, we have seen the emphasis in planning policy shift from one of urban renewal and massive slum clearance (called the federal bulldozer) through a phase emphasizing neighborhood rehabilitation and the conservation of housing to a broad concern with urban revitalization (Burchell and Sternlieb, 1979; Rosenthal, 1980). The latter emphasis has recently been extended to include comprehensive community-wide development, which in theory takes account of social as well as physical needs, the economy, and the necessity for greater energy efficiency (Ridgeway, 1979). In the face of economic recession, incentives have also been extended for the development of locally based strategies to encourage urban economic and industrial growth including, in extreme cases, "private enterprise zones" where all or most land use restrictions are removed. The main point here is not the details of the policies themselves, but rather the emphasis on a community-wide perspective that attempts to integrate social, physical, and economic planning in the city.

There is little question that fundamental changes have taken place and will continue to take place in our cities and in the urban studies literature. Equally clearly, we are uncertain as to what the processes are, why they are happening, or what they will lead to. This disagreement and uncertainty is evident when we compare papers published in a number of recently edited collections on the city (Rose and Gappert, 1975; Romanos, 1979; Soloman, 1980).

Objectives and Rationale

This volume of readings is designed to provide part of the broad background—of ideas, information, experience, and methods of research—necessary to improve our understanding of how and why our cities have reached their current state and where they are likely to be going. In particular, the volume examines how social and economic processes are reflected in the spatial structure and environment of cities and how these in turn condition social, political, and economic behavior.

It is also, like its predecessor, *Internal Structure of the City,* published in 1971 (Bourne, 1971), and its companion volume, *Systems of Cities* (Bourne and Simmons, 1978), a record of research on cities over a decade. Although policy questions appear throughout, this is not principally a policy-oriented or prescriptive collection. Instead, the book is an attempt to bring together a set of high quality academic papers and professional reports that attempt to analyze how cities are spatially organized, how they work, what the problems are, and what we know (and do not know) about possible solutions to those problems.

The specific focus of the readings selected is the spatial structure and changing internal environment of contemporary urban areas. This emphasis is intended both as an organizing device to assist in the selection of papers and as a common denominator for readers that transcends the boundaries of a single discipline or a particular research philosophy. Initially we may define urban spatial structure as comprising the form (shape and internal arrangement), interrelationships (organization), behavior, and evolution of activities (e.g., land uses, the built environment, systems of socioeconomic activities, and political institutions) in the city.

The emphasis is on concepts, theories, and alternative perspectives and on the links between process and pattern. The papers examine current urban forms, historical antecedents, sequences of change, policy issues, and the dynamic properties of urban development. Not all the papers have an explicit spatial focus, but each contributes insights that are directly relevant to untangling the complex puzzle of a continually changing urban form. A detailed bibliography and suggestions for further reading are also provided at the end of the volume.

Initially we can begin with the premise that the spatial structure we observe in urban areas reflects the complex interplay of many diverse forces, some of which are internal, whereas others are external to the city, but none of which can be extracted and studied in isolation. Urban structure is firstly a spatial mirror of society and its historical and organizational principles. That is, it reflects the previous and currently prevailing operating rules—of culture, technology, economy, and social behavior—of the society within which the city has developed. Those societies, for example, that value individualism, a market economy, unrestricted social choice, and high levels of consumption, tend to produce cities that look and function differently from those societies that encourage collective action, a mixed or centrally planned economy, constrained social choice, and high levels of production. Societies that permit wide differences in income and standard of living to exist among social, ethnic, or racial groups usually contain cities with equally marked, if not greater, spatial differentials. The lines of relationship between macro-level (national) socioeconomic and political structures and intra-urban spatial structure, however, are complex and largely undefined.

These societal characteristics can be seen as essentially broad constraints on the historical evolution of a particular urban form, much as a landscape painter begins with a preconceived image and style, a canvas of a given size, and a set of brushes and paints. They do not, it should be stressed, necessarily predetermine the product. Rather a myriad of other mitigating factors intercede to shape, if not overwhelm, the translation of broad societal conditions into specific urban patterns and living conditions. As Harvey (1975) argues, there is a considerable degree of autonomy in the spatial expression of urbanization processes even within the same political system. Differences in the conditions of the site and local topography, in the sequence of building technologies and timing of development, in government policies, in the unique mix of decisions made by individuals, firms, and political groups, as well as differences in community attitudes and preferences within each urban area, to name but a few factors, fundamentally alter how any given set of macro-social and economic forces are reflected in different urban structures.[1] The difficult task for us as students of the city is to identify the relative contributions of such local or internal factors, *in conjunction* with broad external forces, in determining the particular urban structure that emerges in a given country or region and the kinds of living environments that result.

Urban spatial structure is of course not only of interest as an abstract concept. It is also of fundamental importance for a variety of specific social, economic, and political issues. The specific form of any urban area, for example, reflects past investment decisions in transportation, and that form in turn delimits future transportation requirements. The form of the city also sets up particular schedules of land prices, gradients of residential densities, networks of travel flows, and a pattern of social areas. It provides opportunities for and places constraints on the evolution of feelings of community and neighborhood and shapes networks of social interaction and personal support services (Wellman and Leighton, Part IV). It also shapes, as Harvey (1973) and D. Smith (1979) have argued, the allocation or distribution of economic benefits and costs among people and places in our society and enhances or augments nationwide social inequalities. Further, the form of cities does influence levels of environmental pollution, modes of travel, traffic congestion, energy consumption, and the costs of providing welfare services and such physical infrastructures as water and sewerage.

1. These differences are clearly evident in some recent comparisons of Canadian and American cities, which, despite obvious similarities, also have markedly different urban forms and characteristics such as density, inner city conditions, and public transit use (see Mercer, 1979; Goldberg and Mercer, 1980).

Urban structure can also make societal patterns of social segregation and alienation more severe. It can act to trap certain groups and individuals in restrictive environments with poor housing, deteriorating services, and limited accessibility to new jobs in the suburbs. It may also solicit particular kinds of political actions, attitudes, and institutional behavior and thus alter the distribution of political power. Such is often the case in urban areas that are politically fragmented and in those with large disadvantaged minorities (Pack and Pack, 1977). The physical separation of rich and poor, of ethnic and racial groups, also encourages misunderstanding and the development of negative stereotype images of how others live.

An observer from afar might well conclude that if someone wanted to intentionally design an urban structure that would encourage social separation, racial strife, and fiscal warfare, they would be hard pressed to improve on the model of the contemporary American city. The papers reprinted here are intended to demonstrate many of these issues.

Emerging Themes in Urban Research

Every period of academic research brings with it a new wave of ideas, fads, and techniques.[2] Each wave ripples through the field, with differing speed and impact. Some are short-lived, others are more durable, but every one in some way selectively replaces, modifies, or augments what has gone before. In so doing, each wave shifts priorities in research and teaching and less frequently in urban planning or public policy. Each wave sets new ground rules and leaves a revised basic infrastructure of concepts and methods on which participants in the next wave then build. Each wave, as on the beach, also produces a countervailing wave or reaction in the opposite direction. The 1970s were no exception.

These waves represent a response to many different conditions, both internal and external to the city and to any given discipline. These include

2. Each new wave has also brought forth new journals and specialized series of publications. Among the more recent journals that are relevant here are Urban Ecology, Urban Law and Policy, Antipode, Comparative Urban Research, Urban Life and Culture, Urban Education, the International Journal of Urban and Regional Research, Comparative Urban Research, International Review of Regional Science, Urbanism Past and Present, Journal of Urban History, Urban History, Urban History Review, Urban Anthropology, Urban Economics, Progress in Human Geography, Social Networks, Regional and Urban Economics, and Urban Geography. Among those series that provide substantial reviews of the literature are "Geography and the Urban Environment: Progress in Research and Applications" (Herbert and Johnston, 1978, 1979, 1980); the AAG Resource Paper Series (see Wolpert et al., 1972; Muller, 1976), and the Scripta Series in Geography (see Bourne, 1981).

changes in the attitudes, perceptions, and personalities of the actors involved in each discipline; feelings of frustration, particularly among the young, with the failings of established models and research methods; changes in the real or perceived urban problems to which that research has been applied; redirections in administrative and political priorities and policy; shifts in funding for the support of social services and research; and the effects of adopting innovations and copying new paradigms originating from outside any given discipline or country. We can be certain that these same factors will produce frequent and equally rapid waves of change in succeeding decades.

Looking back on the decade of the 1960s, but with an eye cast forward to the 1970s, the introduction to the first edition of *Internal Structure* identified four emerging waves or themes in research on urban structure. These themes, none of which of course were entirely unique to that decade or to urban research, were summarized as (1) the increasing importance of *interdisciplinary* studies, reflecting an attempt at a cross-fertilization of concepts and methods among those disciplines with an urban interest; (2) the rapid evolution of mathematically based theory and *quantitative models,* including innovations in data display and computer processing technology; (3) an expanded *behavioral* emphasis, in which the necessity of small-scale (micro-level) and more socially sensitive studies of individual or group behavior, spatial cognition, and decision-making were widely recognized; and (4) a utilitarian concern with the potential *social relevance* and policy applications of urban research.

These same four themes, in concert with many others, have carried through with renewed vigor into the 1970s and early 1980s. That many of these themes are now firmly in place is evident in most standard textbooks in urban geography (Vance, 1977; King and Golledge, 1978; Yeates and Garner, 1980; Hartshorn, 1980; Palm, 1981; Carter, 1981), but with differing emphases. In some instances, however, the subfields of urban research have become more technical and specialized, and thus more eclectic and divergent, leading some observers to call for a return to more holistic research paradigms (contrast Johnston, 1980 and Berry, 1980a). Others see in this flowering of alternative approaches a strength in diversity that was not there before, if it is assumed that members of each subfield attempt to communicate.

During the 1970s several new emphases in research on cities and urban structure gained strength. The field was buffeted by a flowering of new ideas and by critiques and elaborations of earlier views. Among these emphases at least the following stand out. One is the growing interest in *urban politics and the public sector* generally. This emphasis is a response to a realization that the obvious lack of influence of urban research on policy development was in part due to an inadequate understanding of how the city itself functions and in particular how the political machinery of the city works. It was also due in part to a greater awareness of the important roles played by government policies, public agencies, institutions—that is, the state—and political behavior in shaping our cities. A substantial recent literature attempts to measure the urban and community impacts of government policies (Glickman, 1980). Indeed, it is increasingly recognized that urban development is a political process as well as a socioeconomic or a physical one.

Researchers in geography, for example, have examined urban political structures (Cox, 1973 and 1979), voting behavior and elections (Taylor and Johnston, 1979), the role of public institutions (Vance, 1978), ideology and urban political conflicts (Ley and Mercer, 1980), financial agencies (Williams, 1976; Palm, 1979), and the location of mental health facilities (Dear, 1978, and Part II). The intention to redirect urban research in geography toward *concrete policy evaluations* was particularly evident in the massive comparative project on metropolitan America undertaken by the Association of American Geographers (AAG) (Adams, 1976), in the work of the Applied Geography group of the AAG (Frazier and Epstein, 1979), and in the series of inner city studies in the United Kingdom commissioned by the Social Science Research Council (Hall and Diamond, 1980). Similar efforts are evident in other countries and other disciplines.

This broad interest in politics and policy has been paralleled by a small but growing critique of the established methods, concepts, and theories of mainstream "social scientific" research (Gordon, 1977; Peet, 1977; Johnston, 1980, 1982, and Part I). Those critiques, frequently labeled as "structuralist" or the *political economy approach,* are perhaps best reflected in the work of Harvey (1973, 1978, and Part II), Harloe (1977), Castells (1972, and Part VIII), and Taab and Sawers (1978) on urbanization and urban spatial structure, employing a neo-Marxist perspective.[3] Others have brought similar critical perspectives to a wide range of urban problems: access to housing finance (Williams, 1976; Alcaly and Mermelstein, 1977; Boddy, 1979); profits, government intervention, and the urban economy (Broadbent, 1977; Hill, 1977); the influence of industrial rationalization and corporate reorganization on urban decline (Massey and Meegan, 1979); social pathologies (Peet, 1977); land rent (Scott, 1980); speculation and property development (Ambrose and Colenutt, 1975);

3. An excellent example that examines the macro-level processes of urbanization from a political economy perspective is provided in Harvey (1978).

the urban fiscal crisis (Gordon, 1977); investment capital and neighborhood change (Molotch, 1979); and the variety of planning responses to these problems (Dear and Scott, 1981).

In this context, patterns of urban land use and land values, of social segregation and change, of suburban sprawl and downtown redevelopment may be seen as the spatial manifestation of the operation of a system of monopoly capitalism. This system is viewed as inherently unequal, class-stratified, and eventually socially destructive. They are not, it is argued, the outcome of the working out of individual preferences through an unfettered competitive market, in which government occupies only a peripheral position. Most existing theories, based largely in neoclassical economics or ecology, are found to be wanting from this point of view, primarily because they are not set in a context that encompasses the social structure and the inevitable contradictions of contemporary capitalism. Several examples of this perspective are included in this volume.

One of the implications of the widening interest in the policy, politics, and political economy of urban development is that it explicitly reinforces the need for all researchers, regardless of their initial perspective, to examine the impacts of our existing urban patterns, and our mechanisms (e.g., zoning) for regulating urban development, in terms of their effects on the *distribution of wealth* and social well-being (Pahl, 1975; Knox, 1975). That is, which specific urban forms or spatial organizations contribute to or detract from the overall welfare of urban residents? Questions such as "Who gets what, where, and why?" and "Who benefits and who loses?" are now common currency in the literature (D. Smith, 1979). Similarly, political critiques such as the above require that the role of underlying philosophies and *ideologies* in shaping our research be acknowledged and made more explicit (Gregory, 1978). Clearly, the questions we ask in urban research, and the interpretations we impose on our data, reflect the premises and biases we bring to that research. The combined impact of these initiatives has been to shake to the roots most urban disciplines in a way not experienced since the quantitative revolution in the 1960s. New questions, new assumptions, and reordered priorities for research are now the subject of wide debates and a growing literature.

Considerable evolution has taken place in other areas of urban research. Theoretical and quantitative models of urban structure and growth have become far more sophisticated in both concept and methodology since the 1960s (Colenutt, 1972; Sweet, 1972; Schwirian, 1974; Wilson, 1974). *Mathematical* models are now particularly well developed in the study of urban design (Martin and March, 1972), land use and transportation (Wheaton, 1974; Kain, 1975; Papageorgiou, 1976; Richardson,

1977), planning (Wilson, 1974; Steiss, 1975), neighborhood change (Segel, 1979), residential location (Putnam, 1979), and intra-urban migration (Clark and Moore, 1978). Other approaches have drawn on theoretical constructs from cognate fields, for example, in applying formal systems analysis (Bennett and Chorley, 1978) and information theory (Webber, 1980) to urban and environmental systems. There is now a substantial literature on the concepts and measurement of spatial structure, in general (Cliff *et al.,* 1975), as well as several textbooks on methods of mathematical analysis for planners and geographers (Wilson and Kirby, 1978).

At the same time, however, by the mid-1970s, a requiem had been written for most of the overly ambitious large-scale models of urban development that were popular in the 1960s (Forester, 1969). These models simply became too large, cumbersome, and costly to be maintained by researchers and too complex for decision-makers to use (Batty, 1976, 1979). They also failed because they initially promised too much. They were often too broad to be of immediate practical value and too blunt for specific hypotheses to be tested. Instead, emphasis has shifted to the task of articulating new, *mathematically based* theories of urban structure that are more precise and that will likely lead to smaller, more realistic and testable models. Some of these models, in reduced form, will find wide application in the 1980s through the diffusion of micro-computer and visual display facilities in education, government, and business.

The heightened concern for social welfare and patterns of social justice in cities has been augmented by new thrusts in urban sociology and urban social geography (Herbert, 1972; W. Smith, 1979; Palm, 1981). Cities are indeed social systems comprised of real people rather than numerical quantities (Mercer, 1976). The broad paradigm of humanistic geography (Ley and Samuels, 1979; Ley, 1982), has its parallel in the heightened concern for *cities as humane environments,* as "places" for living and for social enrichment (Strauss, 1976; P. Smith, 1977; Tuan, 1979, and Part I). Clearly, cities are more than places for earning a living or producing goods and services. They are places for living out one's existence, preferably in a positively reinforcing environment.

Here a wide variety of research has extended previous descriptive analyses of the spatial patterns and mix of social characteristics in the city (see Johnston, 1971; Jones and Eyles, 1975; Berry and Kasarda, 1978; Herbert and Johnston, 1978, 1979, 1980). We have indeed come a long way, in both concept and methodology, from the traditional descriptions of urban structure—the concentric, sector, and multiple nuclei models—displayed in Figure 1. These three previously competing generalizations

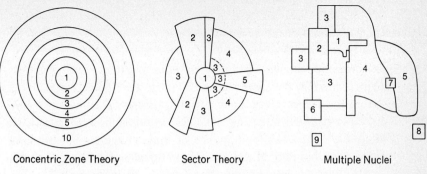

Concentric Zone Theory   Sector Theory   Multiple Nuclei

THREE GENERALIZATIONS OF THE INTERNAL STRUCTURE OF CITIES

DISTRICT:
1. Central Business District   5. High-class Residential   9. Industrial Suburb
2. Wholesale Light Manufacturing 6. Heavy Manufacturing   10. Commuters' Zone
3. Low-class Residential   7. Outlying Business District
4. Medium-class Residential   8. Residential Suburb

Figure 1. Traditional Models of Urban Structure

have recently been brought together, in the form of social area analysis
and through the methodology of factorial ecology, to provide a more
comprehensive view of urban social structure (Herbert and Johnston,
1976). Attempts have also been made to link this structure to the operation of the urban housing market and the behavior of public and private
institutions (Robson, 1975; Bassett and Short, 1980; Bourne, 1981).
Surprisingly, however, these three classic models have remained an essential component in describing and explaining urban social patterns in
the aggregate, although their interpretation varies widely.

Perhaps most interesting is the effort to link changes in the social structure of the city with changes in other aggregate characteristics and with
the actual living *experiences* of particular social groups at a very local
level. Some researchers have looked at stages of neighborhood evolution
(Birch, 1976) and the changing social context within which neighborhoods thrive or decline (Hunter, 1979). Others have examined the changing role of the elderly in urban areas (Golant, 1979, and Part VIII), the
changing role of women within existing and emerging urban forms (Rothblatt, 1979, and Abu-Lughod, Part VIII), and the redefinition of the life-
cycle component in residential mobility (Stapleton, 1980, and Short, Part
II). Still others have examined the political aspects of social change in
urban areas; for example, the origins and effects of collective social movements (Tilly, 1974; Castells, 1977; Pickvance, 1976); the varied experience of community organizations and social participation in planning
(Ley, 1974, and Wolpert *et al.,* Part VII), and the role of neighborhood

activism, local power elites, and political institutions in influencing decisions in planning and the location of public facilities (Wolpert *et al.,*
1972; Kasperson and Breitbart, 1974; Cox and McCarthy, 1980).

Experimentation in *participant observation* of micro-level urban life
and behavior has also increased. The well-known geographical expeditions
into the inner cities of Detroit and Toronto during the 1960s and early
1970s are particularly interesting examples of this approach (see Bunge
and Bordessa, 1975). The importance of these studies is not primarily
their small scale, but rather their attention to the activities of social groups
whose role in the city is commonly ignored (e.g., children) and their sensitivity to unusual but real issues (e.g., traffic accidents, the use of streets
for recreation, litter).

Of particular interest in this context has been the explosion of the behavioral literature in geography (Gold, 1980) and in cognate disciplines,
much of it relevant to urban studies. Substantial studies have appeared of
the processes of *environmental learning* and perception (Moore and
Golledge, 1976), social and environmental planning (Porteous, 1977),
and the detailed activity patterns of urban residents (Chapin, 1974). In
the latter context, such specific research techniques as time budgets have
been used to explore how people actually use their urban landscape and
how their activities change in response to changes in residential location,
type of housing, environment, or life-style (Michelson, 1977). Still others
have examined how the need for interaction and daily contact influences
the location of places of employment, such as offices, manufacturing plants
(Goddard, Part VI; Daniels, 1979) and shopping (retail outlets) (Davies,
1979).

This approach has recently been elaborated into the broader framework
of a *time-space geography* (Pred, 1977, and Hägerstrand *et al.,* 1974,
and Part II; Carlstein, Parkes and Thrift, 1978; Parkes and Thrift, 1980,
and Part IV). In this framework, individuals (or households or firms) are
seen as living in an overlapping set of prisms or activity spaces that encompass their daily, weekly, and seasonal behavior over space and through
time. An example of the typical "daily" pattern of household activities
through time and space is provided in Figure 2. In this illustration, the
activities of a two-adult household with school-age children are mapped,
centered on the location of the home with links to places of work, recreation, and learning.

The aggregate patterns of land use and social structure that we observe
in our cities, it is argued, are but summary indices of these micro-level
activities and the decisions that underlie them. The former can only be
understood by studying the latter. Although relatively little of this re-

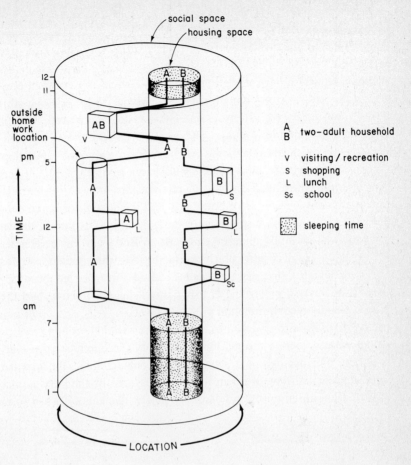

Figure 2. The Daily Prism (time-space geography) of Household Activities

search to date has been applied specifically to intraurban structure, the next decade is likely to see frequent applications.

The 1970s was also the decade of widespread concern for and action on urban *environmental quality* (U.S. Council on Environmental Quality, 1979). Environmental impact assessments are now required on almost all major government programs in the United States and Canada, spawning a formal methodology of assessment (Marsh, 1978) and even a new journal.[4] General texts on the physical environment of cities (Detwyler and Marcus, 1972), on urban environmental management (Berry and Horton, 1974), and especially on pollution provided a considerable library of research in the 1970s. This long-standing interest in the elements of the

4. Environmental Impact Assessment Review, Vol. 1, No. 1, March, 1980.

physical environment has been expanded to include the quality of the built environment (e.g., housing), the social milieu (community ties and neighboring) and the provision of adequate social services (e.g., day care).

Attempts have also been made to define the *relationships* between conditions in the natural environment, such as the types and levels of pollution and urban form (e.g., Berry *et al.,* 1974; Ostro and Naroff, 1979), between amenities and land values (King, 1973), and between environmental quality and health standards and the urban economy. The latter relationships, however, remains relatively unknown territory.

One recent attempt to examine the relationships between urban environmental quality (in terms of pollution) and the spatial form and economic base of the city is displayed in Figure 3. This illustration, drawn from a much larger study undertaken by Brian Berry and his colleagues (Berry *et al.,* 1974), is particularly useful here in that it demonstrates the kinds of linkages that exist between external forces (e.g., the economy) and the internal patterning of urban areas suggested above, and the influence of both on environmental pollution levels.

The relationships are specified as follows. The national economy essentially determines, within broad limits, the city's economic base, size, growth rate, and demographic profile. These characteristics in turn act to create a particular type of urban form, as measured by the internal mix and distribution of land uses and densities. These elements of urban form

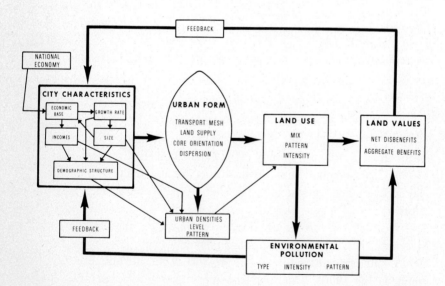

Figure 3. The Links between the Urban Economy, Land Use, and Environmental Pollution

lead to a particular pattern of land values, which then feed-back on and shape the city's aggregate characteristics. In combination these conditions give rise to differences among cities in their levels of pollution—in terms of type, intensity, and location—levels that also subsequently feed-back on the city's growth performance. The result is a view of an urban area as an *interdependent system* (see the following essay) in which urban growth and pollution are both consequences and determinants of urban form and land use.

The final theme, and one that overlaps with those described above, is the systematic and in-depth treatment of particular *topical policy issues* within the context of urban spatial structure. Here the list of topical issues subjected to intensive study is long indeed, selected examples of which are reprinted in Part VII. In-depth studies have been carried out on crime and deviance (Harries, 1980), on aging and the elderly (Wiseman, 1978; Golant, 1979), on the use of vacant land in cities (Mayer, 1979), on urban housing markets (Bassett and Short, 1980; Bourne, 1981), on social deprivation and the inner city (Jones, 1979; Evans and Eversely, 1980), on environmental risk and the use of medical services (Shannan and Spurlock, 1976), on disease and social pathologies (Pyle, 1979), on residential segregation (Peach, 1975), on neighborhood decline (Leven, 1978) and rejuvenation (Cybriwsky, 1978), on poverty (Peet, 1978), on financial institutions (Boddy, 1979), on education, health, and social services (Herbert and Smith, 1979), and on energy and urban form (Corsi and Harvey, 1977; Knowles, 1978), to name only a few.

At the same time there has been a rapid growth in interest in *urban history* and in the evolution of urban form (Morris, 1979; Blumenfeld, 1979, and Part I). In part this research activity has been stimulated by an awareness of the necessity of examining the historical roots of contemporary urban problems and in part by an interest in the historical city itself. Of particular relevance here are those systematic studies of the nineteenth-century industrial city, in North America and western Europe, on such still current issues as social segregation (Ward, 1971, 1975), race and residential location (Radford, 1976), and urban retailing (Conzen and Conzen, 1979).

The majority of the papers in this volume nonetheless are drawn from the main thrust of research on contemporary urban structure—reflecting the empirical and analytical approach. In part this is necessary simply to demonstrate what the city looks like and how it currently functions, and in part it reflects the orientation of the vast majority of the literature. In this context we now have a very extensive literature to draw on both in geography and in related fields. In addition to a wide variety of new text-books in urban geography (Johnston, 1980 and 1982; Palm, 1981), there are now a number of excellent reference volumes and readings collections in cognate disciplines, such as urban economics (Edel and Rothenberg, 1972; Henderson, 1977; Mieszkowski and Straszheim, 1979; Mills, 1980), sociology (Pahl, 1975; Meadows and Mizruchi, 1977; D. Smith, 1979), and planning (Chapin and Kaiser, 1979; Burchell and Sternlieb, 1979; Clavel, Forester, and Goldsmith, 1980). This literature forms part of the background for the papers selected for this volume. It also provides insight into the evolution in our thinking over time about what urban structure is and how it should be studied and a base of reference on recent trends in urban growth, changing patterns of development, and urban policy problems.

On the Selection of Papers

Putting together a volume of readings that is not only internally consistent, but broadly representative of research on urban spatial structure was a difficult if not impossible undertaking in 1970 when the first edition of *Internal Structure* was prepared. At that time the literature was voluminous and diverse, and it lacked the singular focus or consistency in approach and methodology that would have facilitated bringing them together in a single integrated readings volume. By 1980 these same difficulties had multiplied several-fold.

The literature on cities and urban structure, as the preceding discussion suggests, has exploded since 1970. Heterogeneity in content and diversity in research method and philosophy have increased dramatically. Cherished and commonly accepted points of view, as noted earlier, have been widely challenged. This challenge has come not, as in earlier decades, primarily from the quantitative and behavioral revolutions, but increasingly from questions posed by new trends in urban and economic development, by shifts in social attitudes, by changes in the real and perceived roles played by governments and public institutions, and by the emergence of alternative research philosophies and paradigms such as those described above. Moreover, empirical analyses of many urban phenomenon have grown larger and become more sophisticated, making it even more difficult to find papers for a volume such as this that do not assume at least some background knowledge on the part of the reader of the methods and data used. As a result, the emphasis here is on conceptual and theoretical papers rather than on descriptive and empirical papers. Local examples can be introduced by the user to suit the needs of each audience.

A note of caution is necessary here. The reader, particularly the beginning student, should be alert to the very wide divergence in methodology and perspective demonstrated in the following papers. Indeed, the approaches in some papers actually contradict those in other papers, particularly (but not exclusively) in those that involve political interpretations. Other differences represent obvious contrasts in the initial assumptions of the research, the cultural–economic and institutional contexts within which that research is set, and the overlay of "filters" (e.g., the backgrounds, perceptions, and biases) that we, individually or collectively, apply in interpreting the real world. In later sections of this introduction, as well as the papers in Parts I and II, these differences are displayed more clearly for the benefit of the reader.

The basic criterion in the selection of papers for this collection is to set out a representative sample of research on urban spatial structure during the 1970s rather than to favor one approach over any other. Within this framework, however, selection was often limited by the unavailability (publication restrictions or costs) or unsuitability (in form or quality) of papers on some topics. Some publishers are reluctant to approve the reprinting of a paper or section of a book they feel would undercut their own market. Moreover, the emphasis in this volume is on uniformly more substantive papers than was often the case in the first edition, and in most instances on the inclusion of the full text of the paper rather than shortened versions. Nevertheless, the editor has spent considerable effort in eliminating verbose or unnecessary materials from the longer papers. Even so, the result is that fewer papers could be included.

The orientation of the volume is intentionally interdisciplinary. Although admittedly biased toward the geographical literature, contributions are drawn from most of the social sciences, notably economics, sociology, urban planning, and policy analysis, as well as from some of the professions and the private sector. Thus, the beginning reader and the student with a single disciplinary background will often be forced to grapple with concepts and a vocabulary largely outside his or her principal area of expertise.

Any collection of readings on a topic as complex as the modern city, its internal structure and growth, has to leave out more than it includes. Every reader inevitably will find important topics and papers missing. Many of these papers, however, appear in the concluding bibliography. This volume is primarily concerned with the contemporary city in the developed Western and industrial world. Empirical examples are drawn widely from the United States, the United Kingdom, Canada, Australia, and Western Europe. Although frequent references are made to cities in the socialist countries and in a few cases to cities in the Third World, and some papers include specific comparisons of capitalist and socialist cities (see Blumenfeld and Korcelli), no papers are included explicitly in these subject areas. To have done so would have exceeded all practical limits of length, reduced the scope for in-depth analyses, and added even greater diversity and complexity to what is already a very broad frame of reference.

This emphasis should not, however, be interpreted as suggesting that the spatial structures of cities in the socialist countries or Third World are either of secondary importance or a derivative of Western urban patterns. Such is not the case. Although these cities do share a number of common features with Western cities, they differ in equally important ways. Indeed, the framework that was set out earlier stressed the importance of historical and broad socioeconomic and political conditions as determinants of urban structure. Fortunately, there is now a rapidly growing literature on which the interested reader can draw relating to comparative aspects of urban development (Meadows and Mizruchi, 1976; Vance, 1977; Hall, 1979), the spatial structure of socialist cities (French and Hamilton, 1978; Bator, 1980), and urbanization processes and problems in the Third World (Friedmann, 1978; Roberts, 1979; Abu-Lughod and Hay, 1980).

Organization of Papers

The arrangement of papers in any anthology, although of less importance that the actual selection of papers, is nonetheless a significant consideration. That organization inevitably conditions the response of readers to individual papers and tends to emphasize particular topics and perspectives at the expense of others. As a result, and since each paper in this volume is intended to serve several purposes, the organization used here is kept relatively broad and flexible.

The ordering of parts is similar to that followed in the first edition. Papers are arranged under the following headings: (I) a context or introduction, (II) theoretical issues and alternative perspectives, (III) overviews of patterns and processes, (IV) communities and neighborhoods, (V) non-residential activities, (VI) networks of transportation, communication, and interaction, (VII) specific urban problems and planning issues, and (VIII) emerging trends and alternative strategies.

The starting point for most readers, however, should be the following review essay on urban spatial structure, written by the editor specifically as an introduction for this volume. It undertakes to bring together a host of ideas and to synthesize a broad range of literature not adequately represented in the readings. It also attempts to develop an integrated framework of concepts, terminology, and definitional criteria, which can be applied to the city and to the very diverse papers that follow. Students should read it first, but because of the complexity of the ideas involved, they should return to it, after having finished the entire volume, for review.

Part I provides some of the necessary background of historical context, images, and definitions of urban areas. The beginning paper (Blumenfeld) sets the stage with an overview of the site, situation, and cultural bases of urban form as expressed through history and literally across the globe.[5] The second paper discusses the area of interest in the study of the internal structure of the city and reviews various census definitions of metropolitan areas and extended urban areas in the United States, Canada and Britain (Bourne and Simmons). Two subsequent papers provide a review of the diverse images and symbolism of American cities and neighborhoods (Tuan) and a classification of alternative approaches in contemporary urban research (Johnston).[6]

The latter classification, in a provocative paper by R. J. Johnston, differentiates three major paradigms in research on urban geography: (1) the *empirical-analytical* approach, including the quantitative-theoretical or *spatial analysis* approach, which he argues is characteristic of the "mainstream" of urban research and which depends primarily on theories and methods from economics, statistics, ecology, and traditional urban geography; (2) the *behavioral* approach, which sees the city as a behavioral setting, as a product of individual decisions and actions, and which draws heavily on concepts from psychology and sociology; and (3) the *institutional* or political economy approach. The third draws its energy primarily from a critical stance with respect to the first two approaches and its methodology from that of political analysis. It combines an interest in the role of public institutions and agencies in urban development, as discussed earlier in this introduction, with the more radical critiques of political economy. This threefold classification, although much more generalized than that presented earlier in the discussion of emerging trends in urban research, is particularly useful here as a guide in identifying differences in the implicit assumptions, as well as the more obvious contrasts in methods and contents, in the following papers. All three approaches are represented by papers in most sections.

5. The second edition of an extensive collection of essays by Hans Blumenfeld is is available for the interested reader (see Blumenfeld, 1979).
6. Two subsequent articles following up on this discussion also appeared in the journal Progress in Human Geography (see Johnston, 1978, 1979).

Parts II and III contain papers that deal first with alternative theoretical issues and research perspectives and second with descriptive patterns and processes of change within the urban area. These two sections, as in the first edition, are likely to be the most difficult for readers to synthesize. The rationale for putting together what are often diverse papers, rather than dispersing them through subsequent sections (to which the subjects of those papers are often closely linked), is that most are sufficiently important to be prerequisites for all subsequent sections.

Thus, Part II contains reviews of the theoretical literature and examples of the application of alternative theoretical stances to aspects of urban form and growth. The section begins with a unique and comphensive review by Korcelli of research on urban structure (to 1975), including the basic literature on urban ecology, land use, population densities, and spatial interaction. He also draws a number of parallels and contrasts between research styles and subject areas in the study of cities in both market and planned economies. Other papers provide, in sequence, a re-examination of the behavioral determinants of urban structure and the processes of locational decision-making (Horton and Reynolds); a summary of the influence of environment on individual behavior, as an example of the time-space approach to the geography of the city (Häger-strand); recent revisions to the basic micro-economic model of urban structure (Miron); and a classic statement of the political economy approach to urban development (Harvey). The latter paper focuses on the conflict between capital and labor over the "built environment" of cities and the reflection of this conflict in the separation of home and workplace. The final paper (Dear) reformulates public facility location theory, as applied to the specific problem of the location of mental health facilities, which also incorporates the political economy approach.

The obvious difficulty that readers will face with this section is the often high level of abstraction of the theoretical papers. In the case of micro-economic approaches to urban structure, we have witnessed a very substantial evolution since Alonso (1964 and the first edition of *Internal Structure*) in theory and in the level of sophistication of the mathematical modeling. There are now a number of excellent examples of such approaches in the literature, notably Wheaton (1974, 1977) and Muth (1977), but most are far too technical and esoteric to be included here. To fill this crucial gap, John Miron agreed to write a non-technical summary of equilibrium models of urban land use specifically for this volume. For the keen reader, there are also useful and extended summaries of this literature in Richardson's (1977) book on the "new urban economics" and in Mills (1980). Direct criticisms of this literature, and specifically of the assumptions of neo-classical economic models, are provided in Harvey (1973), Ball (1979), and Scott (1980b).

Similar stylistic criticisms can also be leveled at the political economy literature in urban studies. Often this literature is highly technical and convoluted, not in mathematical terms per se, but in concept and language. David Harvey's papers, including the one reprinted here, tend to be an exception to this rule, although they too require a substantial effort in interpretation for those readers unfamiliar with the technical details. This literature also tends to be extremely verbose, and thus it is often unsuitable for inclusion in a readings volume. For this reason, the papers of this genre included here tend to be extracts from much longer papers, and suffer accordingly.

Part III begins with a detailed study of the historical evolution and contemporary structure of American cities (Adams). This paper combines a comprehensive analysis of the imprint on urban form of different building cycles and technological changes in transportation with a schematic model of population densities and development patterns. Subsequent papers examine selected dimensions of urban patterning and examples of the determinants of intra-urban change. These include an extensive review of the principal processes of residential change—household mobility, locational decision-making, search behavior, and filtering in the housing market (Short); patterns of social and political conflict over land use changes and development proposals (Janelle and Millward); and a view of urban spatial structure based on residential preferences and mental maps (Clark and Cadwallader).

The final paper (Morrison) in this part serves two distinct roles in this initial discussion of processes. First it demonstrates the important role played by changes in demographic structure and in net migration rates in shaping our cities. Second, it introduces the broader question of differences between cities that are growing and those that are declining through a comparison of San Jose and St. Louis during the 1960s. As noted earlier in this introduction, there is increasing interest in research on the processes and implications of urban decline and a growing political concern that in an overall slow-growth (or no-growth) environment, the contrasts—and thus the social inequalities—between growing and declining communities will likely increase. This theme is again picked up in papers in the final two sections.

Three subsequent parts examine, in more conventional order, residential communities, social areas, and housing (Part IV); systems of production and distribution, including commercial (retail), industrial, governmental, and social service activities (Part V); and patterns of interaction, transportation, and communication (Part VI). Part IV begins with two overview papers. The first, on different approaches to the study of urban neighborhoods (Wellman and Leighton), introduces the concept of social network analysis as a means of analyzing the question of whether or not communities in the modern city are being lost or saved. The second paper examines the temporal dimensions of urban social structure as revealed through methods of factorial ecology (Taylor and Parkes).[7] Subsequent papers focus on the interaction of social class and religious differences in defining territoriality and patterns of segregation within the city (Boal). Although the example in this paper is Belfast, the processes are by no means unique to that city. Other papers examine the role of information on housing market behavior and images of real estate agents in directing households into different types of housing and different locations (Palm); the role of financial institutions in creating distinct and unequal housing submarkets (Harvey and Chatterjee); and recent evidence on neighborhood revitalization, gentrification, and the return-to-the-city movement and their implications for planning and research (Gale).

Part V brings together papers on the various industrial, commercial, and public sector activity systems that make up the non-residential fabric and productive base of an urban area. Note that we are dealing here with activities with very different locational determinants. The commercial structure of the city, excluding in part the central business district and most public services, are based on local demand. Their composition and location within the city reflect primarily the needs and distribution of the local target population. In contrast, the growth of the industrial base and to a lesser extent the growth of the office sector depend on demands from outside the urban area. For manufacturing industries in particular, their location within the city is not tied to serving the local population, although they are influenced by the distribution of labor supply within the urban area. Questions of labor supply, however, although not well represented in the literature (see Scott, 1980b) are discussed in several papers in the following sections.

The papers in this part review the growth of the downtown through time both as the nucleus of the urban area and the central component in the retail and commercial structure (Bowden); the internal organization of commercial shopping districts in terms of the types of retail outlets and the behavior of consumers (Johnston and Kissling); trends and empirical evidence on industrial location within the city (Struyk); the location and

---

7. An active correspondence followed publication of this article. See B. Brown and M. Boddy, "A Cartesian View of the City" (letter to the Editor) Environment and Planning A, 8, pp. 599–601; and the authors reply in the same journal, pp. 839–841.

distribution of public services in the city, and techniques for locating such facilities, using day-care facilities as an example (Brown *et al.*); and alternative interpretations of the origins and impacts of the political fragmentation of American metropolitan areas (Cox and Nartowicz).

Part VI documents the flows and networks of interaction that act to knit the urban area together: urban transportation systems, the journey-to-work, functional linkages between clusters of activities, the impacts on urban development of public transit, and communication linkages and social interaction. The initial papers review the relationship between transportation and land values (Alcaly); the journey-to-work, as a measure of the changing distribution of employment within an urban area, and as a means of documenting the emergence of subcenters within the suburban fringe (O'Connor and Maher); and patterns of functional linkages among offices in the central city core (Goddard). The two following papers examine the land use impacts of new public transit systems in different cities (Knight and Trygg) and the impact of the telephone on urban form and structure, as a measure of social interaction, and more generally of the relationships between communications and urban form (de Sola Pool). The latter paper also poses questions on the possible future impact of communication innovations on urban travel and patterns of development.

The final two parts examine two broad themes in urban spatial structure: first, social issues and planning problems (Part VII); and second, alternative policy initiatives and emerging factors likely to shape urban structure in the future (Part VIII). In both sections only a very limited number of selective examples could be included. Of course these section headings are also in part artificial. Many of the papers in the preceding sections are concerned directly with urban policy problems. The reader at this point may wish to refer back, for example, to discussions of the provision of mental health care (Dear) and the increasing separation of home from work (Harvey) in Part II; demographic change and population decline (Morrison) and locational conflicts in urban land use (Janelle and Millward) in Part III; the viability of urban communities (Wellman and Leighton), residential segregation (Boal), housing finance (Harvey and Chatterjee) and residential displacement (Gale) in Part IV; industrial decentralization (Struyk), day-care facilities (Brown *et al.*), and government fragmentation (Cox and Nartowicz) in Part V; and employment decentralization (O'Connor and Maher), public transit impact assessment (Knight and Trygg), and communications substitutes for travel (de Sola Pool) in Part VI.

Under the label problems, the papers in Part VII examine the definition and measurement of social (multiple) deprivation in cities (Herbert); the determinants and mechanisms of the widespread housing abandonment in American cities (Sternlieb *et al.*); the effect of industrial decline and corporate restructuring on inner cities, drawing on the U.K. experience (Massey and Meegan); patterns of crime and homicide in Detroit (Rose and Deskins); the question of the degree of control communities have or could have over neighborhood change (Wolpert *et al.*); and the origins and scale of the serious fiscal problems facing some U.S. cities (Urban Institute). The final paper (Alonso) returns to the fundamental theme of demographic and life-style changes introduced earlier in papers by Short and Morrison (Part III). What effects will the massive demographic transition of the last decade have on our cities and on their spatial structure?

Part VIII looks to those factors that will shape the city of the future and to the alternative urban strategies that might emerge. The questions raised are fascinating. Are we in an age in which large cities as such are no longer distinctive or essential elements in our society? How will the massive relocation of jobs and demographic transition of the last decade affect the inner city? Will the urban crisis of the 1960s and 1970s continue and with what results? What new spatial forms will emerge under continued out-migration and zero or slow urban growth overall? How can cities of the future be redesigned to more effectively meet the needs of all citizens, including women and the elderly? What future urban forms are necessary to reduce pollution and to improve environmental quality? Finally, what might be the form of the city look like in an energy short future?

In the first paper Berry provides an overview of the factors that have led to the decline of American inner cities and the problems these cities will face in the future. This paper, published in 1980, should be compared to his earlier paper presented to the same audience a decade earlier (Berry, 1970). His predictions at that time on the rate of metropolitan decline and population decentralization in the United States have turned out to be underestimates. Subsequent papers pick up the various themes identified in the above questions. Castells provides a political economy interpretation of the origins of the current crisis in American urban development. Leven discusses the conditions that will lead to the formation of a new multi-centered form for the post-industrial city and concludes that the urban world of the year 2010 may look more like the world of 1910 than that of 1960. Janet Abu-Lughod offers a personal criticism of the form of the contemporary city (as well as of the attitudes of planners and researchers) in terms of its effects on women, and Golant reviews the changing needs of the elderly in urban areas. The last paper outlines the energy implications of alternative urban forms (van Til). Van Til argues that existing urban forms, and the prevailing directions of change in those forms, are clearly not designed either to reduce pollution levels or promote energy conservation.

At the end of this last part the reader will have absorbed an immense diversity of images on what current trends in urban development will lead to. Some of these images are complementary, others are simply different, and some are contradictory. This diversity is not primarily a function of mistakes in selecting specific papers for inclusion, although in an attempt to select a representative sample of the urban research literature, such misjudgments are certain to be present. Instead, it reflects the reality of widely diverging views on how we arrived at our present state and on what our future urban forms and living environments will probably look like. Our challenge is both to understand these views and to influence the trends and the urban forms that will result.

LARRY S. BOURNE

Urban Spatial Structure: An Introductory Essay on Concepts and Criteria*

Even a casual observer in our cities would notice that there is some order or coherence in the way those cities are laid out. Despite the very wide differences between individual cities, and perhaps allowing for a superficial impression of chaos, things generally are where we expect them to be. When they are not there we ask why not. Moreover, things seem to fit together; buildings and land uses of different types are not scattered randomly throughout the urban area. People and goods do not move equally in all directions. Further, cities seem to work—some obviously work much better than others—but at least they all function as a set of interrelated economic activities, as political institutions, and as a collection of more or less distinct social communities.

What is the logic behind this order? Does everything have its place in the city? What and who determines where things are located and how one activity or part of the city is linked to other activities or areas? What rules or principles govern the ways in which change takes place within urban areas? These simple questions are

* The references for this essay are collected at the end of the volume under the heading "General References and Further Reading."

the central concerns in any study of the internal form and structure of the city and are the focus of this introductory essay.

To date, however, no unified set of concepts or theories of urban form and spatial structure has emerged. Instead, the literature presents a plethora of partial and largely untested theories, hypotheses, and often competing models (Schirwian, 1974; Kain, 1975; Castells, 1977; W. Smith, 1977; Cox, 1978; Mills, 1980; Johnston, 1980). Some of these draw primarily on concepts from economics, others on politics, social psychology, political economy, or human ecology (see Gale and Moore, 1976). Still others draw on physical analogies from information theory, physics, and engineering (Wilson, 1974; M. J. Webber, 1980). Each approach has some validity, within its own terms of reference, but none has universal acceptance. Perhaps not since the publication of *Explorations into Urban Structure* (M. M. Webber *et al.,* 1964) has there been an explicit attempt at formulating a comprehensive theory of urban spatial structure.

This essay does not undertake to set out a new theory or paradigm for urban research. Instead, the objective is considerably more modest: to identify a consistent body of concepts of what urban spatial structure is, and how it might be measured, primarily for the benefit of beginning students. In so doing it draws on a wide range of disciplines and methodologies and attempts to set a basis from which new theories might emerge. The paper provides a series of working definitions, an outline of the components of urban structure and growth, a set of hypotheses on the principles by which cities are spatially organized, and a summary of elementary measurement criteria on which the internal structure of different cities might be examined, compared, and interpreted.

INITIAL DEFINITIONS

The first step then is to provide a set of simple yet broad working definitions that can be used as a basis for our subsequent discussion. There are many different views on how urban form and spatial structure should be defined; indeed, some researchers would prefer not to define the terms at all. Nevertheless, explicit definitions are essential if we are to avoid continued confusion and misinterpretation. In over ten years of reading the literature on cities, this author has encountered an immense diversity—and frustrating inconsistency—in how researchers have used such terms as urban form, spatial structure, and interaction. The result is that many of the otherwise valuable conclusions of this research remain unique to the individual city under study or they evaporate into baseless generalizations.

No definition, however, arises from a vacuum. Each derives from the particular research experience and the—often implicit—theoretical stance of the researcher involved. This essay begins with the language of systems theory, not as an end in itself, but it is relatively clear and precise and because it explicitly emphasizes the simple point that "everything is related to everything else." Interrelationships are undoubtedly the essence of the city and of urban spatial structure.

Systems theory is also relatively neutral in its stance on issues and can be adapted to suit a wide variety of situations, research perspectives, and ideologies. Although some readers may disagree with the premise that systems theory provides a neutral theoretical framework, the important biases and constraints come not from the theory itself, but from how it is applied. Often rejected in the 1970s as too formal and restrictive, systems approaches are now returning to favor, but in more modest and sensitive applications.

In this context, it is argued here that we can most succinctly conceive of the city (or more appropriately, the entire urban area) as a spatial system; that is, as a "city system." This system consists of a complex and bounded whole, encompassing a set of activities or constituent elements and the relationships among those elements, which together make up the system (Berry, 1964; Cliff *et al.*, 1975). The boundaries of the city system are then defined by the extent of these interrelationships, and the system itself can be characterized by the attributes of the elements they encompass. Subsets of elements may, through the strength of their interdependence, form distinct subsystems within the larger urban entity. These subsystems may be defined primarily in aspatial terms, as in the case of hierarchical industrial organizations or administrative agencies, or in spatial terms, as in the case of a small residential area or a retail complex. More likely most subsystems in the city represent a mixture of both.

The immediate and obvious disadvantages of applying a systems approach to urban spatial structure are threefold. First, it may direct our attention to those interrelationships that are visible, that can be easily measured, and that appear to fit most conveniently into the systems framework. These may or may not be the most important relationships. Second, the approach may (and often does) degenerate into an overly simplistic focus on analogies drawn from mechanical or biological systems (e.g., the city as an organism), analogies that are largely inappropriate when applied to such a complex social and economic system as a city. Third, the apparent precision of the language may lead us to assume that we know much more than we actually do about how cities operate and which relationships are dominant in determining their internal structure. The reader will decide whether this writer has fallen victim to these same errors.

With these reservations in mind, three specific terms which are central to this review can now be defined more precisely:

1. *urban form* is the spatial pattern or "arrangement" of individual elements —such as buildings and land uses (or collectively, the built environment), as well as social groups, economic activities and public institutions—within an urban area;
2. *urban interaction* is the underlying set of interrelationships, linkages, and flows that acts to "integrate" the pattern and behavior of individual land uses, groups, and activities into the functioning entities that were described above as subsystems;
3. *urban spatial structure* formally combines an urban form and an overlay of patterns of behavior and interaction within subsystems with a set of "organizational" rules that link these subsystems together into a city system.

A simple illustration may help to clarify these concepts. A map or schematic diagram of, say, land uses in an urban area would qualify as a description, or static photograph, of urban form. We might then add to that picture a map or matrix of the flows of goods, money, or people among types of land uses in different locations within the city—that is, the interactions. If we also add an overall dominant mechanism or organizational principle, such as the existence of a private land market or a centralized planning process, which acts to design or "organize" the pattern or form of urban land uses and interactions across an urban area, the combined result is an "urban spatial structure." If, in addition, we introduce other notions relating to the specific determinants of, for example, land use patterns, notions such as differential location rents or government regulations on land development or factors affecting accessibility and the intensity of interaction, such as the friction of distance (e.g., the gravity model), we have defined a more comprehensive basis for both the description and explanation of urban spatial structure.

Figure 1 provides a simplified schematic example of these three cumulative concepts of urban spatial structure. Figure 1a represents a map showing the broad configuration of land uses in a hypothetical urban area. Figure 1b introduces one possible expression of spatial interaction, perhaps the flows of people from home to work or the pattern of household relocation or shopping behavior, which we would then overlay on the map of land uses. Figure 1c provides an example of the system-wide organizing mechanism that acts to integrate patterns of land use and flows into a distinctive urban structure. The latter mechanism, for purposes of this illustration, is the competitive private market in which different activities bid for different locations within the urban area. This mechanism produces an "ordering" of activities in terms of their location requirements and the rents that each can pay. Other organizing mechanisms could be introduced, as will be done later in this essay. At this point, however, it will suffice to stress that urban spatial structure must include all three elements.

This approach is considerably broader

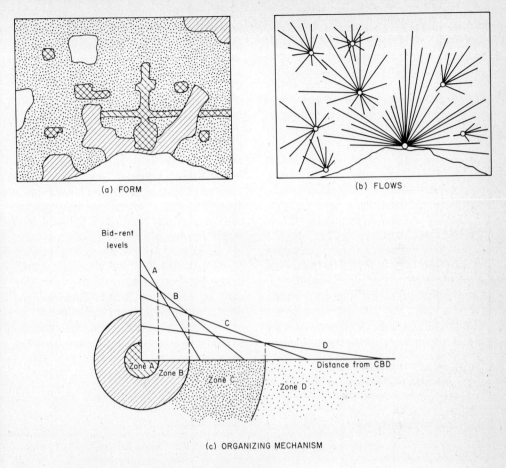

(a) FORM

(b) FLOWS

(c) ORGANIZING MECHANISM

Figure 1. The Components of Urban Spatial Structure

than that in the conventional literature, which tends to equate urban spatial structure with the physical arrangement of land uses (i.e., one part of urban form). It allows one to treat static dimensions of form and interaction as well as some of the properties of complex systems—for example, questions of regulation, control, and interdependence. Further, it allows us to logically incorporate both aspatial and spatial dimensions of the city within the same framework and to speak of urban social structure or the urban economy as necessary ingredients of urban spatial structure.

These definitions also remove the typical, but artificial distinction in the literature between spatial structure and flows. Under the above classification, flows of traffic, people, and services, for example, become an essential ingredient in and a determining factor of what we have defined as urban spatial structure—that is, in producing the "organized" spatial entity we call a city system.

In this framework, space itself can take on different meanings and can be measured in very different ways. The "space" of concern in the study of the internal structure of cities may be physical space, measured strictly in territorial or Euclidian terms, or it may be subjective or preferred space. The latter may include space measured on the basis of social, economic, or political attributes or the actual behavior of different social groups, firms, or institutions. Or it may refer to individual experience, perceptions or mental maps (Tuan, 1977). In both instances, physical and social space may be further broken down into specific units or building blocks, such as edges, boundaries, districts, paths, and landmarks (Lynch, 1960) or into traditional systems elements, such as nodes, networks, flows, gradients, and surfaces (Cliff *et al.,* 1975). These elements in turn may correspond to physical artifacts in the urban landscape, such as political boundaries, transport networks, or high-rise buildings, or to the "bits" of information we all accumulate in learning how to use an urban environment (Moore and Golledge, 1976). In each case we can differentiate between elements that comprise the aggregate or macro-structure of a city and those that represent a more local small-scale or micro-structure.

SYSTEMS COMPONENTS

The preceding definitions also offer a direct link to concepts in general systems theory as well as to the rapidly growing systems applications in geography (Bennett and Chorley, 1978). This literature also provides a useful vocabulary that can be fruitfully applied to urban spatial structure. In any given system, as suggested above, we can identify a number of related elements or components that, in combination, make up that system. For each of these components, Table 1 identifies a parallel element within the fabric of the city defined as a spatial system.

Every system and thus every city has a

Table 1. Systems Components in Urban Spatial Structure

System components	*Corresponding elements in urban spatial structure*
1. Nucleus: the point of system origin and the locus of control	1. The initial settlement (e.g., the confluence of two rivers, or a harbor) and the central business district
2. Geometric area and boundaries of the system	2. The geographic extent and limits of the urban area
3. Elements: the parts, units or bits which form the membership of the system	3. Social groups, land uses, activities, interactions, and institutions
4. Organizational principles: what ties the system together and allocates activities to areas; what "energy" drives the system?	4. The underlying logic or principles of urban structure (e.g., the land market) and the determinants of growth
5. Behavior: how the system acts and changes over time; its routine and non-routine actions	5. The way the city works; its activity patterns and growth performance
6. An environment: the "external" context that influences that system	6. The source and types of external determinants of urban structure
7. Time path: a trend of evolution and change	7. A development sequence; historical profile of building cycles and transport eras

core or *nucleus,* which is usually the original center, a set of member *elements,* a definable *area,* and *boundaries.* These components act to identify the point of origin and physical size of the system, as well as to establish its location, geographic shape, and internal environment. Further, all systems exhibit specific types of behavior; that is, they behave in aggregate and in terms of subsystems in a number of routine (or regular) and irregular, but observable ways over both time and space. Moreover, that behavior (e.g., growth and change) is subject, as argued above, to a dominant set of *principles* (or mechanisms) that underlie its form and determine its temporal pattern of change. These principles may be internal to the system or they may derive from external sources or from a combination of both. For cities we are principally concerned with those organizing mechanisms that are internal, but we must also recognize the importance of external controls and the interrelationships between internal and external influences.

Each system, in addition, has an *external environment* with which it interacts. That environment may be defined as all objects located outside the system and whose behavior influences that system, and whose attributes in turn are affected by changes in the growth and behavior of the system itself. For individual cities that environment may be the immediate territorial hinterland or regional economy or the entire array of political, economic, or cultural spheres of which the city is an integral part. And, finally, at any point in time, the structure and character of a system reflects its current position in a specific historical sequence and *time path* of development. Cities, for instance, clearly show the imprint of different building cycles and transport technologies, each superimposing a new layer of building on and selectively modifying what has been built before, and the actual timing of construction (Adams, Part

III; Whitehand, 1977; Harvey, 1978; Part II).

The characteristics of each of these components could be described at considerable length, but it will suffice here to offer a few brief examples. The nucleus of the city may be considered the location of initial settlement, and in the contemporary city, the commercial and communications center—usually the central business district (CBD). These two points may still be the same, although the current CBD may have shifted slightly away from the original location. The initial settlement location essentially fixes the city to a specific site and landscape, from which it cannot escape and which usually (but not necessarily) shapes the direction of subsequent development. The emergence of a CBD can also be seen as the establishment of a coordinating center or control point for the emerging spatial structure of the entire urban area. As the city grows and spreads out, the influence of the central core tends to decline as prominent sub-centers begin to develop.

The reasons for the establishment of the initial nucleus—usually the original settlement—can be as varied as the cities themselves. There are, however, some common denominators (see Carter, 1977). Although beyond the scope of this essay in any detail, it is useful here to identify the principal types of urban origins, since they set the stage for the city that subsequently develops. Following the terminology of Table 1, we might argue that most cities were established for one or more of the following purposes:

1. *Control:* particularly as military, political, or religious centers intended to subdue a territory or population and to offer protection to local elites;
2. *production:* notably as centers for indigenous crafts or more recently for manufacturing or resource exploitation;

3. *distribution:* as transshipment or break-in-bulk points or as regional centers for the provision of retail or social services;
4. *consumption:* as centers in which the satisfaction of individual or collective needs is paramount.

These become the city-forming processes we subsequently link to city-patterning mechanisms in the following sections. Clearly, most cities serve all these functions at some point in their development, yet the initial stimulus to settlement continues to exert an influence on the urban structure that evolves around it. What we know very little about is how these broad "city-forming" processes translate into the diverse internal structures we observe even among urban areas within the same cultural and economic realm.

Returning to the list of systems components in Table 1, we do know that each system has a more-or-less finite geographic area. In physical or mechanical systems, the boundaries of that area are usually relatively discrete and obvious, but in complex social-spatial systems, such as cities, they seldom are. In the lat-ter case the way we define the extent of the system depends on how we initially define the criteria for membership in, and the organizing principles of, that system.

The factors or events that induce changes in the behavior and evolution of social systems, in general, and in urban structure, in particular, can also be seen as displaying differing frequencies or *periodicities* over time. Each also has a differential impact on the system. Typically, three distinct sets of events and frequencies have been identified, although they clearly represent a continuum in reality. First are those regular or *routine* events that occur frequently, but do not result in substantial changes. Instead they act to maintain the system in its current state. Second are those events that are system-modifying in that they produce gradual or *evolutionary* changes in the path of development of the system under study. Third are those infrequent, but often dramatic events that result in *revolutionary* changes, shifting the system onto a new path and consequently transforming the system itself.

Table 2 summarizes these periodicities with examples of activities and events

Table 2. The Periodicity of Changes in Urban Structure

Type of event	Frequency of occurrence	Impact	Examples in urban structure
Regular or routine	High (predictable)	System-maintaining	Journey-to-work, to shop; provision of services, infrastructure
Evolutionary	Medium (partially predictable)	System-modifying	Demographic change; new transit line; community movements; land use succession
Revolutionary	Low (unpredictable)	System-transforming	Technological change (e.g., steel-frame construction; diffusion of the automobile); social unrest; floods, natural hazards, energy prices

drawn from the changing structure of urban areas. The origins and impacts of these examples are obvious: the daily journey-to-work tends to follow changes in the location of jobs and residences and thus may be seen as system-maintaining. Changes in demographic structure, on the other hand, tend to be more evolutionary and slowly to modify the structure of the city through, for example, changes in the demand for housing, schools, and social services. Community movements, as in the case of neighborhood political organizations, which led the resistence to new expressways, can permanently alter the form and direction of new development.

Other events are less frequent, but more dramatic. Technological innovations, for instance, may very rapidly reorder the form and functioning of the city, as did the introduction of the suburban railway, the automobile, and the telephone. The introduction of steel frame construction, for example, spawned the modern high-rise building and changed the face of our downtown areas. Social unrest can, as it did during the urban ghetto riots of the 1960s, suddenly lay waste large tracts of land; and floods, earthquakes, or other natural events can at a stroke permanently alter the structure of a city.

UNIQUE CHARACTERISTICS OF CITIES

As systems, however, cities display a number of unique attributes and types of behavior. They are perhaps best defined, as Emery and Trist (1973) argue, as *"complex" social systems*. This means that cities are characterized by immense (but nonetheless organized) complexity and internal heterogeneity. They also have a high degree of openness to external influence, often from environments (e.g., the international economy), which are turbulent and highly unpredictable. Moreover, cities are *self-organizing* systems

in that they have the means to internally monitor and "regulate" their own behavior in response to changing conditions. This regulation occurs through the existence of various explicit devices, some not unlike mechanical thermostats (e.g., congestion on roads, high land prices), others are more subtle (e.g., political movements), which feed back information to the relevant decision units. They also change or evolve over time not only through aging, but because they are *cumulative learning systems*. This implies that, unlike physical or mechanical systems, cities can and do learn collectively from past mistakes and successes, and adjust their behavior, perhaps modestly, in response to new information and revised objectives.

The internal organization of cities also exhibits several unusual and more specific characteristics. Four warrant brief mention here. The first characteristic is the immense *heterogeneity* in the elements and constituent parts of the system: that is, the very large number of individual actors, special interest groups, competing firms, and agencies whose actions and decisions shape the growth of the city. This diversity, which tends to increase over time, makes any classification of the actors and elements in the city system an extremely difficult exercise. Second is the high degree of *institutionalization;* that is, the increasing tendency to create sets of formal institutions and procedures to govern how parts of the city work and how they relate to each other. The spatial form of any modern city is overlain with a series of complex institutional meshes, such as building and zoning codes, subdivision regulations, property titles and ownership rights, environmental controls, and traffic regulations and by a myriad of social service delivery districts. These controls often act to freeze areas into certain uses, to channel activities, and otherwise slow the rate of change. These effects in turn influence patterns of individual and collective behavior and help to select from among many alternative paths of urban development the city might follow.

Particularly crucial in this regard is the fundamental role in determining urban patterns played by land and more specifically by *differential rights* of access to use of that land. In our society access to the use of land is primarily determined by ownership, and that, in turn, by income, social position and historical inheritance. This has not always been the case, as Vance (1971) points out for both precapitalist and socialist societies. Throughout most of the history of cities, land has been a collective good, available to everyone. Or at least it has been valued for its functional use rather than for its value for exchange or investment. Urban land in our cities, however, is largely privately owned, primarily by individual households and firms, and is exchanged in the market for profit or pleasure. This means that the city system behaves with respect to land in what is essentially an "atomistic" fashion, that is, with a large number of unrelated decision-makers who often do not know what others will do with their land in the future. This creates uncertainty, which may reduce capital investment, provide opportunities for some owners to reap surplus rents (Harvey, 1975), and leave others bankrupt (Leven, 1977). These conditions in turn may lead to increasing government intervention in the land market, often adding further complexity and uncertainty and perhaps leading to what Scott (1980b) has called the urban land problem or "nexus."

Nevertheless, a significant portion of urban land is owned or directly controlled by a variety of public agencies, non-profit institutions, and other collective bodies. This in turn implies that even in capitalist cities urban land behaves in a fashion that reflects non-market as well as market factors and responds to both individual and collective objectives, making even more complex our exploration of the components and determinants of urban structure.

A fourth characteristic is the presence of pervasive spill-over effects, or environmental *externalities*. These effects link the fortunes of any one individual element, group, or area to that of others in the system, who happen to be located in the immediate vicinity (neighborhood), whether they are functionally related or not. This spatial interdependence acts to alter the behavior of the actors and the relative attractiveness of different locations. In some instances, such as air pollution, or in the case of neighborhood decline and housing deterioration, this interdependence creates its own internal dynamic (Leven, 1977). Once begun, these processes often tend to accelerate and to spread geographically with their leading edge determined by the direction and extent of the externalities. Such conditions are usually made worse in cities in which land is privately owned and in which there is widespread uncertainty over other owners' intentions. There are of course parallels in physical and biological systems, but none have the degree of internal momentum and social imprint that one finds in such complex social systems as cities.

Principles of Urban Structure and Growth

For present purposes, an organizing principle(s) can be defined as a set of *rules* and regulations that determine the arrangement, interrelationships, and behavior of elements within a system. In most instances we can regard such rules as institutionalized practices or social conventions rather than divine edicts. Within our cities, as noted above, these rules most frequently relate to the operation of three processes: (1) the competitive economic land market, (2) the functioning of government and public institutions, and (3) the accepted canons or norms of social behavior.

PROPOSITIONS ON STRUCTURAL GROWTH

What general rules apply to structural growth and how do these apply to cities? Here we can draw on the classic work of Kenneth Boulding (1953) in establishing a set of propositions on the nature of structural growth in systems. These propositions, suitably adapted to an urban context, can be summarized as follows:

1. *Size:* that all systems have some minimum size (or threshold) necessary to ensure their existence and to produce a differentiated internal environment;
2. *inhomogeneity:* that the factors or principles guiding the current (or recent) growth of the system may not be the same as those that initially stimulated the establishment of the nucleus;
3. *non-proportional change:* that a change in the aggregate size of the system must invoke a non-proportional change in the relationships between the various parts of the system;
4. *growth-form dependency:* that the growth of a system determines its initial form, but so too does the form of the system at any given time influence subsequent growth;
5. *designer principles:* that all systems, including cities, have a set of rules, both explicit and implicit, that act to "design" the structure of that system, much as an architect does in designing a building, or a planner, or developer, does in laying out a new neighborhood.

Translated into urban terms, these propositions suggest that cities too have a threshold size, not only to qualify for city "status" in census terms, but in reference to the minimum size necessary to generate a sufficiently differentiated spatial structure. By this we mean the presence of sufficient diversity to allow for the emergence of recognizable subsystems within the urban area. The latter may be reflected in the existence of separate and distinctive functional clusters or social areas or in consistent land value gradients and regular or recurring patterns of interaction. To the extent that these distinct patterns and relationships exist, we have an "organized" urban structure.

The inhomogeneity principle confirms the rather obvious observation that the structure that is built up around an initial nucleus does not have to be homogeneous in form or function with that nucleus. That is, a city initially established as a port, minehead, or fort can subsequently become predominantly an administrative or political center or a retirement spa. The proposition of non-proportional change argues that as any structure grows in size, the proportion of its parts cannot remain constant. This is in part because, in simple terminology, a uniform increase in the linear dimensions of a system also increases its area as a square and its volume as a cube. In addition, increasing city size itself introduces a larger diversity, or heterogeneity, as defined earlier, in almost all aspects of urban structure. The fourth proposition, that growth initially creates a particular form and that form limits subsequent growth, stresses the mutually re-inforcing relationships between the growth and the form of the city, which we examine in more detail below.

DESIGNER PRINCIPLES

The fifth proposition is sufficiently complex that it warrants more detailed discussion. What we have called here designer principles are particularly important in that they pose the basic question of why cities are laid out the way they are? Who then determines or designs the spatial form of the city? And on what criteria? At least three major sets of designer principles are evident in the literature:

1. *Blueprint principles:* this criterion obviously describes a premeditated process of planning, as in the construction of planned new towns, where the layout of the city follows an established set of guidelines and all parts fit together by design. These new towns may be public (e.g., development corporations) or private (e.g., company towns), but in each case they reflect the existence of a complete "monopoly" over the instruments of design and thus over the rules by which uses are allocated to locations within the city;

2. *process principles:* in this case we look to the gradual evolution of urban structure through a sequence of thousands of events, actions, and decisions in which the parts fit together more or less through adaptation, or trial and error, rather than design. The most obvious types of processes are

   i) *competition:* as reflected in a competitive land market (in micro-economics) and in territorial claims by competing social groups (in human ecology). Note here that we are drawing a parallel between two traditionally separate fields because although the vocabularies are different, they share a common emphasis on the process of spatial competition. Within this context, competition generates two contradictory processes that tend to work in directions opposed to that of competition. These two are

      a) *co-operation:* as reflected in collaboration or collusion among collectives (e.g., in planning the socialist city; or the resistance to change among community organizations and political groups) or individuals (e.g., between households and landlords in setting rents); and

      b) *monopoly:* where one set of rules and actors overwhelmingly dominates the direction of events and decisions that determine urban structure (e.g., the property development industry, financial monopolies);

   ii) *socialization/stratification:* as reflected in the process of social clustering, in the partitioning of social contacts and networks of social dependency, in the creation of a particular social organization, and in restricting specific types of behavior;

   iii) *institutionalization:* many of the patterns and rules of behavior in the competitive model and the processes of socialization and stratification have become increasingly routinized, regulated, and formalized in terms of legal agreements, legislation, or the emergence of formal bodies and regulatory agencies;

3. *relational principles:* including those views that see urban spatial structure as based on some physical analog, usually a mechanical analog, which incorporates principles of least effort, minimization of the friction of distance, maximum entropy, allometric principles, or biological analogies.

These approaches are not, despite the impression one receives from the literature, necessarily in conflict, except when they are advanced as "complete" theories of urban structure. All are relevant to particular aspects of the puzzle, depending on the specific context and the combination of circumstances prevailing at that time and place.

Any urban area, at least in contemporary times, is in some part subject to all these rules of design. That is, the internal structure of a city mirrors a complex interplay of pressures that derive from competing—if not contradictory—attempts to "design" a structure that fits someone's image and/or interests. These cities also mirror various combinations of the effects of processes of competition, cooperation, collusion, and monopoly power. Moreover, in some ways that structure also behaves much like a physical system based on frictional (e.g., distance) or proportional change (e.g., allometric) principles.

Whatever the prevailing rules or principles underlying urban spatial structure, we can assume that there are other countervailing forces at work. Whether we argue for the purely competitive market in the economists' equilibrium model of an unconstrained city (Mills, 1980), the monopoly power the political economist sees in the capitalist city (Harvey, 1978), or the centralized design typical of the socialist city (French and Hamilton, 1979), no single explanation of the determinants of urban structure will suffice. In other words, no private enterprise city reflects only a process of pure competition in the land market; no capitalist city is entirely the product of a conspiracy among elites, classes, or power groups or of a monopolistic industrial or property development industry; and no planned or socialist city, even in the best of all worlds, is without the marks of a competitive process among specific activities for space and attractive locations.

Finally, no city designers of any origin or any persuasion can avoid the necessity of considering frictional parameters in planning that city's spatial structure. The latter might, for instance, involve the desire to minimize unnecessary interaction or transportation costs deriving from the excessive separation of land uses or the distances of homes from workplaces or goods and services from the consumers. Thus, in any attempt to study the organizing rules of urban spatial structure, the diversity of possible factors that act to organize that structure must be recognized, and an attempt made to sort out the relative contributions of each.

DEFINING THE AREA OF INTEREST

Clarification of the underlying principles that shape urban spatial structure has the further advantage of allowing us to rephrase an additional set of questions relating to the geographic definition of urban areas. This problem has been a long-standing one in the urban literature (Yeates and Garner, 1980; Hartshorn, 1980). It is also a source of innumerable frustrations for officials in such data-reporting agencies as the census bureau and a veritable nightmare for users of urban data. Since there is a subsequent essay on precisely this subject (Bourne and Simmons, Part I), only a brief summary is necessary here.

The basic question faced by the student of urban spatial structure is: What geographic area is it appropriate to study in terms of urban spatial structure? We do know that the location of the boundaries for an urban area can dramatically alter our initial impressions and the results of any empirical analysis. We can alter such common indices as rates of population or employment growth, changes in land use, housing demand, and rates of out-migration or levels of residential segregation simply by shifting our definition of the boundaries of the urban area. What, for example, is the appropriate definition of metropolitan New York, or Los Angeles? When we say that London is losing population and jobs what spatial concept of London do we have? The farther out from the city center that we draw the boundaries, for example, the more the out-migration of people and jobs to surrounding rural areas becomes simply suburbanization—that is an internal redistribution within the urban area. Boundaries indeed are that important.

Our preceding discussion suggests that these definitional problems can be reordered by turning our initial question around. If we are able to precisely sort out the dominant processes that shape the structure of an urban area, the relevant definition of the area of interest would follow as a logical consequence. That is, an urban area would extend as far from the city center as the processes or organizing principles continued to operate at significant levels. How would we recognize these boundaries? These processes might, for example, extend as far as the competitive market for urban-related land uses was operative, as expressed in a distinct break in the land value gradient and in differential land values above those for agricultural use. Or they may extend as far as the area in which interactions are dominated by urban-centered communications linkages (e.g., newspapers, telephones, television) or by home-to-work or recreational travel patterns. Or they might extend to include that area shaped by urban social patterns and life-styles, as evident in the extension of the social geography of the city into formerly rural districts, or by the expansion of urban-based institutions and regulatory agencies (e.g., water authorities). The latter might include the extent of geographic penetration by city real estate agents, financial institutions, or metropolitan government planning bodies into non-metropolitan areas.

Careful empirical testing of these premises might in fact produce the same results as do the traditional definitions of the city (see Section I), or they might not. In this case, however, they would derive from an improved theoretical base rather than preceding it. This in effect argues that such definitional problems cannot be removed unless and until our theorizing is substantially improved.

CRITERIA FOR URBAN STRUCTURE:
A SUMMARY

Equally apparent is the absence of an agreed-upon set of criteria by which urban form and spatial structure can be measured and comparisons made. Some readers will immediately think of such criteria as defining the boundaries of an urban area, or drawing concentric rings or radiating sectors, or a family of density gradients. Each of these is necessary, perhaps, but are they sufficient? Other readers may well conclude that no consistent set of criteria is possible or even essential. Nonetheless, it is argued here than an enumeration of criteria, bringing together the concepts outlined above, is useful in providing benchmarks for undertaking comparative studies of urban structure and as a framework within which diverse concepts and interpretations can be accommodated and evaluated.

Table 3 provides an example of what such a list might look like based on the concepts in the preceding discussion. Most of the criteria are self-evident in both their intent and application, but a number warrant elaboration. The first section of Table 3 suggests that the internal structure of any city has to be studied *in context;* that is, with particular reference to (1) the age and stage of the city's development and its historical growth or "development path"; (2) the city's functional character, prevailing mode of production, and economic base; (3) its relationships to an external environment; and (4) its situation or location within a system of cities. In other words, the internal structure of urban areas will differ if the building stock, infrastructure, and industrial plant are of different ages—and thus were largely constructed under differing conditions (e.g., financing, demand, technology, and public policy).

Moreover, if cities have dissimilar

Table 3. Criteria for Urban Spatial Structure

Level	Criteria	Description and examples
Context	1. Timing	Time and stage of development
	2. Functional character	Predominant mode and type of production (e.g., service center, mining town)
	3. External environment	The socioeconomic and cultural environment in which the city is embedded
	4. Relative location	Position within the larger urban system (e.g., core-periphery contrasts)
Macro-form	5. Scale	Size: in area, population, economic base, income, etc.
	6. Shape	The geographic shape of the area
	7. Site and topographic base	The physical landscape on which the city is built
	8. Transport network	The type and configuration of transportation system
Internal form and function	9. Density	Average density of development; shape of density gradients (e.g., population)
	10. Homogeneity	The degree of mixing (or segregation) of uses, activities, and social groups
	11. Concentricity	The degree to which uses, activities, etc., are organized zonally about the city center
	12. Sectorality	The degree to which uses, activities, etc., are organized sectorally about the city center
	13. Connectivity	The degree to which nodes or subareas of the city are linked by networks of transportation, social interaction, etc.
	14. Directionality	The degree of elliptical orientation in interaction patterns (e.g., residential migration)
	15. Conformity	The degree of correspondence between function and form
	16. Substitutability	The degree to which different urban forms (e.g., buildings, areas, public bodies) developed for one function can be used (substituted) for another
Organization and behavior	17. Organizational principles	The underlying mechanism of spatial sorting and integration
	18. Cybernetic properties	The extent of feedback; the sensitivity of form to change
	19. Regulatory mechanisms	Internal means of monitoring and control (e.g., zoning, building controls, financial constraints)
	20. Goal orientation	The degree to which urban structure evolves toward a priori objectives

economies and production bases, these will be mirrored in diverse internal structures. Mining towns, for instance, do not look or behave like office centers or university towns. In each case, the city's social and occupational composition, travel patterns, job locations, and land value gradients will differ. As a specific example, mining towns tend to have their major employment centers clustered around the minehead and separated from the downtown area. The journey-to-work pattern is thus biased away from the central area. In contrast, in cities that are office centers, employment tends to be more concentrated in the downtown and thus the prevailing journey-to-work pattern is more core-oriented.

More generally, as has been argued earlier, macro-level urban structure will also differ depending on the political, socioeconomic, and cultural characteristics of the society in which it develops. Cities located in socialist countries, or in the developing world do not generally show the same form as those in the industrialized capitalist world, although there are many common properties. As French and Hamilton (1979) point out, however, the existing literature is not any more precise in suggesting ways to measure and explain the internal structure of the socialist city (at least in Eastern Europe) than it is for the typical Western or capitalist city.

The second series of criteria consist of more traditional and widely known indices and can therefore be dealt with succinctly. First we are aware that the size, shape, and physical landscape of an urban area may significantly affect the internal structure. The principal of nonproportionate change outlined above is one line of argument regarding the effects of city size on form; empirical comparisons of cities of different size is another. Cities, such as San Francisco, built on a rugged peninsula obviously have a different shape and form, as well as a different

spatial organization than have cities, such as Dallas, which have little relief and few barriers to interaction. We also know, for instance, that cities that are linear in shape do not have the same spatial characteristics, in terms of population density gradients or commuting patterns, for example, as the classical circular or semicircular city (e.g., Chicago), which appears in most of our textbooks. Finally, it is apparent that a city (or suburb) that was largely developed during a period of dependence on public transit produces a different urban form—for example, different housing types, higher densities, and on-street shopping—and different patterns of interaction and behavior, than one based entirely on the automobile.

The third set of criteria relates to indices of urban patterning that are more conventional and that submit more easily to empirical measurement and quantitative analysis: (1) density, (2) diversity (homogeneity), (3) concentricity, (4) sectorality, (5) connectivity (linkages), and (6) directionality or directional bias. Although each of these measures is adequately defined in Figure 2 and Table 3, it is worth emphasizing that these criteria can be applied to a wide range of phenomenon. For each index one can also measure several parameters: (a) citywide averages, (b) aggregate internal spatial patterns (e.g., density gradients, transport network lengths, social networks, pollution levels, etc.), and (c) the degree of local or micro-level variability in the indices from place to place within the city. Combined, these indices provide a relatively comprehensive picture of the geometry of the city, but they tell us little about the operation or behavior of the city system itself.

Two other descriptive indices, however, warrant further discussion: conformity and substitutability. These two measures derive from the systems literature discussed above and are of direct relevance in studying the modern city when

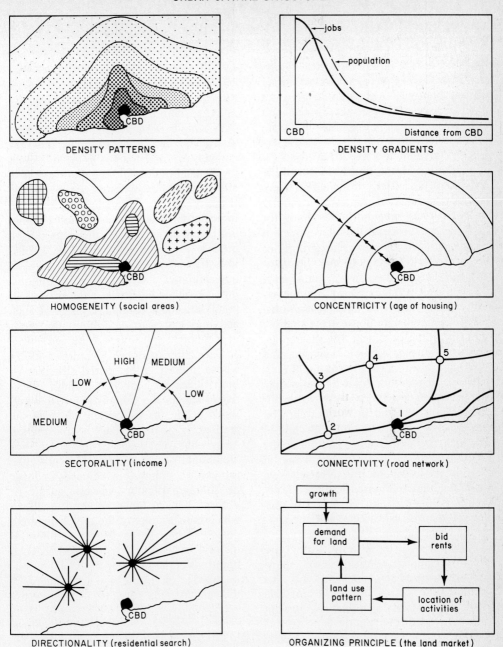

Figure 2. Selected Criteria of Urban Spatial Structure

viewed as a complex social system. Specifically, they refer to the relationship between form and function: that is between the initial rationale for the design and arrangement of elements of urban form—a building, a geographic area, an institution or social service agency—and the specific function they now perform. Historically, cities have been characterized by an immense capability for substitution—that is the ability to substitute a given form, initially designed to serve a particular function, for use by another function. Thus neighborhoods built for the wealthy subsequently filter down to be occupied by lower income groups or the reverse process may occur. Old mansions may become expensive rental units or flophouses or be converted to chic offices. Warehouses become restaurants; industrial plants may house artist studios; soda bars may become crime headquarters; and surplus schools may become community centers or housing for the elderly. Subsequently, social agencies may become welfare advocates. This flexibility has been reduced in recent years by the construction of highly specialized buildings or homogeneous land use districts, as well as by institutional inertia and tighter zoning controls. Nevertheless, it means that we often cannot easily equate form with function or easily predict the nature and direction of the substitution relationship in the future.

The final set of criteria in Table 3 are the most complex and the most difficult to measure empirically. Because of this complexity it is perhaps more realistic to see these criteria as guidelines of what to look for and as aids in devising a strategy for research. These criteria include (1) the underlying mechanism—or principle—that we have assumed (above) to be the prime determinant of urban spatial patterning; (2) cybernetics, including the sensitivity of elements in the urban form to external change and the nature of the feedback linkages between these elements; (3) regulation, the internal devices or instruments available for shaping urban structure and growth; and (4) orientation, the question of whether observed changes in urban structure are directed to specific goals or objectives, and if so, whose objectives?

A simple example might again be of assistance. We might assume that the competitive land market is the dominant mechanism in determining the location of and relationships among activities within the city. Then we might ask How do these activities adjust over time to changing demands and by what means does a growth (or decline) of one activity (e.g., industry) feed-back on the growth of other related activities (e.g., warehousing)? What is involved in the process of regulating the locational choices of such activities and who determines the kinds of regulatory procedures employed?

The latter question in turn asks In whose interest is the spatial structure of the city determined? Is it a single objective, such as the minimization of travel times or the maximization of aggregate land rents, as determined by the market or by what were called earlier physical or "relational" factors? Does this objective represent community-wide needs or those of some particular interest group or groups? Or are there several goals to which the structure of the city is directed, goals that may be conflicting and contradictory? Attempting to respond to such questions is the first step in extending our knowledge of how cities work and why they are spatially "organized" as they are.

CONCLUDING REMARKS

This essay has attempted to set a context of concepts, terminology, and measurement criteria for the discussions that follow. It pulls together in systematic fashion a host of ideas from an immense literature in a variety of academic fields. The language of systems theory has been employed as a guiding framework, as a technique, but not at the expense of alternative approaches. Essentially the essay is intended to pose questions that can be addressed to the often disparate papers in subsequent sections, although many of those papers fail to acknowledge explicitly the underlying assumptions, concepts, and criteria they are employing. The interested reader will almost certainly find that she or he wants to criticize (if not revise) the concepts and definitions and rewrite the criteria outlined above after reading the following papers. If so, then this paper will have served its major purpose.

Perhaps the greatest weakness of the above concepts, aside from their generality, is that they do not tell us how to interpret the empirical measurements we obtain. They may tell us what to look for in urban spatial structure, the kinds of questions to ask, and how to compare and contrast observed spatial patterns, but not necessarily what those observations mean. Those interpretations, as the reprints in this volume demonstrate, depend on our individual and collective philosophies, theories, and ideologies, as well as on the particular vantage point from which we view urban patterns, events, and processes of change. The major advantage of this approach is that it requires that we, as students of the city, at least make our biases known.

I

CONTEXT: Historical Antecedents, Definitions, and Approaches

HANS BLUMENFELD

Continuity and Change in Urban Form

The City's Identity Problem

Sixty years ago, in his perceptive introduction to the catalogue of the International City Planning Exhibition in Berlin, Werner Hegemann remarked that the modern city has little more in common with the historical city than the name. This prophetic insight has been confirmed by subsequent developments. In fact, it can be said that we no longer live in cities, but in a new, much vaster and more dispersed form of human settlement which, for lack of a better word, we call a metropolitan area. It partakes of characteristics of both country and city; but as it is essentially urban, I will identify it with and by the city which is its core.

This is in conformity with common usage. When he is in Detroit or Toronto, a man may say: "I live in Grosse Point" or "in Richmond Hill." But when he is far from home, he will say: "I am from Detroit" or "from Toronto." But what has today's London really in common with medieval London? What constitutes its identity?

For the first time in history these contemporary, vast urban areas contain the majority of the population and are the places where most of the work is done. The historical city was the seat of a small minority, substantially composed of the politico-military, ecclesiastical, and economic elite, and of those who immediately served them. The mass of the population lived in villages, in "urban" as well as in "preurban" cultures. In the latter also the elite lived not in the village, but in a different form of settlement, the castle or manor; or, in Buddhist and Christian countries they lived in a significant variant of the manor, the monastery. The city is a synthesis of the village and the manor.

In the farming village there are a number of basically identical decision-making units, the farm households. They may and do cooperate by addition of identical forces; but they do not interact, do not interchange different goods or services. (This is, of course, a heroic oversimplification.) On the other hand, in the manor there is a differentiation and specialisation of functions, interacting and interdepen-

From **Journal of Urban History**, Vol. 1, No. 2, February 1975, pp. 131–47. Reprinted by permission of the Publisher, Sage Publications, Beverly Hills, Calif., and H. Blumenfeld.

dent; but all its members are subject to one single decision-maker, the lord of the manor.

The city combines the characteristics of the village and of the manor into something uniquely new and different. It is one big unit with its decision-making government—however constituted—which is composed of a number of independent decision-makers—households, corporations, and the like—which perform different functions and are therefore interdependent by an exchange of goods and services.

It is the interplay between the decisions of the community and the decisions of its individual or corporate constituents which creates and recreates the form of the city. Many writers have made a rigid distinction between "planned" and "grown" cities, often identified with "geometric" versus "organic" urban form. But the distinction is not absolute. No living city is built entirely according to plan. Only if and when rigor mortis sets in right after birth, as in Aigues Mortes, may it come close to it. And nothing in any city is ever built that has not been planned by somebody. The real question is: who planned what, and why?

The one big unit, the city government, sees the city primarily as a container. In most historical urban cultures the wall of the city is its primary concern; and even contemporary planners want to "contain" their city by a greenbelt. The wall contains and protects the citizens, their sanctuaries, and last but not least, their goods. As did the manor and the royal palace—as we know from the biblical story of Joseph—so does the city assemble and distribute the goods of the region. It contains and conserves the inventory. It was from keeping record of the inventory that writing developed. All urban cultures are literate; no non-urban culture is. So a second and more important inventory is added: the city becomes the container and transmitter of the accumulated knowledge

and wisdom of the culture, the preserver of its continuity.

Continuity there is, of course, also in the village as well as in the manor. Indeed, both are essentially static; generation after generation follows the same way of life. They are static because they are self-contained. No city is self-contained; it depends on interchange and interaction with other regions and cities; and this interaction is typically, though not exclusively, carried out by many independent decision-makers, individual and corporate citizens. Jane Jacobs is right in defining Catal Hüyük as a "city" because its specialised merchants and craftsmen used materials from afar and presumably sent their products to other places.

As interaction with the outside world expands or contracts, the city grows or shrinks. More, these exogenous forces have their impact on the structure of the city, its internal relation of forces, its functions, and its mores. Change is as much of the essence of the city as is continuity. It is never the same as it was in the "good old days"; not for it the stability of the village.

This instability of the city has disturbed many observers. Plato wanted to prevent it by literally isolating his polis; which, not accidentally, was modeled on rural Lakedaimon. Plato was, of course, a son of the city. So were the mandarins of the Ming dynasty who dismantled China's great merchant fleet, because the impact of foreign trade undermined the stability of the established Confucian order. They, like Plato, regarded identity and change as mutually exclusive.

This appears to be an evident truth by Cartesian logic. How can an entity at one and the same time change and be the same? Yet we know that such entities do exist. Every organism changes constantly, but preserves its identity. More, it preserves its life and identity by change, by metabolism.

A city is not an organism. It is, strictly

speaking, not even an organisation. Certainly there are organisations in and of the city. But, in contemporary North American cities at least, there is not even an organisation of the real city, the socioeconomic system of the metropolis. The city is, or can be defined as, a system. But while every organism is a system, not every system is an organism. The city is a social system and is, as such, not preprogrammed by genetic endowment, as is an organism. An organism can only develop within certain fairly narrow limits of space and time. The organismic view, as represented by Lewis Mumford, postulates that a city must degenerate once it grows beyond a certain size, and that it must end up as a metropolis. But all the evidence is to the contrary.

Determinants of Urban Form

The form of the city results from the interaction of situation, function, and site; from the concepts in the minds of its citizens and from the types of structure they build, both derived from preurban roots; and from the reaction of these on situation, function, and site, and on subsequent human activity. None of these factors is absolutely fixed, all are subject to change. The city is a historical process; its image at any given time is merely a cross-section through a continuous stream. It is not a work of plastic art, not "architecture on a large scale," as a manor or monastery may well be. It may have some similarity with a work of the temporal arts, of poetry or music. There may be a recurrent leitmotif, or at least a basso ostinato.

The situation determines whether there will be a city at all. Cities do not have one common origin. A city may develop from growth of a village, the area around a castle or monastery, or from a temporary camp or fair ground; or it may be consciously established as a "New Town."

But whether it becomes a city or withers on the vine depends on its situation. Geographers define three such situations: the central place, the transfer point, and the specialised city, usually deriving its specialty from a localised natural resource.

The central place as the sanctuary, refuge, and meeting place of the tribe dominates the surrounding tribal territory. A hill rises in the center of the fertile plain known as the Beauce, and a cave at its top became a sanctuary of the great Celtic mother-goddess, venerated far beyond the boundaries of the Beauce. With the Roman Conquest the mother-goddess became Venus Genetrix and with Christianity she became Notre Dame. Directly over the sacred cave stands the high altar, the centre of the great cathedral, which crowns the hill, which is the core of the city of Chartres, which is the centre of the Beauce. Here, the interaction of situation, function, and site, unchanged over millennia, has been made more and more visible by the changing works of man. Chartres has become more itself a great sacred centre.

Similarly, the rock on which the mythical king Erechteus built his house became the dominant central place of the surrounding plain of Attica, its polis. In Homeric Greece polis means the royal castle. At its foot spreads the asty, the settlement of the common people. The inherent duality of the city, being both manor and village, is still separated in space as well as in language. In Athens, where the natural resource of fine clay gave rise to pottery, the asty developed mainly around the Kerameikos, the potter's market. But when the craftsmen and merchants assumed power and constituted themselves as the polis with the Kerameikos as their central agora, the former polis became the Akropolis; deserted by men, it remained the seat of the gods. The city has become the centre of all of Greece as well as Attica, but it is still the glorious rock which proclaims to the world: "This is Athens."

In Athens, as in Chartres, it is a decisive element of the natural site, enhanced by unique works of man, which is the main element of continuing identity. Sometimes it is the natural element alone, as in Montreal where the mountain has given its name to both the city and the island. It may even be a distant mountain which becomes identified with the city, such as Fujiyama with Tokyo and Mount Hood with Portland, Oregon.

But landmarks, natural and/or manmade, are not the only elements of identity and continuity in cities. Toronto is located at the mouth of the small river Humber, from which a short portage was used by the Indians to carry their canoes to the Holland River where they continued through several smaller lakes to the Upper Great Lakes. This situation at the junction of the east-west route along Lake Ontario and the St. Lawrence River with the shortest south-north route to the Upper Lakes continued to influence the growth of the city. When wheeled carts and carriages superseded canoes, the roads to Kingston and Dundas, located at the eastern and western ends of Lake Ontario, respectively, were soon supplemented by a road named Yonge Street leading north to Holland Landing, and becoming the "main street" of Toronto. Urban development followed these three main streets, giving the city the form of an inverted T. All subsequent means of urban transit, horse-drawn, later electric street cars, and finally subways, were first and foremost established on Yonge Street.

This is not the only element that has continuously shaped Toronto. The land of Upper Canada, like that of the United States, was divided by governmental fiat into geometric squares. Here, these were "concessions" of 1,000 acres each, separated by road allowances. These "concession roads" still form the main arterial road system. The area of each concession has been subdivided largely into blocks approaching a square shape.

In Quebec the original land division followed a different system. Starting from the river bank, each settler was allotted a narrow strip which he extended inland as far as he could clear the land. Starting from this basis, Montreal has developed a pattern of long, narrow blocks. The original street and block pattern, far more permanent than buildings, continues to identify the city. It has its roots in the systems of measuring and allotting agricultural land. In Mediterranean countries the parcels were square, and so are the city blocks. In medieval northern Europe, with a different technique of plowing and correspondingly different methods of land measurement—by the chain rather than by the gromma—fields were oblong, and so are the city blocks. The connection, illustrated by the use of the plow to delineate the perimeter of the city, is found in India, Thailand, medieval Bohemia, as well as in ancient Rome. In Rome, as in India and China, the rectangular pattern was tied to the cosmological notion of the four cardinal points which determine the direction of the main streets. Secularized as a principle of order, the cross of main streets dominates the plans of William Penn's Philadelphia as well as Le Corbusier's Ville Radieuse. In Philadelphia the logos spermatikos of the basic cross has generated the cross of the city's two subway lines, and their crossing point is City Hall. The changes made by generation after generation have repeated the basso ostinato with stronger and stronger instruments.

Where the cosmological notion of the axial cross and its correlate, the rectangular pomerium, are absent and the grid is adopted as a purely utilitarian lot and block plan as in most North American cities, there is no predetermined boundary nor a predetermined centre. The cells of the blocks may proliferate in any direction, and the centre of the city may shift.

The classical case is Manhattan, where it is still moving to the north. It is, however, remarkable that the wall of the original core, pregrid Nieuw Amsterdam, has remained the locus of the financial centre. "Wall Street" still stands for New York as the centre of a worldwide financial empire.

Similarly, the other super power is referred to as "the Kremlin." In medieval Russia, as in ancient Greece, the duality of the city exists spatially, as "Kreml" (fortress) and "posad" (settlement). In Novgorod, as in Athens, the Kreml is now a museum of religious monuments. In Moscow, in addition to being a museum, it has again become the seat of power. The original reason for its location was the character of the site. The selection of the site is the first and most important decision of city planning. Where defense is the predominant objective, very frequently a "cape" is chosen. In Moscow it was formed by the acute angle between the Moskva River and the swampy mouth of a small tributary, the Neglinaya Creek. The swamp has long ago been transformed into a park and the creek buried in an underground sewer. Few Moscovites even know that it exists; for them Neglinaya is just a street name.

On the land side of the Kreml triangle, a market place developed known as Red Square. Along the three roads leading to the Kreml, a town developed, called, for unknown reasons, Kitai Gorod (Chinatown). It was enclosed by a wall, which describes a third of a circle from the northeast corner of the Kreml. The city expanded along the roads radiating from Kitai Gorod and the Kreml. This second layer was enclosed in the late Middle Ages by a wall of white stones, describing two-thirds of a circle; it is still known as the "White City." Growth continued along the radial arteries and on a maze of small alleys between them, extending also to the opposite bank of the Moskva. In the seventeenth century this third layer was enclosed by an earthern fortification which, for the first time, describes a full circle, defining what is still called the "Earthen City." The "radiocentric" pattern, which existed only in embryonic form in "Chinatown," was now fully developed and has continued ever since. The places outside the gates of both the "white" and the "earthen" city have been developed as the main squares of Moscow. When railroads were built, their terminals, new forms of the gateway, were located close to the gates of the former earthen wall; and their radial lines were soon connected by a circular railroad. The three concentric walls have all been replaced by broad ringroads. Farther out another ringroad and finally a circumferential expressway were added. In the 1930s the radial arteries were all widened to 200 feet, and the subway lines located under them were supplemented by a circular subway line. Thus, through all the changes of 700 years of history, the radiocentric pattern has become stronger and stronger. Today, Moscow is its classical example.

It is, of course, not the only one. Wherever a city rose as the central place of a relatively uniform plain, its containing wall assumed the form of a circle, the shortest line for enclosing a given area; the roads connecting it with its region radiated in all directions, converging on the market place. The market is the real centre of the medieval city; not the cathedral which often, as in Pisa, Salisbury, and Luebeck, is located at the city's periphery.

Where and when the city grew into an important trading centre, specialised markets for space-consuming goods, such as wood, hay, horses, or cattle, were located outside the gates. People settled outside these gates, and sooner or later these suburbs were taken into the city and protected by a second and sometimes a third circular wall. Later, when these walls were torn down, they were replaced by ringroads. Where they consisted of extensive earthworks and moats of the "Vauban" type, they sometimes also became "greenbelts," separating the older city from its later extensions, as in Vienna. It has been said that the walls have become more significant for the form of the city after they were torn down than while they were standing.

As cities of this type tend to expand in all directions more or less equally, the centre of gravity remains at the original centre. As the city grows, its centrality increases; the centre becomes stronger. It is different in the most typical form of the transfer point, the harbour city, where a large body of water limits expansion to one side. As such "half-cities" grow, the point of gravity moves further and further away from the original centre. The resulting pull weakens the centre, as in St. Louis and Detroit. In Toronto, where the "downtown" centre is still very strong and growing, about a mile further inland a new "uptown" is in the process of formation. The most extreme example of the "moving centre," Manhattan's uptown, has already been referred to.

Not all cities are monocentric. In London the financial centre in the city is separate from the government centre of Westminster, and over the years the specialisation of each has become more pronounced. The street system resulting from this bipolarity, as well as from the autonomous development of the large feudal estates, is rather complex and not easily identified. Probably the strongest element giving continuing identity to this unique city are the tree-planted squares which each of these estates created as focal points of their well-designed residential developments: a "leitmotif" played with many variations.

The embryo of Paris, the Gallic Lutetia Parisiorum, was located on an island in the Seine. The Romans built their town on the left bank, on the "Mountain of Paris" now crowned by the Pantheon.

After the Romans had left, the cathedral and the royal palace were built on the island which thus again became the centre, now known as the "Cité." On the right bank merchants settled. This part, governed by the "Provost des Marchands," became known as the "Ville." On the left bank were several monasteries; from their schools developed the university. Around 1200 this tripartite city was enclosed by a new wall. Outside its western gate, on the right bank of the Seine, the king built a hunting castle, the Louvre. It became the seed of a fourth district, the Paris of aristocratic splendour.

All changes during the succeeding seven centuries have maintained and reinforced the specific character of these four districts. The Cité, while no longer the seat of the government of France, still houses the real government of Paris, the Préfecture, in addition to the courts, the cathedral, and the archbishop. The Ville houses the stock exchange, the banks, and the leading department stores. The "Université" has become the fabled "Left Bank," the Paris of the intellectuals and artists. From the Louvre, via the Tuileries and the Champs Elysées, has developed the Paris of wealth and luxury.

The Renaissance intoned the second theme of the symphony. At the beginning of the fifteenth century a Parisian says of a proposed new street which would open up a long vista toward the Porte St. Antoine, "ce que sera très triomphant." This theme of the triumphant, wide, and straight street leading to an impressive building or monument as "point de vue," is played again and again, moderato under the monarchy, forte by Napoleon, fortissimo by Haussmann. It merges with the subtheme of the axial, geometrically shaped square formed by uniform buildings, which appears first with Henri IV's Place des Vosges.

The same king also gave to Paris the Pont Neuf, of which a writer said: "It is in the city what the heart is in the human body." It is indeed the focal point of Paris, connecting the lower end of the "Cité" with the "Ville" and the "Université," just above the Louvre. The Pont Neuf also was the first open bridge. The previous bridges were lined with buildings, as were the banks of the river. In the following centuries these were gradually displaced by broad quais. Only then did the Seine with its bridges and quais become an integral part of the image of the city to which it had given birth. Now the mature "person" of Paris has fully developed all the characteristics which, one after another, emerged during her childhood and adolescence.

Cities other than Paris also ignored for a long time the inherent characteristics of the site, and sometimes of the situation as well. Peter the Great founded St. Petersburg as a "window to the west" on the river Neva at the point where it branches out into a delta, its two arms enclosing an island. Inherent in this situation were two directions: westward to the sea, and southeast to the Great Russian heartland, to Novgorod and Moscow. Initially only the first direction was recognised. Peter adopted the plan of the French architect Le Blond, which provided for urban development of the entire island by a rectangular grid of canals and streets.

The oval fortification also enclosed a part of the north bank with the Peter-Paul's fortress, but only a narrow sliver on the south bank. Development on the south bank outside the fortifications was expressly forbidden. But on the south bank was the city's biggest employer, the Navy Yard, called the "Admiralty," as well as Peter's modest "winter house." From the southeast came the migrants who were attracted by the new capital city—and they stayed there at its gates. From the southeast also came the country's highest ecclesiastical dignitary, the Metropolit of Novgorod. On his visits to the Imperial Court he stayed at the Alexander Nevsky Monastery, some two miles

from the Winter Palace which soon replaced Peter's little house. For his convenience this road was paved; as the "Nevsky Prospect" it became and remained the main street of the city.

Only two generations after the city's foundation did a new plan recognize the preeminence of the south bank. The Nevsky Prospect was supplemented by two other main arteries, radiating at equal angles from the tower of the Admiralty. This fan-shaped pattern, greatly extended and enlarged, remains the basic arterial system of modern Leningrad.

The island remained a quiet residential district, with its canals filled in and transformed into broad tree-lined avenues. Its eastern tip, the apex of the delta, remained vacant for a long time. Only in the early nineteenth century did this focal point receive its architectural form. St. Petersburg, meanwhile, had also become an important commercial centre, and appropriately, the stock exchange was chosen to occupy this most conspicuous site. It was built in the form of an enormous Doric temple, flanked by two even more enormous columns, with broad granite stairs leading down to the river; the whole on the majestic scale set by the broad river. Only now, with this articulation of its focal point, was the inherent character of the site fully spelled out; only now had the city fully become its unique self.

The site is generally the most permanent element establishing the continuing identity of a city. Where the site is primarily characterised by hills or mountains, it is not substantially changed by man; but human activity may obscure or articulate it. Where water is the characteristic element, modification by man may be substantial. This is evident where water appears mainly in the form of canals, as in Venice, Bruegge, or Amsterdam. But it may also happen with natural watercourses, as in Hamburg.

Hamburg was founded by Charlemagne

as an outpost on the north bank of the Elbe, which here consisted of a shifting maze of watercourses between tidal flats. The site was a typical "cape" site, a slight rise of land protected on both sides by two small tributaries of the Elbe. Charlemagne's son established an archbishopric in the town, and a cathedral was built with a parish church next to it. The main street followed the ridge of the height. For a long time the only paved street, it still retains the name of "Stone Street." Similarly, the Horse and Fish Markets, established outside the land and water gates, respectively, still retain their names.

In the twelfth century the counts of Holstein built a rival town directly adjacent to the bishop's town, by surrounding some mud flats with a dyke and situating a parish church at its centre. With both towns growing rapidly by expanding trade, each soon added a second parish. In the thirteenth century the burghers of the two towns united and obtained the privileges of a "Free and Hanseatic City." They built their city hall on the bridge connecting the two towns. Later, in the sixteenth century, the bourse and the bank were built next to it, a fitting ruling trinity. The four parishes were protected by a common wall, with one of the tributaries, the Alster, serving as its moat on the west side of the city.

Ever since it became a "Free City" Hamburg has controlled the Elbe river. By progressively deepening and widening its northernmost course, Hamburg transformed it into the main channel. Now, with the harbour and shipyards relocated to the opposite side of this wide channel and visible from a broad promenade on the city side, the Elbe has become a much stronger and more integrated part of the city's image than it was in the Middle Ages. Altogether, in this millennial city there are very few structures built before

1800, far fewer than there are in Boston or Philadelphia. But there can be no doubt of the city's continuing identity. The interaction of the inherent element of the site, the two rivers, the outline of the inner city shaped by the wall, and the silhouette have created a strong and unique image. Nobody has planned that image. But each generation, as it changed the city to suit its needs, continued and developed the themes played by its predecessors. It is still the same Hamburg, only more so.

Summary

American cities are rightly concerned about losing their identity by the ruthless destruction of their landmarks. Certainly we should increase our efforts for the preservation of buildings of historical and architectural value. However, it is important to realize that elements other than buildings may be equal or more important factors in the continuity of city form. The natural site is fairly permanent, and it can and should be articulated—made more visible by human action. The astonishing longevity of the street pattern is grounded not only in its increasingly important infrastructure, but even more so in legal notions of property lines in the heads of men; grey matter is harder to move than concrete. The city centre remains in most, though not in all cases, in its original location, strengthened by one transportation system after another. Many districts continue, in ever-changing ways, their characteristic functions.

The words with which Goethe characterizes the human person in the first of his "Orphic Primal Words" entitled "Daimon" may be true of cities as well:

No time, no power ever can dissolve
Created form that living will evolve.

LARRY S. BOURNE AND JAMES W. SIMMONS

Defining the Area of Interest:
Definitions of the City, Metropolitan Areas,
and Extended Urban Regions

Introduction

Every description, analysis, and comparison of the internal structure and growth of cities depends on the validity of the urban definitions employed. Differences in concept and measurement of what is the most appropriate area for study often make comparisons among cities, or of the attributes of areas within any single city, highly suspect. They may even distort our images of spatial patterns and relationships at one point in time.

The first question we must ask is What geographic area is relevant to the study of urban spatial structure? That is, Over what area do the organizing principles that shape the internal structure of cities actually operate? What is, in effect, the "area of interest" in this volume? Most measures of urban growth and change are almost equally vulnerable to definitional differences. Although there is no single solution to these problems, what we need is both a consistent terminology and set of definitions of urban areas as well as an awareness of the effects of modifying those definitions.

One response to the definitional question is to develop a wide spectrum of definitions of the city, each one suitable for different purposes. Then, when patterns and relationships are compared across these differing sets of units we can then evaluate their sensitivity to changes in the size of the areas and the location of boundaries. Ideally this spectrum of urban area definitions should be continuous and additive, with each "nesting" within a larger area. That is, it should be possible to reconstruct any given set of small areal units from the larger basic set and vice versa. In this way flexibility in research is maintained without a greater than necessary loss of information in any artificial subdivision of geographic space.

The Extended City Concept

Most governments and researchers now use some definition of the concept of the "extended" city as a consistent basis for measuring the spatial extent of urban development. In the United States it is the metropolitan statistical area (MSA); in Canada the census metropolitan area (CMA); in Britain the unofficial standard metropolitan labor market area (SMLA) or daily urban system (DUS); in Australia the census expanded urban district; in France the agglomération; in Japan the densely inhabited district (DID) or regional economic cluster

(REC); in West Germany the Stadt region; and in Sweden the labor market area.

All these definitions of extended urban areas share at least three common elements: (1) a minimum population size threshold for designation as a major urban area; (2) a geographic scale large enough to encompass all of the built-up area and small enough to maintain a level of population density that is greater than that which is typical of rural areas in the same region; and (3) the broader area from which a significant proportion of workers are drawn to jobs in the central urban core. The latter effectively delimits the extent of the urban labor market.

The rationale for the widespread application of the concept of an extended city is simply that in most cases the term "city" has become associated with a local political or administrative unit (such as the central city), which is commonly smaller than the area that "functions" as an integrated urban unit. In almost all countries extensive suburban developments have spread far beyond the administrative unit designated as the city. In fact, the existence of such suburbs was recognized in U.S. statistical reports well before the Civil War. Increasingly, in contemporary society, the economy, landscape, and life-styles of an even larger area extending well beyond the limits of the built-up suburbs has become an integral part of the living space and market-place of urban residents, institutions, and firms.

To illustrate the comparative aspects of these definitional questions Table 1 summarizes data on the populations of different urban areas for the United States and Canadian Censuses of 1970 and 1971, respectively. Unfortunately similar statistics from the 1980 and 1981 censuses were not available at the time of writing. Obviously several methods of delimiting urban areas are possible, but it should again be stressed that any relationships specified for one set of urban units do not necessarily carry over to others. In aggregate, however, there is not much disagreement about the total size of the "urban" population in either country, and there is a rather surprising similarity in the average sizes of cities.

The varieties of urban definitions in both countries are worth exploring in detail because of the light they shed on our concepts of the city, of urbanization, and of urbanity and because they provide an essential framework for subsequent papers in this volume. The sections of this paper to follow describe the basic urban definitions used in the United States, and then briefly contrast these first with Canada, and then with Britain.

Approaches to Defining the Urban Areas of the United States

The United States Bureau of the Census pioneered the concept of the extended urban area in its delimitation of the "Metropolitan District" in the Census of 1910. Since that time the concept has been continuously modified and elaborated and in turn has been complemented by a variety of alternative approaches. Probably the best reviews of this evolution of urban definitions are provided in Berry et al. (1968), Berry and Gillard (1977), and Hall and Hay (1978).

THE MUNICIPALITY

The basic spatial building block of every empirical measure of an urban area is the political municipality—the incorporated city, town, township, or corresponding local government area. The simplest approach to defining a city is simply to let the central city—to which place names such as Boston, New York, or Toronto usually refer—represent the entire urban area. Census data compiled for individual households, businesses, and firms are commonly aggregated and published for

Table 1. A Comparison of the Number and Size of Urban Settlements

	United States, 1970			Canada, 1971		
	Number	Total population (in 000s)	Average size	Number	Total population (in 000s)	Average size
Municipalities 10,000 & over	2301[a]	112,451	48,900	207[b]	10,910	52,700
Urbanized areas 50,000 & over	248[c]	118,447	477,600	33[d]	10,754	325,900
Metropolitan areas	243[e]	139,419	573,700	22[f]	11,875	540,000
Urban population	—	149,325[g]	—	—	13,727[h]	—
Total population	—	203,212	—	—	21,568	—

[a] Defined as incorporated urban places. United States, Bureau of the Census, *Census of Population,* 1970, Vol. I, "Characteristics of the Population," Summary, Section I. Table 6.

[b] Defined as incorporated cities, towns, and villages. Canada, Statistics Canada, *1971 Census of Canada,* Bulletin 1.1-8, Table 7.

[c] Includes a central city of 50,000 or more plus surrounding areas that are closely settled, both incorporated and unincorporated. United States, *op. cit.,* Table 20.

[d] Includes the urbanized cores of census metropolitan areas and census agglomerations. Canada, *op. cit.,* Bulletin 1.1-8, Tables 8 and 9.

[e] Standard Metropolitan Statistical Area in 1970 included a central city of 50,000 or more, plus adjacent counties within the laborshed. United States, *op. cit.,* Table 5.

[f] Census Metropolitan Area in 1971 included an urbanized core of 100,000 plus adjacent laborsheds. Canada, *op. cit.,* Bulletin 1.1-8, Table 8.

[g] Includes residents of incorporated and unincorporated places of 2,500 or more plus the urban fringe of urbanized areas. United States, *op. cit.,* Table 3.

[h] Includes population living in incorporated cities, towns, and villages with a population of 1,000 or over; unincorporated places of 1,000 or over having a population density of at least 1,000 per square mile; the built-up fringes of the above having a minimum population of 1,000 and a density of at least 1,000 per square mile. Canada, *op. cit.,* Bulletin 1.1-9, Table 10.

these units, and additional statistics derived by local and state authorities are frequently only available for such municipal areas. The popular press often uses these statistics without even an acknowledgment of the area involved.

The difficulties with the politically defined municipality as a unit of analysis are threefold. Central cities are usually poor fits to most working definitions of the city as a social, economic, or environmental unit: Most often they are under-bounded in that they exclude extensive suburban and exurban areas that are closely integrated with the central city. In less frequent cases, such as Santa Fe or Phoenix, they may be overbounded in that they include vast undeveloped areas. Equally serious is the propensity of some state and local governments to alter these boundaries frequently by annexation of surrounding areas, or on occasion, by the marriage or integration of several municipalities into some form of metropolitan area, regional government, or urban district. The examples of Dade County (Miami), Nashville, Seattle, and the Twin Cities area (Minneapolis–St. Paul) are now well documented. Most major British and Canadian cities, Greater London and Metro Toronto, for instance, now have a two-tier governmental structure of some kind that includes both local governments and a new regional-level government.

Finally, because municipalities are so frequently only partial representations of a laborshed, they can easily generate quite misleading impressions when statistics are calculated. Specialized local municipalities, such as an industrial suburb, an old inner city, or a wealthy residential suburb, will appear as extreme points in any comparative analysis—with characteristics quite unlike those of the larger metropolitan area. It is perhaps only when political variables—such as the distribution of government expenditures or fiscal relationships—are involved, that legal municipalities become a viable definitional unit for urban analysis in their own right, and even these units must be seen as a partner in the larger fiscal system of which that municipality is an integral part.

THE URBANIZED AREA

The most obvious response to the above difficulties has been to define a geographically broader and more functionally based concept of the city. One of the earliest of these concepts, the "urbanized area," was first applied in the U.S. Census of 1950. It is the simplest approximation of the extended urban area concept and the most widely used because of its visual and statistical appeal. Its definition is jointly based on a minimum population size threshold and on the extent of urban land use development. More specifically, in the 1980 U.S. Census User's Guide, the following criteria were used to determine the eligibility and geographic extent of urbanized areas:

1. an incorporated place and adjacent densely settled territory with a combined population of 50,000 or more;
2. the surrounding densely-settled territory consisting of:
   1) contiguous incorporated areas having:
      a) a population of 2,500 or more;
      or b) a population density of 1,000 per square mile or a cluster of 100 housing units;
   2) contiguous unincorporated areas which are connected by road and have a population density of at least 1,000 per square mile;
   3) other contiguous unincorporated areas with a population density of less than 1,000 per square mile but which meet other criteria (e.g., eliminating an enclave);
   4) large concentrations of non-residential land uses (e.g., industrial parks) which have at least one quarter of their boundary contiguous to an urban area.

In addition there are a host of operating rules that have evolved to cover various special cases as well as more specific criteria dealing with such issues as the length of road connections and allowable distances between parts of the built-up area. The most difficult questions relate to the determination of whether or not gaps in the developed landscape have become sufficiently large to preclude their designation as part of one built-up area.

The urbanized area thus embraces the bulk of the built environment of urban areas and of its economic activities (see Table 1). It is particularly useful for cross-sectional comparisons of environmental and land use variables in any given census year, and it is of interest for land use planning purposes. However, precisely because it is delimited by the most rapidly changing boundary in an urban area—the built-up fringe—it tends to be very volatile over time. The real urbanized area boundary changes much more quickly than do census definitions (usually revised every 10 years), and the complex form of the boundary itself makes it largely incompatible with other data sources. By 1980, for instance, the urbanized area for most cities as defined in 1970, already excludes the areas of most rapid physical development and social change within a metropolitan region —the new suburban fringe.

THE METROPOLITAN
STATISTICAL AREA

The next alternative unit of urban aggregation is the "Metropolitan Area," a concept introduced over 60 years ago, which has weathered a number of changes in definition and application. The general concept of a metropolitan area is one ". . . of a large population nucleus, together with adjacent communities which have a high degree of economic and social integration with that nucleus." The definitions used in 1970 were, as in the past, based on three basic requirements: a minimum urban population size, a measure of spatial integration, and a degree of "metropolitan character." The Standard Metropolitan Statistical Area or SMSA as defined in 1970 included (1) a central city, (2) a central county, and (3) the outlying counties that are formally linked with the central city. In the New England states, metropolitan areas were composed of cities and towns rather than counties.

Although the detailed definitions remain essentially as they were in the 1970 Census (Figure 1), preparations for the 1980 Census resulted in innumerable minor adjustments and a few major changes to the basic building blocks and the definitional criteria. At the lowest level, the incorporated local municipality, boundary changes were frequent. For example, nearly 60 percent of all such municipalities annexed territory between 1970 and

1977. Similarly, a number of county boundaries have changed since 1970, through annexation or through the creation of new independent cities. To reduce the possibility of confusion, "unincorporated places" recognized in 1970 and earlier censuses will henceforth be referred to as "census designated places" to emphasize that they are statistical "creatures" of the Census Bureau.

Significant modifications also occurred in the designation of metropolitan areas in 1980. To meet the needs of various interest groups for more flexible definitions, three sets of areas were designated:

1. Metropolitan statistical areas (MSA)
2. Primary metropolitan statistical areas (PMSA)
3. Consolidated metropolitan statistical areas (CMSA)

These were further classified into four levels based on population size: Level A with 1,000,000 or more; Level B with 250,000 to 1,000,000; Level C with 100,000 to 250,000; and Level D with less than 100,000.

Primary metropolitan statistical areas (PMSA) were designated in areas with over 1 million population (Level A) in recognition of the existence of tightly integrated units within larger statistical units. They represent ". . . a large urbanized county or cluster of counties that demonstrates very strong internal economic and social links." When PMSAs are defined, the larger area of which they are component parts is as a result designated as a consolidated metropolitan statistical area (CMSA). In addition, any metropolitan area recognized as a separate metropolitan statistical area prior to 1980, but now part of a consolidated statistical area, will continue to be recognized as a primary statistical area if at a minimum it contains a central county of at least 100,000 population and if there is a relatively low level of commuting

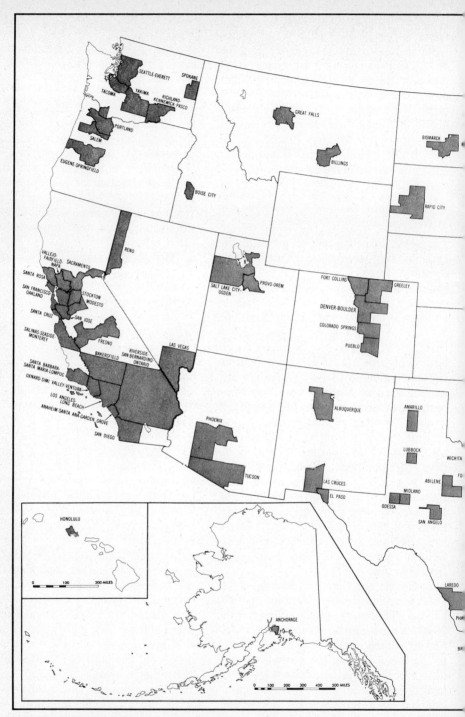

Figure 1. Standard Metropolitan Statistical Areas, as Defined by the
Federal Office of Statistical Policy and Standards, 1979

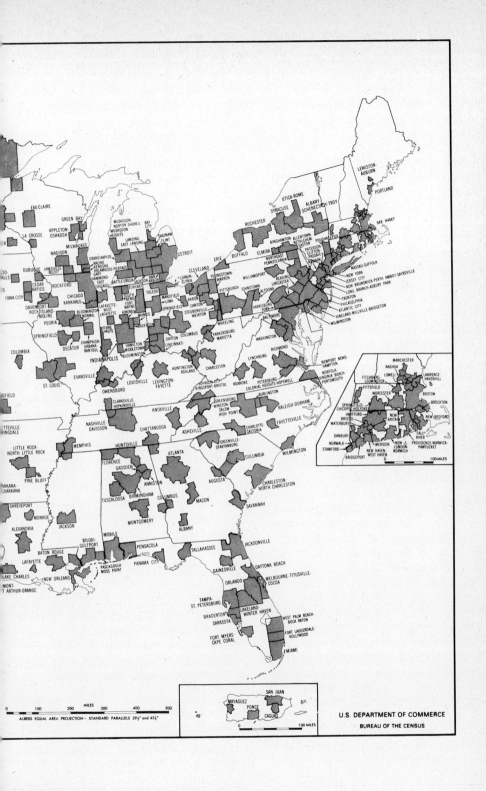

LEWISTON-AUBURN
PORTLAND
SEE INSET
UTICA-ROME
SYRACUSE
ALBANY-SCHENECTADY-TROY
ROCHESTER
BINGHAMTON ALLENTOWN
BETHLEHEM EASTON
POUGHKEEPSIE
BUFFALO ELMIRA NORTHEAST PATERSON-CLIFTON-PASSAIC
ERIE WILLIAMSPORT PENNSYLVANIA NEWARK
CLEVELAND READING NASSAU-SUFFOLK
YOUNGSTOWN- LANCASTER NEW YORK
LORAIN- WARREN JERSEY CITY
ELYRIA PITTSBURGH JOHNSTOWN ALTOONA NEW BRUNSWICK-PERTH AMBOY-SAYREVILLE
WHEELING HARRISBURG- LONG BRANCH-ASBURY PARK
YORK TRENTON
BALTIMORE PHILADELPHIA
STEUBENVILLE- ATLANTIC CITY
WEIRTON VINELAND-MILLVILLE-BRIDGETON
WASHINGTON WILMINGTON

EAU CLAIRE
GREEN BAY
APPLETON- LA CROSSE OSHKOSH
MILWAUKEE
MADISON MUSKEGON-NORTON SHORES MUSKEGON HEIGHTS BAY CITY
DUBUQUE JANESVILLE- GRAND RAPIDS LANSING EAST LANSING SAGINAW FLINT
BELOIT RACINE KENOSHA KALAMAZOO-PORTAGE
CEDAR ROCKFORD GARY EAST EAST CHICAGO BATTLE CREEK JACKSON ANN ARBOR DETROIT
RAPIDS HAMMOND ELKHART
IOWA CITY CHICAGO SOUTH BEND TOLEDO
DAVENPORT- KANKAKEE FORT LIMA MANSFIELD
ROCK ISLAND- LAFAYETTE WAYNE SPRINGFIELD AKRON CANTON
MOLINE BLOOMINGTON- WEST MUNCIE KOKOMO
PEORIA NORMAL LAFAYETTE DAYTON COLUMBUS PARKERSBURG-
SPRINGFIELD TERRE HAUTE ANDERSON MARIETTA
COLUMBIA DECATUR CHAMPAIGN- HAMILTON- MIDDLETON CINCINNATI WHEELING
URBANA- INDIANAPOLIS BLOOMINGTON RICHMOND
RANTOUL
EVANSVILLE HUNTINGTON- CHARLESTON LYNCHBURG
ST. LOUIS OWENSBORO LOUISVILLE LEXINGTON- ASHLAND NEWPORT NEWS-
FAYETTE KINGSPORT-BRISTOL ROANOKE HAMPTON
PETERSBURG- NORFOLK
CLARKSVILLE- JOHNSON CITY- COLONIAL HEIGHTS-HOPEWELL VIRGINIA BEACH-
HOPKINSVILLE KNOXVILLE BURLINGTON PORTSMOUTH
NASHVILLE- GREENSBORO- RALEIGH-DURHAM
DAVIDSON WINSTON-
ATTEVILLE- CHATTANOOGA ASHEVILLE SALEM HIGH POINT FAYETTEVILLE
RINGDALE CHARLOTTE-
LITTLE ROCK- HUNTSVILLE GASTONIA WILMINGTON
NORTH LITTLE ROCK GREENVILLE-
MEMPHIS FLORENCE SPARTANBURG
ARKANA- ATLANTA COLUMBIA
EXARKANA PINE BLUFF GADSDEN
ANNISTON AUGUSTA
SHREVEPORT TUSCALOOSA BIRMINGHAM CHARLESTON-
MONROE COLUMBUS MACON NORTH CHARLESTON
JACKSON
ALEXANDRIA MONTGOMERY SAVANNAH
ALBANY
BILOXI- MOBILE
LAFAYETTE GULFPORT PENSACOLA JACKSONVILLE
BATON ROUGE TALLAHASSEE
LAKE CHARLES PASCAGOULA- PANAMA CITY
MONT- NEW ORLEANS MOSS POINT GAINESVILLE DAYTONA BEACH
T ARTHUR-ORANGE ORLANDO MELBOURNE-TITUSVILLE-COCOA
TAMPA- LAKELAND-
ST. PETERSBURG WINTER HAVEN
BRADENTON WEST PALM BEACH-
SARASOTA BOCA RATON
FORT LAUDERDALE-
FORT MYERS- HOLLYWOOD
CAPE CORAL MIAMI

MANCHESTER
NASHUA
FITCHBURG- LOWELL LAWRENCE
LEOMINSTER HAVERHILL
PITTSFIELD WORCESTER BOSTON
SPRINGFIELD-HOLYOKE BROCKTON
CHICOPEE NEW NEW BEDFORD
HARTFORD BRITAIN FALL
BRISTOL RIVER
WATERBURY MERIDEN NEW PROVIDENCE-WARWICK-
DANBURY LONDON- PAWTUCKET
NORWALK NEW HAVEN- NORWICH
STAMFORD WEST HAVEN
BRIDGEPORT
100 MILES

MILES
0   100   200   300   400   500
ALBERS EQUAL AREA PROJECTION – STANDARD PARALLELS 29½° and 45½°

SAN JUAN
MAYAGUEZ
PONCE
CAGUAS
100 MILES

U.S. DEPARTMENT OF COMMERCE

BUREAU OF THE CENSUS

(less than 50 percent) to jobs outside the county. It is also argued that local opinion must strongly be in favor of the recognition of separate PMSAs.

The *Metropolitan statistical area* (MSA) is now defined on the basis of the following criteria:

A. Population size: each MSA must include at least one central city with at least 50,000 population, *or* an urbanized area of at least 50,000 *and* a total MSA population of 100,000. Smaller cities can be included under certain specific conditions.
B. Central county: the remainder of the county (or counties) to which the central city belongs. These are counties in which at least one-half the population lives in the urbanized area.
C. Outlying counties: in addition to the central county (or counties), an MSA may include one or more outlying and adjacent counties, depending on the level of commuting of its resident workers to the central county-(ies) and the degree of "metropolitan character." The specific requirements on the level of commuting must include one of the following:
   (1) At least 50 percent of the employed workers residing in the county commute to the central county and the population density is at least 25 persons per square mile.
   (2) From 40 to 50 percent commute and the population density is at least 35 persons per square mile.
   (3) From 25 to 45 percent commute and the population density is at least 50 persons per square mile or at least 35 percent of the population is classified as urban.
   (4) From 15 to 25 percent commute, the population density is at least 50 persons per square mile, and the county must also meet two of the following:

a) The population density must be at least 60 persons per square mile.
b) At least 35 percent of the population must be classed as urban.
c) Population growth between 1970 and 1980 must be at least 20 percent.
d) A significant portion of the population (at least 10 percent or 5,000 persons) must live within the urbanized area.

An example of the construction of a metropolitan area from the smallest urban spatial unit, the city block, is provided in Figure 2.

These criteria resulted in the identification (as of 1978) of 34 new MSAs over the 247 (including four in Puerto Rico) defined for the 1970 Census (Figure 1). Over 100 of these initial 247 MSAs have been redefined and expanded by the addition of one or more counties (or towns in New England), while in a few cases others have been reduced in size or merged with adjacent areas.

In recognition of the fact that entire metropolitan areas in close proximity can be closely integrated, the 1960 and 1970 Censuses designated two standard consolidated areas (SCAs) each combining two or more individual SMSAs.

1. New York–North Eastern New Jersey (including the New York SMSA, Newark SMSA, Jersey City SMSA, and Paterson-Clifton-Passaic SMSA, as well as adjoining counties);
2. Chicago–Northwestern Indiana (including the Chicago SMSA and Gary–Hammond–East Chicago SMSA).

In planning for the 1980 Census this concept was extended as the *consolidated metropolitan statistical area* (CMSA).[1]

1. The other areas designed as potential CMSAs in the *Statistical Reporter* of August, 1980 in-

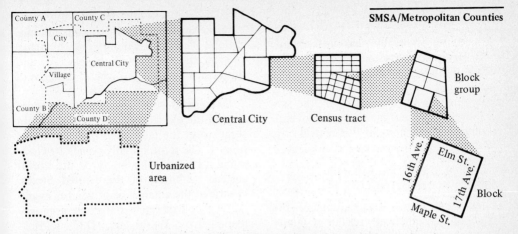

Figure 2. The Building Blocks in U.S. Metropolitan Area Definitions, 1980

The two initial SCAs were redefined and retitled, and (as of 1975) eleven new areas were added. Each of these new CMSAs or consolidated areas was defined as consisting of an MSA of at least 1 million population plus one or more adjoining MSAs linked to it by continuously developed and high density population corridors and/or by extensive inter-metropolitan commuting. The intention of these new CMSAs, as in the case of the earlier SCAs, was not to replace their component metropolitan areas, but to add to them. Generally pairs of MSAs are considered for consolidation if (1) they have a common boundary, (2) they have a commuting interchange of 15 percent, or (3) their urbanized areas have a common boundary.

EVALUATION

All these criteria, although clearly arbitrary, have the primary effect of includ-

cluded Boston, MA-NH; Buffalo, NY; Cincinnati, OH-KY-IN; Cleveland, OH; Dallas, TX; Dayton, OH; Denver, CO; Detroit, MI; Hartford, CT; Houston, TX; Indianapolis, IN; Los Angeles, CA; Miami, FL; Milwaukee, WI; Minneapolis, MN; Philadelphia, PA-NJ-DE; Pittsburgh, PA; Portland, OR-WA; San Francisco, CA; Seattle, WA; Tampa, FL.

ing most of the commuting area or labor shed of the central county, as well as that of the central city, within the MSA. In total, this set of definitions has both strengths and weaknesses, largely stemming from the same source: the simplicity of the county as the basic building block. On the one hand the county is often a crude or unwieldy spatial unit that bears little or no relationship to the way the landscape is organized. In some Western counties (e.g., San Bernardino in California) an enormous area, stretching for hundreds of miles, is covered. A small urban center located in one corner of a county, but linked to an adjacent and larger central city may result in the whole area being included in MSA. In other instances, particularly in the Northeast, the county is inappropriate for designating the boundaries between adjacent urban centers, the cores of which may be only a few miles apart, as in most of New England.

On the other hand, the very crudeness of the metropolitan area delimitation makes them relatively stable over time. They can be more readily linked to other data sources and thus are useful for a wide variety of purposes. These units are also able to absorb and display the effects of decentralization over an extended geographic area. Consequently they have developed into useful information recording units for such purposes as marketing research, housing assessments, labor force studies, and economic base analyses, precisely because they approximate the service area, housing market, and overall labor catchment area of the central city.

THE URBAN FIELD, DAILY URBAN SYSTEM AND MEGALOPOLIS

Beyond the formal designation of the metropolitan statistical area are a family of concepts that define more or less extensive functional urban regions. Among these perhaps the best known are the urban field, the daily urban system, and the megalopolis. The *urban field* concept defines a vast urban region, usually much larger than the metropolitan area, which is essentially the space used by urban residents for their daily (commuting) and weekly (including recreational) activities. The concept, as initially outlined by Friedmann and Miller (1965), reflects both the spread of urban influence outward from the metropolis and the changing life-styles of its residents.

Data gathered on commuting patterns for the first time in the 1960 U.S. Census permitted a detailed exploration of part of the urban field concept. The first comprehensive nationwide examination of these daily trip patterns, by Brian Berry and his associates for 1960 (Berry *et al.,* 1968) and for 1970 (Berry and Gillard, 1977), suggested that the nation could be treated, for most purposes, as fully urbanized. When smaller urban centers of 25,000 population were added to the adjacent metropolitan areas to which they were closely linked, almost every populated area was included within one commuting field or another. To these fields the name *daily urban systems,* initially suggested by C. Doxiadis, has been widely applied

(Berry, 1973) to describe not only commuting, but retail, service, and communication patterns. Later work by Huff (1973), Berry and Gillard (1977), and others has confirmed the basic patterns of these broad functional regions.

The broadest and most popular concept of the extended urban region, but in some ways the least useful, is the *megalopolis.* The term, initially coined by Gottmann (1963) in his study of the northeastern seaboard of the United States, described the emergence of what is essentially a consolidated statistical area extending from Washington, D.C., to Boston. Others have employed the concept as a forecast of future continental-scale urban forms in different parts of the world. Subsequent studies, however, suggest that metropolitan areas have not coalesced on such a large scale and that even within the largest consolidated statistical areas individual urban areas have remained relatively independent. This is exactly what the primary metropolitan statistical area defined in the 1980 U.S. Census was designed to measure.

Canadian Urban Definitions

As in the United States, the basic building block in defining extended urban areas in Canada is the smallest political municipality—the city, town, village, or township—that has the legal responsibility to provide local government services. Differences from the U.S. terminology and practice arise first because of the much smaller geographic area that is intensively settled, and second because of the absence of counties as functional entities in several provinces (Newfoundland and the Western provinces) and the peculiar elongated shapes of counties in Quebec. Consequently counties cannot be used to construct metropolitan regions as conveniently or uniformly as in the United States. Statistics Canada has had to define its own census subdivisions (CSDs) for the presentation of areal data and the delimitation of functional urban regions.

Canada has also been the scene of extensive municipal government reorganization, which has altered the traditional meaning of many urban terms and the nature of the basic municipal blocks. The City of Toronto, for example, is now simply one borough among six comprising the regional municipality of Metro Toronto. Other cities, such as Ottawa, Hamilton, Niagara and Sudbury, are examples of even more dramatic municipal reorganizations that have integrated urbanized cores and extensive rural hinterlands. Western cities, such as Saskatoon, Edmonton and Calgary, on the other hand, have opted for extensive annexation.

Since 1961 Statistics Canada has defined two types of extended urban areas to compensate for this complexity and to ensure compatibility in data sources (Ricour-Singh, 1972). These two areas are

1. The census agglomeration (CA) for delimiting urban centres of less than metropolitan size; and
2. the census metropolitan area (CMA).

Although the purpose of these two has always been approximately the same, their delineation in the past has been quite different. The focus of the former has traditionally been on the presence of a continually built-up or urbanized area that meets certain standards of size and density. To qualify as a CA in the 1971 and 1976 censuses, an area must consist of two adjacent municipalities with an urbanized core of at least 2,000 population and a population density of 1,000 per square mile (385/km²). Those CAs with an urbanized core of 100,000 population or more became census metropolitan areas (CMAs).

For the 1981 Census, the definition of the CA was completely revised, given the availability of data on commuting, for the first time, from the 1971 Census (Parenteau, 1978). These changes made the CA equivalent to the CMA in all but population size. The CAs are now defined as the main labour market area of an urbanized core or continuously built-up area having between 10,000 and 100,000 population. They contain

1. Municipalities or census subdivisions completely or partly inside the urbanized core
2. other outlying municipalities, if
   a) at least 40 percent of the employed labour force living in the municipality works in the urbanized core, or
   b) at least 25 percent of the employed labour force working in that municipality lives in the urbanized core.

The definitional criteria for a census metropolitan (CMA) in 1981 are similar to those outlined above for the CA and to the CMA definitions used in 1976. The CMAs are the main labor market area of an urbanized core having 100,000 or more people, and are comprised of municipalities (or census subdivisions) as defined under 1 and 2 above. Other census subdivisions may be included to maintain the spatial continuity of the designated urban area. The CMA typically consists of four parts: (1) an urbanized core consisting of (a) the largest city and (b), where applicable, a remainder consisting of built-up parts of surrounding municipalities or CSDs in which no discontinuity exceeds 1.6 kilometers; and (2) surrounding municipalities or CSDs consisting of (a) an urban fringe and (b) a rural or an undeveloped fringe. In some instances the city boundary through annexation may be equivalent to that of the CMA (e.g., Calgary).

Applying these criteria to 1976 Census data produced 88 census agglomerations and 23 metropolitan areas. The revisions to the CA definitions for 1981 resulted in the exclusion of 23 CAs as defined in 1971 and the addition of 23 new CAs. The numbers of both CAs and CMAs will likely remain the same when the 1981 Census is published.

The Canadian metropolitan area as a result, although it also emphasizes the main labor market area concept, tends to be both smaller in area and more precisely bounded than its American counterpart. If appropriately defined for a particular problem, the CMA is a consistent and useful unit; but the inflexibility of the definitional criteria makes it difficult to adopt for the study of different kinds of problems or to analyze urban growth over time. Moreover, little work has been done in Canada to develop urban-centred regions similar to those in the United States, although other types of regionalizations have been attempted (Cameron, Emerson, and Lithwick, 1974; Simmons, 1979). This is understandable perhaps, given the small number (23) and diverse locations of metropolitan areas in Canada and the enormous area of the country that is unsettled. Perhaps the most extensive approach is that used by Simmons (1979) in his study of the Canadian urban system. He divided the entire country into 124 urban-centred regions on the basis of patterns of interaction and dependency between small centers and their nearest dominant urban or metropolitan center.

British Urban Definitions

To date Britain has not had an official set of census definitions that approximate the concept of the "extended" urban or metropolitan area. In most instances the boundaries of a bewildering array of local authorities, districts, and boroughs, both urban and rural, have sufficed as statistical reporting units. Local govern-

ment reorganization in the 1970s produced a new and extended set of municipal units—the urban conurbations—which go partway toward meeting the need for consistently defined spatial units for statistical reporting purposes. They were, however, neither sufficiently consistent nor spatially extensive to serve the need. Otherwise the identification of spatial units that more closely approximate the extent of urban–economic integration of the British landscape, has primarily depended on large-scale planning regions (e.g., the South East). It has been argued that these regions, given their size and the relatively high density of population throughout the country, particularly in England, are the most appropriate units for urban research and statistical aggregation. This view has recently been challenged.

One of the first comprehensive attempts at developing a new set of definitions for urban areas in Britain was undertaken in a study by the Political and Economic Planning (PEP) group. Their results were reported in a two-volume report entitled *The Containment of Urban England* (Hall *et al.,* 1973). Using journey-to-work and employment data from the 1961 Census (of England and Wales) this group established two principal types of extended urban units:

1. the Standard Metropolitan Labor Area (SMLA), and
2. the Metropolitan Economic Labor Area (MELA).

The latter area includes the former plus an outer ring of areas more loosely related to the urban core. These definitions were subsequently tested using data from the 1966 and 1971 censuses, and more recently have been extended to include Scotland (Drewett, Goddard, and Spence, 1974; Goddard and Spence 1976). Applying the same criteria in 1971 as in 1961 produced 126 urban labor market areas, compared to 111 in 1961. There was not, unfortunately, and unlike Canada and the United States, a British census in 1976.

THE STANDARD METROPOLITAN LABOR AREA (SMLA)

The SMLA is, as the name suggests, essentially the laborshed of a major urban center. It consists of two parts: (1) a central labor market or core and (2) a surrounding ring of areas strongly linked to the core. The statistical building blocks for these areas are primarily local authorities (municipalities). Over time new metropolitan areas may emerge from either (1) the growth of a nucleus containing sufficient jobs within the outer rings of the metropolitan cores to warrant its separation as a new SMSA or (2) where the growth of free-standing towns passes the population and job thresholds for inclusion as an urban core.

The core areas were defined on the basis of three basic criteria (and a long list of special cases):

1. The density of jobs in a local authority area must exceed 5 per acre (2.12 per hectare);
2. the total number of jobs in those areas constituting the core must exceed 20,000; and
3. local authorities designated as part of the same core must be geographically contiguous.

The criterion for inclusion as part of the metropolitan ring of an urban core is straightforward: a local authority area is so classified if over 15 percent of its resident and economically active population works in the corresponding labor core. Those authorities classified as part of the same ring must be contiguous, either with each other or with the core. The final threshold for inclusion of an urban nucleus as an SMLA is that the combined population of the core and ring must exceed 70,000.

THE 1981 CENSUS DEFINITIONS

At the time of writing, the concept of the functional urban region underlying the SMLA and MELA definitions, after further refinements and extensions, has almost become an official part of governmental data reporting procedures. Drawing on work undertaken by the Centre for Urban and Regional Development Studies (CURDS) at the University of Newcastle-upon-Tyne, agreement has been reached to include a nationwide system of functional urban regions (designated as daily urban systems) in the 1981 Census. Detailed descriptions of the proposed system are provided in Coombes et al. (1978, 1979, 1980).

Although similar in broad outline to the metropolitan area designations used in the U.S. Census, including the emphasis on criteria relating to employment and commuting to work, a number of important differences have been introduced. These differences arise in part because of the types of data and building blocks used, but more importantly because of the size and historical complexities of the British conurbations. The inability of uniform statistical delimitations to compensate for a high density of interactions between adjacent and overlapping urban labor markets, the multinodal character of many urban agglomerations, and the differing travel habits of well-established social classes has raised serious questions regarding the utility of such systems. The U.S. census, as noted above, has responded to many of the same difficulties by defining a primary metropolitan statistical area within the larger consolidated urban regions. But in Britain the scale of the definitional problem is relatively greater.

To accommodate these problems the CURDS study proposed a classification system that allows for a multitude of criteria of urban activity levels and a hierarchy of urban regions and for a distinction between dominant and subdominant

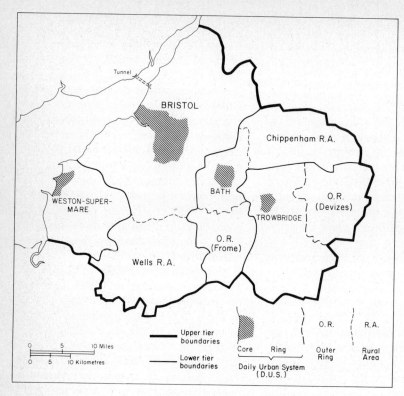

Figure 3. Bristol Metropolitan City Region (after Coombes **et al.**, 1980)

employment centers. Britain was to be divided into 200 functional regions within 75 large city regions. Each functional region consists of as many as four separate parts. Each has a central core surrounded by a suburban or hinterland ring from which many of the residents commute to work in the core. Combined, the core and the hinterland ring form the "daily urban system" (or DUS). Some of the larger regions also have an outer ring in which commuting linkages are less strong and a residual of rural areas that happen to fall within the boundaries of the administrative or statistical building blocks used.

An example of these definitions is provided for the Bristol city region in Figure 3.[1] Note that the classification system

is a hierarchical one. The upper-tier delimitation of the Bristol metropolitan region comprises four lower-tier functional city regions, one (Bristol) of which is classified as dominant, the other three (Weston-Super-Mare, Bath and Trowbridge) as subdominant. These four city regions include an urban core and ring—the daily urban system—and (except for Weston-Super-Mare) an outer suburban ring and adjoining rural area.

Conclusions

Each of these extended urban area definitions has its own advantages and disadvantages. Among the latter perhaps the most important is that each step in ex-

1. Valuable comments were provided on this section of the paper by M. Coombes and

A. Champion of the University of Newcastle-upon-Tyne.

tending the definitional boundaries of the city and the urban area deflates the emphasis given by aggregate statistics to changes within the structure of the older and more densely settled parts of the region. Each extension also introduces a slightly different set of relationships than those contained within preceding delimitations and thus obscures relationships evident only at other smaller scales.

Despite this complexity and the fact that definitional discussions can be boring, urban boundaries are important. We do need consistently defined urban areas for statistical reporting purposes. Extended urban area definitions also play an essential part in understanding and monitoring complex changes in the spatial organization of our cities and of an urbanized society as a whole. Some readers may dispute the need for "formal" urban boundaries and express concern that such boundaries will restrict our analyses. Yet published data sources, such as those of census agencies, do shape our images of what cities are like and how they are changing. In fact they largely predetermine "the area of interest" in our research on urban structure, life-styles, and growth.

A few brief examples will suffice to illustrate the practical significance of the definitional problem, examples that often emerge in the policy concerns identified by municipal governments or local planning agencies. A narrow central city definition commonly delimits only a small portion of the urban landscape, a portion in which there is relatively little new development, frequently a declining population, an older housing stock, and a social environment under stress. The major forms of physical change are a rearrangement of uses within the existing stock or the redevelopment of existing uses.

In contrast, any description or assessment of changes within the entire urbanized or built-up area includes a much greater variety of land uses, built infra-structure, neighborhood types, and more generally a greater mix of processes of change. At this scale the broad-brush models of land use and residential change hypothesized by many authors in this volume become more relevant. The focus of interest has shifted primarily to what is new, to the settling in of neighborhoods, the intensification of uses, and the provision of social services in new suburban areas. Clearly, in terms of the total land area, capital investments, and the number of families or economic activities involved, these changes are of greater significance than the more visually striking decay or redevelopment of the core.

The daily urban system includes an even larger land area, much of it essentially undeveloped, but which is nonetheless strongly affected by the urban core. Significant processes visible at this geographic scale include extensive commuting and migration flows; haphazard development in the urban fringe, land speculation, and the replacement of agriculture by recreational facilities for urban residents and exurbanites. Policy concerns also differ. In addition to those identified above, they include land use regulation, agricultural land preservation, and the conservation of natural resources.

Thus, each geographic scale generates a somewhat different image of urban spatial structure. Each captures a unique mix of processes of change and brings forth its own policy issues and policy initiatives. These differences cannot be ignored.

References

Berry, B. J. L. 1973. *Growth Centers in the American Urban System.* Vol. 1. Cambridge: Ballinger.

Berry, B. J. L., Goheen, P. G. and Goldstein, H. 1968. *Metropolitan Area Definition: Reevaluation of Concept and Statistical Practice.* Working Paper No. 28. Washington, D.C.: United States Bureau of the Census.

Berry, B. J. L. and Horton, F. eds. 1970. *Geographical Perspectives on Urban Systems.* Englewood Cliffs, N.J.: Prentice Hall.

Berry, B. J. L. and Lamb, R. 1974. "The Delineation of Urban Spheres of Influence: Evaluation of an Interaction Model." *Regional Studies,* Vol. 8, pp. 185–190.

Berry, B. J. L. and Gillard, Q. 1977. *The Changing Shape of Metropolitan America, 1960–1970. Commuting Patterns Urban Fields and Decentralization Process.* Cambridge, Mass.: Ballinger.

Bourne, L. S. and Simmons, J. W. eds. 1978. *Systems of Cities.* New York: Oxford University Press.

Canada, Statistics Canada, 1979. "Census Agglomerations: Revision of the Concept and Criteria for the 1981 Census," *Working Paper No. 10*–Geo 79, Ottawa.

Cameron, D., Emerson, D. L. and Lithwick, N. H. 1974. "The Foundations of Canadian Regionalism," *Discussion Paper 11,* Economic Council of Canada, Ottawa.

Coombes, M. G. *et al.* 1978. "Towards a More Rational Consideration of Census Areal Units: Daily Urban Systems in Britain," *Environment and Planning A,* Vol. 10, pp. 1179–1185.

Coombes, M. G. *et al.* 1979. "Daily Urban Systems in Britain: From Theory to Practice," *Environment and Planning A,* Volume 11, pp. 565–574.

Coombes, M. G. *et al.* 1980. "Functional Regions for the 1981 Census of Britain: A User's Guide to the CURDS Definitions," *Discussion Paper 30,* CURDS, University of Newcastle-upon-Tyne, England.

Drewett, R., Goddard, J. and Spence, N. 1974. "Urban Change in Britain: 1966–71," *Working Paper No. 1,* Department of Geography, London School of Economics and Political Science.

Friedmann, J. and Miller, J. 1965. "The Urban Field," *Journal of the American Institute of Planners,* Vol. 31, pp. 312–320.

Goddard, J. and Spence, N. 1976. "British Cities: Urban Population and Employment Trends 1951–71," Department of Environment *Research Report No. 10,* London.

Gottmann, J. 1963. *Megalopolis.* New York: Twentieth Century Fund.

Hall, P. *et al.* 1973. *The Containment of Urban England.* Vol. 1. London: Allen and Unwin.

Hall, P., Hansen N. and Swain, H. 1975. "Urban Systems: A Comparative Analysis of Structure, Change and Public Policy," *Research Memorandum RM-75-35.* Laxenburg, Austria: International Institute for Applied Systems Analysis.

Hall, P. and Hay, D. 1978. *European Urban Systems.* Department of Geography, Reading University.

Huff, D. 1973. "The Delineation of a National System of Regions on the Basis of Urban Spheres of Influence," *Regional Studies,* Vol. 7, pp. 323–329.

Linge, G. J. R. 1965. *The Delimitation of Urban Boundaries.* Canberra: Australian National University.

Neutze, M. 1977. *Urban Development in Australia.* Sydney: Allen and Unwin.

Parenteau, R. F. 1978. *Census Metropolitan Areas: Revision of the Delineation Criteria.* Working Paper No. 7–GEO 78. Ottawa: Statistics Canada.

Phillips, P. D. 1976. "The Changing Standard Metropolitan Statistical Area," *Journal of Geography,* Vol. 75, pp. 165–173.

Ricour-Singh, F. 1972. "Census Metropolitan Areas: Revision of the Concept, Criteria and Delineations for the 1971 Census," Statistics Canada, Ottawa (mimeo).

Simmons, J. W., 1977. "The Canadian Urban System: an Overview." *Research Paper No. 104,* Centre for Urban and Community Studies. University of Toronto.

Thompson, G. 1975. "United States Census County Divisions as a Geographical Data Base," *Professional Geographer,* Vol. 27, pp. 467–469.

U.S. Department of Commerce, Bureau of Census, 1980. *Census 1980: Introduction to Products and Services.* Washington, D.C.: U.S. G.P.O.

U.S. Department of Commerce, Office of Federal Statistical Policy and Standards. 1980. "Metropolitan Statistical Area Classification," *Federal Registrar,* Washington, D.C. January 3, 1980.

Yamaguchi, T. 1980. "The Japanese Urban System," IGU Reports on National Settlement Systems," Commission on National Settlement Systems, Tokyo.

YI-FU TUAN

American Cities: Symbolism, Imagery, and Perception

Image, Experience, and Class[1]

In any large metropolis people of different income and social status live in separate parts of the city. The rich very rarely see the poorer quarters except perhaps on slumming tours inside air-conditioned limousines. They may have a clear mental map of the city but it is largely abstract knowledge. Their own residential areas they know intimately: the rich are as isolated by their wealth in their exclusive compounds as the poor in their slums and ethnic ghettos. The poor know little of the metropolis outside their own districts. They are the urban villagers, suffering many of the city's ills but enjoying few of its compensating amenities. The poor, however, do have a "backstairs" experience of the outside world. When ill they may be taken to a distant hospital for free or low-cost service, and when they run afoul of the law they spend time in a distant reformatory or jail. The poor thus become aware of alien places that seem threatening even when the pur-

1. This reprint excludes the first paragraph of the section in the original text (p. 207).

pose of the institution, as with the hospital, is benign. One result of these alarming, involuntary trips to the outside world may be to increase their awareness of the identity of their own neighborhood. On a day-to-day basis, the female poor know well-to-do residential areas as maids, gaining a perspective on the world of wealth very unlike that of their employers. In contrast to lower-class housing, the front and back regions of middle-class residences are sharply differentiated. The front tends to be tidy and formal, the rear unprepossessing. Social adults enter the house through the front, while the socially marginal—the domestics, delivery men, and children—enter through the rear. In the middle- and upper-class business world, janitors and scrubwomen perceive and work in environments that differ appreciably from those of executives and their retinue of well-pressed assistants. The uniformed workers perceive the small doors that lead to the back regions of business buildings; they see and smell the "guts" of the building exposed in the basement store and heating rooms; they are well aware of the profane trans-

From Yi-Fu Tuan, **Topophilia: A Study of Environmental Perception, Attitudes, and Values,** © 1974, pp. 207–15. Reprinted by permission of Prentice-Hall, Inc., Englewood Cliffs, N.J., and Yi-Fu Tuan.

portation system that moves the dirty cleaning equipment, the large stage props, and themselves.[2]

The upper-middle- and upper-class white American male lives in sylvan suburbia and works in a steel-and-glass tower downtown. The route he traverses daily is the freeway or road that passes through the better residential and business districts. The social character of the parts of the city—nodes and connecting routes—that he experiences in person is essentially homogeneous. Business trips take him to other towns but the places he visits are of the same general physical and social character. Vacations to Europe lead him to urban milieus that are different only superficially if he continues to circulate at the same socioeconomic level. True novelty is jarring, even painful; the pleasant vacation combines the security of the familiar with mere tokens of adventure. What is true of the well-to-do probably holds also for the less affluent middle and lower-middle classes: their experiences of the city are tied to places that, however physically distinctive, tend to have similar social standing. Descent to quarters of a lower level occur as infrequent visits—to shop for specialty foods and to eat in ethnic restaurants. The emphasis here is on the very narrow range of urban experience for most city dwellers. When a family moves into a new town there is usually a brief period of exploration to become oriented to the larger setting, to locate the shopping areas, and decide on the shortest and most pleasant paths between home and places of work. But soon a routine is established that deviates very little from one work week to the next.

Perhaps a member of the professional middle class—a doctor, lawyer, or journalist—has greater opportunity to experience a broad range of environments and

cultures than either the very rich or poor. William Stringfellow noted with surprise this unexpected bonus of freedom when, as a young graduate of Harvard Law School, he went to Harlem to live, to work as a lawyer, to take part in neighborhood politics, and to be a layman in the local church. He lived in the slum but as a well-educated white man he was not bound to the environment. In suburbia he might have submitted to its mores but in Harlem he was free and able to transcend barriers that otherwise separated people. In the course of a day, Stringfellow might spend the morning in court with an addict, then have lunch with a law professor at Columbia, "interview clients back at 100th Street during the afternoon, have a drink with some of Harlem's community leaders at Frank's Chop House on 125th Street, have dinner with clergy friends or with fellow parishioners at a midtown restaurant, stop for a bull session with some law students or seminarians, or spend the evening talking with friends from the Harlem neighborhood." Or he might "return to the tenement to read or write; or, more often than not, do a little more work in rehabilitating the place, go out late to get the *Times,* and visit with people on the street."[3]

St. Clair Drake and Horace Cayton's study of Chicago's black ghetto suggests that the "upper shadies" also experience an exceptionally broad spectrum of life styles. Upper shadies are wealthy blacks who acquired their wealth and the social status in their community that goes with it through illegal means, for example, by operating syndicates that control lottery and gambling. They also establish legal businesses in the ghetto, partly to serve as fronts and partly to earn the approval of respectable citizens. Being black and hence ostracized by the white community, the upper shadies can identify emo-

2. Erving Goffman, *The Presentation of Self in Everyday Life* (Garden City, N.Y.: Doubleday, 1959), pp. 123–24.

3. William Stringfellow, *My People is the Enemy* (Garden City, N.Y.: Doubleday, 1966).

tionally with the ghetto poor; they are recognized by the poor as Race Men, that is, supporters of black causes. Being shady they are familiar with the underground world. Being wealthy they lead lives characteristic of wealth and engage in such social rituals as formal dinners, attending the races, and horseback riding. Upper shadies like to travel, and are continually shuttling between Chicago and New York. They visit friends on the West Coast; they have summer homes in the lake regions of Michigan and northern Illinois, and they vacation in Europe. They thus live and work in a wide range of environments and can transcend many social barriers. Only racial barriers, in the period before the second world war, confined their mobility.[4]

The Urban Neighborhood

RECOGNITION

"Neighborhood" and "community" denote concepts popular with planners and social workers. They provide a framework for organizing the complex human ecology of a city into manageable subareas; they are also social ideals feeding on the belief that the health of society depends on the frequency of neighborly acts and the sense of communal membership. However, Suzanne Keller has shown that the concept of neighborhood is not at all simple.[5] The planner's idea of neighborhood rarely coincides with that of the resident. A district well defined by its physical characteristics and given a prominent name on the city plan may have no reality for the local people. The words "neighborhood" and "district" tend to evoke in the outsider's mind images of simple geometrical shape, when in fact

the channels of neighborly acts that define neighborhood may be extremely intricate and vary from small group to small group living in close proximity. Moreover, the perceived extent of neighborhood does not necessarily correspond with the web of intense neighborly contacts. "Neighborhood" would seem to be a construct of the mind that is not essential to neighborly life; its recognition and acceptance depend on knowledge of the outside world. The paradox can be put another way: residents of a real neighborhood do not recognize the extent and uniqueness of their area unless they have experience of contiguous areas; but the more they know and experience the outside world the less involved they will be with the life of their own world, their neighborhood, and hence the less it will in fact be a neighborhood.

Distinctive neighborhoods have well-defined boundaries that tend to separate them from the mainstream of urban life. They are isolated for economic, social, and cultural reasons. The districts of the extremely wealthy and the extremely poor, the exclusive suburbs and the slums, the racial and immigrant ghettos stand out sharply in the urban mosaic. However, the residents of these locales do not recognize their own uniqueness to the same degree. The very rich are well aware of the bounds of their world: "We keep ourselves to ourselves." Middle-class suburbanites can be even more sensitive of their territorial integrity, for their world, in comparison with that of the established rich, is more vulnerable to invasion by "uppity" outsiders. Colored residents of ghettos are compelled to develop an awareness of their home ground for they encounter unmistakable hostility beyond it. On the other hand, slum dwellers and residents of white ghettos (the quarters of recent European immigrants, for example) may show little appreciation of the fact that they occupy districts of any special character with definable

4. St. Clair Drake and Horace R. Cayton, *Black Metropolis*, II (New York: Harper & Row, 1962), 547.
5. Suzanne Keller, *The Urban Neighborhood* (New York: Random House, 1968).

boundaries. Let us look at these generalizations more closely.

Beacon Hill, Boston, is a famous upper-class neighborhood. For a long time it has been a world to itself, marked off from its contiguous areas by tradition, culture, social standing, and economic power. It is keenly aware of its own distinction, a claim that is widely accepted by outsiders. In self-awareness, in the sense of community based on culture and tradition, Beacon Hill is perhaps matched by certain ethnic quarters; but the psychological differences are very great, since the one seeks isolation through its presumption of superiority whereas the other takes isolation to be the best means to cope with threat. New middle-class suburban communities try to achieve something of Beacon Hill's exclusiveness; but without the sanction of history and tradition they must depend on economic fences or walls of racial prejudice to keep out the undesirable elements. Yet Beacon Hill began as suburbia. After the Revolution upper-class families turned to the then rural and out-of-the-way Beacon Hill district. Moreover, Beacon Hill did not simply grow: it was planned to be a fashionable quarter for people of position and means. For a century and a half it was able to maintain its high status, although next to it a working class quarter (the West End) sprang up to accommodate the successive waves of poor immigrants. The fence that Beacon Hill raised about itself was not simply economic: poor relations and indigent students of the right background could live in it, but high-paying business establishments and exclusive apartment-hotels were not welcome. In the course of time Beacon Hill has become far more than a piece of real estate; it is a symbol for a mellow world that whispers rather forbiddingly of old family lineages, distinguished residents, old family houses, local antiquities, and venerable neighborhood traditions. It is as effective symbol that Beacon Hill, in

the mid-twentieth century, can continue to attract and retain certain upper-class families that would not otherwise live there. Many houses on Beacon Hill belonged to famous people and carry their names. Such domiciles are permeated by the ghostly presence of an illustrious past and can bestow instant standing to people who currently live in them.

Residents of Beacon Hill are keenly aware of their neighborhood identity. The place has a rich literary heritage, and some of the energy for composition seems to have gone into pamphleteering. Articles and pamphlets in profusion have been written by residents of the Hill, extolling its charm and sacredness. Newer communities may wish to advertise themselves likewise, but since they lack the historical reality that begets self-confidence their voices tend to be somewhat shrill. The historical theme in Beacon Hill is not only an objective fact that any scholar can uncover: it lives in the minds of the residents. Two types of organization, formal and informal, contribute to neighborhood solidarity. Formally, the Beacon Hill Association exists to represent the specialized interests of the residents as a whole. Its declared objective is "to keep undesirable business and living conditions from affecting the hill district." Formed on December 5, 1922, the existence of the Association suggests that the informal means for maintaining the Hill's character have not been adequate. It is, however, the informal organizations that give vitality to the neighborhood. In Beacon Hill they center mainly around kinship ties and visiting relationships. Of a less routine and intimate nature are certain annual ceremonies on the Hill. The principal ceremony takes place on Christmas Eve and involves caroling and candle lighting. An old custom, it had lapsed during the Civil War and was revived in the present century. Eventually the ceremony attracted city-wide attention and thousands of outsiders would flock to Beacon Hill on a Christmas Eve to observe and participate. In 1939 an estimated 75,000 persons took part in the carol singing, and nearly all the dwellings on the Hill displayed lighted candles. Such events accentuated local self-awareness and enriched the public image of the neighborhood.[6]

Beacon Hill is an example of a place where the local resident and the outsider tend to agree on its essential character and limits. The resident himself easily acts the role of the passing observer who views the district from a knowledge of the world beyond. Behind the image is the reality of the neighborhood in its historical continuity and cultural distinctiveness, in its formal and informal organization. Few urban districts are communities in all the senses that Beacon Hill is a community. The internal and external images do not normally coincide: the area perceived as neighborhood by the resident is often only a fraction of that perceived by the outsider as homogeneous social space. In a study of West Philadelphia, researchers have found that the area name familiar to social workers and informants was not widely known among the inhabitants, the majority of whom (seven-tenths) considered the area simply as part of West Philadelphia in general. The lack of prestige of the name was possibly a factor in its denial, for in a racially mixed area in the same city the inhabitants of one district might adopt the name of an adjoining district if it had greater prestige.[7] Neighborhood concept seems also a vague spatial idea to the residents of a southern town. Fewer than one out of ten respondents thought of "this part of town" as "having any par-

ticular boundaries or limits." However, 29 percent of the sample could supply some kind of a neighborhood name in response to the question: "If someone you meet elsewhere in Greensboro asks you where you live, what do you tell him?" An equal proportion supplied a street name, but when pressed for a neighborhood designation they were able to provide it.[8]

Boston's West End illustrates the multifaceted and often ambiguous nature of the neighborhood concept. The West End was a working-class district of Italian Americans of the first and second generation, mixed with Irish and Jewish elements that at one time dominated the area. Before its destruction under a Federal renewal program, West End, in both physical characteristics and in the life style of the people, provided a colorful contrast to its neighbor, the high-class Beacon Hill. From the economic, sociological, and cultural points of view both West End and Beacon Hill are clearly defined neighborhoods. But whereas Beacon Hill dwellers are highly conscious of their own culture and geography, this seems less true of West Enders. Trained observers of the West End scene reach conclusions that appear, at first glance, to be contradictory. Fried and Gleicher say that "the sense of the West End as a *local region,* as an area with a spatial identity going beyond (although it may include) the social relationships involved, is a common perception." To the question, "Do you think of your home in the West End as part of a local neighborhood?" eighty-one percent of those interviewed replied in the affirmative.[9]

6. Firey, *Land Use in Central Boston,* pp. 45–48, 87–88, 96.
7. Mary W. Herman, *Comparative Studies of Identification Areas in Philadelphia* (City of Philadelphia Community Renewal Program, Technical Report No. 9, April 1964, mimeographed); quoted in Keller, *Urban Neighborhood,* p. 98.

8. Robert L. Wilson, "Liveability of the City: Attitudes and Urban Development," in F. Stuart Chapin, Jr. and Shirley F. Weiss (eds.), *Urban Growth Dynamics in a Regional Cluster of Cities* (New York: Wiley, 1962), p. 380.
9. Marc Fried and Peggy Gleicher, "Some Sources of Residential Satisfaction in an Urban Slum," *Journal of the American Institute of Planners,* 27, No. 4 (1961), 308.

By contrast, Herbert J. Gans notes that "the concept of the West End as a neighborhood was foreign to the West Enders themselves. Although the area had long been known as the West End, the residents themselves divided it up into many *subareas,* depending in part on the extent to which the tenants in one set of streets had reason or opportunity to use another."[10] Residents of this working-class district never used the term "neighborhood." Until they were threatened with eviction so that the district could be redeveloped, the West End as a neighborhood was not important to them. They lacked interest in it as a physical or social unit. Comments about it were rarely colored by emotion. The imminence of redevelopment made many of them aware of the existence of the West End as a spatial and cultural entity, but few protested its destruction. Some felt sure until the end that while the West End as a whole was coming down, their street would not be taken.[11]

DEGREE OF SPATIAL EXPERIENCE
AND CONCERN

These apparently conflicting views concerning the West Ender's awareness of neighborhood can be reconciled if we recognize the degrees of spatial experience and concern. The middle-class homeowner has an intimate experience of his house. At the same time he has an abstract but intense interest in his neighborhood as a piece of real estate the quality of which directly affects the market value of his house. Beyond economic considerations the homeowner values the neighborhood and will defend its integrity because it represents a desired way of life. The artist or intellectual, like the middle-class homeowner, is keenly aware of the special quality of his district and

will defend it against encroachment. However, he is not likely to possess much property and is more apt to attach value to his neighborhood for aesthetic and sentimental reasons. Herbert Gans observed that in the campaign to save the West End the Italian Americans who participated were limited to a handful of artists and intellectuals.[12] Although the artists and writers shared many of the activities of their age and kin groups in the West End, their talents and careers set them psychologically apart. Through knowing something of the greater world they could see the West End as a whole and value its distinctive traits.

The great majority of West Enders are people of the working class. Their awareness of neighborhood seems to be made up of concentric zones, highlighted in varying degrees by the type and intensity of experience they have of them. The core of awareness centers on the home and the street or a segment of the street. Within this small locale the working class of West End socialize informally with great frequency, generating in time a warmth of feeling for place rarely attained in middle-class communities. Besides the home base working-class people may identify strongly with a few other spots, usually within walking distance of home. These are the favorite recreation areas, the local bars, and perhaps the settlement houses. Sentiment is unromantic and unverbalized but real and pervasive over these fuzzily bounded areas and the web of short linking routes. By contrast, people of the urban middle class are highly selective in the use of space, and the areas familiar to them are far flung. Another difference is that their sense of home has sharp limits. To a middle-class person home may extend to a lawn or garden for which he pays taxes, but beyond it the space is impersonal. As soon as he steps on the street he is in a public

10. Herbert J. Gans, *The Urban Villagers* (New York: Free Press, 1962), p. 11.
11. Ibid., p. 104.

12. Ibid., p. 107.

arena in which he feels little sense of be-
longing. To a working-class man the
boundary between his dwelling and its
immediate environs is permeable. All
channels between dwelling and environment, such as open windows, closed windows, hallways, even walls and floors,
serve as a bridge between inside and outside.[13]

In Boston's West End, territory is differently bounded for different people. To
most residents it is quite small. The
boundary between the dwelling unit and
the street may be highly permeable but
few people venture to include much of
the public realm as their private space.
The street is a common unit of neighborhood sentiment. Politicians recognize this
fact, for when they campaign they not infrequently trim their talks to appeal to
the passions of each street. It is instructive to note that the perceived size of the
neighborhood bears little relation to the
extensiveness of the West End kin- and
friendship net. The conclusion would
seem to be that although sentiment for
place is strongly influenced by the availability and satisfactoriness of interpersonal ties, it does not depend entirely on
the social network.

13. Fried and Gleicher, "Residential Satisfaction," p. 312.

Neighborhood is the district in which
one *feels* at home. Another more abstract
sense of neighborhood is that it is the district one knows fairly well both through
direct experience and through hearsay.
Most West Enders claim familiarity with
a large part or most of West End; and
many have knowledge of contiguous areas.
A quarter of the people interviewed report familiarity with some distant sector
of the Boston region. In other words,
many residents are aware of an inner
world of the West End, surrounded by a
somewhat hostile outer world. We should
not expect the West Enders to be able to
delimit the boundaries on maps, nor that
their inner worlds be much alike. They
have experienced certain differences between their world and what lies beyond,
and their consciousness of these differences is intensified by their perception of
the outside world as not only rich and
powerful, cold and lonely, but threatening. In the mid-fifties the vague sense of
threat turned into reality when plans for
redevelopment were announced. For a
time West Enders became fully conscious
of the unique character of their district,
but (as we have noted earlier) with the
exception of a few intellectuals and artists, their concern for the survival of
West End sufficed to generate only an occasional flurry of uncoordinated protests.

RONALD J. JOHNSTON

Urban Geography: City Structures

Introduction

Kuhn's (1962) model of the progress of scientific disciplines comprises two main components—the relatively long periods of continuity when most research is organized within an accepted paradigm, or basic philosophy methodology, and the occasional interruptions to this continuity when an accumulation of new findings suggests anomalies and demands a new paradigm. Both Haggett and Chorley (1967) and Harvey (1973, chapter 4) have applied this model to human geography, identifying major periods of discontinuity in the early 1960s and the early 1970s respectively. An alternative model suggests that the new approaches which occasionally develop do not lead to overthrow of the existing paradigm. Rather a new branch of the discipline is set up, focusing either on new approaches to traditional subject matter or on new subject matter in the context of accepted philosophies. With time, the radical fervour of such branches becomes spent, and its salient elements are incorporated with the main body of the subject (Mulkay, 1975). This continuity with evolution is stressed by Chisholm (1975) and

its sociology has been essayed by Harvey (1973, chapter 4) and Taylor (1976).

Although there have been major changes in the emphasis of human geography in recent decades, notably away from the humanities with their focus on the past and into the social sciences which are more future-oriented and also in a greater volume of work on urban rather than rural topics, the branching model seems the more valid. Three branches are identifiable in the current literature of urban geography. The first is a quantitative approach to description, based on a nomothetic philosophy in which the geographer's role is to document the spatial organization of society. Its explanatory models are derived in part from those of neoclassical economics, that emphasize price-fixing through competition in free markets and into which the geographer has introduced the extra costs of crossing distance [Berry, Conkling, and Ray (1975) give a useful summary of this position], and also, often only implicitly, from the functional sociology of Talcott Parsons, producing "a demographic notion of social structure" (Pahl, 1967, 223). Second is the so-called behavioural approach, propounded

From **Progress in Human Geography**, Vol. 2, No. 1, 1977, pp. 118–29. Reprinted by permission of Edward Arnold Publishers, Ltd, London, and R. J. Johnston.

in the mid-1960s as an attack on the models of the first branch, and which proposed as an alternative the study of individual activities within their perceived worlds. Finally there is the approach variously termed "radical" and "structuralist" which stresses the constraints that society as a whole, and particularly certain groups within it, imposes on the behaviour of individuals. All three of these have developed as reactions to stimuli from the wider worlds of academia and "reality," and each has developed a concern with inequalities within and between societies; the models of social action which they propose differ widely, however, and are strongly ideological.

All three branches are well represented in the current literature, with each having its own journals (*Environment and Planning* and *Geographical Analysis* for the first, *Environment and Behavior* the second, and *Antipode* the third). The first two now have many of the characteristics of what Kuhn calls "normal science," having been generally accepted as important segments of geographical scholarship and education. The major trends have been set, and the problems isolated; most publications comprise one or more of:

1. Applications of existing theories and methods to a range of locales
2. Sophistication of techniques
3. Articulation of new findings into existing models and theories.

The third branch is much newer and much less accepted (Chisholm, 1975, 175). In this very brief review of the large current literature on city structure, therefore, major emphasis is laid on the novel arguments.

Neoclassical–Functional Description

Description of urban land use patterns in this branch is based on models relating location and accessibility through the price mechanism. It is assumed that lower prices in less accessible places represent a trade-off against increased travel costs, an axiom which has been recently investigated (Ball and Clark, 1975). Most current interest is in the effects of changing land values on particular underprivileged population groups (e.g., Berry, 1975) and in the effects of pollution and other negative externalities on the price of land (Bednarz, 1975; Mercer, 1975); the latter interest reflects an increasing refusion of human and physical geography focusing on environmental issues, with the neoclassical (Berry *et al.*, 1974), the behavioural (Detwyler and Marcus, 1972), and the institutional (Harvey, 1974a) approaches all represented.

Early work in this branch emphasized commercial land use patterns, based on the neoclassical economics of von Thünen, Christaller, and Lösch, but this area is now relatively ignored. Of recent publications, only Wilson's (1976) reinterpretation of Hotelling's classical location model oriented towards consumer welfare (in terms of travel costs) rather than the more usual entrepreneurial profits, and Beavon's (1974a, 1974b, 1975, 1976) applications of Löschian theory to the pattern generally interpreted in Christallerian terms have added new insights.

Urban residential areas continue to attract much research, most of it concerned either with expanding the range of places studied, in both time and space, or with sophistication and criticism of techniques (e.g., Davies, 1975; Giggs and Mather, 1975; Sanders, 1976; Palm, 1976c; van Valey and Roof, 1976; Woods, 1976). In this genre, only the simulation by Taylor and Parkes (1976) of probable social patterns at different times of the day and night carries much novelty effect. Dwyer (1975) has provided a valuable general overview of the literature on Third World squatter settlements, however, and Peach (1976) has edited a collection of major papers on spatial segregation, notably of ethnic groups—an ever-interesting topic (Trlin, 1976). Linked with the study of residential patterns is the analysis of intra-urban migrations; again there has been some modification of existing theory (e.g., Poulsen, 1976). One major study, Pritchard's (1976) thesis on mobility in Leicester over the last century, which shows that mobility rates have declined, has important value for the growing interest in urban historical geography (Ward, 1975, 1976).

Residential areas act as neighbourhood contexts for various forms of socialization, and there has been some debate on the processes and their measurement (Giggs, 1975; Gudgin, 1975; Johnston, 1976b). Patterns of crime and of health related to neighbourhood structures have been reported (Pyle *et al.,* 1974; Corsi and Harvey, 1975; Herbert, 1975; Pyle, 1976) and methods of locating public facilities in neighbourhoods to maximize welfare, according to the neoclassical attribution of accessibility with cheapness and availability, have been sought (e.g., Feldman and Gonen, 1975; Shannon *et al.,* 1975; Wagner and Falkson, 1975; Hodge and Gattrell, 1976; McAllister, 1976; ReVelle *et al.,* 1976). Of considerable interest and novelty has been C. J. Smith's (1976) measurement of the association of neighbourhood type with success rates in the rehabilitation of the mentally ill, with findings which, if repeated elsewhere, may be of considerable value in the planning of health care (see also Wolpert *et al.,* 1975).

Comprehensive models of intra-urban spatial order are of two main types, and both, especially the second, have received attention in the characteristic format of "normal science." The first type are part of the wider field of regional science, with descriptions and predictions based on the "distance minimizing = cost minimizing" equation (Moore, 1973). The other, exemplified by Wilson's (1974)

entropy based models, focuses on interaction patterns within given constraints and attempts to reproduce various flow patterns, usually as an input to transport planning (e.g., Anas, 1975; Evans, 1975a; Batty and March, 1976).

The Behavioural Approach

Workers in this branch criticize the research orientation of the first, which they claim is based on normative assumptions that bear no relationship to the ways in which location decisions are really made, especially regarding the information they are based on and how this is interpreted. Thus the suggested alternative approach focuses on the collection of data about decision-making.

There are two main strands to this work, neither of which has claimed a large amount of research effort. The first is very similar to the neoclassical–functional branch in its methodology, using sophisticated quantitative techniques to analyse large data sets collected from individual respondents. Two particular decisions have been stressed in studies of the internal structure of the city—where to shop and where to live—providing a bank of empirical analyses and techniques, many of them testing hypotheses derived from the neoclassical approach, notably that people aim to travel as short a distance as possible (Cadwallader, 1975; Fingleton, 1975, 1976; Higgs, 1975; Hudson, 1975, 1976; Schneider, 1975; Barrett, 1976; Beck and Wood, 1976; G. C. Smith, 1976; Svart, 1976). Some potentially seminal work is beginning to appear regarding the joint constraints of space and time (Parkes and Thrift, 1975).

Work in the second strand focuses much more on the understanding of individual decisions, and has strong ties with phenomenological and idealism philosophies. The ways in which people experience the world around them are emphasized, in a verbal rather than quantitative presentation (Tuan, 1975, 1976; Hugill, 1975; Buttimer, 1976), although the concept of a mental map has also been investigated by the study of aggregate response patterns (Downs and Stea, 1974). The sources of inspiration are varied, as in Ley's (1974, 1975) work. His monograph on a black neighbourhood in Philadelphia looks at the reactions of its residents to their uncertain environment by way of a model of frontier outposts, derived from Caesar's *Gallic wars*. He portrays the area as the residents do, rather than through the stereotyped white American view, and found that whereas outsiders see the ghetto as a single block of given character, in fact the locals refer to it as a disordered jungle.

Institutional Approaches

The birth of this branch can probably be dated from the events of the 1969 AAG meetings at Ann Arbor, at which the radical journal *Antipode* was launched. A major boost and publicity drive came with Harvey's (1973) book *Social justice and the city,* and there has been fruitful contact with a group of French marxist scholars, some of whose essays have recently been translated (Pickvance, 1976a).

Protagonists of the institutional approaches accuse both of the other two branches of ignoring the realities of human decision-making. The positivism of the neoclassical–functional branch is pilloried because it focuses only on statistical associations between various aspects of the socioeconomic system and presents models which emphasize individual choice regardless of the institutional constraints on this (Gray, 1975; see also the exchange between Boddy, 1975 and Evans, 1975b). Similarly, the behavioural approach is condemned because by studying only the perceived worlds of individuals it ignores the constraints imposed on them by society, and which at best they may well be only dimly aware of. As an alternative, it is argued that the main determinant of locational behaviour is power, particularly economic power, so that geographical analysis has to be firmly based in the relevant political economy: "The structural analysis of capitalism and its various spatial manifestations is the core problem facing geographers" (Gray, 1975, 232).

By far the major focus in this work has been on the operation of urban housing markets. Three types of work can be identified. The first comprises the general essays concerning the structure of capitalist housing markets, in which a series of important essays by Harvey (1973, chapter 5, 1975b, 1975c, 1975d) is outstanding (see also Duncan, 1976; Kirby, 1976). Second, and most numerous, is a series of empirical studies of the roles of different power-holders in determining urban socio-spatial patterns. The activities of speculators and the "property industry" in general (Ambrose and Colenutt, 1975; Davidson, 1975; Carey, 1976; Colenutt, 1976; Johnston, 1976a), and with especial reference to the current inflation of land values and property prices; the roles of private landlords (Elliott and McCrone, 1975), of managers of public housing (Baldwin, 1974, 1975; Harloe *et al.,* 1974; Niner, 1975; Bird, 1976; Byrne, 1976; Gray, 1976), of real estate agents (Palm, 1976a, 1976b), and of the personnel of institutions such as building societies (Harvey, 1974b; Ashmore, 1975; Ford, 1975; Stone, 1975; Boddy, 1976a, 1976b; Williams, 1976) as gatekeepers who control the allocation of housing as part of the system of capitalist reproduction (Pickvance, 1976b); the use of public money to restructure parts of the housing market, often for considerable personal gain (Duncan, 1974; Bassett and Hauser, 1975); and the encouragement which the planning process gives to capitalist accumulation (Ambrose, 1976; Preteceille, 1976): all have come under scrutiny and have introduced much valuable new material to our understanding of the city. Finally, there is the work of Batty (1974a, 1974b, 1975, 1976), who is developing mathematical models of power relationships in urban planning, based on coalition theory (Coleman, 1973), and of the influence which various groups are likely to have on the urban design process.

Conflict is a salient concept in the institutional approaches; often this is conflict between unequals. The nature and consequences of some of the conflicts which have spatial parameters have been investigated (e.g., Ernst *et al.,* 1974; Stetzer, 1975; Fisch, 1976; Isserman, 1976; Janelle and Millward, 1976), indicating how various social groups attempt to structure space for their own ends (Short, 1976) in the political game of "who gets what *where,* and how" (Smith, 1974).

Most urban conflict has a strong class basis, and so it is not surprising that many of the supporters of the institutional approaches have taken ideological stances, especially with regard to the production of future intra-urban patterns. Anti-capitalist, often marxist, arguments are common, as in Harvey's (1975a) review of Berry's (1973) work and in an exchange over geographical studies of crime (Peet *et al.,* 1975, 1976); a general view is that because of their implicit "belief that people are free to prefer and choose . . . urban geographers have, by default, accepted, aided, and supported the existing structure of society and hindered a true understanding of reality" (Gray, 1975). Among other ideologies, Bunge (1973, 1975) continues to advance a child-centred humanism; his latest work on Toronto (Bunge and Bordessa, 1976) is a powerful statement of all that he finds wrong in urban society—notably the hegemony of the motor car, the personal stress of much architecture, and the rampant pollution—which he backs up with a variety of novel research inquiries.

Conclusions

Development of the third and most recent branch has generated vibrant debate within geography which is reminiscent of the onset of quantification two decades ago [see King (1976) for some pondering on this]. Some of the explanatory poverty of the other two branches has been exposed, which is not to deny their value as descriptive procedures in the educational process and as normative planning devices within stated ideologies. For those advancing the institutional approaches, there is a need to exemplify the explanatory power of their models. They must, for example, face a contrafactual question; would different patterns have developed in contemporary cities which lacked the current capitalist institutions, or does innate selfishness in man (original sin: Johnston, 1975) mean that exploitation involving a spatial order will invariably unfold?

In a discipline with very little of a "radical" tradition and with relatively weak links with other social sciences, it is not surprising that many of the studies in the institutional mould have abstracted small elements of the total political economy as their foci. Yet, as Harvey has shown in his marxist-oriented essays, and as is clear in much of the structuralist approach to social science, the part cannot be divorced from the whole. Harvey (1973, chapter 5) illustrated this in his work on use valuation and exchange valuation of property, suggesting that housing problems in urban areas can only be understood in the context of the dynamic of capitalist reproduction. Similar arguments have been advanced by French writers (Lamarche and Lojkine, both in Pickvance, 1976a), but detailed research has rarely taken such an integrative view. When it does, it may be that there will be a partial return to the neoclassical modelling, for study of the political system in the context of the grants economy, which now controls so large a portion of the GNP (Boulding, 1973; Blair *et al.*, 1975), suggests that the models of *homo economicus* are valuable as aids to understanding the actions of *homo politicus* (Tullock, 1976; Johnston, 1976c). And meanwhile, as the research effort proceeds, new teaching material will be needed, for only Robson's (1975) brief text conveys much of the institutional approaches to the undergraduate audience.

References

Ambrose, P. J. 1976: British land use planning: a radical critique. *Antipode* 8(1), 2–14.

Ambrose, P. J. and Colenutt, R. J. 1975: *The property machine.* Harmondsworth: Penguin Books.

Anas, A. 1975: The empirical calibration and testing of a simulation model of residential location. *Environment and Planning* A 7, 899–920.

Ashmore, G. 1975: *The owner-occupied housing market.* University of Birmingham, Centre for Urban and Regional Studies Research Memoranda 41.

Baldwin, J. 1974: Problem housing estates—perceptions of tenants, city officials and criminologists. *Social and Economic Administration* 8, 116–35.

1975: Urban criminality and the "problem" estate. *Local Government Studies* No. 1, 12–20.

Ball, N. R. and Clark, M. J. 1975: Private sector housing in south east England. *Tijdschrift voor Economische en Sociale Geografie* 66, 75–83.

Barrett, F. 1976: The search process in residential relocation. *Environment and Behavior* 8, 169–98.

Bassett, K. and Hauser, D. 1975: Public policy and spatial structure: housing improvement in Bristol. In Peel, R., Chisholm, M. and Haggett, P., editors, *Processes in physical and human geography: Bristol essays,* London: Heinemann, 20–68.

Batty, M. 1974a: Social power in plan-generation. *Town Planning Review* 45, 291–310.

1974b: A theory of Markovian design machines. *Environment and Planning* B 1, 125–46.

1975: Design as collective action. *Environment and Planning* B 2, 151–76.

1976: *A political theory of planning and design.* University of Reading, Department of Geography, Geographical Papers No. 45.

Batty, M. and March, L. 1976: The method of residues in urban modelling. *Environment and Planning* A 8, 189–214.

Beavon, K. S. O. 1974a: Interpreting Lösch on an intra-urban scale. *South African Geographical Journal* 56, 36–59.

1974b: Generalising the intra-urban model based on Lösch. *South African Geographical Journal* 56, 137–54.

1975: *Christaller's central place theory: reviewed, revealed, revised.* Johannesburg, University of the Witwatersrand, Department of Geography and Environmental Studies, Occasional Paper 15.

1976: The Lösch intra-urban model under conditions of changing cost functions. *South African Geographical Journal* 58, 36–9.

Beck, R. J. and Wood, D. 1976: Cognitive transformation of information from urban geographic fields to mental maps. *Environment and Behavior* 8, 199–238.

Bednarz, R. S. 1975: *The effect of air pollution on property value in Chicago.* University of Chicago, Department of Geography, Research Paper 166.

Berry, B. J. L. 1973: *The human consequences of urbanization.* London: Macmillan.

1975: Short-term housing cycles in a dualistic metropolis. In Gappert, G. and Rose, H. M., editors, *The social economy of cities,* Beverly Hills: Sage Publications, 165–82.

Berry, B. J. L., Conkling, E. C. and Ray, D. M. 1975: *The geography of economic systems.* Englewood Cliffs, New Jersey: Prentice-Hall.

Berry, B. J. L. *et al.* 1974: *Land use, urban form and environmental quality.* University of Chicago, Department of Geography, Research Paper 155.

Bird, H. 1976: Residential mobility and preference patterns in the public sector of the housing market. *Transactions of the Insti-*

tute of British Geographers, New Series 1, 20–33.

Blair, J. P., Gappert, G. and Warner, D. C. 1975: Rethinking urban problems: inequality and the grants economy. In Gappert, G. and Rose, H. M., editors. *The social economy of cities,* Beverly Hills: Sage Publications, 471–506.

Boddy, M. J. 1975: Theories of residential location or castles in the air? *Environment and Planning* A 7, 109–11.

— 1976a: The structure of mortgage finance: building societies and the British social formation. *Transactions of the Institute of British Geographers, New Series* 1, 58–71.

— 1976b: Political economy of housing: mortgage-financed owner-occupation in Britain. *Antipode* 8(1), 15–23.

Boulding, K. E. 1973: *The economy of love and fear: a preface to grants economics.* Belmont, California: Wadsworth.

Bunge, W. 1973: Ethics and logic in geography. In Chorley, R. J., editor, *Directions in Geography,* London: Methuen, 317–31.

— 1975: Detroit humanly viewed: the American urban present. In Abler, R., Janelle, D., Philbrick, A., and Sommer, J., editors, *Human geography in a shrinking world,* North Scituate, Mass.: Duxbury Press, 147–82.

Bunge, W. and Bordessa, R. 1976: *The Canadian alternative: survival, expeditions and urban change.* York University, Downsview, Ontario, Department of Geography, Geographical Monographs No. 2.

Buttimer, A. 1976: Grasping the dynamism of lifeworld. *Annals of the Association of American Geographers* 66, 277–92.

Byrne, D. S. 1976: Allocation, the council ghetto, and the public economy of housing. *Antipode* 8(1), 24–9.

Cadwallader, M. 1975: A behavioral model of consumer spatial decision making. *Economic Geography* 51, 339–49.

Carey, G. W. 1976: Land tenure, speculation and the state of the aging metropolis. *Geographical Review* 66, 253–65.

Chisholm, M. 1975: *Human geography: evolution or revolution.* Harmondsworth: Penguin Books.

Coleman, J. S. 1973: *The mathematics of collective action.* London: Heinemann.

Colenutt, R. J. 1976: The political economy of the property market. *Antipode* 8(2), 24–9.

Corsi, T. and Harvey, M. E. 1975: The socio-economic determinants of crime in the City of Cleveland: the application of canonical scores to geographic process. *Tijdschrift voor Economische en Sociale Geografie* 66, 323–36.

Davidson, B. R. 1975: The effects of land speculation on the supply of housing in England and Wales. *Urban Studies* 12, 91–100.

Davies, W. K. D. 1975: Variance allocation and the dimensions of British towns. *Tijdschrift voor Economische en Sociale Geografie* 66, 358–71.

Detwyler, T. R. and Marcus, M. G., editors, 1972: *Urbanization and environment.* North Scituate, Mass.: Duxbury Press.

Downs, R. M. and Stea, D., editors, 1974: *Image and environment.* London: Edward Arnold; Chicago: Aldine.

Duncan, S. S. 1974: Cosmetic planning or social engineering? Improvement grants and improvement areas in Huddersfield. *Area* 6, 259–70.

— 1976: Research directions in social geography: housing opportunities and constraints. *Transactions of the Institute of British Geographers, New Series* 1, 10–19.

Dwyer, D. J. 1975: *People and housing in Third World cities.* London: Longman.

Elliott, B. and McCrone, D. 1975: Landlords in Edinburgh: some preliminary findings. *Sociological Review* 23, 539–62.

Ernst, R. T., Hugg, L., Crooker, R. A. and Ayorre, R. L. 1974: Competition and conflict over land use change in the inner city: institution versus community. *Antipode* 6(2), 70–97.

Evans, A. W. 1975a: Rent and housing in the theory of urban growth. *Journal of Regional Science* 15, 113–26.

— 1975b: Theories of residential location or castles in the air?–a reply. *Environment and Planning* A 7, 601–3.

Feldman, S. and Gonen, A. 1975: The spatio-temporal pricing of some urban public services: urban ecology, equity, and efficiency. *Environment and Planning* A 7, 315–23.

Fingleton, B. 1975: A factorial approach to the nearest centre hypothesis. *Transactions of the Institute of British Geographers* 65, 131–40.

1976: Alternative approaches to modelling varied spatial behavior. *Geographical Analysis* 7, 95–102.

Fish, O. 1976: The social cost of through traffic: contribution to the suburban–central city exploitation thesis. *Regional Science and Urban Economics* 5, 263–78.

Ford, J. R. 1975: The role of the building society manager in the urban stratification system: autonomy versus constraint. *Urban Studies* 12, 295–302.

Giggs, J. A. 1975: The distribution of schizophrenics in Nottingham: a reply. *Transactions of the Institute of British Geographers* 65, 150–56.

Giggs, J. A. and Mather, P. M. 1975: Factorial ecology and factor invariance: an investigation. *Economic Geography* 51, 366–82.

Gray, F. 1975: Non-explanation in urban geography. *Area* 7, 228–34.

1976: Selection and allocation in council housing. *Transactions of the Institute of British Geographers, New Series* 1, 34–46.

Gudgin, G. 1975: The distribution of schizophrenics in Nottingham: a comment. *Transactions of the Institute of British Geographers* 65, 148–9.

Haggett, P. and Chorley, R. J. 1967: Models, paradigms and the new geography. In Chorley, R. J. and Haggett, P., editors, *Models in geography*, London: Methuen, 19–42.

Harloe, M., Ischaroff, R. and Minns, R. 1974: *The organization of housing*. London: Heinemann.

Harvey, D. 1973: *Social justice and the city*. London: Edward Arnold.

1974a: Population, resources, and the ideology of science. *Economic Geography* 50, 256–77.

1974b: Class-monopoly rent, finance capital, and the urban revolution. *Regional Studies* 3, 239–55.

1975a: Review of B. J. L. Berry, *The human consequences of urbanization. Annals of the Association of American Geographers* 65, 98–103.

1975b: Class structure in a capitalist society and the theory of residential differentiation. In Peel, R., Chisholm, M. and Haggett, P., editors, *Processes in physical and human geography: Bristol essays,* London: Heinemann, 354–72.

1975c: The geography of capitalist accumulation: a reconstruction of the Marxian theory. *Antipode* 7(2), 9–21.

1975d: The political economy of urbanization in advanced capitalist societies: the case of the United States. In Gappert, G. and Rose, H. M., editors, *The social economy of cities,* Beverly Hills: Sage Publications, 119–64.

Herbert, D. T. 1975: Urban deprivation: definition, measurement and spatial qualities. *Geographical Journal* 141, 362–72.

Higgs, G. 1975: An assessment of the action component of action space. *Geographical Analysis* 7, 35–50.

Hodge, D. and Gattrell, A. 1976: Spatial constraint and the location of urban public facilities. *Environment and Planning* A 8, 215–30.

Hudson, R. 1975: Patterns of spatial search. *Transactions of the Institute of British Geographers* 65, 141–54.

1976: Linking studies of the individual with models of aggregate behaviour: an empirical example. *Transactions of the Institute of British Geographers, New Series* 1, 158–74.

Hugill, P. J. 1975: Social conduct on the Golden Mile. *Annals of the Association of American Geographers* 65, 214–28.

Isserman, A. M. 1976: Interjurisdictional spillovers, political fragmentation and the level of local services. *Urban Studies* 13, 1–12.

Janelle, D. G. and Millward, H. A. 1976: Locational conflict patterns and urban ecological structure. *Tijdschrift voor Economische en Sociale Geografie* 67, 102–14.

Johnston, R. J. 1975: Regarding bourgeois geography and original sin. *New Zealand Geographer* 31, 192–3.

1976a: Spatial and temporal variations in land and property prices in New Zealand: 1953–72. *New Zealand Geographer* 32, 30–55.

1976b: Areal studies, ecological studies, and social patterns in cities. *Transactions of the Institute of British Geographers, New Series* 1, 118–22.

1976c: Territorial injustice and political campaigns: notes towards a methodology. *Policy and Politics* 5, 181–99.

King, L. J. 1976: Alternatives to a positive economic geography. *Annals of the Associa-*

tion of American Geographers 66, 293–308.

Kirby, A. M. 1976: Housing market studies: a critical review. *Transactions of the Institute of British Geographers, New Series,* 1, 2–9.

Kuhn, T. S. 1962: *The structure of scientific revolutions.* Chicago: University of Chicago Press.

Ley, D. 1974: *The black inner city as frontier outpost.* Washington, DC: Association of American Geographers.

Ley, D. 1975: The street gang in its milieu. In Gappert, G. and Rose, H. M., editors, *The social economy of cities,* Beverly Hills: Sage Publications, 247–74.

McAllister, D. M. 1976: Equity and efficiency in public facility location. *Geographical Analysis* 7, 47–64.

Mercer, J. 1975: Metropolitan housing quality and an application of causal modelling. *Geographical Analysis* 7, 295–302.

Moore, E. G., editor, 1973: *Models of residential location and relocation in the city.* Northwestern University, Evanston, Studies in Geography 20.

Mulkay, M. J. 1975: Three models of scientific development. *Sociological Review* 23, 509–26.

Niner, P. 1975: *Local authority housing policy and practice: a case study approach.* University of Birmingham, Centre for Urban and Regional Studies, Occasional Paper 31.

Pahl, R. E. 1967: Sociological models in geography. In Chorley, R. J. and Haggett, P., editors, *Models in geography.* London: Methuen, 217–42.

Palm, R. 1976a: *Urban social geography from the perspective of the real estate salesman.* University of California, Berkeley, Institute of Urban and Regional Development, Center for Real Estate and Urban Economics, Research Report 38.

1976b: Real estate agents and geographical information. *Geographical Review* 66, 266–80.

1976c: An index of household diversity. *Tijdschrift voor Economische en Sociale Geografie* 67, 194–201.

Parkes, D. N. and Thrift, N. 1975: Timing space and spacing time. *Environment and Planning* A 7, 651–70.

Peach, G. C. K., editor, 1976: *Urban social segregation.* London: Longman.

Peet, J. R. 1975: The geography of crime: a political critique (with comments by K. D. Harries, P. D. Phillips and Yuk Lee). *The Professional Geographer* 27, 277–85.

1976: Further comments of the geography of crime. *The Professional Geographer* 28, 96–100.

Pickvance, C. G., editor, 1976a: *Urban sociology: critical essays.* London: Tavistock.

1976b: Housing, reproduction of capital, and reproduction of labour power: some recent French work. *Antipode* 8(1), 58–68.

Poulsen, M. F. 1976: Restricted lateral movement: an initial test of the locational attachments hypothesis. *Environment and Planning* A 8, 289–99.

Preteceille, E. 1976: Urban planning: the contradictions of capitalist urbanisation. *Antipode* 8(1), 69–76.

Pritchard, R. M. 1976: *Housing and the spatial structure of the city.* Cambridge: Cambridge University Press.

Pyle, G. F. *et al.* 1974: *The spatial dynamics of crime.* University of Chicago, Department of Geography, Research Paper 159.

Pyle, G. F., editor, 1976: Human health problems: spatial perspectives. *Economic Geography* 52.

ReVelle, C., Toregas, C. and Falkson, L. 1976: Applications of the location set-covering problem. *Geographical Analysis* 7, 65–76.

Robson, B. T. 1975: *Urban social areas.* London: Oxford University Press.

Sanders, R. A. 1976: Bilevel effects in urban residential patterns. *Economic Geography* 52, 61–70.

Schneider, C. H. P. 1975: Models of space searching in urban areas. *Geographical Analysis* 7, 173–86.

Shannon, G. W., Spurloch, G. W., Gladin, S. T. and Skinner, J. L. 1975: A method for evaluating the geographic accessibility of health services. *The Professional Geographer* 27, 30–36.

Short, J. R. 1976: Social systems and spatial patterns. *Antipode* 8(1), 77–82.

Smith, C. J. 1976: Residential neighbourhoods as humane environments. *Environment and Planning* A 8, 311–26.

Smith, D. M. 1974: Who gets what *where,* and how: a welfare focus for human geography. *Geography* 59, 289–97.

Smith, G. C. 1976: The spatial information

fields of urban consumers. *Transactions of the Institute of British Geographers, New Series* 1, 175–89.

Stetzer, D. F. 1975: *Special Districts in Cook County: towards a geography of local government.* University of Chicago, Department of Geography, Research Paper 169.

Stone, M. E. 1975: The housing crisis, mortgage lending, and class struggle. *Antipode* 7(2), 22–37.

Svart, L. M. 1976: Environmental preference migration: a review. *Geographical Review* 66, 314–30.

Taylor, P. J. 1976: An interpretation of the quantification debate in British geography. *Transactions of the Institute of British Geographers, New Series* 1, 129–42.

Taylor, P. J. and Parkes, D. N. 1975: A Kantian view of the city: a factorial-ecology experiment in space and time. *Environment and Planning* A 7, 671–88.

Trlin, A. D. 1976: Toward the integration of factors affecting the immigrant intra-urban residential patterns. *New Zealand Geographer* 32, 56–89.

Tuan, Yi-Fu, 1975: Images and mental maps. *Annals of the Association of American Geographers* 65, 205–13.

Tuan, Yi-Fu, 1976: Humanistic geography. *Annals of the Association of American Geographers* 66, 266–76.

Tullock, G. 1976: *The vote motive.* Hobart Paperback 9, London: Institute of Economic Affairs.

Van Valey, T. L. and Roof, W. C. 1976: Mea-suring residential segregation in American cities: problems of intercity comparison. *Urban Affairs Quarterly* 11, 453–68.

Wagner, J. L. and Falkson, L. M. 1975: The optimal nodal location of public facilities with price-sensitive demand. *Geographical Analysis* 7, 69–83.

Ward, D. 1975: Victorian cities: how modern? *Journal of Historical Geography* 1, 135–51.

1976: The Victorian slum: an enduring myth? *Annals of the Association of American Geographers* 66, 323–36.

Williams, P. R. 1976: The role of institutions in the inner London housing market: the case of Islington. *Transactions of the Institute of British Geographers, New Series* 1, 72–82.

Wilson, A. G. 1974: *Urban and regional models in geography and planning.* London: John Wiley.

1976: Retailers' profits and consumers' welfare in a spatial interaction shopping model. In Masser, I., editor, *Theory and practice in regional science,* London Papers in Regional Science 6, London: Pion, 42–59.

Wolpert, J., Dear, M. and Crawford, R. 1975: Satellite mental health facilities. *Annals of the Association of American Geographers* 65, 24–35.

Woods, R. I. 1976: Aspects of the scale problem in the calculation of segregation indices: London and Birmingham 1961 and 1971. *Tijdschrift voor Economische en Sociale Geografie* 67, 169–74.

II

CONCEPTS: Theoretical Issues and Alternative Perspectives

PIOTR KORCELLI

Theory of Intra-Urban Structure: Review and Synthesis. A Cross-Cultural Perspective

The literature on intra-urban structure and growth has been expanding rapidly in recent years, which is a typical feature in the case of complex, interdisciplinary problems. This expansion is well testified by the increasing number of reviews and theoretical syntheses such as those by B. J. Garner (1967), C. L. Leven (1969), R. Colenutt (1970), R. J. Johnston (1972), B. Greer-Wootten (1972) and M. L. Senior (1973).

The present article has two specific objectives. The first aim is to reduce the multitude of generalizations found in the contemporary literature on intra-urban structure into a set of basic theoretical statements and postulates. The second aim is to demonstrate to what extent individual theories and statements reflect particular social, political and cultural contexts and to show which approaches, and why, may be regarded as of a more or less universal range of applicability.

It is possible to identify six major approaches which have contributed to the existing body of theory on urban spatial structure and growth. These include:

1. Ecological concepts,
2. theories of urban land market and land use,
3. urban population density models,
4. models of intra-urban functional patterns (or spatial interaction models),
5. settlement network (or system) theories,
6. models of spatial diffusion on an intra-urban scale.

In terms of origin, those theoretical approaches are related to various disciplines, such as sociology (1), economics (2), demography (3), urban planning (4) and geography (5, 6). Until very recently they developed largely independently of each other. The trends towards an integration are mainly a product of the present decade. Even as late as 1969/ 1970 some leading authors could deplore the state of urban and regional research which was "more of a market place where various ideas are traded than a building ground where brick is placed on brick in an orderly fashion" (Hägerstrand, 1969, p. 62), and was characterized by a lack

From **Geographica Polonica**, Vol. 31, 1976, pp. 99–131. Reprinted by permission of PWN– Polish Scientific Publishers and Piotr Korcelli.

of an "interdisciplinary framework for thinking let alone theorizing" and split into a number of "confined conceptual worlds" (Harvey, 1970, p. 47).

Ecological Concepts

There are two reasons for starting the discussion with the urban-ecological school. First, this approach has so far commanded great interest among representatives of "urban science," a fact which is reflected by the immense and still rapidly expanding literature. Second, the question of cross-cultural differences comes out in ecological studies more explicitly than elsewhere. The crux of the matter lies in whether or not within the urban residential space there are pronounced variations in terms of median family income, level of education, demographic characteristics and other related variables. In the case of an affirmative answer, ecological forces are assumed to operate and made responsible for the variations identified. The next question is whether those variations tend to become more intensive with the passage of time or, otherwise, tend to level-out. The third basic question refers to the spatial pattern. This can be: (a) concentric with a positive or negative relationship between the distance from the city centre and neighbourhood quality, (b) sectoral, (c) mixed (some variables showing a concentric, others—a sectoral pattern), (d) mosaic-like, or (e) other. Comparative factorial ecology (Berry, 1971), seeks answers to the above questions and it has produced a number of important generalizations (Timms, 1971; Rees, 1970; Robson, 1969). These, however, when seen in the world-wide scale, are still quite partial and sometimes inconclusive.

Thus, according to Berry (1971, p. 219) the findings of factorial urban ecology demonstrate that detailed comparisons based on uniform methods and concepts, appear appropriate only within:

(a) Western, industrial societies, (b) societies of planned development, (c) traditional, or pre-industrial societies. Other evidence suggests the actual divisions to be still more complicated and related to:

1. Level of economic development and technological advancement,
2. social and economic systems,
3. cultural systems,
4. degree of ethnic heterogeneity,
5. size, age, rate of growth, and functions of the city.

In Pahl's (1967) opinion the dividing lines can be found even within individual urban communities as various social groups differ in respect to the level of spatial mobility and the degree of freedom in selecting residential location. Similar notions are also expressed by Vance (1969).

One of the problems which bear heavily on factor ecological studies and conclusions reached in such studies, is that the principal theoretical basis of urban factorial ecology i.e., the social area theory, explicitly pertains to contemporary Western societies. It should be emphasized that this fact is well reflected in the results of empirical work. Thus, the social area model which postulates the three basic dimensions of differentiation of the urban community: socio-economic status, family status, and ethnic status, has been generally confirmed by factor ecological studies of those Western cities with a high degree of ethnic heterogeneity (see Murdie, 1969; Rees, 1970; Salins, 1971; Timms, 1971), as well as by studies of some other Western industrialized cities (Pedersen, 1967; Janson, 1971) in which factors corresponding to the first two axes have been identified. In the case of Mediterranean and Latin American cities (McElrath, 1962; Morris and Pyle, 1971) these factors could also be derived, though they seldom formed distinctly separate spatial patterns. On the other hand, analyses for Asian and African cities (Abu-Lughod, 1969; Linday, 1971) show a high correlation between socio-economic and demographic variables and a clear presence of the ethnic status factor.

Few factor ecological studies exist for the cities of socialist countries and therefore it is not easy to discuss their patterns in terms of the social area model. However, empirical work based on other concepts and methods largely suggests that the Shevky-Bell hypothesis may be invalid in this case. For instance, V. V. Pokshishevsky (1973) has demonstrated a gradual increase in the spatial integration of various ethnic groups in the large cities of the USSR. Planning is a factor which was in fact disregarded by social area theory. Robson (1969) has already noted that in his study of Sunderland. When equipped with such tools as housing assignment policies and the control over a bulk of housing construction, planning has proved to be a very effective vehicle in eliminating sharp differences within urban residential space.

Studies of Polish cities (Pióro, 1962), although displaying a persistence of spatial differentiation in a number of ecological variables, show a substantial decrease in such differentiation since World War II. A recent factor ecological study of Warsaw (Węcławowicz, 1975) has proved that while in the 1930s residential variations within the city closely corresponded to the one postulated by the social area model, the contemporary (1970) structure was much less pronounced and could yield to an interpretation mostly in terms of the evolving housing policies. Although the image of high or low prestige attached to individual districts has not fully disappeared, the motivations of individuals to change residence concern in most cases, the apartment itself (i.e., its size) rather than its location within the urban social space. This is an effect of the basic policy idea, followed since

World War II, which has been to achieve a more or less homogeneous socio-economic structure and a similar standard of services, especially of educational, transportation, and recreational facilities throughout the city.

In contrast to the problem of dimensions and intensity of residential differentiation, the question of its spatial patterns has been subject to hypotheses whose scope extends to a cross-cultural scale. There exist in fact two competing concepts, both formulated in quasi-dynamic terms. Reference is made here to Schnore's (1965) model and to the scheme developed by Johnston (1972). The first one combines the "reverse Burgess" and "Burgess-type" patterns into an evolutionary sequence where transition from one into the other is attributed to the change in economic and technological conditions which in turn determine locational preferences of those social groups which are characterized by the highest degree of spatial mobility. Johnston's concept which stems from a criticism of Schnore's model, sees the emergence of a mosaic-like pattern as an outcome—both in developed and developing countries—of the growing role of the intermediate social strata.

It has been proved that certain elements of the concentric pattern, together with some sectoral components, can be found in cities representing all the major contemporary socio-political and cultural systems (see Tanabe, 1970), although in the socialist city they are more closely related to the arrangement of land uses than to the differentiation of residential space (Werwicki, 1973). One may agree with Johnston that present patterns are reflecting a stage of transition, and that they are, at least temporarily, becoming more complex or "mosaic-like." (A good example of this trend is Warsaw; see Węcławowicz, 1975). It seems to be a general rule that when technological conditions (mostly transportation) allow, groups with growing incomes tend to seek residence near the edge of a city. Nevertheless, proportions between those moving towards an outer zone and those selecting a central location greatly differ. This rule, therefore, is not strong enough to suggest whether the existing patterns are now converging or whether they are still evolving in divergent directions.

The question is closely related to the ecological succession which remains one of the least developed aspects in comparative urban ecology. Most studies pertain to the succession of ethnic groups and, more recently, to the life-cycle succession (Simmons, 1968). They all are characteristic of American cities and, in the case of the latter, also of some other large Western cities (Johnston, 1969). Other types of succession, such as those connected with urban redevelopment, are probably more universal in scope and they should be subjected to comparative study on an international scale.

Succession (along with competition in space and dominance) belongs to those basic notions of human ecology which were directly borrowed from plant ecology. In fact, the definition of human succession by Park[1] closely resembles a standard biological definition. The notion of invasion–succession lay also at the base of the dynamic interpretation of the Burgess model. There it referred both to population change and the evolution of an urban landscape. Later on this notion became chiefly restricted—at least in sociological literature—to the movement of social groups, particularly ethnic minorities, over space and over time.

In the traditional interpretation, phases of succession were determined in reference to stages of community organization and the intensity of change. Cressey (1938), for example, divided the succession cycle into the phases of invasion, conflict, recession, and reorganization, while Duncan and Duncan (1957) identified the phases of penetration, invasion, consolidation, and saturation. It was established empirically that the succession cycle might be depicted by a normal, unimodal curve if its change of intensity over time was taken as a measure, and by a S-shaped curve, well known in innovation diffusion studies, if the degree of its accomplishment was considered. A high regularity of the succession cycle led sometimes to a narrow, deterministic interpretation (and related action) often referred to as a "self-fulfilling prophecy" (Wolf 1957, quoted by Bourne, 1971).

In a cross-cultural perspective data on change of residence within urban areas are rather scarce and, if available, they rarely allow the isolation of the individual migration factors (some authors prefer to speak of bundles of factors). Therefore, it is possible to propose other general hypotheses relating intra-urban migrations to social and economic mobility or to changes in the urban environment. Those are, in fact, indirect factors acting through housing market systems and various institutional factors. Their differentiation in the contemporary world restricts considerably the range of generalizations on intra-metropolitan migrations.

The geographical concept of sequent occupance, closely corresponding to a broad interpretation of ecological succession, was rediscovered by Hoover and Vernon (1959) who formulated a model of the morphological succession cycle for a large metropolitan area. Individual concentric zones, according to Hoover and Vernon, tend to experience the following sequence of occupance: (1) development of single-family houses (corresponding to primary succession), (2) spread of multi-

---

1. ". . . an orderly sequence of changes through which a biotic community passes in the course of its development from a primary and relatively unstable, to a relatively permanent or climax stage. . . ." In the course of this development the community moves through a series of more or less clearly defined stages (after Timms, 1971, p. 87).

family housing, (3) influx of minority ethnic groups and/or economically disadvantaged groups, and conversion of residential buildings, (4) deterioration of housing and decline of overall densities, (5) redevelopment. This model has been empirically confirmed by Duncan, Sabagh, and Van Arsdol (1962) who observed a regular pattern of population growth (with rapid growth in the first stage, slower—in the second stage and negative increase in the remaining stages) for cohorts of census tracts developed during subsequent time periods; and by Birch (1971) who found a statistical relationship between the population growth rate of an individual zone and its position on the time axis of the morphological cycle, as well as between the age of buildings and a phase of that cycle.

Theories of Urban Land Market and Land Use

Theories conceiving urban structure as the reflection of spatial patterns of transport costs and urban land rent, share with ecological theories a number of basic notions, such as competition in space and dominance. The relationships are genetic since Hurd (1903) is recognized as the forerunner of both groups of theoretical concepts. In addition, the "neo-classical" ecological theory (Hawley, 1950) assumes a given pattern of rent values as a framework for the development of social patterns over urban space. This was already noted by Timms (1971, p. 94) with respect to the classical urban–ecological models.

There are fundamental differences between the role of land rent in the contemporary Western city and in the socialist city. The "Western" theory of the capitalist city explicitly links land use and urban rent patterns and looks upon allocation as a process based on competition where individual decision-making units aim at occupying locations with the

highest utility level (Ratcliff, 1949) or, in the case of the residential sector, the highest level of satisfaction (Alonso, 1964). Garner (1967, pp. 335–36) gives a simplified account of this process: "Each activity has an ability to derive utility from every site in the urban area; the utility of a site is measured by the rent the activity is willing to pay for the use of the site. . . . In the long run, competition in the urban land market . . . results in the occupation of each site by the "highest and best" use, which is the use able to derive the greatest utility from the site and which is, therefore, willing to pay most to occupy it. As an outgrowth of the occupation of sites by the "highest and best" uses, an orderly pattern of land uses results in which rents throughout the systems are maximized and all activities are optimally located."

In the theory and planning of the socialist city the notion of land rent is not formally applied. Instead, urban land development is based upon principles of investment effectiveness, the productivity of agricultural land (if urban territorial expansion is involved), technical and economic requirements of different uses, and the functional organization of urban space. During recent years a number of concepts of determining urban land prices were proposed. It has been suggested that a uniform and theoretically based system of land prices should aid planning and land development policies. The major concepts, put forth by Polish authors, are comparatively presented and analysed by Kolipinski (1970). In most of the methods proposed accessibility is treated implicitly through such variables as the value of investments and the productivity per unit of land (Chołaj, 1966).

Haig (1927), who laid the foundations of the economic theory of urban spatial structure, considered site rent and transportation costs as complementary values, summing up to total costs of friction. He identified site rent with the value of savings resulting from the accessibility of a given site to the remaining sites within an urban area. Locations with low aggregate transportation costs, because of their limited supply, are becoming occupied by those activities which are able to take advantage of high accessibility most effectively. "The layout of a metropolis— the assignment of activities to areas— tends to be determined by a principle which may be termed the minimizing of the costs of friction" (Haig, 1927, p. 39). The resulting land use pattern, with assumptions simplifying the structure of transportation costs, corresponds, in fact, to that portrayed by von Thünen. Haig based his analysis mainly on the location of business and manufacturing oriented to the local market, but he extended his assumptions concerning the role of aggregate transport costs to all kinds of activities, the residential sector included. He considered locations (sites) in terms of points rather than portions of territory.

The latter omission was filled in by Alonso (1964) whose theory emphasizes the substitution of transport inputs and lot size. He assumes that in the land development process individual decision-makers, be it firms or households, aim at minimizing rent and transportation costs and maximizing the area occupied. A crucial concept in Alonso's theory—the bid rent curve is defined as a set of combinations of rent and transport inputs which represent an equal satisfaction level for an individual. Alonso proves that users with steep bid rent curve gradients tend to occupy locations close to the city centre. This allows him to reinterpret the classical urban–ecological models. The Burgess-type pattern, in terms of Alonso's theory, is the case when for higher income groups the rate of decrease of the marginal rate of substitution is less than the rate of the increase of land (Alonso, 1964, p. 108). The reverse pattern represents a different scale of preferences; factors other than income, influencing preferences are, however, beyond the scope of Alonso's theory. Other concepts of urban land use, which also apply the principle of substituting space for transport inputs, and which explicitly pertain to a competitive, free-market economy, were developed by Wingo (1961) and Muth (1969).

The theory of urban land market has been criticized for its static–equilibrium form and the assumptions drastically simplifying reality, such as the location of all service and employment opportunities at a single city centre, a symmetric pattern of transport costs and the condition of perfect competition. Angel and Hyman (1972) have demonstrated that the substitution of rent and transport costs leads eventually, at a certain distance from the city centre, to negative rent values. The assumption of a constant rent may be a solution but then the condition of a single centre (or a single trip destination point) becomes impossible. The same assumption is questioned by Boyce (1965) and Wheeler (1970) who show a poor correspondence between empirical data on directions and length of trips for various socio-economic groups and the pattern postulated by the urban land market theory.[2] Another simplification in the theory which deserves criticism and further study is that it disregards all components of differential rent, other than site rent. Numerous studies (Brigham, 1965) have empirically established the importance of such factors as topography, directions of urban growth, environmental quality, and historical factors.

In the present context the question of the generality of urban land market and land use theory over time and space is of primary importance. Vance (1971) came to the conclusion that the theory can be applied, with some limitations, to an

---

2. Attempts of W. Alonso (1964, pp. 134–141) as well as G. Papageorgiou and E. Casetti (1971) to construct polycentric urban rent models should be noted at this point.

analysis of the spatial structure of the capitalist city, but he denies its relevancy in the case of both the precapitalist (or feudal) and the post-capitalist city. To the latter categories one should add the socialist city. Vance notes that in the feuday city land utilization was of a functional rather than an economic character and the land assignment basis related to the social status of the users rather than the rent-paying ability. In the capitalist city, to continue Vance's arguments, the principle of land inputs—transportation inputs substitution mainly pertains to man's economic activity, while the spatial structure of the housing market is shaped mostly by social factors, such as the class structure of the society, status models and symbols, discrimination (i.e., ethnic ghettos), and others.

In the socialist city, as represented by a large Polish city, the substitution principle is actually of marginal importance.[3] New housing is characterized by practically uniform standards not only in terms of materials and equipment but also in density. Since the overwhelming majority of new dwelling units are in multi-family buildings, net residential densities in housing estates, located in city peripheral zones, do not greatly differ from those in centrally situated residential districts. Although central locations are generally preferred, this does not usually produce a growth in population concentration within the inner city districts as, because of the communal ownership of land and the centralization of investment rights, the land development process is largely of a non-competitive character. At the same time, diseconomies associated with both urban sprawl and congestion are recog-

nized by the planners and decisionmakers. With the spread of single-family housing the substitution rule may grow in importance, although the terms opposite to transportation costs would be the existing structure of housing and amenity factors (particularly relating to air quality and noise disturbances) rather than land rent.

This leads to another critical question which is the implicit time dimension of the urban land market and land use theory. Of particular interest is the effect of changes in the site rent gradient upon land use patterns. If technological progress in transportation and the related decrease in the friction of space lead to the equalization of accessibility values (or aggregate transport costs) throughout the city, their consequence is definitely a flattening site rent gradient. Not every improvement in transportation technology however brings such effects; while some improvements may promote spatial concentration (in a punctual or a linear form), others aid deconcentration. If one assumes, as one finds some empirical evidence,[4] that those trends follow one another, then changes in accessibility and in site rent gradients may be of a cyclical character.

Urban Population Density Models

The Clark's (1951) rule[5] describing an intra-urban population density pattern in terms of a negative exponential function of distance from the city centre, has often been recognized as the most universal statistical generalization in urban geography. Although tested by numerous authors, in-

---

3. Recently P. Lentz (1973) applied Muth's model to an analysis of land use and population densities in Warsaw. She found some general similarities between the spatial patterns of Warsaw and of American cities, although as she admitted, those patterns were produced by different processes.

4. During the rail transportation era the accessibility of the central districts increased faster than that of the remaining city areas. Motor transportation brought a more uniform growth in accessibility, with the most substantial additions in the marginal zones.
5. An earlier formulation is given by H. Bleicher in 1892.

cluding Berry *et al.* (1963), Romashkin (1967), and Lentz (1974) for cities of varied size, origin, socio-political and cultural milieu, the rule has never been invalidated. In addition, Berry (1964) has found that for most of the cases investigated the density gradient declines with the city size. On this basis he postulated a relation between the density rule and the rank-size rule.

Empirical material suggests that the density gradient (the *b* parameter) and the central density (d_0) substantially vary between cities (of comparable class categories) located in different countries and different parts of the world, as well as between cities of different age, shape and functions. Those observations prompted many authors to build formulae describing individual types of density patterns more precisely than does the Clark's formula. Thus Sherratt (1960) put forth a quadratic exponential function:

$$d_x = d_0 \exp(-bx^2)$$

while Medvedkov (1968) proposed a function with the *b* values differing—depending on the direction from the city centre:

$$d_x = d_0 \exp[-b(\phi)x]$$

Gurevich and Saushkin (1966) described several hypothetical density patterns, including one with the gradient value constant in all directions but varying with distance from the centre. Kostrubiec (1970) identified that pattern with the generalized density profile constructed by Korzybski (1952), whose work was parallel to, and independent of, Clark's contributions. The pattern is in fact similar to the one derived by Ajo (1965) for London, in which densities in subsequent concentric zones are described by different formulae. Attempts have also been made to build formulae taking into account the central density crater, and to build density models for polycentric patterns, both for a single city (Gurevich, 1967; Dacey, 1968) and a regional urban system (Papageorgiou and Casetti, 1971). In this latter approach the density rule is treated as a general model of population distribution.

Although the urban population density concept appeared originally as an "inductive generalization in search of a theory" (Berry, 1964), its explicative layer is now not much thinner than that of any other concept pertaining to intraurban structure and growth. Most frequently the density profile is explained in terms of transportation costs and site rent structure; however, Casetti (1967), Papageorgiou (1971), and Sevostyanov (1972) have attempted more general interpretations, avoiding the notion of land rent. A decline in the population density with distance from the city centre logically follows from the Alonso (1964) theory. When accessibility values decline from the centre the amount of space occupied by individual households increases, and the residential density decreases in a similar manner, with a correction made for variations in family size. The negative exponential decline of density with the distance does not follow directly from the theory, but Niedercorn (1971) and Casetti (1971) derived that function using such assumptions as a concave transportation costs curve and uniform household preferences.

In an earlier study Casetti (1967) treated population distribution within a city as an outcome of two opposite locational factors: the centrality preference and the preference for noncongested sites. He demonstrated that the equilibrium density pattern generated by a competitive process is higher than the optimum density. This difference is supposed by Casetti to form a basis for the so-called "deglomeration" policies which have been followed in the socialist countries.

Equivocal differences between various density models, in their empirical and theoretical performance, suggest that this problem may only be solved within a dynamic framework. Here, theoretical analyses are much less developed than in the case of the equilibrium density patterns. The available data series for the b values show, in a very consistent manner, the progressive flattening of density profiles over time. This may imply that: (1) with the passage of time and with the growth in size, cities are subject to a deconcentration, and/or (2) the deconcentration processes, which are tied to certain technological, economic, and cultural factors, are a contemporary feature of cities (of all size categories) in the developed countries. The former hypothesis can be ascribed to Winsborough (1963), Berry (1964), and Newling (1966, 1969), while the latter was exposed mainly by Bogue (1950), Hawley (1956), and Schnore (1957, 1959).

However, contemporary changes in urban density patterns are relatively well documented and on this basis some fragmentary generalizations, on a cross-cultural scale, were attempted by several authors. It has been already asserted that the existing studies pertaining to West European, North American, and Australian cities, consistently show, over time, the parallel decrease of density gradients and of central (as well as maximum) densities. Studies for socialist cities contain findings basically analogous to those noted above. Thus, Golc (1972) indicated that in the case of Moscow both the maximum density value and the b value have substantially declined during the last decades. In addition, Romashkin (1967) found a further decline in population densities within the central districts of Moscow over the 1963–65 period, and a substantial growth of densities in its marginal zones, with inter-sectoral differences becoming more pronounced. The density profiles for Cracow, compiled by Bromek (1964) for the 1880–1950 period show the emergence of the central

crater about 1920 and a progressive flattening of the density curve since 1930. Over the whole 70-years-long period the maximum density zone moved from the distance of about 0.4 km to 1.5 km from the historical centre of Cracow. Trends in density patterns are often more complicated when a city is subject to a large-scale redevelopment, as has been the case of Warsaw after its nearly-total destruction during the Second World War. Large portions of the central zone in Warsaw were put to residential construction in the 1960s, after the surrounding areas had been already developed. New, centrally situated housing is often in the form of residential towers, a fact which adds to the recent increase of net population densities within the central part of Warsaw.

Although the density patterns in cities of the Third World countries remain weakly recognized, Berry et al. (1963) ventured a generalization according to which the patterns in question, when seen over time, are characterized by growing d_0 values and a stability of b values. This also suggests a general increase of central densities with growing city size. Berry's graphical model found a confirmation in more recent empirical analyses, although they do not answer the fundamental question of whether the recent flattening of density profiles and a parallel increase of maximum densities in cities of Asia and Latin America, follow the principle of a gradual density decline with the growing urban scale or whether those trends are symptomatic of the early stages of deconcentration processes.

The conclusion that under given conditions city growth is accompanied by city deconcentration calls for determining the limits of the process. Duncan et al. (1962, p. 428; also quoted by Winsborough, 1962) sees the limits in the following way: . . . growth tends to take the form of outward expansion until the spread of the city begins to present a barrier to internal transportation and communication, at which juncture growth takes the form of upward expansion near the metropolitan core." If therefore, one may assume that urban density patterns pass through subsequent stages of concentration and deconcentration, then it is possible to describe their transformations as a cyclical process, connected with the cycles of occupancy and succession, and related to changes in accessibility patterns, which were discussed in the previous section.

Models of Intra-urban Functional Patterns

The theoretical background of models and research approaches labelled here "functional" are concepts of social physics (Wilson, 1969A), more precisely the concept of human interaction in space. These concepts, introduced to spatial analysis during the 1940s (Stewart, 1947; Zipf, 1949) have found numerous applications in studies of migrations, settlement network and intra-urban structure. Since models of functional patterns were often developed by planners in connection with particular studies of individual cities or metropolitan areas, they are predominantly of an operational character, and in this respect they differ from the models discussed so far.

Models of intra-urban functional patterns describe spatial relations between individual spheres of man's activity from the point of view of the location of individuals and firms, or the differentiation and succession in land use patterns. Sometimes both approaches are used concomitantly. A "typical" model (see King 1972, p. 4) contains the so-called exogenous variables, such as size and distribution of basic employment, which serve to generate the total employment figure, the economic structure and the population total of a city, or a metropolitan area. These endogenous variables are distributed over space using particular allocation functions. The structure of land use within individual subareas is derived by the use of land-requirement functions for the different allocated variables.

The allocation functions are based upon accessibility formula, the notion of spatial accessibility being here of no less importance than in the case of urban land market theories and the population density concepts. While in the latter approaches this notion pertains to relations between all the structural units of a city, in models of functional patterns it refers only to those elements which are, or may become, functionally interconnected; in other words, it refers to potential interactions. The role of spatial accessibility concepts stems also from the fact that models of functional patterns originated from metropolitan transportation models, and are often called the second generation transportation models. In metropolitan transportation models, for example in the well-known CATS study, the land use pattern was assumed as given and as a basis for the estimation of spatial variations in the demand for transportation. In contrast, models of functional patterns assume the location of certain land use elements, but the derived variations in predicted trip patterns serve to generate the remaining components of land use.

Two general characteristics of the allocation models have been subject to numerous critical evaluations. One of the characteristics are the methods of measuring spatial accessibility and spatial interaction, the other is the way the temporal dimension is usually handled. For example, Stegman (1969) strongly questions the concept of locational choice exclusively based on the spatial accessibility factor. To support his argument he submits data which attest to dependencies of intra-metropolitan migrations on variations in the quality of the urban environment, the social differentiation of urban communities, and the structure of housing markets, rather than on the location of workplaces, shopping centres, or other focal points of social interaction. It should be admitted that similar data are supplied by many ecological studies.

As far as the problem of time dimension is concerned, it is frequently noted that even the so-called quasi-dynamic models do not take account of changes in the nature of interactions, the evolution of the attractiveness criteria and the development of transportation means. It is possible that studies on individual activity patterns, both spatial and temporal, such as those advanced by Chapin (1968) and Hägerstrand (1970) would produce new inputs for the allocation models meeting the requirements of higher theoretical, rather than technical, sophistication.

Settlement Networks Theories

At least three different theoretical approaches originally developed on the scale of regional or inter-regional settlement networks have been subsequently extended to an interpretation of intra-urban growth and structure. These include: the central place theory, the concepts of linear settlement patterns, and the theory of metropolitan area. All three approaches have been mainly concerned with principles of the spatial distribution of functions and with the hierarchical organization of space.

The possibility of transferring the central place theory onto an intra-urban scale was suggested in the late 1950s by Garrison and Berry, while the first explicit, detailed analysis along this line was the study by Carol (1960) who found three hierarchical levels in the structure of the retail trade in Zurich and identified those levels with three out of the several orders in Christaller's hierarchy. Later, Berry (1963) proposed a comprehensive classification of shopping centres within a metropolitan area connecting the morphological and functional approaches. In addition to five hierarchical levels of centres he described two types of non-hierarchical retail clusters, namely commercial ribbons and specialized clusters. Berry found the following explanations of the hierarchical arrangement of business within a city: (1) different commercial functions have different conditions of entry (threshold) and thus demand minimum trade areas measured in size of population for their support, (2) goods and services differ in terms of the demand they generate and in terms of the frequency with which they are bought. In consequence, high threshold functions that meet sporadic needs, or are demanded by a small portion of the population, are found in higher level nucleations serving larger trade areas. These centres also perform lower order functions (as various kinds of goods may be purchased on one shopping trip) and for their lower order goods serve larger areas (population) than centres which are exclusively of that lower level. Thus, according to Berry the hierarchical structure of business centres within cities is generated by the same factors which are responsible for the emergence of central place systems on the regional scale.

It follows from the above that when incomes increase and transportation costs fall, the explanatory power of the central place theory gradually diminishes, at least on an intra-urban scale. Nevertheless, some of its elements retain validity. They include the non-hierarchical Lösch (1944) model of market areas for individual goods, the areas which according to Olsson (1967) may also be treated as changeable over time. Another argument in favour of the theory is that the territorial expansion of urban areas and the decline in overall population densities may counterbalance the decrease in transportation costs, hence the role of physical distance in hindering spatial mobility even on the intra-metropolitan scale. With the trend towards an increase in size of firms, units, and centres, this may lead to the emergence of a new, relatively regular pattern of business centres, although lacking hierarchy and differing in spatial scale from the traditional patterns.

In contrast to the central place models which apply to one of the components of urban spatial structure, i.e., to commercial and service patterns, models of linear patterns are usually intended to be comprehensive in scope. Their origin is sometimes traced to Lösch (1944) who postulated that central place forces produce what are called city-rich and city-poor sectors. Isard and Reiner (1962) described the mechanism of expansion within such a pattern. In an early phase growth of the main centre occurs in those portions of its peripheral zone which offer the advantages of low transportation costs and scale economies. Such areas, of course, happen to be located in the city-rich sectors. With a further expansion coming from the centre, consecutive rings of former central places are engulfed by the emerging metropolis. In city-poor sectors growth is relatively retarded; thus the shape of the metropolitan area tends to repeat the original pattern of settlement within the region.

The last of the three groups of concepts discussed in this section, namely, the theory of metropolitan area, can be traced back to the theory of metropolitan dominance and the theory of urban regions (Geddes, 1915). The functional approach of the former and the morphological approach of the latter concept were integrated in the theory of metropolitan community and in the related theory of metropolitan region (Bogue, 1949; Duncan et al. 1960).

It was McKenzie's (1933) contribution to demonstrate the interrelations between the growth of a city as an economic organism and its territorial expansion and internal rearrangement of functions, leading to the state in which a metropolis becomes identified with the former hinterland of its principal centre and the population occupying the whole territory becomes functionally integrated to form one metropolitan community. According to McKenzie, the rapid development of transportation during the first decades of the 20th century and the resulting growth of the spatial mobility of people, followed by the mobility of institutions, were the principal factors of metropolitan development. Similar interpretations prevail in the contemporary literature. For example, Lappo (1969) proposed a verbal model of the sequence of urban growth starting from a concentrated pattern, typical of the railway era, and ending up in a polycentric city-region pattern. Here again the dominant means of transportation determine to a large extent the major features and parameters of the urban structure.

Several authors have observed that monocentric and polycentric agglomerations evolve towards analogous spatial and functional forms. Thus, Bogorad (1968) distinguished two routes for the development of an urban agglomeration. In the first case a single large city, in the course of its expansion, encroaches upon surrounding settlements which become transformed in terms of both functions and physiognomy. New settlements, linked with the main city, are also established, and the rural-urban fringe continuously expands. In the second case the development of an industrial settlement complex proceeds via concentration and a parallel growth of its constituent parts. Individual mining and industrial towns gradually coalesce to form larger cities of dispersed, and later on, a more concentrated structure. An urban cluster is converted into a continuous urbanized territory, and, subsequently, into an urban agglomeration with a well-developed core area and morphologically diversified outer zones. Dziewoński (1973) adds another stage to the growth sequence, namely the stage of modernization and change of the economic base of a conurbation. Its expanding potential attracts new functions, particularly tertiary and quaternary activities which replace the original functions, eliminated by new technological requirements and/or the exhaustion of local resources.

Models of Spatial Diffusion on the Intra-urban Scale

Many of the models and concepts discussed so far in the paper emphasized spatial patterns rather than the processes responsible for their formation. Models of spatial diffusion pertain first of all to the process itself while treating existing or simulated patterns as possible outcomes of the development process. In turn, spatial diffusion is recognized as a basic process shaping locational patterns, consisting in a spread of phenomena on a given territory over time (Brown, 1968B).

Models of spatial diffusion can be traced back to the concepts of the spread of cultures and plants, the sequent occupancy, and the movement of colonization frontiers. Later, they were usually identified with innovation diffusion models (Hägerstrand, 1952). From there, via models of migrations (Hägerstrand, 1969) and of the development of local settlement networks (Morrill, 1965A) stem those approaches which treat urban spatial growth and the change of urban structure as specific types of diffusion processes. Despite dissimilarities between the nature of innovation diffusion on the one hand, and urban growth on the other, the two kinds of models share many common notions. These include the notion of the so-called neighbourhood effect, the notion of the resistance of the environment, and, first of all, the basic concepts of mean information field and physical barriers to diffusion. Brown (1968A) pointed out market organization and the structure of contact networks as factors largely determining the course of both innovation diffusion and the change in settlement net-

works. R. L. Morrill (1965A) in his early empirical study on the province of Småland attempted to demonstrate that the existing settlement system was a product of the complex historical process which, evolving irregularly over time and over space, took place in physically restricted and differentiated environments, whose mechanism included random factors, representing locational decisions based on criteria other than economic-man criteria, insufficient information, birth and decay, and technological change.

To place properly the process of urban expansion in relation to other diffusion processes it is instructive to quote Beckmann (1970, p. 109) who classified objects of diffusion into states (e.g., information) and physical objects. While changes in state may be reversible or irreversible, physical objects are subject to a law of conservation, or continuity. According to this criteria technical innovations and urban growth belong to the same category of diffusion phenomena. A different classification was proposed by Brown (1968B) who identified a relocation-type and an expansion-type of spatial diffusion. In the case of relocation a phenomenon or elements of population actually move over space between t and $t + 1$. Expansion, on the other hand, consists in a growth of population over the given time span, and the spread of the territory occupied. An interpretation of the expansion-type of diffusion may not be unequivocal if it is associated not only with states but also with physical objects, as Brown himself suggests, since, in the latter case a real transfer over space is taking place.

A specific regularity in the change of intensity forms one of the most distinctive features of diffusion processes and it supports hypotheses according to which some fundamental features are common to all types of diffusion. Thus, the innovation diffusion cycle, described by Hägerstrand (1952), consisted of the following stages:

(1) the primary stage, when new centres of innovation acceptance appeared, (2) the proper diffusion stage, when the existing centres became consolidated and the innovation began to spread out from the centres into the surrounding territory, (3) the condensing stage, when the phenomenon in question was commonly known and the number of new accepting units diminished. The condensing stage was followed by the saturation stage (4) when diffusion reached a certain ceiling and could not proceed further under the existing conditions.

A rural settlement diffusion cycle, presented by Hudson (1969) in the plant-ecological jargon possessed similar characteristics. In both cases an S-shaped curve represents a cumulative increase of population, while a closed unimodal curve describes the change of intensity of the process over time. Its shape, in fact, prompted Hägerstrand to introduce the notion of innovation waves, for which Morrill (1968, 1970) substituted later the more general term of diffusion waves. Morrill observed, however, that only certain diffusion processes have wave-like properties, as some (e.g., immigration into a region) may consist of a gradual intensification of a relatively constant pattern over time. On the other hand, urban spatial growth was found to possess many characteristics of a wave-like process (Korcelli, 1970, 1972).

Conclusions

It seems that theories and concepts which represent first of all what may be called the aggregate approach to the study of urban structure and growth, are largely universal in scope. This category includes settlement network theories, population density concepts, and the concepts of functional patterns. On the other hand, theories which emphasize the disaggregation of the metropolitan community into status, income, or ethnic groups, and analyse individual decision making processes, are usually specific to different socio-economic and cultural systems. To the latter group belong general ecological concepts, urban land market theories and, to some extent, diffusion concepts of urban growth.

As far as research frontiers are concerned, three major developments, already conspicuous, are likely to grow further in importance. First, there is a trend towards an expansion of the functional patterns concepts, mostly in the direction of activity systems and contact networks analysis. This is hardly accidental since the second major development is the growing emphasis on the relevancy of research and its applicability to urban and regional planning. Finally, one may perceive a growing share of theoretical studies pertaining to urban structure in the developing countries and in the socialist countries.

Bibliography

Abu-Lughod, J., 1969, Testing the theory of social area analysis: the ecology of Cairo, Egypt, *Amer. Soc. Rev.,* 34, pp. 198–212.

Ajo, R., 1965, On the structure of population density in London's field, *Acta Geogr.,* 18, 4.

Alonso, W., 1964, *Location and land use,* Harvard University Press, Cambridge, Mass.

Angel, S., Hyman, G. M., 1972, Urban transport expenditures, *Papers, Reg. Sci. Ass.* 29, pp. 105–123.

Beckman, M. J., 1970, The analysis of spatial diffusion processes, *Papers, Reg. Sci. Ass.,* 25, pp. 109–118.

Berry, B. J. L., 1963, *Commercial structure and commercial blight,* University of Chicago, Department of Geography, Research Paper 85.

Berry, B. J. L., 1964, Cities as systems within systems of cities, *Papers, Reg. Sci. Ass.,* 13, pp. 147–164.

Berry, B. J. L., 1967, *Geography of market*

centers and retail distribution. Foundations of Economic Geography Series, Prentice-Hall, Englewood Cliffs, N. J.

Berry, B. J. L., 1971, The logic and limitations of comparative factorial ecology, *Econ. Geogr.,* 47, 2 (Suppl.), pp. 209–219.

Birch, D. L., 1971, Toward a stage theory of urban growth, *J. Amer. Inst. Planners,* 37, pp. 78–87.

Bogorad, D. J., 1968, Zadachi i metody regulirovanya rosta gorodskikh aglomeratsii, in: *Gradostroitelstvo. Rayonnaya planirovka; gorodskiye aglomeratsii,* Budivelnik, Kiev, pp. 10–19.

Bogue, D. J., 1949, *The structure of the metropolitan community. A study of dominance and subdominance,* Institute for Human Adjustment; Social Research Project, University of Michigan, Ann Arbor.

Bourne, L. S., 1971, Physical adjustment processes and land use succession: a conceptual review and central city example, *Econ. Geogr.,* 47, pp. 1–15.

Boyce, D. E., 1965, The effect of direction and length of person trips on urban travel patterns, *J. Reg. Sci.,* 6, pp. 65–80.

Brigham, E. F., 1965, The determinants of residential land values, *Land Econ.,* 41, pp. 325–334.

Bromek, K., 1964, *Rozwój demograficzny regionu Krakowa w okresie od 1869 do 1950* (Sum.: The development of the demographic region of Cracow), Zesz. Nauk. U. J., 85, Prace Geogr., 9, Prace Inst. Geogr. 31, Kraków.

Brown, L. A., 1968A: *Diffusion dynamics. A review and revision of the quantitative theory of the spatial diffusion of innovation,* Lund Studies in Geography, Ser. B, Human Geography, 29, C. W. K. Gleerup, Lund.

Brown, L. A., 1968B: *Diffusion processes and location. A conceptual framework and bibliography,* Regional Science Research Institute, Bibliography Series 4.

Bucklin, L. P., 1971, Retail gravity models and consumer choice: A theoretical and empirical critique, *Econ. Geogr.,* 47, pp. 489–497.

Carol, H., 1960, The hierarchy of central functions within a city, *Annals, Ass. Amer. Geogr.,* 50, pp. 211–237.

Casetti, E., 1967, Urban population density patterns: an alternative explanation, *Canad. Geogr.,* 11, pp. 96–100.

Casetti, E., 1969, Alternative urban population density models: an analytical comparison of their validity range, in: *Studies in Regional Science,* 1, A. J. Scott, ed., Pion, London.

Casetti, E., 1971, Equilibrium land values and population densities in an urban setting, *Econ. Geogr.,* 47, pp. 16–20.

Chapin, F. S., Jr., 1968, Activity systems as a source of inputs for land use models, in: *Urban development models,* Special Report 97, Highway Research Board, Washington, D.C.

Chojnicki, Z., 1966, *Zastosowanie modeli grawitacji i potencjału w badaniach przestrzenno-ekonomicznych* (Sum.: The application of gravity and potential models in spatial economic research), Studia KPZK PAN, 15, Warszawa.

Cholaj, M., 1966, *Cena ziemi w rachunku ekonomicznym* (Land price in economic calculation), Warszawa, PWE.

Clark, C., 1951, Urban population densities, *J. Roy. Statist. Soc.,* 64, Ser. A, pp. 490–496.

Colean, M. L., 1953, *Renewing our cities,* The Twentieth Century Fund, New York.

Colenutt, R. J., 1970, Building models of urban growth and spatial structure, in: *Progress is Geography,* 2, Arnold, London, pp. 109–152.

Cressey, P. F., 1938, Population succession in Chicago, 1898–1930, *Amer. J. Soc.,* 44, pp. 59–69.

Curry, L., 1962, The geography of service centers within towns: the elements of an operational approach, in: *Proceedings of the IGU Symposium in urban geography,* Lund Series in Geography, Ser. B, Human Geography, 24, Lund, pp. 31–53.

Dacey, M. F., 1968, A model for the areal distribution of population in a city with multiple population centers, *Tijd. Econ. Soc. Geogr.,* 59, pp. 232–236.

Domański, R., 1967, Konstruowanie teorii w geografii ekonomicznej (Sum.: Construction of theories in economic geography), *Przegl. Geogr.,* 39, pp. 85–102.

Duncan, B., Sabagh, G., Van Arsdol, M. D.,

1962, Patterns of city growth, *Amer. J. Soc.,* 67, pp. 418–429.

Duncan, O. D., Duncan, B., 1957, *The Negro population of Chicago. A study of residential succession,* University of Chicago Press.

Duncan, O. D., Scott, W. R., Lieberson, S., Duncan, B., Winsborough, H. H., 1960, *Metropolis and region,* Resources for the Future, Johns Hopkins University Press, Baltimore.

Dziewoński, K., 1973, The geographical differentiation of contemporary urbanization, *Geogr. Pol.,* 27, pp. 31–41.

Garner, B. J., 1967, Models of urban geography and settlement location, in: R. J. Chorley, P. Haggett, eds., *Models in geography,* Methuen, London, pp. 303–360.

Garrison, W., 1962, Toward a simulation model of urban growth and development, in: *Proceedings of the IGU Symposium in Urban Geography,* Lund Studies in Geography, Ser. B., 24, Lund 1960, pp. 91–108.

Geddes, P., 1915, *Cities in evolution,* London.

Golc, G. A., 1972, Vliyanye transporta na prostranstvennoe razvitye gorodov i aglomeratsii, in: *Problemy sovremennoy urbanizatsii,* Statistika, Moskva, pp. 159–190.

Greer-Wootten, B., 1972, *Metropolitan regional analysis,* Progress in Geography, 4, Edward Arnold, London.

Gurevich, B. L., 1967, Plotnost naseleniya goroda i plotnost veroyatnosti sluchaynoy velichiny, *Vestn. Mosk. Univ., Ser. Geogr.,* 1, pp. 15–21.

Gurevich, B. L., Saushkin, J. G., 1966, Matematicheskii metod v geografii, *Vestn. Mosk. Univ., Ser. Geogr.,* 1, pp. 3–28.

Hägerstrand, T., 1952, *The propagation of innovation waves,* Lund Studies in Geography, Scr. B, Human Geography, 4.

Hägerstrand, T., 1969, Methods and new techniques of urban and regional research, in: *Urban and regional research,* Economic Commission for Europe, 2, United Nations, New York, pp. 61–72.

Hägerstrand, T., 1970, What about people in regional science, *Papers, Reg. Sci. Ass.,* 24, pp. 7–21.

Haig, R. M., 1927, *Major economic factors in metropolitan growth and arrangement,* Regional Plan of New York and its Environs, 1, New York.

Hansell, Ch. R., Clark, W. A. V., 1970, The expansion of the Negro ghetto in Milwaukee: a description and simulation model, *Tijd. Econ. Soc. Geogr.,* 61, pp. 267–277.

Harvey, D. W., 1970, Social processes and spatial form: an analysis of the conceptual problems of urban planning, *Papers, Reg. Sci. Ass.,* 25, pp. 47–70.

Hawley, A. H., 1950, *Human ecology. A theory of community structure,* Ronald Press Co., New York.

Hoover, E. M., Vernon, R., 1959, *Anatomy of a metropolis. The changing distribution of people and jobs within the New York Metropolitan Region,* Harvard University Press, Cambridge, Mass.

Hudson, J. C., 1969, A location theory for rural settlement, *Annals, Ass. Amer. Geogr.,* 59, pp. 365–381.

Hurd, R. H., 1903, *Principles of city land values,* New York, The Record and Guide.

Isard, W., Reiner, T. A., 1962, Regional science and planning, *Papers, Reg. Sci. Ass.,* 8, pp. 1–36.

Janson, C. G., 1971, A preliminary report on Swedish urban spatial structure, *Econ. Geogr.,* 47, No. 2 (Suppl.), pp. 249–257.

Johnston, R. J., 1969, Some tests of a model of intra-urban population mobility: Melbourne, Australia, *Urban Studies,* 6, No. 1.

Johnston, R. J., 1972, *Towards a general model of intra-urban residential patterns: some cross-cultural observations,* Progress in Geography, 4, Edward Arnold, London.

King, L. J., 1972, Models of urban land-use development, in: *Models of urban structure.* D. C. Sweet, ed., Lexington, Mass., pp. 3–26.

Kolipiński, J., 1970, *Metody rachunku efektywności w miejscowym planowaniu przestrzennym w Polsce (Studium krytyczne),* (Sum.: Methods of the efficiency calculation in spatial planning—applied in Poland), Studia KPZK PAN, 32, PWN, Warszawa.

Korcelli, P., 1970, A wave-like model of metropolitan spatial growth, *Papers, Reg. Sci. Ass.,* 24, pp. 127–138.

Korcelli, P., 1972, Urban spatial growth: a wave-like approach, *Geogr. Pol.,* 24, pp. 45–55.

Korcelli, P., 1973, Urban growth: some models and generalizations, *Geogr. Pol.,* 27, pp. 133–141.

Korzybski, S., 1952, Le peuplement des grandes agglomérations urbaines, Londres et Paris aux XIXe et XXe siècles, *Population*, 3, pp. 485–520.

Kostrubiec, B., 1970, Badania rozwoju przestrzennego aglomeracji miejskiej metoda profilów (Sum.: Spatial expansion of the urban agglomeration investigated by means of the method of profiles), *Przegl. Geogr.*, 42, pp. 235–248.

Lappo, G. M., 1969, *Geografia fiorodov s osnovami gradostroitelstva*, Izd. Mosk. Univ., Moskva.

Lentz, P., 1973, *The influence of a socialist economic environment on intra-urban residential spatial structure*, Clark Univ., Worcester, Mass. Ph.D. thesis.

Leszczycki, S., Eberhardt, P., Herman, S., 1971, Aglomeracje miejsko-przemysłowe w Polsce, 1966–2000 (Sum.: Urban-industrial agglomerations in Poland, 1966–2000), *Biuletyn KPZK PAN*, 67, Warszawa.

Leven, Ch. L., 1969, Determinants of the size and spatial form of urban areas, *Papers, Reg. Sci. Ass.*, 22, pp. 7–28.

Linday, S., 1971, The ecology of Islamic cities: the case for ethnocity, *Econ. Geogr.*, 47, No. 2 (Suppl.), pp. 303–313.

Lösch, A., 1944, *Die räumliche Ordnung der Wirtschaft*, Gotha.

Lowry, I. S., 1964, *A model of metropolis*, The Rand Corporation, RM-4035-RC, Santa Monica, California.

Lowry, I. S., 1968, Seven models of urban development: a structural comparison, in: *Urban development models*, Special Report 97, Highway Research Board, Washington, D.C.

McElrath, D. C., 1962, The social areas of Rome: a comparative analysis, *Amer. Soc. Rev.*, 27, pp. 376–391.

McKenzie, R. D., 1933, The metropolitan community, McGraw-Hill, New York.

Medvedkov, Yu. V., 1971, Internal structure of a city: an ecological assessment, *Papers, Reg. Sci. Ass.*, 27, pp. 95–117.

Morrill, R. L., 1965A, *Migration and the spread and growth of urban settlement*, Lund Studies in Geography, Ser. B, Human Geography, 26.

Morrill, R. L., 1965B, The Negro Ghetto: problems and alternatives, *Geogr. Rev.*, 55, pp. 339–361.

Morrill, R. L., 1965C, Expansion of the urban fringe: a simulation experiment, *Papers, Reg. Sci. Ass.*, 15, pp. 185–202.

Morrill, R. L., 1968, Waves of spatial diffusion, *J. Reg. Sci.*, 8, pp. 1–18.

Morrill, R. L., 1970, The shape of diffusion in space and time, *Econ. Geogr.*, 46 (Suppl.), pp. 259–268.

Morris, F. B., Pyle, G. F., 1971, The social environment of Rio de Janeiro in 1960, *Econ. Geogr.*, 47, No. 2 (Suppl.), pp. 286–299.

Murdie, R. A., 1969, *Factorial ecology of metropolitan Toronto, 1951–1961.* The University of Chicago, Department of Geography, Research Paper 116, Chicago.

Muth, R., 1969, *Cities and housing*, Chicago.

Newling, B. E., 1966, Urban growth and spatial structure: mathematical models and empirical evidence, *Geogr. Rev.*, 56, pp. 213–225.

Newling, B. E., 1969, The spatial variation of urban population densities, *Geogr. Rev.*, 59, pp. 242–252.

Niedercorn, J. H., 1971, A negative exponential model of urban land use densities and its implications for metropolitan development, *J. Reg. Sci. Ass.*, 11, pp. 317–326.

Olsson, G., 1967, Central place systems, spatial interaction, and stochastic processes, *Papers, Reg. Sci. Ass.*, 18, pp. 13–45.

Pahl, R. E., 1967, Sociological models in geography, in: R. J. Chorley, P. Haggett, eds., *Models in geography*, Methuen, London.

Papageorgiou, G. J., 1971, A theoretical evaluation of the existing population density gradient functions, Econ. Geogr., 47, pp. 21–26.

Papageorgiou, G. J., Casetti, E., 1971, Spatial equilibrium residential land values in a multicenter setting, *J. Reg. Sci.*, 11, pp. 385–389.

Pederson, P. O., 1967, *An empirical model of urban population structure. A factor analytical study of the population structure in Copenhagen.* Proceedings of the First Scandinavian-Polish Regional Science Seminar, Studia KPZK PAN 17, pp. 193–216.

Pióro, Z., 1962, *Ekologia spoleczna w urbanistyce* (Social ecology in urban planning), Arkady, Warszawa.

Pokshishevski, V. V., 1973, Urbanization and ethnographic processes, *Geogr. Pol.*, 27, pp. 79–85.

Ratcliff, R. U., 1949, *Urban land economics,* McGraw-Hill Publishing Co., New York.

Rees, P. H., 1970, The factorial ecology of Metropolitan Chicago. Chapter 10, in: B. J. L. Berry, F. E. Horton, eds., *Geographic perspectives on urban systems,* Prentice-Hall, Englewood Cliffs, N.J.

Robson, B. T., 1969, *Urban analysis,* Cambridge University Press, Cambridge.

Romashkin, V. J., 1967, Matematicheskaya model raspredeleniya plotnosti naseleniya Moskvy, *Vestn. Mosk. Univ., Ser. Geogr.,* 3, pp. 54–58.

Salins, P. D., 1971, Household location patterns in American metropolitan areas, *Econ. Geogr.,* 47, No. 2 (Suppl.), pp. 234–248.

Schmitt, R. E., 1956, Suburbanization: statistical fallacy?, *Land Econ.,* 32, pp. 85–87.

Schnore, L. F., 1957, Metropolitan growth and decentralization, *Amer. J. Soc.,* 63, pp. 171–180.

Schnore, L. F., 1965, On the spatial structure of cities in the two Americas, in: P. H. Hauser, L. F. Schnore, eds. *The study of urbanization,* Wiley and Sons, New York, pp. 347–398.

Senior, M. L., 1973, Approaches to residential location modelling; Urban ecological and spatial interaction models (A review), *Environment and Planning,* 5, pp. 165–197.

Sevostyanov, V. I., 1972, Plotnost naseleniya kak kharakteristika protsessa razvitiya goroda, *Vestn. Mosk. Univ.,* 2, *Ser. Geogr.,* pp. 40–46.

Sherratt, G. G., 1960, A model for general urban growth, in: C. W. Churchman, A. Verhulst, eds., *Management sciences, models and techniques,* New York, Pergamon Press, pp. 147–159.

Simmons, J. W., 1968, Changing residence in the city: a review of intra-urban mobility, *Geogr. Rev.,* 58, pp. 622–651.

Stegman, M. A., 1969, Accessibility models and residential location, *J. Amer. Inst. Planners,* 35, pp. 22–29.

Stewart, J. Q., 1947, Empirical mathematical rules concerning the distribution and equilibrium of population, *Geogr. Rev.,* 37, pp. 461–548.

Tanabe, K. 1970, Intra-regional structure of Japanese cities, in: *Japanese cities: a geographical approach,* Special Publication 2, The Association of Japanese Geographers, Tokyo.

Timms, D. W. G., *The urban mosaic,* The Cambridge University Press, Cambridge, 1970.

Vance, J. E., 1969, Urban structure and the geography of choice, *Annals, Ass. Amer. Geogr.,* 59 (abstract of a paper prepared for 64th Annual Meeting AAG).

Vance, J. E., 1971, Land assignment in the precapitalist, capitalist, and postcapitalist city, *Econ. Geogr.,* 47, pp. 101–120.

Werwicki, A., 1973, *Struktura przestrzenna średnich miast ośrodków wojewódzkich w Polsce* (Sum.: Internal structure of Polish medium size towns, voivodship capitals), Prace Geogr. IG PAN, 101, Warszawa.

Węcławowicz, G., 1975, *Struktura przestrzeni społeczno-gospodarczej Warszawy 1931 i 1970 w świetle analizy czynnikowej* (Sum.: The structure of socio-economic space of Warsaw of 1931 and 1970 in the light of factor analysis), Prace Geogr. IG PAN, 116, Warszawa.

Wheeler, J. O., 1970, Transport inputs and residential rent theory: an empirical analysis, *Geogr. Analysis,* 2, pp. 43–54.

Wilson, A. G., 1969A, Notes on some concepts in social physics, *Papers, Reg. Sci. Ass.,* 22, pp. 159–193.

Wilson, A. G. 1969B, Developments of some elementary residential location models, *J. Reg. Sci.,* 9, pp. 373–385.

Wingo, L., Jr., 1961, *Transportation and urban land,* Resources for the Future, Washington, D.C.

Winsborough, H. H., 1962, City growth and city structure, *J. Reg. Sci.,* 4, pp. 35–50.

Winsborough, H. H., 1963, The ecological approach to the theory of suburbanization, *Amer. J. Soc.,* 68, pp. 565–570.

Zipf, G. K., 1949, *Human behavior and the principle of least effort,* Addison-Wesley, Reading.

FRANK E. HORTON AND DAVID R. REYNOLDS

Effects of Urban Spatial Structure on Individual Behavior

The term *spatial structure,* although apparently never defined explicitly in the geographical literature, has been implicitly defined in a number of ways by geographers. For some, spatial structure is used as a shorthand description of the geometric concepts of interest in geography, such as pattern, distance, and morphology [2]; while for others, spatial structure is used as a synonym for spatial arrangements or relative location [7]. In all cases, however, spatial structure is viewed as an abstract or generalized description of the distribution of phenomena in geographic space.

Although geographers have turned from a predilection for the examination of individual elements of spatial structure to analyses of the spatial, causal, and functional relationships between elements [8], these elements must still be identified before such relationships can be examined. Typical elements included in a "macro" depiction of urban spatial structure include linear features (e.g., transportation networks and commercial "ribbons"), nodes (e.g., shopping centers, individual manufacturing plants, retail and wholesale outlets) and surfaces (e.g., residential population densities in general and densities of population subgroups, rent surfaces). In short, the geographer tends to view an urban area as a geometrically (spatially) organized whole. The modern urban geographer undertakes not only the description of this organized whole—via generalized statements of spatial structure—but also the explanation and prediction of changes in structure over time.

Several methodological orientations have been adopted by geographers to achieve explanation and prediction. The one of interest here is the so-called "behavioral approach." In broad terms, this approach can be described as an attempt to arrive at a set of empirically valid statements about individual, group, or mass behavior which can form the postulates in a theory yielding statements of spatial structure as logical outputs [*12*, p. 594].

It is the contention of this paper that an urban area cannot be viewed as one geometrically organized whole, *if* the researcher adopting a behavioral mode of empirical and theoretical analysis recognizes the existence of a large number of

From **Economic Geography**, Vol. 47, No. 1, 1971, pp. 36–41. Reprinted by permission of Economic Geography, Clark University, F. E. Horton, and D. R. Reynolds.

actors at varying geographical locations. Even if each actor has perfect information concerning opportunities and their locations, the urban spatial structure of the city would differ from actor to actor. At this level of analysis, one vital, if not central, element in urban spatial structure, which by necessity is not considered in the "macro" view, is the home. For many types of behavior, it is the origin from which the "macro" spatial structure of the urban area is utilized. Hence researchers attempting to develop behavioral theory might find it advantageous to view urban spatial structure in terms of the location of elements of the urban environment relative to the individual whose behavior is being studied.[1]

The behavioral approach adopted in the research reported on here possesses a different perspective from that described above. The concern is not with explaining changes in urban spatial structure, but rather in providing a basis from which to evaluate the impacts of exogenously induced changes in urban spatial structure on the spatial behavior of individuals. Collective changes in spatial preferences and behavior no doubt contribute to changes in the generalized geometrical organization of cities. However, in a majority of cases the individual actor has no direct control over the spatial organization of his environment. For the purposes of this research effort, changes in spatial behavior at the individual level are viewed as adjustments to changes in urban spatial structure rather than the active agents of structural change.

Specifically, this paper has three aims: (1) to specify and relate several concepts that appear to be important vehicles for tackling the problem of assessing impacts of changing urban spatial structures on spatial behavior, (2) to outline the authors' ongoing research in this problem area, and (3) to present two empirical

1. Essentially the same argument is made in *Moore* [15].

analyses which form a part of this research.

Basic Concepts

Before proceeding further, it is necessary to define several basic concepts utilized throughout the paper. The term *objective spatial structure* refers to the location of a household relative to the actual locations of all potential activities and their associated objective levels of attractiveness within an urban area. *Action space* is the collection of all urban locations about which the individual has information and the subjective utility or preference he associates with these locations. The subjective utility or preference is evaluated with regard to both potential and actual spatial behavior. Geometrically, action space is characterized by two components: first, its spatial extent as defined by the set of locations; and, second, a generalized surface (discrete and continuous) specifying the utility or preference level associated with each location.[2] An individual's *activity space* is defined as the subset of all urban locations with which the individual has direct contact as the result of day-to-day activities.[3] Geometrically, activity space is

2. This definition is a slight reformulation of the concept as it was originally presented by Wolpert [22], and is isomorphic to the concept of "awareness space" as utilized by Brown and Moore [1], if one assumes that there is a one-to-one correspondence between subjective utility or preference level and information level.
3. The term activity space is also similar to the notion of *activity system*. As defined by Chapin and Hemmins, an activity system is the sum of activities engaged in by individual urban inhabitants. The methodology chosen by Chapin and Hemmins attempts to develop taxonomies of urban residents based on similarities in the utilization of time and choice of activity and extending these group similarities to the analysis of how urban inhabitants interact with their environment. The approach taken here differs in that we are attempting to define the area for potential interaction with the environment (action space) and are seeking

characterized as a surface (again both discrete and continuous) descriptive of the intensity of actual spatial behavior over portions of the action space.

Although the individual has access to a broad range of environmental information, such information is not complete and varies considerably in both quality and quantity. Hence, discounting individual variations in information storage and retrieval capacities and capabilities, and assuming the objective spatial structures of any subset of individuals are approximately the same, variations in the cognitive images of objective spatial structures will still exist. Since, at any moment in time, the structure of an individual's action space is a direct function of his cognitive image, variations in action spaces will also be manifest. The degree to which the individual's activity space corresponds in form to the objective spatial structure of his urban environment depends upon his efficiency in collecting and assimilating information concerning it. Differences in race, sex, education, income, and social status are all likely to represent early and salient factors contributing to the individual's efficiency in receiving and weighing such information and may also induce distinctive biases in his spatial behavior. In this regard Meier [14] has convincingly argued that the individual's action space also evolves from birth through maturity.

While environmental perception is almost certainly affected by group memberships of the individual, or by his position and role in networks of social interaction, and by his stage in the life cycle, it will also be affected by his geographical location [22]. Through personal observation, the individual is likely to be more familiar with local areas (the areas in the vicinity of his residence and his workplace, in particular) than those points and areas at greater distances from him and about which available information is limited.

Since no two individuals perceive an environment from exactly the same location simultaneously, and since each bases his interpretation of received information on past experience, the cognitive images of the objective spatial structure of environments vary between individuals to an extent greater than anticipated by variations in geographical locations alone. Nevertheless, a useful hypothesis to test is that images and the resultant action spaces are, to a large extent, shared by groups of people in close geographical propinquity. In this regard, the work of some social scientists, sociologists, and social psychologists in particular contain several useful insights, albeit indirect, into the formation of the individual action space and the extent to which these are shared [18]. The importance of social groups in affecting individual behavior has been especially well studied [6]. Studies of the networks of interpersonal contacts have provided empirical evidence to suggest a close relationship between social and spatial propinquity [6, 16]. The flow of information through the networks of interpersonal communication forms the basis for images shared by individuals in social networks. Although group membership fosters development of shared images, it may also inhibit the flow of information to the individual from other sources. In this regard, Deutsch [5] has commented on the manner in which groups of people may be "marked off from each other by communicative barriers, by 'marked gaps' in the efficiency of communication."

Even though we may derive interesting research hypotheses from investigations such as Lynch's empirical examinations of how individuals in several areas perceive the "macro" spatial structure of their home cities, the present state of knowledge regarding the manner in

---

quantitative relationships which will yield both the activity space within a particular urban environment and expected changes in that activity space given changes have taken place within the urban environment [4, 3, 9, 10].

which objective spatial structures, the images of such structures, and travel preferences interact to form the action space is meager [13]. The research reported on below is directed towards overcoming this deficiency.

A Conceptualization of the Learning Process

An individual's action space and his perception of the urban environment cannot be viewed as being static, but rather as changing via a complex learning process. As indicated earlier, the nature of this process has not yet been investigated, and hence, is ill understood. However, predicated upon the preliminary findings of the authors' ongoing research, tentative hypotheses of the stages in the learning process, at least for the new in-migrant, can be outlined.[4]

It should be stressed that in the following it is assumed that the new in-migrant has already made a residential site selection, although in reality this decision is likely to be biased by his initial perception of his new urban environment. As presently conceived, it is not clear whether these stages are discrete or what the relative time duration is for each.

STAGE I—DISTANCE BIAS

The initial travel patterns established by the individual are highly unstable except for the journey to work, which is likely to become routinized early in his residential history. Other forms of spatial behavior are greatly influenced (1) by the new in-migrant's visual experience incurred on the journey to work and that derived from his immediate residential area, and (2) by his set of expectations of goal satisfaction at certain types of des-

4. In our framework, an individual's relocation within the urban area may be viewed as a change in urban spatial structure, e.g., when the individual is completely displaced from his former activity space.

tinations (e.g., chain department stores, national food and gasoline chains) and his preferences for travel—both of which have been developed elsewhere, whether in rural areas or in another urban place. At this stage, the individual's action space is fast expanding and his activity space is undergoing rapid change from week to week. However, both his action and activity spaces are dominated by two major nodes—the residence and the place of work—while other nodes are being subjected to what may be referred to as a spatial discounting procedure. Nodes near the residence and work place are "learned" first, then those at increasing distances. The in-migrant frequents more distant nodes and subjectively compares these with nodes learned earlier. If the more distant nodes are perceived as the more desirable, then the "local" nodes are discounted. (That is, they are dropped from the individual's current activity space, but are retained as component points in the action space even though they are negatively responded to, and vice-versa when perceived as less desirable.) Spatial behavior, although perhaps overtly characterized by utility maximization and distance minimization, is *suboptimal* as a result of previously learned expectations and preferences as well as locational biases in the receipt of environmental information induced by the location of home and work places and their location vis-à-vis one another.

STAGE II—COMMUNITY SOCIALIZATION

At the onset of the second stage, the individual has established temporary equilibrium between his spatial behavior and his direct and vicarious environmental experience which, as suggested above, has been affected by distance and directional biases. He has now become acquainted with neighbors and members of his work group from whom he learns of other potentially satisfactory destinations within the city. If these are located near the perimeter of his action space, he is more likely to investigate their desirability—and again, perviously satisfactory destinations are subject to spatial discounting. Newspapers and other forms of mass media now exert more impact upon spatial behavior than in the distance bias stage when too little of the urban environment was within the individual's action space and he rejected a major portion of the informational content of these media due to his lack of sufficient locational information.

STAGE III—SPATIAL EQUILIBRIUM

At this stage the individual's activity space is in spatial equilibrium with his perception of opportunities within his action space, and for many individuals the learning process becomes very slow with only occasional new pieces of information being absorbed (such as learning from new neighbors, and so on).[5] For these individuals, spatial behavior has become routinized and habitual (i.e., the activity space is stable). Any increase in the size of the action space is independent of the activity space; in fact, the action space is likely to become smaller as a result of lack of reinforcement of earlier perceptions.

For others, the environmental learning process, although proceeding at a reduced rate, continues largely as a result of their continued attention to information channels (interpersonal, and mass media). For these individuals, provided that no change of residence takes place and provided that they do not perceive change in the environment itself, their behavior can be expected to approach so-called rational economic behavior as their action spaces become congruent with the total metropolitan area. The spatial *extent* of the activity space, by definition,

5. Equilibrium is used here reflects a stable pattern of movement linkages produced by the individual's satisfaction with his current set of urban activities and their location.

is less than the extent of the action space. The "surface" characterizing the activity space is interrupted since many points and areas in the action space have been discounted relative to those points and areas in the activity space. Further, the individual's prior expectations and preferences for travel have changed as a result of his new environmental experience.

It should be stressed that this conceptualization of the environmental learning process presupposes that objective spatial structures of the urban environment itself do not change, or at least that any changes are not perceived by the individual. In point of fact, however, objective spatial structures and their components (i.e., retail structure, location of employment opportunities, residential quality, and so on) are constantly undergoing change, which results in the continuous reordering of perceived urban spatial structure. Ever present technological change also plays an important role in extending an individual's action and activity spaces and in modifying their morphology, but concomitantly impedes the tendency of the individual's spatial behavior toward the economically rational. One example of this is the increase in the use of private transportation which has, without doubt, made it possible for the individual to extend the perimeter of his action and activity space. At the same time, however, continual increases in the use of this mode of transportation has affected spatial distortions and place "disutilities" within the areally increased activity space by yielding penalties in the form of congestion with all its concomitant psychological and physiological effects. Therefore, continuous technological change and perceptual lags would seem to preclude the possibility of the individual achieving spatial equilibrium and economically rational behavior, although they may be approached. Herein lies at least a partial explanation of why deterministic, non-behavioral models have met with little success in explaining or even

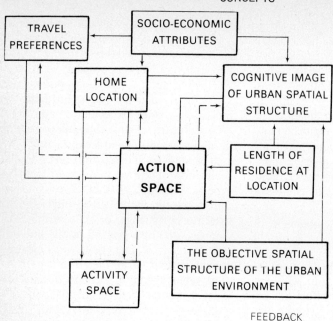

Figure 1. Conceptual Model for Action Space

forecasting spatial behavior, except at a highly aggregative level.

Although urban change results in a continuous reordering of the perceived urban environment, this reordering is likely to differ markedly by locational and socioeconomic groups. For example, despite rapid environmental change in parts of metropolitan areas, urban ghetto life would seem to generate a cramped view of the urban environment due, in part, to the spatial concentration of environmental experience [19]. Also, the construction of expressways through low income, central city areas to date seems to have a greater effect in expanding the activity and action spaces of suburbanites than those of the central city residents.

RESEARCH OVERVIEW

There are several ways in which one could proceed with an examination of individual action spaces and the isolation of those factors which are important

inputs to their formation and change. The conceptualization of the learning process specified earlier leaned heavily on the importance of a temporal dimension. In essence, our lack of knowledge of the relationship among components deemed important in the action space formation process and the direct inputs of these components to individual action spaces has limited the current research strategy to a cross-sectional analysis. Figure 1 illustrates in diagrammatic form our present conceptualization of the important inputs to the formation of an individual's action space. The total research effort encompasses the definition of relationships among components and between components and the urban resident's action space.[6]

The specific objectives of the total research effort can be thought of as consisting of three closely related tasks.

6. The specific empirical example is not reprinted here since there are others in the book (Ed. note).

(1) The definition and measurement of urban individuals' action spaces, and the manner in which urban spatial structures are perceived by urban residents in such a way as to permit testing of hypotheses.

(2) The construction and testing of a behavioral model which can be utilized to define the urban household's action space.

(3) The development of a coherent methodology for assessing how the individual's perception of his objective spatial structure is affected by changes occurring within his environment.

Literature Cited

1. Brown, L. A. and E. G. Moore. "The Intra-Urban Migration Process: A Perspective," *Geografiska Annaler,* Ser. B, 52 (1970).

2. Bunge, W. *Theoretical Geography.* Rev. ed. Lund: Gleerup, 1966.

3. Chapin, F. S., Jr. "Activity Systems and Urban Structure: A Working Schema," *Journal of the American Institute of Planners,* 34 (January, 1968), pp. 11–18.

4. Chapin, F. S., Jr. and T. H. Logan. "Patterns of Time and Space Use," *The Quality of the Urban Environment.* Edited by H. S. Perloff. Baltimore: Johns Hopkins Press, 1969, pp. 305–32.

5. Deutsch, K. M. *Nationalism and Social Communication.* Cambridge, M.I.T. Press, 1960.

6. Festinger, L., S. Schacter, and K. Back. *Social Pressures in Informal Groups.* New York: Harper and Brothers, 1950.

7. Garrison, W. L. "Spatial Structure of the Economy: I," *Annals of the Association of American Geographers,* 49 (June, 1959), pp. 232–39.

8. Haggett, P. and R. J. Chorley. "Models, Paradigms and The New Geography," *Models in Geography.* Edited by R. J. Chorley and P. Haggett. London: Methuen, 1967, pp. 19–41.

9. Hemmins, G. C. "Analysis and Simulation of Urban Activity Patterns." Paper presented at the Annual Symposium on Application of Computers to the Problems of Urban Society, New York, October 18, 1968.

10. Hemmins, G. C. "Experiments in Urban Form and Structure," *Highway Research Board Record,* No. 207 (1968), pp. 32–41.

11. Horton, F. E. and D. R. Reynolds. "An Investigation of Individual Action Spaces: A Progress Report," *Proceedings, Association of American Geographers,* 1 (1969), pp. 70–75.

12. King, L. J. "The Analysis of Spatial Form and Its Relation to Geographic Theory," *Annals of the Association of American Geographers,* 59 (September, 1969), pp. 573–95.

13. Lynch, K. *The Image of The City.* Cambridge: M.I.T. Press, 1960.

14. Meier, R. "Measuring Social and Cultural Change in Urban Regions," *Journal of The American Institute of Planners,* 25 (1959), pp. 180–90.

15. Moore, E. G. "Some Spatial Properties of Urban Contact Fields," *Geographical Analysis* (forthcoming).

16. Merton, R. K. "The Social Psychology of Housing," *Current Trends in Social Psychology.* Pittsburgh: University of Pittsburgh Press, 1950, pp. 163–219.

17. Peterson, G. L. "Subjective Measures of Housing Quality: An Investigation of Problems of Codification of Subjective Values for Urban Analysis." Unpublished Ph.D. dissertation, Northwestern University, 1965.

18. Rubenstein, A. H. and C. J. Haberstrol. *Some Theories of Organization.* Homewood, Illinois: Richard D. Irwin, 1964.

19. Suttles, G. D. *The Social Order of The Slum.* Chicago: University of Chicago Press, 1968.

20. Torgeson, W. S. *Theory and Methods of Scaling.* New York: John Wiley and Sons, 1958.

21. Wachs, M. "Evaluation of Engineering Projects Using Perceptions of and Preferences for Project Characteristics." Research Report, The Transportation Center, Northwestern University, 1967.

22. Wolpert, J. "Behavioral Aspects of The Decision to Migrate," *Papers, The Regional Science Associations,* 15 (1965), pp. 159–69.

TORSTEN HÄGERSTRAND

The Impact of Social Organization and Environment upon the Time-Use of Individuals and Households

We need some pervading structure and predictability in society in order to secure cooperation between people and things. Industrial society has worked out its own way to accomplish this task. The system shows an overwhelming power to provide articles for private consumption. At present it is not so friendly with other aspects of life and it has difficulties in giving public goods a sufficient share.

Two dimensions have become rather overlooked in the development process. One is the need of the human being to experience coherence and continuity in his activities and relations both in a practical and in a mental sense. The other is the costs related to certain environmental constraints of a more fundamental nature than the available amount of critical raw materials in a purely quantitative meaning. Both omissions could be the outcome of two corresponding circumstances working together. One is the fact that the general philosophy behind traditional industrial organization has been permitted to extend throughout the rest of society. The other is the lack of a conceptual frame or language, suitable to lay bare events in society which should have been

noted long ago as problems to be counteracted.

Impressed by the immense efficiency of manufacturing industry we have been led into the belief that such key concepts as "increased division of labour" and "specialization of function" ought to be applied without reservation to almost all spheres of human activity. A growing bureaucracy, a vast number of technical specialists and a multiplicity of powerful interest organizations try to look after more and more narrowly defined sets of events. The built environment and the uses of natural resources take shape in the hands of an army of separated experts. It makes little difference if we examine economic, social or cultural activities. And what is more serious, the individuals as patients, pupils or students have likewise come to be treated more and more piecemeal as if they were factory products. Age-groups and generations are directed into separate clusters. Small children lose sight of the adult world in day nurseries and old people learn how to die properly away from the rest of society. Oddly enough the logic of chopping up activities of all sorts in

From **Plan International,** 1972, Swedish Society for Town and Country Planning. Reprinted by permission of the Society and T. Hägerstrand.

smaller and smaller parcels leads to bigger and bigger firms, institutions, unions, buildings and cities to contain them.

To our great astonishment this tremendous accumulation of specialized competence and administrative ambition is on its way to creating an aggregate outcome which is much less than satisfactory. As already indicated the explanation could be simple enough. It is hard to go on dividing up tasks along systematic lines and still keep in mind and respect that the human being is indivisible and that there are needs and wants which can never be satisfied with money transactions or professional intervention. Secondly, it tends to go unnoticed that things and processes in the real world do not only hang together in the manner the expert thinks to be important. They also interact in all sorts of unexpected and unwanted configurations because of their coexistence in time and terrestrial space. Like other natural resources time and space have particular scarcity characteristics. It is inevitable that unlike phenomena engage in a packing process, full of disturbing consequences (of which pollution is just one). Few are trained to appreciate this point.

Now, both conditions—the indivisibility of the human being and the limitations of time-space to accommodate things and events—do not come out well, perhaps hardly at all, in the language of descriptive statistics which today is the dominating kind of information behind decision-making. The descriptive task is really not numerical but topological in nature. But so far no convenient language is available to meet the challenge.

It is easy to see why this fundamental language problem, or conceptual problem, has not been solved a long time ago. In an earlier, less complicated society, both conditions were intuitively clear. The peasants of the preindustrial village understood perfectly well how their settlement functioned in terms of manpower, social relations, technical equipment, working procedures and landuse. They could all literally see all this at work from childhood. There was no need for a particular language to deal with a closed situation of this kind. The same cannot be said of today's city-fathers nor of their advisors. As everything has become broken up into small pieces of knowledge, responsibility and action and as connections between events have become more and more invisible for the locally based observer, we have lost touch with the kind of direct information which is needed for intuitive understanding.

Our very different cognitive situation may have invited us to think that the loosening of local ties has given us an altogether free personal choice of events to engage ourselves in. It is true that the assortment of possible combinations is vastly greater than it ever was, but certain fundamental limitations are still there. Just as we can achieve only a limited rationality so is only a limited freedom attainable when it comes to action. A vast number of situations which the individual becomes involved in are of a kind that he cannot avoid or counteract. A reorientation of the pattern of risks and opportunities must be worked out on some system level above him as far as the matter can be influenced at all by human intervention. This is quite clear where pollution and traffic hazards are concerned. But also circumstances like availability of employment, dwellings, education, health care, recreation, kind of social contacts and transportation beyond walking distance are among environmental resources outside immediate control by the average citizen. He can sometimes migrate, of course, to some other setting. But when he is there he will again find himself hooked up in a pre-existing arrangement which largely has to be taken as it is.

As pointed out by Harvey (1970), the manner in which urban areas are structured and the ways urban activities

are organized have deepgoing consequences for the distribution of real income among the urban population. By
real income is then understood not only
money income in a narrow sense but also
access to environmental resources and
opportunities of all kinds. If this is true
of urban areas it is as well true of the
wider regions which make up nations
and continents.

Given this outlook one comes to the
conclusion that a population, organized
in a certain way and contained in a physical setting, partly immutable and partly
only slowly rearrangable, sends its individual members into sequences of events
which by their distributions and characteristics describe the performance of the
set-up as a whole. One kind of effort to
estimate performance in a comprehensive
way is well known: the national income
account is a widespread instrument for
the purpose since a couple of decades.
Experiments are under way to break down
the national measure into corresponding
regional income accounts. But it is clear
that the transactions included in the accounts do not exactly measure what is
under discussion here. They cannot show
how roles become divided between individuals in the process, seen in cross-
section, and how events thereby tend to
fall out upon individuals in a longitudinal
perspective. A step in the latter direction
is taken more clearly in surveys collecting
so called social indicators. The growing
interest in time budgets as a research tool
is an indication of a further move towards
a less aggregated and abstract form of
observation.

The trends in research just mentioned
are clear advancements. But still one
should not overlook that empirical approaches of this kind also entail those
disadvantages which always follow measurement without theory. It is true that by
observing the behaviour of members of a
population, one learns something about
their living conditions as they have been
understood by the actors. But this information does not clearly separate what are
wants and needs from what are various
degrees of necessities. Behaviour does
not reveal in full the underlying pattern
of constraints which shapes the situations
in which action takes place. And this also
means that no good clues are provided
for how to reshape the living conditions
if that seems to be called for. We must
look for latent structure and latent processes to find the clues. Purposeful
changes of the distribution of opportunities and risks among individuals require
first of all an understanding of how constraints interact and how the choice potential is affected by relaxation or tight-
ening of one or more of those which can
be influenced at all. If we assume—as the
above reasoning implies—that people survive in "niches" of possible actions then
the shapes and volumes of these niches
are more fundamental objects for research than actual behaviour at a certain
moment. The latter is just a sample from
the universe of permitted events—permitted taken in a much broader sense
than the legal. It also includes the physical and physiological side of the matter.
The pattern of niches as formed by constraints in operation describes something
different. It renders the map of potential
events. The notion of potentials contains
a more general measure of performance.
The big question is how to go about finding the map.

A way out which has seemed worth trying is to translate all necessary concepts,
old or new, into a strictly "physical"
language. In this procedure it is essential
that the unity of time and space is fully
respected. What that means can be indicated by a simple figure (Figure 1). For
the sake of illustration three-dimensional
space has been collapsed into a two-
dimensional map. This trick leaves the
third dimension for representing time.
The acting individual describes an un-
broken "path" in time-space. It is easy to

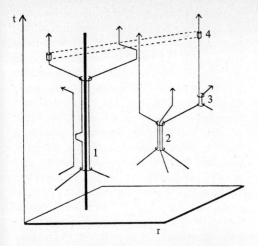

Figure 1. The Time-Space Paths of a Group of Individuals Bound Up in a Day's Activity System.

r represents geographical space and t represents time. 1, 2, 3 and 4 indicate different kinds of activity bundles. I is connected with some fixed installation, 2 and 3 are meetings with different durations. All three kinds of bundles require movements before and after in order to be formed. 4 stands for a telephone call which does not require movement but still binds two individuals together in one activity. It is evident that time-use would be affected by a change of locations. It is also clear that every new bundle put in eliminates some preexisting potential combinations. Thus, the time budget of an individual is not a wholly private affair. It is subordinated to some sort of collective arrangement and this is so even if only "market forces" are at work

imagine how a population of interacting individuals form a network of paths but with the fundamental property that identity is retained. In the same way, the environment in which the population network is embedded comes out either as paths described by mobile objects or as time-space pattern of walls and channels or—on a more aggregate level—as localized probability densities. The picture makes it immediately clear that cooperation between individuals, buildings, tools, materials and signals require both synchronization and synchorization in order to work. In other words, time and place

hang together. Seen as a whole, the system exhibits a skeleton of meeting-times and meeting-places. Much of the skeleton has been built up in advance, frequently very far in advance.

It is not the intention to describe the model further in the presentation (cf. Hägerstrand, 1970, Cullen and Godson, 1971, Bullock, 1971). But let us consider a little more a few points related to human cooperation. It should be kept in mind that this is a complicated matter already in a space-free timetable sense. Even if members of a population do nothing else than engage in sending messages of different length by telecommunication media (so that transportation for all practical purposes is instantaneous), the indivisibility of the human being is a severe constraint on what can happen. As soon as a communicating group has come into being, the duration of its activity inevitably creates waiting-times among those who want to come into contact with one or more members of the group. The conflicts that arise will become a more and more obvious difficulty as we move towards a society in which the handling of information develops into the main activity, whether for economic, educational, political, personal service or recreational purposes.

To think of the problems of a big and exclusive communication society is to take the case to the extreme. But it is clear that already in the society we have, there is much headache related to time-use. One can safely assume that much of the trouble is associated with coupling constraints which have been left unanalyzed as to their broader implications. Still, it is necessary to remember that more than coupling between time-uses goes into the problem.

To illustrate, let us assume that the population network (Figure 1) has been preplanned in the best conceivable way in terms of just time-use in order to take care of some defined set of tasks. That sort of planning is never done for open society of course (except perhaps in times of war), but certain big organizations like universities and hospitals at least try to carry out planning in that direction. It follows from the earlier discussion that even the best arrangement which can be made contains much human time which has to be left out. It is rather arbitrary what part of this comes to be called unemployment or hidden as blank hours. One cannot come around a conflict between the internal logic of tasks to perform and the indivisibility of persons involved. Let us further assume that the preplanned time-table is imposed over a population as an ideal pattern and that this population is immersed in an area with ordinary irregular geographic characteristics. This latter exercise will then add some further complexities.

It is first of all unavoidable that facilities where sub-operations of the program have to take place are separated by distances. This adds time for movement. How much depends on the program. As a rule, the more of division of labour and specialization of function one has foreseen, the more bits of transportation will have to be provided. It is further unavoidable that facilities will have certain capacity limitations. These produce waiting-times in queues. It is unavoidable that people, when moving from location to location in the area, become involved in unforeseen events depending upon how things and activities happen to get packed together in the limited space. In short, the ideal space-free time-table does not work.

Adjustments can take place in many ways. People have to change roles. Tasks have to be given up or it has to be accepted that they are carried out at a slower pace than originally planned. In a long-term perspective people will have to migrate out from and into the system in order to satisfy their private time-use needs. Technology comes in and tries to speed up transportation and manufacturing procedures. The physical infrastructure is slowly reshaped in terms of locations and/or capacities. Some enterprising people will find out that as soon as certain tasks cannot be accommodated, some new ones with a different time-space structure might go in. In short, just that process will develop which we witness in today's urbanization, a process which is kind and rewarding to some groups and not so kind and rewarding to other groups.

What has just been said is not a historical account. Social and economic organization does not develop as distortion of a preplanned master time-table. But reality still contains enough of thinking and acting as if it worked that way. Therefore it comes to mind as a reasonable proposition to structure research concerned with the pattern of constraints in steps going from idealization to distortion. The fact is that industrial organizers, welfare administrators and individuals frequently present their ideas in forms which imply ideal time-tables. It seems to be closest at hand to think in the linear time dimension as soon as we leave the still more convenient money dimension. Strong decision-makers impose their schemes (say industry and school) and the weaker ones have to find their places, if any, in spaces left between. In the never-ending battle between time-tables it is no longer clear to anybody how the system actually works. We have lost sight of the indivisibility condition and the fact that a space-less economy and society are impossible. It seems worth trying to wind up the question of the impact upon the individual of social organization and environment from the time-use end but at the same time doing so in a deductive fashion.

In a couple of research projects, related to the Swedish regional policy program, some aspects of the problems mentioned above have been taken up for closer examination. The focus has been placed upon how events fall out upon the single individual and the household group depending on interaction between timetables and geographical environments. It is not possible to go into technical details showing how this analysis can be done. Computer simulation is so far the most important device. The basic scheme is the following:

1. Assume a population and a related sequence of actions in time-table terms;
2. sieve the population-and-action system through an environment;
3. register the outcome as it is distributed among individuals in the given population.

A considerable part of the work is basic research dealing with computer modelling as such. A second component covers empirical testing of the patterns of constraints and opportunities inherent in typical present-day urban and other environments in the country. The sample includes the sparsely populated area, the small and the middle-sized town, both with their immediate hinterlands, the big city and finally the urban system as a whole.

Two time scales have been chosen. One part of the work deals with daily and weekly activities. The other part takes a long-term perspective. Questions are asked about how life chances and environments are related. In neither case are broad statistical surveys of actual behaviour essential. Emphasis is laid upon the working of constraints. And these are in various ways sensed with the aid of idealtypical sequences of actions which are confronted with actual or model environments. Questions are asked about how these various environments perform as providers of jobs, training, services, recreation, care, social communication and time at free disposal—to mention only the most important items looked for.

Beside investigations turning on the individual and household, a related project (Törnqvist *et al.*) is applying a similar approach in order to try out how far location of economic activity is dependent upon direct personal contacts between individuals. The main purpose so far has been to test how well the present national transportation system functions as part of the daily environment for co-operating individuals in industry, business and public administration. The first step has been to estimate the "contact potential" under existing circumstances. The second step was to measure how a relocation of base-points within the urban system affects the contact potential if at the same time no change takes place in the network and timing of passenger transportation. The third step, finally, is intended to show what happens to the potential if one goes on to reorganizing transportation as well as location.

Thus what the researchers are moving towards are methods to test in advance the probable outcome of policies and plans but all the time in terms of potentials, not in terms of actual events.

References

Bullock, N.: An approach to the simulation of activities: a university example. Land Use and Built Form Studies, Working Paper 21, Cambridge 1970.

Cullen I. and Godson, V.: The Structure of Activity Patterns. Joint Unit for Planning Research, Research Paper No. 1, London 1971.

Harvey, D.: Social processes, spatial form and the redistribution of real income in an urban system. Regional Forecasting (ed. Chisholm-Frey-Haggett), Colston Research Symposium Bristol, London 1971.

Hägerstrand, T.: What about people in regional science? Regional Science Association, Papers vol. XXIV, 1970.

Törnqvist, G.: Kontaktbehov och resemöjligheter. Några Sverigemodeller för studier av regionala utvecklingsalternativ (in print).

JOHN R. MIRON

Economic Equilibrium in Urban Land Use

Why are certain land uses found extensively in certain parts of a city, but not in others? This question has been at the heart of urban geography for many decades. As one might expect, a variety of theories have been advanced during this time. This paper describes one theory that sees urban land use as a spatial equilibrium pattern generated by economic principles. The essence of the theory is that the allocation of urban land to various uses is determined in a competitive land market in equilibrium, where each parcel of land is allocated to the highest bidder. In this theory, the question "Why is a land use found on a certain parcel of land?" reduces to the question "Why is this land use the highest bidder for that parcel?" This paper argues that the land market theory is important and that it does provide valuable insights about urban spatial structure. At the same time, there are some very real limitations to the theory as currently formulated.

Here is a guide to the rest of this paper. In Section 1, some important terms and concepts are defined. A land market theory of the spatial pattern of commercial and industrial land uses is described in Section 2. In Section 3, some problems in applying this theory to residential land

use are raised. In Section 4 a "simple" theory of residential land use patterns is described. This is followed in Section 5 by a review of different recent elaborations of this simple theory. Finally, some conclusions are drawn in Section 6 about the validity and usefulness of this approach.

1. Of Definitions and Concepts

This paper is based on some terms and concepts that must be carefully defined. One pair of such terms are the "market price" for a parcel of land and the "market rent" for it.

The market price of land: The asset value of a unit of land. The amount paid in the market for legal ownership of that unit of land.

The market rent for land: An amount paid in the market for the exclusive use of a unit of land for a specified, short period of time, such as a month or year.

The ensuing discussion focuses almost exclusively on the "rent" as opposed to the "price" for land. In other words, we ask how much a household or firm is willing to pay to occupy a parcel of land for one time period. How much someone is willing to pay to obtain legal ownership is not considered.

In the theory outlined in this paper, rent and price are assumed to be separable. The theory suggests that each landowner in effect "leases" land to the highest bidder in that time period, even though the highest bidder may actually be the landlord (thus introducing the possibility that no cash rent is actually paid). In effect, ownership is deemed to be irrelevant in determining who will actually occupy or use the land during a given time period.

This is a stringent assumption, but one which greatly simplifies any analysis. If the time period of a lease is fairly short, the rent a potential user is willing to bid for a parcel of land will depend only on the use to which that parcel is to be put during that time. That bid rent specifically will not depend on the bidder's perception of future market trends in price or rent. However, if the user is bidding for a long-term lease (or ownership as the extreme version of this), the possibility of capital gains or losses accruing on a subsequent sublease (or sale in the case of ownership) cannot be ignored. This dimension of future returns or losses is ignored where rents are considered rather than prices. This is the simplification purchased by ignoring ownership.

Next, let us define for a commercial firm some notions about profits.

The "normal profit" of a firm: That flow of profit to a business enterprise which must be maintained in the long run for that firm to find it worthwhile to remain in business. It is usually thought of as a set of normal rates of return applied to invested capital and other unpriced or underpriced factors.

The "excess profit" of a firm: The amount if any by which the actual profits of a firm exceed the normal

profit before land rent has been subtracted out.

The "net excess profit" of a firm: The excess profit of the firm after land rent has been subtracted out.

In these definitions, it is assumed that the disposition of a firm's total revenues can be split into four components: (1) the amount paid for inputs other than land and including taxes, (2) the amount paid for land, (3) the normal profit, and (4) a residual net excess profit. If the sum of the first three components is greater than total revenues, net excess profit will be negative.

In this theory, households "consume" land and other goods. The leasing of a parcel of land for a given time period for the household's place of residence is assumed to help generate a certain level of utility or satisfaction.[1] This concept is defined as follows.

A "utility level": An index, $U(W)$ measuring the relative desirability of a certain choice (W). If a household has a choice between W and X and chooses W, then $U(W)$ is larger than $U(X)$.

Let us consider a household that is competing for a given parcel of land. Suppose the household is considering offering either $150 or $200 per month for this parcel. We could represent these two choices as $W = \$150$ and $X = \$200$. Clearly our household is not indifferent between these two choices. Given a choice, this household would prefer W to X because the additional $50 per month that would be saved could be used for other purposes. In other words, $U(W) > U(X)$. Thus, we can draw a correspondence between a bid rent by a household

---

1. Readers unfamiliar with terms such as utility or profit should consult a standard introductory text in economics.

for a certain parcel and the utility level associated with this bid. A household may have any number of bid rents for a parcel, each associated with its own utility level.

In a similar manner, a firm that makes a certain bid for a certain parcel of land can measure the desirability of this bid by the net excess profit which it implies. A low "bid rent" implies a larger net excess profit and a high bid a low net excess profit. On the basis of the above two paragraphs, let us now define a bid rent.

> The "bid rent" for land: An amount someone is willing to bid for the exclusive use of a unit of land for a specified, short period of time given a certain prescribed utility level (households) or a certain level of net excess profits (firms).

Suppose there are two different sites being considered by the same firm or household. Suppose that a bid rent is being considered for each site that would give the household (or firm) the same utility (or net excess profit) level. Why would not the bid rents at the two sites be necessarily identical? Clearly, different sites may generate different utilities or different net excess profits. Commonly, these differentials are attributed to two sets of factors: "site advantage" and "locational advantage."

> The "site advantage" of a parcel of land: The portion of a bid rent attributable to the internal characteristics of that site. This may, for example, be associated with the cost of developing that parcel as having to do with topographical grade, soil load-bearing capacity, or drainage characteristics.

> The "locational advantage" of a parcel of land: The remaining portion of a bid rent assumed to be attributable to its locational characteristics, e.g., its accessibility to markets or proximity to good transportation facilities.

2. Commercial and Industrial Land Use Theory

Any explanation of urban land use patterns should as a first test be able to explain the spatial pattern of the dominant land use, the residential sector. This however is precisely where early attempts at a land market theory failed. If land is allocated to the highest bidding renter, why is a certain kind of residential use the highest bidder at a given site? More specifically, what determines the rent that a residential user is willing to bid for that site? A given site may be very desirable—e.g., be in a pleasant neighbourhood, have good public facilities, or be accessible to work, school, or shopping facilities—but what determines whether a household with a given income and other characteristics bids $100, $1,000, $10,000, or $100,000 per time period for that site? As Alonso (1964, pp. 1–17) points out in his review of earlier work, a number of earlier writers ignored the residential sector altogether because of the intractability of this question.

By contrast, the land market explanation is much more easily applied to commercial and industrial land uses. Consider a site that is desired by such firms either for its site advantages or its locational advantages. Suppose that many identical firms are competing for this same parcel of land. The price of that parcel will be bid up. Where will the bidding stop? There is a rent at which the attractiveness of that parcel—usually its locational advantage—is exactly nullified. In more exact terms, there is a rent at which the net excess profit is driven to zero. Thus a firm ends up paying a rent that permits it to just achieve a normal profit at that site, neither more nor less. If the rent were any less, another firm could step in and bid away the site by offering a marginally higher rent. If the rent were any larger than the excess profit, no firm could remain there and still earn a normal profit.

Imagine for a moment that this fierce competition for one parcel of land is simultaneously going on as well for all other parcels in the area. On each parcel, the rent would rise to the amount of the excess profit that could be earned at that site. Of course, on some parcels of land a firm might not be able to earn even normal profits, let alone excess profits, so that no firm will bid for such a parcel. Thus, the spatial pattern of land rents, where these are zero or positive, reflects the excess profit attainable at each site.

This model can easily be extended to allow for more than one kind of firm provided that there are enough firms of each kind to make for competitive bidding for each site. Suppose for example that there are two kinds of firms; kind "a" and kind "b." At a given site an "a" firm will have an excess profit of r_a and a "b" firm r_b. These firms will thus have bid rents of r_a and r_b, respectively. Landlords, in maximizing rental revenue would choose the larger of r_a or r_b. Thus, the market rent at a given site is the maximum excess profit any kind of firm could bid for that site (or zero if the excess profit is negative for all possible kinds of firms).

This model breaks down, however, when there are not a large number of competitive firms of each kind. Imagine the following scenario in which you are the only firm of kind "b." There are many firms of kind "a" competing for each different site. In your absence there would be a market rent of r_a at a given site (or zero if r_a is negative). Let us suppose that you have calculated your excess profit, r_b, at each site and picked out that site where $r_b - r_a$ is a maximum. You might approach the landlord of that site and offer r_a (i.e., what the other firms are willing to pay) plus a minute amount to secure that site for yourself. The following dialogue might ensue.

You: How about r_a plus a little bit to rent this site?

Landlord: How about a little more, say, r_b?

You: That's outrageous. I can always go down the street. . . .

Landlord: But down the street, your best net excess profit (after rents) there, i.e., $r_b - r_a$, is smaller than it would be here.

You: I can see you've done your homework. Let's work out a deal. . . .

The exact nature of the "deal" would be determined in the ensuing bargaining, but it is clear that the market price for this site would settle somewhere between r_a and r_b.

We can now formally state the land market explanation of spatial (commercial and industrial) land use patterns. At each site in our region, the market rent for land will be bid up to at least the maximum excess profit earnable by a *competitive* firm and to no more than the maximum excess profit of *any* firm, or zero if this is negative. The land use allocated to that site will be that highest bidder. Thus, the allocation of land uses to sites is seen as a dual to the problem of determining market rents.[2] Market rents, in turn, are related to excess profit levels, and these vary from site to site for a given firm with changes in site advantage or locational advantage. The firm whose excess profit level is the highest for that site is the one who can use that site most advantageously.

3. Residential Land Use Theory: Bid Rents and Utility Levels

Let us return to the problem posed at the outset of Section 2. How do we develop

2. We use the term "dual" here in its economic sense. Any allocation problem can be phrased in terms of the quantities allocated or of the prices necessary to sustain the allocation. Thus either problem (solving for prices or quantities) is the dual of the other.

a theory of residential land use comparable to that for commercial and industrial use? The crux of the problem is that there is no bid rent function for households that corresponds to the zero net excess profit function of competitive firms. With such firms there is a bid rent level beyond which they cannot go and still earn a normal profit and below which they will be outbid by competing firms.

A household has instead a utility level associated with each bid rent. If forced to bid a larger amount, the household's utility level would decline. However, there is no such thing as a zero utility level in the sense of a rent above which it would not bid and below which other households would step in and outbid it. But, without such a level, how can we determine the bid rent a household will offer and assess whether or not that household is in fact the highest bidder for that parcel?

Alonso provided the clue to the answer to this question. Imagine a large number of identical households competing for residence sites in an urban area. Each household will bid up the rent for a site where the attainable utility level is high and will draw back from competing for sites which are "too expensive," i.e., where the attainable utility level is lower than elsewhere. The result should be a spatial equilibrium in which the bid rent at each parcel is just large enough to ensure that the utility level attainable at every site is exactly the same. Notice that we have not specified what that utility level is. We have merely asserted that, whatever that utility level is, a spatial pattern of bid rents will emerge to preserve it everywhere in the urban area.

Wheaton (1974) was among the first to recognize that there are two different ways in which to specify the utility level that will be achieved. He called these the "open" and "closed" versions.

In the open version, Wheaton sees the urban area as just one element in a national urban system. Suppose that households could move in or out of this particular urban area costlessly and at will. Presumably, households would move in when the utility level in this urban area was higher than in the rest of the nation and move out when it was lower. If so, Wheaton argues that the utility level in the urban area will eventually move to the national average. As far as this particular urban area is concerned, being just one small part of a nation, it cannot affect the utility level that is arrived at. The utility level is exogenously determined in other words. At the same time, the number of households in the urban area is endogenous; it fluctuates up or down to keep the local utility level similar to that found in the rest of the nation.

In the closed version, Wheaton assumes an opposite case. Here, the number of households in the region is fixed. In other words, there is no movement of households into or out of the urban area. The utility level is arrived at by finding a bid rent for each available site such that every household is located and such that at least one household (the marginal household) bids no more than the next best (i.e., a nonresidential) land use.[3] In the closed version, the number of households is exogenous, but the utility level is endogenous.

The "closed" and "open" versions are two polar cases. They illustrate how a utility level can be found when an urban area is either completely open to household inmigration or outmigration or completely closed to such movements. Presumably most urban areas would be somewhere in between these two cases with a certain amount of household migration but not likely quite enough to

3. A lower bid rent function (i.e., a higher level of utility) would not permit enough households to locate in the area. The same number of households could of course still be accommodated on a higher bid rent function (i.e., a lower utility level), but households would then be bidding more than the amount required to take enough land away from other uses.

completely eliminate utility level differentials between urban areas.

As in commercial and industrial land use theory, there is no problem in handling different groups of identical households (e.g., different income groups) provided there are enough households of each kind to make for competitive bidding.[4] As before, landlords will allocate land to the highest bidder, which will be either one of the groups of households or some non-residential use. In equilibrium, every household in a certain group is identical and will achieve the same level of utility. However, the utility level achieved by the households in one group need not bear any relationship to that achieved by another group. The utility level for each group would have to be found separately. This could be done for instance by solving a closed or open version separately for each group.

4. Residential Land Use Theory: The Fundamental Model

In Section 3, an overview has been presented of a residential land use theory. In this section, a more-detailed model based on this theory is introduced. This model is sometimes called the Alonso Model, although in fact it is somewhat simpler than Alonso's original version. I prefer to call it the "fundamental model" because much of the published work since Alonso has used this model as a starting point.

In the fundamental model, we begin by assuming N identical households. Each household has a utility level U defined as a function of the consumption of two commodities: land (L) and other goods or services (X).

$$U = f(X,L) \qquad (1)$$

4. A variety of different groupings of households have been considered. See Section 5, (2) below.

"Other goods and services" consists of all nonland purchases by the household, including items such as food and clothing as well as a physical dwelling unit and equipment such as furniture, appliances, wallpaper, and landscaping. These other goods and services are in aggregate positively valued, i.e., an increase in X produces an increase in U.

In the above equation, L is the lot size of the parcel occupied by a household. Land is also positively valued in the fundamental model; a larger lot size produces a higher U. Putting L into the utility seems reasonable when a household lives in a conventional detached dwelling. However, in what sense can we specify L when a household lives in an apartment. Alonso argued that every residential building has to occupy a certain amount of land and that if that building has, say, 50 apartments then each apartment effectively consumes 1/50 of that area. Thus, in Alonso's view, every household effectively occupies some amount of land for its residence and this amount is L in its utility function (1) above.[5]

Let us assume next that each of our N identical households has the same monthly income (Y). This income is expended on three items: the rental of land, the purchase of other goods and services, and the cost of commuting. Let us suppose that this household is bidding for land at point "s" in the urban area. Suppose that

5. I accept Alonso's argument that every household effectively occupies a certain amount of land. I do question, however, whether this amount enters into a household's utility function as he argues. I suspect that a household values a number of attributes of a parcel of land, e.g., the amount and quality of outdoor recreation space, the degree of privacy afforded, or the access to sunlight. To some extent, lot size may act as a proxy for several of these attributes. However, for apartment residents in particular, the ratio of parcel size to number of apartments may bear little relationship to such attributes. Let us ignore this problem for the time being though and consider the rest of the fundamental model.

it wants to make an offer for land of $R(s)$ per square meter. If it rents L square meters, rental payments will be $R(s) \cdot L$ per month. If X is the amount per month and P_x is the unit price of other goods and services purchased, total expenditures on that component will be $P_x X$ per month. Finally, assume total monthly commuting costs at site s are $k(s)$ per month. The monthly budget constraint is now

$$Y = R(s) \cdot L + P_x X + k(s) \qquad (2)$$

Note in the above that $R(s)$ and $k(s)$ vary with the choice of location "s"; i.e., they are spatially variant. On the other hand, income (Y) and the price of other goods or services (P_x) are assumed to be the same no matter where the household locates; i.e., they are spatially invariant.

The household's problem is the following. What is the bid rent at site "s"? In other words, what rent per square meter at "s" will just permit the household to achieve a certain level of utility, say, U^*? This question can be approached graphically. In Figure 1 is presented a diagram showing the indifference curve (U^*ABU^*) for our household corresponding to a utility level of U^*. On the vertical axis, the amount of other goods and services (X) is drawn. The amount of land is shown on the horizontal axis. The curve U^*ABU^* shows all the combinations of X and L that yield the same level of utility U^*.[6] No matter where our household locates, be it at "s" or somewhere else, U^* must be obtained. Thus wherever the household locates, it must choose one of the combinations of X and L along U^*ABU^*.

On this same figure, let us now draw the household's budget constraint at "s" given a bid rent $R(s)$. Equation (2) can be rewritten as

6. This curve is convex with respect to the origin of the graph reflecting the assumption that both goods are positively valued and that both are subject to diminishing marginal utility.

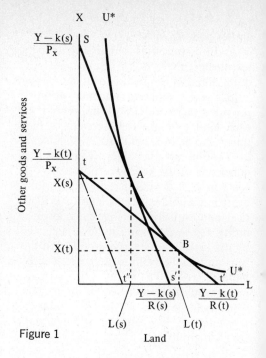

Figure 1

$$X = [Y - k(s)]/P_x - [R(s)/P_x] \cdot L \qquad (3)$$

This is the equation of a straight line with intercept $[Y - k(s)]/P_x$ and slope $- R(s)/P_x$. It crosses the horizontal (or L) axis at $[Y - k(s)]/R(s)$. Such a straight line is labeled SAS' in Figure 1. The household can, given its budget constraint, consume any combination of X and L along this line. It can be shown that this household maximizes its utility at point A where the budget line is just tangent to the indifference curve U^*ABU^*. In other words, when the household bids an amount $R(s)$, it is just able to reach the required utility level U^*.

If the bid rent had been higher the budget line would still pass through S but have a steeper (more negative) slope; i.e., it would lie below or to the left of point A. In that case, the utility level U^* could not be reached as this budget line would not touch U^*ABU^*. On the other hand, if the bid rent were lower than $R(s)$, the budget line would flatten although still passing through S. Such a budget line would cut $U*ABU*$ at possibly two points, meaning $U*$ is achievable. However at this lower bid rent, a level of utility higher than $U*$ is also attainable. Thus only at $R(s)$ can the household at best achieve a utility level of exactly $U*$.

Consider another location "t," which has higher commuting costs than "s"; i.e., $k(t)$ is larger than $k(s)$. Suppose our household were to make the same bid $R(s)$ for land at this site. Its budget line would be given by tt″ a line parallel to the old budget line SAS', but with a smaller intercept; $[Y - k(t)]/P_x$ is smaller than $[Y - k(s)]/P_x$. However, such a budget line would never allow the household to reach $U*ABU*$. Therefore the bid rent is too high. As the bid rent is reduced, the budget line flattens (slope tends towards zero) until a bid rent $R(t)$ is reached where the budget line (now tBt') just comes tangent to $U*ABU*$ at some point (here B).

In the fundamental model, changes in bid rent are thus linked to changes in commuting cost.[7] A location such as "t" with higher commuting costs will have a lower bid rent than a location such as "s." Note also though that at "t" the household consumes more land $[L(t)$ vs. $L(s)]$ and less of the other goods or services $[X(t)$ vs. $X(s)]$. At t the household has a lower income net of commuting costs $[Y - k(t)$ vs. $Y - k(s)]$. For the household to be as happy at "t" as "s," the rent on land at "t" must be sufficiently smaller than at "s" to compensate for the reduction in net income.

Using calculus, a formal condition can be established for the bid rent function. It asserts the following

7. In the fundamental model there is no site advantage and locational advantage is defined solely in terms of relative commuting costs.

$$L \cdot dR(s)/ds + dk(s)/ds = 0 \quad (4)$$

Here $dR(s)/ds$ is the rate at which the bid land rent per square meter is declining with increasing distance (s) from the job site. Note that $dR(s)/ds$ is negative. Thus $L \cdot dR(s)/ds$ is the total savings in land rent (area consumed $\times$ bid savings/m²) to a household from this move and this again is negative. On the other hand, $dk(s)/ds$ is the rate at which commuting costs increase with increasing distance from the job site. The household thus generates a bid rent for a nearby site so that rent savings are exactly offset by increased commuting costs.

Note that equation (4) above does not tell us what rent will be bid at s. It merely asserts that the differential in bid rents between s and a nearby point will satisfy equation (4). To determine the actual bid rent at any point we must specify either the utility level (open version) or the number of households (closed version).

Let us suppose that commuting costs are proportional to the distance traveled. This would be the case, for example, if there is a flat cost of say $0.20 for each kilometer traveled. From equation (4), it can be shown that $R(s)$ will fall but at a decreasing rate. This pattern is illustrated in Figure 2 where the bid rent curve is shown as $R(s|U)$ to illustrate the assumption of a particular utility level, U. Before Alonso, several people including Wingo (1961) argued that the bid-rent curve should mirror $k(s)$. In other words, they said that $R(s|U)$ should decline linearly if $k(s)$ is increasing linearly. Alonso argued differently. He said $R(s|U)$ declines at a declining, not a fixed linear rate because of the substitution of land for other goods by the consumer. In moving for example from "s" to "t" as in Figure 1, the household compensates for its reduced net income at "t" by consuming more land. The increase in commuting

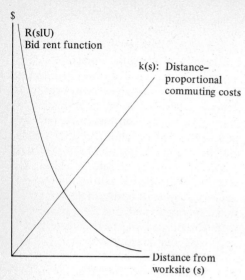

$

R(s|U)
Bid rent function

k(s): Distance-
proportional
commuting costs

Distance from
worksite (s)

Figure 2

costs is thus "spread" over an increasing lot size as "s" increases. $R(s)$, the bid rent per square meter, therefore declines at a decreasing rate.

This last observation is very important. Land rents are commonly observed to be sharply peaked in space. They change quite quickly with distance near the center of the region, but more slowly near the fringe. Alonso's model explains this "peaking" as a consequence of the substitution by a household between land and other goods.

5. Residential Land Use Theory: Extensions of the Fundamental Model

There have been at least several hundred papers and books written to date that extend this fundamental model in one direction or another. The interested reader will find extensive technical reviews of this literature in several places: Anas and Dendrinos (1976), Goldstein and Moses (1973), McDonald (1979, pp. 7–33), Richardson (1977), Senior (1974), Solow (1973), and Wheaton (1979). Here, a brief and highly selective non-

technical overview of six areas of extension is presented. These extensions cover the introduction of (1) housing, (2) differentiated populations, (3) transportation policy issues, (4) a variety of other public policy issues, (5) externalities, and (6) dynamics into the fundamental model.

HOUSING

In the fundamental model, households demand land but not housing as such. A number of analysts beginning with Muth (1969) have introduced housing directly into the household's utility function. In such models, the household values certain housing characteristics such as floor area, quality of construction, or lot size. There are usually two sets of actors; households who are consumers and builder-landlords who supply the various housing units. The builder-landlords typically take the bid rents of households and determine the most profitable housing form at each location. This form in turn dictates both the intensity of land use and the rent that the builder-landlord is willing to pay for land at that site. The owner of the site thus faces a "derived" demand for her land by households, which she would then compare against the bids of other types of land uses.

DIFFERENTIATED POPULATIONS

All households are assumed to be identical in the fundamental model. There is no problem in extending the model to cover distinct groups of identical households as long as each group is large enough to ensure competitive bidding for land. Several kinds of groupings have been considered: by income class, place of work (as in the central city or suburb), number of wage earners in the household, or household type (as in the presence or absence of children). In each case, the groupings have been chosen to identify households who may have distinctive preferences for particular locations or lot sizes and thus have distinctive bid rent patterns.

Some interesting work has been done on the comparative statistics of such differentiated population models. Suppose that we have a two-group model (closed version) which is in equilibrium with N_1 households of the first type and N_2 of the second. What happens to this equilibrium if we introduce one more household of either type? How does the spatial pattern of land use change for each group? Hartwick et al. (1976) present an elegant, intuitive analysis of this type.

TRANSPORTATION POLICY ISSUES

A variety of issues have been addressed under this general title. One facet of this has been the allocation of land for transportation. In planning a city, how much land should be set aside for transportation. In cost-benefit studies of transportation projects, how should one measure the opportunity cost of the land so used? These are questions that can be addressed to some extent using variants of the fundamental model. These variants commonly make use of a mathematical technique called Calculus of Variations to find not the equilibrium pattern of land use, but rather the pattern that is most efficient or optimal in economic terms. This Calculus of Variations approach can also be used to study the effects of traffic congestion on equilibrium and optimal land use patterns. Representative of this work are two papers by Averous and Lee (1973, 1978).

Another group of analysts have studied the relationships between land use patterns and the availability of various modes of transportation. Haring et al. (1976), for example, undertake simulations with a model wherein households choose between public and private transportation modes in their journeys-to-work. In such work, the household's simultaneous decisions as to how much to

bid for land and how much of each good to consume are extended to cover a choice of travel mode as well.

Another problem that has received attention is the impact of transportation investment on land values in urban areas. As one example, Getz (1975) has developed a model of an urban area including both firms and households. The impacts of a change in transportation costs on the spatial equilibrium pattern of land uses and land rents as well as on the aggregate size of the urban area are examined.

A final issue considered in this area is the valuation of travel time and its impact on bid rents. Casetti and Papageorgiou (1971) consider an extension to the fundamental model wherein the household values leisure time. Commuting is seen by them to involve not just monetary costs but also a reduction in available leisure time. They show how the loss of additional leisure time at more remote locations shapes the household's bid rent function.

OTHER PUBLIC POLICY ISSUES

In addition to the transportation issues above, the fundamental model has been extended to look at other questions of public concern. One such question concerns the impact of zoning on land values and land use. Another concerns the efficiency of property taxes versus other forms of revenue generation for local governments. Still another concerns the efficient and equitable provision of different kinds of public goods such as parks where both usage and bid rents are related to proximity of residence sites. An example of this type of analysis is found in Thrall (1979).

EXTERNALITIES

It has been argued that cities exist, grow, and die because of externalities. An externality, according to economists, is an unpriced, or possibly mispriced, transaction that affects others. Traffic congestion is often thought to be a classic example. When you use a crowded roadway, you also slow down everyone by a small amount. When you are deciding whether to make that trip, you will likely consider the time cost to yourself. It is unlikely though that you will also consider how much you slow down others by your presence. In this sense, you impose a time loss "cost" on those other users (as they do you) for which you did not have to pay (as in a congestion tax). Thus your decision to use that roadway is an unpriced transaction that affects others; i.e., an externality.

We have already pointed out that the fundamental model has been extended to look at congestion in particular. Tolley *et al.* (1979) have looked at several other kinds of externalities. These include economies of scale in production and in the provision of public services as well as pollution. These four kinds of externalities are commonly used to explain why cities are sometimes very attractive to new firms and at other times very repugnant. In all cases, the fundamental model can be extended to some degree to consider these.

DYNAMICS

In the fundamental model, we assume the existence of a spatial equilibrium. This is of course a long-run equilibrium viewpoint that assumes that households have had sufficient time to adjust their lot size and consumption bundles to a given set of conditions. Critics argue that in fact a set of conditions in reality does not stay "given" for very long. Also, they assert that the durability of buildings and the difficulty of changing lot sizes at will make land uses slow to adapt to new conditions. Instead of being in a state of equilibrium, it is thus argued that land

use patterns are in disequilibrium, partly reflecting historical trends and partly reflecting emerging equilibrium conditions. If so, any explanation of current land use patterns must be based on a dynamic, rather than an equilibrium model.

Attempts have been made to extend the fundamental model in this direction. Evans (1975) and Fujita (1976) identify a number of the problems inherent in any approach of this type. The central difficulty is that a spatial equilibrium must be matched with a temporal equilibrium on top of which one must put some kind of adaptive behavior rule to describe how households and firms react when in disequilibrium. This is by no means a simple task.

6. Conclusion

I have presented here a nontechnical overview of the land market theory of urban land use, the fundamental model of residential land use, and recent extensions of this fundamental model. Virtually all the writing in this area is, however, reasonably technical in that it assumes at least a moderate knowledge of Calculus. Because of this, many of the conclusions reached in these papers are quite specific in both meaning and context. My purpose has been to expose and I hope interest new readers in the potential of this area of inquiry rather than to formally review in detail its current frontiers. The interested reader should pursue the references listed at the outset of Section 5.

What can we expect to learn in the future from a continued study of the land market theory? I am guardedly optimistic here. I think that there are important additional insights to be gained in each of the six broad areas outlined in Section 5. I do not accept the view of some critics that the land market theory is inappropriate, incorrect, infertile, or unrealistic and therefore should be abandoned. Let me outline what I think are the most common criticisms of the land market theory and my responses to them.

The land market theory is faulted by a reliance on a competitive land market. There are, to begin with, certain land uses, such as government, schools, hospitals, and parks that are not allocated by a land market. Further, even residential and commercial land uses are increasingly being allocated not by competitive forces, but by fiat. Examples of the latter include both zoning restrictions and the recent growth of large monopolistic land development corporations who can dictate emerging land use patterns.

I agree with the criticism that not all land uses can be analyzed with this theory. Other theories, as outlined at the start of this paper, have been developed and will continue to be needed to explain certain aspects of urban land use patterns. However, I disagree that land allocation by fiat is very widespread or that, to the extent that it exists, it necessarily obviates the need for a land market theory. As outlined in Section 5 on other public policy issues, for example, the land market theory can be used to look at household choice behavior in the presence of zoning or other locational restrictions.

The reliance on equilibrium in the land market theory is incorrect. With constantly changing conditions and sticky land uses, the spatial pattern of land uses is in disequilibrium. Further, there is no apparent evidence that land uses are even equilibrium-seeking.

This criticism has been responded to by some analysts working on the dynamics of land use equilibrium and change. As noted in Section 5 (dynamics), above, progress there has been slow and has been hampered by severe conceptual and methodological problems. However, advances are being made and one can look forward to a time when both spatial and temporal features of the land market theory are more adequately outlined.

Whereas the land market theory as originally formulated by Alonso and others is insightful, much of the recent analysis has suffered from diminishing returns. Development of the land market theory has now reached a point where there is little point in undertaking further work.

Because of the difficult technical nature of much of what is written in this area, it is easy and tempting to come to this kind of conclusion. However, I am continually surprised at the number of new formulations, extensions, and policy applications of the land market theory and the fundamental model. In my mind, these insights make the analyses worthwhile. As with most ideas, these innovations will eventually run their course, but I do not foresee an end to useful work in this area in the near future.

The land market theory is patently unrealistic. It is an oversimplified view of how land uses are allocated. Households and firms are not utility or profit-maximizers, but instead follow complex behavioral decision rules. A correct theory of land use must be based on more realistic models of these two sets of actors.

I agree with the spirit of this criticism, but object strenuously to the setting up of the land market theory as a "straw man." Any theory, of necessity, abstracts from (i.e., simplifies) reality. This is unavoidable. Whether or not a theory is "oversimplified" depends on whether you think the insights to be gained from it are worth the price of the abstraction. As stated above, I feel that to date the insights gained have been worthwhile. At the same time, there is a need for new ways of looking at household and firm behavior. Both areas of analysis can and should co-exist.

References

Alonso, W. (1964). *Location and Land Use: Toward a General Theory of Land Rent.* Harvard University Press.

Anas, A., and D. S. Dendrinos (1976). The New Urban Economics: A Brief Survey. In G. J. Papageorgiou (ed.), *Mathematical Land Use Theory.* Lexington Books, pp. 23–51.

Averous, C. P., and D. B. Lee (1973). Land Use and Transportation: Basic Theory. *Environment and Planning, 5*:491–502.

Averous, C. P., and D. B. Lee (1978). Land Allocation and Transportation Pricing in a Mixed Urban Economy. *Journal of Regional Science, 13*:173–185.

Casetti, E., and G. Papageorgiou (1971). A Spatial Equilibrium Model of Urban Structure. *Canadian Geographer, 15*:30–37.

Evans, A. W. (1975). Rent and Housing in the Theory of Urban Growth. *Journal of Regional Science, 15*:113–125.

Fujita, M. (1976). Toward a Dynamic Theory of Land Use. *Papers of the Regional Science Association, 37*:133–165.

Getz, M. (1975). A Model of the Impact of Transportation Investment on Land Rents. *Journal of Public Economics, 4*:57–74.

Goldstein, G. S., and L. N. Moses (1973). A Survey of Urban Economics. *Journal of Economic Literature, 11*:471–495.

Haring, J. E. *et al.* (1976). The Impact of Alternative Transportation Systems on Urban Structure. *Journal of Urban Economics, 3*:14–30.

Hartwick, J. *et al.* (1976). Comparative Statics of a Residential Economy with Several Classes. *Journal of Economic Theory, 13*: 396–413.

McDonald, J. F. (1979). *Economic Analysis of an Urban Housing Market.* Academic Press.

Muth, R. F. (1969). *Cities and Housing.* University of Chicago Press.

Richardson, H. W. (1977). *The New Urban Economics and Alternatives.* Academic Press.

Senior, M. L. (1974). Approaches to Residential Location Modelling: Urban Economic Models and Some Recent Developments. *Environment and Planning, 6*:369–409.

Solow, R. M. (1973). On Equilibrium Models of Urban Location. In J. M. Parkin (ed.) *Essays in Modern Economics.* Longmans, pp. 2–16.

Thrall, G. (1979). Public Goods and the Derivation of Land Value. Assessment Schedules within a Spatial Equilibrium Setting. *Geographical Analysis, 11*:23–35.

Tolley, G. S. *et al.* (1979). *Urban Growth Policy in a Market Economy.* Academic Press.

Wheaton, W. C. (1974). A Comparative Static Analysis of Urban Spatial Structure. *Journal of Economic Theory, 9*:223–237.

Wheaton, W. C. (1979). Monocentric Models of Urban Land Use: Contributions and Criticisms. In P. Mieskowski and M. Straszheim (eds.) *Current Issues in Urban Economics.* Johns Hopkins, pp. 107–129.

Wingo, L. (1961). *Transportation and Urban Land.* Resources for the Future.

DAVID HARVEY

Labor, Capital, and Class Struggle around the Built Environment in Advanced Capitalist Societies

In this paper, I will seek to establish a theoretical framework for understanding a facet of class struggle under advanced capitalism. The conflicts that will be scrutinized are those that relate to the production and use of the built environment, by which I mean the totality of physical structures—houses, roads, factories, offices, sewage systems, parks, cultural institutions, educational facilities, and so on. In general I shall argue that capitalist society must of necessity create a physical landscape—a mass of humanly constructed physical resources—in its own image, broadly appropriate to the purposes of production and reproduction. But I shall also argue that this process of creating space is full of contradictions and tensions and that the class relations in capitalist society inevitably spawn strong cross-currents of conflict.

I shall assume for purposes of analytic convenience that a clear distinction exists between (1) a faction of capital seeking the appropriation of rent either directly (as landlords, property companies, and the like) or indirectly (as financial intermediaries or others who invest in prop-

erty simply for a rate of return), (2) a faction of capital seeking interest and profit by building new elements in the built environment (the construction interests), (3) capital "in general," which looks upon the built environment as an outlet for surplus capital and as a bundle of use values for enhancing the production and accumulation of capital, and (4) labor, which uses the built environment as a means of consumption and as a means for its own reproduction. I shall also assume that the built environment can be divided conceptually into *fixed capital* items to be used in production (factories, highways, railroads, and so on) and *consumption fund* items to be used in consumption (houses, roads, parks, sidewalks, and the like).[1] Some items, such as roads and sewer systems, can function both as fixed capital and as part of the consumption fund depending on their use.

The domination of capital over labor

1. This distinction derives from Marx. See Karl Marx, *Capital* (New York: 1967), 2: 210; and idem, *The Grundrisse* (Harmondsworth, Middlesex: 1973), pp. 681–7.

From **Politics and Society,** Vol. 6, No. 3, 1976, pp. 265–79; 290–94. Reprinted by permission of the publisher.

is basic to the capitalist mode of production—without it, after all, surplus value could not be extracted and accumulation would disappear. All kinds of consequences flow from this and the relation between labor and the built environment can be understood only in terms of it. Perhaps the single most important fact is that industrial capitalism, through the reorganization of the work process and the advent of the factory system, forced a separation between place of work and place of reproduction and consumption. The need to reproduce labor power is thus translated into a specific set of production and consumption activities within the household, a domestic economy that requires use values in the form of a built environment if it is to function effectively.

The needs of labor have changed historically and they will in part be met by work within the household and in part be procured through market exchanges of wages earned against commodities produced. The commodity requirements of labor depend upon the balance between domestic economy products and market purchases as well as upon the environmental, historical, and moral considerations that fix the standard of living of labor.[2] In the commodity realm, labor can, by organization and class struggle, alter the definition of needs to include "reasonable" standards of nutrition, health care, housing, education, recreation, entertainment, and so on. From the standpoint of capital, accumulation requires a constant expansion of the market for commodities, which means the creation of new social wants and needs and the organization of "rational consumption" on the part of labor. This last condition suggests theoretically what is historically observable—that the domestic economy must steadily give way before the expansion of capitalist commodity production. "Accumulation for accumulation's sake, production for

production's sake," which jointly drive the capitalist system onwards, therefore entail an increasing integration of labor's consumption into the capitalist system of production and exchange of commodities.[3]

The split between the place of work and the place of residence means that the struggle of labor to control the social conditions of its own existence splits into two seemingly independent struggles. The first, located in the work place, is over the wage rate, which provides the purchasing power for consumption goods, and the conditions of work. The second, fought in the place of residence, is against secondary forms of exploitation and appropriation represented by merchant capital, landed property, and the like. This is a fight over the costs and conditions of existence in the living place. And it is this second kind of struggle that we focus on here, recognizing, of course, that the dichotomy between *living* and *working* is itself an artificial division that the capitalist system imposes.

Labor Versus the Appropriators of Rent and the Construction Interest

Labor needs living space. Land is therefore a condition of living for labor in much the same way that it is a condition of production for capital. The system of private property that excludes labor from land as a condition of production also serves to exclude labor from the land as a condition of living. As Marx puts it, "the monstrous power wielded by landed property, when united hand in hand with industrial capital, enables it to be used against laborers engaged in their wage struggle as a means of practically expelling them from the earth as a dwelling

2. See Marx, *Capital,* 1: 171.

3. This condition can be derived directly from Marxian theory by bringing together the analyses presented in Marx, *Capital,* 1: 591–640, 2: 437–48, 515–16.

place."[4] Apart from space as a basic condition of living we are concerned here with housing, transportation (to jobs and facilities), amenities, facilities, and a whole bundle of resources that contribute to the total living environment for labor. Some of these items can be privately appropriated (housing is the most important case) while others have to be used in common (sidewalks) and in some cases, such as the transportation system, even used jointly with capital.

The need for these items pits labor against landed property and the appropriation of rent as well as against the construction interest, which seeks to profit from the production of these commodities. The cost and quality of these items affect the standard of living of labor. Labor, in seeking to protect and enhance its standard of living, engages in a series of running battles in the living place over a variety of issues that relate to the creation, management, and use of the built environment. Examples are not hard to find—community conflict over excessive appropriation of rent by landlords, over speculation in housing market, over the siting of "noxious" facilities, over inflation in housing construction costs, over inflation in the costs of servicing a deteriorating urban infrastructure, over congestion, over lack of accessibility to employment opportunities and services, over highway construction and urban renewal, over the "quality of life" and aesthetic issues—the list seems almost endless.

Conflicts that focus on the built environment exhibit certain peculiar characteristics because the monopoly power conferred by private property arrangements generates not only the power to appropriate rent but also yields to the owners command over a "natural monopoly" in space.[5] The fixed and immobile character of the built environment

entails the production and use of commodities under conditions of spatial monopolistic competition with strong "neighborhood" or "externality" effects.[6] Many of the struggles that occur are over externality effects—the value of a particular house is in part determined by the condition of the houses surrounding it and each owner is therefore very interested in seeing to it that the neighborhood as a whole is well-maintained. In bourgeois theory, the appropriation of rent and the trading of titles to properties set price signals for new commodity production in such a way that a "rational" allocation of land to uses can be arrived at through a market process. But because of the pervasive externality effects and the sequential character of both development and occupancy, the price signals suffer from all manner of serious distortions. There are, as a consequence, all kinds of opportunities for both appropriators and the construction faction, for developers, speculators, and even private individuals, to reap windfall profits and monopoly rents. Internecine conflicts within a class and faction are therefore just as common as conflict between classes and factions.

We are primarily concerned here, however, with the structure of the three-way struggle between labor, the appropriators of rent, and the construction faction. Consider, as an example, the direct struggle between laborers and landlords over the cost and quality of housing. Landlords typically use whatever power they have to appropriate as much as they can from the housing stock they own and they will adjust their strategy to the conditions in such a way that they maximize the rate of return on their capital. If this rate of return is very high, then new capital will likely flow into landlordism, and, if the rate of return is very low, then we will likely witness disinvestment and aban-

4. Marx, *Capital,* 3: 773.
5. Ibid., chap. 37.

6. See David Harvey, *Social Justice and the City* (London and Baltimore: Edward Arnold, 1973), chaps. 2, 5.

donment. Labor will seek by a variety of strategies—for example, moving to where housing is cheaper or establishing rent controls and housing codes—to limit appropriation and to ensure a reasonable quality of shelter. How such a struggle is resolved depends very much upon the relative economic and political power of the two groups, the circumstances of supply and demand that exist at a particular place and time, and upon the options that each group has available to it.[7]

The struggle becomes three dimensional when we consider that the ability of appropriators to gain monopoly rents on the old housing is in part limited by the capacity of the construction interest to enter the market and create new housing at a lower cost. The price of old housing is, after all, strongly affected by the costs of production of new housing. If labor can use its political power to gain state subsidies for construction, then this artificially stimulated new development will force the rate of appropriation on existing resources downwards. If, on the other hand, appropriators can check new development (by, for example, escalating land costs), or if, for some reason, new development is inhibited (planning permission procedures in Britain have typically functioned in this way), then the rate of appropriation can rise. On the other hand, when labor manages to check the rate of appropriation through direct rent controls, then the price of rented housing falls, new development is discouraged, and scarcity is produced. These are the kinds of conflicts and strategies of coalition that we have to expect in such situations.

But the structure of conflict is made more complex by the "natural monopoly" inherent in space. For example, the monopoly power of the landlord is in part

modified by the ability of labor to escape entrapment in the immediate environs of the work place. Appropriation from housing is very sensitive to changes in transportation. The ability to undertake a longer journey to work is in part dependent upon the wage rate (which allows the worker to pay for travel), in part dependent upon the length of the working day (which gives the worker time to travel), and in part dependent upon the cost and availability of transportation. The boom in the construction of working-class suburbs in late nineteenth-century London, for example, can in large degree be explained by the advent of the railways and the provision of cheap "workman's special" fares and a shortening of the working day, which freed at least some of the working class from the need to live within walking distance of the work place.[8] The rate of rental appropriation on the housing close to the centers of employment had to fall as a consequence. The "streetcar" suburbs of American cities and the working-class suburbs of today (based on cheap energy and the automobile) are further examples of this phenomenon.[9] By pressing for new and cheap forms of transportation, labor can escape geographical entrapment and thereby reduce the capacity of landlords in advantageous locations to gain monopoly rents. The problems that attach to spatial entrapment are still with us, of course, in the contemporary ghettos of the poor, the aged, the oppressed mi-

7. For a more detailed argument see David Harvey, "Class-Monopoly Rent, Finance Capital and the Urban Revolution," *Regional Studies* 8 (1974): 239–55.

8. John R. Kellet, *The Impact of Railways on Victorian Cities* (London: Routledge & K. Paul, 1969), chap. 11.

9. G. R. Taylor, "The Beginnings of Mass Transportation in Urban America," *The Smithsonian Journal of History* 1, nos. 1–2: 35–50, 31–54; J. Tarr, "From City to Suburb: The 'Moral' Influence of Transportation Technology," in *American Urban History*, ed. Alexander B. Callow (New York: Oxford University Press, 1973); David R. Ward, *Cities and Immigrants* (New York: Oxford University Press, 1971).

norities, and the like. Access is still, for these groups, a major issue.[10]

The struggle to fight off the immediate depredations of the landlord and the continuous battle to keep the cost of living down do much to explain the posture adopted by labor with respect to the distribution, quantities, and qualities of all elements in the built environment. Public facilities, recreational opportunities, amenities, transportation access, and so on, are all subjects of contention. But underlying these immediate concerns is a deeper struggle over the very meaning of the built environment as a set of use values for labor.

The producers of the built environment, both past and present, provide labor with a limited set of choices of living conditions. If labor has slender resources with which to exercise an effective demand, then it has to put up with whatever it can get—shoddily built, cramped, and poorly serviced tenement buildings, for example. With increasing effective demand, labor has the potential to choose over a wider range and, as a result, questions about the overall "quality of life" begin to arise. Capital in general, and that fraction of it that produces the built environment, seek to define the quality of life for labor in terms of the commodities that they can profitably produce in certain locations. Labor, on the other hand, defines quality of life solely in use value terms and in the process may appeal to some underlying and very fundamental conception of what it is to be human. Production for profit and production for use are often inconsistent with each other. The survival of capitalism therefore requires that capital dominate labor, not simply in the work process, but with respect to the very definition of

the quality of life in the consumption sphere. Production, Marx argued, not only produces consumption, it also produces the mode of consumption and that, of course, is what the consumption fund for labor is all about.[11] For this reason, capital in general cannot afford the outcome of struggles around the built environment to be determined simply by the relative powers of labor, the appropriators of rent, and the construction faction. It must, from time to time, throw its weight into the balance to effect outcomes that are favorable to the reproduction of the capitalist social order. It is to this aspect of matters that we must now turn.

The Interventions of Capital in Struggles over the Built Environment

When capital intervenes in struggles over the built environment it usually does so through the agency of state power. A cursory examination of the history of the advanced capitalist countries shows that the capitalist class sometimes throws its weight to the side of labor and sometimes on the side of other factions. But history also suggests a certain pattern and underlying rationale for these interventions. We can get at the pattern by assembling the interventions together under four broad headings—private property and home-ownership for the working class, the cost of living and the value of labor power, managed collective consumption of workers in the interest of sustained capital accumulation, and a very complex, but very important, topic concerning the relation to nature, the imposition of work discipline, and the like. A discussion of the pattern will help us to identify the underlying rationale, and in this manner we can identify a much deeper meaning in the everyday struggles in which labor engages in the living place.

10. The McCone Commission Report on the Watts rebellion in Los Angeles in 1964 attributed much of the discontent to the sense of entrapment generated out of lack of access to transportation.

11. Marx, *Grundrisse,* Introduction.

PRIVATE PROPERTY AND
HOMEOWNERSHIP FOR LABOR

The struggle that labor wages in the living place against the appropriation of rent is a struggle against the monopoly power of private property. Labor's fight against the principle of private property cannot easily be confined to the housing arena, and "the vexed question of the relation between rent and wages . . . easily slides into that of capital and labor."[12] For this reason the capitalist class as a whole cannot afford to ignore it; they have an interest in keeping the principle of private property sacrosanct. A well-developed struggle between tenants and landlords—with the former calling for public ownership, municipalization, and the like—calls the whole principle into question. Extended individualized homeownership is therefore seen as advantageous to the capitalist class because it promotes the allegiance of at least a segment of the working class to the principle of private property, promotes an ethic of "possessive individualism," and brings about a fragmentation of the working class into "housing classes of homeowners and tenants.[13] This gives the capitalist class a handy ideological lever to use against public ownership and nationalization demands because it is easy to make such proposals sound as if the intent is to take workers' privately owned houses away from them.

The majority of owner-occupants do not own their housing outright, however. They make interest payments on a mortgage. This puts finance capital in a hegemonic position with respect to the functioning of the housing market—a position that it is in no way loath to make use of.[14] The apparent entrance of workers into the petit form of property ownership in housing is, to a large degree, its exact opposite in reality—the entry of money capital into a controlling position within the consumption fund. Finance capital not only controls the disposition and rate of new investment in housing, but controls labor as well through chronic debt-encumbrance. A worker mortgaged up to the hilt is, for the most part, a pillar of social stability, and schemes to promote homeownership within the working class have long recognized this basic fact. And in return the worker may build up, very slowly, some equity in the property.

This last consideration has some important ramifications. Workers put their savings into the physical form of a property. Obviously, they will be concerned to preserve the value of those savings and if possible to enhance them. Ownership of housing can also lead to petty landlordism, which has been a traditional and very important means for individual workers to engage in the appropriation of values at the expense of other workers. But more importantly, every homeowner, whether he or she likes it or not, is caught in a struggle over the appropriation of values because of the shifting patterns of external costs and benefits within the built environment. A new road may destroy the value of some housing and enhance the value of others, and the same applies to all manner of new development, redevelopment, accelerated obsolescence, and so on.

12. Quoted in Counter Information Services, *The Recurrent Crisis of London* (CIS, 52 Shaftesbury Ave., London, W.1).
13. C. B. McPherson, *The Political Theory of Possessive Individualism* (Oxford: Clarendon Press, 1962); J. Rex and T. Moore, *Race, Community and Conflict* (London: Oxford University Press, 1975).

14. M. Stone, "Housing and Class Struggle," *Antipode,* vol. 7, no. 2 (1975); David Harvey, "The Political Economy of Urbanization in Advanced Capitalist Societies: The Case of the United States," in *The Social Economy of Cities,* ed. G. Gappert and H. Rose (Beverley Hills: Urban Affairs Annual, no. 9 (1975).

THE COST OF LIVING AND
THE WAGE RATE

Marx argued that the value of labor power was determined by the value of the commodities required to reproduce that labor power. This neat equivalence disappears in the pricing realm, but nevertheless there is a relation of some sort between wages and the cost of obtaining those commodities essential to the reproduction of the household.[15]

An excessive rate of appropriation of rent by landlords will increase the cost of living to labor and generate higher wage demands that, if won, may have the effect of lowering the rate of accumulation of capital. For this reason capital in general may side with labor in the struggle against excessive appropriation and attempt also to lower the costs of production of a basic commodity such as housing. Capitalists may themselves seek to provide cheap housing, as in the "model communities" typical of the early years of the industrial revolution, or they may even side with the demands of labor for cheap, subsidized housing under public ownership, provided that this permits the payment of lower wages. For the same reason the capitalist class may seek to promote, through the agency of the state, the industrialization of building production and the rationalization of production of the built environment through comprehensive land use planning policies, new town construction programs, and the like. Capitalists tend to become interested in such things, however, only when labor is in a position, through its organized collective power, to tie wages to the cost of living.

15. The relation between values and prices in Marxian theory is highly problematic and involves us in the celebrated "transformation problem." To avoid making silly mistakes it is important to bear in mind that the value of labor power is not automatically represented by the wage rate.

These considerations apply to all elements in the built environment (and to social services and social expenditures also) that are relevant to the reproduction of labor power. Those that are publicly provided (which means the bulk of them outside of housing and until recently transportation) can be monitored by a cost-conscious municipal government under the watchful eye of the local business community, and, perhaps, in an emergency situation such as that experienced in New York both in the 1930s and the 1970s, even under direct supervision by the institutions of finance capital. In the interests of keeping the costs of reproduction of labor power at a minimum, the capitalist class as a whole may seek collective means to intervene in the processes of investment and appropriation in the built environment. In much the same way that the proletariat frequently sided with the rising industrial bourgeoisie against the landed interest in the early years of capitalism, so we often find capital in general siding with labor in the advanced capitalist societies against excessive appropriation of rent and rising costs of new development. The coalition is not forged altruistically but arises organically out of the relation between the wage rate and the costs of reproduction of labor power.

"RATIONAL," MANAGED, AND
COLLECTIVE CONSUMPTION

Workers mediate the circulation of commodities by using their wages to purchase means of consumption produced by capitalists. Any failure on the part of workers to use their purchasing power correctly and rationally from the standpoint of the capitalist production and realization system will disrupt the circulation of commodities. In the early years of capitalist development this problem was not so important because trade with noncapitalist societies could easily take up any slack in effective demand. But with the transition to advanced capitalism, the internal market provided by the wage-labor force becomes of greater and greater significance. Also, as standards of living rise, in the sense that workers have more and more commodities available to them, so the potential for a breakdown from "irrationalities" in consumption increases. The failure to exercise a proper effective demand can be a source of crisis. And it was, of course, Keynes's major contribution to demonstrate to the capitalist class that under certain conditions the way out of a crisis manifest as a falling profit rate was not to cut wages but to increase them and thereby to expand the market.

This presumes, however, that workers are willing to spend their wages "rationally." If we assume, with Adam Smith, that mankind has an infinite and insatiable appetite for "trinkets and baubles," then there is no problem, but Malthus voiced another worry when he observed that the history of human society "sufficiently demonstrates [that] an efficient taste for luxuries and conveniences, that is, such a taste as will properly stimulate industry, instead of being ready to appear the moment it is required is a plant of slow growth."[16] Production may, as Marx averred, produce consumption and the mode of consumption, but it does not do so automatically, and the manner in which it does so is the locus of continuous struggle and conflict.[17]

Consider, first of all, the relationship between capitalist production and the household economy. In the United States in 1810, for example, "the best figures available to historians show that . . . about two thirds of the clothing worn . . . was the product of house-

hold manufacture," but by 1860 the advent of industrial capitalism in the form of the New England textile industry had changed all that—"household manufactures had been eclipsed by the development of industrial production and a market economy."[18] Step by step, activities traditionally associated with household work are brought within the capitalist market economy—baking, brewing, preserving, cooking, food preparation, washing, cleaning, and even child-rearing and child socialization. And with respect to the built environment, housebuilding and maintenance become integrated into the market economy. In the United States in the nineteenth century a substantial proportion of the population built their own homes with their own labor and local raw materials. Now almost all units are built through the market system.

The advent of the factory system was a double-edged sword with respect to the household economy. On the one hand it extracted the wage earner(s) from the home. In the early years of industrial capitalism it did so for 12 or 14 hours a day and, under particularly exploitative conditions, forced the whole household —women and children as well as men— into the wage labor force (in this manner the wages of the *household* could remain stable in the face of a falling wage rate). Of these early years E. P. Thompson writes: "Each stage in industrial differentiation and specialization struck also at the family economy, disturbing customary relations between man and wife, parents and children, and differentiating more sharply between 'work' and 'life.' It was to be a full hundred years before this differentiation was to bring returns,

18. Thomas Bender, *Toward an Urban Vision: Ideals and Institutions in Nineteenth Century America* (Lexington, Kentucky: University Press of Kentucky, 1975), pp. 28–29; R. M. Tryon, *Household Manufacturers in the United States, 1640–1860* (Chicago: University of Chicago Press, 1917).

16. T. R. Malthus, *Principles of Political Economy* (New York: Kelley Reprint, 1836), p. 321.
17. Marx, *Grundrisse,* Introduction.

in the form of labour-saving devices, back into the working woman's home."[19]

This "return" of commodities to the household is the other edge of the sword. The factory system produced use values for consumption more cheaply and with less effort than the household. The use values may be in the form of standardized products, but there should at least be more of them and therefore a material basis for a rising standard of living of labor. In the early years of industrial capitalism this did not in general happen. Laborers certainly worked longer hours and probably received less in the way of use values (although the evidence on this latter point is both patchy and controversial).[20] But the rising productivity of labor that occurs with accumulation, the consequent need to establish an internal market, and a century or more of class struggle have changed all of this. Consumer durables and consumption fund items (such as housing) have become very important growth sectors in the economy, and the political conditions and the material basis for a rising standard of living of labor have indeed been achieved.

The experience of labor in substituting work in the factory for work in the household has, therefore, both positive and negative aspects. But such substitutions are not easily achieved because they involve the nature and structure of the family, the role of women in society, culturally entrenched traditions and the like. The substitutions are themselves a focus of struggle. The rational consumption of commodities in relation to the accumulation of capital implies a certain balance between market purchases and household work. The struggle to substitute the former for the latter is significant because its outcome defines the very meaning of use values and the standard of living for labor in its commodity aspects. The construction of the built environment has to be seen, therefore, in the context of a struggle over a whole way of living and being.

Techniques of persuasion are widely used in advanced capitalist societies to ensure rational consumption. Moral exhortation and philanthropic enterprise are often put to work "to raise the condition of the laborer by an improvement of his mental and moral powers and to make a rational consumer of him."[21] The church, the press, and the schools can be mobilized on behalf of rational consumption at the same time as they can be vehicles for genuinely autonomous working-class development. And then, of course, there are always the blandishments of the ad-men and the techniques of Madison Avenue.

It would be idle to pretend that "the standard of living of labor" has been unaffected by these techniques. But, again, we are dealing with a double-edged sword. They may in fact also exert what Marx called a "civilizing influence" on labor and be used by labor to raise itself to a new condition of material and mental well-being that, in turn, provides a new and more solid basis for class struggle.[22] Conversely, the drive by labor to improve its condition may be perverted by a variety of stratagems into a definition of use values advantageous to accumulation rather than reflective of the real human needs of labor. The human demand for shelter is turned, for example, into a process of accumulation through housing production.

Rational consumption can also be ensured by the collectivization of consump-

---

19. E. P. Thompson, *The Making of the English Working Class* (Harmondsworth, Middlesex: 1968), p. 455.
20. Ibid., chap. 10; E. J. Hobsbawn, *Labouring Men* (London: Weidenfeld and Nicolson, 1964), chap. 7.

21. Marx, *Capital,* 2: 516; Dickens satirized the role of bourgeois philanthropy in relation to workers' consumption in *Hard Times.*
22. Marx, *Capital,* p. 408.

tion, primarily, although not solely, through the agency of the state.[23] Working-class demands for health care, housing, education, and social services of all kinds are usually expressed through political channels, and government arbitrates these demands and seeks to reconcile them with the requirements of accumulation. Many of these demands are met by the collective provision of goods and services, which means that everyone consumes them whether he or she likes it or not. Capitalist systems have moved more and more towards the collectivization of consumption because of the need, clearly understood in Keynesian fiscal policies, to manage consumption in the interests of accumulation. By collectivization, consumer choice is translated from the uncontrolled anarchy of individual action to the seemingly more controllable field of state enterprise. This translation does not occur without a struggle over both the freedom of individual choice (which generates a strong antibureaucratic sentiment) and the definition of the use values involved (national defense versus subsidized housing for the poor, for example).

The built environment has a peculiar and important role in all of this. The bundle of resources that comprise it—streets and sidewalks, drains and sewer systems, parks and playgrounds—contains many elements that are collectively consumed. The public provision of such public goods is a "natural" form of collective consumption that capital can easily colonize through the agency of the state. Also, the sum of individual private decisions creates a public effect because

of the pervasive externality effects that in themselves force certain forms of collective consumption through private action—if I fail to keep my yard neat then my neighbors cannot avoid seeing it. The built environment requires collective management and control, and it is therefore almost certain to be a primary field of struggle between capital and labor over what is good for accumulation and what is good for people.*

Class Consciousness, Community Consciousness, and Competition

The phrase, "the standard of living of labor," plainly cannot be understood outside of the context of actual class struggles fought over a long period in particular places around the organization of both work and living. This continuously shifting standard defines the needs of labor with respect to use values—consumption fund items—in the built environment. Individual workers have different needs, of course, according to their position in the labor force, their familial situation, and their individual requirements. At the same time, the processes of wage rate determination in the work place yield different quantities of exchange value to workers in different occupational categories. The social power that this money represents can be used to procure control over certain use values in the built environment. The way this money is used affects the appropriation of rent and the functioning of the price signals that induce the flow of capital into the production of new consumption fund items. We can envisage three general situations.

Consider, first, a situation in which each worker seeks independently to command for his or her own private use the best bundle of resources in the best loca-

23. The theme of collective consumption has been examined in some detail by the French urbanists. See E. Preteceille, *Equipements Collectifs, Structures Urbaines et Consommation Sociale* (Paris: Centre de Sociologie Urbaine, 1975); and M. Castells, "Collective Consumption and Urban Contradictions in Advanced Capitalist Societies," in *Patterns of Advanced Societies,* ed. L. Lindberg (New York: 1975).

* Due to the length of this article, the middle section of the paper on the socialization of labor has not been reprinted here. (Ed. note.)

tion. We envisage a competitive war of all against all, a society in which the ethic of "possessive individualism" has taken root in the consciousness of workers in a very fundamental way. If the use values available in the built environment are limited, which is usually the case, then individuals make use of their market power and bid for scarce resources in the most advantageous locations. At its most elemental level this competition is for survival chances, for each worker knows that the ability to survive is dependent upon the ability to secure access to a particular bundle of resources in a reasonably healthy location. There is also competition to acquire "market capacity"— that bundle of attitudes, understandings, and skills that permits the worker to sell his or her labor power at a higher wage rate than the average.[24] Symbols of status, prestige, rank, and importance (even self-respect) may also be acquired by procuring command over particular resources in prestigious locations. These symbols may be useful in that they help a worker gain an easier entry into a particularly privileged stratum within the wage labor force. And finally we can note that if the relation to nature in the work place is felt to be as degrading as it truly is, then there is a positive incentive to seek a location far enough away that the "facts of production" are in no way represented in the landscape. In other words, workers may compete to get as far as possible away from the work place (the automobile proves particularly useful for this purpose).

The competitive situation that we have here outlined is in most respects identical to that assumed in neoclassical models of land use determination in urban areas.[25]

Individual households, such models assume, attempt to maximize their utility by competing with each other for particular bundles of goods in particular locations subject to a budget constraint. If it is assumed that the two most important "goods" being competed for are locations with lower aggregate transportation costs and housing space, then it can be shown with relative ease that individuals will distribute themselves in space according to (1) the distribution of employment opportunities, usually assumed to be collected together in one central location, and (2) the relative marginal propensities to consume transportation services and living space in the context of the overall budget constraint. Competitive bidding under these conditions will generate a *differential rent surface* that, in the case of a single employment center, declines with distance from the center at the same time as it distributes individuals by income in space. In this case the ability to appropriate differential rent is entirely created by competitive behavior within the working class. Also, if new development is typically distributed in response to the pricing signals set by such differential rents, then it is easy to show *that a spatial structure to the built environment will be created that reflects, to a large degree, social and wage stratifications within the labor force.*

The second situation that we wish to consider is one in which collective action in space—community action—is important. The pervasive externality effects and the collective use of many items in the built environment mean that it is in the self-interest of individuals to pursue modest levels of collective action.[26] Workers who

24. See Anthony Giddens, *The Class Structure of the Advanced Societies* (London: Harper and Row, 1973), p. 103.
25. See, for example, W. Alonso, *Location and Land Use* (Cambridge: Harvard University Press, 1964); and E. S. Mills, *Studies in the*

Structure of the Urban Economy (Baltimore: Johns Hopkins Press, 1972).
26. The theory of self-interested collective action is laid out in Mancur Olson, *The Logic of Collective Action* (Cambridge: Harvard University Press, 1965), but the theory of community is a mess that will require a good deal of sorting out.

are homeowners know that the value of the savings tied up in the house depends on the actions of others. It is in their common interest to collectively curb "deviant" behaviors, bar "noxious" facilities, and to ensure high standards of public service. This collectivization of action may go well beyond that required out of pure individual self-interest. A consciousness of place, "community consciousness," may emerge as a powerful force that spawns competition between communities for scarce public investment funds, and the like. Community competition becomes the order of the day.

This process relates to the appropriation of rent in an interesting way. Community control enables those in control to erect barriers to investment in the built environment. The barriers may be selective—the exclusion of low-income housing, for example—or more or less across the board, a ban on all forms of future growth. Actions of this sort have been common in suburban jurisdictions in the United States in recent years. The cartel powers of local government are in effect being mobilized to control investment through a variety of legal and planning devices. Homeowners may use these controls to maintain or enhance the value of their properties. Developers may seek to use such controls for rather different purposes. But "community consciousness" typically creates small legal "islands" within which monopoly rents are appropriatable, often by one faction of labor at the expense of another faction. This latter situation gives rise to internecine conflicts within the working class along parochialist community-based lines. The spatial structure of the city is very different under these conditions compared to the product of individual competition.

The third kind of situation we can envisage is that of a fully class-conscious proletariat struggling against all forms

of exploitation, whether they be in the work place or in the living place. Workers do not use their social power as individuals to seek individual solutions; they do not compete with each other for survival chances, for ability to acquire market capacity, for symbols of status and prestige. They fight collectively to improve the lot of all workers everywhere and eschew those parochialist forms of community action that typically lead one faction of labor to benefit at the expense of another (usually the poor and underprivileged).

Under such conditions the appropriation of rent cannot be attributed to the competitive behavior of individual workers or of whole communities. It has to be interpreted, rather, as something forced upon labor in the course of class struggle. A differential rent surface may arise in an urban area, but it does so not because labor automatically engages in competitive bidding, but because the class power of the appropriators is used to extract a rent to the maximum possible, given that resources are scarce and that they exist in a relative space. Because we witness a consequent social stratification (according to income) in space, and a development process that exacerbates this social ordering, we cannot infer that this is simply a reflection of individual workers expressing their "subjective utilities" through the market. Indeed, it may express the exact opposite—the power of the appropriators to force certain choices on workers no matter what the individual worker may think or believe. The power to appropriate rent is a class relation and we have to understand it that way if we are to understand how residential differentiation emerges within cities and the degree to which this phenomenon is the outcome of free or forced choices.[27]

27. I have attempted a preliminary analysis on this theme in David Harvey, "Class Structure in a Capitalist Society and the Theory of Resi-

A Conclusion

The capitalist mode of production forces a separation between working and living at the same time as it reintegrates them in complex ways. The superficial appearance of conflict in contemporary urban industrial society suggests that there is indeed a dichotomy between struggles in the work place and in the living place and that each kind of struggle is fought according to different principles and rules. Struggles around the consumption fund for labor, which have been the focus of attention in this paper, seemingly arise out of the inevitable tensions between appropriators seeking rent, builders seeking profit, financiers seeking interest, and labor seeking to counter the secondary forms of exploitation that occur in the living place. All of this seems self-evident enough.

But the manner and form of such everyday overt conflicts are a reflection of a much deeper tension with less easily identifiable manifestations—a struggle over the definition and meaning of use values, of the standard of living of labor, of the quality of life, of consciousness, and even of human nature itself. From this standpoint, the overt struggles between landlord-appropriators, builders, and labor, which we began by examining, are to be seen as mediated manifestations of the deep underlying conflict between capital and labor. Capital seeks definitions, seeks to impose meanings, conducive to the productivity of labor and to the consumption of the commodities that capitalists can profitably produce. Like Dickens's *Dombey and Son,* capital deals "in hides but never in hearts." But labor seeks its own meanings, partly de-

rived out of a rapidly fading memory of artisan and peasant life, but also out of the ineluctable imperative to learn what it is to be human. "Human nature" has, then, no universal meaning, but is being perpetually recast in the fires of restless struggle. And even though capital may dominate and impose upon us a predominantly *capitalist* sense of human nature, the resistances are always there, and the internal tensions within the capitalist order—between private appropriation and socialized production, between individualism and social interdependency —are so dramatic that we, each of us, internalize a veritable maelstrom of hopes and fears into our present conduct. The human nature that results, with all of its complex ambiguities of desire, need, creativity, estrangement, selfishness, and sheer human concern, forms the very stuff out of which the overt struggles of daily life are woven. The manner in which these struggles are fought likewise depends upon a deeper determination of consciousness—individual, community, or class-based as the case may be—of those who do the struggling. From this standpoint it must surely be plain that the separation between working and living is at best a superficial estrangement, an apparent breaking assunder of what can never be kept apart. And it is at this deeper level, too, that we can more clearly see the underlying unity between work-based and "community"-based conflicts. They are not mere mirror images of each other, but distorted representations, mediated by many intervening forces and circumstances, which mystify and render opaque the fundamental underlying class antagonism upon which the capitalist mode of production is founded. And it is, of course, the task of science to render clear through analysis what is mystified and opaque in daily life.

dential Differentiation," in *Processes in Physical and Human Geography,* ed. M. Chisholm, P. Haggett, and R. F. Peel (London, 1975).

MICHAEL DEAR

Planning for Mental Health Care: A Reconsideration of Public Facility Location Theory

Ten years ago, Michael Teitz published an important paper which advocated the development of a distinctive theory for urban public facility location (Teitz 1968). In the decade that followed, a considerable literature has appeared around this theme (Freestone 1977). That the majority of this subsequent research has remained within the bounds of the initial paradigm is a tribute to the synthesis achieved by Teitz. The contention of this essay is, however, that a fundamental realignment of the public facility location theory paradigm is necessary. There are two reasons for this assertion. First, in spite of the richness of the paradigm defined by Teitz, his paper has served to restrict the range of topics considered in the public facility literature. Hence, several important features of a comprehensive public facility location theory have been ignored, especially the political dimensions of location. Second, most efforts directed toward operationalizing the Teitz model have opted for some form of a mathematical programming model. While this approach led initially to many important insights, it has tended to discourage experiment with other analytical formats.

In addition, such models have not been successful in operationalizing such important concepts as equity in public facility location.

The purpose of this paper is to promote a critical reconsideration of public facility location theory. In its first section, the paper provides a brief critique of the major themes which have developed in the ten years since the appearance of Teitz's paper. It should be emphasized that this is not a comprehensive review of the state-of-the-art in public facility location theory. Instead, the literature is used selectively in order to indicate the significant advances and remaining limitations of that theory. From this critique, a simple statement on the requirements of a comprehensive public facility location theory is derived. The second part of the paper is devoted to an examination of recent empirical evidence on mental health facility location.

Theory of Public Facility Location

Public facilities are those units whose primary function is to deliver goods and services which fall wholly or partly within the domain of government. Such

From **International Regional Science Review**, Vol. 3, No. 2, 1978, pp. 93–111. Reprinted by permission of the **Review** and M. Dear.

facilities have an important impact on urban form and environmental quality. The basis for a distinctively *public* facility location theory lies in the fact that decisions regarding such facilities are political decisions on public spending, in response to a social welfare criterion in a mixed market/non-market setting. In contrast, a private sector location theory emphasizes individual choice, and utility- or profit-maximizing in a predominantly market context (Teitz 1968, pp. 37–38). As a consequence of the public dimension, public facility location theory is not likely to be solely concerned with locational efficiency. Instead, as Teitz emphasizes, such questions as the distributive impacts of the facility system and the influence of the political dimension on public decisions will be of paramount importance. In addition, the theoretical problem is complicated by the need to consider the dynamic interactions within multiple-facility systems.

Analytical approaches to these fundamental precepts of public facility location have been varied. Teitz's own attempts at alternative model formulations are indicative of many highly intractable problems. For instance, his simple static model was aimed at consumption-maximization of a zero-priced good supplied from a *given* spatial distribution of service facilities. Only the briefest sketch is given of a dynamic model (Teitz 1968, pp. 45–50). Perhaps the greatest single advance made by later researchers was to convert Teitz's microeconomic-based model into a more tractable mathematical programming framework. This allowed for a variety of improvements in modelling, including a more specific incorporation of the location variable, a wider range of social welfare surrogates as objective functions, and the addition of a hierarchical organization in the facility set (see the reviews by Freestone 1977 and Lea 1973).

Most public facility programming models have been derived from the private sector analogue. The typical plant problem views location as a trade-off between facility and transport costs; hence, the greater the number of facilities, the lower the distribution costs, although this is only achieved by increased facility costs (ReVelle *et al.* 1970). This model has been converted to a public sector equivalent simply by substituting an objective function which represents "social utility." Characteristically, the problem of location in the public sector is expressed as designating m out of n sites as service locations, so as to minimize aggregate distance travelled by clients (ReVelle and Swain 1970).

Several variations on this theme have been suggested. They reflect the search for a more adequate specification of the reality of the public sector location process. For instance, the realization that "accessibility" is only one aspect of social welfare has led to a search for a better surrogate in the objective function. Alternatives have included maximizing the demand created by the facility set and minimizing the distance-decay in utilization rates (Calvo and Marks 1973). Others have been content merely to tamper with the constraints of the model. Rojeski and ReVelle (1970), for example, replace the constraint of a fixed number of facilities with an upper limit on investment in facility costs.

In recognition of the political nature and redistributive consequences of public facility location, more recent papers have begun to explore the equity dimension of the location problem. For instance, Wagner and Falkson (1975) have suggested maximizing the sum of producers' and consumers' surpluses for a given facility set, while McAllister (1976) has treated the equity-efficiency trade-off in facility location. In McAllister's model, efficiency is measured by the quantity of service demanded for a given budget; the principal source of inequity is distance, as represented by the size and spacing of centers. As might be anticipated, the equity and efficiency goals are in conflict. Equity is high and efficiency low in a system of closely-spaced centers; and equity is low and efficiency high in a widely-spaced system. As McAllister indicates, there is no en-dogenous criterion for assessing the trade-off between efficiency and equity in his model.

The introduction of an equity dimen-sion in public facility location theory re-quires that some *exogenously-derived* equity or justice criterion be introduced into the optimizing framework. This is the reason that many researchers are continuing to explore an heuristic ap-proach to public facility location. For example, McGrew and Monroe (1975) defined pure-efficiency and pure-equity solutions for a locational problem, and utilized a Tornquvist-like search pro-cedure to improve system equity subject to an efficiency constraint. In addition, Hillsman and Rushton (1976) have de-vised an algorithm which allows decision makers to depart from a globally opti-mum locational solution in order to use their local knowledge and preferences to devise a "better" local plan. The need to consider elements of decision-making discretion in the model has also stimu-lated specific studies of the nature of public decision-making. Thus, increas-ing attention is being directed toward the conflict which arises when communities oppose the siting of controversial public facilities as a consequence of the external effects of the facility set.

A clear statement on the need to in-corporate externality-induced compensa-tion principles in locational analysis is provided by the dynamic programming approach of Austin *et al.* (1970). This model minimizes the costs of a "facility package" which includes the sum of the fixed costs of the facility set, plus costs of modifying the facilities to offset com-munity opposition. This latter group of costs refers to "auxiliary facilities" which are designed to modify the external effects of a noxious public facility, e.g., a barrier to insulate residents from ex-pressway noise. The facility package ap-proach is an important variation on the traditional themes not only because it emphasizes a balance between efficiency and equity in public location decisions, but also because it recognizes the sig-nificance of externalities in the location process. It is important to observe that equity in location is thus composed of two elements (Dear 1976): a direct im-pact which is related to the delivery of service to a client population (where tra-ditional concerns of equity in access are of paramount importance) and an indi-rect impact which affects the wider, non-client population through the externality fields of the facility set (where infringe-ments of amenity rights cause commu-nity opposition).

Such prominent departures from the traditional efficiency concerns of loca-tional theory represent attempts to incor-porate the public aspect of location deci-sions more specifically in the analysis. At the core of a public sector theory is the concept of a public good or service. In the absence of a clearly-defined demand function for public goods, collective ac-tion by state agencies becomes necessary in response to the perceived needs of the populace. Otherwise, these goods are underprovided or are not produced at all. The degree of intervention to provide public goods and services in a capitalist economy falls between the extremes of a completely spontaneous private process and a perfectly controlled public process. It is, of course, unlikely that any good is produced at either extreme of the con-tinuum. Different degrees of intervention may be anticipated (1) according to the degree of private market failure; and (2) according to decisions made in the polit-ical arena. As a consequence, the provision of public goods and public facilities can only be explained as a consequence of two distinct components: first, a *substantive* component, which is solely concerned with the characteristics of demand and supply of a particular good or service, and second, a *procedural* component, which emphasizes the political and administrative procedures which govern decisions about the provision of the good or service.

The relevance of these observations for public facility location theory is immediately obvious. Although Teitz and others have been aware of the political (i.e., procedural) aspects of public decisions, their analytical formulations have almost entirely focused upon the substantive aspects of the location problem. Thus, the relevance of the economic base and its superstructure has been almost totally ignored. Yet the procedural/substantive dichotomy is logically unsupportable, since the nature of public intervention cannot be separated from the socio-economic and political context within which it is embedded. Procedural and substantive aspects inevitably act as mutual constraints. Hence, a public facility location theory must also be a theory of society, and it can only be understood as a manifestation of a given social order.

Requirements of a Comprehensive Theory of Public Facility Location

At the outset, an important distinction must be made between the "level of appearances" in society and the "social reality" underlying those appearances. Such a distinction is a central part of Marxist epistemology (Wright 1978). The preferable scientific method is one which allows underlying structural processes to be linked systematically to empirically observable phenomena. This requirement, though simply stated, is one of the most difficult methodological hurdles in social science. It is also a core issue in social science theory and philosophy (e.g., Habermas 1974). Hence, some digression into these wider issues is unavoidable.

It has recently been suggested that geography and other spatial sciences have been overly committed to a positivist epistemology. This has tended to isolate researchers from society and its cultures, making ". . . social science an activity performed *on* rather than *in* society" (Gregory 1978, p. 51). Progress away from the "empirical-analytic" traditions of positivism depends upon the application of the "historical-hermeneutic" approach in social science (Habermas 1974). This approach rejects the possibility of an autonomous science, insisting instead that concepts of science are contingent upon determinate social contexts and practices. Thus, scientific progress depends upon an emancipatory dialogue between our internal and external theoretical frameworks. The reciprocal dialectic between these two frames of reference is, according to Habermas, the source of knowledge (cf. Gregory 1978, Chs. 2, 5).

In developing an appropriate mode of analysis in public facility location theory, the choice between the empirical-analytic and historical-hermeneutic approaches is crucial. The former offers a well-defined analytical methodology which succeeds only in describing the superficial level of appearances of locational processes; the latter offers a complex but powerful heuristic for interrogating the relationship between the empirical reality of public facility location and the underlying social formation. However, it is important to note that the historical-hermeneutic approach proceeds by debate and contradiction, and is not conducive to the establishment of scientific "findings" or "facts." This is clearly illustrated by recognizing that the criterion of validity in empirical-analytic knowledge is a successful *prediction;* in historical-hermeneutic knowledge, the criterion is a successful *interpretation* (Gregory 1978).

In spite of the difficulties presented by the historical-hermeneutic method, it is the key concept in the public facility location theory developed in the remainder of this paper. This is because it requires a derivation of theory from the wider social formation (cf. Hindess and Hirst 1975, pp. 13 ff). It implies that spatial structure should be interpreted as an expression of social process; hence, analysis of the spatial expression of public intervention insists upon a theory of society as well as a theory of space.

We may now clarify the fundamental requirements of a comprehensive public facility location theory. First, such a theory should be self-consciously embedded within the context of the wider social organization, in order that the forward and backward linkages may be clarified among the social formation, its concomitant public policy, and the spatial outcomes of that policy. Secondly, spatial outcomes, which form the focus of analysis, should be disaggregated into two components: the direct (anticipated) outcomes of the policy decision and the indirect (unanticipated, externality-induced) outcomes. Both the direct and indirect outcomes of public decisions are a major source of environmental quality and social well-being. The substantive impact of these outcomes therefore is an important source of procedural (i.e., political) debate in the public decision process.

Any comprehensive theory of public facility location should seek to explain spatial outcomes in terms of the dual (direct and indirect) impact of public decisions on social welfare and to situate the public decision-making process within the wider social formation. Hence, three analytical components are essential in such a theory: (1) location as access; (2) location as externality; and (3) lo-cational decisions in the context of the wider social formation. In what follows, the importance of these three themes are illustrated by reference to the example of mental health care.

Location as Access

One of the major current policy objectives in mental health care in North America is to decentralize service units into relatively small scale community facilities. This has the dual objective of making care more readily accessible to the client population, and of placing care units in a milieu which is likely to facilitate the "normalization" of the patients (Dear 1977b). The policy has had a major impact in shifting the locus of treatment away from the mental hospital and into the community.

THE "MARKET" FOR MENTAL
HEALTH CARE

The most immediate problem facing mental health care planners is to derive reliable estimates of the size of the client population for a decentralized network. Most of the difficulties in analyzing the *demand* for mental health care stem from problems and ambiguities in defining the good and its consumers. Five specific constraints should be noted. (1) Mental illness is generally involuntary and unpredictable; the decision to "consume" care is usually taken on the patient's behalf by some other person. (2) For consumers to seek care themselves requires recognition of symptoms and an acceptance of the "sick" role. (3) Except in a minority of cases, consumers are rarely required to make payment for services; hence, in public mental health care, the concept of "purchasing" services is often redundant. (4) Consumer behavior in the market-place is essentially irrational, due to the inability of consumers to assess the quality of service received, their inability to choose amongst service providers (largely through lack of expert knowledge), and their failure to use preventive services. (5) Finally, mental health care has a wide range of external benefits, which accrue to society as a whole; for example, it is clearly in society's interest that a potentially harmful patient be detained in custodial care. One important consequence of such external effects is that non-consumers frequently have an important procedural voice in the kinds of services provided.

In the absence of the traditional demand signposts, it is unsurprising that the response on the *supply* side of mental health has been ambiguous. The difficulties involved in measuring mental health outcomes, and thus, of developing appropriate pricing policies, have effectively removed profit as a factor in many sectors of mental health care. Even when private care is possible, strict regulation and licensure procedures are generally involved. Without an effective demand and a traditional supply-side response, the "market" for mental health care remains undeveloped. The market has tended to be replaced by a public decision mechanism. For present purposes, the most important consequence of collective action is that traditional efficiency criteria in decision-making are frequently replaced by alternative equity or justice criteria. Decisions on service delivery in mental health tend to be based upon the concept of client *need* rather than demand. Need is a complex notion, embracing political and professional judgments about the preferred level of community health for a population at risk. Hence, analysts have tended to retreat both from the technical difficulties involved in estimating demand and from the political judgments involved in calculating needs. Instead, they have chosen to focus on the *utilization* variable, as a suitable surrogate for demand. It has been argued that it is possible to observe "typical" utilization patterns for a given set of facilities and a given population.

THE ROLE OF LOCATION IN UTILIZATION

The influence of location on the utilization of health services has been widely conceded, although its specific role remains ambiguous. For instance, Weiss *et al.* (1966) have shown that the further patients reside from a mental hospital, the more rigorous the diagnostic criteria which doctors exercise before discharging them. On the other hand, Smith (1976) emphasizes the "miniscule" effect of distance upon a patient's ability to stay out of hospital once discharged. As a point of departure in this analysis, it is important to emphasize that many public facility services are vital to the potential consumer. The availability of a service may literally mean the difference between life and death. Consequently, a dual hypothesis seems necessary for the analysis of public facility utilization: (1) that location has little measurable impact on the overall utilization of services by the population at risk (i.e., the decision to seek care); and (2) that location has a significant effect on a user's choice of a particular facility.

Previous research has suggested that three groups of characteristics influence the utilization of mental health services: the characteristics of the *service* being provided; the characteristics of the *client* population; and the *location* of the service (Dear 1976). The utilization decision of any consumer is viewed as a function of fifteen variables (Table 1). Different consumer responses represent differential weightings on some or all of the fifteen characteristics. It is unlikely that all variables will be relevant at all times. More commonly, the variables will enter and leave the individual's decision calculus with differential weights attached, according to a specific situation. It should be emphasized that this formu-

Table 1. Variables Influencing Utilization of Mental Health Care Facilities

---

Service Characteristics
  Intake policy, including facility opening times
  Quality and type of service
  Physical amenity of the service facility
  Size of facility
  Capacity of facility
  Price of service

Client Characteristics
  Demographic factors
  Income
  Education
  Religion
  Presenting symptoms

Location Characteristics
  Physical distance, accessibility
  Location as catchment[a]
  Social distance[b]
  Relative location[c]

---

[a] In which rules governing the administrative area where clients may obtain service may force the clients to ignore more accessible service alternatives.
[b] The "distance" placed between client and service by referral patterns.
[c] The set of intervening service opportunities and why they may be ignored or accepted.

lation of the utilization decision is not intended as an operational model, descriptive of (for example) consumer choice. Hence, no functional relationships amongst the variables has been specified. In its present form, the model should be viewed as an heuristic tool for analyzing client behavior in mental health care. The task of operationalizing the model is relatively straightforward, however. For example, in an exercise designed to predict mental health needs in Hamilton, Ontario the utilization function was expressed as a linear multiple regression equation.

The functional form of the distance-decay relationship suggests a relatively strong relationship between utilization rate and increasing distance from the mental health facility. The strength of this relationship, together with the previous multiple regression results tends to confirm a two-level interpretation of the role of location in utilization of mental health care facilities: location seems to play a minor role in overall client access to care, but has a major impact on client choice behavior with respect to individual facilities. This finding parallels that of Abernathy and Schrems (1971) in the public health field and clarifies the ambiguity in the location variable noted by others (e.g., Dear 1977b; Smith 1976).

Location as Externality

The primary emphasis on delivering a service to the consumer, or on making services accessible to consumers, detracts from the important range of external effects generated by the location variable. Such externalities may affect both consumers (users) and nonconsumers (nonusers) of the facility's services. The former group may be designated as user-associated externalities, the latter group as neighborhood-associated externalities.

The set of *user-associated* external effects is related to the concept of agglomeration economies. While the traditional emphasis on accessibility encourages a dispersed facility pattern, agglomerative criteria might warrant a concentrated pattern. The consumer will obviously benefit if all internal scale economies have been captured in a facility's operation. However, more significantly, urbanization and localization economies might encourage clustering of service facilities, such that users might be able to take advantage of choice or make multiple-purpose visits (Wolch 1978).

There is increasing empirical evidence indicative of the significance of user-associated external effects in social service systems. In his study of three U.S. metropolitan areas, White (1976) noted strong "co-locational" patterns for mental health, mental retardation, and social support facilities. Such patterns were, in fact, composed of two discrete (but overlapping) locational tendencies: one strong agglomeration was defined for mental health and linked services; and another looser agglomeration for social support and public health services. Other research has shown that the service facility agglomeration provides a highly supportive environment for the disadvantaged person. In many parts of the U.S. and Canada, small "ghettos" of recently-discharged mental hospital patients are appearing, usually in the downtown areas of major cities (Dear 1977a). Within the ghetto, patients help each other to find accommodation, to locate a job referral center, or to run local newsletters (Wolpert and Wolpert 1976). A systematic analysis of the positive (beneficial), negative (harmful), and neutral facility interactions emphasizes that interaction is only possible up to some crucial distance threshold. Thereafter, all interaction will be neutralized by the fact of excess distance (Dear 1976).

It is vital to note that while user attitudes toward service facility clusters are usually positive, nonuser attitudes are almost universally negative. The same facility set generates external effects which are perceived differently as *neighborhood-associated externalities* by the "host" community. Residents often appear to be concerned with the possible saturation of service facilities in their neighborhood. A "tipping" effect has already occurred in some cities, transforming what was once an area of residential land use into one of predominantly institutional uses. In Philadelphia, for example, the proliferation of outreach facilities, dormitories, parking lots, and street signs had caused one area to take on the appearance of an "outpatient ward" for the whole city.

Locational conflict over public facility location is usually based upon the perceived negative external effects of a facility or of a multiple-facility complex. Two groups of external effects have been noticed: tangible effects, which are based upon clearly recognizable, usually quantifiable, impacts of the facility in question; and intangible effects, referring to a wide range of non-quantitative effects. The former group includes property value decline and increased traffic in the vicinity of the facility. The latter group includes fear for personal security, the stigma attached to mental illness, and dislike of loitering clients. While there is little to prevent tangible external effects from being incorporated into planning decisions, the systematic analysis of intangible effects poses a considerable analytical challenge. Two distinct components of this task have been recognized: (1) the identification of the *attributes* by which externalities are perceived by the observer; and (2) the measurement of *respondent rating* of a facility with respect to these designated attributes. Preliminary experiments using multidimensional scaling for the first task, and semantic differential measurements for the second, suggest that mental health centers may be judged by non-users in terms of their attractiveness, condition, and neighborhood impact (Dear et al. 1977).

In response to extensive community opposition to substantive plans for mental health facility siting, planners have developed numerous procedural strategies to avoid conflict. One of two approaches tends to be adopted: the "low profile" approach, which educates and coerces the community into accepting a facility before it is introduced, or the "fly-by-night" strategy, which involves setting up a facility secretly, and hoping that it will not be noticed until its operation can demonstrably be shown to be harmless (Wolpert et al. 1975). However, since both strategies are hazardous, a third "risk aversion" strategy has become common. This involves seeking out locations where no community opposition is anticipated or where controversial facilities would go unnoticed. Such locations tend to proliferate in transient, rental accommodation areas of inner cities. As well as making location/siting concessions toward potentially opposing community groups, planners have also made financial concessions to impacted communities and have altered facility design to cope with specific objections.

The planning problem is complicated by lack of foresight in developing the community health program. Enormous pressures have been placed upon community aftercare facilities by the large volume of patients being discharged from mental hospitals. The acute pressure on the aftercare system has meant, however, that an accelerated, haphazard discharge program has caused a significant proportion of discharged patients to be "lost" to the system. Such patients frequently filter through the urban space to areas of cheap private rental accommodation, thus reinforcing the trend toward ghettoization of the mentally ill. These tendencies were very clear in a recent study of 169 patients who were discharged from Hamilton Psychiatric Hospital (Ontario) during the first quarter of 1975. Of this total, 75% were discharged into noninstitutional settings (e.g., family or friends) and 25% to other institutional settings (e.g., nursing homes). Within six months of discharge, no less than 25% of the 169 patients had made at least one change of address. The movers were traced through a sequence of addresses: 9 merely changed location; 7 were readmitted to the hospital; and 21 were "lost." The losses are typical of the problem patient, who probably filters down into the transient ghetto situation. They usually did not leave forwarding addresses, left without notifying the landlord, and were often alcoholic. Of the 21 patients, 4 were lost after release from the criminal justice system; 10 dropped out of sight immediately; and 7 were lost only after an extensive search through subsequent addresses. It is worth noting that only 3 out of the 21 were discharged to their families; the majority of losses were discharged in their own recognizance, i.e., to selfcare (Dear 1977a).

In summary, the development of the mental health patient ghetto—the new asylum without walls—is a product of three major forces, all of which have their source in location as externality:

1. The formal assignment of mental patients to institutional aftercare facilities which tend to proliferate in downtown locations because of planners' actions and because of the availability of large convertible properties;
2. the extent of community opposition to mental health facilities in other neighborhoods; and
3. an informal process of spatial filtering by which a volatile minority of mobile patients tend to gravitate toward the transient areas of rental accommodation in the inner urban core.

Social Context for Mental Health Care

The two dimensions of location (as access and as externality) have produced two entirely different treatment settings in mental health care. The first, based on access, has resulted in a (frequently suboptimal) decentralized system of community mental health centers. The second, a consequence of aggregate external effects, has led to the organic creation of a ghetto of the mentally disabled. In order to plan for the future of these two important service modalities, it is essential to place mental health in its proper policy context. For example, the ghetto is already being dismantled by zoning ordinances in a number of U.S. cities; this is in pragmatic response to community opposition to such ghettos, irrespective of their potentially positive service impact. In order to proceed with the analysis of public facility location, it must be conceded that the pattern of provision is inextricably determined by the contemporary socio-economic and political context. This can be demonstrated by reference to both historical and current sources.

In his historical study of the "geography of haunted places," Foucault (1973) traces the birth of the asylum in the Classical Age in Europe. He notes the progressive exclusion of the mentally disabled outside city walls to their confinement in the "Ship of Fools." Subsequently, in seventeenth century France began the "great confinement" of poor, sick, and mentally ill. This continued until the ultimate development of special places solely intended to contain the mentally ill—the true birth of the asylum. Foucault emphasizes the link between the developing policy toward the mentally disabled and the contemporary philosophies of social control in these formative centuries. Rothman (1971) was also concerned with the discovery of the asylum, but within the context of postcolonial America. He notes that psychiatrists at this time were more American than scientific, and that the simultaneous growth of asylums, prisons, poorhouses, and orphan asylums suggested society's concern with a broad range of social problems. Mental illness was regarded as a social problem; and since the penitentiary would reform the criminal and the almshouse rehabilitate the poor, so would the insane asylum cure the mentally ill (Rothman 1971, p. 80).

Just as the historical development of the asylum cannot be understood without reference to the wider contemporary social context, so current planning efforts cannot be divorced from the policy context within which they are embedded.

The current trend toward community-based mental health care began in the mid-sixties in North America. Impetus for the movement derived from several sources, most notably the beliefs that long-term incarceration in hospital did more harm than good and, thereby, infringed upon civil liberties; that a community-based care would aid in the resocialization of the disturbed patient; and that cost savings could be achieved through transfer of patients to treatment settings outside hospitals. In short, an alliance between civil rights libertarians and fiscal conservatives was achieved. Their objectives were facilitated by contemporary advances in psychiatric treatment, particularly in chemotherapy, through which the extremes of behavior disorders could be controlled. As a consequence, a massive shift in treatment setting has occurred: mental hospitals have been closed, or reduced in operation, and many community mental health centers opened. The trends are similar in Canada, the U.S., and parts of western Europe. The last decade has witnessed a strong increase in active caseloads of community-based facilities and, to a lesser extent, of psychiatric units in general hospitals. In contrast, the active caseload of mental hospitals has declined to about one-third of its 1965 rate. At the same time, a much larger turnover in psychiatric hospital census is evident in the growing volume of admissions and discharges (Dear 1977a).

The impact of the changing mental health policies has been profound. Wolpert and Wolpert (1976) summarize the major impacts as follows:

Fewer new hospitals are being built and a number have been closed down in recent years; an undetermined, but significant proportion of ex-hospital patients have benefitted from release; the economic spillover effects of treatment programs and facilities, positive and negative, have been shifted from the generally remote and rural sites of the state hospitals to more urban locations; and service activities are more prominently focused upon prevention aspects and the out-patient mode of treatment (p. 40).

The most prominent outcome of the shifts in treatment practice has been upon the cost accounts. On a superficial level, there seems little doubt that the change to community care has resulted in savings on a per patient basis. However, what is not so commonly conceded is that the true burden of payment has been *shifted,* in the U.S. at least, from the state and local health sector to the federal welfare sector. In California, for example, the decline in state hospital utilization can be exactly correlated with the introduction of federal reimbursement schemes for local social service programs. Wolpert and Wolpert (1976) estimate that the share of such local programs in the California state mental health budget increased from 1.1% (1957–58) to 49.2% (1971–72).

What is the prospect for the future? In Canada and the United States, there is little likelihood of any immediate retreat from a community-based mental health care program, although the need for a continuing hospital network for chronic patients is now conceded. Perhaps the greatest single factor in the future development of the service network is the status of mental health as a public good, especially in the light of current restraints on public spending. The costs of mental health are enormous, especially if the total budgets of the welfare and aftercare support systems are included. Any requests for restraint in future spending could severely affect service plans. This was demonstrated in one recent study of a psychiatric hospital in Ontario (Dear *et al.* 1979). In a period of economic expansion followed by recession plus inflation (1960–77), the hospital (1) reduced its bed capacity; (2) discharged large numbers of patients; and (3) subsequently stabilized admission and discharge rates to maintain a low hospital census.

References

Abernathy, W. J., and E. L. Schrems. 1971. *Distance and Health Services: Issues of Utilization and Facility Choice for Demographic Strata.* Graduate School of Business, Research Paper No. 19, Stanford University.

Austin, M., Smith, T. E., and J. Wolpert. 1970. The Implementation of Controversial Facility-Complex Programs. *Geographical Analysis* 2: 315–329.

Calvo, A. B., and D. H. Marks. 1973. Location of Health Care Facilities: An Analytic Approach. *Socio-Economic Planning Sciences* 7: 407–422.

Dear, M. 1976. Spatial Externalities and Locational Conflict. *London Papers in Regional Science* 7: 152–167.

Dear, M. 1977a. Psychiatric Patients and the Inner City. *Annals, Association of American Geographers* 67: 588–594.

Dear, M. 1977b. Locational Factors in the Demand for Mental Health Care. *Economic Geography* 53: 223–240.

Dear, M., Fincher, R., and L. Currie. 1977. Measuring the External Effects of Public Programs. *Environment and Planning A* 9: 137–147.

Dear, M., Clark, G., and S. Clark. 1979. Economic Cycles and Mental Health Care. *Social Science and Medicine.* (forthcoming)

Foucault, M. 1973. *Madness and Civilization: A History of Madness in the Age of Reason.* New York, Vintage Books.

Freestone, R. 1977. *Public Facility Location.* Council of Planning Librarians Exchange Bibliography 1211.

Gregory, D. 1978. *Science, Ideology and Human Geography.* London, Hutchinson U.P.

Habermas, J. 1974. *Theory and Practice.* Boston, Beacon Press.

Hindess, B., and Hirst, P. Q. 1975. *Pre-Capitalist Modes of Production.* London, Routledge and Kegan Paul.

Hillsman, E. L., and G. Rushton. 1976. Solutions for Multi-Attribute Location Problems. Paper read at the North American

Conference of the Regional Science Association, Toronto.

Lea, A. C. 1973. *Location-allocation Systems: An Annotated Bibliography*. Department of Geography Discussion Paper 13, University of Toronto.

McAllister, D. M. 1976. Efficiency and Equity in Public Facility Location. *Geographical Analysis* 8: 47–63.

McGrew, J. C., and C. B. Monroe. 1975. Efficiency, Equity, and Multiple Facility Location. *Proceedings, Association of American Geographers* 7: 142–146.

ReVelle, C., Marks, D., and J. Liebman. 1978. An Analysis of Private and Public Sector Location Models. *Management Science* 16: 692–708.

ReVelle, C. S., and R. W. Swain. 1970. Central Facilities Location. *Geographical Analysis* 11: 30–42.

Rojeski, P., and C. S. ReVelle. 1970. Central Facilities Location Under an Investment Constraint. *Geographical Analysis* 2: 343–360.

Rothman, D. J. 1971. *The Discovery of the Asylum: Social Order and Disorder in the New Republic*. Boston, Little, Brown & Co.

Smith, C. J. 1976. Distance and the Location of Community Mental Health Facilities: A Divergent Viewpoint. *Economic Geography* 52: 181–191.

Teitz, M. B. 1968. Toward a Theory of Urban Public Facility Location. *Papers Regional Science Association* 21: 35–52.

Wagner, J. L., and L. M. Falkson. 1975. The Optimal Nodal Location of Public Facilities with Price-Sensitive Demand. *Geographical Analysis* 7: 69–83.

Weiss, P., Macaulay, J., and A. Pincus. 1966. Geographic Factors and the Release of Patients from State Mental Hospitals. *American Journal of Psychiatry* 123: 408–412.

White, A. N. 1976. Locational Analysis for Public Facilities: Reassessing the Role of Accessibility. Paper read at the North American Conference of the Regional Science Association, Toronto.

Wolch, J. 1978. Residential Location of Service-Dependent Households. Unpublished Ph.D. dissertation, Princeton University, Princeton.

Wolpert, J. 1977. Social Income and the Voluntary Sector. *Papers, Regional Science Association* 39: 37–59.

Wolpert, J., Dear, M., and R. Crawford. 1975. Satellite Mental Health Facilities. *Annals, Association of American Geographers* 65: 24–35.

Wolpert, J., and E. Wolpert. 1976. The Relocation of Released Mental Hospital Patients into Residential Communities. *Policy Sciences* 7: 31–51.

Wright, E. O. 1978. *Class, Crisis and the State*. London, New Left Books.

III

PATTERNS AND PROCESSES: Determinants of Urban Structure and Change

JOHN S. ADAMS

Residential Structure of Midwestern Cities

Two classes of urban models provide a framework for studying urban residential patterns. Berry and others demonstrated that a factor analysis of urban census-tract data yields contemporary support for traditional ideas about sectors, rings, and neighborhoods of different land use types.[1] At the same time, population density models presented by Colin Clark and others describe how population densities decline with distance from city centers.[2]

This study examines residential land use in Midwestern cities as a function of American construction history. A hypothetical model residential pattern is generated using housing construction statis-

tics from 1889 to 1960. Residential patterns produced with the model are consistent with patterns expected based on the population density models. Evaluation of the model in terms of the sector-ring-neighborhood framework is more difficult but the model is consistent with it. Finally, the model is clearly in agreement with distance-density decline interpretations of American urban population structure, especially within Midwestern cities.

The Sector–Ring–Neighborhood Framework

Twentieth century social science literature contains several attempts to describe in a general model the spatial patterning of land uses within the American city.[3] Hurd's study of neighborhoods, incomes, and rentals described patterns created by central and axial growth. Burgess emphasized outward growth from the center and described the well-known concentric zone hypothesis of urban structure. Ac-

1. B. J. L. Berry, "Internal Structure of the City," *Law and Contemporary Problems,* Vol. 31 Winter, 1965), pp. 111–19.
2. The best recent summary of these studies, with all the important literature cited, is B. J. L. Berry, J. W. Simmons, and R. J. Tennant, "Urban Population Densities: Structure and Change," *Geographical Review,* Vol. 53 (1963), pp. 389–405. Additional material and some later research appears in B. E. Newling, "Urban Growth and Spatial Structure: Mathematical Models and Empirical Evidence," *Geographical Review,* Vol. 56 (1966), pp. 213–25.

3. This discussion borrows from Berry, *op. cit.,* footnote 1.

From the **Annals** of the Association of American Geographers, Vol. 60, 1970, pp. 37–60 (excluding Figs. 2, 3, 7, and 16). Reprinted by permission of the Association of American Geographers and J. S. Adams.

cording to this argument the city expanded outward, led by successively lower income groups in a continuing process of invasion and succession.

McKenzie argued in favor of a pattern of axial movements, and Hoyt put the argument in the form of his celebrated sector hypothesis. According to this idea, income and status differences develop around the edge of the urban core very early in the history of the city. As the city expands in size and area the various economic activities and social-economic groups expand their territories outward from the center creating pie-shaped wedges of distinct land use types. Certain transportation and industrial uses preempt land in one set of sectors. The rich bid up the price of residential land which offers high amenity value, and the lower economic classes build their neighborhoods on the land remaining after superior purchasing power has taken what it wants.

Empirical evidence was massed to support both models of urban land use. Both were general land use hypotheses, with residential land classes delineated as part of larger arguments. Amid the discussions of sectors and rings the literature in sociology, geography, real estate, economics, and planning drew attention to the phenomenon of neighborhood segregation, particularly with respect to racial-ethnic ghettos in all large cities. Since ghettos were usually compact and isolated in terms of intraurban movement patterns from the rest of the city, they did not appear to conform to either the sector or ring hypotheses of urban spatial organization.

The existence of segregation in cities, conforming neither to the ring nor sector models prompted additional research for new generalizations. Foremost among the efforts is the multiple nuclei idea advanced by Harris and Ullman in 1945. For a long time it was thought that the three constructs must necessarily be mu-

tually contradictory. The fact that they have endured so long in the literature means that there must be a remarkably large kernel of truth in each of them, or that there is no promising alternative to the three constructs.

Recent research supports the first claim.[4] There is substantial empirical support for all three constructs. The evidence is that each has validity but in each case the validity depends on the set of variables examined. Berry reports that a succession of large scale factor analytic studies conducted since the 1940's supports the idea that the three models are independent and additive explanations of the way in which residential neighborhoods are structured. Depending on the set of characteristics chosen for analysis, sectors can be delineated, rings can be delineated, and homogeneous residential neighborhoods can be identified independent of the rings and sectors. Within the urban residential landscape, nonresidential nuclei can be discerned easily.

The factor analyses disclose three dimensions of variation. This means that three distinct sets of spatially distributed attributes can be distinguished. Within each set or cluster of variables things change together, and they vary independently from the variables present in the other clusters. Axial variation in the sectors depends on a cluster of variables describing neighborhoods on the basis of socioeconomic rank. Concentric variation in the rings depends on family structure, the life cycle, and neighborhood age. Each residential neighborhood itself can be distinguished on the basis of its racial and ethnic composition. (Nonresidential nuclei are identified by their category of economic activity and by nodal position on transport nets.) The three dimensions of residential variation, and the three

4. Berry, *op. cit.,* footnote 1; elaborated in B. J. L. Berry and F. Horton, *Geographic Perspectives on Urban Systems* (Englewood Cliffs, N.J.: Prentice-Hall, 1970).

models of spatial composition and arrangement, are independent and additive.

If any Midwestern city is overlaid with both the concentric scheme and the axial pattern, neighborhoods can be defined. Within each of them remarkable uniformity in social and economic characteristics will exist. Moving around any ring, residential neighborhoods will vary in their income characteristics, but will have largely the same patterns of density, tenure, and family patterns. Moving out from the center within a particular residential sector, income and education patterns will be fairly consistent, with variations encountered ring by ring owing to family structure and stage in the life cycle. Accordingly, a set of polar coordinates, centered on the city center, is sufficient to describe most of the socio-economic variation in the Midwestern city. According to Berry, the sector-ring-neighborhood scheme offers a promising framework for further research on the spatial structure of urban land use patterns.

Population Density Models

Clark published evidence that regardless of time or place, population densities within cities conform to a simple empirically derived expression:[5]

$$d_x = d_0 e^{-bx} \qquad (1)$$

where d_x is population density at any distance x from the city center, d_0 is the extrapolated population density at the city center, e is the base of the natural logarithms, and b is the density gradient describing the way in which density decreases with distance. With thirty-six examples Clark showed that if the dis-

5. C. Clark, "Urban Population Densities," *Journal of the Royal Statistical Society,* Series A, Vol. 114 (1951), pp. 490–96; and "Urban Population Densities," *Bulletin of the International Statistical Institute,* Vol. 36 (1957), pp. 60–90.

tance and density data were put through a simple logarithmic transformation they would fit the linear expression:

$$\ln d_x = \ln d_0 - bx \qquad (2)$$

In other words, the population density at a distance x from the city center depends on the central density and the rate at which density diminishes with distance from the center. From (1) it follows that the population residing within a distance r from the city center is a function of central density d_0 as well as the density gradient b. If r is increased to its limit, then:

$$P = 2\pi d_0 b^{-2} \text{ or } P = 2\pi \cdot \frac{d_0}{b^2} \qquad (3)$$

where P is the population within radius r of the city center. If P is held at some constant value, then the central density d_0 can be expressed as a function of the density gradient b:

$$d_0 = \frac{b^2}{2\pi} \qquad (4)$$

Equation (4) appears to conform with evidence presented by Muth and derived from 1950 census data on forty-six American cities.[6] When city size is held constant central density increases as a function of the square of the density gradient b (Figure 1). Berry presented Muth's data in the form of a scatter diagram. The effects of holding city size constant can be evaluated by noting the relationship between central densities and density gradients for each city size class. Isolines representing a sample of city sizes were estimated using the scatter of points based on the 1950 data. The isolines trended upward with the appropriate slope. Equa-

6. R. F. Muth, "The Spatial Structure of the Housing Market," *Papers and Proceedings of the Regional Science Association,* Vol. 7 (1962), pp. 207–20.

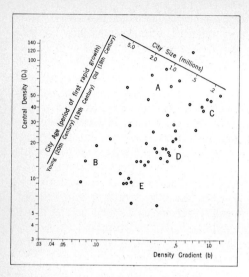

Figure 1. Estimates of Central Density and Density Gradients for Forty-six American Cities in 1950. Suggested stratifications based on city size and city age. Based in part on Berry **et al.**, footnote 2, and estimates by Muth, footnote 6

tion (4) expresses the relationship concisely, and accounts for a large part of the variation within the data plotted in Figure 1.

Equation (4) conflicts with evidence from other sources. Weiss discovered that for American cities in 1950 the density gradient b could be calculated using the expression:[7]

$$b = (10^5/P_m)^{1/3} \qquad (5)$$

where b is given in people per mile, and P_m is the population of the metropolitan area. From (5) it follows that:

$$P_m = \frac{10^5}{b^3} \qquad (6)$$

Now if population is a function of the density gradient b according to equation

7. H. K. Weiss, "The Distribution of Urban Population and an Application to a Servicing Problem," *Operations Research*, Vol. 9 (1961), pp. 860–74; cited by Berry, *op. cit.*, footnote 2.

(6), and population is also a function of central density d_o as indicated in (3), the two expressions can be combined to relate central density d_o and the density gradient b in a different way:

$$d_o = \frac{(10^5/2\pi)}{b} \qquad (7)$$

In expression (7) central density varies inversely with the density gradient. In (4) central density varies directly with the squared value of the density gradient. How can the apparent contradiction be resolved? Berry suggested that (4) applies to cities within a size class, whereas (7) applies to cities classified or stratified on another basis. Some possible bases are city site (plain, lake side, and valley), factors influencing central density, age of the city, or location in the United States.

Consider the group of large cities in Figure 1. Cities in position A (Boston, Baltimore, Philadelphia) have much higher central densities than the newer cities in position B (Los Angeles, Detroit, Cleveland). Type A cities also have steeper density gradients than the newer Type B cities. Within the smaller cities (C, D, and E) similar variations exist. The stratification by age, however, does not yield such sharp results. The cities in position C have higher central densities and steeper density gradients than cities of Type D. I think it is reasonable to expect that port cities on the New England and Middle Atlantic coastal estuaries would tend to be found in group C, Midwestern cities in group D, and perhaps the new cities along the Florida and Gulf coasts and the Southwest plotted in Group E. Muth's estimates are inconclusive, neither rejecting nor confirming the expectation that there is systematic variation in central density and density gradients with age of smaller cities (Figure 1). It seems that additional variation is present in the data, perhaps depending on the value of the ratio:

$$\frac{P_m \text{ in } 1960}{P_m \text{ in } 1860} \qquad (8)$$

where P_m is the population of the metropolitan area. The ratio is 1.0 for a city that did not grow at all, and for such a city the density gradient will be steeper and the extrapolated central density higher than for other cities of similar age but with ratios of 5.0 or 10.0 or higher.

The present study examines these possibilities by suggesting four ages of city building. Midwestern cities are products of the second and third periods of American city building. They are neither the oldest nor the youngest cities. If Midwestern cities are evaluated as a separate class of cities, central densities are fairly high, but not as high as older cities. Density gradients are steeper than those prevailing in recently settled parts of the United States.

Additional insight about the distance-density profiles of Midwestern cities lies hidden within Figure 1. According to Figure 1 the population-density profile of a city depends on central density, the density gradient, the age of the city, and the size of the metropolitan area.

Central density is related to city age. The general relationship is positive, with variations from the average depending partly on the size class of the city, as shown, and partly on the density gradient. Central density is an extrapolated value.

Central density is related to city size. Within any age class of cities, the larger the city the higher the central density. Variations in density gradients and other factors introduce unexplained variation.

Density gradients depend in part on the age of the city. The older cities have higher gradients than the young cities. Variation from the average relationship derives from size variations of cities and other factors.

Using data from London and other cities Clark showed that density gradients

for a given city declined over time, especially if city population grew. The relationship between population and density gradients is complex but, at a given date (say 1960), large old cities have lower density gradients than small new cities, but new cities have generally lower density gradients than old cities (Figure 2). If an earlier year is chosen for comparison (say 1900), density gradients are greater for all size classes, yet even in early years old cities had higher gradients than their newer counterparts.

City size cannot be meaningfully related to city age. Large and small cities are present in every age class. Yet when age and size data are plotted some general locational regularities can be displayed. The old cities of the East coast occupy one section and the new cities of the west, southwest and the Gulf Coast

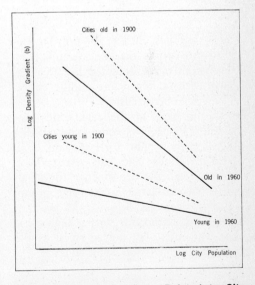

Figure 2. Density Gradients Related to City Size. As cities increase in population and area their density gradients drop. Cities of different ages show different initial gradients, different paths of gradient decline as population changes, as well as variations in these relationships from one time period to another, for example 1900 and 1960

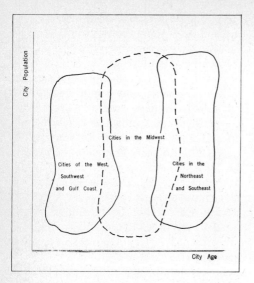

Figure 3. City Size and City Age Related Only as a Function of the Advance of the Urban Frontier across the United States. When age-size data pairings are plotted, typical cities in each region cluster approximately as shown

occupy another cluster (Figure 3). Between the two is the zone occupied by Midwestern cities, founded in the nineteenth century during the middle period of American urban history.

On the basis of the regularities displayed in Figure 1–3 some expected distance-density profiles for large and small cities of different ages can be described. Density gradients are steeper for small cities than for large in each age group. Within a size class, however, Midwestern cities display gradients steeper than those of newer cities, but not so steep as the old cities founded in colonial times.

Growth Rates and Growth Rings

What would be the residential age structure of a model city in the United States if it faithfully reflected every significant trend in residential construction activity throughout a century of city building? It

is convenient to work out the answer to the question with some hypothetical cases before developing a model representing the Midwestern city and based on the construction history of the past hundred years.

Consider a city with a commercial and industrial center located at a point and serving as an employment and shopping core for an adjacent residential area that is ten units in size. Assume also that:

1. All dwelling units constructed as additions to the city are single family detached houses;
2. the size of lot allocated to each new dwelling unit remains unchanged over the construction period;
3. the city offers a transport surface with equal ease of movement away from the core in any direction;
4. all new residential development occurs on the margin of the previously built up ten-unit area; and sites are improved (built up) in order of their distance from the core; and
5. all houses last indefinitely, that is, they are not destroyed and replaced by newer houses.

Under these asumptions, the city area will assume a different residential age structure depending on its rate of growth through successive growth periods. Consider the following cases.

Case 1. The city area equals ten square units in size. The city is circular in shape with a radius of 1.78 (Figure 4). Case 1 is a special case in which growth during time periods two through five equals zero. At the end of five time periods the city area is older but no larger. The edge of the built up area forms a fixed perimeter through time. Throughout the five time periods the change in area equals zero and the change in radius of the city equals zero. Under these assumptions total area and radius of the city

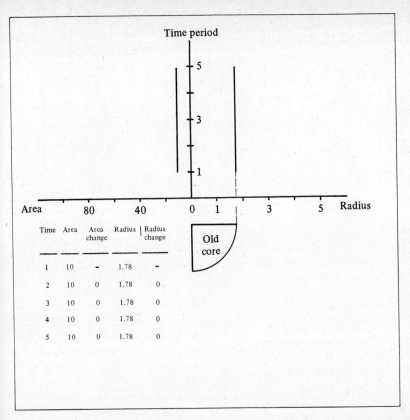

Figure 4. Case I. City area and radius are unchanged through five time periods

through time remain fixed; there is zero growth.

Case 2. At the end of the first time period the built up city area covers ten square units. In each succeeding period the absolute rate of areal growth is halved. The radius of the city increases in each time period but at a sharply decreasing rate. Each growth ring added is narrower than the preceding ring (Figure 5).

Case 3. Beginning with a built up area of ten units at the end of period one the city adds additional area at the constant arithmetic rate of ten areal units per time period. The radius of the built up area again increases but at a gradually de-creasing rate. Each new growth ring is somewhat narrower than the preceding ring (Figure 6).

Case 4. Again the city expands from a base of ten areal units at the end of the first time period. In this case, however, the perimeter moves away from the center at a constant rate through time. When the radius increases at a steady arithmetic rate through time (0.6 per time period) the city area grows larger at a slightly increasing rate. Each growth ring has the same width as the preceding ring, but the larger diameter corresponds to a larger increment to the city area in each successive growth period. In the second growth period the radius increased by

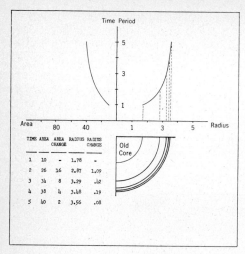

Figure 5. Case 2. Areal growth in each period following Time 2 is half the growth of the previous period

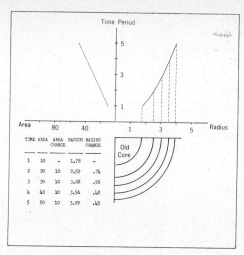

Figure 7. Case 4. The urban area adds ten units of land in each growth period

0.6, while the area of the city expanded by 7.8 square units. In the fifth growth period the radius again increased by 0.6 but this time the area increased by 14.6 units (Figure 7).

Case 5. In the fifth case the radius of the city expands at an increasing arith-

metic rate through successive time periods. Each growth ring is wider than the preceding growth ring. Over time the city area grows at a rapidly increasing rate (Figure 8).

Regardless of the rate of growth at any period, the growth ring from each period faithfully records the styles, tastes, and

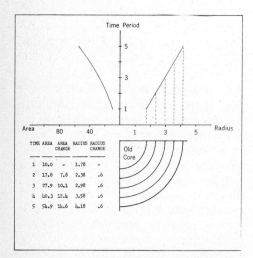

Figure 6. Case 3. Following time period one the radius of the city increases at a constant amount per time period. The urban area therefore increases at an increasing rate

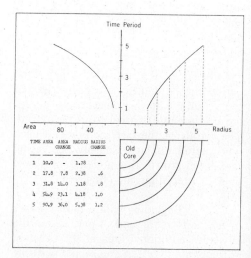

Figure 8. Case 5. The radius of the city changes at an increasing rate and the area of the city expands at a rapidly increasing rate

arrangements demanded and supplied in the new housing market during that period. The width of a particular growth ring is a function of the rate of growth during that period and the radius of the city at the start of the growth period. The more rapid the growth rate the wider the growth ring in the growth period, provided that other things remain equal.

Implications and Alternative Assumptions

Consider now the assumptions that determined the outcomes illustrated by the five growth cases. It is clear that a growth process over time will produce an urban residential landscape and that variations in the process become manifest in a city's residential age structure. Different kinds of variations are introduced into the models by loosening the assumptions.

If we relax the first assumption and permit a mixture of structures instead of only single family detached dwellings, a particular growth ring will reflect the mix characteristics of its construction era. In actual fact residential construction history discloses fads in dwelling types, with some growth stages composed mostly of multiple family buildings, whereas other building eras depended mainly on single family house construction.

If the average size of lot associated with each dwelling unit changes over time or with the type of structure (single, double, multiple) an additional source of variation in the width of growth rings is introduced. In American urban development dwelling units in single family structures typically use more land than the same size unit in a multiple structure. It follows, therefore, that if a construction period emphasizes single family units rather than doubles or multiples, the average lot size for all dwelling units built during that period increases and the size of the growth ring for that period is correspondingly larger. Conversely, a shift to multiples, and away from single family units, has

the opposite effect and narrows the growth ring for a fixed number of new dwelling units in a certain time period. Similarly, construction styles may change and larger sites may be used for singles, multiples, or both. In either way, then, by construction mix (singles, doubles, or multiples) and construction styles (larger or smaller lots per dwelling unit), the width of growth rings can be modified from one residential development era to the next.

If the city's transport system represents a network rather than an isotropic surface of movement the concentric circle growth pattern will be distorted. Areal growth will proceed faster along arterials leading to the center. Along such routes movement-cost gradients are less severe. Growth will be retarded in interstitial areas where movement costs are higher. Movement surfaces promote a concentric circle movement pattern. Movement networks foster a star-shaped pattern of urban spread.

American cities were built up during a series of intraurban transport eras.[8] Some eras provided a transport surface whereas others depended on a sharply defined network of movement routes. Whichever transport era is considered, we can see its unmistakable mark on the shape of the residential growth rings from that era. The model developed in this paper assumes four significantly different transport eras:

1. The walking/horsecar era: up to the 1880's;
2. the electric streetcar era: 1880's–World War I;
3. the recreational auto era: 1920's–1941; and
4. the freeway era: Post World War II.

8. Suggested by a short discussion in Hoyt, *op. cit.*, footnote 3; elaborated in A. J. Krim, *The Innovation and Diffusion of the Street Railway in North America* (unpublished M. A. Thesis, Department of Geography, University of Chicago, 1967).

The transport systems of the first and third eras provided a movement surface, whereas those of the second and fourth periods exhibit the channels and nodes associated with sharply delineated movement networks.

To assume that residential development occurs at sites on the margins of built-up urban areas fits the facts well. In the recent period there has been some leapfrogging owing to land speculation at the built-up margins of the city, but as the radius of the city increases, the supply of available sites increases exponentially. No land holder can acquire a monopoly position by cornering the market on all building sites on the edge of the built-up area. Away from the built-up margin total site costs rise faster than land and other costs drop so there is little incentive to develop residential land beyond the margin.

In the freeway auto era, the margin of the city is progressively redefined in terms of time-distance from previously built-up areas. Conventional maps depict such growth like beads on a string. A suitable isochronic map based on the city center would account for the space distorting features of modern limited access highway systems. Such a map would demonstrate that sites on the time-distance margins of a city are built up prior to sites beyond margins defined this way. The leap-frogging is real only in a restricted sense, as the crow flies rather than as the high speed auto moves.

Since the vast majority of the housing built in the United States during the past century is still in existence there is no reason to evaluate alternatives to the fifth assumption that housing lasts indefinitely.

Urban Residential Construction

Although none of the five hypothetical growth cases (Figures 4–8) represents the history of urban residential construction in the United States or the Midwest,

each one sheds some light on at least one construction era. In our cities, residential construction activity has been subjected to wild ups and downs. Let us explore some of the human and economic causes and consequences of the fluctuation in urban construction activity.

The production of new residential buildings has followed effective demand for them. When larger urban populations needed more living space, if they could pay for additional housing they were soon supplied by small speculative builders who put up one or a few houses and sold them for whatever the market would bear. Natural population change, coupled with migration into and out of the city, modified changes in demand for shelter space traceable to high wages and full employment. Changes in birth rates, fluctuations in death rates owing to war and disease (influenza), and irregular rates of marriage and family formation wielded a major impact on the secular demand for new housing. In the past century fluctuations in the level of economic opportunity present in cities were tied to national and regional waves of prosperity and depression. In good times people flocked to the cities from rural areas, small towns, and foreign countries.

For most of the past hundred years, American residential construction activity has been a boom or bust proposition.[9]

9. The residential construction record has been extensively reported and analyzed in: U.S. Bureau of the Census, *Housing Construction Statistics: 1889–1964* (Washington, D.C.: Government Printing Office, 1966); G. H. Beyer, *Housing and Society* (New York: MacMillan, 1965); J. S. Dusenberry, *Business Cycles and Economic Growth* (New York: McGraw-Hill, 1958); L. Winnick, *American Housing and Its Use: The Demand for Shelter Space* (New York: John Wiley and Sons, 1957); D. Blank, *The Volume of Residential Construction: 1889–1950,* Technical Paper No. 9 (New York: National Bureau of Economic Research, 1954); M. Colean and R. Newcomb, *Stabilizing Construction: The Record and Potential* (New York: McGraw-Hill, 1952); M. Colean, *Ameri-*

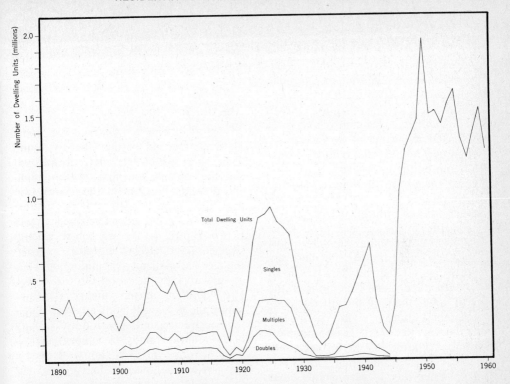

Figure 9. Estimated Number of Dwelling Units Started Each Year, 1889–1960. Dwelling units are built as single family houses, in double houses, or in multiples. Estimated detail by type of structure is not available for units built before 1900 or after 1944. Source: United States Bureau of the Census: **Housing Construction Statistics:1889–1964** (Washington, D.C.: Government Printing Office, 1966), Table A-1

Construction levels fluctuated violently between 1889 and 1960, with each new building cycle introducing novel housing styles and new consumer preferences (Figure 9). Single family dwellings account for almost all structures in some construction cycles, while at other times a large fraction of structures are doubles and multiples. As an example of wild fluctuations in residential building cycles Hoyt reported that in Chicago between 1852 and 1932 (eighty years), five-sixths of all the buildings erected were put up

in the forty most active building years.[10] If the prosperity connected with business expansion in a period of national boom was not fully shared by an individual city, the growth ring from that era is proportionately narrow. Chicago participated in all the booms of the past century. In one cycle its population rose from 2.6 million in 1919 to 3.4 million in 1927. That rise contributed to a building boom with annual permit values of new buildings increasing from a low of $35 million in 1918 to $367 million in 1926. When Chicago's population dropped slightly be-

can Housing: Problems and Prospects (New York: 20th Century Fund, 1944); J. B. Derksen, "Long Cycles in Residential Building," Econometrica, Vol. 10 (1940), pp. 97–116.

10. H. Hoyt, One Hundred Years of Land Values in Chicago (Chicago: University of Chicago Press, 1933), Figure 99, cited in Hoyt, op. cit., footnote 3, p. 93.

tween 1927 and 1932 the annual volume of new construction fell ninety-nine percent to $4 million in 1932.[11] Other evidence clearly links economic and population growth to building booms. Newman showed that from 1875 to 1933 in seventeen American cities population growth regularly anticipated major changes in building activity by one or two years.[12]

When new houses were built they were usually put on the urban fringe bypassing whatever vacant lots there were scattered throughout the inner city. Hoyt argued that this practice reduced the risk that a new structure might lose part of its value in unattractive surroundings.[13] Alternative explanations might be that sites cost less on the fringe, or that builders perceived more favorable demand conditions on the edge of town than in the interior. Although these ideas about peripheral growth seem to square with common knowledge, I know of no formal study of several cities testing such generalizations. Neither has it been shown that neighborhoods of houses homogeneous with respect to age are more or less stable in their physical or price maintenance, or socio-economic character of residents, than neighborhoods with buildings of many ages.[14]

A succession of business-construction cycles means that residential areas grow by spurts, adding a growth ring to represent each cycle. Periods of business depression produced steep age gradients as one moves outward from the center of town. Such abrupt age gradients separate growth rings created during times of boom. When other correlates of age are legible and identifiable the edges and homogeneous inner bands of each ring are easily recognized.

The Old Core and the Walking-Horse Car Era

Between the end of the Civil War and 1960 there were eight major residential building booms. The first two generated the present Old Core of the Midwestern city. The former ended with the depression of 1873; the second reached a peak in the 1880's. In the era before electric streetcars and electric elevators a growing city had difficulty expanding outward or upward from the core. Growth of the city therefore meant higher densities within the previously built-up area. Housing constructed in that period was usually of the multiple family (tenement) variety with densities up to a thousand people per acre for the lower income groups, and three and four story row houses on fifteen, eighteen, and twenty foot lots for the middle classes who could afford the luxury of rather low density buildings. The rich, of course, have always been able to use their superior buying power to gain access to the countryside. They could afford in both time and money a life of ease and amenity on an estate beyond the congested urban core.[15] High density patterns based on movement constraints continued through the first postbellum cycle. The only important exceptions were the commuter towns located along rail spokes out from large centers like New York, Boston, and Philadelphia. In the Mid-

11. Hoyt, op. cit., footnote 3, p. 93.
12. W. H. Newman, "The Building Industry and the Business Cycle," The Journal of Business of the University of Chicago, Vol. 8 (July, 1935), pp. 32–39.
13. Hoyt, op. cit., footnote 3, p. 95.
14. Whether or not this is so has captured the attention of several researchers, especially in the light of present possibilities for rebuilding neighborhoods with urban renewal funding.

15. C. N. Glaab and A. T. Brown, A History of Urban America (New York: Macmillan, 1967), especially Chapter 4, "The Urban Milieu," pp. 83–106; and D. Ward, "A Comparative Historical Geography of Streetcar Suburbs in Boston, Massachusetts, and Leeds, England: 1850–1920," Annals, Association of American Geographers, Vol. 54 (1964), pp. 477–89.

west, Chicago is the best example. Owing to the vertical movement constraint, a large fraction of the housing from the first cycle was destroyed when central business districts expanded during the following period of boom.

The boom of the 1880's reached a peak shortly before the depression of 1893. Housing constructed then constitutes a large fraction of what I refer to as the Old Core. The housing resembles that of the postbellum cycle but is distinctive because most of it still remains on the urban scene, although urban renewal schemes have eliminated some of it recently.[16] Downtown areas halted their outward expansion when new construction techniques permitted taller buildings and when steam and electric elevators promoted expansion upwards. In 1880 the core of Chicago consisted of six story buildings. The full impact of the elevator and the electric streetcar, which were introduced on a wide scale in the 1880's, was not felt in the location and design of new residential construction until the next cycle of feverish building activity. Four and five story walkup apartment buildings, visible for mile after mile in places like Harlem, Brooklyn, South Chicago, and the north side and south side of St. Louis, represent the transportation and housing technology of the period in which they were built. Horse car lines were used for several decades in many cities but they were of small scale importance. In the biggest cities small-gauge steam railways and cable cars were a temporary response to intraurban transport needs. But even in the few cities operating transit systems the typical resident walked in the 1880's.[17]

Cycles 1 and 2: The Streetcar Era

The electric streetcar was responsible for the character of residential areas developed in the two-cycle building epoch which reached a peak in 1905 and trough at the end of World War I (Figure 9). In a few exceptional cases the biggest and busiest cities inherited extensive cores with narrow streets held over from the foot travel era. Some Eastern cities and Chicago were forced to increase the carrying capacity of downtown streets using elevated rail systems and subways. Away from the urban core, wherever streetcar tracks were laid, residential development was possible, a fact that did not escape the attention of land speculators, especially those in a position to influence the location of new streetcar lines.[18]

Urban houses constructed in the streetcar era resemble farm houses constructed at the same time. Fads in house architecture are very pervasive. The large frame houses, often more than two stories, were placed on relatively narrow lots. Land prices were high near the streetcar lines because travel costs were too high for the person with average or below average income if the distance from home to the streetcar lines became too great. The lots usually lacked alleys, garages, or sheds. The houses reflected the family life of the era. Women were still at home, kitchens and dining areas were large, and family sizes, although already smaller than rural

16. For bibliography and discussion see D. W. Griffin and R. E. Preston, "A Restatement of the 'Transition Zone' Concept," *Annals*, Association of American Geographers, Vol. 56 (1966), pp. 339–50. For discussion of characteristic housing patterns of pre-1890 vintage see: N. N. Foote, *et al. Housing Choices and Housing Constraints* (New York: McGraw-Hill, 1960), pp. 84–85.

17. For many decades statistics of transit systems were published by the American Transit Association. See, for example, their *Transit Operating Reports—1950*, Part I (New York: American Transit Association, 1951).

18. S. B. Warner, *Streetcar Suburbs: The Process of Growth in Boston, 1870–1900* (Cambridge: Harvard University Press, 1962); and Krim, *op. cit.*, footnote 8.

counterparts, were large enough to fill the many rooms.

Cycles 3 and 4: The Recreational Auto Era

The building boom of the twenties (cycle 3) reached a peak in 1925 and a trough at the bottom of the depression in 1933 (Figure 9). It differed fundamentally from preceding cycles. New architectural styles, the automobile, and a new role in life for American women are reflected in the residential growth ring from this period. Houses are smaller and built on larger lots because land prices dropped relative to purchasing power. With the use of the automobile the effective supply of urban land rose dramatically without a proportionate expansion in demand. Alleys and garages were installed along with the houses. Houses had fewer rooms reflecting smaller family sizes and a change in family living tastes. Kitchens and dining areas in the house were reduced in size as women as well as the rest of the family spent more time outside the home for business and recreation. The speculative binge of the twenties contributed mightily to the large number of double and multiple family dwellings built during the period. It was a common expectation that since real estate values were rising rapidly, to own one's own house while renting out one or several units in the same building, meant that the house could be paid for with the rental proceeds and the owner could protect himself from the inflation of that bullish period. The growth ring of the twenties, then, is a mute commentary on the expectations and activities of urban America in the 1920's.

During the last half of the 1930's, up to the entry of the United States into World War II, the next building boom was under way (cycle 4). Many housing characteristics of the twenties were retained but new forms appeared which anticipated some of the postwar characteristics of residential neighborhoods. Relatively few multiples were built, and the single family dwellings seem larger than the average of the twenties. Evidently the demand for housing is rather income-elastic in certain middle income groups, that is, as a consumer's disposable income rises by a certain fraction, the amount of housing he chooses to purchase rises by a larger fraction.[19] In the later 1930's, after the middle and upper classes had saturated themselves with consumer durables, many put their extra income into housing. The housing built in the few years before World War II was remarkably well designed and constructed, compared to what followed in the five to ten years after the war. This particular growth ring, apparent in almost every American city, although relatively narrow because it was choked off by the war, is a prominent and attractive record of prewar construction activity.

Automobile ownership by middle and upper income groups in the 1920's had many recreational aspects to it. Yet by the late 1930's the widespread use of cars by commuters had begun. Residential areas built in the late 1930's display garages and paved alleys, wider lots and sidewalks, and a general recognition that the family car was becoming indispensable. The first extensive development of automobile-oriented, planned shopping centers dates from this period, although the prototype had been created by Nichols' Country Club Plaza in Kansas City in the 1920's. High-speed limited-access intraurban highways for commuter travel came into general use shortly be-

19. L. Winnick, "Housing: Has there been a Downward Shift in Consumer Preferences?" and S. J. Maisel and L. Winnick, "Family Housing Expenditures: Elusive Laws and Intrusive Variances," in Wheaton, Milgram and Meyerson, *op. cit.,* footnote 3, pp. 139–62.

fore World War II as another manifestation of the central importance of the automobile for everyday living.

Cycles 5 and 6: The Freeway Auto Era

The freeway era includes the two most recent building cycles (Figure 9). Associated with the freeway are the ranchette and urban sprawl. An irregularly shaped ring of residential suburbs surrounds any city that underwent any significant growth since World War II. After 1950 average annual increments to the urban housing supply exceeded a million dwelling units. The majority of these units were built at low densities in single family units on the margins of the cities. The completely planned shopping center is the commercial adjunct of the residential growth ring in this period.[20]

Before turning to the model of residential age structure, some additional background comments on urban growth rings and secular growth processes are in order. The various sectors of the urban economy grew at different rates during the past century. The national economy entered its industrial takeoff phase in the 1840's. By the turn of the twentieth century the drive to industrial maturity was well under way. The period following World War I was an age of high mass consumption and widespread sharing of national income and wealth.[21] Rapid increases in median income per capita produced dramatic changes in the consumption habits of urban Americans. As higher incomes were spent on goods and services beyond the basic necessities of life, new industries were stimulated. They responded by pouring forth their wares and services in an ever-increasing torrent. To produce and dispense this output new sales and service arrangements were needed in the city.

In early phases of urban growth a large fraction of urban land was assigned to manufacturing, transportation, and merchandise businesses. Recent growth rings involve mainly residential and transportation land use. Overall, most urban land today is residential in character. Bartholomew estimated that the proportion was as high as eighty percent in some cities.[22] Improved communications and transportation systems permitted the widespread replacement of warehousing activity with direct factory shipments. Communication and transport efficiency did not diminish the absolute importance of warehousing activity or related urban land use, but it did curtail expansion rates while the rest of the urban economy grew.

Each successive growth ring captured the flavor of the living styles, income levels, transport technologies, spending habits, and tastes of its period. The landscape increment of each growth era remained remarkably stable in structure and layout during successive growth periods. The only exception to the persistence of prior arrangements was the slow yet steady migration of the shopping core of the central business district toward the most fashionable high income sector of the city. The movement of the shopping district core toward the peak of the city's buying power potential surface was documented for several cities and is especially evident in Chicago, Minneapolis, Kansas City, and Manhattan.

On the basis of trends in residential construction and urban spatial development, we can now ask: what is the average or typical pattern? Presented below is a model of the Midwestern city which

20. H. Hoyt, "Classification and Significant Characteristics of Shopping Centers," *The Appraisal Journal*, Vol. 26 (1958), pp. 214–22.
21. W. W. Rostow, *The Stages of Economic Growth* (Cambridge: University Press, 1961).

22. H. Bartholomew, *Land Uses in American Cities* (Cambridge: Harvard University Press, 1955); and Hoyt, *op. cit.*, footnote 3, p. 24.

takes account of the salient features of each construction cycle. Viewed through the model, the city becomes more legible.

Assumptions and the Model

Recent estimates of the volume of residential construction in the United States between 1889 and 1960 reveal six distinct construction cycle peaks and an equal number of troughs. In several periods of building depression (1900, 1913, 1918, and 1944) construction virtually ceased. Three urban transportation eras followed the demise of the walking and horse-car period in the 1880's. For purposes of the model I assumed that the electric streetcar era extended from the end of the 1880's to the end of World War I; that the recreational auto era was in full swing after 1920; and that the freeway era was fully underway after 1945.

Comprehensive age-of-housing data was collected by the Censuses of 1940, 1950 and 1960. In the 1940 Census for each census tract and city block, dwelling units were assigned to one of four age categories depending on the year the structure was built: pre-1900, 1900–1919, 1920–1929, 1930–1940.[23] The 1960 Census published similar data by census tract and identified whether structures were built before 1940, 1940–1949, 1950–1960.[24] Since a chronic housing

shortage has plagued American cities since the end of World War II, most of the housing that was in existence in 1940 and described in the census of that year was still around to be enumerated in 1960. This was verified by carefully inspecting the data by census tract from the two censuses for several cities. Little error is introduced into our analysis by assuming that the pre-1940 housing described in the 1960 Census can be disaggregated using the detail provided in the 1940 Census. For most census tracts in most cities, therefore, the fraction of housing erected during each of the six construction cycles can be easily determined as of 1960.

Only two minor problems remain to be spelled out. The building boom of the late 1930's continued through 1940 and into 1941. Census data records these post-1939 but pre-war structures as built between 1940 and 1949. But as a fraction of all the housing built in the 1940's, the pre-war portion, which really belongs to the fourth construction cycle of the late 1930's, is small. Another minor problem is created by the Census age class: pre-1900. In testing the model, for purposes of calculating median age of housing in census tracts, I assumed that half of the pre-1900 housing in a tract was built before 1890 and the rest between 1890 and 1900. More detailed information supported this procedure, especially for Midwestern cities.[25]

Assume a model Midwestern city in existence since pre-Civil War times, and growing every year at average national

23. United States Bureau of the Census, *Sixteenth Census of the United States: 1940, Reports on Housing*, Vol. 1, Supplement: Block Statistics for cities—name of city (Washington, D.C.: Government Printing Office, 1942), especially Table 2, "Characteristics of Housing by Census Tracts: 1940." For a summary and bibliography of earlier compilations of age of housing data see Work Progress Administration, Division of Social Research, *Urban Housing: A Summary of Real Property Inventories Conducted as Work Projects—1934–36* (Washington, D.C.: Government Printing Office, 1938).

24. United States Bureau of the Census, *U.S. Census of Population and Housing: 1960, Census Tracts,* Final Report PHC (1)—Separate

report for each S.M.S.A. (Washington, D.C.: Government Printing Office, 1962), especially Table H-1, "Occupancy and Structural Characteristics of Housing Units, by Census Tract: 1960."

25. United States Bureau of the Census, *Sixteenth Census of the United States: 1940, Special Reports,* Housing; Characteristics by Type of Structure, Regions, States, Cities and Principal Metropolitan Districts (Washington, D.C.: Government Printing Office, 1945), especially Tables A-1.

rates of economic expansion and urban population increase through the nineteenth and twentieth centuries. If such a model city expanded at rates neither faster nor slower than the average for all urban places, then its internal urban structure and spatial organization would reflect in correct proportions the impact of each national epoch of national prosperity and decline, transportation innovation, trade and service locational structure, and fads in residential architecture. We can construct such a model from urban residential construction estimates.

Assume that at the start of cycle one (1889), the Old Core of the model city had an area of 5,000 units. (The model could be constructed in symbolic terms but no generality is sacrificed using a numerical example and fewer people are frightened.) Assume also that the number of units of land allocated per dwelling unit varied by type of structure and by construction cycle (Table 1). On the basis of construction estimates for 1889, therefore, the area of the model city would have grown at a rate slightly greater than ten percent if it participated

in one-tenth of one percent of the national construction activity and expanded from a base area of 5,000 units.

If we combine the construction data into six groups corresponding to the six construction cycles already identified, we can specify the number of dwelling units in each type of structure (singles, doubles, multiples) produced in each of the six construction eras (Figure 9). By applying the estimate of land allocation per dwelling unit (lot size) by type of structure from Table 1 we can arrive at an estimate of areal growth of the model city for each building cycle (Table 2). For example, in 1889, 222,000 dwelling units were constructed in single family dwellings in United States cities, and 120,000 units were erected in double or multiple family structures. If we assume that each single family dwelling used two units of land and that each dwelling unit in a double or multiple family structure only used one unit of land, then the model city grew by 564 units assuming that one-tenth of one percent of the national construction effort occurred in the model city.

If we assume that new housing was always added on the fringe of the previously built-up area, then the radius of the original city (the Old Core) was forty, whereas the radius of the built-up city at the end of cycle one was fifty-eight (Table 3). The change in radius, which is of course the width of the growth ring from cycle one, is eighteen. Similarly, the areal growth was estimated for the six construction cycles and the width of the growth ring from each cycle was calculated.

Once the radius of the model city has been calculated for the end of each construction cycle it is an easy matter to draw a map to illustrate the relative widths of the growth rings from each construction period together with the zones of influence of each urban transport era (Figure 10). The pre-1890 Old Core of the city corresponds to the era of foot travel and the horse car. The first

Table 1. Units of Land Allocated per Dwelling Unit, by Type of Structure, by Construction Cycle

	Units of Land per Dwelling Unit in		
Cycle	Singles	Doubles	Multiples
1	2	1[a]	1[a]
2	3	2	1
3	4	3	2
4	5	3	2
5	6	6[b]	6[b]
6	7	7[b]	7[b]

[a] Applies to estimated detail by type of structure.

[b] Doubles and multiples treated the same as singles since detail by type of structure is not available for testing.

Source: Estimated by author.

Table 2. Areal Growth per Construction Cycle in a Model Midwestern City: 1889–1960[a]

Building Cycle	Singles Dwelling Units	Singles Estimated Area	Doubles Dwelling Units	Doubles Estimated Area	Multiples Dwelling Units	Multiples Estimated Area	Estimated Areal Growth Per Cycle
1889	222	444	120[b]	120[b]			564
1: 1889–99	2,134	4,268	1,149[b]	1,149[b]			5,417
2: 1900–19	4,720	14,160	1,056	2,112	1,423	1,423	17,695
3: 1920–29	4,272	17,008	1,090	3,270	1,673	3,346	23,704
4: 1930–39	2,127	10,635	153	459	454	908	12,002
5: 1940–49	7,442[c]	44,655					44,652
6: 1950–60	16,320[c]	114,394					114,394

[a] With a core area of 5000 and in which 0.1 percent of all United States residential construction activity occurred each year.
[b] The non-singles, estimated on the basis of 1900–1905 averages.
[c] Detail by type of structure (i.e., single, double, multiple) not available.
Source: United States Bureau of the Census, *op. cit.*, footnote 9, Table A-1.

and second building cycles (peaks in 1892 and 1905) occurred under the influence of the electric streetcar. The third and fourth construction cycles (peaks in 1925 and 1941) correspond to the age of the recreational automobile, and the fifth and sixth post World War II construction cycles (peaks in 1950 and 1954) show the unmistakable sprawl related to the high-speed auto and the freeway.

Table 3. Radius Change in the Model City by Residential Construction Cycle: 1889–1960

End of Cycle	Areal Growth	Model City Total Area	Model City Radius	Radius Change: Growth Ring Width
0	—	5,000	40	—
1	5,417	10,417	58	18
2	17,695	28,112	95	37
3	23,704	51,816	128	33
4	12,002	63,818	142	14
5	44,652	108,470	186	44
6	114,394	222,864	266	80

Model Spatial Arrangements and Internal Appearances

The first transport era coincided with the founding and early growth of the city. A transport surface based on foot and horsecar movement surrounded a high density focal center of nonresidential activities. A high density residential zone circled the core. Lower and middle classes lived in close-packed three to five story stone, brick, or wood tenements. Single family dwellings for upper income groups, described and illustrated by Rickert, included classic revival types (1830–1850), classic Gothic transition styles (1850–1865), or Gothic Balloon houses (1865–1880's).[26]

The electric streetcar era imposed a transport network on the city and the concentric residential growth rings of the

26. J. E. Rickert, "House Facades of the Northeastern United States: A Tool of Geographical Analysis," *Annals,* Association of American Geographers, Vol. 57 (1967), pp. 211–38. An excellent review of nineteenth century residential architecture appears in J. M. Fitch, *American Building: I. The Historical Forces That Shaped It* (Boston: Houghton Mifflin, 1966).

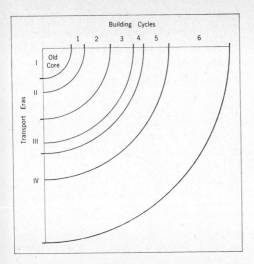

Figure 10. Spatial Structure of a Quadrant of the Model City. Six post-1889 building cycles produced growth rings around the Old Core: 1890's, 1900–1919, 1920's, 1930's, 1940's, and 1950–1960 cycles

city assumed star-like shapes as a result. The commercial and industrial pre-eminence of the core persisted. It was still the point of easiest access for the greatest number of city residents although a few outlying streetcar intersections emerged as important secondary nodes of business concentration. The intolerably high densities of the old residential areas near the core subsided as new neighborhoods sprang up along transit arteries. Single family houses became the modal style when the streetcar introduced the possibilities for low density housing. The first construction cycle after 1890 peaked in 1892. The Victorian gingerbread castle was the characteristic residential style of the period. Houses from the second cycle which peaked in 1905 were described by Rickert as "eclectic cubes," a conservative reaction to the stylistic excesses of the Victorian period.

The recreational automobile permitted even greater intraurban mobility and lower residential densities than the streetcar. The third construction cycle which ran its course in the 1920's created a ring of "boxes and bungalows," and the fourth cycle brought spacious lots and "neo-colonial" houses in the 1930's. The house types are helpful in identifying the rings of growth from each cycle.

What is more important, though, is the way in which transport technologies determined densities and spatial arrangement in each of the growth rings. Automobiles could move easily on a transport surface of city streets in contrast to the highly articulated streetcar system. Interstitial areas between the radial spokes of growth along streetcar lines were filled in as the isotropic movement that became possible with the automobile permitted concentric growth once more. Extensions of transit lines in the era of the recreational auto took the form of motorbuses in flexible routes on city streets. Buses permitted easy movement across a transport plane in public transportation which paralleled the impact of the private car on the spatial character of residential growth rings. Buses could go wherever the demand warranted. Thus, buses followed residential development, whereas streetcars directed it.

The fifth construction cycle introduced the "cape cod" and "ranch house" styles and the sixth cycle emphasized three more types: the "split level, the functional modern, and the colonial copy."[27] The extremely low densities created by single family housing on lots up to an acre in size meant movement requirements that could be serviced only with high-speed automobiles and limited ac-

27. See Rickert, *op. cit.,* footnote 26, for treatment of the house types. For transport arrangements see R. E. Dickinson, "The Journey to Work," in J. Gottmann and R. Harper (Eds.), *Metropolis on the Move: Geographers Look at Urban Sprawl* (New York: John Wiley and Sons, 1967), pp. 69–83.

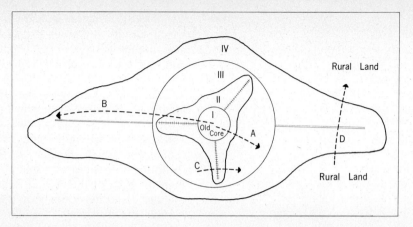

Figure 11. Expected Distortions from Concentric Growth Patterns. The highly articulated urban transport networks of transport eras two (streetcar lines) and four (freeways) promoted star shaped deviations from concentricity. Transport eras one (foot travel) and three (recreational auto) promoted transport surfaces and compact, circular urban forms. Traverses A through D indicate the variety of contrasting age gradients

cess highways. In the last transport era the city could not spill out from its prewar boundaries with equal ease in every direction. Good highway arteries leading out of the city were limited in number, but along such highways one location was pretty much like another. Isochrones were widely spaced along high speed channels. Residential growth rings jutted out along the major highways into desirable suburban living areas. Growth rings narrowed in the direction of areas difficult of access. Once again, a network of high-speed channels instead of a surface of equal movement-ease in all directions guided the spatial extensions of the city. In schematic terms, the growth rings from the second and fourth cycles departed from concentricity (Figure 11).

Verification of the Model

The model of urban residential age structure can be verified with census tract data from the Census of Housing of 1940 and of 1960. Of the sixty cities enumerated in both censuses Minneapolis was picked to test the model. The site of that city presents few barriers to urban expansion in any direction. It is dotted with small glacial lakes on a relatively flat till plain, broken only by the Mississippi River and a few pleasant hilly areas of recessional morain in the high class residential areas. Minneapolis was founded long before the Civil War with settlers clustering between St. Anthony Falls and a convenient river crossing point a half mile above the falls at Nicollet Island.[28]

The median age of housing in each tract was estimated from census data. Some error was introduced by interpolating but for any tract I estimated the chances as better than even that the error is less than three years. For example, if a tract contained a thousand dwelling units in 1960, and the data showed that 400 were erected before 1920 and another 400 were built after 1929, I esti-

28. See R. Hartshorne, "The Twin City District: A Unique Form of Urban Landscape," *Geographical Review*, Vol. 22 (1932), pp. 431–42; and J. S. Adams, *Urbanization Processes, Urban Economic Systems, and the Allocation of Urban Land for Industry* (Ph.D. Dissertation, University of Minnesota; Ann Arbor: University Microfilms, 1966).

mated the median age of housing in that tract as 35 years in 1960 by assuming that the 500th dwelling unit was built in 1925. No problem arose in the pre-1900 age category. I had already assumed that in every tract half of the pre-1900 housing was built from 1890 through 1899. With such a stipulation, therefore, it was impossible for the median year built to be estimated as prior to 1890.

Following these procedures Figure 11 was constructed. Isolines were plotted at intervals corresponding to boundaries used in the model (Figure 10). There were more than 120 census tracts in the central city of fifty-five square miles.*

Striking similarities with the model are readily apparent (Figure 10). Distortions from concentricity owing to streetcar lines during cycles one and two are obvious. Cycles three and four, representing housing from the 1920's and 1930's, filled in the spokes of growth from previous cycles and created growth rings that were roughly concentric. In cycle five thrusts of residential development to the south, west, and northwest are clearly visible. In the last growth era, the star-shaped pattern of the fifth growth ring has continued.

The widths of the various growth rings record construction rates and density styles of each building cycle. From the narrow band of housing built in the 1930's, to the sprawling tongues of growth representing the last two cycles, the patterns anticipated by the model are faithfully reproduced. Closer measurement would reveal departures, of course, but the general pattern is one of close correspondence.

Several traverses across the city were plotted (Figure 11 A-D). Along traverse A one moves rapidly from the old walking-horse car core down a steep age gradient to newer neighborhoods of the 1920's

and 1930's. Along traverse B, on the other hand, the age gradient per unit distance is more gradual. Traveling route C one moves up an age gradient approaching the old streetcar route, then down the gradient to newer housing on the other side of the route. Traverse D illustrates a similar pair of gradients that are more obvious from common experience. From rural land the traverse intersects residential areas of the recent construction era only, then passes into rural land once more. Age gradients of varying severity can be predicted and verified with maps. Moreover, with a model of urban residential age structure legibility of the Midwestern city is vastly improved.

Mean Age of Housing and Age Variability within Tracts

If the assumptions of the model were met in the case of Minneapolis construction history, additional inferences about the age structure of the city can be made. Specifically, if houses added during a construction cycle were added on the edge of the previously built up city neighborhoods, then neighborhoods should be homogeneous with respect to age. A traverse through the core of the model city provides an ideal disaggregated pattern of residential age structures (Figures 10 and 12). Immediately adjacent to the commercial-industrial core, 100 percent of the housing dates from the original construction period (pre-1889) and cycle one (1889–99). Next is housing from cycle two and only cycle two, and so forth for other cycles for every point along a traverse through the core of the model city (Figure 12). The greater the amount of construction in a cycle, or the smaller the radius of the city being added to, the wider is the ring of growth from a construction cycle.

How well does the model predict the facts about age variance in the Minneapolis case? Two series of data were

---

* Due to space limitations several of the original illustrations are not repeated here (Eds. note).

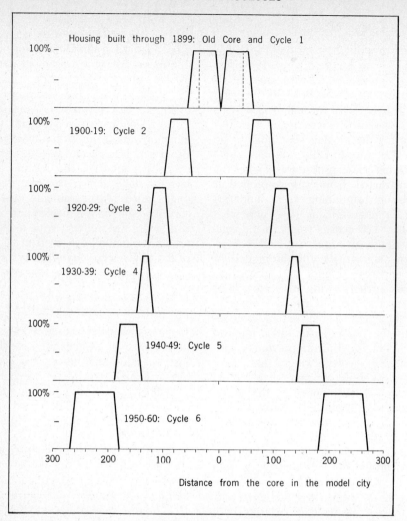

Figure 12. Patterns of Residential Age Structures. Age characteristics of residential areas along a traverse through the core of the model city, showing the percent at each point that was built during each construction cycle

charted for two traverses extending outward from the core of the city into the suburbs (Figure 13). The particular traverses chosen intersect a maximum number of census tracts and, therefore, yield a maximum amount of detail.

Pre-1889 housing plus the ring from cycle one dominate the inner residential zone. In that zone there is less mixing of housing from different cycles than in any

zone except that created by the sixth cycle. The percentage curve drops sharply away from the peak indicating that the oldest housing is immediately adjacent to the core (which we knew) and is virtually absent a short distance away from the central housing ring.

Housing from the second cycle encroaches on the core. No doubt this represents limited replacement of older

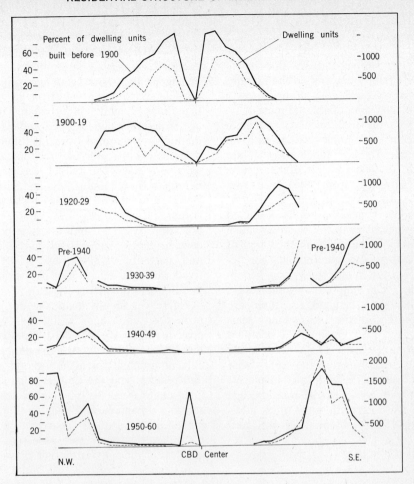

Figure 13. Patterns of Housing Tract Age Structures. Age characteristics of housing in census tracts along a northwest-southeast traverse through the core of Minneapolis. For each construction cycle the solid curve describes for each tract along the traverse the percent of housing built during that cycle. The dashed line indicates the number of dwelling units in each tract. Housing density per unit area is ignored

housing. We know that there was little vacant land within the built up city at the start of cycle one. The major additions to the housing stock in cycle two were located beyond the inner ring (Figure 13). Housing from the 1920's, built on larger lots for lower density living, created a definite ring at the edge of the cycle two increment.

Although the suburban portion of the growth ring from the 1930's is difficult to

plot owing to limitations in the census, the pre-war building boom (1940–1941) and the first part of the post-war boom (1946–1949) show up clearly with double peaks (Figure 11). The former increment (1940–1941) was mostly individually built housing whereas the post-war additions were tract housing, almost mass produced.

There were two kinds of housing booms in the 1950's. The first consisted of urban redevelopment and public housing efforts aimed at replacing deteriorated neighborhoods around the core of the central city. The second was the ring of new single family housing on the margins of the fifth growth ring. Every growth ring is clearly identifiable (Figure 13). Rings from the first, second, and sixth cycles seem most homogeneous with respect to age. Detailed block statistics are available to test this inference more closely. Housing from the third and fourth cycles (1920's and 1930's) is found today in neighborhoods of mixed housing ages. This owes to the relative lack of major constraints on the siting of housing when the automobile, supplemented by the motor bus, was widely introduced. The supply of available sites rose faster than demand for their use and at the end of the 1930's many scattered vacant lots remained to be filled during the first part of the fifth cycle (1940's). Accordingly, the ring from the fifth cycle is rather diffuse in places. Together with mean age of housing, age variance within growth rings sheds additional light on residential growth and aging processes.

Conclusions

This study recognizes that a better understanding of urban spatial structures cannot ignore the age and density composition of urban residential areas. Legibility of the Midwestern city depends on adequate models of residential land use arrangements. Working deductively with housing construction data from six building cycles, a model of urban residential age structure was developed and six residential growth rings were identified and described with reference to four urban transport eras. The model was verified with data from Minneapolis and suburbs. Based on annual housing construction volumes, the structure of urban transportation systems, and housing density considerations, the model agrees with and partially explains empirically derived distance-decay models of urban population structure.

Inferences about mean age of neighborhoods and age variations within growth rings were tested to demonstrate insights provided by the model. Some current problems of neighborhood aging and renewal and the obsolescence of related commercial districts emphasize that sensible urban renewal programming demands more adequate theoretical models of urban structures and processes. Regardless of the age of different cities, adequate models of urban residential structure permit a better diagnosis of their ills, and promote clearer thinking about curative measures.

JOHN R. SHORT

Residential Mobility

The movement of households within urban areas, defined as residential mobility or intraurban migration, is the predominant form of population movement in the developed world. In the United States and Great Britain, for example, two thirds of all moves are made within cities. The amount of movement is considerable. About 10 per cent of British households and 20 per cent of North American households move each year. There has been a tremendous growth in recent years in the number of papers devoted to discussing and explaining various aspects of this movement and the aim of this paper will be to review this literature so that our current knowledge can be critically assessed and the directions of future research tentatively charted. Three areas of interest present themselves; general theories of residential mobility, a consideration of the relationship between residential mobility and urban structure and an examination of the behavioural aspects of the decision to move.

The Background to the Study of Residential Mobility

Until recently residential mobility was a neglected topic. In part this omission reflected the wider neglect of population movement in human geography. An early beginning was made by Ravenstein (1885) in the form of seven "laws" of migration but this lead was not followed up and almost fifty years later Crowe (1938) was chiding his fellow geographers for their static view of human population and their lack of concern with population movements. This call to action was effectively ignored and even by the mid-sixties Haggett (1965) could note that population movement was not receiving sufficient attention. When population movement was studied the emphasis was on interregional mobility. This is well illustrated in Trewartha's (1953) scheme for population geography in which interregional, seasonal and even diurnal movements are considered, but not residential mobility, and more recently in Shaw's (1975) general review of migration which scarcely mentions movement within cities. The neglect of this topic was also partly due to the paucity of data (Welch, 1970) but since this drawback still afflicts this area of study we need to consider two trends in human geography, and urban geography in particular, to explain the recent interest in the topic.

First, there has been a change in hu-

From **Progress in Human Geography**, Vol. 2, No. 1, October 1978, pp. 419–47. Reprinted by permission of Edward Arnold (Publishers), Ltd., London, and J. R. Short.

man geography's focus from an emphasis on form and pattern to an awareness of, and then an emphasis on, the process which shape spatial structures. Within urban geography this changing emphasis can be seen in the movement of research away from the analysis of the static structure of towns and cities. In the 1960s the main interest in urban geography was factorial ecology. To simplify, this consisted of selecting a number of variables for areas of the city and subjecting them to a principal components (or less commonly, factor) analysis. The components were then identified by the pattern of component loadings, the component scores mapped and the resultant spatial distribution compared with various theories of urban structure (see Rees, 1971 and Johnston, 1976 for comprehensive reviews). Such studies provided valuable guidelines but gave only limited intimations of how the ecological patterns were created and maintained. As attention turned to relevant processes, the importance of residential mobility was being identified. Robson (1973, viii) suggested that, "one avenue which does appear to offer considerable potential in throwing light on the structure of residential areas, however, is the study of mobility."

Second, linked to this concern with process, there was a corresponding change in the scale of analysis from the aggregate to the individual. The so-called behavioural focus grew from an awareness that aggregate patterns studied in human geography derive from the perception, evaluation and decisions of individuals, and developed into attempts to examine the individual decision-making process. These two changes in emphasis provided a background in which the study of research mobility was afforded an important role. Residential mobility was a *process* involving household *decisions* and consequently, by common consensus, had been designated an important research topic for the understanding of urban residential patterns.

INVASION AND SUCCESSION

Burgess's (1925) conceptualizations of urban structure, composed of identifiable concentric rings, contain an implicit theory of residential mobility. Burgess assumed that urban growth was maintained by immigrants arriving in the central city who then tried to make their way to the suburbs. In this model, movement began in the central area of the city, the main point of immigrant arrival, and spread out towards the suburbs (see Figure 1). The analogy of this model is of a pebble dropped into calm water where the pat-

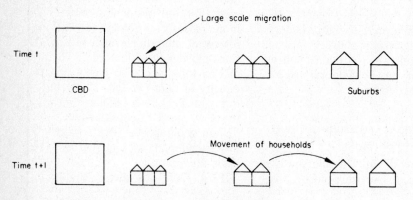

Figure 1. Invasion and Succession; A Simplified Model

tern formed is one of concentric waves reaching out to the water's edge. Burgess termed this outward movement, invasion and succession. The newly arrived immigrants "invade" tracts of the city closest to the city centre succeeding (displacing) the previous population. This initiates a chain reaction with each population group moving a little closer to the edge of the city.

The theory was formulated in the context of Chicago in the first part of the twentieth century when the city was experiencing massive inmigration, both from within the United States and from overseas. Most of these migrants were relatively poor, only able to gain a foothold in the city by renting the cheap inner-city properties. Subsequent increases in the standard of living were translated into the ability to rent or buy better housing and the consequent movement towards the suburbs. When these conditions are replicated the invasion/succession model does seem an adequate description of reality. For example, in the rapidly growing nineteenth-century city of Sunderland, Robson (1969) found that there was an identifiable pattern of inmigration to the central city and subsequent outmovement, and in his study of population movement in London between 1960 and 1961, Johnston (1969a) found that immigrants from abroad were concentrated in the inner-city areas and continued outward movement from this core area did appear to be initiating the process of invasion and succession. However, the assumptions of the Burgess model are less than realistic for many modern cities. In the first place the interurban moves of middle-income families from one suburban location to another are beginning to dominate migration flows in both the United States (Schwind, 1971) and Great Britain (Johnson et al., 1974) and moves by low income households into the central city constitute a declining proportion of total movement (Boyce, 1969). Second, the assumption

that newly arrived immigrants can easily move from their initial point of entry towards the suburbs is negated by the continued concentration of black households in the inner parts of many North American cities (Deskin, 1972) and of New Commonwealth immigrants in the inner cities of Britain (Richmond, 1973). Burgess's model does not take into account the obvious constraints affecting many immigrants and was derived from a context in which the newly arrived immigrants could easily increase their standard of living. For some households the escalator of rising real incomes and increased housing opportunities moves very slowly, if at all. Third, the model assumes that housing is allocated entirely through market forces. This assumption is clearly unrealistic in countries such as Britain where many low-income households can obtain public housing on the periphery of the city (Jennings, 1962).

The continued use of the Burgess model, both as a teaching device and as a focus for research, derives not only from the fact that the invasion/succession process does sometimes occur but also from the correspondence between the model and contemporary reality in terms of aggregate patterns of movement. Burgess's postulated pattern was one of outward movement from the central city and in the major cities of the developed world there has been a continued suburbanization of the population. However, the processes underlying this suburbanization are often more complex than is depicted in the invasion-succession thesis.

FILTERING

The process of filtering is an implicit part of Hoyt's (1939) sector model of urban form and growth. This model hinges around the growth of high-status residential areas. Hoyt suggested that the expansion of this land use occurs because of the obsolescence of existing housing and a

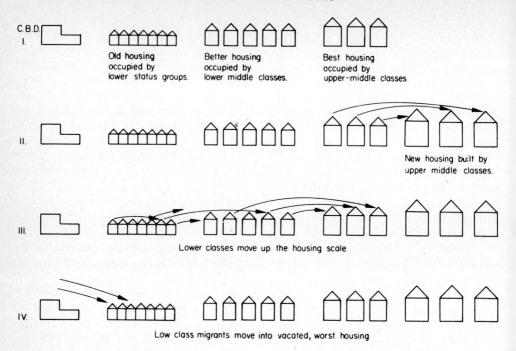

Figure 2. The Filtering Process

desire of high-status households to buy new housing in order to maintain this status. The expansion of these high-status residential areas occurs in the opposite direction from industrial areas, utilizing natural routeways and hilly land, towards the homes of community leaders. In the wake of this continual outmovement of high-status households, housing is left vacant and is subsequently occupied by lower-status households. In effect the housing stock filters down the social hierarchy (see Figure 2).

Over the long term the process of filtering has obviously occurred. In some areas of many British cities the once-fashionable large houses of the rich have been subdivided into flats and bedsitters and the areas no longer house the local élite. In the short and medium term there is evidence to suggest that the high-status households are not as mobile as Hoyt suggests. In an oft-quoted study, Firey

(1945) draws attention to the role of cultural factors in vitiating the filtering process. He found that, although the housing in Beacon Hill, Boston, was ageing, the strength of sentimental attachments to the areas precluded the outmovement of high-status households. The stability of élite location has also been noted elsewhere; in Melbourne (Australia) and in Christchurch (New Zealand) by Johnston (1966; 1969b). The strength of sentimental ties with an area and the ability of high-status households to maintain the exclusive nature of an area by restrictive covenants and land-use controls reduce the desire and the need for high-status households continually to move.

Hoyt's model is formulated for an aggressively capitalist society in which new housing is only available to the higher-income households while middle- and lower-income households only obtain housing through the vacancies created by high-income households' movement. This is an inadequate description of housing allocation in many contemporary capitalist societies. In Britain many low-income households can obtain new housing through the public sector and in a number of countries, such as New Zealand, middle-income households are able to purchase new housing through state funding. Where the housing market is not totally dominated by market forces, the process of filtering is likely to be less important than Hoyt imagined.

Hoyt's initial model of filtering has stimulated research into the study of housing chains (White, 1971). Housing chains, sometimes known as vacancy chains, result from the addition of new housing units to the housing market. Some of the households who move into these new units leave behind vacancies in the housing market, and some of the households who move into these new vacancies move from existing accommodation, and so other vacancies arise. The movement of households into new housing produces a chain reaction, creating vacancies throughout the housing market. The chain ends when a vacancy is taken by a household from outside the city, by a newly established household or when a vacant dwelling is demolished or changed into non-residential use (see Figure 3). Research into this area has focused on discovering the extent to which housing filters down the income scale and measuring the number of household moves associated with the addition of each new housing unit. Results from the United States (Lansing et al., 1969) have shown that inmovers to any one dwelling tend to have lower incomes than the outmovers. In this respect the housing associated with housing chains would seem to filter down the income scale. The results have more than academic interest since they can be used to justify a housing policy which concentrates on the construction of new housing for the wealthy in the belief that the less

wealthy benefit from the consequent movement in housing chains. But house construction for the rich does not always benefit the poor. In their analysis of housing chains resulting from the construction of expensive housing in Windsor (Canada), Dzus and Romsa (1977) have shown that none of the chains penetrated into the poor residential areas of the city and even at the end of a chain the mean annual income of the incoming household was comparatively high, about $10,000.

In terms of the number of moves associated with new housing, Lansing et al. found that the average number of moves associated with new housing in 17 standard metropolitan areas in the United States was 3.5, with most chains terminating in the movement of immigrants or with the establishment of new households. In Clydeside, Watson (1973) discovered that new private dwellings averaged 2.0 moves while new public houses averaged 1.6 associated moves. The chains resulting from new private housing were terminated mainly in the establishment of new households, while the public housing chains were terminated in 55 per cent of new cases by demolition. This high demolition figure is related to the very poor housing conditions found in this part of Scotland.

Variations on the theme of filtering are the processes of gentrification and blowout. Gentrification is the reverse of filtering, namely higher-income households moving into the inner city and buying or renting houses previously occupied by lower-income households. This process, which has been examined in Islington, London (Williams, 1976) and Toronto (Maher, 1974), is initiated by two factors. First, the appraisal by some high-income households of the inner city as a place to live as the costs of commuting continue to rise and second, as Williams admirably shows, by the action of estate agents and various financial institutions

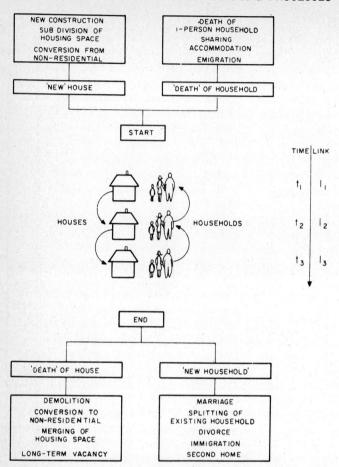

Figure 3. A Simple Model of Housing Chains. **Source:** Robson, 1975

eager to profit from the consequent increase in turnover and rise in house
prices. The term "blow-out" was coined
by Harvey (1973) with reference to the
movement of middle-income households
from the city to the suburbs. He suggests
that the existence of the poor in American cities, by their very presence, create
negative externalities which can be overcome by the higher-income households,
by virtue of their political and economic
power, but not by the middle-income
households who are forced to move to
the suburbs.

The three processes of filtering, gentrification and blow-out are variations on
the theme of social and income classes,
their differential access to housing and
the resultant mobility patterns. Filtering
describes high-income households moving outwards; gentrification describes and
explains the movement of high-income
households into the inner city; and blow-
out refers to the suburbanization of middle-income households. In any one city
all three processes may be occurring at
the same time in different residential
areas.

THE LIFE-CYCLE MODEL

On the basis of a study of movers in Philadelphia, Rossi (1955, 4) came to the conclusion that "the major function of mobility is the process by which families adjust their housing to the housing needs that are generated by the shifts in family composition that accompany life cycle changes." This life-cycle model of residential mobility in the private housing market has been elaborated in a number of subsequent studies (Abu-Lughod and Foley, 1960; Johnston, 1971) and is summarized in Table 1.

The changes in the life cycle both precipitate movement and determine the destination of this movement. The overall direction of movement, as in the Burgess and Hoyt models, is outwards towards the suburbs. In reality, households may not make all the moves associated with each of the life-cycle changes and in many smaller cities the housing stock may not be as differentiated as the model suggests, but, notwithstanding these comments, the model does provide a useful framework for comparing the actual movement patterns of middle-in-

Table 1. Housing Needs Associated with Different Stages of the Life Cycle

Stage in Life Cycle	Housing Needs/ Aspirations
1 Pre-child stage	Relatively cheap, central city apartment
2 Child-bearing	Renting of single family dwelling close to apartment zone
3 Child-rearing	Ownership of relatively new suburban home
4 Child-launching	Same areas as (3) or perhaps move to higher status area
5 Post-child	Marked by residential stability
6 Later life	Institution/apartment/live with children

come households in a large city. It is important to note, however, that the model is restricted to middle-income households in the private housing market. For those households in public housing and for those with restricted housing choices, because of racial or income discrimination, the proposed life-cycle model is largely irrelevant.

THE TRADE-OFF MODEL

The trade-off model of residential mobility is implicit in the neoclassical, microeconomics theory of the city (Alonso, 1960; Muth, 1961). Put simply, the theory assumes a city, located in a homogeneous plain, in which all jobs are located in the city centre. Competition for central sites causes rents to rise towards the city centre. Households are assumed to live as close to their workplace as possible and when they move they are assumed to substitute travel costs for housing costs or vice versa, subject to an overall budget constraint. If households move outwards from the city centre they are assumed to substitute increased travel costs for decreasing housing costs, with the level of substitution governed by the households' preferences for high or low density living and their valuation of time. The relationship between this model and the life-cycle is clear, and Evans (1973) has suggested that a life-cycle change, such as an increase in the number of children, shifts the least-cost location of households away from the city centre, for with every increase in the number of children the quantity of space demanded increases but the travel costs remain the same.

In criticism of this model, most empirical evidence (e.g. McCracken, 1973; Short, 1976a) suggests only a minor role for accessibility to workplace as a determinant of residential mobility. It seems that most moves are made with only minor consideration being given to the length, in distance and time, of the journey to work. In defence of the model it could be argued that the spatial scales of these studies are within an indifference space as regards accessibility considerations. In larger or more dispersed cities, accessibility may be a more important factor in influencing movement. A more basic criticism of the model comes from Richardson (1971), who argues that the model assumes freedom of choice, perfect knowledge and near perfect competition, which may add to the elegance of the model but do not exist in the real world. He goes on to suggest that household location is more adequately described in terms of households maximizing their housing costs subject to the constraints of their income rather than in terms of accessibility consideration.

As descriptions, rather than explanations, of the aggregate pattern of mobility in the city, the four general models with their different perspectives provide a useful starting point for any analysis of residential mobility. In this respect their main value has been in stimulating subsequent research. But it is important to emphasize that as explanatory models their applicability is at best limited. They are cast in a demand-oriented analysis of the private housing market of the United States, indeed their specificity extends to an analysis of mainly middle and upper-income households in this housing market. If the nineteenth-century image of the United States is of immigrants moving towards the untamed west, then, on the basis of these models, the twentieth-century motif is of households eventually making their way to the promised land of the suburbs. Their lack of explanatory power lies not only in that they are specific to one country, prompting one writer to note that for British cities the game of hunt-the-Chicago-model is dead (Robson, 1969), but in their lack of consideration of housing supply and allocation.

The nature of housing supply and allocation confers and imposes a variety of housing opportunities and housing constraints on different types of households and more generally structures the type of housing decision which households can make. If residential mobility is viewed as one expression of the supply/allocation-demand relationship operating in the housing market then these models, as initially postulated, fail to provide us with a useful basis for evaluating the role of supply and allocation in structuring residential mobility patterns.

Residential Mobility and Urban Structure

Patterns of residential mobility both create and reflect the social structure of residential areas. The movement of households can maintain and change the ecological patterns of the urban mosaic. There is a relationship between residential mobility and urban structure which is at once both obvious and yet difficult to disentangle. The complexity of this relationship, therefore, dictates a variety of perspectives.

MOBILITY AND THE EVOLVING CITY

In a wider historical perspective patterns of mobility reflect large-scale social and economic changes. Three models relating to Britain, North America and cross-cultural comparisons can briefly be considered. Rex (1968) confines his analysis to a study of British cities from the mid-nineteenth century to the present day. To simplify his analysis, in British cities by 1880 social classes were aligned into two main categories, the working class and the bourgeoisie. The captains of industry, as Rex sometimes calls them, lived in the rural outskirts of the city, while the working classes were huddled together in the central city, often in appalling housing conditions. From 1880 to 1939 the growing middle classes, anxious to maintain their distance from the working classes and eager to escape the squalor of the central city, began to move to suburban locations. After 1945 the political power in the cities of the working class was reflected in the new public housing estates on the peripheries. This development initiated the game of urban leapfrog with the middle classes moving outwards away from the council estates.

While Rex sees the expansion of the middle class as an important factor in initiating movement away from the central city, Edel (1975) focuses on the growth of working class consciousness in North American cities. In the late nineteenth century the development of the working-class political machine in American cities filled the predominantly white middle- and upper-income classes with feelings ranging from a vague sense of fear to undiluted panic. Suburbanization was the outcome of this conflict. Johnston (1972) describes patterns of mobility in terms of sequences of urban growth. He develops a model of urban growth which has modernization of society (perhaps a euphemism for the rise of capitalism as the dominant mode of production) and resultant social change as the independent variables. During the period of industrial take-off, higher-status households move away from the central city and lower-status households obtain housing through filtering, from employers, from speculative builders or by self-help organizations. With the growth of the economy the middle classes grow and attempt to translate their rising incomes into housing consumption. Two main types are identified—the upper-class mimickers who move as close as possible to the upper classes, and the satisfied suburbanites who move to the less fashionable areas. Into this basic model Johnston fits the experience of several countries: in the United States, the middle classes attain their housing aspirations through accumulated savings; in New Zealand, state funding is more important, while in Latin America the satisfied suburbanites have emerged earlier in the modernization process and can be found in the self-made residential areas of the city.

CONTEMPORARY PATTERNS OF MOBILITY

The existence of household movement raises the general questions of who moves? Why do they move? What are the origin and destination of these movements?

Residential mobility is a selective process. Most moves are made at the early stages of the life cycle; the predominant age category for the head of moving households is 20–30 (Simmons, 1968; Butler et al., 1969; DOE, 1972). The typical intra-urban migrant is in a newly established household setting up a house for the first or second time. Increasing age brings increasing residential stability. We can suggest three reasons for this marked age bias. First, the propensity to move declines with age since increasing age and length of residence in one dwelling lead to strong emotional attachments to the dwelling (Land, 1969). Second, this selectivity is also due to the fact that the early stages of the life cycle are characterized by a relatively large number of changes in space requirements which prompt movement. The setting up of a new household, the birth and growth of children, occur within a comparatively short period while subsequent change in space requirements are infrequent. Third, and to my mind a previously neglected aspect, age selectivity of movement is a function of the nature of the housing market. Many young households are unable or unwilling to move either into owner-occupation or public housing and tend to live in privately rented accommodation. Their subsequent move into the other tenure categories, as they collect enough points for public housing or save up enough money for owner-occupation, affects their ease of mobility. Movement into and within the private rented sector does not entail the administrative and financial barriers found in the other tenure categories (Murie *et al.,* 1976). Two other types of movers are those households at the middle and later stages of the life cycle who are moving due to changes in space requirements associated with the growth and departure of children, and those households who have little option but to move. Included in this latter category are those households whose accommodation has been purchased compulsorily, and those households trapped in privately rented accommodation. For those, mainly low income, households unable to afford owner-occupation and denied access to public housing, because of an insufficient supply, cheap private renting provides the only available form of housing. The movement of these households is precipitated by eviction, increasing rents and the physical deterioration of the dwellings.

As a generalization it can be stated that voluntary movement arises from the changing space requirements associated with changes in the life cycle (Rossi, 1955; Sabagh *et al.,* 1969). Residential mobility can be seen as the process whereby households move in order to obtain housing in conformity with their new space requirements. Added to this many moves are also stimulated by a desire to move into a particular tenure category, mainly owner-occupation. Because of the obvious financial incentives in owner-occupation, including tax relief and the possibility of exchange-value as well as use-value, households who have the choice prefer to move into owner-occupation rather than private renting and, although many of the moves by young middle-income households living with parents or in privately rented accommodation are primarily influenced by space

requirements, the desire for owner-occupation is an added incentive to movement. This "changing space requirements" explanation of movement is specific to those households able to express their space requirements in appropriate forms of housing consumption and to those households not prompted to move because of stress or threat. It ignores those households who are effectively forced to move by the perceived deterioration of the surrounding neighbourhood and those households whose movement in the public housing section is primarily determined by housing officials. The explanations of these types of movement need to incorporate more than the changing space requirements schema of the life-cycle model or the desire for owner-occupation. For example, to explain the blow-out movement referred to by Harvey we need to consider the perceived threat by middle-income households of low-income, predominantly black, households, the consequent fear of a decline in house prices and the associated activities of estate agents (Harvey, 1975), while to understand the movement of households in the public housing sector we need to consider the power and activities of local public housing officials in selecting and allocating households to dwellings (Gray, 1976).

Spatial patterns of movement have been considered with respect to three components. First, there is a considerable literature describing and attempting to explain the distance, direction and sector bias of residential mobility (Clark, 1970; 1971; Adams, 1969; Adams and Gilder, 1976; Greer-Wootten and Gilmour, 1972; Whitelaw and Robinson, 1972). Second, there have been attempts to model spatial patterns of mobility with respect to vacancy rates, accessibility and propensity-to-move indicators (Moore, 1972). Third, there have been attempts to relate the spatial patterns of movement to the broad patterns of social segregation within the city. Since the first two approaches deal with phenomena largely dependent on the type of relationship discussed in the third approach, only this approach will be discussed in this section.

It is possible to identify migration channels, or subsystems, within the private housing market of cities which maintain the pattern of socio-economic status segregation. Residential mobility maintains this segregation insofar as movement by different socio-economic groups is within distinct migration channels, as expressed in the similar status categories of the origin and destination areas. Goldstein and Mayer (1961), for example, showed that within Rhode Island (USA) the majority of residential moves are made within silimar status areas. This finding has been reported elsewhere (Brown and Longbrake, 1970; Willmott and Young, 1973; Simmons and Baker, 1972; Clark, 1976; Short, 1977a). Both choice and constraint factors can be invoked to explain this pattern.

Given an unequal distribution of income and dwellings of different prices, clustered together in distinct residential areas, households of differing incomes have differential house bidding functions which are reflected in migration channels when movement occurs. Low-income households are restricted to house purchase or renting in the cheaper areas of the city, while the higher-income households can afford to live in the more expensive housing areas. Assuming no large change in income or house prices, when movement occurs it tends to be within similarly priced housing areas. This of course does not explain why higher-income households do not preempt the cheaper housing or why some higher-income households do not buy or rent cheaper properties. The income/housing relationship provides a basic framework to which we must add considerations of housing consumption as a method of maintaining status in the community, the financial benefits of a mortgage commensurate with income and the preferences of some households with effective choice. In some cases the relationship between income and house purchasing ability can be modified by the allocation policies of financial sources lending money for house purchase—as in Britain, where the building societies lend more to non-manual households than manual households even when incomes are similar.

When spatial patterns of residential mobility are seen as reflections of the house purchasing (renting) ability/house price nexus then the whole range of institutions which affect this relationship can be considered in the analysis. In Britain, for example, the allocation policies of building societies and local authority mortgage schemes, affecting the house purchasing abilities of certain types of households and the credit rating of certain inner city areas, have important consequences for the structure of the housing market and specific implications for patterns of residential mobility (Boddy, 1976).

POPULATION TURNOVER IN THE CITY

The analysis of the ecological correlation between population turnover and selected variables was an important focus for the very early papers on residential mobility (Lund, 1925; McKenzie, 1923). A major theme of this research was the search for, and explanation of, significant correlations between turnover and social disorganization indices such as the number of mentally ill. Population turnover was seen as a surrogate for the strength of community bonds and high turnover rates were seen as symptomatic of "anomie." A secondary feature of this research was a concern with possible data sources (telephone directories, school registration forms, etc.) and their relative effectiveness for ascertaining the amount of turnover. More recent studies of turnover have moved away from this Wirthian-type framework in favour of an analysis of the spatial covariance between turnover and various ecological variables. Moore (1969; 1971) in his partial and multiple regression analysis of population turnover in Brisbane, Australia, found that turnover was significantly correlated with age of the population, percentage of single females, percentage of owner-occupied dwellings and distance from the city centre. The highest rates of turnover were found in the inner-city renting areas and the lowest rates were found where there was a large percentage of owner-occupiers. This type of analysis is not without its difficulties. Apart from the obvious danger of the ecological fallacy, variable selection has to be careful to avoid multicollinearity, and the relationship between turnover and the independent variables may not be linear. It might be more appropriate to use a form of cohort analysis which denotes the residence duration of households and allows the estimation of the mover:stayer ratio (Ravetz, 1971). Although this method is data intensive it is more useful in Britain than relying on the census figures.

Morrison (1973), elaborating on the simple mover:stayer dichotomy proposed by Wolpert (1966), suggested that the population can be regarded as a continuum of moving potential. At one end of the continuum are the more mobile households with low decision thresholds (it does not take much to make them move), while at the other end are the virtually immobile households with high decision thresholds. Position in the life cycle, tenure type and duration of residence are three characteristics which structure a household's position on the continuum. Younger households move more frequently than older households, private renters tend to move more frequently than households in other tenure categories and, according to the principle of cumulative

inertia (Cave, 1969; Speare, 1970), the longer a household remains in a dwelling the less likely it is to move.

Behavioural Aspects of Residential Mobility

In the general models of residential mobility it was tacitly assumed that a move to the suburbs was the goal for all urban residents. This is clearly an over-generalization since some households do not want to move, or cannot move, to the suburbs. Those households with effective housing choice can be classified with reference to preference classes. Bell (1958) suggests that four distinct "ideal" preference classes exist—family types, careerists, consumerists and community seekers. Family oriented people may spend much of their spare time with their children and many of their moves are made "for the sake of the children." Bell found that 83 per cent of the households in his sample who had moved to suburban locations in Chicago had moved for this reason. In Britain some middle- and upper-income households move in order to be within the catchment area of a school with a good reputation. The explicit aim of this type of move is to increase the children's educational opportunity. Careerism is the life-style asociated with a high commitment to work and career advancement. High mobility rates are associated with this group. Mushgrove (1963) terms them the migratory élite, since movement is often a necessary part of their career advancement. Movement occurs between different cities as the careerist moves either between jobs and/or up the hierarchy of a particular company. Bell uses the term consumers to refer to those households whose interest predisposes them to a central city location. Households who have the ability to move to the suburbs but prefer tó live in the central city place greater emphasis on accessibility to central city facilities (Rapkin and Grigsby, 1960). As the name suggests community seekers move to locales where they feel there is community feeling and identity. This quest for community can be seen as an integral part of the decision by some high-income households to move to quasi-agricultural villages in the exurban areas (Pahl, 1965).

These preference clauses are not mutually exclusive and many households can be considered to straddle the different categories: households may move to a small village outside the city in the quest for community and for the sake of the children. Households are not permanently located in one or two preference classes. Households at the early stages of the life cycle may prefer central-city location but with the arrival and growth of children they may place less emphasis on accessibility and more emphasis on an environment conducive to the rearing of children (Michelson, 1977).

Although the preference classes are useful categories in outlining the background to the residential moves of middle- and particularly higher-income households, they are inappropriate for discussing the residential moves of those in public housing or those in the private housing market with more restricted housing options. Previous research, by concentrating on higher-income households, has consequently focused on the choice element in residential mobility with little discussion or analysis of the constraints affecting many households in the housing market.

THE DECISION-MAKING PROCESS

In a seminal paper, Brown and Moore (1970) outlined a scheme for the analysis of moving decisions. They presented a two-stage model consisting of the decision to move, comparable with the Wolpert (1965, 1966) framework, and the decision to relocate. The relocation decision was viewed, in general accordance with the actual sequence of events, in terms of the evaluation of vacancies, the search for vacancies and the choice of a specific dwelling (see Figure 4). Since the reasons behind movement have already been considered, this section will focus on aspects of the relocation decision.

Evaluation of vacancies. Flowerdew (1973) provides a theoretical model of the process by which households evaluate vacancies, but this has proved difficult to calibrate and, as yet, stands untested. Other studies have focused on discovering the criteria by which households evaluate vacancies (Troy, 1973; Herbert, 1973a). The studies suggest that the most important criteria in defining a household's aspiration region (i.e. the type and location of housing which it desires and can afford) are cost, dwelling characteristics, location, quality of the physical environment and the social status of the neighbourhood. These factors are not equally important for all households. Those with restricted housing opportunities may have to take what is available while those with more effective choice may stress the social status of the neighbourhood, and/or attempt to maximize their predilection for specific dwelling types. For those with more effective choice a hierarchically structured aspiration region can be suggested; households have a broad aspiration defined by the average price, location, and the social and physical attributes of residential areas and within these "acceptable" areas households have a more detailed aspiration region relating to the size and design of dwellings.

Search behaviour. Having defined an aspiration region the potential migrant must then search for vacancies. This search behaviour can be considered in terms of initial information, the use of various information sources and the utili-

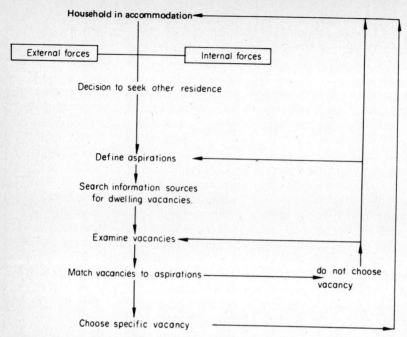

Figure 4. The Decision-Making Process

zation of this information. Two hypotheses related to the role of initial information have been suggested. First, Roseman (1971) has suggested that moves based on only a partial knowledge of the housing market are unlikely to fulfil a household's aspiration. This lack of knowledge is mainly found in households who have recently moved to a city. The discussion arising from Roseman's initial article (Adams *et al.,* 1973; Roseman, 1973) provided empirical results which showed that an immigrant to the city was more likely to move again than an established resident. In other words, a proportion of intraurban moves can be seen as the second-stage adaptive move, based on better knowledge of the housing market, after an initial interurban move.

Secondly, Brown and Moore have postulated that households have a distinct awareness space, i.e. areas of the city with which they are familiar, and that the search for vacancies and the ultimate destination is within this awareness space. This is similar to the notion proposed by Adams (1969) but differs in that a sectoral-shaped awareness space radiating out from the city centre is not assumed. Despite the obvious difficulties in eliciting and measuring "familiarity" or "knowledge of an area," subsequent studies have verified this hypothesis. Barrett (1973) and McCracken (1973) have shown that over 70 per cent of households in their respective samples of movers in Toronto and Edmonton searched and indeed relocated within their awareness spaces, although the latter study does suggest that households moving into private renting and those households who have been forced to move are more likely to move outside their awareness spaces. These results can be used to explain the distinct distance bias of household movement in the city. Most households have a dome of knowledge concerning areas in the city, centring on their present residence. This knowledge is gained in the process of living in the area and may be reinforced by the nearby location of friends, local shops and schools. When households decide to move they will tend to search in the surrounding area for, as Silk (1971) points out, faced with a space searching problem most people tend to search in the best known areas. The net result is for search and ultimately movement to be contained within the local area.

The information sources which a potential migrant can use when searching for vacancies are formal channels such as newspapers and estate agents and informal contacts such as friends, workmates and relations. Flowerdew (1976) provides a theoretical framework for discussing search strategies while more empirical research has been reported in Rossi (1955) and Herbert (1973b). Rossi found that newspapers and personal contact were the most extensively used sources of information with personal contact being the most effective. Herbert stratified his sample of movers in Swansea into those moving into high-cost and low-cost areas, and found a greater use of informal contacts by the latter group.

Estate agents are one of the most important channels of information. From a sample of movers in Toronto, Michelson (1977) found that estate agents were consulted by over 90 per cent of the households moving to a downtown house, by over 60 per cent of those moving to suburbs and were the most effective source of information for those moving from one house to another. Their importance can extend beyond the passive role of providing information on housing vacancies. In his analysis of estate agents in New Haven, USA, Palmer (1955) found that some agents controlled the entry of households into select residential areas by either not informing or misinforming households they considered "not suitable." Hatch (1973), in a survey of estate agents in Bristol, found that some estate agents

steered black households away from housing vacancies in predominantly white areas even when no discriminatory instructions were given by the vendor.

The most comprehensive account of search behaviour is given by Barrett (1973). For a sample of home-owning movers in Toronto, obviously a well studied city, he derived three indices of search behaviour based on how long the search lasted, the actual number of vacancies seriously considered and the spatial extent of search. His findings show that searching is not a thorough process but consists of a fairly brief consideration of a few vacancies within a familiar area. At first glance the findings may seem strange; after all, buying a house is likely to be the single biggest expenditure any household is likely to make. Given its importance, why is the process of house searching a relatively inefficient procedure? First, Barrett suggests that deciding to move causes uncertainty and that the patterns of search can be seen as a form of uncertainty reduction. Households reduce uncertainty by considering seriously only a small number of vacancies over a limited area in a short time period. Second, it can be suggested that this search behaviour is only inefficient if a wide variety of choice and/or a weakly defined aspiration region are assumed. If households can afford all vacancies and if they do not know what type of area or type of dwelling they require, then all vacancies have to be considered. This is clearly not the case since, for any household, some vacancies are not considered because they are too expensive while other vacancies, by virtue of location and other characteristics, fall below their aspiration levels.

Choice of specific dwelling. When potential migrant households have set up an aspiration region and searched for vacancies they may then decide not to move, reconsider their aspiration or choose a specific dwelling. Cost and dwelling characteristics are the main criteria on which households choose a specific dwelling (McCracken, 1973). In some cases the aspiration region may be so tightly structured that only one or two vacancies are seriously considered and if there is a choice between two comparable vacancies the actual choice may be based on some minor feature of the dwelling. If households are forced to move, or if they have time constraints, then quick entry may be an important consideration.

The Brown-Moore model of residential mobility stops at the point where a specific dwelling is chosen, but in reality households do not stay in one dwelling forever. Residential mobility has to be seen as a continual process. Kennedy (1975) models the post-move situation in three stages: reflection of the previous image of the new dwelling as it does or does not coincide with actual experience, evaluation of experience in the new dwelling as compared with experience in the former dwelling, and a final evaluation of experience in the new dwelling in terms of opportunities and constraints. Kennedy further suggests that in the light of this final evaluation, houeholds may either experience satisfaction and decide to stay or experience dissatisfaction and attempt to move again.

Conclusions

The study of household movement and of the relationship between this movement and urban structure demands a variety of time and scale perspectives. The complex nature of residential mobility is not revealed through any one temporal or scale perspective, indeed there is a danger that to adopt one perspective is to reach a restricted set of conclusions. This is apparent in the current emphasis on the short-term process of individual household decision-making. While this research has considerably added to our knowledge of why and how individual households move,

it leads to an emphasis on the independent status, in explanatory terms, of household movement. From a wider historical perspective patterns of residential mobility are more adequately treated as a dependent variable reflecting larger-scale social processes crystallized in the changing access to housing of different socio-economic groups.

The focus on behavioural aspects of residential mobility has consisted predominantly of the analysis of middle- and upper-income households. Apart from the obvious neglect of the study of households with less effective choice, this research has tended to treat the allocation of housing as a constant, given variable; and to view variations in household decisions as variations in household preferences. However, a study of a range of households has shown that household decisions are strongly influenced by households' access to housing and, more specifically, the reasons for movement, the structure of the aspiration region, the evidence of choosing a specific dwelling and search behaviour were found to vary between households with different positions in the housing consumption stakes (Short, 1977b). This suggests that households are not autonomous decision-making units and that behavioural aspects of residential mobility are more realistically explained as a form of adaptive behaviour to the system of housing supply and allocation, which is, of course, dependent on the structure of the wider society. The explanatory links between the nature of society, the structure of the housing market and the adaptive behaviour of households need to be developed.

The most important conclusion to be drawn from this review is that if residential mobility is viewed as one aspect of the supply/allocation-demand relationship operating in the housing market, then previous studies have almost entirely focused on the demand side. It has been consistently argued throughout this paper that we need to understand more fully the role of housing supply and allocation in structuring mobility patterns. More specifically it was argued that a consideration of the institutions and the factors affecting the relationships between income and housing may provide us with a suitable reference point for studying both mobility patterns and the dynamics of the housing market.

References

Abu-Lughod, J. L. and Foley, M. M. 1960: Consumer strategies. In Foote, N. N., Abu-Lughod, J. J. Foley, M. M. and Winnick, L., editors, *Housing choices and housing constraints,* New York: McGraw-Hill.

Adams, J. S. 1969: Directional bias in intra-urban mobility. *Economic Geography* 45, 302–23.

Adams, J. S., Caruso, D. J., Norstrand, E. E. and Palm, R. 1973: Intra-urban migration. *Annals of the Association of American Geographers* 63, 152–5.

Adams, J. S. and Gilder K. A. 1976: Household location and intra-urban migration. In Herbert, D. T. and Johnston, R. J., editors, *Social areas in cities; volume 1,* Chichester: John Wiley.

Alonso, W. 1960: A theory of the urban land market. *Papers and Proceedings of the Regional Science Association* 6, 149–57.

Barrett, F. A. 1973: Residential search behaviour: a study of intra-urban relocation in Toronto. Toronto: *York University, Geographical Monographs no. 1.*

Bell, W. 1958: Social choice, life styles and suburban residence. In Dobriner, W., editor, *The suburban community,* New York: Putman.

Boddy, M. 1976: The structure of mortgage finance, building societies and the British social formation. *Transactions of the Institute of British Geographers, New Series* 1, 58–71.

Boyce, R. 1969: Residential mobility and its implications for urban spatial change. *Proceedings of the Association of American Geographers* 1, 338–43.

Brown, L. A. and Longbrake, D. B. 1970: Migration flows in intra-urban space:place utility considerations. *Annals of the Association of American Geographers* 60, 368–87.

Brown, L. A. and Moore, E. G. 1970: The intra-urban migration process: a perspective. *Geografiska Annaler* 52B, 1–13.

Brown, L. A. and Holmes, J. 1971: Search behaviour in an intra-urban migration context: a spatial perspective. *Environment and Planning A* 3,307–26.

Burgess, E. W. 1925: The growth of the city. In Park, R. E., editor, *The city,* Chicago: University of Chicago Press.

Butler, E. W., Chapin, F. S., Hemmens, G. C., Kaiser, E. J., Stegman, M. A. and Weiss, S. F. 1969: *Moving behaviour and residential choice.* Washington, D.C.: Highway Research Board. Highway Research Program Report 81.

Cave, P. W. 1969: Occupancy duration and the analysis of residential change. *Urban Studies* 6, 58–69.

Clark, W. A. V. 1970: Measurement and explanation in intra-urban residential mobility. *Tijdschrift voor Economische en Sociale Geografie* 61, 49–57.

— 1971: A test for directional bias in residential mobility. In McConnell, H. and Yasheen, W. W., editors, *Models of spatial variation,* Illinois: Illinois University Press.

— 1976: Migration in Milwaukee. *Economic Geography* 52, 48–60.

Crowe, P. R. 1938: On progress in geography. *Scottish Geographical Magazine* 54, 1–19.

Department of the Environment 1972: West Yorkshire movers survey 1969. London: *Housing Survey Report No. 8.*

Deskins, D. R. 1972: *Residential mobility of negroes in Detroit, 1837–1965.* Ann Arbor: Michigan Geographical Publication No. 5.

Doucet, M. J. 1972: *Nineteenth-century residential mobility: some preliminary remarks.* York University, Toronto: Department of Geography Discussion Paper no. 4.

Dzus, R. and Romsa, G. 1977: Housing construction, vacancy chains and residential mobility in Windsor. *Canadian Geographer* 21, 223–36.

Edel, M. 1975: *The origin of American suburbanisation patterns.* University of Bristol, Department of Economics, seminar paper.

Evans, A. W. 1973: *The economics of residential location.* Edinburgh: Macmillan.

Firey, W. 1945: Sentiment and symbolism as ecological variables. *American Sociological Review* 10, 140–8.

Flowerdew, R. T. N. 1973: Preference working on several attributes: applications in residential site selection. *Environment and Planning* 5, 601–11.

1976: Search strategies and stopping rules in residential mobility. *Transactions of the Institute of British Geographers, New Series* 1, 47–57.

Goldstein, S. and Mayer, K. B. 1961: *Metropolitanisation and population change in Rhode Island.* Providence: Rhode Island Development Council.

Gray, F. 1976: Selection and allocation in council housing. *Transactions of the Institute of British Geographers, New Series* 1, 34–46.

Greer-Wootten, B. and Gilmour, G. M. 1972: Distance and directional bias in migration patterns in depreciating metropolitan areas. *Geographical Analysis* 4, 92–8.

Haggett, P. 1965: *Locational analysis in human geography.* London: Edward Arnold.

Harloe, M. 1977: *Captive cities.* Chichester: John Wiley.

Harvey, D. 1973: *Social justice and the city.* London: Edward Arnold.

1975: The political economy of urbanisation in advanced capitalist countries: the case of the United States. In Gappert, G. and Rose, M., editors, *The social economy of cities. Urban Affairs Annual Review,* Volume 9, Beverly Hills: Sage Publications.

Hatch, S. 1973: *Estate agents as urban gatekeepers.* Paper delivered to the British Sociological Association, Urban Sociology Group, University of Stirling.

Herbert, D. T. 1973a: Residential mobility and preference: a study in Swansea. In Clark, B. D. and Gleave, M. B., editors, *Social patterns in cities,* Special Publication no. 5, Institute of British Geographers.

1973b: The residential mobility process: some empirical observations. *Area* 5, 44–8.

Hoyt, H. 1939: *The structure and growth of residential neighbourhoods in American cities.* Washington, D.C.: Federal Housing Administration.

Jennings, H. 1962: *Societies in the making: a study of development and redevelopment within a county borough.* London: Routledge and Kegan Paul.

Johnson, J. H., Salt, J. and Wood, P. A. 1974: *Housing and the migration of labour in England and Wales.* Farnborough: Saxon House.

Johnston, R. J. 1966: The location of high status residential areas. *Geografiska Annaler* 48B, 23–35.

1969a: Population movements and metropolitan expansion: London, 1960–61. *Transactions of the Institute of British Geographers* 46, 69–91.

1969b: Process of change in the high status residential districts of Christchurch, 1951–64. *New Zealand Geographer* 25, 1–15.

1971: *Urban residential patterns.* London: Bell.

1972: Towards a general model of intra-urban residential patterns: some cross cultural observations. In Board, C., Chorley, R. J., Haggett, P. and Stoddart, D. R., editors, *Progress in Geography,* Volume 4, London: Edward Arnold.

1976: Residential area characteristics: research methods for identifying urban subareas—social area analysis and factorial ecology. In Herbert, D. T. and Johnston, R. J., editors, *Social areas in cities,* volume 1, Chichester: John Wiley.

Kennedy, L. W. 1975: *Adapting to new environments: residential mobility from the movers point of view.* University of Toronto, Centre for Urban and Community Studies, Major Report no. 3.

Land, K. 1969: Duration of residence and prospective migration: further evidence. *Demography* 6, 133–40.

Lang, C. D. 1940: *Building cycles and the theory of investment.* Princeton: Princeton University Press.

Lansing, J. B., Clifton, C. W. and Morgan, J. N. 1969: *New homes and poor people: a study of chains of moves.* Ann Arbor: University of Michigan, Institute for Social Research.

Lewis, J. P. 1965: *Building cycles and Britain's growth.* London.

Lund, A. W. 1925: *A study of mobility of populations in Seattle.* University of Washington, Publication in the Social Sciences 3, 1.

Maher, C. A. 1974: Spatial patterns in urban housing markets: filtering in Toronto, 1953–71. *Canadian Geographer* 18, 108–24.

McCracken, K. W. J. 1973: *Patterns of intra-urban migration in Edmonton and the residential relocation process.* Unpublished PhD Thesis, Department of Geography, University of Alberta.

McKenzie, R. D. 1923: *The neighbourhood: a study of local life in the city of Columbus, Ohio.* Chicago: University of Chicago Press.

Michelson, W. 1977: *Environmental choice, human behaviour and residential satisfaction.* New York: Oxford University Press.

Moore, E. G. 1969: The structure of intra-urban movement rates: an ecological model. *Urban Studies* 6, 17–33.

1971: Comments on the use of ecological models in the study of residential mobility in the city. *Economic Geography* 47, 73–84.

1972: *Residential mobility in the city.* Washington, D.C.: Association of American Geographers, Commission on College Geography Resource Paper no. 13.

Morrison, P. A. 1973: Theoretical issues in the design of population mobility models. *Environment and Planning* 5, 125–34.

Murie, A., Niner, P. and Watson, C. 1976: *Housing policy and the housing system.* London: Allen and Unwin.

Mushgrove, F. 1963: *The migratory elite.* London: Heinemann.

Muth, R. 1961: The spatial structure of the housing market. *Papers and Proceedings of the Regional Science Association* 7, 207–20.

Pahl, R. E. 1965: *Urbs in rure.* London School of Economics, Department of Geography, Geographical Paper no. 2.

Palmer, R. 1955: *Realtors as social gatekeepers, a study in social control.* Unpublished PhD Thesis, Yale University.

Pritchard, R. M. 1976: *Housing and the spatial structure of the city.* Cambridge: Cambridge University Press.

Rapkin, C. and Grigsby, W. 1960: *Residential renewal in the urban core.* Philadelphia: University of Pennsylvania Press.

Ravenstein, E. G. 1885: The laws of migration. *Journal of the Royal Statistical Society* 48, 167–227.

Ravetz, A. 1971: Tenancy patterns and turnover at Quarry Hill Flats, Leeds. *Urban Studies* 8, 181–201.

Rees, P. 1971: Factorial ecology: an extended definition, survey and critique of the field. *Economic Geography* 47, 220–33.

Rex, J. A. 1968: The sociology of a zone transition. In Pahl, R. E., editor, *Readings in urban sociology,* London: Pergamon.

Richardson, H. W. 1971: *Urban economics.* Harmondsworth: Penguin.

Richmond, A. H. 1973: *Migration and race relations in an English city; a study in Bristol.* London: Institute of Race Relations/Oxford University Press.

Robson, B. T. 1969: *Urban analysis.* Cambridge: Cambridge University Press.

1973: Foreword. In Clark, B. D. and Gleave, M. B., editors, *Social patterns in cities,* Special Publication no. 5, Institute of British Geographers.

1975: *Urban social areas.* London: Oxford University Press.

Roseman, C. C. 1971: Migration as a spatial and temporal process. *Annals of the Association of American Geographers* 61, 589–98.

1973: Comment in reply. *Annals of the Association of American Geographers* 63, 155–6.

Rossi, P. H. 1955: *Why families move.* Glencoe: Free Press.

Sabagh, G., van Arsdol, M. D. Jr., and Buttler, E. W. 1969: Some determinants of intra-urban residential mobility: conceptual consideration. *Social Forces* 48, 88–97.

Schwind, P. J. 1971: *Migration and regional development in the US, 1950–60.* University of Chicago, Department of Geography, Research Paper no. 133.

Shaw, R. P. 1975: *Migration theory and fact.* Pennsylvania: Regional Science Research Institute, Bibliography series no. 5.

Short, J. R. 1976a: *Aspects of residential mobility in Bristol.* Unpublished PhD Thesis, Department of Geography, University of Bristol.

1976b: Social systems and spatial patterns. *Antipode* 8, 77–82.

1977a: *Patterns of residential mobility in the private housing market.* University of Bristol, Department of Geography, Bristol Housing Studies no. 2.

1977b: The intra-urban migration process: comments and empirical findings. *Tijdschrift voor Economische en Sociale Geografie* 68, 362–70.

Silk, J. 1971: *Search behaviour.* University of

Reading, Department of Geography, Geographical Paper no. 7.

Simmons, J. W. 1968: Changing residence in the city: a review of intra-urban mobility. *The Geographical Review*, 58, 621–51.

Simmons, J. W. and Baker, A. M. 1972: *Household movement patterns.* University of Toronto, Centre for Urban and Community Studies, Research Report No. 54.

Speare, A. 1970: Home ownership, life-cycle stage and residential mobility. *Demography* 7, 449–58.

Trewartha, G. T. 1953: A case for population geography. *Annals of the Association of American Geographers* 43, 71–97.

Troy, P. N. 1973: Residents and their preferences: property prices and residential quality. *Regional Studies* 7, 183–92.

Watson, C. J. 1973: *Household movement in West Central Scotland.* University of Birmingham, Centre for Urban and Regional Studies, Occasional Paper no. 26.

Welch, R. L. 1970: *Migration research and migration in Britain.* University of Birmingham, Centre for Urban and Regional Studies, Occasional Paper No. 14.

White, H. C. 1971: Multipliers, vacancy chains and filtering in housing. *Journal of the American Institute of Planners* 37, 88–94.

Whitelaw, J. S. and Robinson, S. 1972: A test for directional bias in intra-urban migration. *New Zealand Geographer* 28, 181–93.

Williams, P. R. 1976: The role of institutions in the inner London housing market, the case of Islington. *Transactions of the Institute of British Geographers, New Series* 1, 72–82.

Willmott, P. and Young, M. 1973: Social class and geography. In Donnison, D. and Eversley, D., editors, *London: urban patterns, problems and politics,* London: Heinemann.

Wolpert, J. 1965: Behavioural aspects of the decision to migrate. *Papers of the Regional Science Association* 15, 159–69.

1966: Migration as an adjustment to environmental stress. *Journal of Social Issues* 22, 92–102.

DONALD G. JANELLE AND HUGH A. MILLWARD

Locational Conflict Patterns and Urban Ecological Structure

The existing and ever-changing geography of the city and its region is the end-product of innumerable conflicts over locational issues. The provision of public services, attempts to close schools, the enforcement and modification of zoning codes and the alteration of traffic patterns are familiar examples of the types of locational issues which confront most large and growing cities. Although planners and policy makers may seek to avert such conflicts, it is generally regarded (particularly in the North American case) that market forces play the dominant role in the eventual siting of private and public investments and in the spatial allocation of noxious and amenity features.[1] As a consequence, it is not surprising that the spatial distributions of the costs and benefits associated with changes in the city's physical structure accord well with the geographic patterns of its citizens' status

1. Even though most large North American cities now have planning departments and seek to enforce zoning codes, the residual patterns of land uses developed prior to the adoption of planning, plus the opportunities to seek variances from the zoning bylaws tend to force actual decisions into agreement with the market dictates.

and political power. Indeed, the varying abilities of people and communities to command a voice in designing, maintaining (protecting) and enhancing their local areas have facilitated a spatial polarization which has prompted questioning of the marketplace ethic (Bunge, 1975; Harvey, 1971).

In this paper locational issues are viewed as resulting from divergent interpretations of "best interest" with respect to such matters as the spatial allocation of amenity (e.g., a park) and noxious (e.g., an incinerator) facilities, the delimitation of jurisdictional boundaries for administering to the needs and desires of people, and the spatial mismatch between resources and needs. Locational conflicts are characterized by a strong spatial basis to the arguments advanced by the conflict participants, and they conform with Boulding's general definition of conflict ". . . as a situation of competition in which parties are *aware of the* incompatibility of potential future positions and in which each party *wishes to* occupy a position that is incompatible with the wishes of the other" (Boulding, 1962, p. 5).

Noteworthy conceptual contributions to

From **Tijdschrift voor Economische en Sociale Geographie**, Vol. 67, 1976, pp. 102–12. Reprinted by permission of The Royal Dutch Geographical Society KNAG, D. G. Janelle, and H. A. Millward.

the study of intra-urban and regional locational conflict are evident in the works of Cox, Isard and Wolpert. Cox (1973) has considered the role of disparities between resources and needs as a generator of conflicts within American cities, Isard (1969) has illustrated the conceptual linkage between general game theory and classical location problems, and Wolpert has drawn attention to the strategy formulations of participants in the conflict process.[2] As a general observation, most of the empirical analyses of intra-urban locational conflict have focused either on individual issues (e.g., the attempt by officials to close a school against neighborhood opposition) or on a specific type of issue (e.g., in the American case, conflicts resulting from the fiscal disparities between the inner city and its independently incorporated suburbs).

This paper departs from the individual-issue tradition by attempting to consider the geographic pattern for the aggregate of all locational conflicts operative within a city over a given period of time. This macro-view of intra-urban locational conflict complements previous work by making possible

1. Specific recognition of the interdependencies among the many ongoing issues which condition city development, and
2. a direct conceptual linkage between city conflict patterns and classical models of the social, demographic and physical components which characterize urban ecological structure.

These possibilities provide the overall research objectives within which the present work is couched. Specific viewpoints related to them are the following:

2. Of particular interest are the many discussion papers, *Research on Conflict in Locational Decisions* (Philadelphia, Pa.: Regional Science Department, University of Pennsylvania), published between 1970 and 1973.

1. There exists for any urban region an identifiably distinct spatial pattern to the distribution and intensity of locational conflicts which cannot be explained by an assumed random process.
2. Although individual locational conflicts may possess characteristics unique to themselves, all such issues occurring at a given point in time combine in contributing to the surface of conflict intensity for the city as a whole.
3. The spatial bases of particular conflicts are, in part, products of their positions within the conflict surface of the total urban-region.
4. The composite pattern of conflict intensity is an expression of the changes occurring in a city's structural and population attributes and, in this sense, conflict is viewed as contributing to the adaptation of the urban environment to changing human needs and expectations.

With the above viewpoints in evidence, a general model illustrating relationships between locational conflict and urban ecological structure is suggested. An evaluation of this model is then attempted through an analysis of the three year conflict pattern within a representative Canadian city.

An Ecological Model of Intra-urban Locational Conflict

The model presented in Figure 1 suggests how, in response to the indicated environmental forces, specific types of locational conflict are spatially distributed to form a concentric pattern of urban ecological zones. Although this model possesses a simple linear structure (having no feedback linkages among the model components), the complex interdependencies existing among the conflict generating

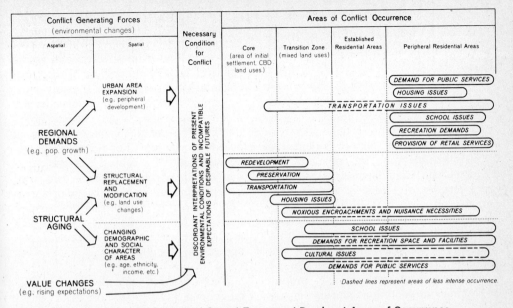

Figure 1. Conflict Types by Suggested Causal Forces and Dominant Areas of Occurrence

forces and the conflict patterns are recognized in the discussion which follows. The assumptions underlying this model are derived directly from statements on the classical models of urban ecological structure—notably from the work of Park and Burgess (Park *et al.*, 1925). Thus, the model assumes a uninodal city experiencing substantial population growth and areal expansion. Its pattern of spatially segregated but functionally related land uses and socio-demographic areas is representative of a mature, fairly large city. And, any changes in this pattern are judged to be a consequence of a competitive ethic operating within a free market economy. Land is regarded as a private commodity. In this context, the spatial sorting of land uses and people is a continuous process which accords with the ecological assumptions of outward expansion and invasion-succession. Dominance within such a system is regarded as a function of buying power which allocates people to their "proper" social areas and land to its "highest and best use."

Conflict generating forces. The model in Figure 1 depicts *regional demand* and *structural aging* as two of the primary forces of environmental change. These are derived from the previously stated ecological assumptions of growth, outward expansion and maturity. Regional demands, owing to external and city-wide growth, frequently force mandatory expansion for a range of utility facilities, such as streets and sewage, and they frequently provide threshold requirements to accommodate the entry of new public services and economic establishments. In contrast, structural aging is evidenced by the deterioration and obsolescence of existing facilities. In response to profit (possibly aesthetic and sometimes social) motivations, land use changes, urban renewal and renovation are options customarily considered for replacing the existing pattern with more efficient and profitable (or "socially acceptable") facilities and activities. Spatially, the forces of structural aging and regional demand are equatable with the locationally differentiated patterns of (1) urban area expansion, (2) structural replacement and modification, and (3) changes in the demographic and social characteristics of neighborhoods.

The emergence of conflict patterns. Individually or in concert, these forces generate conflict situations only if a demanded or proposed change is perceived in incompatible ways by the many participants who align themselves as either proposers or objectors of change. The transfer of these basically latent forces for generating conflict into actual conflict situations presupposes the existence of a *necessary condition*. This necessary condition is considered to be "the existence of discordant interpretations of present environmental conditions and incompatible expectations of desirable future states."

Such interpretations and expectations are, of course, influenced by diverse information inputs, by different sets of values and by value changes (the third primary force identified in the model for generating conflicts). For example, increasing evidence on the association between contaminated air and various diseases may result in higher expectations of air quality standards and in heightened levels of conflict between the contributors of contaminants and those who feel threatened.

Given the spatially variant incidence of environmental change, and given the assumptions built into this model, it is then possible to suggest the likely zones of occurrence for specific types of locational conflict. The area labels (Core, Transition zone, Established Residential Areas and Peripheral Residential Areas) accord in a general way with the concentric zonal concept of urban ecological theory, and the conflict categories refer primarily to the dominant land use characteristic of the issues. Exceptions include preservation, public service and cultural issues.

Although the typology's categories are neither always mutually exclusive nor completely independent of one another, as a group they exhaustively represent the range of locational conflicts likely to occur in urban environments. In many ways, functional and spatial interdependencies among issues make some element of redundancy in the classificatory scheme an acceptable feature. For instance, the redevelopment of a central city could initiate a chain of related conflicts associated with housing, transportation and preservation of historic structures. Most issues, however, have dominant features which establish the relevance of one category as opposed to others.

Rationalization of the model. The model depicts only the more highly probable zones of occurrence for each type of conflict. These hypothesized locational patterns were arrived at through rationalizations relying heavily upon other interpretations of macro-patterns within urban areas. For example, particular attention is called to the relationships between conflict patterns and the population density gradient (Clark, 1951, Newling, 1966), the land value surface (Alonso, 1964) and the associated degree of competitiveness over real estate, the age of existing city infrastructure (assumed to increase towards the city center and to be accompanied by an outwardly moving wave of renewal efforts), and family structure as suggested by the urban factorial ecology models (Berry, 1971). With these considerations in mind, definitions and model rationalizations are now presented for each conflict grouping.

Redevelopment issues are generally equatable with structural change brought about by obsolescence, rising expectations on the part of both property owners and the public, and by increasing regional demands for retail and service expansion. They are generally dominant in areas where the competitive ethic of the marketplace is strongest and where the antiquity of buildings is greatest. Thus, a central city and uninodal distribution, with the degree of potential conflict tapering-off rapidly beyond the transition zone, is suggested. Redevelopment efforts often give rise to conflicts over other issues such as preservation, transportation and housing.

Preservation issues usually concern the continued existence of areas or buildings and other artifacts judged to have historical, architectural or sentimental value. Such conflicts are most prevalent in the older and more central portions of the city. Whereas money is usually regarded as a suitable exchange for the transfer of land from agricultural to other uses, in the city center money value is often compounded or exceeded by psychic and aesthetic considerations associated with the city's past.

Transportation issues are expected to exhibit a bi-modal distribution with peaks of conflict intensity in the areas of peripheral expansion and in the region immediately surrounding an expanding city core. However, demands for transport improvements to accommodate the increasing levels of interaction between these functionally interdependent areas can be expected to generate conflict situations within the intervening zones as well. Typical issues develop over attempts to widen and extend streets, to provide parking, to construct railroad overpasses, bridges and so forth. The environmental expectations of residents affected by such developments often conflict with the growing accessibility needs associated with suburban growth and core area redevelopment.

Housing issues are dominant in the transition zone in association with core area expansion and in the suburban zone in association with lags over the provision of basic public services and amenity facilities. Housing conflicts are often generated by disparities between the regional demand for housing and the availability of serviced land. Attempts to meet these demands through construction of high-rise apartments and public housing projects are also prominent conflict generators.

Noxious encroachments and nuisance necessities refer to manufacturing and processing land uses interpreted to include such activities as industrial plants, gravel pits, scrap yards, pollution control plants, land fill sites and so forth. Conflicts result owing largely to opinions on the compatibility of such land uses in residential areas. These perceptions may stem from more exacting expectations generally, or, locally, from changes in population characteristics. Local opposition to these "encroachments" often conflicts with regional demand and fails to recognize the constraints on the locational options available for many such activities.

Public services and utilities such as libraries, health centers, bus routes and paved streets are usually regarded as either desirable amenities or necessary infrastructure. They are demanded through perceptions of their maldistribution (rising expectations), or through the changing needs resulting from modifications in an area's population structure. Conflicts over the provision of required utilities and services, such as sewerage mains and fire protection, occur principally in the newly developing zone of peripheral residential expansion; but, as a result of rising standards, they may also occur in areas previously developed without the full gamut of currently-expected utilities.

Retail related issues frequently accompany efforts at inner-city redevelopment and retail expansion in suburban areas. In suburban zones, conflict situations frequently reflect the incompatible requirements for serving peripherally expanding residential regions and for maintaining perceived environmental quality through the segregation of land uses. In general, the spatially dispersed nature of commercial land uses in most cities (commercial ribbons along major arterials, community and neighborhood shopping centers, and more or less regularly-spaced convenience stores) suggests the possibility of a rather dispersed pattern to retail-related conflicts. Such conflicts might concern the physical expansion of a store into a residential area, problems over customer parking and conflicts over requested variances from official zoning bylaws. Conflicts of this nature are often highly localized in their significance; but, occasionally, conflicts over such issues as the development of a large regional shopping center can be wide-ranging in their significance.

School issues occur dominantly in the transition zone and in the newest subdivisions; however, their presence is likely throughout the city. Inner-area demographic change is largely responsible for conflicts over school closings and over proposals for the busing of students to achieve an efficient use of facilities. These proposals are often regarded as threats to community integrity. Also, a city's peripheral development may engender dispute over lags in school provision and through competition among communities for school expansion.

Recreational parks and facilities cater to demands at a range of scales. Hence, locational conflicts over recreational issues may be brought about by a combination of regionally and locally generated forces. Such issues may relate to "threat" situations caused, for instance, by inner-area redevelopment, or they may result from rising expectations of, for example, acceptable parkland/population ratios. Since most cities have greater per capita recreation space at their peripheries than near their cores, one may expect higher conflict intensities over such issues in the more densely populated transition zone than in the generally lower density areas more distant from the city center.

Cultural issues (for example, the encroachment of one ethnic group upon the residential area occupied by another) are expected to decline in number and intensity with increasing distance from the city core. Such a pattern would reflect a combination of factors, including greater population densities and greater likelihood of ethnic diversity with increasing proximity to the city core. In contrast, the more culturally homogeneous middle class suburbs would be expected to exhibit less internal conflict. Nonetheless, as in the American case, conflict between the inner city and the suburban ring looms as a possibility having wide impact on the potentialities for resolving a large number of urban issues. It is, of course, often the case that ethnic distinctions carry with them distinctions of income, class and political power as well.

Having illustrated how the suggested typology of conflict is related to the model's assumptions of ecological structure and to its component forces of environmental change, the remainder of this paper presents an evaluation of the model.

An Example: Locational Conflict in London, Canada, 1970–1972

A principal problem in exemplifying the spatial pattern of urban conflict is the identification of a meaningful surrogate value for conflict intensity—a problem not unrelated to the availability of data and to the choice of study area.

The data base. Based on a page by page review of the local newspaper, articles were assembled according to locationally identifiable conflicts satisfying the following criteria: (1) the issue had a locational component which could be mapped as an area, line or point pattern; (2) conflicting interest among two or more parties (individuals or groups, private or public) was evident; and (3) city-wide issues which could not be related to specific locations were eliminated for purposes of this study. These included such issues as the proposal and implementation of regional government, relationships between the city and neighboring townships and attempts to locate a freeway through the city. By applying these criteria, 153 locational issues were identified to form the empirical base for this analysis.

A measure of conflict intensity. The surrogate value of conflict intensity was taken as column inches of newspaper coverage (including letters to the editor, editorials and news reports) for each of the issues. The advantages of this proxy variable are simplicity of computation, ease of comparison and the supposed consistency of its bias. Its principal disadvantage is its selective bias in terms of assumed reader interest, editorial policy and reporter competency. Notwithstanding these difficulties, it is believed by the authors that London's news is not overly-managed and therefore constitutes an acceptable data source.[3]

The Study Area. London, Ontario is a city of 230,000 people with a population growing until recently at a rate of about three per cent a year. It exhibits a range of life-styles fairly representative of other middle-size North American cities. Its basically simple radial structure about a dominant central business area, combined with its relatively uncomplicated topography and its isolation from other major population centers, make it a particularly suitable setting for this case study. However, in interpreting London's pattern of locational conflict, certain of its rather unique features should be considered. First, it is unusual by North American standards that a central business district

3. Alternative and augmentative surrogates might include minutes of the City Council, the Planning Board and of other semi-autonomous agencies such as the city's Public Utilities Commission, the Transportation Commission and the Board of Education. Also, data could be collected on location through systematic monitoring of the activities of various community associations.

in a city of this size should account for over sixty per cent of the metropolitan area's retail sales. This dominance is maintained by an aggressive downtown merchants' association and is undoubtedly associated with London's position as a financial and administrative center of regional significance in one of Canada's most prosperous agricultural and manufacturing areas. A second distinction is that, consequent to an extensive annexation of land in 1961, nearly ninety per cent of the urban region's developed properties are within the city limits. Thus, London falls in a different class of cities than those American cities, studied by Cox (1973), where jurisdictional conflict was of prime significance in generating financial disparities between the incorporated suburbs and the central city. Finally, planning efforts to "optimally" design the use of space have a long tradition here and they are supported by strong planning controls at both the local and provincial levels. In general, however, London approximates many of the assumptions built into the model.

A descriptive analysis of the conflict pattern. This analysis is limited to testing the spatial correspondence of conflicts in London with the pattern suggested in the model. Causal links between the pattern and the specification of conflict generating forces are treated only subjectively.

Gradients of conflict intensity. The procedures adopted for testing the model are based on data provided in Figure 2. The 153 conflicts satisfying the study criteria are mapped according to the conflict typology with circles proportionate to the newspaper coverage. A visual correlation of the location, type and intensity of conflict is possible from this map. However, a more direct indicator of the average position of given conflict categories is provided for by a form of gradient analysis relating a measure of conflict intensity

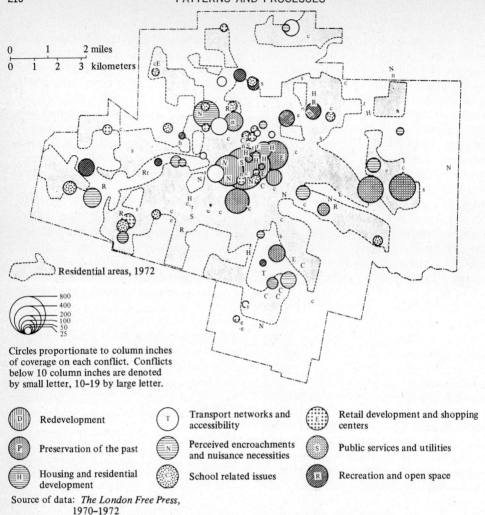

Figure 2. Type and Intensity of Locational Conflicts, London, Ontario, 1970–1972

Residential areas, 1972

800
400
200
100
50
25

Circles proportionate to column inches
of coverage on each conflict. Conflicts
below 10 column inches are denoted
by small letter, 10–19 by large letter.

(D) Redevelopment	(T) Transport networks and accessibility	(E) Retail development and shopping centers	
(P) Preservation of the past	(N) Perceived encroachments and nuisance necessities	(S) Public services and utilities	
(H) Housing and residential development	(C) School related issues	(R) Recreation and open space	

Source of data: *The London Free Press,*
1970–1972

against distance from the city center. In Figure 3, the data are aggregated cumulatively by conflict type according to concentric zones one mile in width. In general the results agree with the model.

Redevelopment and preservation conflicts occur almost exclusively within two miles (3.2 km) of the city center. But, housing and transportation issues exhibit bi-modal cross-sections with peaks dominant in the transition area and towards the periphery. Beyond three miles (4.8 km), the graph seems to mirror the environmental adaptation of peripheral lands to urban, and particularly residential, uses. Conflicts in this area usually result from time-lags in the provision of public and retail services and from perceived needs to segregate these new services and often pre-existing "noxious and nuisance" facilities from the newer residential tracts. In contrast, school and recreation related issues are dominant within the older, more established residential area in the roughly two to three mile zone (3.2–4.8 km). Such conflicts are frequently in response to proposals for land use changes which are perceived as threats to community character; but, changes in the area's demographic and social structure can also be instrumental in generating conflict. Interestingly enough, cultural issues were not identifiable from the newspaper data base. Although one might suspect a newspaper bias here, the general absence of such issues in London could be attributed to a comparatively homogeneous English-Canadian population base and to a lack of well-defined ethnic or other cultural group enclaves.

Frequency of conflict and scale of concern. From Table 1 and from Figure 3, it is evident that the number of issues occurring within each conflict category is quite different from the proportions of total newspaper coverage. Those issues which are most common (schools, noxious and nuisance, recreation and retail) receive, on average, the least newspaper coverage. This highlights the essentially local character of these problems. In contrast, redevelopment and preservation issues have city-wide importance. Although they accounted for only five and four per cent respectively of the city's total issues, they garnered twenty-eight and thirteen per cent respectively of the newspaper space devoted to locational conflicts.

Additional evidence on the regional versus local significance of issues is provided by considering the areal extent of occurrence for specific types of locational conflict.

By dividing the city into 79 square mile (1 sq mile = 2.59 sq km) grid cells, it was noted that 67 per cent of the urban area was affected by some form of locational conflict during the three year period. The more spatially scattered conflicts are related to school issues (affecting 34 per cent of the total city) and noxious facilities (33 per cent). In contrast, all redevelopment and preservation issues are confined to six per cent of the city's area. Taking the proportion of grid cells in which each conflict type is dominant, controversy over noxious facilities and nuisance necessities receives most coverage in almost a quarter of all areas experiencing conflict, compared with school issues in one-sixth.

These descriptive findings on the areal extent, number, intensity and average positions of locational conflicts lend support for the basic spatial structure of the model. However, an assessment of the degree of spatial associations among conflict types might be more revealing of potential causal links and interdependencies.

Spatial associations among conflict types. An understanding of the interdependence among conflict types would, as a minimum, require detailed investigations of individual issues with respect to their participant and functional linkages. However, correlations among conflict types by ecological units and the application of a principal components analysis are at least broadly suggestive of such associations. Using newspaper coverage by grid cells as the data base, simple linear least-square coefficients of correlation between each pair of conflict types were computed. The strongest relationships, as revealed by the highest coefficients, were between redevelopment and retail, retail and schools and preservation and transport. Figure 4 graphically illustrates the linkages among the conflict types as represented by correlation coefficients equal to or greater than 0.2. These linkage clusters are also identified by the first two components of a principal components analysis on the nine conflict variables (components rotated to normal varimax position in order to approximate the notion of simple factor structure). In

Table 1. Summary Statistics on the Occurrence of Locational Conflict, by Type, London, Canada, 1970–1972

Type of Locational Conflict	Newspaper Coverage (col. ins.)	Propn. of Coverage	Propn. of Issues	Mean Conflict Size (col. ins.)	Weighted Mean Dist. from City Center (mls.)	Propn. of City Affected	Propn. of City Dominant	Avg. Distribution of col. ins. over 79 Grid Cells	Coefficient of Variation (Per cent)
Redevelopment	2231	.28	.05	300	0.3	.06	.04	29.7	576
Preservation	995	.13	.04	166	1.1	.06	.03	13.5	461
Provision of services	864	.11	.10	61	4.1	.23	.08	12.4	487
Noxious and nuisance	848	.11	.17	34	3.0	.33	.16	12.7	211
Recreation	728	.09	.13	38	2.6	.20	.07	9.9	333
Housing	713	.09	.09	55	1.6	.14	.08	10.2	421
School issues	590	.08	.24	17	3.3	.34	.11	10.2	196
Transportation[a]	573	.07	.06	63	1.8	.18	.07	8.1	232
Retail	372	.05	.11	23	2.5	.18	.04	6.3	248
All issues	7914	1.00	1.00	52	—	.67	—	100.18	

[a] Excludes London Freeway controversy, this being a regional rather than intra-urban issue.

Source: Data gathered by authors

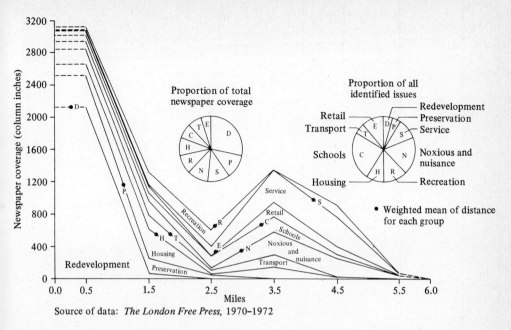

Source of data: *The London Free Press,* 1970–1972

Figure 3. Cumulative Graph of Conflict Intensity against Distance from City Center, London, Ontario, 1970–1972

all, five components (specified by eigenvalues equal to or greater than 0.8), as illustrated in Figure 4, accounted for 83 per cent of the variance in the original data. Component I, accounting for 31 per cent of the data variance, has high loadings on preservation (0.84), transportation (0.77) and housing (0.61). When its component scores are mapped, it comes across strongly as the transition zone factor. The area immediately surrounding the city's central business core forms a prominent ridge of high scores. Hence, in agreement with the model, the transition zone is recognized as a clearly defined ecological unit which is important in the interpretation of the city's conflict pattern.

The second principal component accounted for fifteen per cent of the data variance and, in contrast to the first component, it scored only moderately high in the transition zone. Its highest scores were

in the center of the city itself and in the peripheral areas of recent urban growth. High loadings for schools (-0.82), retail (-0.79) and redevelopment (-0.68) are suggestive of a central city redevelopment and peripheral expansion factor. The remaining three components are easily identified by high loadings for single variables—namely, recreation, public services and noxious-nuisance. These components have their high scores scattered throughout the city and, hence, are less spatially cohesive than components I and II.

An attempt to group the grid cells according to the similarity of standardized factor scores by Ward's algorithm[4] did not result in the simple pattern suggested in the model of Figure 1. However, it is note-

4. This clustering technique groups cells so as to minimize the overall estimation of variance within groups and to maximize the distinction between groups. See Ward (1963). Computer program derived from Veldman (1967).

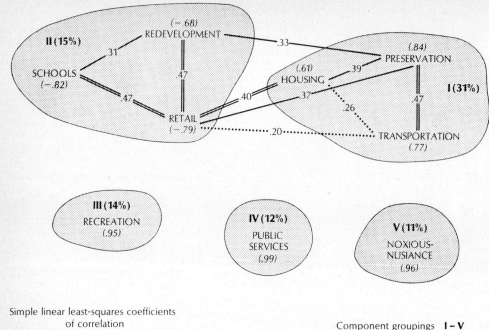

Simple linear least-squares coefficients
of correlation

════════════════════════════ ⩾ .40

─────────────────────────── ⩾ .30 < .40

·· ⩾ .20 < .30

Based on column inches of newspaper
coverage, aggregated according to type
of locational conflict for seventy-nine
one square mile units.

Component groupings **I – V**

are indicated along with the proportion
of variance accounted for by each
component (e.g., **I (31%)**), and the
loading of each variable on the factor
(e.g., SCHOOLS (–.82)).

Figure 4. Spatial Associations among Conflict Types, London, Ontario, 1970–1972

worthy that of the final two groups to emerge from the analysis (at 79% unexplained variance), one was a spatially contiguous grouping of central city cells covering seven square miles. Redevelopment, preservation, transportation and housing were the most prominent conflict issues in this area.

Inferred from the spatial associations identified in the above analysis, the highest degree of conflict interdependence occurs in the city's central area, including the transition zone of mixed land uses. This region has clearly dominated Lon-

don's conflict history over the three years in question. Central dominance was, of course, a key feature of early concepts on urban ecological structure and this study offers evidence in confirmation of its role.

Conclusions

This study has focused on a spatial description of the aggregate of locational conflicts operative within a given city for a three-year period. The correspondence between the mapped pattern of these conflicts and that of a proposed ecologically-based model has been basically confirmed as to geographic pattern but not as to process. As to geographic pattern, this study offers evidence in support of the ecological concept of central-city dominance and for the propensity of certain types of locational issues to show relatively stronger locational associations than others (e.g., preservation and transportation issues).

Inferential judgements relating these general geographic patterns to the model's suggested process of intra-urban locational conflict may be possible. However, the causal links between the suggested forces of environmental change and the spatial pattern of conflicts have not been directly evaluated in this research. It is anticipated that investigations in this direction may prove useful. In this regard, work is proceeding on an analysis of a four-year pattern of locational conflicts according to categories which are in closer agreement with the determinant forces specified in the model. Instead of focusing on static land use categories, this analysis will allow discrimination of the conflict pattern according to the proposed environmental changes and according to the characteristics of conflict participants.[5]

While acknowledging several possible shortcomings in this analysis (such as the problem of selecting a viable surrogate measure of conflict intensity, the hazards of ecological fallacy and the limitations of a test based on a sample of one), it is hoped that this exploratory effort will be suggestive of further research. Certainly, the significance of locational conflict in shaping the emergent form of the urban area warrants its inclusion as a high priority in our research agenda.

5. These categories refer to the proposed land use changes which generate the conflict situations and not to static land use categories as employed here.

References

Alonso, W. (1964), Location and Land Use. Cambridge, Mass.: Harvard University Press.

Austin, M., T. E. Smith, & J. Wolpert (1970), The Implementation of Controversial Facility-Complex Programs. *Geographical Analysis* 2, pp. 315–329.

Berry, B. J. L., ed. (1971), Comparative Factorial Ecology. *Economic Geography* 47, no. 2 (supplement).

Boulding, K. (1962), Conflict and Defense: A General Theory. New York, Harper and Brothers.

Bunge, W. (1975), Detroit Humanly Viewed: The American Urban Present. *In:* R. Abler, D. G. Janelle, A. K. Philbrick, & J. Sommers, eds., Human Geography in a Shrinking World. North Scituate, Mass.: Duxbury Press.

Clark, C. (1951), Urban Population Densities. *Journal of the Royal Statistical Society, Series A* 114, pp. 490-496.

Cox, K. R. (1973), Conflict, Power and Politics in the City: A Geographic View. New York: McGraw-Hill Book Co.

Harvey, D. (1971). Social Process, Spatial Form and the Redistribution of Real Income in an Urban Area. *In:* M. Chisholm, A. Frey & P. Haggett, eds., Colston Papers No. 22: Regional Forecasting. London: Butterworths, pp. 267-300.

Isard, W. (1969), General Theory: Social, Political, Economic, and Regional, with Particular Reference to Decision Making Analysis. Cambridge, Mass.: The M.I.T. Press.

Newling, B. E. (1966), Urban Growth and Spatial Structure: Mathematical Models and Empirical Evidence. *Geographical Review* 55, pp. 213-225.

Park, R. E., E. W. Burgess, & R. D. McKenzie, eds. (1925), The City. Chicago: The University of Chicago Press.

Veldman, D. J. (1967), Fortran Programming for the Behavioral Sciences. New York: Holt, Rinehart and Winston.

Ward, J. H. Jr. (1963), Hierarchical Grouping to Optimize an Objective Function. *American Statistical Association Journal* 58, pp. 236-244.

WILLIAM A. V. CLARK AND M. CADWALLADER

Residential Preferences: An Alternative View of Intraurban Space

This paper is concerned with the intra-urban residential preferences of a sample of residents from the Los Angeles metropolitan area. Most of the previous investigations of space preferences have emphasized the relationship between preferences and the spatial behavior of individuals or institutions (Gould, 1967; Johnston, 1972). This conceptual relationship between preferences and behavior is intuitively appealing, since it can be readily acknowledged that individuals respond to the environment as they perceive it, rather than as it objectively exists. In this paper, however, the intent is to emphasize that residential preferences can be regarded as an alternate way of viewing intraurban space.

In the literature there has been a major concern with the development of factorial ecological models of the internal structure of North American and, to a lesser extent, non-Western cities (Berry, 1971). These studies, which are part of the general area of investigation described as social area analysis, are becoming increasingly undertaken as computers increase in size and are more generally available. It is not our intention to launch a major discussion of these descriptions of the internal structure of the city, except to point out that almost all the factorial studies have been based on such input variables as measures of socioeconomic status, housing quality, and ethnicity, at the census tract level. The maps which have been created from these studies are viewed as "objective" descriptions of urban space. In contrast, the maps created from a residential-preference analysis give a picture of the city based on a set of respondents' subjective evaluations of the communities within that city. It is suggested that these maps provide an alternative, and equally important, perspective of the city. Indeed, in terms of explaining spatial behavior within the city, they may well prove to be more appropriate than those derived from factorial ecological studies.

In the present investigation we are not concerned with the actual choice mechanism; rather, our aim was to produce and interpret a series of residential-preference maps of the Los Angeles metropolitan area. Firstly the analysis presents the first, second, and third choices of the respondents in three preference maps. Secondly

From **Environment and Planning A,** Vol. 5, 1973, pp. 693–703. Reprinted by permission of Pion Limited, London, W. A. V. Clark, and M. Cadwallader.

the locational characteristics of individuals choosing particular communities are examined. Thirdly preference maps of different income groups are analyzed; and finally the preference maps of two distinctive ethnic groups, Blacks and Mexican-Americans, are examined.

Data and Methodology

The data used in the analysis consist of interviews with 1024 respondents within the Los Angeles metropolitan area. The sample data used in the present study was collected as part of the Los Angeles Metropolitan Area Survey, conducted by the Survey Research Center at U.C.L.A. The sample is a multistage stratified probability sample, in which Los Angeles is divided into ten geographic regions, and census-block groups in each region are stratified by housing value and percent owner occupied. A total of 199 census-block groups was sampled, and within each group two clusters of households were chosen. The method of choosing the households is discussed in Kish (1965).

Each individual was shown a map of the Los Angeles metropolitan area which included the extensive freeway system and the Santa Monica Mountains. In addition, approximately 180 communities were indicated by name on the map, although their boundaries were not given. Respondents were allowed to identify additional communities, and a list of these was kept by the interviewers. (Table 1 indicates the extent to which other communities were identified.) The actual question asked of each individual was: "Taking your family income into consideration, please show me on this map the three neighborhoods where you would most like to live, starting with the one you would like to live in most." Information was recorded as to whether the respondent indicated that he or she could read the map, and only two respondents replied that they were unable to use the map. Coordinate

Table 1. Frequency of Community Choice

Community Choice	Number of Sample Respondents
Community on the map	820
Other Los Angeles City community	53
Other Los Angeles County community	87
Other Southern Californian counties	19
Other Californian counties and out-of-state	25
Did not know	13
No answer or refused	7

locations were established for all communities and, using the SYMAP mapping routine, space preference maps were generated, based on the respondents' choice patterns.

At this point in the paper it is pertinent to discuss some of the technical aspects of our investigation. Firstly we have simplified the respondent's task by only asking him to rank his first three choices. In other experiments subjects have been asked, for example, to rank on a map, in terms of residential desirability, the 48 contiguous states of the United States (Gould, 1967). This methodology immediately raises the question, however, as to whether individuals can really discriminate among the 48 states, or whether in reality they just view some states as being very desirable, others as being very undesirable, and the rest simply somewhere in the middle. It is noteworthy in this context that 29.4% of the respondents in our study were unable or unwilling to rank even three communities. Johnston (1972), in an analysis of preferences within cities, asked the subjects to order a list of districts, according to residential desirability, on a five-point scale. This again requires the respondent to make judgments about every district in the study. In contrast to these two methods, our question appears to be conceptually simpler and less demanding of the subjects, although we do not presume to have completely solved the problem.

More important, methodologically, is the introduction of an income constraint in the residential-preference question. Until now, in this type of experiment, the respondent has been given complete freedom of choice. For example, in Gould's (1967) study at the national scale, it was argued that the widespread preference for California implies that the state is still the land of opportunity. While we would not disagree with this view, it does seem that the introduction of some kind of constraint might be useful. In a study of residential preferences it seems particularly appropriate to ask the respondents to take their family income into consideration when stating their preferences, as income is undoubtedly the most important constraint when choosing a community in which to live. In the present study,

for example, without the income constraint many individuals could have chosen such obviously attractive, but realistically unattainable, communities as Beverly Hills, Bel Air, or Palos Verdes. Similarly, in a study at the national scale, the choice of California may only represent the fantasies of an individual, and bear little relation to future behavior. It seems to the present authors that constraints of one kind or another should be an essential part of further investigations of residential preferences.

Results

The analysis of residential preferences is summarized in three maps which represent the responses of all 1024 respondents in the survey as regards their first-, second-, and third-choice communities (Figures 1, 2, and 3). On each of the

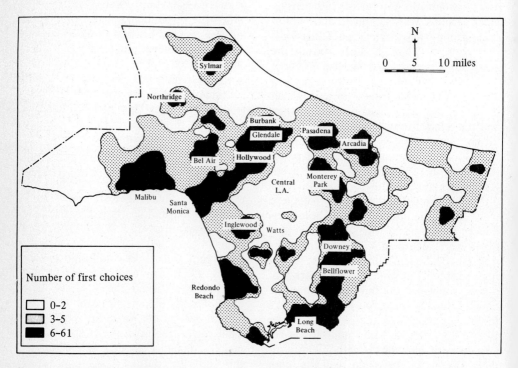

Figure 1. First-Choice Preferences of Sample Respondents in the Los Angeles Metropolitan Area (redrawn from SYMAP output)

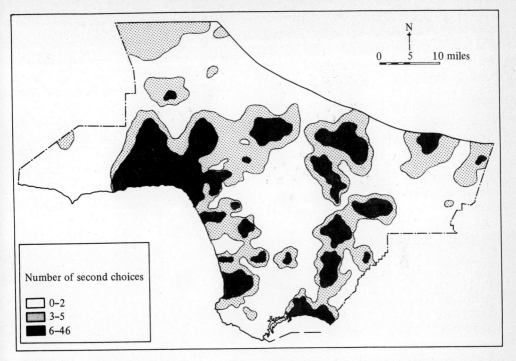

Figure 2. Second-Choice Preferences of Sample Respondents in the Los Angeles Metropolitan Area (redrawn from SYMAP output)

maps the communities are mapped with an intensity according to the number of times they were chosen by the respondents. Thus, for each of the maps, the most heavily shaded areas represent communities which were chosen by the greatest number of people. In mapping the intensities of choice, a minimum of six respondents choosing a particular community was used as the highest cutoff point, as this is the number of choices (~1024/180) which we would expect every community to receive if they were all perceived as being equally attractive.

The highly preferred communities comprise a number of distinctive regions. First, there is a ridge extending from Santa Monica in the west to Hollywood in the east. The following communities (with number of people choosing them in parentheses) are included: Santa Monica (61), West Los Angeles (23), West-wood Village (13), Beverly Hills (18), and Hollywood (11). The reasons for choosing these communities can be related to the quality of life in this region. The area is physically attractive, with large amounts of open green space and good access to the ocean and mountains. Several well-developed employment centers exist within the region, and there is a wide variety of shopping and entertainment facilities. The incidence of smog is generally less than elsewhere in the Los Angeles Basin, and the overall attractiveness of the area is reflected in higher rents and house values (Brigham, 1965). A similarly attractive area, chosen by 49 respondents, includes the beach towns of Redondo Beach (12), Manhattan Beach (13), and Hermosa Beach (6), and the inland community of Torrance (18). The attraction in this case is related to the life style associated with beach communities.

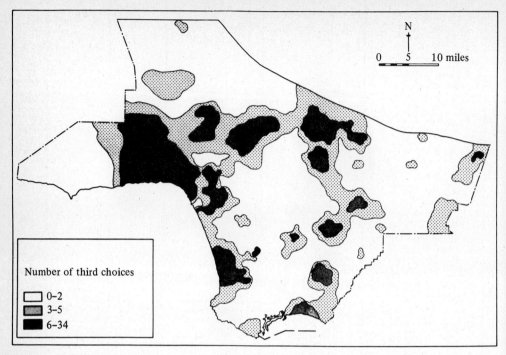

Figure 3. Third-Choice Preferences of Sample Respondents in the Los Angeles Metropolitan Area (redrawn from SYMAP output)

A highly preferred area comprised of several communities in the eastern portion of the Los Angeles Basin is less easily understood. The communities of Pasadena (16), Monterey Park (12), Alhambra (10), and Arcadia (29) were all chosen by large numbers of respondents. The explanation for this is probably traceable to several different sources. The choice of Pasadena almost certainly relates to its preeminence as a residential area in times past, while that of Arcadia is related to newer housing opportunities. Alhambra is a middle-income white community, and Monterey Park is a community preferred by Mexican-American households.

A fourth area which was identified by a significant number of respondents is a belt of communities extending from Long Beach (41) in the south, to Bellflower (11) and Downey (16) in the north. The northward extension of this belt, which includes the poorer quality housing (in objective terms) located in the central part of the basin, is related to the residential preferences of lower-income whites, Blacks, and Mexican-Americans. The same reasoning applies to the choice of Inglewood (30) near the Los Angeles airport.

The least preferred areas are those near the center of the city, and large portions of the San Fernando Valley. Despite the smog problem associated with much of the Valley, the rapid expansion of the housing stock, especially in the last twenty years, would lead one to believe that the Valley would be a more highly preferred area. This paradox is obviously of some interest to planners and developers.

The maps illustrating the second and third choices of the sample respondents are structurally similar to the first-choice map. The preferred western communities, including Santa Monica, West Los Angeles, and Hollywood, and the eastern axis from Long Beach to Monterey Park, are clearly defined in both the second- and third-choice maps. A minor difference between the second-choice map and the first-choice map can be noted in the development of a highly preferred area in the far eastern part of the county, including the communities of Glendora (8), and Covina–West Covina (6). The overall conclusion to be drawn from the second- and third-choice maps is that several more distant communities within the county are chosen as second and third choices, but that the basic pattern established in the first-choice map is not materially altered.

In order to gain a deeper understanding of the preference pattern, we attempted three preliminary investigations of the preference structure. More sophisticated analysis is precluded by the simplicity of the data which has been collected to date. One analysis focuses on the spatial distribution of the respondents' choices of particular communities, while another is concerned with the preference maps associated with four different income groups. Finally the preference maps of two minority groups, Blacks and Mexican-Americans, are analyzed.

The results of an investigation of which respondents chose particular communities are summed up in Figures 4 and 5, and Table 2. In a large number of cases the majority of respondents choosing a particular community were already residents of that community. This happened regardless of whether or not the communities were, in objective terms, high valued areas. For example, of the 16 people who chose Pasadena, 12 were already living

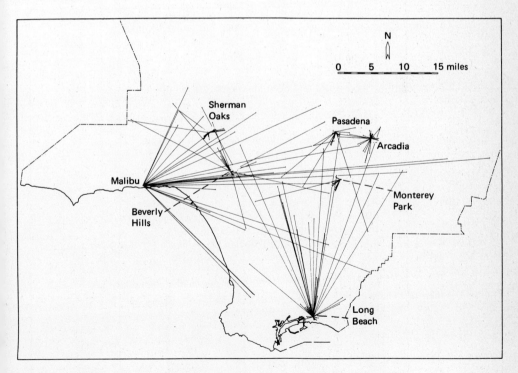

Figure 4. Location of Sample Respondents Who Chose a Particular Community

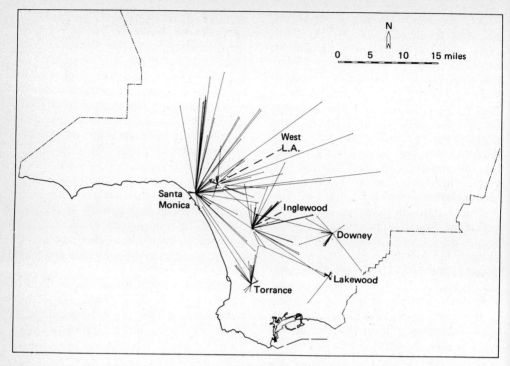

Figure 5. Location of Sample Respondents Who Chose a Particular Community

Table 2. Relationship between First and Second Choices for Sample Communities

Community	Number of First Choices Recorded	Second Choice Communities[a] and Numbers Choosing Them
Arcadia	29	Temple City (5), no choice (2)
Beverly Hills	18	Brentwood (6), no choice (2)
Inglewood	30	Compton (3)
Long Beach	41	Bellflower (3), Downey (3), no choice (12)
Malibu	30	Santa Monica (6), Topanga (3), no choice (2)
Santa Monica	61	Malibu (7), West Los Angeles (6)
Sherman Oaks	14	Encino (5), Woodland Hills (4), no choice (2)
West Los Angeles	23	Santa Monica (7), no choice (4)

[a] These are the second choices of respondents who have chosen the community in column 1 as their first choice.

there; and of the 15 people who chose Sherman Oaks, 13 were already living there. In addition, many of those who did not choose their own community chose one nearby (see Figures 4 and 5). Even communities like Santa Monica and Long Beach, which attracted preferences from widely scattered segments of the Los Angeles Basin, were most often chosen by respondents who lived nearby. The exceptional pattern associated with Malibu is in part a function of the "imageability" of this well-known and attractive beach community, and in part a result of the sample, which did not include any residents of Malibu. Table 2, which indicates the relationship between first and second choices for sample communities, offers some support for this local community effect. For example, of the respondents who identified West Los Angeles as their first preference, seven indicated that Santa Monica, a nearby community, was their second choice. However, in many cases second choices were not indicated, and the large number of nearby communities which were identified by at least one person precludes their complete listing.

In order to examine the preferences of the sample when the respondents are divided into income classes, four income groups were identified: under $5000; $5000–$9999; $10,000–$14,999; and $15,000 and over. Preference maps were developed for each of these four income groups. Given the income constraint imposed in the original question, it can be argued that different income groups should exhibit different preference maps. However, on a general level, these preference maps reflect the preference map of the whole sample. Cities such as Santa Monica and Long Beach appear as highly preferred on almost all the maps. This is because the housing stock in these cities is sufficiently variable to provide housing opportunities for both high- and low-income families.

Superimposed on this general pattern, however, are some interesting differences, especially in terms of the transition from the low-income choices to the high-income choices. The choices of the lowest income group essentially form a pattern of centrally located communities, with the addition of Long Beach, Santa Monica, and Hollywood. The maps for this group also show some preference for communities such as Inglewood and Downey, in the south-central part of the basin. This in part reflects the preferences of minority households, which are generally confined to the lower income groups. The preferences of the next two income groups, which might loosely be described as middle-income families, include a large number of communities which are outside the central area of the city. These tend to form a suburban ring of communities, including concentrations in the San Fernando Valley. The highest income group has the simplest and most restricted preference pattern of all the income groups. The communities of Bel Air, Malibu, Pasadena, Westwood, and Santa Monica dominate the map. Overall the transition of choices with increasing income is an interesting documentation of, and argument for, the use of constraints and stratifications in describing residential preferences.

Preference maps were also constructed for the two major ethnic groups in the area: Blacks and Mexican-Americans. There were 107 Black families included in the sample, and the preference map constructed from their answers is shown in Figure 6. Overlaid on this map are the areas containing large numbers of Black households. The preference pattern is not surprising, as there is a high degree of correspondence between it and the present distribution of Blacks. This adds weight to the frequently heard statement that, even given the choice of more attractive surroundings, the ethnic ties on the one hand and the fear of discrimination on the other, are very strong forces.

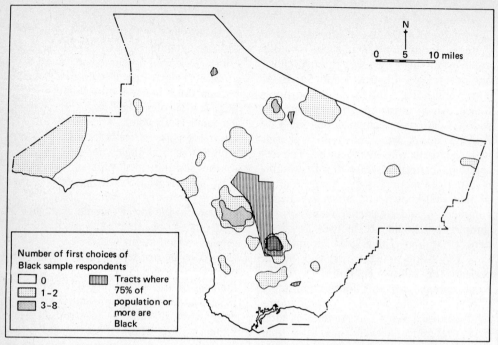

Figure 6. First-Choice Preferences of Black Respondents in the Lost Angeles Metropolitan Area (redrawn from SYMAP output)

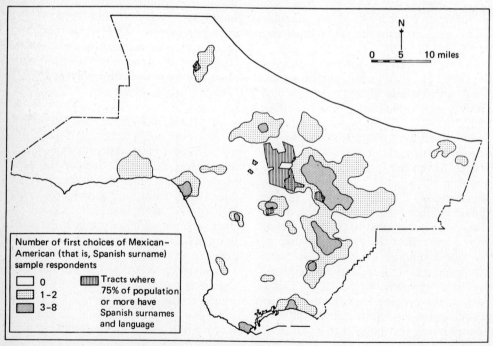

Figure 7. First-Choice Preferences of Mexican-American (Spanish Surname) Respondents in the Los Angeles Metropolitan Area (redrawn from SYMAP output)

Despite the fact that an income constraint was imposed, there are other, seemingly more attractive, low-income areas in the city that the Black households might have chosen. A similar pattern can be discerned in the preference map of Mexican-Americans (see Figure 7), which was constructed from the responses of 136 families. Again the ridge of highly preferred communities is in an area already containing large numbers of Mexican-Americans.

Conclusion

In this paper we have shown the nature of the residential-preference pattern for the Los Angeles metropolitan area, and have suggested the value of this as an alternative representation of urban space. Like the factorial ecological studies, it is still only a classification of urban space, but we do believe that this particular mode of analysis is more relevant in terms of urban planning, the establishment of social indicators, and spatial be-havior within cities. Also of interest in this context would be the development of a negative-preference surface. This would highlight those areas where people do not wish to live. Finally the implications of these preference patterns as regards spatial information levels are of some interest, although we suspect that the development of a true information surface is still some way off.

References

Berry, B. J. L. (Ed.), 1971, "Comparative factorial ecology," *Economic Geography,* 47 (2) (supplement).

Brigham, E. F., 1965, "The determinants of residential land values," *Land Economics,* 41, 325–334.

Gould, P. R., 1967, "Structuring information on spacio-temporal preferences," *Journal of Regional Science,* 7, 259–274.

Johnston, R. J., 1972, "Activity spaces and residential preferences: some tests of the hypothesis of sectoral mental maps," *Economic Geography,* 48, 199–211.

Kish, L., 1965, *Survey Sampling* (John Wiley, New York).

PETER A. MORRISON

Urban Growth and Decline:
San Jose and St. Louis in the 1960's

This article presents an analysis of the sharply contrasting demographic trends in two U.S. metropolitan areas and discusses the implications of these trends for public policy. San Jose, California, exemplifies rapid population growth in the low-density mode typical of the 1950's and 1960's. The city of St. Louis exemplifies central-city population decline within the core jurisdiction of metropolitan St. Louis.

If we studied San Jose and St. Louis as isolated cases and sought to explain their population changes, historically unique processes that have shaped each city probably would occupy our attention and prevent us from seeing them as variations of common demographic processes. It is therefore advantageous to take a broad view of the two as opposite extremes of a growth-decline continuum. If we can perceive common demographic processes at work in such contrasting settings, our generalizations about these processes should be all the firmer.

San Jose: Growth and Migration Flows

Early in this century, population in urban centers grew mainly through rural-to-urban and international migration. These large migrations from outside the metropolitan system, along with a substantial amount of natural increase, afforded all urban centers some measure of growth. In recent years, however, the intensification or reversal of some long-standing trends has altered the growth and redistribution of the U.S. population.

For one thing, net growth from international migration has diminished both absolutely and as a percentage of the U.S. population. During the era of major immigration—1908 to 1915—the population increased 0.6 percent annually through net international migration; more recently, this increase has been only about 0.2 percent.

The rate of rural-to-urban migration has also diminished. The rural population has declined over recent decades, leaving a limited reservoir of potential migrants in the countryside. Equally significant is the fact that rural areas now retain a much higher proportion of their population growth than formerly.

Finally, the national fertility rate has declined. The "average" woman in 1960 would eventually bear 3.7 children over a lifetime; in 1973, her completed fertility would be only 2.0 children.

As these traditional growth forces weakened, migration flows among metropolitan areas emerged as the principal determinants of urban growth. But inter-metropolitan migration favors a certain few metropolitan centers with most of the available migratory growth.[1]

No metropolis demonstrates this effect more clearly than San Jose, whose rapidly expanding aerospace and service industries have attracted an extraordinary influx of new residents over the last two decades. During the 1960's, metropolitan San Jose's population increased 66 percent, a rate surpassed by only four other standard metropolitan statistical areas (SMSA's) in the United States. One-third of this growth was due to natural increase, two-thirds to net in-migration. In 1965, fewer than seven of every thousand metropolitan Americans were residents of San Jose, but San Jose received 55 of every thousand net migrants arriving in metropolitan areas between 1960 and 1970.

Having more than tripled in population between 1950 and 1970, San Jose today bears the cumulative hallmarks of selective in-migration: its population is young and highly migratory, and its age distribution, enriched through additions of young adults of childbearing age, gives rise to many more births than deaths.

But this remarkable growth cannot be comprehended strictly in local terms, San Jose's experience is part of the expansion of California's entire metropolitan structure through migration to and within it.[2]

California draws migrants from great distances. The vast majority of them enter the state through Los Angeles, San Francisco, or San Diego. Table 1 shows that these centers act as national magnets, drawing migrants mostly from out of state.[3] (Los Angeles and San Francisco also draw significant numbers of foreign immigrants.) The ten other California metropolises in Table 1 draw migrants primarily from within the state.

But large numbers of people use these cities only as gateways. Consider the flows in and out of San Francisco. Between 1965 and 1970, San Francisco received 269,000 out-of-state migrants and sent only 204,000 migrants to other states—a net population gain of 65,000 for San Francisco (and California). But San Francisco kept little of this gain: 249,000 of its residents moved to other places in California, but only 191,000 Californians moved to San Francisco; so the city lost 59,000 migrants to the rest of the state of whom 23,000 ended up in San Jose. In fact, San Jose lures nearly as many migrants away from San Francisco and Los Angeles combined as it does from the remainder of the entire nation (Table 2). This abundant supply of new growth funneled into California through San Francisco and Los Angeles has undoubtedly been an important factor in San Jose's 44 percent increase through migration during the 1960's.

Repercussions of Rapid Migratory Growth

Rapid growth causes a number of repercussions, one of which is the youth-weighted age distribution that heavy immigration typically confers. (Nationally, nearly a third of all migrants are in their 20's, the peak child-bearing age, and 16 percent more are children aged 1 to 6

1. W. Alonso and E. Medrich, in *Growth Centers in Regional Economic Development,* N. M. Hansen, Ed. (Free Press, New York, 1972), p. 229.

2. D. L. Foley, R. L. Drake, D. W. Lyon, B. A. Ynzenga, *Characteristics of Metropolitan Growth in California,* vol. 1, *Report* (Center for Planning and Development Research, Institute for Urban and Regional Development, Berkeley, Calif., 1965).

3. U.S. Bureau of the Census, *Census of Population, 1970: Subject Reports,* Final Report PC (2)-2E, *Migration between State Economic Areas* (Government Printing Office, Washington, D.C., 1972).

Table 1. Domestic Migration Streams into and out of California's Metropolitan Areas, 1965 to 1970. These data exclude foreign migration. The Salinas-Monterey and Vallejo-Napa SMSA's are not shown, since they cannot be approximated with the data for the state economic areas used here (see footnote 3).

Metropolitan Area[a]	Migrants to Metropolitan Area from		Migrants from Metropolitan Area to		Net Migration to Metropolitan Area	
	California	Out of State	California	Out of State	California	Out of State
San Francisco	190,931	268,824	249,495	204,149	−58,564	+64,675
Los Angeles	265,500	649,166	414,096	516,019	−148,596	+133,147
San Diego	124,578	223,001	88,544	139,130	+36,034	+83,871
San Jose	132,223	102,416	92,875	67,043	+39,348	+35,373
Sacramento	67,055	52,245	77,359	50,631	−10,304	+1,614
Stockton	29,601	13,808	29,658	11,609	−57	+2,199
Fresno	39,296	15,731	47,972	18,704	−8,676	−2,973
San Bernardino–Riverside	150,470	112,553	107,600	91,728	+42,870	+20,825
Bakersfield	35,097	23,451	42,314	24,328	−7,217	−877
Santa Barbara	41,296	31,879	32,576	29,529	+8,720	+2,350
Santa Rosa	51,516	15,201	29,834	14,178	+21,682	+1,023
Modesto	35,493	21,793	31,797	20,801	+3,696	+992
Oxnard-Ventura	68,157	37,366	39,973	29,183	+28,184	+8,183

[a] These are SMSA's, with the following exceptions: San Francisco here includes Solano County, Los Angeles combines the Los Angeles SMSA and the Anaheim–Santa Ana–Garden Grove SMSA, Sacramento excludes Placer and Yolo counties, Santa Rosa includes Napa County, and Modesto includes Merced County.

years.) One can see the difference between a place that grows through migration and another that declines by comparing the San Jose SMSA with the city of St. Louis. While San Jose's population more than tripled between 1950 and 1970, mostly because of migration, St. Louis's declined 27 percent as heavy out-migration more than canceled out its natural increase. Thus, compared with that of St. Louis, San Jose's age distribution shows a comparative surplus in the under-44 age brackets and a comparative deficit in the over-45 range (Figure 1). With relatively more potential parents, San Jose's population grew faster than that of St. Louis. San Jose's rate of natural increase during 1960 to 1970 was 21.6 per hundred residents in 1960; St. Louis's was only 7.3.

San Jose's rapid migratory growth also makes its population hypermobile. Since people who migrate tend to do so repeatedly, a population built up by waves of past in-migration is heavily weighted with chronically mobile people and, therefore, is subject to high rates of subsequent out-migration.[4] Consequently, there is a continual flow of migrants through San Jose. Annual net migration into metropolitan San Jose averaged nearly 4 percent during the 1960's. This net flow was composed of about 21 arrivals and 17 departures each year per hundred residents (or nearly 10 actual moves for each "net migrant" added).[5] About 7 of these

4. Evidence on this point is given in P. A. Morrison, Demography 8, 171 (1971).
5. Based on data from the Social Security Continuous Work History Sample. These data, which are furnished by the Social Security Administration, Washington, D.C., and cover

Table 2. Domestic Migration Streams into and out of the San Jose SMSA, 1965 to 1970. Foreign migration is excluded, and the Salinas-Monterey and Vallejo-Napa SMSA's are not shown (see Table 1). [Data from footnote 3]

Metropolitan Area[a]	Migrants from Metropolitan Area to San Jose	Migrants to Metropolitan Area from San Jose	Net Migration to San Jose
San Francisco	55,674	32,241	+23,433
Los Angeles	23,741	15,363	+8,378
San Diego	5,553	4,008	+1,545
Sacramento	6,646	2,443	+4,203
Stockton	2,160	1,616	+544
Fresno	3,954	1,897	+2,057
San Bernardino–Riverside	3,219	2,504	+715
Bakersfield	1,970	968	+1,002
Santa Barbara	2,881	2,169	+712
Santa Rosa	2,340	2,875	−535
Modesto	2,788	2,428	+360
Oxnard-Ventura	1,265	1,452	−187
Rest of California	20,032	22,911	−2,879
Rest of United States	102,416	67,043	+35,373

[a] See footnote to Table 1.

17 out-migrants, though, had moved into San Jose only 1 year before. Indeed, fully one-third of the migrants attracted to San Jose had moved away a year later.

Thus, San Jose's rapid population growth rests on a rather precarious arithmetic balance between in-migration and out-migration. Although many of its in-migrants subsequently leave, San Jose manages to grow by attracting more than enough new arrivals each year to offset

this considerable loss. Any moderate decline in the rate of gross in-migration could easily bring net migration down to a small fraction of its present level. For example, if San Jose attracted only 16 (instead of 21) in-migrants per hundred residents, its net migratory gain would stand at less than 1 percent (instead of 4 percent) annually.[6]

On the other hand, because it is highly mobile, San Jose's population can probably accommodate change quite quickly. Adjustment to changes in the overall demand for labor, or to shifts in the mix of required skills, can occur promptly because of the brisk inflow and outflow of

nine out of ten wage and salary workers nationally, are not directly comparable to the census figures (in ftn. 3). The Social Security data shown here refer only to employed civilians in Social Security—covered jobs—a subset of the entire population 5 years and older to which the census data refer. Thus, the Continuous Work History Sample excludes completely self-employed and unemployed workers, persons not in the labor force, and certain classes of workers (principally civilian employees of the federal government, some state and local government employees, and railroad workers). We have also excluded migrants entering or leaving military service.

6. This estimate is a rough approximation only. It assumes that the lower rate of in-migration would, by reducing the stock of chronic movers, lower the rate of subsequent out-migration from 17 to 15 per hundred residents. All estimates here refer to the period to which these Continuous Work History Sample data apply (1957 through 1966) and to San Jose residents working in Social Security-covered jobs.

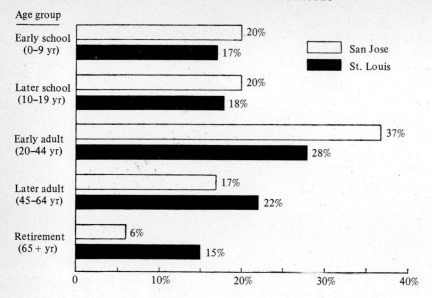

Figure 1. Contrasting Age Distributions: San Jose SMSA and St. Louis, 1970

workers. For this reason, San Jose's labor market is likely to show an uncommon resiliency to change.

St. Louis: Population Decline and Its Consequences

The St. Louis SMSA encompasses the city of St. Louis and six counties lying on both sides of the Mississippi River: the counties of St. Louis, St. Charles, Franklin, and Jefferson in Missouri and the counties of St. Clair and Madison in Illinois. The city of St. Louis is entirely separate in area and jurisdiction from St. Louis County. (Hereafter, St. Louis will refer to the city, while St. Louis County will be so designated.) The closest metropolitan area of comparable size is the Kansas City SMSA, about 275 miles (440 kilometers) to the west.

In 1970, the population of metropolitan St. Louis stood at about 2.4 million. It had increased by 12 percent since 1960, a rate lower than the average national metropolitan increase of 17 percent. After 1970, population in metro-

politan St. Louis, like that in 21 other formerly growing SMSA's, began to decline.

St. Louis attained a peak population of 880,000 in the early 1950's. But by 1972 it had dwindled to a city of less than 590,000. During the 1960's, St. Louis's population declined 17 percent while its metropolitan ring population increased 29 percent. The central-city decline was acute, compared with that of most cities. Examination of the demographic change components reveals why[7] (see Table 3).

The white population declined mostly because of massive outward migration, chiefly to the suburbs. Between 1960 and 1970, a net 34 percent of the white city dwellers moved away. But whites also declined because their death rate steadily approached their birth rate, and

7. U.S. Bureau of the Census, *Census of Population and Housing: 1970; General Demographic Trends for Metropolitan Areas, 1960 to 1970,* Final report PHC(2)-1, tables 10–12; PHC(2)-27, table 3; PHC(2)-15, table 3 (Government Printing Office, Washington, D.C., 1970).

Table 3. Components of Population Change in St. Louis, 1960 to 1970 (see footnote 7). Data are expressed as rates of change per 100 residents in 1960

Area	Total Change	Natural Increase[a]	Net Migration
Both races			
St. Louis SMSA	12.3	11.5	0.8
St. Louis city	−17.0	7.3	−24.4
Remainder of SMSA[b]	28.5	13.8	14.7
Whites			
St. Louis SMSA	9.4	10.1	−0.7
St. Louis city	−31.6	2.4	−34.0
Remainder of SMSA[b]	26.6	13.3	13.3
Nonwhites[c]			
St. Louis SMSA	28.2	20.2	9.7
St. Louis city	18.6	19.5	−0.4
Remainder of SMSA[b]	53.8	22.0	37.2

[a] Rate of increase attributed to excess births over deaths.
[b] Metropolitan ring.
[c] In this section of the table, "total change" applies only to the black population. "Natural increase" and "net migration" apply to the nonwhite population as a whole, but virtually all nonwhites in the St. Louis SMSA are blacks.

since 1965 has exceeded it. Those who remained in the city added only 2 percent to their numbers (nationally, the increase in the white metropolitan population for that decade was 11 percent).

It was a different picture for blacks. There was no gain or loss through net migration during the 1960's, but the black population rose 19.5 percent through natural increase, very close to its national rate of 21.6 percent. Annual population estimates, however, show St. Louis's nonwhite population to have peaked in 1968 at around 269,000.[8] By 1972, it is estimated to have dropped below 250,000. In view of the black population's positive natural increase, the only explanation is that blacks have been migrating out of the city since at least 1968 (and almost certainly before).

The number and composition of households in the city also changed during the decade. The number of households declined somewhat more slowly than the population (13 versus 17 percent), and the average size of a household went down slightly. Households with only one person increased from 21 percent in 1960 to 28 percent in 1970, a reflection primarily of the growing frequency of elderly widows.

Demographic trends were somewhat more uniform outside the city (Table 3). Natural increase and net migration contributed equally to the white population's 26.6 percent increase during the 1960's. The black population's 53.8 percent suburban growth was attributable more to net migration than to natural increase.[9] St. Louis's suburbs attracted migrants largely from the city but also from outside the metropolitan area. Increasingly, migrants of both races entering the St.

8. In St. Louis, blacks make up 99 percent of the nonwhite population. Hence the terms "nonwhite" and "black" are used synonymously in the following discussion.

9. Suburban blacks registered a high overall rate of growth between 1960 and 1970 because their 1960 base was minuscule.

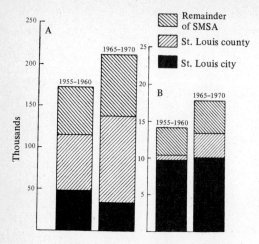

Figure 2. Destinations of Migrants Entering the St. Louis SMSA, 1955 to 1960 and 1965 to 1970 (persons 5 years old and over, residing outside the SMSA or abroad 5 years previously). (A) Total. (B) Blacks (data shown for 1955 to 1960 refer to nonwhites)

Louis SMSA bypassed the city and settled in the suburbs (mainly in St. Louis County). It can be seen in Figure 2 that the total stream of new arrivals to St. Louis between 1965 and 1970 was smaller (both absolutely and relatively) than it had been a decade earlier. For blacks, the inbound stream was numerically about the same; but in relative terms, newly arriving blacks increasingly favored the suburbs.

Persistent and severe migration away from St. Louis has altered the structure of its population. These changes bear heavily on the city's capacity to meet the needs of the increasingly disadvantaged population that remains and on this population's very capacity to regenerate itself.

Diminished replacement capacity. The white population's capacity to replace itself diminished during the 1960's. Heavy and prolonged out-migration among

whites drew away potential parents and left behind an elderly population that no longer replaces itself.

We can gauge the severity of out-migration by young white adults by following individual age cohorts from 1960 to 1970 (Figure 3). For example, in the absence of migratory change, people 5 to 14 years old in 1960 would reappear as the same number of people 15 to 24 years old in 1970, less a small allowance for mortality. Since this allowance is negligible below age 45 (at most 5 percent), any sizable discrepancy between 1960 and 1970 indicates the extent of migration that has taken place in that cohort. Figure 3 gives stark evidence of extensive out-migration from St. Louis in the early adult years. For example, in 1960 there were 37,900 white females aged 15 to 24, but by 1970 only 17,900 aged 25 to 34 remained—a 53 percent reduction. There were 31,100 white males 25 to 34 in 1960, but only 15,900 aged 35 to 44 in 1970—a 49 percent reduction. Overall, 46 percent of whites 15 to 34 in 1960 were gone by 1970, leaving St. Louis with a sharply diminished pool of prospective parents.

The resultant modifications in replacement capacity are illustrated more directly in Table 4, from which we can see that:

1. Women in the middle and later child-bearing years had grown more scarce. In 1960, white women aged 25 to 44 made up 22.1 percent of all white women in the city; by 1970 the figure had dropped to 17.6 percent. (Part of this drop stemmed from the changing national age distribution; for white women nationally, this age group declined from 26.4 to 23.5 percent of the total population between 1960 and 1970.)

2. The proportion of elderly whites had risen. Whites 65 and over made up

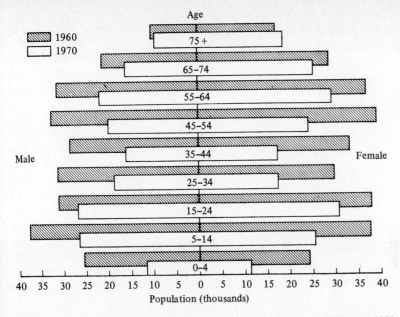

Figure 3. Age Distribution of the White Population in St. Louis, 1960 and 1970

14.5 percent of the population in 1960, but 19.2 percent in 1970. (The corresponding figure nationally was 10 percent in both years.)

3. Partially as a result of these changes in age structure, the crude birth rate per thousand whites declined from 22.1 in 1960 to 12.0 in 1972; and the crude death rate per thousand whites rose from 14.8 to 18.0 (Part of the decline in the birth rate, of course, was a consequence of the national trend in the birth rate, which dropped nearly 25 percent during the 1960's.)

Since 1965, the white population has ceased to replace itself, its death rate having exceeded its birth rate. By 1972, the services of the undertaker exceeded those of the obstetrician by a margin of 3 to 2. Since it is now undergoing natural decrease, St. Louis's white population will continue to shrink whether or not net out-migration continues. Only a dra-

matic rise in fertility or a massive influx of childbearing families can alter this situation.[10]

The city's black population has not undergone severe migratory change and retains its strong replacement capacity: in 1972 its crude birth rate was 24.9 per thousand, but its crude death rate was only 11.2. In 1969, however, the black population began to decline, indicating a net migratory loss severe enough to offset its natural increase. This recent shift could signify an increase in departing migrants, a reduction in entering migrants, or a combination of both. Indications favor the first of these explanations.[11]

10. Because changes in fertility are difficult to forecast, a dramatic rise cannot be entirely ruled out, although it seems highly unlikely at this time. Foreseeable changes in mortality have no appreciable bearing on the population's replacement capacity.

11. Data in Fig. 2 indicate that the gross number of black migrants entering St. Louis between 1965 and 1970 was about the same as

Table 4. Indices of Change in Replacement Capacity for St. Louis's Black and White Population, 1960 to 1972

Indicator	1960	1970	1972
Percentage of women in later childbearing years (age 25 to 44)			
White	22.1	17.6	—a
Black	27.1	22.7	—a
Percentage of population age 65 and over			
White	14.5	19.2	—a
Black	6.8	8.3	—a
Crude birth rate per thousand			
White	22.1	14.5	12.0
Black	34.4	25.1	24.9
Crude death rate per thousand			
White	14.8	17.7	18.0
Black	11.4	11.3	11.2

a Data not available.

Accumulation of disadvantaged citizens. As migration has changed the metropolitan-wide distribution of population, St. Louis has come to be composed disproportionately of those citizens who are disadvantaged or have special needs, as the following comparisons show:

1. Between 1960 and 1970, the black percentage of the city's population rose from 29 to 41 percent; it increased only from 6 to 7 percent in the rest of the metropolitan area.
2. The city's residents aged 65 years and older increased from 12 percent to constitute 15 percent of the population; they stayed at 8 percent in the rest of the metropolitan area.
3. For families and unrelated individuals, median income in the city was 79 percent of that for the St. Louis SMSA in 1959; by 1969 city income was only 68 percent of the SMSA income.

between 1955 and 1960—around 10,000. Thus only an increase in gross out-migration could account for the change in net migration.

4. The proportion of relatively high income families declined sharply. In 1959, 11 percent of families in the city had incomes at least double the city's median family income; 10 years later, only 4 percent had incomes double the 1969 median.
5. The proportion of relatively low income families rose slightly. In 1959, 16 percent of families in the city had incomes less than half the city's median family income; 10 years later, 21 percent had incomes less than half the 1969 median.

Through selective out-migration, then, problems of dependency and poverty—not exclusively problems *of* St. Louis—have come increasingly to be located *in* St. Louis.

The Dilemma of Policy: Coping with Decline

The degree of population decline in St. Louis may be exceptional, but St. Louis is no exception to the rule. The phenomenon of local population decline is widespread now—a characteristic of entire metropolitan areas, not just their central cities. The policy dilemma in coping with decline and its local consequences is likely to intensify during the 1970's.

The dilemma is this. The local official responsible for what happens in a place like St. Louis is understandably alarmed by severe population loss and the bleak future in store for the city if it continues. The city's boundaries, which have not changed since 1876, separate the problems within St. Louis from resources in its suburbs. But from the standpoint of individual welfare, it can be argued that the people who left St. Louis now enjoy living conditions they prefer, and those who remain have benefited from a thinning out of people from formerly overcrowded areas.[12] Even the widespread abandoned housing in St. Louis can be viewed as a positive sign that many people have upgraded their living conditions, leaving behind a residue of housing no longer competitive within the market. Both views have validity, the choice depending on whether one's perspective is that of a local policy-maker or of a freely mobile citizen.

But that line of argument may amount to no more than a confusing piece of sophistry for the policy-maker, or even the objective student of urban affairs, who looks at careful statistics from respectable sources telling him unequivocally that St. Louis is much worse off than it used to be. Part of the confusion is due to the paradox that statistics can be deceptive even when they are accurate. They can mislead us here, for example, if they beguile us into confining our attention to the plight of *places,* whereas our central concern is with the well-being of *people.* It is hard to escape that situation, however. A major difficulty in our way is that standard social and economic statistics are compiled and organized mostly by areas rather than by groups of people. Consequently, we can observe the experience of places, but not of people. These experiences can differ sharply. For instance, black in-migrants from impoverished rural areas in states like Mississippi may be less affluent or employable, on the average, than the mostly white population they join in St. Louis. If this is true in St. Louis as it is in other cities,[13] then area indicators (for

example, unemployment or poverty in St. Louis) may register a worsening of local conditions. But measures of individuals' experiences (for example, their unemployment or poverty now, compared with what it was before they came to St. Louis) may show marked improvement. In short, the place we call St. Louis may be worse off because of in-migration while the in-migrant people are better off than they were.

Summary and Conclusions

The population changes in San Jose and St. Louis between 1960 and 1970 exemplify the two broad trends—urban formation followed by metropolitan dispersal—that have shaped 20th-century urbanization in this country. The fact that these developmental trends were expressed through demographic processes found to be common to both cities, despite their contrasting recent experiences, suggests that generalizations can be made about the complex forces underlying urbanization.

The formation of metropolitan San Jose's population parallels the traditional process whereby a region's growth comes to be focused, through migration, on a few urban centers. The modern variant is not characterized by a rural-to-urban shift, however, but by migration flows among urban areas, and particularly to a few most-favored areas, such as San Jose.

Migratory growth has left a powerful demographic legacy in San Jose. This legacy is also instructive for studying the migratory formation of any new city's population. Its demographic character determines its demographic destiny, whose

12. If the number of persons per room is taken as the conventional index of overcrowding, census data show that only 12.7 percent of all occupied housing units in St. Louis contained more than one person per room in 1970, compared with 16.4 percent in 1960.

13. Evidence on this point is reviewed by P. A. Morrison "The impact and significance of rural-urban migration in the United States," in *Hearings before the Subcommittee on Migra-*

tory Labor, Senate Committee on Labor and Public Welfare, on Land Ownership, Use and Distribution, held in San Francisco, 11 January 1972 (Government Printing Office, Washington, D.C., 1972), part 3A, p. 1039.

likely variations we can now perceive with some clarity. San Jose's population is both youthful and chronically migratory. The presence of many prospective parents and relatively few elderly persons lays a broad foundation for the population's continued growth through natural increase, despite the national downturn in fertility.[14] Even without further net in-migration, the population of new cities like San Jose would continue to grow at an above-average rate.

The hypermobility of San Jose's population (that is, its propensity for further migration) also has an important bearing on the future. With about 21 migrants entering and 17 departing each year per hundred residents, San Jose's rapid migratory growth rests (as it would in other new cities) on a precarious arithmetic balance. A significant dip in local employment growth could easily reduce net migration to a small fraction of its present high level. Even a slight decline would result in the inflow's no longer exceeding the high volume of outflow. Demographic analysis alone cannot foresee such an employment downturn, but if it happened, the migratory downturn probably would be swift. Hypermobility also works the other way; and given San Jose's focal position in California's expanding metropolitan structure (with its virtually endless supply of migratory growth), net migration could resume with equal swiftness.

The outward dispersal of population from central cities that has occurred in St. Louis has been accelerating in other cities as well, and will remain a prominent feature of U.S. urban growth. It may seem paradoxical that in a period noted for something called "urban growth" there are so many declining central cities, but that is merely one indication that the "central city" no longer is the real city, except in name. Real city or not, the central city can expect to come into political conflict with other jurisdictions created in the process of dispersion. In cities like St. Louis, where population is dispersing but old political boundaries are fixed, the problems of the central city are separated from the resources in the suburbs. Transitional problems associated with persistent and severe out-migration also arise: accumulation of disadvantaged citizens, declining demand for city housing, and a diminished replacement capacity in the population.

Carried far enough, the last of these problems results in natural decrease, and thereafter the population's decline acquires its own dynamic. As noted earlier, the white population in St. Louis has reached this point: The number of persons dying now exceeds the number being born.

For two reasons, this natural decrease can do little other than intensify. First, a substantial proportion of whites are either entering or already within the high-mortality age brackets. The white population's crude death rate therefore will continue to rise. Second, prospective parents are becoming scarce among St. Louis's whites, and the national evidence that parents in general will choose to have smaller families continues to mount. The white population's crude birth rate is therefore likely to fall, barring a dramatic increase in fertility or a strong and sustained inflow of childbearing families. Nor is St. Louis's black population likely to grow substantially. It is expanding steadily through natural increase, but black migration out of the city is more than enough to cancel that increase.

14. The exact rate of San Jose's natural increase, although dependent on the future course of U.S. fertility, will remain above the national metropolitan average.

IV

COMMUNITIES: Residential Areas, Neighborhood Change, and Housing

BARRY WELLMAN AND BARRY LEIGHTON

Networks, Neighborhoods, and Communities: Approaches to the Study of the Community Question

Urban sociology has tended to be *neighborhood sociology*. This has meant that analyses of large-scale urban phenomena (such as the fiscal crisis of the state) have been neglected in favor of small-scale studies of communities. It has also meant that the study of such communities has been firmly rooted in the study of neighborhoods, be they the "symbiotic" communities of Park (1936) or the "street corners" of Liebow (1967). It is to the sorting out of this second tendency, the merger of "neighborhood" with "community" that we address this paper.

There are a number of reasons why the concept of "neighborhood" has come to be substituted for that of "community": First, urban researchers have to start somewhere. The neighborhood is an easily identifiable research site, while the street corner is an obvious and visible place for mapping small-scale interaction. Second, many scholars have interpreted the neighborhood as the microcosm of the city and the city as an aggregate of neighborhoods. They have emphasized the local rather than the cosmopolitan in a building block approach to analysis which has given scant attention to large-scale urban structure. Third, administrative officials have imposed their own definitions of neighborhood boundaries upon urban maps in attempts to create bureaucratic units. Spatial areas, labeled and treated as coherent neighborhoods, have come to be regarded as natural phenomena. Fourth, urban sociology's particular concern with spatial distributions has tended to be translated into local area concerns. Territory has come to be seen as the inherently most important organizing factor in urban social relations rather than just one potentially important factor. Fifth, and most important, many analysts have been preoccupied with the conditions under which solidary sentiments can be maintained. The neighborhood has been studied as an apparently obvious container of normative solidarity.

For these reasons at least, the concentration on the neighborhood has had a strong impact on definitions of, research on, and theorizing about community. Neighborhood studies have produced

From **Urban Affairs Quarterly,** Vol. 14, No. 3, March 1979, pp. 363–90. Reprinted in revised form by permission of the Publisher, Sage Publications, Inc., Beverly Hills, Calif., B. Wellman, and B. Leighton.

hundreds of finely wrought depictions of urban life, and they have given us powerful ideas about how small-scale social systems operate in a variety of social contexts. But does the concept of "neighborhood" equal the concept of "community"? Are the two really one and the same?

Definitions of community tend to include three ingredients: *networks of interpersonal ties* (outside of the household) which *provide sociability and support* to members, residence in a *common locality,* and *solidarity sentiments and activities* (see Hillery, 1955). It is principally the emphasis on common locality, and to a lesser extent the emphasis on solidarity, which has encouraged the identification of "community" with "neighborhood."

THE COMMUNITY QUESTION

With its manifest concerns for the activities of populations in territories (Tilly, 1974), urban sociology has often seemed to stand apart from broader theoretical concerns. Yet its concentration on the study of the neighborhood-as-community is very much a part of a fundamental sociological issue. This fundamental issue, which has occupied much sociological thinking, is the *community question:* the study of how large-scale divisions of labor in social systems affect the organization and content of interpersonal ties.

Sociologists have been particularly concerned with that form of the community question which investigates the impact the massive industrial bureaucratic transformations of North America and Europe during the past two hundred years have had on a variety of primary ties: in the home, the neighborhood, the workplace, with kin and friends, and among interest groups. Have such ties attenuated or flourished in contemporary societies? In what sort of networks are they organized? Have the contents of such ties remained as holistic as alleged to be in preindustrial societies or have they become narrowly specialized and instrumental?

The community question thus forms a crucial nexus between macroscopic and microscopic analysis. It directly addresses the structural integration of a social system and the interpersonal means by which its members can gain access to scarce resources. We urge, therefore, that the study of the community question be freed from its identification with the study of neighborhoods.

NEIGHBORHOOD ≠ COMMUNITY

The entangling of the study of community ties with the study of the neighborhood has created a number of problems for the analysis of the community question.

First, the identification of a neighborhood as a container for communal ties assumes the a priori organizing power of space. This is spatial determinism. Even if we grant that space-time costs encourage some relationships to be local, it does not necessarily follow that all communal ties are organized into solidary neighborhood communities. These neighborhood ties may exist because of the attraction of ready accessibility to a few people and not because of a tangible neighborhood social organization.

Second, even the presence of many local relationships does not necessarily create discrete neighborhoods. There may well be overlapping sets of local ties, the range of these ties being affected by the needs and physical mobility of the participants.

Third, the identification of neighborhood studies with community studies can omit major spheres of interaction. There are important ties outside of the neighborhood even in the most "institutionally complete community" (Breton, 1964). Perhaps work relationships are the most serious and prevalent omission from community studies: residents tend to disappear from view in the morning and mysteriously reappear at dusk.

Fourth, the focus on the neighborhood may give undue importance to spatial characteristics as causal variables. Are cities just concrete and concentrated manifestations of larger structural forces? For instance, Castells (1976) argues that most Western urban sociology can be explained by studying capitalist modes of production.

Fifth, many analyses of neighborhoods have been preoccupied with the conditions under which solitary sentiments can be maintained. Consequently, when there has been an observed lack of locally organized behavior and sentiments, the assumption has easily been made that community has decayed. When not found in the neighborhood, community is assumed not to exist.

The Network Perspective

We suggest that the *network analytic perspective* is a more appropriate response to the community question in urban studies than the traditional focus on the neighborhood.[1] A network analysis of community takes as its starting point the search for social linkages and flows of resources. Only then does it enquire into the spatial distribution and solidary sentiments as-

1. Network analysis is essentially a perspective which focuses on structured relationships between individuals and collectivities. As yet there is no commonly agreed definition. We believe that network analysis's salient characteristics are that it gives attention to: (1) structured patterns of relationships and not the aggregated characteristics of individual units, analyzed without reference to their interrelationships; (2) complex network structures and not just dyadic ties; (3) the allocation of scarce resources through concrete systems of power, dependency, and coordination; (4) questions of network boundaries, clusters and cross-linkages; (5) structures of reciprocal relationships and not just simple hierarchies (see Wellman, 1981).

sociated with the observed linkages. Such an approach largely frees the study of community from spatial and normative bases. It makes possible the discovery of network-based communities which are neither linked to a particular neighborhood nor to a set of solidary sentiments.

However, the network perspective is not inherently antineighborhood. By leaving the matter of spatial distributions initially open, this perspective makes it equally as possible to discover an "urban village" (Gans, 1962) as it is to discover a "community without propinquity" (Webber, 1963). A network analysis might also tell us that strong ties remain abundant and important, but that they are rarely located in the neighborhood. With this approach we are then better able to assess the position of neighborhood ties within the context of overall structures of social relationships.

The community question has been extensively debated by urban scholars. In this paper, we evaluate three competing scholarly arguments about the community question from a network perspective. The first two arguments to be discussed both focus on the neighborhood: the *community lost,* asserting the absence of local solidarities, and the *community saved* argument, asserting their persistence. The *community liberated* argument, in contrast, denies any neighborhood basis to community. General tendencies in each argument are summarized, although not every article making each argument neatly fits into the analytic categories we have imposed on them.

Community Lost

The community lost argument contends that the transformation of Western societies to centralized, industrial bureaucratic structures has gravely weakened primary ties and communities, making the individual more dependent on formal organizational resources for sustenance (see the reviews in Stein, 1960; Nisbet, 1962; Gusfield, 1975; Castells, 1976; Mellor, 1977). The first attempts to deal with the community question (e.g., Tönnies, 1887) were, at the turn of the century, closely associated with broader sociological concerns about the impact of the Industrial Revolution on communal ties and normative integration (e.g., Durkheim, 1893; Simmel, 1908).

Scholars working in the lost tradition have initiated the analysis of the impact of large-scale social changes upon community structures. A number of such significant changes have been suggested, although not all analysts proposing them would necessarily agree that the loss of community was the ultimate outcome:

1. An increase in the scale of the nation-state's activities, with a concomitant decrease in local community autonomy and solidarity;
2. the development of bureaucratic institutions for production and reproduction, which have taken over many family, neighborhood, and friendship activities;
3. the large size of cities, which provides a basis for the population and organizational potential for more, and diverse, interest groups;
4. the high social density of interactions among segments of the population (even where spatial density is decreasing), with the ensuing complexities of ecological sorting and social arrangements;
5. the diversity of people with whom city dwellers can come into contact under conditions of heightened physical mobility;
6. the proliferation of cheap, efficient, and widespread transportation and communication facilities, increasing the ease with which contact can be made and enabling urbanites to be less tied to the neighborhood.

The lost argument has had continuing academic attention. It underlay much of the 1920s–1930s theoretical writing of the dominant "Chicago school" of urban studies (although the Chicago scholars found much evidence of communal organization in their empirical work). Robert Park's early programmatic statement asserted that "the growth of cities has been accomplished by the substitution of indirect 'secondary' for direct, face-to-face 'primary relations' " (Park, 1925a, p. 23). Over a decade later, Louis Wirth (1938) summarized the lost argument well in his now classic statement of "urbanism as a way of life." Primary ties are recognized as still existing, but in a weaker, more narrowly instrumental fashion than those which had flourished in traditional solidary communities.

Lost scholars have seen modern urbanites as alienated isolates who bear the brunt of the transformed society on their own. Many research procedures have reinforced this perspective by using survey techniques which lump together individuals *qua* individuals in analytically imposed categories which do not take into consideration their structural connectedness (i.e., the statistical assumption of independence elevated to a world view). Such individual-as-unit oriented research techniques have been particularly suited to social psychologistic explanations which see internalized attitudes as determining social activity; they have not been nearly as well-suited towards the direct study of social-structural effects.

LOST NETWORKS

The community lost argument makes a number of specific assertions about the kinds of primary ties, social networks, and community structures that will tend to be present under its assumptions. By casting the lost argument in network analytic terms, we shall be better able to evaluate it in comparison with the community saved and community liberated arguments:

1. Rather than being a full member of a solidary community, urbanites are now *limited members* (in terms of amount, intensity, and commitment of interaction) of *several social networks.*
2. Primary ties are *narrowly defined;* there are *fewer strands* in the relationship.
3. The narrowly defined ties tend to be *weak in intensity.*
4. Ties tend to be *fragmented* into isolated *two-person* relationships rather than being parts of extensive networks.
5. Those networks that do exist tend to be *sparsely knit* (a low proportion of all potential links between members actually exists) rather than being densely knit (a high proportion of potential links exists).
6. The networks are *loosely bounded;* there are few discrete clusters or primary groups.
7. Sparse density, loose boundaries and narrowly defined ties provide *little* structural basis for *solidary activities or sentiments.*
8. The narrowly defined ties dispersed among a number of networks create *difficulties in mobilizing assistance* from network members.

IMAGERY

Community lost imagery has had a good deal of scholarly impact, appealing to radical (e.g., Engels, 1845; Castells, 1976), liberal (e.g., Woodsworth, 1911; Stein, 1960; Slater, 1970), and conservative (e.g., Nisbet, 1962; Banfield, 1968; Grant, 1969) concerns. Lost scholars of all political persuasions have been con-

cerned about the upheavals caused by the large-scale transformation of industrial bureaucratic societies and the social disorganization and depravity allegedly let loose by the weakening of traditional communal bonds. Running through many lost analyses has been the implicit assumption that human beings are fundamentally evil (or easily capable of being driven to evil by industrialism, bureaucraticism, or capitalism), and that where restraining communal structures have been destroyed by the Industrial Revolution, riot, robbery, and rape have swept the city.

POLICY IMPLICATIONS

The community lost argument has significantly affected urban policy in North America and Western Europe. There have been extensive "community development" programs designed to end alienation and to grow urban roots, such as the putative War on Poverty. The desired community ideal in such programs has been the regeneration of the densely knit, tightly bounded, solidary neighborhood community. When, despite the programs, a return to the pastoral ideal has not seemed achievable, then despair about social disorganization has led to elaborate social control policies, designed to keep in check the supposedly alienated, irrational, violence-prone masses. When even the achievement of social control has not seemed feasible, policies of neglect—benign or otherwise—have developed. Administrators have removed services from inner-city neighborhoods, asserting their inability to cope with socially disorganized behavior and leaving the remaining inhabitants to fend for themselves.

CURRENT STATUS

The principal scholarly value of the community lost argument has been the attention it has focused on some important theoretical issues. First, it has sharpened perceptions of the ways in which industrial bureaucratic social systems can affect the nature of traditional communities. Second, it has raised the problem of the impact of residential and social mobility on the maintenance of community ties. Because it has seen community as only existing in neighborhoods, the lost argument has interpreted such mobility as a loss of community. However, if community becomes redefined in non-spatial terms, then the lost argument has served as an important precursor of the more recent community liberated argument (see below).

Despite its tenacity, the lost argument has received little empirical confirmation. Indeed, much of the impetus behind the saved and liberated arguments since World War II has been to disprove the loss of community contention (see the reviews in Craven and Wellman, 1973; Feagin, 1973; Hunter, 1975; Fischer, 1976). A modified version of the lost argument has recently emerged, taking into account the extensive documentation of primary ties that has been performed by saved and liberated scholars (see below). This modified lost version acknowledges the persistence of primary ties but contends that they are now markedly narrower in scope: the former wide range of content in kinship, neighborhood, and friendship ties has been reduced to sociability and emotional support, with formal institutions and the nuclear family now taking over much of the former content of such relationships (e.g., Sennett, 1970).

Community Saved

The community saved argument maintains that neighborhood communities have persisted in industrial bureaucratic social systems as important sources of support and sociability. It argues that the very formal, centralizing tendencies of bureaucratic institutions have paradoxically encouraged the maintenance of primary ties as more flexible sources of sociability and support. The saved argument contends that urbanites continue to organize safe communal havens, with neighborhood, kinship, and work solidarities mediating and coping with bureaucratic institutions.

The saved argument shares with the lost argument the identification of "community" with "neighborhood." However, saved scholars have reacted against the tendency of some lost scholars to write secondary analyses *about* the neighborhood community rather than primary analyses *of* neighborhood communities.

In marked contrast to the lost argument scholar's proclivity for armchair theorizing, much of the saved argument's case has rested on the sheer empirical demonstration of the continued vitality of those urban primary ties which had been pronounced lost. Since World War II, hordes of scholars have presented carefully documented community studies, using systematic survey and field-work techniques, to make the saved argument. These studies have concentrated on delineating the social structure of neighborhood communities and have not just presented urbanites as aggregates of unconnected individuals. They have shown that urbanites still neighbor, still have a sense of local community, and still use neighborhood ties for sociability and support (see the reviews in Keller, 1968; Wellman and Whitaker, 1974; Warren and Warren, 1976; Fischer, 1976; Warren, 1978).

SAVED NETWORKS

The saved argument, cast into network analytic terms, is quite different from the lost argument:

1. Urbanites tend to be *heavily involved members* of a *single neighborhood community,* although they may combine this with membership in other social networks.
2. There are *multiple strands* of relationships between the members of these neighborhood communities.
3. While network ties vary in intensity, many of them are *strong.*
4. Neighborhood ties tend to be organized into *extensive networks.*
5. Networks tend to be *densely knit.*
6. Neighborhood networks are *tightly bounded,* with few external linkages. Ties tend to loop back into the same cluster of network members.
7. High density, tight boundaries, and multistranded ties provide a structural basis for a good deal of *solidary activities and sentiments.*
8. The multistranded strong ties clustered in densely knit networks *facilitate* the *mobilization* of assistance for dealing with routine and emergency matters.

IMAGERY

Saved scholars have tended to regard human beings as fundamentally good and inherently gregarious. They are viewed as apt to organize self-regulating communities under all circumstances, even extreme conditions of poverty, oppression, or catastrophe.

Hence the saved argument has shared the neighborhood community ideal with the lost argument, but it has seen this ideal as attainable and often already existing. Neighborhood communities are valued precisely because they can provide small-scale loci of interaction and can effectively mediate urbanites' dealings with large-scale institutions. Densely knit, tightly bounded communities are valued as structures particularly suited to the tenacious conservation of its internal resources, the maintenance of local autonomy, and the social control of members (and intruders) in the face of powerful impinging external forces (e.g., Jacobs, 1961; Newman, 1972).

POLICY IMPLICATIONS

Public acceptance of the saved argument has greatly increased during the past two decades. Active neighborhood communities are now valued as antidotes to industrial bureaucratic societies' alleged impersonality, specialized relationships, and loss of comprehensible scale. "Streetcorner society" (Whyte, 1955), "the urban village" (Gans, 1962), and "Tally's Corner" (Liebow, 1967) have become exemplars of saved communities.

The neighborhood unit has been the twentieth-century planning ideal for new housing. Saved ideologues have also argued the necessity for preserving existing neighborhoods against the predations of ignorant and rapacious institutions. The saved argument has been the ideological foundation of the neighborhood movement which seeks to stop expressways, demolish developers, and renovate old areas (e.g., Powell, 1972). Some neighborhoods have been successfully rescued from "urban renewal," although Gans' West End in Boston (1962) and Clairmont and Magill's Africville in Halifax (1974) have been lost.

Many saved social pathologists have encouraged the nurturance of densely knit, bounded communities as a structural salve for the stresses of poverty, ethnic segregation, and physical and mental diseases (see the review in Caplan and Killilea, 1976; Ratcliffe, 1978). Getting help informally through neighborhood communities is alleged to be more sensitive to peculiar local needs and protective of the individual against bureaucratic claims. Furthermore, such programs have been welcomed by administrators as more cost-effective (or, as some critics allege, merely cheaper to operate) than the formal institutional intervention implied by the lost argument.[2]

CURRENT STATUS

In the early nineteen-sixties the saved argument became the new orthodoxy in community studies with the publication of such works as Gans' *The Urban Villagers* (1962), Greer's (1962) synthesis of postwar survey research, and Jacob's (1961) assertion of the vitality of dense, diverse central cities. Such case studies as Young and Willmott's (1957) study of a working-class London neighborhood, Gans's (1967) account of middle-class, new suburban networks, and Liebow's (1967) portrayal of inner-city blacks' heavy reliance on network ties helped clinch the case.

The rebuttal of the lost argument's assertion of urban social disorganization has therefore been accomplished, theoretically and empirically, by studies emphasizing the persistence of neighborhood communities. In the process, though, the lost argument's useful starting point may have come to be neglected: that the industrial bureaucratic division of labor has strongly affected the structure of primary ties. Saved scholars have tended to look only for—and at—the persistence of functioning neighborhood communities.[3] Consequently we now know that neighborhood communities persist and often flourish, but we do not know the position of neighboorhood-based ties within overall social networks.

Many recent saved analyses have rec-

ognized this difficulty by introducing the "community of limited liability" concept, which treats the neighborhood as just one of a series of communities among which urbanites divide their membership (see Janowitz, 1952; Greer, 1962; Suttles, 1972; Kasarda and Janowitz, 1974; Hunter, 1975; Warren, 1978). Hunter and Suttles (1972, p. 61), for example, portray such communities as a set of concentric zones radiating out from the block to "entire sectors of the city." However, while such analyses recognize the possibilities for urbanites to be members of diverse networks with limited involvement in each network, the "limited liability community" formulation is still predicated on the neighborhood concept, seeing urban ties as radiating out from a local, spatially defined base.

Community Liberated

The third response to the community question, the liberated argument, agrees with the lost argument's contention that the industrial bureaucratic nature of social systems has caused the weakening of neighborhood communities. But the liberated argument also agrees with the saved argument's contention that primary ties have remained viable, useful, and important. It shares the saved argument's contention that communities still flourish in the city, but it maintains that such communities are rarely organized within neighborhoods.

The liberated argument contends that a variety of structural and technological developments have liberated communities from the confines of neighborhoods and dispersed network ties from all-embracing solidary communities to more narrowly based ones: (1) cheap, effective transportation and communication facilities; (2) the separation of workplace and kinship ties into nonlocal, nonsolidary networks; (3) high rates of social and residential mobility (e.g., Crump, 1977).

2. One mental health technique, questionably labeled "network therapy," has as a principal goal the "retribalization" of those with whom the patient is in close contact (see Speck and Attneave, 1973).

3. Perhaps only Banfield (1958) and Vidich and Bensman (1958) have set forth in search of solidary communities and not found them.

The liberated argument, like the other two arguments, begins with the concept of space. Yet where the other arguments see communities as resident in neighborhoods, the liberated argument confronts spatial restrictions only in order to transcend them. Although harkening back to some of the more optimistic writings of Simmel about the liberating effect of urban life (e.g., 1902–1903: last portion; 1908, p. 121) and Park (e.g., 1925b, pp. 65 ff.), the argument has become prominent only in the past two decades following the proliferation of personal automotive and airplane travel and telecommunications in the Western world. It contends that there is now the possibility of "community without propinquity" (Webber, 1964) in which distance and travel time are minimal constraints (e.g., Hiltz and Turoff, 1979).

LIBERATED NETWORKS

With its emphasis on aspatial communities, the liberated argument has been methodologically associated with network analytic techniques (e.g., Kadushin, 1966; Walker, 1977; Wellman, 1979). However, it must be emphasized that network analysis does not necessarily share the liberated argument's ideological bias and can be used to evaluate the existence of *all three* community patterns: lost, saved, and liberated.

In network terms, the liberated argument contends that:

1. Urbanites now tend to be *limited members of several social networks,* possibly including one located in their neighborhood.
2. There is *variation in the breadth of the strands* of relationships between network members; there are multi-stranded ties with some, single-stranded ties with many others, and relationships of intermediate breadth with the rest.

3. The ties range in intensity: *some* of them are *strong,* while others are weak but nonetheless useful.
4. An individual's ties tend to be organized into a *series of networks with few connections* between them.
5. Networks tend to be *sparsely knit* although certain portions of the networks, such as those based on kinship, may be more densely knit.
6. The networks are *loosely bounded, ramifying* structures, branching out extensively to form linkages to additional people and resources.
7. Sparse density, loose boundaries, and narrowly defined ties provide *little structural basis for solidary activities and sentiments* in the overall networks of urbanites, although some solidary clusters of ties are often present.
8. *Some network ties can be mobilized* for general-purpose or specific assistance in dealing with routine or emergency matters.

IMAGERY

The liberated argument is fundamentally optimistic about urban life. It is appreciative of urban diversity; imputations of social disorganization and pathology find little place within it. The argument's view of human behavior emphasizes its entrepreneurial and manipulative aspects. People are seen as having a propensity to form primary ties, not out of inherent good or evil, but in order to accomplish specific, utilitarian ends.

The liberated argument, as does the lost argument, minimizes the importance of neighborhood communities. But where the lost argument sees this as throwing the urbanite upon the resources of formal organizations, the liberated argument contends that sufficient primary ties are available in nonneighborhood networks to provide crucial social support and sociability. Furthermore, it argues that the diverse links between these networks organize the city as a "network of networks" (Craven and Wellman, 1973) to provide a flexible coordinating structure not possible through a lost formal, bureaucratic hierarchy or a saved agglomeration of neighborhoods.

The liberated argument recoils from the lost and saved arguments' village-like community norm. The argument celebrates the structural autonomy of being able to move among various social networks (e.g., Cox, 1966). It perceives solidary communities as fostering stifling social control and of causing isolation from outside contact and resources. Multiple social networks are valued because the cross-cutting commitments and alternative escape routes limit the claims that any one community can make upon its members.

POLICY IMPLICATIONS

Liberated analysts have called for the reinforcement of other social networks in addition to the traditional ones of the neighborhood and the family. Whereas industrial power considerations have worked against the development of solidary networks in the workplace, much attention has been paid recently to fostering "helping networks" that would prevent or heal the stress of physical and mental diseases (e.g., Caplan and Killilea, 1976; Hirsch, 1977; Ratcliffe, 1978). No longer is the neighborhood community seen as the safe, supportive haven; no longer are formal institutions to be relied on for all healing attempts. Instead, networks are to be mobilized, and where they do not exist they can be constructed so that urbanites may find supportive places.

The liberated argument has had an important impact on thinking about political phenomena, especially that related to collective disorders. Research by Tilly (e.g., 1978) and associates, in particular, has shown such collective disorders to be integral parts of broader contentions for

power by competing interest groups. In addition to the internal solidarity emphasized by the saved argument, a contending group's chances for success have been shown to be strongly associated with the capacity for making linkages in external coalitions that crosscutting ties between networks can provide (e.g., Gans, 1974a, 1974b; Granovetter, 1974b).

Recent British New Town planning (e.g., Milton Keynes) has been predicated on the high rates of personal automotive mobility foreseen by the liberated argument. However, the argument's contention that there are minimal costs to spatial separation has come up against the increase in the monetary costs of such separation associated with the significant rise in the price of oil within the last decade. One response has been to advocate increased reliance on telecommunications to maintain community ties over large distances. New developments in computer technology foreshadow major increases in telecommunications capabilities, such as "electronic mail" and "computer conferencing" (see Hiltz and Turoff, 1979). Yet the strength of the liberated argument does not necessarily depend on technological innovations. Recent research in preindustrial social systems has indicated that long-distance ties can be maintained without benefit of telephone or private automobiles, as long as such ties are structurally embedded in kinship systems or common local origins.[4]

The strength of the liberated argument

4. Contemporary studies making the liberated argument have proliferated in the past decade. They have examined the nature of membership in multiple social networks (e.g., Kadushin, 1966; Laumann, 1973; Boissevain, 1974; Breiger, 1976; Bell and Newby, 1976; Shulman, 1976), the use of network ties to obtain needed resources (e.g., Cohen, 1969; Lee, 1969; Granovetter, 1974a; Jacobson, 1975), and the ways in which links between social networks can structure social systems (e.g., Granovetter, 1973; Wireman, 1978; Laumann, Galaskiewicz, and Marsden, 1978).

is that it can account for, and at the same time propose, socially close communities which stretch over large distances. "Community" need no longer necessarily be tied to "neighborhood." However, in propounding the virtues of nonlocal communities the liberated argument may have unduly neglected the usefulness of quick local accessibility and the advantages of the solidary behavior that can come with densely knit, tightly bounded, multistranded ties.

Communities: Lost, Saved, or Liberated?

Are communities lost, saved, or liberated? Too often, the three arguments have been presented as (1) competing alternative depictions of the "true" nature of Western industrial bureaucratic social systems, or (2) evolutionary successors, with preindustrial saved communities giving way to industrial lost, only to be superseded by postindustrial liberated.

In contrast, we believe that all three arguments have validity when stripped of their ideological paraphernalia down to basic network structures. Indeed their structural character might be highlighted by thinking of them as sparse, dense, and ramified network patterns. Different network patterns tend to have different consequences for the acquisition and control of resources (see the discussion of kinship systems in Wolf, 1966). We might then expect to find the prevalence of lost, saved, and liberated communities to vary according to the kinds of societal circumstances in which they are located.

SAVED COMMUNITIES/DENSE NETWORKS

In saved networks, densely knit ties and tight boundaries tend to occur together. This may be because network members have a finite lump of sociability, so that if they devote most of their energies to within-network ties, they do not have much scope for maintaining external linkages. Conversely, tight boundaries may also foster the creation of new ties within the community, as internal links become the individual's principal hope of gaining access to resources.

Such dense, bounded saved networks, be they neighborhood, kinship, or otherwise based, are apt to be solidary in sentiments and activities. They are well-structured for maintaining informal social control over members and intruders. The dense ties and communal solidarity should facilitate the ready mobilization of the community's resources for the aid of members in good standing. But because solidarity does not necessarily mean egalitarianism, not all of the community's resources may be gathered or distributed equally.

Community studies have shown the saved pattern to be quite prevalent in situations in which community members do not have many individual personal resources and where there are unfavorable conditions for forming external ties. Certain ethnic minority and working-class neighborhoods clearly follow this pattern (e.g., Liebow, 1967). In such situations, concerns about conserving, controlling and efficiently pooling those resources the beleaguered community possesses also resonate with its members' inability to acquire additional resources elsewhere. A heavy load consequently is placed on ties within the saved community.

LIBERATED COMMUNITIES/RAMIFIED NETWORKS

If saved network patterns are particularly suited to conditions of resource scarcity and conservation, liberated network patterns are particularly suited to conditions of resource abundance and acquisition. Such sparsely knit, loosely bounded networks are not structurally well-equipped for internal social control. Implicit assurance in the security of one's home base is necessary before one can reach out into new areas.

Loose boundaries and sparse density foster networks that extensively branch out to link up with new members. These ramifying liberated networks are well-structured for acquiring additional resources through a larger number of direct and indirect external connections. Their structure is apt to connect liberated network members with a more diverse array of resources than saved networks are apt to encounter, although the relative lack of solidarity in such liberated networks may well mean that a lower proportion of resources will be available to other network members.

It may well be that the liberated pattern is peculiarly suited to affluent sectors of contemporary Western societies. It places a premium on a base of individual security, entrepreneurial skills in moving between networks, and the ability to function without the security of membership in a solidary community. However, its appearance in other social contexts indicates that it reflects a more fundamental alternative to the saved community pattern.

LOST COMMUNITIES/SPARSE NETWORKS

What of circumstances where no alternative network sources of escape or retreat are possible? It is in such situations that the lost pattern of direct affiliation with formal institutions can become attractive: the army, the church, the firm, and the university (see Shorter, 1975). However, the lost pattern may always be unstable for individuals and communities as formal institutional ties devolve into complex primary network webs. Therefore, as primary ties develop between the within organizations, we may expect to find networks taking on the patterns of saved or liberated communities.

PERSONAL COMMUNITIES

When studying neighborhoods and communities, we are likely to find diversity rather than a universal pattern to either local or personal networks. We have proposed that dense saved network patterns are better suited for internal control of resources while ramified liberated patterns are better suited for obtaining access to external resources. Although we have suggested that each of these patterns should be more prevalent in one sort of a society than another, it is quite likely that the total network of a community will comprise a mixture of these two patterns in varying proportions. That is, some of the ties within a network will be densely knit and tightly bounded, while others will be sparsely knit and ramified. The different patterns are useful for different things.

Our own research in the Borough of East York, Toronto, has revealed that individuals, too, may be simultaneous members of both saved and liberated pattern networks.[5] Some of an urbanite's ties tend to be clustered into densely knit, tightly bounded networks, their solidarity often reinforced by either kinship structures or residential or work-place propinquity. Such saved networks are better able to mobilize help in emergencies through efficient communication and structurally enforced norms. Their density and boundedness tend to give these clusters more of a tangible collective image, so that network members have a sense of solidary attachment.

Yet we have found (Wellman, 1979) that such clusters are likely to comprise only a minority of one's important net-

5. The data were collected in a 1968 random-sample, closed-ended survey of 845 adult East Yorkers, directed by Donald B. Coates, with Barry Wellman as coordinator. East York (1971 population = 104,646) is an upper working-class, lower middle-class, predominantly British-Canadian inner-city suburb of Toronto.

work ties. The other ties tend to be much less densely connected. Instead of looping back into one another within boundaries, they tend to be ramified, branching out to encounter new members to whom the original network members are not directly connected. These sparsely knit, loosely bounded liberated networks are structurally not as efficient in mobilizing collective assistance for their members, but their branching character allows additional resources to be reached. Furthermore, the liberated ties, while not as conducive to internal solidarity as the saved clusters, better facilitate coalition building between networks.

NEIGHBORHOOD AND COMMUNITY

Neighborhood relationships persist but only as specialized components of the overall primary networks. The variety of ties in which an urbanite can be involved —with distant parents, intimate friends, less intimate friends, coworkers, and so on—and the variety of networks in which these are organized can provide flexible structural bases for dealing with routine and emergency matters.

In sum, we must be concerned with neighborhood *and* community rather than neighborhood *or* community. We have suggested that the two are separate concepts which may or may not be closely associated. In some situations we can observe the saved pattern of community as solidary neighborhood. In many other situations, if we go out and look for neighborhood-based networks, we are apt to find them. They can be heavily used for the advantages of quick accessibility. But if we broaden our field of view to include other primary relations, then the apparent neighborhood solidarities may now be seen as clusters in the rather sparse, loosely bounded structure of urbanites' total networks.

References

Banfield, E. (1968) The Unheavenly City. Boston: Little, Brown.

—— (1958) The Moral Basis of a Backward Society. New York: Free Press.

Barnes, J. A. (1972) Social Networks. Reading, MA: Addison-Wesley.

Bell, C. and H. Newby (1976) "Community, communion, class and community action," pp. 189–207 in D. T. Herbert and R. J. Johnston (eds.) Social Areas in Cities II: Spatial Perspectives on Problems and Policies. London: John Wiley.

Belshaw, C. (1965) Traditional Exchange and Modern Markets. Englewood Cliffs, NJ: Prentice-Hall.

Bender, T. (1978) Community and Social Change in America. New Brunswick, NJ: Rutgers Univ. Press.

Boissevain, J. (1974) Friends of Friends. Oxford: Basil Blackwell.

Breiger, R. L. (1976) "Career attributes and network structure: a blockmodel study of a biomedical research specialty." Amer. Soc. Rev. 41 (February): 117–135.

Breton, R. (1964) "Institutional completeness of communities and the personal relations of immigrants." Amer. J. of Sociology 70 (September): 193–205.

Caplan, G. and M. Killilea (1976) Support Systems and Mutual Aid. New York: Grune & Stratton.

Castells, M. (1976) The Urban Question. London: Edward Arnold.

Clairmont, D. and D. Magill (1974) Africville. Toronto: McClelland & Stewart.

Cohen, A. (1969) Custom and Politics in Urban Africa. Berkeley: Univ. of California Press.

Cox, H. (1966) The Secular City. New York: Macmillan.

Craven, P. and B. Wellman (1973) "The network city." Soc. Inquiry 43 (December): 57–88.

Crump, B. (1977) "The portability of urban ties." Paper presented at the Annual Meetings of the American Sociological Association, September, Chicago.

Durkheim, E. (1893, 1933) The Division of Labor in Society. New York: Macmillan.

Engels, F. (1845, 1969) The Condition of the Working Class in England. St. Albans, Herts.: Panther Books.

Feagin, J. R. (1973) "Community disorganization: some critical notes." Soc. Inquiry 43 (December): 123–146.

Fischer, C. S. (1976) The Urban Experience. New York: Harcourt Brace Jovanovich.

Freeman, L. C. (1976) A Bibliography of Social Networks. Monticello, IL: Council of Planning Librarians, Exchange Bibliographies Nos. 1170–1171.

Gans, H. J. (1974a). "Gans on Granovetter's 'Strength of Weak Ties.'" Amer. J. of Sociology 80 (September): 524–527.

——— (1974b) "Gans' response to Granovetter." Amer. J. of Sociology 80 (September): 529–531.

——— (1967) The Levittowners. New York: Pantheon.

——— (1962) The Urban Villagers. New York: Free Press.

Granovetter, M. (1974a) Getting a Job. Cambridge, MA: Harvard Univ. Press.

——— (1974b) "Granovetter replies to Gans." Amer. J. of Sociology 80 (September): 527–529.

——— (1973) "The strength of weak ties." Amer. J. of Sociology 78 (May): 1360–1380.

Grant, G. (1969) "In defence of North America," pp. 15–40 in Technology and Empire. Toronto: Anansi.

Greer, S. (1962) The Emerging City. New York: Free Press.

Gusfield, J. R. (1975) Community: A Critical Response. New York: Harper & Row.

Hillery, G. A., Jr. (1955) "Definitions of community: areas of agreement." Rural Sociology 20 (June): 111–123.

Hiltz, R. S. and M. Turoff (1979) The Network Nation: Human Communication via Computer. Reading, MA: Addison-Wesley.

Hirsch, B. (1977) "The social network as a natural support system." Paper read at the Annual Meetings of the American Psychological Association, August, San Francisco.

Howard, L. (1974) "Industrialization and community in Chotanagpur." Ph.D. dissertation. Cambridge, MA: Harvard Univ.

Hunter, A. (1975) "The loss of community: an empirical test through replication." Amer. Soc. Rev. 40 (October): 537–552.

——— and G. Suttles (1972) "The expanding community of limited liability," pp. 44–81 in G. Suttles (ed.) The Social Construction of Communities. Chicago: Univ. of Chicago Press.

Jacobs, J. (1961) The Death and Life of Great American Cities. New York: Random House.

Jacobson, D. (1975) "Fair-weather friend: label and context in middle-class friendships." J. of Anthropological Research 31 (Autumn): 225–234.

Janowitz, M. (1952) The Community Press in an Urban Setting. New York: Free Press.

Kadushin, C. (1966) "The friends and supporters of psychotherapy: on social circles in urban life." Amer. Soc. Rev. 31 (December): 786–802.

Kasarda, J. D. and M. Janowitz (1974) "Community attachment in mass society." Amer. Soc. Rev. 39 (June): 328–339.

Keller, S. (1968) The Urban Neighborhood. New York: Random House.

Laslett, P. (1971) The World We Have Lost. London: Methuen.

Laumann, E. O. (1973) Bonds of Pluralism. New York: John Wiley.

———, J. Galaskiewicz, and P. Marsden (1978) "Community structures as interorganizational linkages." Annual Rev. of Sociology.

Lee, N. H. (1969) The Search for an Abortionist. Chicago: Univ. of Chicago Press.

Liebow, E. (1967) Tally's Corner. Boston: Little, Brown.

Marx, L. (1964) The Machine in the Garden. New York: Oxford Univ. Press.

Mellor, J. R. (1977) Urban Sociology in an Urbanized Society. London: Routledge & Kegan Paul.

Newman, O. (1972) Defensible Space. New York: Macmillan.

Nisbet, R. (1962) Community and Power. New York: Oxford Univ. Press.

Park, R. E. (1936) "Human ecology." Amer. J. of Sociology 42 (July): 1–15.

——— (1925a) "The city: suggestions for the investigation of human behavior in the urban environment," pp. 1–46 in R. E. Park, E. W. Burgess, and R. D. McKenzie (eds.) The City. Chicago: Univ. of Chicago Press.

——— (1925b) "The urban community as a spatial pattern and a moral order," pp. 55–68 in R. H. Turner (ed.) Robert E. Park on Social Control and Collective Behavior. Chicago: Univ. of Chicago Press.

Popenoe, D. (1977) The Suburban Environment. Chicago: Univ. of Chicago Press.

Powell, A. [ed.] (1972) The City: Attacking Modern Myths. Toronto: McClelland & Stewart.

Ratcliffe, W. (1978) "Social networks and health." Connections 1 (Summer): 25–37.

Ross, M. H. and T. S. Weisner (1977) "The rural-urban migrant network in Kenya." Amer. Ethnologist 4 (May): 359–375.

Scott, J. and L. Tilly (1975) "Women's work and the family in nineteenth century Europe." Comparative Studies in Society and History 17 (January): 36–64.

Sennett, R. (1970) Families Against the City. Cambridge, MA: Harvard Univ. Press.

Shorter, E. (1975) The Making of the Modern Family. New York: Basic Books.

Shulman, N. (1976) "Network analysis: a new addition to an old bag of tricks." Acta Sociologica 19 (March): 307–323.

——— (1972) "Urban social networks." Unpublished Ph.D. dissertation, Department of Sociology, Univ. of Toronto.

Simmel, G. (1908, 1971) "Group expansion and the development of individuality," pp. 251–293 in D. N. Levine (ed.) Georg Simmel: On Individuality and Social Forms. Chicago: Univ. of Chicago Press.

——— (1902–1903, 1950) "The metropolis and mental life," pp. 409–424 in K. Wolff (ed.) The Sociology of Georg Simmel. Glencoe, IL: Free Press.

Slater, P. E. (1970) The Pursuit of Loneliness. Boston: Beacon.

Speck, R. V. and C. Attneave (1973) Family Networks. New York: Pantheon.

Stein, N. (1960) The Eclipse of Community. Princeton, NJ: Princeton Univ. Press.

Suttles, G. D. (1972) The Social Construction of Communities. Chicago: Univ. of Chicago Press.

Tilly, C. (1978) From Mobilization to Revolution. Reading, MA: Addison-Wesley.

——— (1974) "Introduction," pp. 1–35 in C. Tilly (ed.) An Urban World. Boston: Little, Brown.

——— (1973) "Do communities act?" Soc. Inquiry 43 (December): 209–240.

Tönnies, F. (1887, 1955) Community and Association. London: Routledge & Kegan Paul.

Vidich, A. J. and J. Bensman (1958) Small Town in Mass Society. Princeton, NJ: Princeton Univ. Press.

Walker, G. (1977) "Social networks and territory in a commuter village, Bond Head, Ontario." Canadian Geographer 21 (Winter): 329–350.

Warren, D. I. and R. B. Warren (1976) "The helping role of neighbors: some empirical findings." Unpublished paper, Department of Sociology, Oakland Univ. December.

Warren, R. (1978) The Community in America. Chicago: Rand McNally.

Webber, M. (1964) "The urban place and the nonplace urban realm," in M. Webber et al. (eds.) Exploration into Urban Structure. Philadelphia: Univ. of Pennsylvania Press.

——— (1963) "Order in diversity: community without propinquity," pp. 23–54 in L. Wingo, Jr. (ed.) Cities and Space: The Future Use of Urban Land. Baltimore: Johns Hopkins.

Wellman, B. (1981) "Network analysis: from method and metaphor to theory and substance." Sociological Theory 1 (forthcoming).

——— (1979) "The community question." Amer. J. of Sociology (March):1201–31.

Wellman, B. and M. Whitaker (1974) Community–Network–Communication: An Annotated Bibliography. Toronto: Centre for Urban and Community Studies, Bibliographic Paper No. 4, Univ. of Toronto.

Whyte, W. F. (1955) Street Corner Society. Chicago: Univ. of Chicago Press.

Wireman, P. (1978) "Intimate secondary relations." Paper presented at the Ninth World Congress of Sociology, August, Uppsala, Sweden.

Wirth, L. (1938) "Urbanism as a way of life." Amer. J. of Sociology 44 (July): 3–24.

Wolf, E. R. (1966) "Kinship, friendship, and patron-client relations in complex societies," pp. 1–22 in M. Banton (ed.) The Social Anthropology of Complex Societies. London: Tavistock.

Woodsworth, J. S. (1911, 1972) My Neighbour. Toronto: Univ. of Toronto Press.

Young, M. and P. Willmott (1957) Family and Kinship in East London. London: Routledge & Kegan Paul.

PETER J. TAYLOR AND DONALD N. PARKES

A Kantian View of the City: A Factorial-Ecology Experiment in Space and Time

Introduction. "Absolute" Space and Time

David Harvey (1969) has characterised the treatment of space by geographers as being either "relative" or "absolute" in approach. In the relative approach to space, the researcher is interested in the uses made of the space by people engaged in some specified activity. The approach employing "absolute space," on the other hand, views space simply as an abstract frame of reference within which objects occur and events take place. These approaches towards space can be readily transferred to the treatment of time in social research. Thus several researchers have been interested in the uses made of time by different groups of people (Chapin and Hammer, 1972; Szalai, 1972) and in how time affects their activities. In contrast, the research approach developed by Hägerstrand (1970, 1974) and Carlstein (1974) treats time as an "absolute" property of the system through which individuals pass.[1] Hägerstrand's

[1]. The origin of this study is a direct result of this contrast in approaches, and follows from the first author's comments on the "relative" time research presented in Parkes (1974).

space-time prisms represent an integrated treatment of both time and space as the joint "containers" of activities. This absolute approach to space and time is usually traced back to Emmanual Kant's *Doctrine of Transcendental Idealism*[2] (as given in Popper, 1963) in which time and space are treated as the basic underlying framework of the universe. Popper neatly summarises Kant's doctrine as follows:

. . . space and time themselves are neither things nor events: they cannot even be observed: they are more elusive. They are a kind of framework for things and events: something like a system of pigeon-holes, or a filing system, for observations. Space and time are not part of the real empirical world of things and events, but rather part of our mental outfit, our apparatus for grasping this world. Their proper use is as instruments cf observation . . . (Popper, 1963, p. 179).

Harvey (1969) has been critical of Kant's influence on geographical methodology and argues strongly for a relative ap-

[2]. The doctrine is "transcendental" in the sense that Kant argued that time and space cannot be empirically observed—they are beyond our perceptions—and only objects and events can be observed "within them."

From **Environment and Planning A**, Vol. 7, 1975, pp. 671–88. Reprinted by permission of Pion Limited, London, P. J. Taylor, and D. N. Parkes.

proach to space (and by implication, to time also). At the practical level of research it seems to us that either approach may be employed depending on the purpose of the investigation. Thus the "container" view of time and space would certainly seem to be the most obvious way of treating these concepts in any preliminary descriptive investigations. This is our justification for applying an absolute approach to time and space in this paper. In fact we explicitly follow Kant's instructions, as stated by Popper above, and use space and time as our "instruments of observation." We apply these instruments in the context of urban factorial ecology and this constitutes our Kantian view of the city.

The City in Space and Time

The city that has been described in the factorial-ecology literature is essentially static. The major source of data has been the various national population censuses, which tell us about the characteristics of the inhabitants of the city as they appear in the middle of the night. However, every workday morning people commute from their homes to other parts of the city to carry out their daytime activities.[3] Thus conventional factorial ecologies only tell us about one aspect of the city's social geography. In this study we wish to illustrate the changing social geography through the day by using the same basic procedure. Since "real" data are not available we do this experimentally by

3. It is of interest to note that daytime activities have tended to be studied by economic geographers as, for instance, in their analyses of commercial and industrial land-use patterns. There is, thus, almost a strange time-based distinction in subject matter between economic and social geography. However, there are, of course, some demographic studies concerning urban-population patterns "around the clock," but these have not attempted to be more comprehensive in terms of social attributes (see Breese, 1949; Chapin and Stewart, 1963; Foley, 1954; Schmitt, 1956).

using artificial data. In the next section we shall describe the generation of this experimental data and this is followed by a description of the results obtained by applying the common-factor-analysis model to the data. We conclude with a brief discussion of the procedure and the specific implications of this type of space–time study.

The Experimental Data

In essence, we attempt to construct a factorial ecology of a typical working day, in summer, in a medium-sized British city. One reason why social geographers have concentrated on nighttime patterns has been the ready availability of data from census sources. There is no other equivalent systematic enumeration of people at any time during the day. Where researchers have wanted to consider the activities and locations of people during the day, they have had to resort to collecting their own data. The result has been the publication of a number of specific space- and specific time-budget surveys (Chapin and Hammer, 1972; Szalai, 1972). These studies form a useful source of background information to the present study without explicitly furnishing our data needs. For this preliminary study the strategy adopted is the establishment of a hypothetical city as an experimental "laboratory,"[4] within which we design both the base units and the variables. The resulting data matrix is the input of our subsequent "space–time factorial ecology."

We begin by defining our base units— the individuals of our subsequent analysis. This involves integrating a taxonomy

4. Although our hypothetical city is "British" in character, much of the basic data used to make it reasonably realistic has been American in origin, for example, the American time surveys in Szalai (1972), and the land-use patterns described in Browning (1964), and Niedercorn and Hearle (1964).

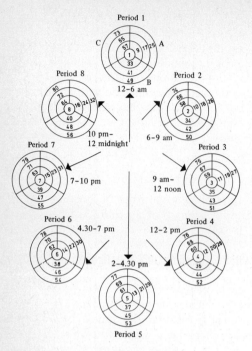

Figure 1. The Space–Time Units

periods, each reflecting predominant *activity bundles*.[5] These periods are set out in Table 1.

Our space–time units now consist of districts of the city at specific periods of time. Since everyone of the ten districts is operating through each of the eight periods, we have eighty space–time units in all. These are all illustrated in Figure 1 and numbered 1–80. The central zone constitutes the first 8 space–time units as it progresses through the day. The final space–time unit, number 80, is the outerzone in sector C, between 10 pm and midnight. We have argued that factorialecology studies have only dealt with nighttime locations and these constitute just one-eighth of our data units. The conventional factorial ecology would belong in space–time units 1, 9, 17, 25, 33, 41, 49, 57, 65, and 73, as shown in period 1, Figure 1.

Having produced the space–time units of our hypothetical city, we face the much more difficult task of generating variables over these units. This involves two problems. First, there is the problem of what variables to include, and second, there is the difficulty of allocating values to the variables in space–time. We shall consider each in turn.

Several criteria were involved in choosing the variables to describe our hypothetical city. First of all we wanted to maintain the comparison with the conventional factorial-ecology approach, and so we chose a high proportion of variables that have already appeared in factorial studies; for instance, employed females, age-related data, marital status, etc. Exact parallels were not always possible nor indeed does the factorial-ecology approach always use the most diagnostic variables, hence a number of the variables

of the city's social geographic space with a taxonomy of diurnal "social" time. This really involves deciding on a crude classification of sequence. The taxonomy of space is derived directly from schematic representations of the findings of factorial ecology (Murdie, 1969). As Figure 1 shows, the city is divided into ten "districts": a central zone, not to be confused with the functional centre of the city (the CBD which is strictly defined) and nine other districts. These are defined by the interaction of the three sectors, A, B, and C, with three concentric rings. Following the findings of many factorial-ecology studies, we specify variations in terms of "economic status" to the sectors, and variations in terms of "family status" to the rings or zones. Thus we have upperclass (A), middle-class (B), and lowerclass (C) sectors, and increasing "familism" or suburbanism away from the central district. Time is divided up into eight

---

5. Distinctions between obligatory activity time and discretionary activity time have not been made here. They do form an important part of the time-budget literature, especially in Chapin's work.

Table 1. Daily Activity Periods

Period	Duration	Activity Bundle
1	12 midnight to 6 am	Sleep
2	6 am to 9 am	The transfer to worktime
3	9 am to 12 noon	Morning phase of worktime
4	12 noon to 2 pm	Lunchtime
5	2 pm to 4:30 pm	Afternoon phase of worktime
6	4:30 pm to 7 pm	The transfer to residential-time
7	7 pm to 10 pm	Early evening discretionary-time
8	10 pm to 12 midnight	Late evening and bedtime

employed are unique to this study. Secondly, of course, we must not forget that the objective of the present study is to "see what happens" when we take the factorial approach beyond a purely residential framework. Therefore we need some additional variables not normally associated with factorial-ecology studies. The result is a compromise between familiar nighttime social-geographic variables and "daytime"-oriented variables. Thus, social-status and demographic-structure variables have been included along with land-use and transport variables. We have "produced" 22 variables: 6 are land-use variables, 9 are fairly typical demographic variables, 4 are social-status variables, and 3 are transport-movement variables. Each variable is allocated eighty values corresponding to each of the eighty space–time units, and we shall now consider each of these variables in turn.

1. *Residential land use.* Since we are operating in a space–time context the emphasis in all the land-use categories is on the term "use." Thus we do not consider an empty house, say in the afternoon, as constituting residential land use. The values which we have allocated to the space–time units represent percentages of the total land area of the district which is being used for residential purposes in a particular time period.

2. *Retail and commercial-service land use.* This includes shops, banks, and other "high-street" land use.

3. *Other commercial land use.* All those other office functions not included in variable (2), because they are primarily administrative rather than servicing the public directly.

4. *Industrial land use.* This includes factories, warehouses, transport depots, and other industrially-oriented land use.

5. *Entertainment land use.* This includes all cinemas, clubs, public houses, theatres, and other forms of indoor-entertainment facilities.

6. *Open-space land use.* Typically parks, sports fields, and golf courses would make up this category.

7. *Population.* This is a simple enumeration of population.

8. *Persons per dwelling.* The average number of people in each occupied dwelling.

9. *Male adults.* The percentage of male adults in the population.

10. *Age 0–4 years.* The number of children under 5 as a percentage of the population.

11. *Age 5–17 years.* The children aged between 5 and 17 as a percentage of total population. It is assumed that the children all go to local schools and so do not leave their district during the day.

12. *Age 18–29 years.* The young adults,

many of whom are unmarried or are married and childless, as a percentage of the total population.

13. *Age over 65 years.* Old people as a percentage of the total population.[6]

14. *Married adults.* The percentage of adults who are married.

15. *Employed females.* The percentage of the adult females who are gainfully employed.

16. *Upper class.* The percentage of the population of this class for the city as a whole was set at 15%. They were largely allocated to sector A at nighttime, although they become somewhat dispersed during the day.

17. *Lower class.* These represented 60% of the population of the city as a whole and were largely allocated to their nighttime sector, C.[7]

18. *Professional (personal) services.* Personal services include legal and medical services in particular. The variable has been defined as the number of "professional-service units" operating in a space–time unit. Since medical services are available throughout the night this attribute is reflected in the values assigned to the variable.

19. *Manual and other personal services.* These services are also often available through the night, for instance gas and electricity services, various emergency services such as firefighting, and highly mobile services such

as taxis. Many of these services have the distinctive attribute of being at their peak intensity in the early morning period: deliveries of milk, mail, newspapers, etc. The variable has been defined as the number of "manual-service units" available in the space–time units.

20. *Private transport.* This variable measures the number of people actually travelling in private transport in each space–time unit.

21. *Public transport.* This variable measures the number of people actually travelling in public transport in each space–time unit.

22. *Access.* This is an index of the degree of access which households have to vital services in the city. Thus, if a medical emergency occurs during the middle of the night, those parts of the city where cars and telephones are more numerous have better access to qualified help. The highest accessibility scores occur in the central district, where the population is physically near to the major services in the city.

We thus have a description of our city in terms of an 80 × 22 matrix of space–time data.*

A Factorial Ecology in Space and Time

Factorial ecology comprises the application of factor analysis to data describing the residential differentiation of the population, generally the urban population (Timms, 1971, pp. 53–54).

Obviously this is so because factor analysis has been applied almost exclusively to the residential population, but there is absolutely no acceptable conceptual reason for this restriction even if we trace

6. In producing these four "age" variables a further variable, "percentage aged 30–64 years," was in fact developed so that percentages added up to 100 in every space–time unit. However, this variable was omitted from the analysis since its information content is contained in the four age variables listed here.

7. These class variables were augmented in the initial data production by a "middle class" variable containing 25% of the total population. As in the case of the age variables, this extra variable involved the class percentages adding up to 100 in each space–time unit, and only the two variables listed were in fact used in our analyses.

* This matrix is reproduced in full in the original paper (Ed. note).

factorial studies back to the origins of social area analysis.

In this experiment we have used the common-factor model (Rummel, 1970), with communalities estimated by iteration, and the varimax criteria employed to obtain a rotated simple structure. The output which we shall present consists of the loadings on the rotated factors, and the estimated-factor scores for the space–time units. Unlike conventional factor ecological studies, interpretation of the rotated factors was not based solely on the structure of the loadings. Factor scores were mapped for each of the 80 space–time units, and this spatio-temporal schema provided essential information for the labelling of factors.

The basic starting point in any factor-analysis interpretation is the matrix of loadings for the rotated factors and these are shown in Table 2. As can be seen, seven factors have been extracted and rotated. The initial choice of rotating just the first seven factors, is, of course, a subjective one. Although the convention of accepting only factors which add at least 5% to the explained variance, and which also have an eigenvalue 1.0, is a useful rule of thumb, we felt that factors 6 and 7 were sufficiently "informative" to warrant their being kept in the rotation. There is also a marked drop in the size of the eigenvalues between factors 7 and 8, from 0.63 to 0.28, and this provided a further reason for using the first seven

Table 2. Varimax Rotated Factor Matrix

	Factors						
Variables	1	2	3	4	5	6	7
1. Residential	−0.41	0.24	−0.42	0.42	−0.35	−0.32	0.39
2. Retail and service	**0.84**	0.10	0.03	−0.15	−0.13	0.23	−0.16
3. Other commercial	**0.96**	0.11	0.36	−0.06	0.05	0.09	−0.04
4. Industrial	0.06	−0.33	−0.11	−0.06	0.24	0.24	**−0.85**
5. Entertainment	0.13	−0.00	**0.83**	−0.08	0.07	0.00	0.03
6. Open space	0.14	0.38	−0.01	0.10	**−0.68**	−0.11	−0.07
7. Population	**0.78**	0.05	0.23	0.15	0.31	0.37	0.12
8. Persons/dwelling	−0.43	−0.13	−0.37	**0.57**	−0.16	−0.34	0.35
9. Male adults	0.12	−0.07	0.14	−0.02	**0.89**	−0.08	−0.22
10. Age 0–4	−0.22	−0.22	−0.47	0.28	**−0.68**	−0.23	0.15
11. Age 5–17	−0.33	−0.08	−0.44	0.37	**−0.65**	−0.27	0.17
12. Age 18–29	0.32	−0.02	**0.82**	0.25	0.30	0.21	0.06
13. Age over 65	−0.07	0.24	−0.19	**−0.92**	0.10	0.04	−0.04
14. Married adults	0.08	0.00	**−0.60**	**0.72**	−0.25	−0.12	−0.06
15. Employed females	**0.85**	0.05	0.18	0.01	0.19	0.25	−0.32
16. Upper class	0.12	**0.92**	0.00	−0.09	−0.05	−0.03	0.15
17. Lower class	0.01	**−0.88**	0.10	0.07	0.13	0.04	−0.09
18. Professional services	**0.92**	0.08	0.24	0.05	0.14	0.20	0.12
19. Manual services	0.45	−0.11	0.34	−0.15	−0.11	**0.65**	−0.18
20. Private transport	0.37	0.22	0.12	−0.20	0.11	**0.82**	0.06
21. Public transport	0.27	−0.15	−0.02	0.01	0.15	**0.83**	−0.34
22. Access	0.39	**0.68**	0.37	−0.33	0.04	0.32	0.02
Eigenvalues	9.05	3.42	2.82	1.90	1.23	0.93	0.63
Cumulative percentage of total variance	41.1	56.7	69.5	78.1	83.7	88.0	90.8

Loadings greater than ±0.5 are shown in bold type

factors which, in fact, accounted for 91% of the total variance.

Considering the rotated factor matrix initially in general terms, two or three points might be mentioned. First of all, variable (1), the *percentage of residential land use,* loads reasonably highly on all the 7 dimensions. This is to be expected since the city is, above all, a residential system as far as land use is concerned. One other variable has a similar sort of pattern to variable (1) and this is (19), manual services; the reasons for this will be outlined below. Second, every attribute loads reasonably highly on at least one dimension and there is a healthy distribution of near-zero values on each factor.

Factor 1 is a white-collar workday cycle dimension and accounts for 41% of the total variance, thus emphasising the importance of tertiary and quaternary activity in the city. Other commercial (0.96), professional (personal) services (0.92), retailing with "high street" commerce (0.84), and percentage of females employed (0.85) are the most important variables. However, population size (0.78), in space–time units remember, is also critical because it summarises the shifting population mass of the city during the day. With such a high proportion of the variance accounted for, labelling is difficult, but the factor score space–time scheme simplifies the issue somewhat (Figure 2). Other variables which contribute at ±0.4 are manual or other services (0.5), percentage residential (−0.4), persons per dwelling (−0.4), access (0.4) and private transport (0.4). Clearly all of these, apart from manual services perhaps, are readily associated with a workday cycle. It is because the manual or other services are primarily concerned with the servicing of residential areas, that we find they have a fairly even spread over a number of dimensions. They form a general urban–suburban space–time variable. However, they tend to be somewhat out of phase with many of the activities, which are nonresidential, in the rest of the city. The number of residential service activities which occur early in the morning is responsible, to a considerable degree, for the relative lack of synchronisation that there appears to be. In fact, of course, these activities are finely timed to the needs of the residential area.

The factor scores have been mapped in Figure 2. Conventional factorial ecologies would be accommodated in the uppermost time period 1, and only in that time period. What is the general pattern of this factor in space–time? Most obviously there is a clear dichotomy in the urban structure between residential space–time (periods 6–2) and employment space–time (periods 3–5), with some break across the lunch period (12–2 pm). In the central-area it is the working-day, space–time units which dominate the pattern with their large positive scores.

Factor 2 identifies class segregation in space–time and accounts for a further 15.5% of the variance. Two variables dominate and make interpretation quite straightforward. The spaces and times of the city are continuously being structured and restructured according to attributes of social status: social status is not simply a nighttime phenomenon. Upper class (0.92) and lower class (−0.88), readily identified as spatially segregated by conventional factorial ecologies, remain as important structuring attributes throughout the day, but as will be seen from Figure 3, there is some degree of mixing and a dilution of class segregation during the working day.[8] This is self-evident in workplaces and in retail areas, for instance. The association of the *access* variable with the two "status" variables is en-

8. This does not, of course, imply intimate social contact but merely that, on the scale of analysis attempted here, social classes tend to be less physically isolated from one another during the day.

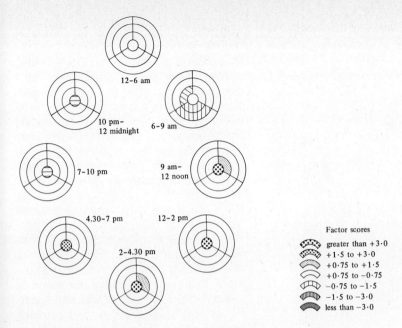

Figure 2. Factor 1: The White-Collar Workday Cycle

tirely acceptable and indicates a "welfare" component in the dynamic ecology of the city. Loading 0.68, it is positively associated with space sector A and, although it loads above 0.3 on four of the other six rotated factors, it is most informative (given our present level of understanding) on the second dimension, where it helps to emphasise the segregation of sectors A and C at nighttime and also points to the relative "de-urbanization" of sector C during the nighttime period. This results from lack of linkage with the services of the urban system, such as hospitals, fire brigades, police, doctors, taxi-services, etc. Discrimination of social space in terms of "access" has been discussed elsewhere (Parkes, 1974).

Because the social-status variables, upper and lower class, dominate the dimension we find the conventional economic-status dimension of factorial ecologies at period 1, shown in Figure 3. This pattern is, in fact, held from 7 pm to 6 am and

fits in with the primary function of residential space, which is to satisfy obligatory time demands related to biological rhythms (sleep and eat). The dilution of status differentials is most marked in periods 3 to 5 (9 am to 4.30 pm). Only in the outermost suburban spaces is segregation fully maintained in space–time. In the late-afternoon phase of the daily cycle we note a strengthening of the segregation, and by 9 pm (period 6) this is almost complete again. The central zone remains undifferentiated throughout the day. At night, however, lower-order service factors maintain the city core, and there is some shift in the status of this area towards a sector C type.

Factor 3 is the "bright lights" dimension. It is often hard to find an illustrative and descriptive title for a factor, and this one is no exception. It accounts for 13% of variance and variable (5), *entertainment land use,* has the highest loading (0.83). The positive relationship

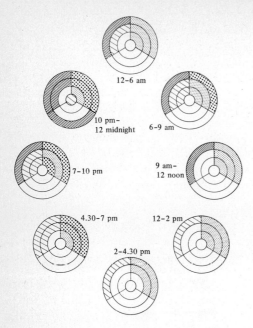

Figure 3. Factor 2: Class Segregation (Key as for Figure 2)

the urban area. In general, the conventional factorial-ecology dimension of "family status" relates inversely to the bright-lights dimension in a space–time ecology of the city. In the 12 noon to 2 pm phase of the daily cycle, however, many of the activities which are used more intensively in the evening period are "operational," though at a lower level of intensity, and this is shown by a positive score for the core area. A simple day–night dichotomy would be an oversimplification, but a marked structural difference is certainly suggested between "daytime" and "nighttime."

Factor 4 is an old-age dependency dimension and it accounts for 8.5% of the variance. In the space–time ecology of the city it identifies a distinctive dimension in urban social structure, as well as indicating an area of need for welfare-oriented studies and policy formulation. Many planning strategies have been too concerned with the "where" of old age rather

with variable (12), *age group 18–29,* brings together two attributes of the ecology of the city which are patently a characteristic of urbanism. Their inverse relationship with variables (10), (11), and (14), emphasises the nonfamilistic associations of the dimension. Conventional factorial ecologies do not isolate this sort of relationship at all. *Access* is again a part of the dimension and relates positively to entertainment and the 18–29 age group. Maximum use of entertainment facilities in space–time is associated with private transport, variable (20), rather than with public transport, variable (21), and this is just as expected.

By early evening, 7 pm (period 6) the central area is clearly exerting its greatest influence on urban space–time for "passive" recreation activity (Figure 4). Right through into the early morning phase, people in age group 18–29 are "packed" into the central zone in disproportionate numbers to their overall distribution in

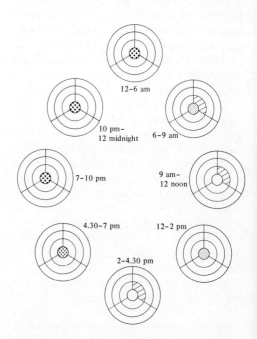

Figure 4. Factor 3: "Bright Lights" (Key as for Figure 2)

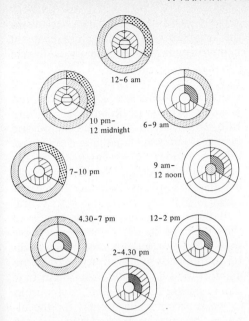

Figure 5. Factor 4: Old-Age Dependency (Key as for Figure 2)

than the "when." A retiming of space is likely to be more to the point rather than the more simplistic relocation in space, which must involve retiming of individual activity systems.[9] Variable (13), *people over the age of 65* (−0.92), establishes the nature of the dimension, and the inverse relationship—with *percentage married* (0.72), *persons per dwelling* (0.57), and *age group 5–17* (0.37)—emphasises spatio–temporal segregation of the old from the "family-based" and "young" space–time units. This segregation is less extreme at nighttime, however, unlike the situation for class segregation (Figure 5), though, it should be noted, of course, that segregation in these terms need not necessarily relate to social contact. Thus the old-age dependency zones of the city are isolated much more efficiently when a

9. For a development of this theme see Parkes and Thrift (1975), and for a range of perspectives on the space–time approach see Carlstein *et al.* (1978).

space–time structure is used than when conventional analyses are undertaken, because it is during the daytime that most younger adults are at work. In fact, during period 1 the negative factor scores which locate the old-age concentrations are particularly weak. By periods 2 to 6, however, the map is quite different, and major relative concentrations of old people occur especially in the inner zone of sector A. However, the important thing is the spatial variation in factor domination over a temporal cycle; in this case, the day.

Factor 5 is a breadwinner–young dependants dimension and is conceptually closely related to factor 4. Although it only accounts for 5.5% of the total variance it is an important factor to have isolated. The highest loading variable is the proportion of *male adults* (0.89), and it is in negative association with variables (10) and (11), *age group 0–4* (−0.68) and *age-group 5–17* (−0.65). The *open space* variable lends further weight to the coherence of the dimension (−0.68). During the day the suburbs are "female" and "young," the inner city "male" and "older." The factor scores in space–time clearly show this structural variability (Figure 6). During the workday phase a suburban high-family-status environment is dominant in all outer zones from periods 3 to 5. Only in the transition zone of sector C and the central area is the male adult population dominant at these times. This is a function of the location of employment, especially the industrial, transportation, and warehousing activities which are concentrated in the transition zone.

Factor 6 is a journey-to-work factor. This dimension is conspicuous by its absence from traditional factorial ecologies. Though only 4.2% of total variance is explained, it is an important space–time dimension, absolutely dominating one phase of the daily cycle. In the experiment the morning "rush hour" com-

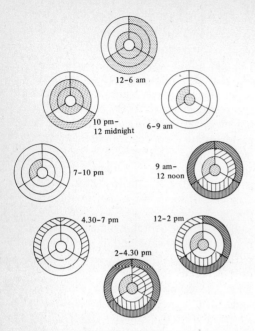

Figure 6. Factor 5: Breadwinner-Young Dependency (Key as for Figure 2)

singularly geographical characteristic in the complex web of the city's ecology. From this analysis the primary *ecological characteristic* of journey to work, in the space–time scheme, is its intensity. The temporal elements are tightly packed into a single period. It becomes an "event" with strong but finely limited boundaries in space–time over a daily cycle. On one side is residential space–time, on the other side the work space–time, and journey to work splices itself into this structure.

Between 6 am and 9 am the change in the rhythm of the city is unparalleled, see Figure 7. In period 1 there are no structural differentials at all in terms of movement-to-work locations. From 6 am to 9 am, in period 2, "all is flux," and journey to work becomes the process for the dilution or further concentration of the other dimensions which we have identified in the city's ecology. During the

pletely dominates its late-afternoon–early-evening complement. This is due to two basic reasons: (1) the return journeys are spread over two periods (4 and 5); (2) this particular factor incorporates an extra element beyond the simple journey to work. This is the early morning non-professional service provision which operates concurrently with the morning rush hour in period 2, and is thus represented in this particular factor.

The highest loading variables are (20) and (21), *private transport* (0.82) and *public transport* (0.83), and they are supported by variable 19, *manual and other services* (0.65). As will be seen from Table 2 there are four variables on this dimension with loadings around ±0.3, and apart from *access* they relate to residential characteristics, including *population size*. Obviously, "journey to work" drains some areas of the city and fills others at specific times. This is its

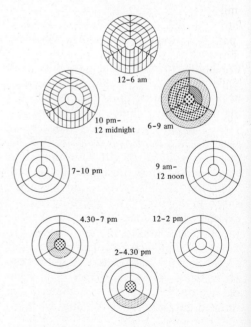

Figure 7. Factor 6: Journey-to-Work (Key as for Figure 2)

hours of the normal working day, say "9 to 5," the cadence of all residential sub-areas is more or less the same,[10] and a less intense "flux" is identified in periods 5 and 6. From 7 pm through to midnight (periods 7 to 1) there is a gradual slowing down of the movement system. By midnight this is over (that is, the movement shifts) and all residential areas achieve a similar status—they are asleep!

Factor 7 complements factor 1; it is the blue-collar workday cycle, and is the last of the factors which we considered. It accounts for only 2.1% of the variance but has one high-loading variable which has not loaded above 0.33 on any other dimension; this is *industrial land use* (−0.85). Recall that by "land use" we mean just that—in *time* as well as in *space*. The second variable on this factor is *residential land use* and this relates inversely (0.39), meaning that when industrial activities are *on*, residential activities tend to be *off*, by space–time units. *Public transport* (−0.34) correlates positively with industrial activity space–time, whereas there is no relationship with private transportation (0.06). For the white-collar workday cycle, it will be recalled that *private transport* (0.37) and *public transport* (0.27) were associated.

Sector C is the only one which experiences any sort of structural change in this dimension, apart from the innermost zone of sectors A and B, see Figure 8. These sectors have an input of blue-collar workers and female service labour.

10. Specifically in terms of these experimental data. Elsewhere it has been argued that urban residential space is marked by variety in activity cadence (Parkes, 1973, 1974). To have identified this aspect of the city's ecology by means of an analysis such as this one would obviously have required additional activity variables. This can be achieved when we know more about activity structure and sequence (see Chapin and Hammer, 1972; Stone, 1972; Cullen and Godson, 1972).

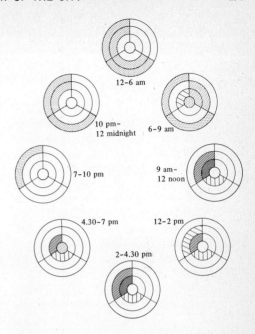

Figure 8. Factor 7: Blue-Collar Workday Cycle (Key as for Figure 2)

During the day the space–time pattern complements that generated for sector A in factor 1, the white-collar cycle, and this is as we should expect.

Thus the varimax-factor solution from our original artificial-data matrix has produced an interesting set of dimensions for characterising the city in space and time. We have been able to isolate seven factors which are both interpretable in terms of the input variables and, more important, in terms of our *a priori* knowledge of how the city works and operates over a typical twenty-four-hour cycle. However, one word of caution should be offered at this stage. The varimax solution produces orthogonal factors, and we have no real justification for assuming that the underlying dimensions in the complex ecology of the city, in time and space, are in fact independent of one another. In order to meet this point an oblique-rotation procedure (Oblimin) was employed on the data, and this gave essentially the same seven factors produced by using the varimax criteria.

Discussion

Let us begin with the obvious problems relating to the use of artificially-created data. This is not, of course, unknown in other areas of research; for example, in plant ecology where Greig-Smith (1952) conducted his classical scale experiments on artificial plant communities. Hägerstrand (1968) in his modelling of the diffusion of innovations has also employed artificial conditions which are part of his experimental trials. The important feature of these examples and our own study is that the results are not meant to be substantive empirical findings but rather are simply illustrative of an approach. Thus, as our title suggests, the results are from an "experiment" based on our perception or "view" of the city. Of course, we believe our view of the city is not too far removed from reality but that research requires a completely new design and effort.

We can deal with the use of abstract space–time units based on zones and sectors in the same way. Since we are familiar with the traditional factorial-ecology studies (Murdie, 1969), we have a view of the city which incorporates zones and sectors. Similarly the time periods are arbitrary but do coincide with our experience of the activities in the city. As long as it is remembered that our space–time diagrams are meant to be suggestive about how the complex space–time ecology of the city is structured, then no confusion need arise and our approach, although atypical, is nonetheless justifiable. One final point should be emphasized at this juncture, however: where a strategy of creating artificial data is employed this must be kept entirely separate from the subsequent analysis of the data. Obvi-

ously it is not permissible to keep modifying the data input to produce a "required" output.

Finally, if we concede that the study is "simply illustrative," let us consider exactly what it is that this study is attempting to illustrate. Basically we are calling attention to the limitations of conventional ecological studies with their nighttime bias. This is not to argue that nighttime urban patterns are not important indicators of social processes, but rather that they only tell part of the story. Time is every bit as important as space in the organization of the modern city.[11] There are distinctive time patterns just as there are distinctive spatial patterns. Space and time can be studied separately, but it is clear that very many problems of the city can only be fully specified in an integrated space–time framework. The most obvious example is the problem of congestion associated with the journey to work, but equally relevant are problems of isolation—one cannot be isolated in either space or time alone, but only in both simultaneously. It is towards the consideration of such problems that this experiment was aimed.

11. It is of interest to note finally that much "bed-time" social geography has drawn inspiration from Social Area Analysis (Shevky and Bell, 1955). Their study purports to derive three residential dimensions of urban structure as society increases in "scale." Major criticisms have been levelled at this "theory" because of the very weak links between general societal aspects of changing scale and their expression in urban residential dimensions. The seven dimensions produced in this study seem to fit Shevky and Bell's proposals for societal change much more clearly than the traditional economic, family, and ethnic-status trilogy. If this is so, it simply reflects the fact that "modernization" has involved reorganization of time as much as space. In general this argument lends support to the contention of Hawley and Duncan (1957), that these "basic" urban-structure dimensions were not derived from the theory, but that the theory was an attempted rationale for empirically observed patterns of census data which were readily available.

References

Breese, G. W., 1949, *The Daytime Population of the Central Business District of Chicago* (University of Chicago Press, Chicago).

Browning, C. E., 1964, "Selected aspects of land use and distance," *Southeastern Geographer*, 4, 29–40.

Carlstein, T., 1974, "Time allocation," Department of Geography, University of Lund, Sweden.

Carlstein, T., Parkes, D. N., Thrift, N., 1978, *Timing Space and Spacing Time* (Edward Arnold, London).

Chapin, F. S., Stewart, P. H., 1963, "Population densities around the clock," in *Readings in Urban Geography*, eds H. M. Mayer, C. F. Kohn (University of Chicago Press, Chicago), pp. 180–182.

Chapin, F. S., Hammer, P. G., 1972, *Human Time Allocation: A Case Study of Washington DC*, Center for Urban and Regional Studies, University of North Carolina, Chapel Hill.

Cullen, I., Godson, V., 1972, *The Structure of Activity Patterns*, Joint Unit for Planning Research (University College, London School of Economics, London University, London).

Engel-Frisch, G., 1948, "Some neglected temporal aspects of human ecology", *Social Forces*, 22, 43–47.

Foley, D. L., 1954, "Urban day-time populations: a field for demographic–ecological research", *Social Forces*, 32, 323–330.

Greig-Smith, P., 1952, "The use of random and contagious quadrants in the study of the structure of plant communities", *Annals of Botany* (new series), 16, 293–316.

Hägerstrand, T., 1968, *The Diffusion of Innovations* (University of Chicago Press, Chicago).

Hägerstrand, T., 1970, "What about people in regional science?", *Papers and Proceedings of the Regional Science Association*, 24, 7–21.

Hägerstrand, T., 1974, "On socio-technical ecology and the study of innovations," paper No. 10, Department of Geography, University of Lund, Sweden.

Harvey, D., 1969, *Explanation in Geography* (Edward Arnold, London).

Hawley, A., 1950, *Human Ecology* (Ronald Press, New York).

Hawley, A., Duncan, O. D., 1957, "Social area analysis: a critical appraisal," *Land Economics*, 33, 286–302.

Moore, W. E., 1963, *Man, Time and Society* (John Wiley, New York).

Murdie, R. A., 1969, *Factorial Ecology of Metropolitan Toronto, 1951–61*, research paper 116, Department of Geography, University of Chicago, Chicago.

Niedercorn, J. H., Hearle, E. F. R., 1964, "Recent land use trends in 48 large American cities," *Land Economics*, 40, 105–110.

Parkes, D. N., 1973, "Timing the city: a theme for urban environmental planning," *Royal Australian Institute Journal*, 12, 130–135.

Parkes, D. N., 1974, "Themes on time in urban social space: an Australian study," seminar paper No. 26, Department of Geography, University of Newcastle Upon Tyne, Newcastle, England.

Parkes, D. N., Thrift, N., 1975, "Timing space and spacing time", paper presented at the 46th Congress of ANZAAS, Section 21, Canberra.

Popper, K. R., 1963, *Conjectures and Refutations* (Routledge and Kegan Paul, London).

Rummel, R. J., 1970, *Applied Factor Analysis* (Northwestern University Press, Evanston, Illinois).

Schmitt, R. C., 1956, "Estimating daytime populations," *Journal of the American Institute of Planners*, 22, 83–85.

Shevky, E., Bell, W., 1955, *Social Area Analysis: Illustrative Application and Computational Procedures* (Stanford University Press, Stanford).

Stone, P. J., 1972, "The analysis of time-budget data," in *The Use of Time*, ed. A. Szalai (Mouton, The Hague), pp. 89–112.

Szalai, A. (ed.), 1972, *The Use of Time*, Proceedings of the World Time-Budget Study (Mouton, The Hague).

Timms, D. W. G., 1971, *The Urban Mosaic: Toward a Theory of Residential Differentiation* (Cambridge University Press, Cambridge).

FRED W. BOAL

Close Together and Far Apart: Religious and Class Divisions in Belfast*

In many cities, in many parts of the world, people have a marked tendency to live among "their own kind." "Their own kind" may be defined in terms of social class, race, ethnic group or religion. Thus any one residential area in a city may be inhabited by people who display a high degree of uniformity in terms of one or more of the above criteria. For instance the residents may be all of the one religious denomination or of the same race. Given this type of situation where people of differing characteristics live apart, the question may be asked whether separate living is also associated with lack of contact between people of the differing groups.

The two studies[1] reported on below were carried out in Belfast in the winter of 1967–8.* The first study examines two

areas with very distinct religious[2] "affiliations" though quite similar in social class terms, while the second examines two areas with marked social class differences, but very similar in terms of religious affiliation. Since we wish to examine the influence of social class and religious differences on the degree of interaction, we also selected areas that were very close to each other, so that any lack of contact between the areas could not be explained in terms of physical distance.

Shankill-Springfield: The Religious Divide

Residents in an area lying between the Springfield and Shankill Roads were interviewed. It became immediately clear that the area could be divided into two on the basis of the religious affiliation of the residents. One part (Clonard) was

1. The two studies are fully reported in the following publications: F. W. Boal "Territoriality on the Shankill-Falls Divide, Belfast", *Irish Geography* 6, No. 1, 1969, pp. 30–50, and F. W. Boal "Territoriality and Class: a study of two residential areas in Belfast", *Irish Geography,* 6, No. 3, 1971, pp. 229–248.
* It should be pointed out that the data for this paper were gathered in 1967–68, prior to the

outbreak of violent conflict in August, 1969 and which, unfortunately, continues to this day. Needless to say, religious and class conflicts are not unique to Belfast. (Ed. note).
2. Obviously the term religious has strong political connotations in the Northern Ireland context.

From **Community Forum,** Vol. 3, No. 2, 1972, pp. 3–11. Reprinted with modifications by permission of F. W. Boal.

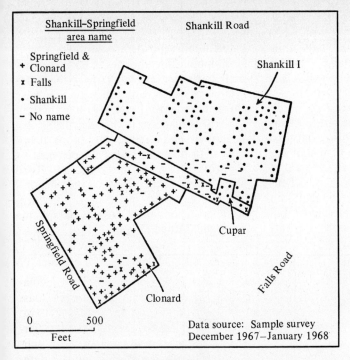

Shankill–Springfield
area name

Shankill Road

+ Springfield &
  Clonard

x Falls

• Shankill

– No name

Shankill I

Springfield Road

Cupar

Clonard

Falls Road

0   500
└─────────┘
   Feet

Data source: Sample survey
December 1967–January 1968

Figure 1. Shankill-Springfield Area Name

overwhelmingly Catholic (98 per cent), the other (Shankill 1) overwhelmingly Protestant (99 per cent). The two areas met in a very narrow band of "mixed" housing along Cupar Street. At the time of the survey the mixed area was about two-thirds Protestant (Figure 1).

The people living in Clonard and Shankill I were very conscious of the existence of their own areas and of the line where their area ended and somebody else's began (Cupar Street). The people in Clonard almost universally used the terms "Springfield," "Clonard" or "Falls" for their area, while those in Shankill I almost universally used the term "Shankill." The only confusion about area name occurred in the religiously-mixed Cupar Street where about a third used the Springfield-Clonard-Falls name, a third called the area Shankill, and one-third did not think the area had a name at all.

We can now pose the question, to what extent did the people in the two areas interact? Obviously there are many possible activities that could be examined in order to provide an answer. Only a few are discussed here, but it can be claimed that those examined are all important. The activities described are church membership, school attendance, grocery shopping and social visiting.

The very nature of the religious affiliations of the residents of Clonard and Shankill I ensure considerable interaction within each area, but practically none at all between them. Separate churches in different parts of the city are attended (or no church is attended at all). Thus the residents do not partake in religious activities in common, and thus do not meet at any church related social events.

In the sample of households interviewed there were 99 children attending primary school. All the Shankill children were attending County (state) Primary Schools while all the Clonard children were attending Voluntary (church) Schools. Forty-seven children in the sample were attending secondary school. All the children in Clonard attended church schools; all the children save one in Shankill attended County schools. That one child was the only Catholic of school age in our sample who lived in the Shankill area. She attended a church school. Thus except for this one child, the children from the two areas were completely separated in terms of the schools they attended. Not only did they attend separate schools, the schools themselves were located in different parts of the city.

Shopping for groceries is an important activity for housewives. Trips to the shops familiarises them with the areas they pass through and with those who live there, if the trip is made on foot. Socialising also occurs in and around the shops themselves. In Shankill I area 93 per cent of the trips were made to the Shankill Road shops or to local shops in the Shankill Road area. Four per cent of the trips were to shops in Clonard or on the Springfield Road (Figure 2).

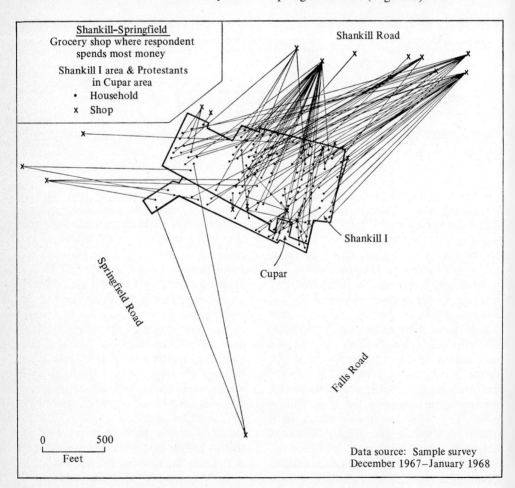

Figure 2. Shankill-Springfield. Grocery shop where respondent spends most money

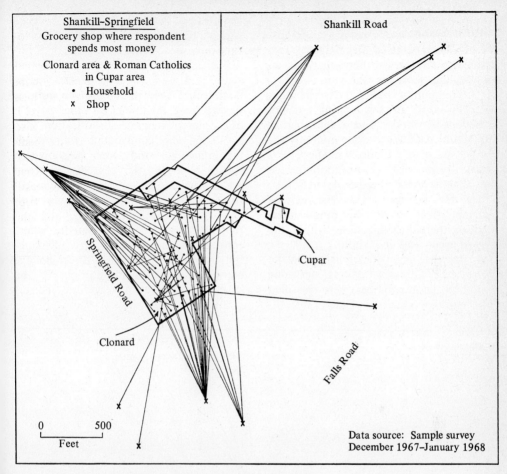

Figure 3. Shankill-Springfield. Grocery shop where respondent spends most money

In Clonard, on the other hand, 90 per cent of the trips were to the Springfield Road and local shops in Clonard while 10 per cent were to the Shankill Road (1968) (see Figure 3).

Thus, in both instances, a strong focusing of each area on its own main road can be observed, though at the time of the survey the shops on the Shankill were drawing a significant number of people across from Clonard, confirming to some extent the locally held opinion that the Shankill Road was a more attractive shopping area than the Falls/Springfield.

While grocery shopping displayed a considerable degree of segregation between the Clonard and Shankill areas, when we examined social visiting, an even more segregated pattern emerged. In the survey 450 visits within the study area were recorded, but only *one* of these was between the Shankill and Clonard areas. All the rest were either within Clonard, within Shankill I or were linked to Cupar Street. Broadening the view beyond the immediate study area, we find that about half of all the Shankill I visit connections fell within the Shankill Road Protestant sector, 66 per cent of these being with relatives, while 53 per cent of the Clonard connections were within the general Falls Road Roman Catholic sector, in this case 35 per cent being with relatives. Two comments are relevant here, first that we are dealing with the standard working class community pattern described by Marc Fried as "an over-lapping series of close-knit networks," and second that we are dealing with two almost mutually exclusive sets of such networks. There were practically no visitor connections across the religious divide (Figures 4 and 5).

The visit connections analysis can be extended out beyond the purely local level to include connections within the Belfast urban area as a whole.

In this case point locations, being the addresses of persons visiting or being visited by the interviewee, were classified according to whether they were associated with a Protestant or a Roman Catholic in the study area. The points were then further classified as being segregated or unsegregated using a first nearest neighbour technique whereby a given point is unsegregated if the nearest other point is of a different religious classification. The result for point connections lying outside the immediate study area is shown in Figure 6. Eighty per cent of the points are segregated. These segregated connections coincide with the better known religiously segregated residential areas of the city. Thus, with an activity where connections are socially very meaningful, there is effectively no direct linkage between the two main portions of the study area and even very little indirect

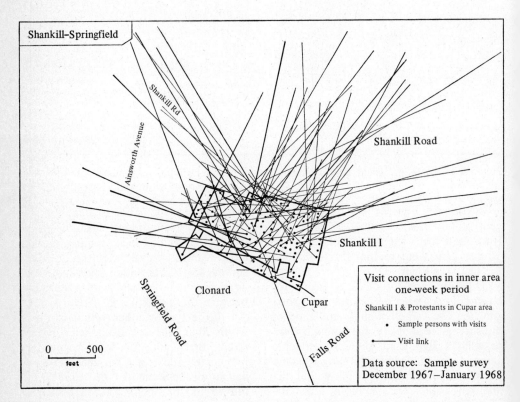

Figure 4. Shankill-Springfield. Visit connections in inner area, one-week period, Shankill I and Protestants in Cupar area

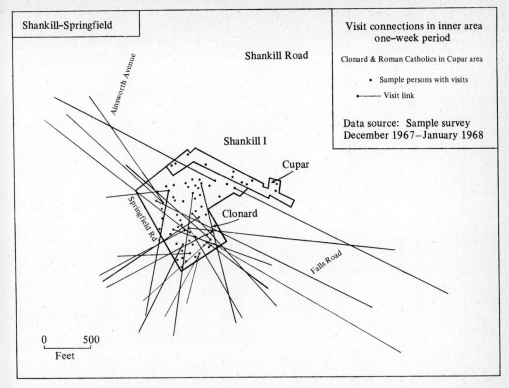

Figure 5. Shankill-Springfield. Visit connections in inner area, one-week period, Clonard and Roman Catholics in Cupar area

linkage in the urban area in general. This high level of activity segregation in terms of visiting is further accentuated, and probably in part caused by the separate school systems.

Although newspaper readership is not the same type of activity as those described above, in a situation where there appears to have been little direct contact between people in the two areas (at least through those activities described here) readership of the same newspapers could at least be one common link. The readership of the three local dailies was examined. The most interesting distribution to emerge was the readership of the morning Irish News which was read by 83 per cent of the sample in Clonard, but only 3 per cent in Shankill 1. The alternative local morning paper, the Belfast News-

letter, was not widely taken in either area. Evidence from elsewhere suggests that the Newsletter is more of a middle class paper in appeal. Morning newspaper readership in Shankill I concentrated on the English-based popular dailies. Irish News readership is a very distinguishing feature of the two religious subdivisions of the study area. The strong Catholic loyalty to the paper is not surprising in that it takes an anti-Unionist line in politics and gives substantial cover to Gaelic games and Roman Catholic church news. The third local daily, the evening Belfast Telegraph had, spatially, a much more uniform readership, in that it was read by 58 per cent in Clonard and 68 per cent in Shankill I. This common readership gives to the Telegraph an important role as a potential integrator op-

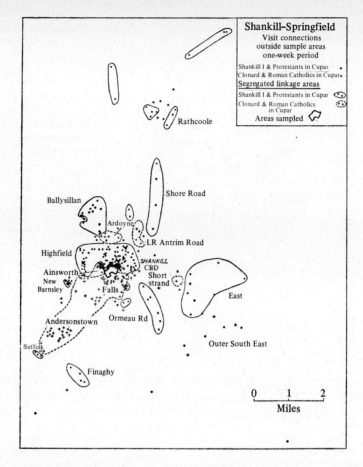

Figure 6. Shankill-Springfield. Visit connections outside sample areas, one-week period

erating across the religious community boundary.

The above discussion is an attempt to define on the basis of the religious affinities of residents, distinctive areas within a working class portion of Belfast, and then to see to what extent selected activity characteristics correspond with the underlying religious pattern. The cumulative evidence indicates the presence of two very distinct territories. This distinctiveness has been even further accentuated by events subsequent to 1968, and the boundary between the two areas has been given a physical reality in the form of the "Peace Line" erected along the

Cupar Street location in the autumn of 1969.[3]

Upper Malone-Taughmonagh: The Class Divide

In this case residents on either side of the Upper Malone Road were interviewed. On one side of the road lay a Belfast Cor-

3. The historical context of the Cupar Street location and events there subsequent to 1969 are provided in F. W. Boal, "Territoriality on the Shankill-Falls Divide: the perspective from 1976" in David A. Lanegran and Risa Palm (eds.), *Invitation to Geography* (Second Edition), McGraw-Hill, New York, 1978, pp. 58–77.

Table 1. Religious and Socio-economic
Status of the Study Units

	Taugh-monagh	Upper Malone
N^a	92	66
Religious composition (per cent		
Roman Catholic)	13.1	7.6
Socio-Economic Status of Head of Household (per cent)		
Social Class I		
Managerial and Professional	0	72.7
Social Class II		
Intermediate and non-manual	31.5	16.7
Social Class III		
Skilled manual	30.4	0
Social Classes IV and V		
Semi- and unskilled manual	29.3	0
Others		
retired	0	10.6
full-time housewife	1.1	0
unemployed	7.7	0

a N, size of sample.

poration (public) housing estate called Taughmonagh, on the other side an area of detached dwellings in the higher price range. Very considerable social class differences existed between the two areas, as Table 1 shows. On the other hand, just as class differences between Clonard and Shankill I were small, so religious differences between Upper Malone and Taughmonagh were insignificant, both areas being about 90 per cent Protestant.

As was done in the Shankill-Clonard area, the residents were asked what name they had for their area. "Taughmonagh" was the most frequently used name by residents in the Corporation estate (73 per cent) while "Upper Malone" was the most frequent name used by residents of the private housing area (67 per cent). None of the Upper Malone residents used the term Taughmonagh, though 5 per cent of the Taughmonagh people used the term Upper Malone. Unlike the residents in the vicinity of Cupar Street, those on either side of the Upper Malone

Road did not reach mutual agreement on the boundary between their two areas. The Taughmonagh residents saw the Upper Malone Road itself as the boundary but the Upper Malone residents did not reciprocate. They did not define out of their area the Taughmonagh estate. They seemed not to recognise its presence at all.

The religious affiliation differences between Clonard and Shankill I were such that the segregated patterns in regard to church and school attendance disclosed in the survey could not be considered surprising in the context of Belfast. Where religious affiliation differences in terms of the Protestant-Catholic dichotomy were small, as in the Upper Malone-Taughmonagh situation, one would expect a much lower degree of segregation for these two activities. In fact the survey data demonstrates that this is far from being the case.

Figure 7 shows the church membership distribution of adherents of the Church of Ireland (Episcopalian) and Presbyterian traditions. In Taughmonagh most are members of the nearest church of their own denomination (74 per cent of all Church of Ireland members, 73 per cent of Presbyterians). In Upper Malone however church membership is dispersed amongst a greater number of churches. The principal church for Taughmonagh Presbyterians has no Upper Malone members, despite it being the nearest Presbyterian church to Upper Malone, while the principal church for Taughmonagh Church of Ireland members has only one Upper Malone member in the sample population, again despite it being the nearest Episcopal church to Upper Malone. Thus a remarkably high degree of segregation was, in fact, observed.

The school attendance pattern is complex. This is due to the existence of state primary, Catholic primary and grammar school preparatory departments for children under the age of eleven, and of state secondary, Catholic secondary, Catholic grammar, state grammar and partly inde-

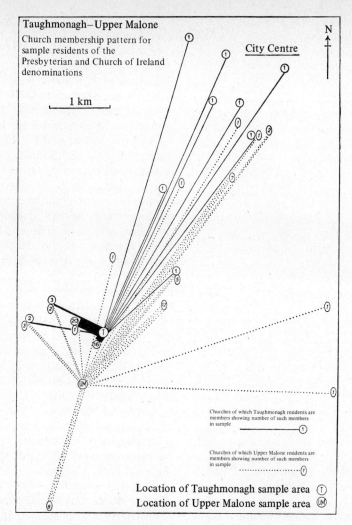

Figure 7. Taughmonagh-Upper Malone. Church membership pattern for sample residents of the Presbyterian and Church of Ireland denominations

pendent (Protestant) grammar schools for children over the age of eleven. The most striking feature of the school attendance pattern is the contrast between the two sample areas. All the primary age children from Taughmonagh attended state or Catholic primary schools. Fifty-six per cent of the Upper Malone children likewise attended state or Catholic primary schools but a further 44 per cent attended grammar school preparatory departments. In addition it may be noted that of the non-preparatory primary school children in the sample, only one Upper Malone child attended a school to which Taughmonagh children go and only two Taughmonagh children attended that school.[4]

4. A Local Education Authority boundary separates Upper Malone and Taughmonagh. This

Subsequent to the selection tests at the age of eleven, 86 per cent of Taughmonagh children went to state or Catholic secondary schools and 14 per cent went to grammar schools. All the post-primary Upper Malone children attended grammar schools. In addition, of the eight Taughmonagh children in the sample households who attended grammar school, only three attended ones to which Upper Malone children went.

The education of the children from the two sample areas is spatially highly segregated, partly by attendance at separate schools of the same type and partly by attendance at schools of different type (the preparatory school-primary school split and the grammar school-secondary school split). Overall the result is to make the school attendance division between the low and high status areas almost as sharp as that existing between the Catholic and Protestant Falls-Shankill area of west Belfast.

As in the Shankill-Clonard area residents were asked about their social visiting patterns. From a spatial viewpoint two features of these patterns in the Upper Malone Road area are paramount. First of all no visiting whatsoever was recorded across the socio-economic divide, and second the visiting patterns for the two sample populations show very little spatial overlap within the urban area as a whole (Figure 8). Clearly the visiting patterns are constrained by the areas of origin of the interviewees, with Taughmonagh connections being with the inner city and the Upper Malone connections being with the Malone sector. Thus there was practically no social visiting, in a spatial sense, across the socio-economic divide either locally or at the scale of the urban area. This shows a remarkable similarity to the lack of social visiting

across the religious divide recorded in the previous study in the Shankill-Falls area.

As in the study of the Cupar Street area, it is possible to classify each visit point as being either segregated or unsegregated. (See above.) The principal concentrations of segregated points are indicated in Figure 8. The Taughmonagh segregated concentrations correspond with the inner low status Protestant parts of Belfast, while the Upper Malone concentrations go some way towards depicting the high status residential areas of the city.

Patterns of newspaper readership were examined (Table 2).

Much could be made of the differences between the two areas. However in this case perhaps the outstanding feature was the importance of the Belfast Telegraph which had a very high readership in both areas. This paralleled the situation across the religious divide in west Belfast where the comment was previously made that "this common readership gives to the Telegraph an important role as a potential integrator operating across the religious community boundary." The same comment could be made in the context of the socio-economic class boundary.

The full significance of newspaper readership as a divisive or integrative factor could only be pinpointed if one carried out a content analysis of the papers and also if one was able to specify exactly what was read by each group in each paper.

Comment

The activity patterns analysed in this paper show high levels of integration within each of the separate study units but practically no interaction between them. If we define a territory as being an area within which there are a high number of linkages between occupants and which is consciously perceived as a unit distinctive

_____

affects the "state" primary schools attended but does not currently affect the locations of secondary or grammar schools attended.

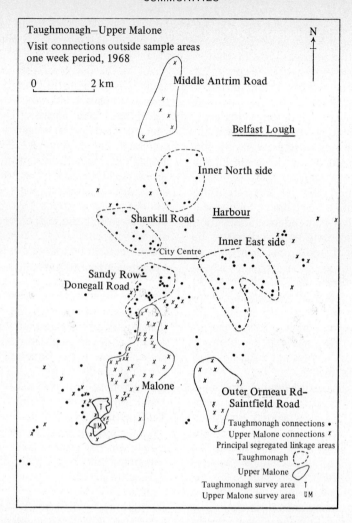

Figure 8. Taugmonagh-Upper Malone. Visit connections outside sample areas, one-week period, 1968

Table 2. Percentage of Sample Residents Reading Particular Newspapers

		Taughmonagh N = 92 Per Cent		Upper Malone N = 66 Per Cent	
Daily papers		Belfast Telegraph	82	Belfast Telegraph	76
		Daily Mirror	33	Belfast Newsletter	39
		Belfast Newsletter	15	Daily Express	12
Sunday papers		The People	45	Sunday Times	39
		News of the World	28	Sunday Express	23
				Observer	18

from surrounding areas, then the Taughmonagh, Upper Malone, Clonard and
Shankill I areas all qualify. However, a
further feature of territory is that boundaries must be maintained. In the case
of the religious territorial boundary of
the Shankill-Falls, boundaries have been
maintained by considerable pressures for
uniformity of residents in terms of religious persuasion on each side of the line.
Sometimes these pressures have been indirect but from time to time they have
been most direct, taking the form of
forced eviction of minority group members. Boundaries have also been visually
demonstrated by suitable flags, bunting
and wall slogans.

In the instance of the socio-economi-
cally based territories of the Upper Malone road, boundary maintenance is not a
problem, because residential invasion of
one area by people from the other is
highly unlikely—Upper Malone residents
will have no desire to live in Taughmonagh, and Taughmonagh residents will
be economically incapable of moving into
a house in Upper Malone. The elaborate
boundary maintenance procedures of the
Shankill-Falls are quite unnecessary in
Malone.

The lack of contact across the socio-
economic divide of the Upper Malone
Road would appear to be almost as great
as the lack of contact across the religious
divide in west Belfast. This is true both
for the activity patterns in the Taughmonagh-Upper Malone area itself and in
the urban area at large.

The almost total absence of contact
observed in the case of the Shankill-Falls
area has been the subject of considerable
comment. People who are not resident in
these areas have been surprised at the
low contact situation there and this has
raised the whole question of religious residential segregation and the concomitant
segregation of activity systems. The Upper Malone Road data indicate almost
the same degree of segregation for that

area, where the division appears to have
a class bias rather than a "religious" one.

Before anyone throws up their hands
in horror at the degree of class and religious segregation reported above, it
would be useful to affirm that such residential segregation fulfils many positive
functions. Living in areas that are homogeneous in class or "religious" terms provides like-minded neighbours. It provides
insulation against undesirable or potentially embarrassing contact. It provides a
means of group support in the face of a
hostile environment and may well provide a degree of physical protection. Belfast is not unique in this respect. It has
recently been written that residential differentiation characterises both the pre-
industrial and the industrial city, both
the laissez-faire and the planned, both the
capitalist and the socialist. "The physical
isolation of differing populations seems
an inevitable concomitant of urbanism as
a way of life."[5]

Nonetheless, despite the positive attributes of segregated living, concern
must be expressed at the low contact between the class and religious groups in
the areas studied. We don't really know
what the effects of this are, but studies
elsewhere would suggest that such low
contact tends to reinforce prejudice. There
is very much of a chicken-and-egg situation in all this however. Segregation may
perpetuate and reinforce prejudice; prejudice may reinforce segregation. If a value
judgement is made that the extremely low
degree of inter-group contact is undesirable, how does one break into this vicious
circle? One solution, usually emanating
from middle class sources, is that the religious segregation in working class Belfast be broken down by a policy of forced
integration, making use of urban redevelopment and the large scale provision of
publicly owned housing. The feasibility

5. D. Timms, *The Urban Mosaic,* Cambridge
University Press, 1971, p. 2.

or indeed the desirability of such a policy is highly questionable, not least because those proposing it are more than likely themselves to be living in a highly class segregated situation.

Forced integration is potentially disastrous. Equally, segregation that is forced is highly undesirable. What we need is a widening of people's choices, the opportunity to make contact with individuals who differ in religious or class terms. The possibility that such contact can be fostered through attendance at the same schools, shopping at the same local shops, or taking part in certain joint communal activities suggests the need to provide such opportunities. In the end many people may still opt for homogeneous neighbourhoods and mixing strictly with their own kind; others however may well grasp the opportunities for contact outside their own group. Only the dogmatic will have pat answers to the questions raised by segregation. All of us, however, need to ask a lot of questions about the causes and effects of the low contact situations reported here. Unbiased answers to them will help illumine future policy decisions.

RISA PALM

Real Estate Agents and Geographical Information

A substantial empirical literature on intra-urban mobility has accumulated over the past ten years. In these studies, the city or metropolitan area is considered to be the "whole" within which such descriptors as directional bias, sectoral patterns, distance bias, and search space are applied. However, the specification of the whole defines the nature and valence of its parts[1]: the assumption that the urban area acts as the whole within which mobility behavior takes place gives rise to patterns, generalizations, and even descriptions of behavior that may differ from those which would be derived from another framework. Any structural-functional analysis of mobility requires the specification of its frame, and any behavioral study must ensure that this frame be behaviorally meaningful to the persons involved in the process under study. To study mobility from a behavioral perspective, it is thus essential to specify the nature of the geographical information field.[2]

The purpose of this paper is to demonstrate that even in a relatively homogeneous, medium-sized metropolitan area there is no single information field. Not one but many information spaces, sometimes overlapping, sometimes disjunct, operate even for households with equivalent means and preferences. The thesis herein is that the metropolitan area cannot be considered as a whole within which individuals choose locations. Even if the home buyer makes use of those information sources that should provide the broadest and least spatially biased sources of information—real estate agencies who are members of the Multiple Listing Service[3]—he is exposed to only a small portion of the market in any price range.

Home Buyers and Their Information Sources

The household seeking to purchase a single-family detached house searches for

---

1. F. Lukermann: Geography: De Facto or De Jure, *Journ. Minnesota Acad. of Sci.*, Vol. 32, 1965, pp. 189–196.
2. Peter Gould: Acquiring Spatial Information, *Econ. Geogr.*, Vol. 51, 1975, pp. 87–99.

3. The Multiple Listing Service is a cooperative listing service conducted among a group of member realtors. A member company that accepts a listing promises to turn it over to a central bureau, from which it is distributed to all members who then have the right to sell the property. Commissions are divided between the selling office and the listing office, with a small percentage returned to the MLS office itself.

From **Geographical Review,** Vol. 66, July 1976, pp. 266–88. Reprinted by permission of the American Geographical Society and R. Palm.

particular characteristics of the housing unit, such as number of rooms, style of the dwelling unit, age of the unit, and landscaping.[4] In several surveys recent buyers were asked to evaluate the importance of such features in their purchase decision, and answers were found to vary by the respondent's income and sex.[5] The household also has to make a decision about the location of the house, involving such factors as tax rates, reputation of local schools, and distance from shopping, relatives, or place of work. The potential house buyer thus seeks a wide variety of information, not all of which can be obtained through direct observation. Although the means by which the household gains information about the house itself is of interest, we shall focus on the ways in which potential buyers obtain information about the area in which the house is located.

For many people, the choice of area is affected by an information network that is strongly influenced by family ties, ethnic group membership, previous experience with the neighborhood, or information from friends and colleagues. Other people are more dependent on formal or public sources of information, including newspaper advertisements, on-site notices, and real estate agency files. For example, a third of the approximately 32,000 people sampled in a recent survey by the National Opinion Research Center (NORC) claimed that they had used such public information sources as real estate agencies and newspaper advertisements to find their current residence, and another third said that friends, relatives, and co-workers

had been their most important information source. A perhaps surprising similarity in the use of various information sources exists across socioeconomic classes and ethnic groups: when responses were stratified into four socioeconomic categories and four ethnic or racial categories, there was less than 5 percent difference in the use of each of the information sources, with the exception of newspaper advertisements.

Empirical work on mental maps of urban areas and on the nature of space-searching behavior provides strong inferential evidence that households do not possess a very large portion of the total available information about existing vacancies.[7] Tuan has suggested that research findings on spatial images may not be related to an understanding of spatial behavior.[8] In any case, further work will be required if we are to understand the ways in which people use the information that is available to them. But for the moment we may turn our attention to the overall limitations on the availability of information. In other words, although individual choices are interesting to study, they are difficult to specify and perhaps less useful for planning purposes than the nature of the overall constraints on human choice.[9]

4. Donald J. Hempel: A Comparative Study of the Home Buying Process in Two Connecticut Housing Markets (Center for Real Estate and Urban Economic Studies, Univ. of Connecticut, Storrs, Conn., 1970).
5. "Buyers Profile Analysis of Factors Relating to the Home Buying Decision" (School of Bus. Admin., Calif. State Polytech. Coll., Pomona; Calif. State Dept. of Real Estate, Sacramento; 1971).
7. J. S. Adams: Directional Bias in Intra-Urban Migration, Econ. Geogr., Vol. 45, 1969, pp. 302–323; Lawrence A. Brown and Eric G. Moore: The Intra-Urban Migration Process: An Actor-Oriented Approach, Geografiska Annaler, Vol. 52B, 1970, pp. 1–13; D. J. Caruso: Neighborhood Search, Residential Evaluation and the Housing Market (Ph.D. dissertation in progress, Dept. of Geography, Univ. of Minnesota, Minneapolis).
8. Yi-Fu Tuan: Images and Mental Maps, Annals Assn. of Amer. Geogrs., Vol. 65, 1975, pp. 205–213.
9. Torsten Hägerstrand (The Domain of Human Geography, in Directions in Geography [edited by Richard J. Chorley; Methuen and Co., Ltd., London, 1973], pp. 67–87) presents a cogent argument for analyzing constraints on human behavior rather than investigating preferences which are already environmentally constrained.

Home buyers have a limited amount of time and resources which they are willing to expend in their search for a house. They must continually reevaluate the options of choosing from the information they have at hand or of possibly losing a "bird in the hand" as the house they have tentatively settled on is sold to someone else while they continue their search. Lease expiration dates, problems of timing and financing the coordination of buying a home while selling a previous home, or the excessive costs of living in a hotel while looking for a permanent home in a new city may further constrict the search. Furthermore, some houses never reach the general market.

In general, information that purchasers may consider necessary for an optimum practical decision is scattered in such places as real estate company files, newspapers, on-property "for sale" signs, and personal contacts. The greatest constraints in information face newcomers to the city who lack access to private information sources. The information source that should be most complete is the large, multibranched realty office, subscribing to a metropolitan-area-wide Multiple Listing Service (MLS) and perhaps affiliated with one of the several intercity realty company chains. This source should not be spatially biased in the sense of systematically excluding listings in low-income or nonwhite areas.[10] Therefore one may expect that as a single information source, large, MLS-affiliated realty companies show the least territorial or price bias in representing the housing market. It is this kind of agency that provides us with a portrait of the most complete information readily available to the home buyer from a single source. If we can demonstrate that these real estate agents are not providing information on

the entire city, but instead are focusing on systematically selected segments of the housing market, we will conclude that the entire metropolitan area cannot be considered as a whole in the home selection process and that structural-functional statements such as those about directional bias must be redefined.

The Real Estate Agent as Information Source

The role of the realtor as a source of information in the home purchase process has been studied chiefly through survey research. In some studies, recent movers have been asked to list those sources of information they consulted during the move process and to evaluate the relative importance of each source.[11] Other studies have attempted to isolate the type of information that real estate agents provide to home buyers[12] and the methods agents use to encourage or discourage buyers from considering particular neighborhoods.[13] Survey information exists on the proportions of persons who consult with real estate agents and on their evaluations of the importance of agents on their final decision. In general, newcomers to the city, especially those who have come to the city because of job transfers, are highly dependent on the real estate agent as an information source.[14] The

10. Boris William Becker: Selected Economic Aspects of Real Estate Brokerage (unpublished Ph.D. dissertation, Dept. of Business Administration, Univ. of California, Berkeley, 1970).

11. Donald J. Hempel: The Role of the Real Estate Broker in the Home Buying Process (Center for Real Estate and Urban Economic Studies, Univ. of Connecticut, Storrs, Conn., 1969); D. T. Herbert: The Residential Mobility Process: Some Empirical Observations, *Area*, Vol. 5, 1973, pp. 44–48; and Frank A. Barrett: Residential Search Behavior, *York Univ. Research Monographs, No. 1,* Toronto, 1973.
12. Hempel, Role of the Real Estate Broker [see footnote 11 above].
13. Charles M. Barresi: The Role of the Real Estate Agent in Residential Location, *Sociol. Focus,* Vol. 1, 1968, pp. 59–71.
14. Caruso, *op. cit.* [see footnote 7 above]; and Hempel, Role of the Real Estate Broker [see footnote 11 above].

less familiar the mover is with the metropolitan area, the more dependent he is on the agent for information, not only on the location of vacancies but also on the desirability of various neighborhoods. This dependence is affected by the length of the search, as well as by the previous experience of the home buyer with using real estate agents in the home purchase process.[15]

Well-meaning real estate agents may intentionally or even unintentionally provide information that limits the search of prospective buyers by advising clients on the social character of neighborhoods and on the likelihood of property resale. Although most agents do not provide so blatant a social evaluation of parts of the city, the newcomer may be assaulted with printed literature even as he arrives at the metropolitan airport:

So the "good" residential areas extended South and a little West from the loop (by the river)—First Lowry Hill, then Kenwood —Lake of the Isles. . . . Edina is one of the very logical places for newcomers. There is usually quite a little turnover. Making new friends in Edina is easy—many other "new" families are also seeking, and the constant come-and-go keeps the community fairly uncliquish.[16]

One has no doubt that if the newcomer follows the advice of the pamphlet and contacts this well-established realty firm he will get quite definite guidance on which areas of the city are best for his family and for their life-style. Not even the best tourist guidebook or most careful social geography of a city will provide the newcomer with as many opinions about communities that are or are not "appropriate."

The membership of a real estate office in the Multiple Listing Service should in some ways offset the local effects of company territoriality on agents' views. Each member company is provided with specifications of houses for sale in all price brackets and in all areas of the city in which member companies sell houses. Although the agent may still be tempted to sell his own company listings first (to enjoy a greater commission), he should at least be aware of listings in all parts of the city. Ideally, what we might call his awareness space should coincide with the limits of the areas governed by his board of realtors.

To confirm the thesis that even real estate agents affiliated with the largest realty companies and associated with the Multiple Listing Service have limited knowledge and biased opinions of local areas within the metropolitan area, three hypotheses were tested: that realty companies cover limited parts of the housing market in their listings; that the overall evaluations of realtors correspond to the actual vacancy pattern; and that individual real estate agents vary significantly in their evaluations of areas "appropriate" for certain types of home buyers, an evaluation which is associated with market territorialization. In other words, an attempt was made to ascertain the limits of information, especially the local variances one might find from the aggregate picture.

The Minneapolis Study

Minneapolis, Minnesota, and its suburbs were selected as the study area. St. Paul and its suburbs were excluded from this study on the grounds that its residential housing market operates in an independent fashion despite its proximity to Minneapolis.[17] In addition, by limiting the

15. Becker, Real Estate Brokerage [see footnote 10 above].
16. "What's it Like to Live in Minneapolis?" (Rees, Thomson, Scroggins, Inc., Minneapolis, n.d.)

17. Richard Hartshorne (The Twin City District: A Unique Form of Urban Landscape, Geogr. Rev., Vol. 22, 1932, pp. 431–442) observed the functional independence of the two cities in shopping behavior, travel patterns, and

study to Minneapolis and its suburbs, we could ignore the very real barriers to information flow imposed by two competing sets of realty boards.

Minneapolis is a particularly good study area because of its structural simplicity. Its housing stock is distributed according to the classic (Chicago) model of regular accretions of new housing around the central business district, and socioeconomic groups are arranged sectorally.[18] Areas of upper-income residence have traditionally focused on the lakes to the west and southwest of the central business district, at present including parts of the Kenwood neighborhood within Minneapolis and parts of the suburbs of Golden Valley, Edina, Minnetonka, and West Bloomington (Figure 1). Low-income areas spread from the near north and near south sides of the central city to the flat countryside to the north and south of the city, including Columbia Heights, Crystal, Robbinsdale, and parts of Richfield. The central business district has maintained itself as a focus of office and business activity, making it a plausible employment center for persons in a variety of occupational classes. Although the Mississippi River divides the city north of the central business district, relatively few sharp physical breaks or climatic contrasts interrupt the settlement pattern or add to its complexity. Moreover, the population is fairly homogeneous in ethnic structure, permitting us to set aside, to a large extent, questions of the effects of the predominance of a particular ethnic or racial group in a local neighborhood on realtor evaluations of that area. Because this structural simplicity makes Minneapolis an excellent laboratory for testing such concepts as directional bias and sectoral structure, it should also be an excellent test case for measuring the range of the geographical information field.

MARKET COVERAGE

The first hypothesis was that even the largest realty companies vary in the degree to which their listings are representative of the price range and areal extent of the actual vacancy surface. A 20 percent stratified random sample was drawn of all houses listed for sale by the thirty-eight largest member companies of the Minneapolis Board of Realtors. Each of the companies studied was a member of the Multiple Listing Service, and three of them were affiliated with national intercity relocation offices. This list of houses for sale in early August, 1973, was a sample of approximately 70 percent of all the houses offered for sale through the Multiple Listing Service at that time.[19] The offices of the thirty-eight companies studied were located throughout Minneapolis and its suburbs. The locations of houses for sale were plotted, and a mean center and a standard deviation ellipse were calculated for the listings for each agency.[20]

support of cultural events. Hildegard Binder Johnson (An Introduction to the Geography of the Twin Cities [Dept. of Geography, Macalester College, St. Paul, Minn., 1970]) elaborated on this theme in noting the separate newspapers, television stations, and real estate advertisements in the two cities. Finally, even intracity telephone call frequencies in a toll-free area show substantial independence (see Risa Palm: The Concept of Community: A Geographical Perspective [unpublished Ph.D. dissertation, Dept. of Geography, Univ. of Minnesota, Minneapolis, 1972]).
18. John S. Adams: Residential Structure of Midwestern Cities, *Annals Assn. of Amer. Geogrs.*, Vol. 60, 1970, pp. 37–62.

19. There were more than the usual number of houses for sale during this particular period than there would usually be in the late summer, because of a shortage of mortgage money. However, this should not distort the pattern of house listings for particular companies, nor should it affect the results of the survey, except to emphasize the territorial patterns of real estate company coverage.
20. The standard (deviation) ellipse has been widely used as a measurement of spatial dis-

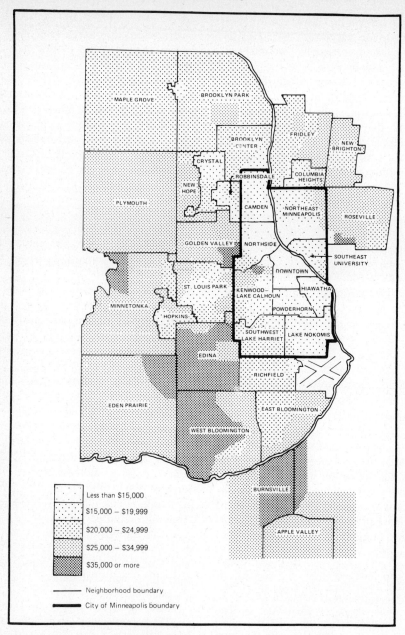

Figure 1. Median Value of Housing, Minneapolis, 1970. Compiled from data in the United States Census of Population, Census Tracts, 1970

Listings for the largest companies showed variation in areal coverage and in average price and price specialization (Table 1). Areal coverage was approximated by measuring the area included within the standard ellipse. These areas varied from 2.7 square miles to 94.8 square miles, although it must be noted that these sizes were distorted by the uneven spatial distribution of the listings. Variation in the extent to which listings were localized within sectors of the city was estimated with a rough index of directional bias, the extent to which the listings were circular or linear in areal distribution (the ratio of the length to the width of the standard deviation ellipse). Coverage varied from almost circular (index of approximately 1.00) to strongly linear (index of 7.67). The relationship between the size of the area covered by real estate company listings and the extent to which coverage was circular ($r_s = -0.15$) was weak. This absence of association indicates great variation in the sizes and patterns of company sales areas.

Agencies also showed marked variation in price specialization. Some companies specialized either in high-priced or in low-priced homes, and others handled a variety of price classes. The mean price of houses listed by the companies ranged from $17,700 to $67,800. In addition, the within-company variance in prices of house listings, indexed by a coefficient of variation (standard deviation/mean price), ranged from 0.96 to 0.18. There was a fairly strong inverse relationship between size of the area covered by the listings and price specialization as in-

dexed by the price coefficient of variation ($r_s = 0.63$), and also between number of listings (company size) and price specialization ($r_s = 0.60$). There was little association, however, between average price and price specialization ($r_s = 0.28$), indicating that those companies which listed higher-priced houses tended to be no less specialized than those which listed lower-priced houses. The average price of houses listed was positively related to the areal size of company coverage ($r_s = 0.40$) and to the total number of listings the company had during the study period ($r_s = 0.51$). We can conclude that real estate agents had widely varying direct contact spaces, in the sense that some handled listings throughout the urban area while others dealt with a territory little larger than a single census tract.

The effects of real estate company specialization on home-buying behavior are difficult to specify without studying the consumers themselves. Nevertheless, it is clear that there is great variation in the so-called awareness space of the realty agents and that potential home buyers, and certainly newcomers to the city who are dependent on real estate agents for information, will find themselves dealing initially with a highly variable information market, limited by the nature of the real estate company with which they happen to make contact first.

EVALUATIONS OF NEIGHBORHOODS BY AGENTS

If agents are to act as sources of information without a spatial bias, it must be assumed that they provide buyers with essentially similar evaluations of the character of neighborhoods. Any deviation from this relative homegeneity in the provision of information must be seen as a second, and perhaps even more important, constraint on the information set of the home buyer.

---

persion, and is described in Roberto Bachi: Standard Distance Measures and Related Methods for Spatial Analysis, *Papers Regional Sci. Assn.*, Vol. 10, 1963, pp. 83–132; and Lawrence A. Brown and John Holmes: Intra-Urban Migrant Lifelines: A Spatial View, *Demography*, Vol. 8, 1971, pp. 103–122.

Table 1. Market Coverage of Minneapolis Realtors

Company	Number of Listings	Area of Coverage (in square miles)	Directional Bias of Listings (length of main axis in standard ellipse/width)	Mean Price of Listings	Price-Coefficient of Variation (standard deviation/mean price)
1	110	58.3	1.79	$49,100	0.96
2	305	51.2	1.37	40,600	0.55
3	110	39.9	1.07	37,300	0.45
4	115	94.8	1.58	39,700	0.63
5	385	45.2	1.06	48,000	0.65
6	80	17.5	1.05	55,600	0.50
7	115	18.1	1.93	39,600	0.41
8	135	33.3	2.00	67,800	0.92
9	80	39.8	1.14	36,900	0.39
10	170	30.2	1.16	29,100	0.36
11	265	36.7	2.00	28,700	0.55
12	115	20.0	2.13	37,100	0.36
13	135	56.2	1.85	33,500	0.75
14	36	7.0	1.00	20,200	0.41
15	19	13.3	1.25	45,000	0.18
16	14	2.7	1.00	28,700	0.31
17	13	7.9	1.90	27,400	0.34
18	11	50.7	2.52	29,100	0.49
19	10	16.8	2.39	23,900	0.30
20	40	38.9	1.38	39,400	0.55
21	14	14.4	1.53	31,600	0.26
22	21	41.2	2.05	23,300	0.33
23	50	46.7	1.03	36,500	0.49
24	39	11.4	2.27	21,900	0.34
25	20	2.7	1.83	17,700	0.28
26	39	27.9	1.34	30,000	0.45
27	26	29.9	2.39	21,000	0.49
28	12	11.5	7.67	47,500	0.35
29	28	31.4	1.12	28,200	0.48
30	31	13.9	2.33	23,700	0.38
31	26	21.0	2.57	26,100	0.30
32	25	45.4	1.62	23,900	0.60
33	15	19.3	1.81	25,600	0.46
34	21	15.0	3.60	29,400	0.49
35	33	17.2	1.28	24,700	0.72
36	56	33.7	1.11	34,400	0.53
37	11	21.0	1.55	30,500	0.33
38	16	34.9	2.10	31,200	0.31

Source: Calculated from information in Multiple Listing Service files.

Evaluations of neighborhoods were elicited from more than 250 realtors, at least five and as many as ten from each of the thirty-eight largest companies. The questionnaire consisted of a schematic map of Minneapolis and its suburbs, divided into typical real estate districts compiled from a composite of newspaper real estate want ad divisions and planning department delimitations of community areas. Eight hypothetical families, each headed by a male who worked in the central business district, and whose occupation was selected from one of four positions along a composite of occupation status rating scales, were to be matched with these districts. In each of the hypothetical families the female spouse was a housewife not employed outside the home. Each social status was represented by two families at different stages in their life cycle: one childless and one with two children of school age. The realtors were directed to indicate one or more areas of the city where they, as agents for their companies, would advise such families to look for a home to buy.

Considering all agents together, recommendations to each of the family types corresponded remarkably well with the current pattern of vacancies at appropriate price ranges, inasmuch as this pattern could be reconstructed from the locations of houses advertised for sale in the classified advertisements of the Sunday newspaper and from the total listings available from the Multiple Listing Service (Figure 2). Agents seemed to have no difficulty in and virtually no objection to responding to a questionnaire in which they were provided with a minimum of information about a family and were asked to recommend any number of neighborhoods to them. The highest degree of consensus, not surprisingly, centered on those neighborhoods most appropriate for upper-income households. But in all price ranges the recommendations of all of the realtors taken together

and the pattern of houses offered for sale showed considerable coincidence.

Recommendations to the hypothetical family at the second highest socioeconomic status position, that of the accountant, converged on Edina and Golden Valley, with West Bloomington added for the family without children. Houses advertised for sale in the $46,000–$60,000 range (using the real estate rule of two and a half times the yearly income as a suitable home value) are located in these areas and also in Minnetonka, recommended by fewer of the realtors for this family type. Other areas with houses for sale in this price bracket but which received few recommendations include Eden Prairie, Plymouth, Richfield, Lake Nokomis, and some of the northern suburbs. Realtors seem to favor the southwestern suburbs here, to the disadvantage of areas within the city limits (such as the Lake Nokomis area) and north of the city.

St. Louis Park was recommended for the bookkeeper, a good choice in view of the distribution of houses for sale in the $24,000–$28,000 price range. The scatter of houses in this price bracket in East Bloomington, Richfield, Southrest–Lake Harriet, Crystal, and Robbinsdale is reflected in the agreement of a smaller number of realtors on these as appropriate areas. Northeast, Camden, and Brooklyn Center were omitted, however, again reflecting a general bias in favor of the southern and western suburbs.

A variety of areas were recommended to the family of lowest socioeconomic status. To the deliveryman's family, the North Side was most frequently recommended, followed closely by Northeast, Powderhorn, and Hiawatha. These areas, however, accounted for only a small portion of the areas with houses for sale for less than $24,000, which included, in addition, Camden, St. Louis Park, Southwest–Lake Harriet, Lake Nokomis, Richfield, and East Bloomington.

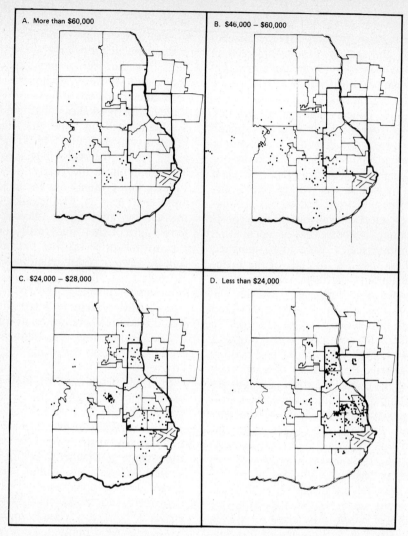

Figure 2. Houses Listed for Sale in the Minneapolis **Sunday Tribune** during the Month of August, 1973

REAL ESTATE AGENTS' VIEWS
OF THE URBAN AREA

Deviation from the overall association between areas recommended by realtors
and location of houses for sale within an
appropriate price range is considerable
when one focuses on recommendations
made by realtors from individual companies. For example, some realtors rec-

ommended that the high-income dentist
move to areas near the inner city or to
the northeastern suburbs, and some realtors recommended that the low-income
deliveryman move to Edina or to West
Bloomington.

To assess the strength and nature of
individual company recommendation patterns, a matrix of "expected" neighborhood frequencies per company was

constructed against which observed frequencies could be compared. Expected frequencies were computed based on the proportion of total responses recommending the particular neighborhood.[21] An expected cell entry was computed for each of the thirty-eight companies, for thirty-two neighborhoods, for each of the eight family types. To assess the extent to which the location of company listings was associated with the overrecommendation of a neighborhood, a matrix of observed minus expected frequencies was calculated.[22]

The pattern of individual areas strongly overrecommended is clearly local. Realtors within companies have a strong tendency to recommend areas close to their offices and their own company listings, regardless of the social class or family status of the hypothetical family (Figure 3). Of the seventeen companies strongly recommending neighborhoods to the dentist, fourteen recommended neighborhoods in which the company had houses for sale. Thirteen of fourteen companies overrecommended local areas to the accountant, and fourteen of seventeen recommended local areas to the deliveryman and to the bookkeeper. It should be em-

phasized that the survey presented the realtors with hypothetical families to be matched with hypothetical housing opportunities. Unlike the situation which realtors confront in attempting to satisfy actual customers, there was no economic incentive to recommend areas or houses within the realty company territory, for there was no commission to be gained or lost from their recommendations. We cannot, therefore, explain the localized view of the realtors in terms of mere financial self-interest, but rather must consider these patterns of responses to be actual reflections of realtors' knowledge and opinions of various areas of the city. Furthermore, of all Minneapolis agents, it was these who should have had the broadest view of the availability of housing, since they were employed by the largest, most well-connected agencies, all of which were members of the Multiple Listing Service.

The Hypotheses Confirmed

There is positive evidence to confirm each of the hypotheses. First, realty companies do cover limited portions of the housing market in both price and area. Areal coverage varies from those companies that list houses in a single neighborhood to those with branches throughout the urban area that list houses in large portions of the metropolitan area. No single company covers the entire metropolitan area, however. Similarly, price coverage varies from those companies that specialize in high-priced or low-priced houses to those that list houses in all price brackets.

Second, the overall evaluations of realtors taken together provide a generally accurate portrayal of the houses listed for sale throughout the metropolitan area, inasmuch as this can be reconstructed from a combination of Multiple Listing Service and newspaper information. Exceptions to this general statement occur

21. For example, if there were 1,000 total responses in which realtors recommended some of the thirty-two neighborhoods to a given type of family and if Company A accounted for 100 of these responses, we would expect Company A to account for 10 percent of the responses for each of the neighborhoods. If Neighborhood 1 were recommended 50 times, Company A would be expected to have made 5 of those recommendations, and the 5 would be entered in the cell for Neighborhood 1, Company A. Similarly, if Neighborhood 2 were recommended 70 times, Company A would be expected to have provided 7 of these recommendations. Each cell entry was thus computed for each of the companies and each of the neighborhoods.

22. An area was classed as overrecommended if it had a score of 2.0 or more; in other words, if it received at least two more than the expected number of recommendations it was considered to be overrecommended.

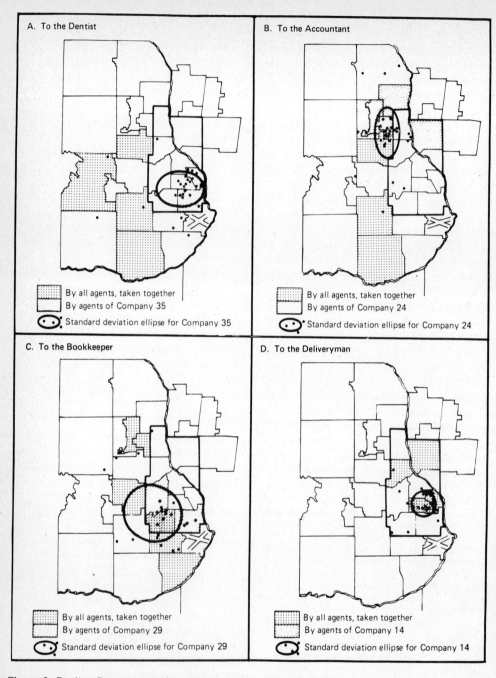

Figure 3. Realtor Recommendations, Minneapolis, 1973. Examples of recommendations by individual companies that "overrecommended" their local territories. Those areas recommended by "all agents taken together" represent areas recommended by at least 35 percent of all the respondents. Overrecommendations for selected companies are indicated, with the listings which that company offered for sale during August, 1973, and along with a generalized estimate of company territory (the standard deviation ellipse)

in an underevaluation of the northern sector of the city and an overevaluation of the western and southwestern sectors by all realtors taken together. The pattern of underevaluation or overevaluation of particular areas of the city does not seem to be related to the relative numbers of houses for sale, the turnover rate, or the relative quality of houses in these areas. Indeed, many of the housing developments in Brooklyn Center, New Hope, and Plymouth were constructed and sold by the same companies that built up large portions of West Bloomington, Burnsville, and Eden Prairie. Rather, it seems that the description by developers and realtors of the southern and southwestern suburbs as highly mobile areas with rapidly increasing house prices has become a self-fulfilling prophecy; overevaluation by realtors and developers leads to an increase in demand, the upward bidding of prices, rapid sales, and a further round of relative increases. The realtor evaluations are, in fact, reflected in the relative costs of housing: often the "same" houses, constructed by the same firm, and with the same apparent amenities, have prices that vary as much as $10,000 to $20,000.

Third, individual agents show marked differences in their evaluations of those neighborhoods that are most appropriate for certain types of home buyers. When agent responses are considered by a company, one notes a clear pattern of over-recommendations for neighborhoods in which company offices are located and in which the company has listings. Real estate agents have a tendency to bias their recommendations in favor of the territories with which they are most familiar, giving a strong local effect to the pattern of neighborhood recommendations. Thus not only the buyers but also the real estate agents have limited awareness spaces. It is no doubt true that these limitations in agents' views of the city have some effect on the decision-making process of the home buyer with respect to the neighborhood on which he focuses his search.

The information surface of even those professionals who are involved on a daily basis in the sale of property and who have connections with similar sales agents throughout the metropolitan area is localized, falling far short of covering the entire urban area. That such localization prevails in a relatively homogeneous urban area must lead us to suspect that a discontinuous pattern of information sets is even more prevalent in larger and more physically complex metropolitan areas, which are frequently even further segmented by separate and competing boards of realtors.

The home buyer finds himself in an even more limited situation. Since he is one step removed from an already incomplete informational whole, he inevitably is constrained to an even smaller portion of the information available, as biases and filters simplify information about housing vacancies and neighborhoods.

The description of the city in terms of metropolitan-wide patterns of rings, wedges, sectors, or an overall directional bias in spatial behavior is logically linked to the view that the metropolitan area constitutes a behavioral whole. When one considers the set of housing opportunities as filtered through restrictions on information, this whole appears to be arbitrarily bounded, for it has been defined by such criteria as commuting patterns and residential densities and not directly linked to the set of housing opportunities which a potential migrant considers in his decision to move.

If there is no single geographical information field, there is no common and continuous territory in which intra-urban migration as a process of geographical knowledge acquisition and decision-making can be discussed. In this sense directional bias becomes meaningless; although there is no doubt that moves may occur within a limited portion of the city, we cannot logically establish a directional pattern to these moves if we do not have agreement on a behaviorally meaningful, common territory which we are dividing into directions. Similarly, we cannot divide the urban pie into wedges or rings of opportunities unless we can first specify that there is a single, common, geographical information pie to divide. As in the familiar problem of the delimitation of regions, we must give attention to the effects of bounding some area for study on the results of subsequent analysis.[23] In the present case, we have little reason to believe that the metropolitan area constitutes a ready-made region within which

locational information is evenly available. Informational wholes should be delimited empirically, and with a specific purpose in mind.

Geographers need to heed Peter Gould's plea for a return to the exploration and mapping of new spaces and landscapes of the information environment.[24] We should not, then, merely assume the formulation of awareness spaces within which moves, tautologically, take place. We cannot understand the landscape of knowledge about place merely by asking questions about the places people visit or recognize. Rather, we must seek to discern how people learn about places and focus our attention on institutions that facilitate or limit access to geographical information.

23. Fred Lukermann: Empirical Expressions of Nodality and Hierarchy in a Circulation Manifold, *East Lakes Geogr.*, Vol. 5, 1969, pp. 17–44.

24. Gould, *op. cit.* [see footnote 2 above].

DAVID HARVEY AND LATA CHATTERJEE

Absolute Rent and the Structuring of Space by Governmental and Financial Institutions

In this paper we sketch the answers to two questions: (1) How do the macro and micro features of housing markets relate to each other in theory and in practice? (2) How is absolute rent realized in the housing markets of large metropolitan areas? We can afford the luxury of two questions because the same materials suffice to answer both.

The Macro and Micro Features of Housing Markets

There is a considerable body of theory and a mass of empirical information on the macro-economic aspects of housing markets. The same can be said with respect to the micro-economic modelling of housing choices—including locational choices through which residential differentiation of metropolitan areas is thought to be achieved. But there is little theory or information on the relationship between these two aspects of housing markets. What there is usually gets lost in the formalism of aggregation theory in which it is assumed that the relationship between national aggregates and local indi-vidual behaviours is a technical problem that has a formal (usually mathematical) solution. In the face of problems of this kind. We believe that it is imperative to investigate human practice, for that practice will likely reveal what formal analysis seems helpless to resolve. Economies do not stop working because of the aggregation problem and there are innumerable procedures in practice which serve to link decisions made at the national level to decisions made at lower levels. Elaborate devices exist to integrate the national and local aspects of economies. These devices are to a large degree embedded in the structure of governmental and financial institutions. In order, therefore, to understand the links between the national and the local, we have to examine in detail the structure of these institutions.

It is important to establish at the outset an appropriate methodological stance for such an investigation. We require a methodology capable of dealing with the relationship between the individual and society viewed as a totality of some sort. The methodology appropriate to this purpose has been generally neglected in the

From **Antipode**, Vol. 6, No. 1, April 1974, pp. 22–36. Reprinted in revised form by permission of **Antipode**, D. Harvey, and L. Chatterjee.

social sciences and much of our inability to deal with the "aggregation-problem" must be traced to that eclecticism and methodological myopia of which Barnbrock[1] speaks, which insists that we have to understand phenomena through conventional filters of cause-and-effect, functionalism and the like. The relations which we need to understand are, however, *contextual relations* or, as Ollman and others have proposed, *internal relations* through which the social totality is structured and transformed by individuals or entities (such as corporations) simultaneously exhibiting both "learning" behaviours which sustain the social structure as a whole and "instructing" behaviours—through which the social structure is itself transformed.[2] This conception of things is neither widely accepted nor even understood. But from it we gain an immediate object for enquiry—viz., the *processes* of structuring and transformation together with the determinate structures that mediate these processes.[3] We will now adopt such a methodological stance with respect to the housing market.

Typical concerns of housing policy at the national level are:

1. The relationship between construction, economic growth, and new household formation (population growth);

2. the behavior of the construction industry and the housing sector as a Keynesian regulator through which cyclical swings in the economy at large are ironed out;

3. the relationship between housing provision and the distribution of income (welfare) in society.

Since the 1930s, these concerns have generated aims that have, by and large, been successfully met.[4] Economic growth has been accompanied and to some degree accomplished by rapid suburbanization—a process that has been facilitated by national housing policies. Much of the growth in GNP (both absolute and per capita) since the 1930s is wrapped up in the suburbanization process (taking into account the construction of highways and utilities, housing, the effective demand generated by the automobile, etc.). Cyclical swings have been broadly contained since the 1930s and the construction industry appears to have functioned effectively as one of several major countercyclical tools. The evident social discontent of the 1930s has to some extent been successfully defused by a government policy that has created a large wedge of middle income people who are "debt encumbered homeowners" and who are unlikely to rock the boat because they are both debt-encumbered and reasonably well satisfied with their housing. The discontent of the 1960s exhibited by blacks and the poor provoked a similar political response to that of the 1930s in the housing sector a response that has not been particularly successful in obtaining "a decent house in a decent living environment" for many of the poor and the black, although

1. "A prologomenon to a methodological debate on location theory—the case of von Thunen," *Antipode,* Vol. 6, No. 1.
2. See Harvey, D., *Social Justice and the City* (Johns Hopkins University Press, Baltimore; 1973) chapter 7; Ollman, B., *Alienation: Marx's Conception of Man in Capitalist Society* (Cambridge University Press, London; 1971) and "Marxism and political science: prologomenon to a debate on Marx's method" (Department of Politics, New York University; 1972).
3. The concept of structure which we adopt is set out in detail by Godelier, M., *Rationality and Irrationality in Economics* (NLB, London; 1972). See also Piaget, J., *Structuralism* (Harper, New York; 1970).

4. The views set forth in this paragraph can be documented in detail from The Douglas Commission Report, *Building the American City* (Government Printing Office, Washington, D.C.; 1968). More detailed analyses of cyclical swings are collected together in Page, A. N. and Seyfried, W. R., *Urban Analysis* (Scott Foresman, Glenview, Illinois; 1970).

social instability of the 1960s appears to have been defused. At the national level, then, policies are designed to maintain an existing structure of society intact in its basic configurations, while facilitating economic growth and capitalist accumulation, eliminating cyclical influences, and defusing social discontent. Housing provides a vital and effective tool for stabilizing and perpetuating the social structure of a market-based, capitalist system.

How are these general programs and policies transmitted to the local level and ultimately to individuals making choices with respect to housing services in different locations? The mechanisms are very complex and we can do no more than sketch-in some of the basic relations between financial and governmental institutions, through which policies are filtered and transmitted to the local level. State Savings and Loans, Federal Savings and Loans, mortgage bankers, savings banks and commercial banks all operate in the housing market. The operations of State and Federal S&Ls are confined to housing and these institutions are designed to "promote the thrift of the people *locally* to finance their own homes and the homes of their neighbors."[5] The rules and regulations vary but in general State S&Ls tend to be small scale, community based and depositor controlled, whereas the larger Federal S&Ls tend to be "professionally" managed.[6] But Federal S&Ls are usually restricted to financial operations within 100 miles of their head office. Import and export of funds for housing from one market to another cannot occur through these institutions unless depositors shift their funds. The Federal S&Ls are, for the most part, under the control and guidance of the Federal Home Loan Bank Board which has tended in the past to regulate the flow of funds into the mortgage market in a counter-cyclical fashion with respect to the economy as a whole. FNMA and GNMA (the government institutions that buy up mortgages from the financial institutions to provide the latter with the liquidity for further investment in housing) on the other hand, operate usually to dampen cycles in housing construction which means that two sets of governmental institutions tend to follow contradictory policies.[7]

How do all of these financial and governmental complexities relate to the individual? In the typical micro-economic models of residential differentiation and housing markets, it is assumed that income is the relevant determinant of housing choice.[8] In fact, it is the ability to obtain credit and a mortgage that is, for most people, the immediate determinant. This ability is income-related, of course, but the ability to obtain a mortgage under suitable terms is also a function of the policies of financial and governmental institutions. Because servicing costs are constant no matter what the price of a house, financial institutions (particularly those geared to profit-making) prefer to finance the more expensive housing. In Baltimore, for example, savings banks rarely finance transactions in the price range below $20,000. Mortgage bankers have not gone below $7,000 very often and have recently decided as a matter of policy to try and stay above the $15,000 mark. Different institutions have distinctive policies with respect to downpayments, credit-worthiness, and the like, while government policies (particularly those of the FHA) also intervene in these respects and play a major role in those

5. *See Homeownership and the Baltimore Mortgage Market* (Draft Report of the Homeownership Development Program, Department of Housing and Community Development, Baltimore City; 1973).
6. The management characteristics of Federal S&Ls are documented in Rose, S., "The S&Ls break out of their shell," *Fortune*, 86, No. 3, pp. 152–70.

7. The details can be documented from the Douglas Commission Report (*op. cit.*).
8. For a general critical evaluation of these models see Harvey, D. (*op. cit.*) chapter 5.

Table 1. Distribution of Mortgage Activity in Different Price Categories by Type of Institution Baltimore City, 1972

	Under $7,000	$7,000–$9,999	$10,000–$11,999	$12,000–$14,999	Over $15,000
Private	39	16	13	7	7
State S&Ls	42	33	21	21	20
Federal S&Ls	10	22	30	31	35
Mortgage Banks	7	24	29	23	12
Savings Banks	—	3	5	15	19
Commercial Banks	1	1	2	3	7
Per cent of City's transactions in category	21	19	15	20	24

Source: "Homeownership and the Baltimore Mortgage Market," Draft Report of the Home Ownership Development Program, Department of Housing and Community Development, Baltimore City, 1973.

sectors of the population with moderate to marginal incomes or slender resources for down payment. There are also distinctive policies with respect to the nature of the housing stock which financial institutions are willing to finance (above and beyond the general operating rule, that appears to have held good for the last decade or so, that "new means better and safer" investment). There is also no question that different institutions, both financial and government, exhibit strong "neighborhood biases" (both pro and con) over and beyond that inherent in the community basis found in the State and some Federal S&Ls.

We will now describe some of the ways in which all of these factors coalesce in the Baltimore housing market. Consider first of all the behaviour of the different institutions with respect to house sales in different price categories (Table 1). There is clearly a structured relationship that leads the "commercial" institutions to operate in the higher price ranges while the State S&Ls, which tend not to be very strongly profit oriented, take up the housing in the lower price categories. The health of the housing market in this lower price category appears to be attached entirely to the fate of the

State S&Ls and a perpetuation of their community-based non-profit orientation. Should these institutions collapse, or come to have a strong profit orientation (as seems to be happening), then the housing market in the below $15,000 price range will suffer irreparable damage, particularly if the mortgage bankers implement a policy of a $15,000 minimum. There is, clearly, a highly structured relationship between household characteristics (particularly income) and the availability of mortgage funds (in appropriate price categories).[9]

This structured relationship has a geographical manifestation.[10] To demonstrate this we have divided the housing market in Baltimore City into 13 sub-markets which can be further aggregated to eight primary sub-market types (see Figure 1). We have tabulated data concerning the financing of housing in each of these sub-markets (see Table 2). We have also tabulated some information on house

9. See Homeownership and the Baltimore Mortgage Market (op. cit.).
10. This material is summarized from Harvey, D., Chatterjee, L., and Klugman, L., Effects of FHA Policies on the Housing Market in Baltimore City (Draft Report to the Urban Observatory, 222 E. Saratoga St., Baltimore, Md.; 1973).

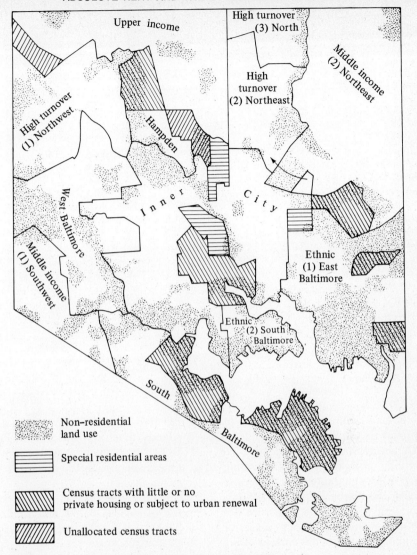

Figure 1. Sub-markets in Housing Finance, Baltimore City 1970

prices and socio-economic composition in the sub-markets. It is plain that the housing market in Baltimore City is highly structured geographically in terms of institutional involvement and FHA insured mortgage activity. The main features in this structuring are:

1. The inner city is dominated by cash and private transactions (with scarcely a vestige of institutional or governmental involvement) accompanied by a low purchase price, low incomes and a high proportion of tenants and blacks.

2. The ethnic areas are dominated by small community and neighborhood State S&Ls which circulate money within the community and in some cases finance migration to, for exam-

Table 2. Housing Sub-Markets, Baltimore City, 1970 (Census data)

	Total Houses Sold	Sales per 100 Properties	% Transactions by Source of Funds:							
			Cash	Pct	Fed S&L	State S&L	Mtge Bank	Comm Bank	Savings Bank	Other[a]
Inner City	1,199	1.86	65.7	15.0	3.0	12.0	2.2	0.5	0.2	1.7
East	646	2.33	64.7	15.0	2.2	14.3	2.2	0.5	0.1	1.2
West	553	1.51	67.0	15.1	4.0	9.2	2.3	0.4	0.4	2.2
Ethnic	760	3.34	39.9	5.5	6.1	43.2	2.0	0.8	0.9	2.2
E. Baltimore	579	3.40	39.7	4.8	5.5	43.7	2.4	1.0	1.2	2.2
S. Baltimore	181	3.20	40.3	7.7	7.7	41.4	0.6			2.2
Hampden	99	2.40	40.4	8.1	18.2	26.3	4.0		3.0	
West Baltimore	497	2.32	30.6	12.5	12.1	11.7	22.3	1.6	3.1	6.0
South Baltimore	322	3.16	28.3	7.4	22.7	13.4	13.4	1.9	4.0	9.0
High turnover	2,072	5.28	19.1	6.1	13.6	14.9	32.8	1.2	5.7	6.2
Northwest	1,071	5.42	20.0	7.2	9.7	13.8	40.9	1.1	2.9	4.5
Northeast	693	5.07	20.6	6.4	14.4	16.5	29.0	1.4	5.6	5.9
North	308	5.35	12.7	1.4	25.3	18.1	13.3	0.7	15.9	12.7
Middle income	1,077	3.15	20.8	4.4	29.8	17.0	8.6	1.9	8.7	9.0
Southwest	212	3.46	17.0	6.6	29.2	8.5	15.1	1.0	10.8	11.7
Northeast	865	3.09	21.7	3.8	30.0	19.2	7.0	2.0	8.2	8.2
Upper income	361	3.84	19.4	6.9	23.5	10.5	8.6	7.2	21.1	2.8

a Assumed mortgages and subject to mortgage.

ple, the middle income sub-market of Northeast Baltimore.

3. Black residential areas are serviced mainly by mortgage bankers operating under FHA guarantees (a response to the social discontent of the 1960s). Community-based State S&Ls are absent and without a strong sense of community will be difficult to bring into being. The Federal S&Ls apparently are reluctant to become involved in financing black ownership.

4. Mortgage bankers using the FHA guarantees (often of the no-down payment sort) are the predominant source of finance in areas of high turnover and racial change.

5. The white middle class, largely brought into homeownership through the FHA programs of the 1930s, occupies a solid area of northeast and southwest Baltimore as well as much of Baltimore County (which surrounds much of the City). Federal S&Ls here dominate with FHA guarantees supporting the market in traditional fashion.

6. The more affluent groups make greater use of savings banks and commercial banks and rarely make use of FHA guarantees.

This geographical structure forms a "decision environment" in the context of which individual households make housing choices. These choices are likely, by and large, to conform to the structure and to reinforce it. The structure itself is a product of history. Attempts to change the structure can in fact generate considerable social conflict. For example, middle-income buyers, disillusioned with the suburban dream, have to fight the institutional policies of the lending industry and

% Sales Insured:		Average Sale Price ($)b	Median Incomec	% Black Occupied Units	% Units Owner Occupied	Mean $ Value of Own. Occ.	% Renter Occupied	Mean Monthly Rent
FHA	VA							
2.9	1.1	3,498	6,259	72.2	28.5	6,259	71.5	77.5
3.4	1.4	3,437	6,201	65.1	29.3	6,380	70.7	75.2
2.3	0.6	3,568	6,297	76.9	27.9	6,963	72.1	78.9
2.6	0.7	6,372	8,822	1.0	66.0	8,005	34.0	76.8
3.2	0.7	6,769	8,836	1.2	66.3	8,368	33.7	78.7
0.6	0.6	5,102	8,785	0.2	64.7	6,504	35.3	69.6
14.1	2.0	7,059	8,730	0.3	58.8	7,860	41.2	76.8
25.8	4.2	8,664	9,566	84.1	50.0	13,842	50.0	103.7
22.7	10.6	8,751	8,941	0.1	56.9	9,741	43.1	82.0
38.2	9.5	9,902	10,413	34.3	53.5	11,886	46.5	113.8
46.8	7.4	9,312	9,483	55.4	49.3	11,867	50.7	110.6
34.5	10.2	9,779	10,753	30.4	58.5	11,533	41.5	111.5
31.5	15.5	12,330	11,510	1.3	49.0	12,726	51.0	125.1
17.7	11.1	12,760	10,639	2.8	62.6	13,221	37.5	104.1
30.2	17.0	12,848	10,655	4.4	48.8	13,470	51.2	108.1
14.7	9.7	12,751	10,634	2.3	66.2	13,174	33.8	103.0
11.9	3.6	27,413	17,577	1.7	50.8	27,097	49.2	141.4

b Ground rent is sometimes included in the sales price and this distorts the averages in certain respects. The relative differentials between the sub-markets are of the right order however.
c Weighted average of median incomes for census tracts in sub-market.
Source: City Planning Department Tabulations from Lusk Reports; 1970 Census.

the FHA if they wish to renovate an inner-city neighborhood.[11] Likewise, low-income blacks cannot be turned into "debt encumbered homeowners" painlessly. By struggles of this sort the structure can be transformed. In practice, therefore, we find that the geographic structure is continuously being transformed by the ebb and flow of market forces, the operations of speculators and realtors, the changing potential for homeownership, the changing profitability of landlordism, the pressures emanating from community action, the interventions and disruptions brought about by changing governmental and institutional policies, and the like. It is this process of transformation of and within a structure that must be the focus for

understanding residential differentiation and, as we will later show, provides the basis for understanding how absolute rent is realized in the housing market. We will examine two facets of this transformation process in Baltimore very briefly.

THE FHA IN BALTIMORE CITY[12]

Since the 1930s the Federal Housing Administration has administered a variety of programs designed to facilitate homeownership by making institutional investment in housing risk-free. Until the 1960s these programs serviced the needs of middle-income buyers and were instrumental in financing the suburbanization process. During the 1960s various programs with "social" objectives were initiated as the government attempted to

11. A typical struggle of this sort is documented by the Citizens Planning and Housing Association, *FHA: an Unsatisfactory Status Quo* (Baltimore, Md.; 1973).

12. This material is summarized from Harvey, D., Chatterjee, L. and Klugman, L. (*op. cit.*).

create a debt-encumbered, socially stable class of homeowners amongst the poor and the black. A mix of old and new programs were applied for this purpose and these—together with administrative directives to end, for example, the discriminatory "red-lining" of low-income and black neighborhoods—led to the creation of FHA-insured black and low-income housing sub-markets during the 1960s. The main tool in Baltimore was the 221 (d) (2) program (D2s) which permits the financing of home purchase for moderate- or low-income people of housing below $18,000 with negligible or no downpayment. A map of FHA insured mortgages indicates areas of high concentration within Baltimore City in 1970, while Table 2 indicates the extent of FHA involvement in the different sub-markets.

The creation of such a housing sub-market has not been without its problems, although Baltimore has not suffered from the speculative intervention that proved so disastrous in Detroit (where redistributive rent, in the sense that Walker argues for it,[13] was extracted with a vengeance). Foreclosure rates have been low in Baltimore compared to Detroit. The main problems in Baltimore have arisen from supporting the movement of a low-income and predominantly black population into middle class white neighborhoods, from forming a specific geographical sub-market within which a specific kind of financing and population are confined, and from risk-aversion practices, designed to prevent a high rate of foreclosure, which effectively deny government insurance to inner-city neighborhoods. These problems arise for a variety of reasons. The FHA programs, particularly the D2s are a "last resort" for housing finance—they are only made use of when conventional sources of financing

are unavailable. The FHA has to "draw a line" somewhere in administering these programs (a line set up in terms of credit characteristics of the purchaser, the nature of the housing and its physical conditions, etc.). This "drawing of the line somewhere" in fact means a line between mortgage finance and cash transactions which becomes, by design or accident, a "red-line" on the map of housing market activity. Within this line, in the inner city, mortgages cannot be obtained and immediately outside of it the FHA supports the market. The jump of housing prices across this line is clearly evident (see Table 2).

The net effect is that FHA programs and policies create a plateau of house prices between the "disinvestment sink" of the inner city and the stable middle income areas. On this plateau we find a mixture of low-income and predominantly black homeownership and landlordism. At the edges of the plateau we find social conflict as processes of "filter-down" and "blow-out" erode the geographical structure of housing sub-markets.[14]

LANDLORDISM AND THE BALTIMORE CITY HOUSING MARKET[15]

There are many different types of landlord varying from the individual who has one house to the professional who owns a large number, uses professional management techniques, and is very sensitive

13. Walker, R. A., "Urban ground rent—building a new conceptual framework," *Antipode,* Vol. 6, No. 1.

14. The concepts of filter-down and blow-out are discussed in detail in Harvey, D. (*op. cit.*) and their relevance to the Baltimore housing situation is discussed in detail in Harvey, D., Chatterjee, L., Wolman, M. G., Klugman, L. and Newman, J., *The Housing Market and Code Enforcement in Baltimore* (The Baltimore Urban Observatory, 222 E. Saratoga St., Baltimore, Md.; 1972).

15. This material is derived from Chatterjee, L., *Real Estate Investment and Deterioration of Housing in Baltimore* (Doctoral Dissertation, Department of Geography and Environmental Engineering, The Johns Hopkins University; 1973).

to profits, losses and the rate of return on capital. We will ignore the complexities and confine attention to professional landlords who own and manage about a quarter of Baltimore City's rental inventory. These professional landlords make their decisions in terms of a structured decision environment and closely gear their operations to the characteristics of sub-markets as they perceive and experience them.

We asked four landlords to distinguish areas in the city which they regarded as "good," "moderately good," "moderately bad," or "bad" for investment. We aggregated their maps of perceived investment opportunity to form a composite map and analyzed their costs, expenditures, rates of return, etc., across these different perceived investment situations. It was found that there was a rational adjustment of landlord operations to sub-market characteristics and that this adjustment had certain important consequences for the maintenance of the housing stock, rent levels, and the like. We will not discuss the details here, but the most important element in the landlord's decision is the availability or non-availability of landlord finance. In areas where the landlords can obtain mortgage funds they work on the basis of "leverage" which works as follows. A $10,000 house is purchased with a $1,000 down payment and a $9,000 mortgage at, say, a 6 per cent interest rate. The landlord manages the property to yield an overall 8 per cent rate of return on the $10,000 (which is $800), pays off the interest of $540, which leaves $260 to be applied to the landlord's investment of $1,000 which yields an effective return of 26 per cent on the landlord's part of the capital. This calculation is more complicated when worked out over the lifetime of the mortgage, of course, but the principle of leverage operates over each round and the average rate of return is much higher for the landlord (it usually comes to between

15 and 18 per cent) than is indicated by the rate of return calculated against the total value of the house. The tenant is also advantaged by this, for the tenant lives in a $10,000 house for a rent that yields only 8 per cent on that value, while the landlord, interested in capital accumulation in the physical form of the house, will keep it well maintained.

If the landlord cannot obtain mortgage finance, the story becomes rather different. The landlord has to obtain a "satisfactory" yield on the total value of the house. What is meant by a "satisfactory" yield is set by convention on the part of professional landlords but it is obviously sensitive to the rate of return possible in the capital market in general.[16] Professional landlords in Baltimore, in fact, look for a 20 per cent rate of return on their capital, regard 15 per cent as "normal" and will still stay in operation at 11–12 per cent (this is *after* all expenses are met including interest payments *and* an imputed managerial wage to the landlord as manager). Using leverage, landlords can gain a 15 per cent rate of return for themselves by taking, say, an 8 per cent rate of return on the total value of the property. Without leverage they have to take a 15 per cent rate of return directly. Leverage is not possible in the inner city because mortgage funds are not generally available; so tenants here have to pay a much greater rent relative to the total value of the property than would be the case if mortgage finance were available. But the inner city is the worst sub-market in terms of quality of housing stock, etc. Landlords therefore find it difficult to dispose of their properties in this sub-market, except through urban renewal schemes (which landlords

16. Exactly how a "satisfactory" rate of return on capital is defined in general is, of course, a subject of dispute. We follow in general the view put forward by Rhaduri, A., "Recent controversies in capital theory: a Marxian view," *Economic Journal*, 79, 1969, pp. 532–9.

frequently actively promote as a means of bailing out of the worst sub-market). If profit levels fall or if there is even an expectation that they will fall below the limit of, say, 11–12 per cent (because of oversupply of poor housing, rising management costs, vandalism, and the like), then landlords will seek to get their money out through a disinvestment process (economizing on maintenance, milking properties, etc.). Hence there arises a housing sub-market characterized by landlord disinvestment, housing abandonment, and severe neighborhood decay. Landlords will still, on occasion, purchase in this sub-market, but if they do so, it is at a very low market price (note the prices in Table 2) for a good quality dwelling which they operate to regain their outlay over a short time-horizon.

It is evident that landlords "structure" their behavior according to their decision environment. There is a "rational" (profit maximizing) adjustment of landlord behaviour to sub-market characteristics. This behaviour, in turn, structures outcomes with respect to the renter, the maintenance of the housing stock, reinvestment and disinvestment, neighborhood decay and the like. This structuring activity is not without its implications for the way in which financial institutions and government institutions together formulate, in turn, rationales for investment and intervention.

The Realization of Absolute Rent

The category of absolute rent has been completely ignored in locational analysis until recently.[17] We will not discuss its theoretical aspects here, but will attempt to explain the actual processes whereby it is realized in the housing markets of a large urban area. It is important to re-

17. See Harvey, D. (*op. cit.*) and Walker, R. A. (*op. cit.*) for recent attempts to explicate the rental concept in a contemporary context.

alize, however, that rent essentially represents a *transfer payment* between individuals, interest groups or classes and that it does not represent any increase in value through production.

Absolute rent implies class monopoly power of some sort. By a "class monopoly" we mean a class of producers (or consumers) who have power over a class of consumers (or producers) in a situation of structured scarcity.[18] We have first to define the basis for such class monopoly power in the housing market. The materials we have assembled in the first part of this paper in fact provide a description of this necessary basis. Through the structuring activity of governmental and financial institutions, urban space is differentiated into specific sub-markets. If absolute rent is to be realized we have to show that there are absolute limits of some sort operating over different segments of the housing market. These absolute limits can be set by the joint attributes of housing, of financiers, of housing suppliers and of consumers. To become a low-income owner of a $5,000 house in Baltimore, for example, means

18. The use of the word "class" here may generate some confusion. We use the word flexibly to mean any group of individuals who find themselves collectively in opposition to any other collectivity of individuals with respect to the transfer payment that rent represents. The "class distinctions" which we here make use of are not, therefore, of the sort that stem from the organization of production and the division of labour (for a modern examination of these see Poulantzas, N., "Marxism and social classes," *New Left Review*, 78, 1973, pp. 27–55). We do not believe our use of the concept of class in this special sense is inconsistent with Marx's relational definition and usage of this concept. Certainly, the concept of class monopoly power is explicitly formulated in Marx, K., *Capital,* Volume 3 (International Publishers Edition, New York; 1967) pp. 194–5, while it is clear from Marx's various analyses of the rental concept that distinctive classes (such as that of the rentier) may emerge outside of the process of production to reflect the various transfers that can occur in the circulation of the surplus.

either a cash transaction or access to a community based State S&L. A low or moderate income black will purchase a $10,000 house through a mortgage banker operating under an FHA guarantee. An upper-income person will typically go through a savings bank or a Federal S&L and purchase a house priced above $25,000. In each of these cases, the opportunities are restricted in terms of the structure. But the absolute limits are also set geographically through the structured pattern of housing sub-markets within which specific conditions hold. "Absolute limits" means in this case the creation of absolute urban spaces within which producers and consumers of housing services face each other as classes in conflict.[19] What transpires within each sub-market depends (1) on the internal conditions within that sub-market and (2) on the interaction between sub-markets.

The processes are evidently complex when we take into account the relationships both within and between sub-markets, and as we introduce more actors into the housing drama (financial and governmental institutions, the construction industry, and so on). But the principle remains the same. The geographical and social structure creates conditions within which absolute rents can be realized to varying degrees depending upon the relative power of those supplying housing and those consuming it, as that relative power is mediated by institutional policies (legal, political, financial, governmental, etc.).

In all of these situations—and we could specify the situation in detail with respect to each sub-market if we so wished—the rates of return and the potential for obtaining absolute rent are structured by the opposing forces within each sub-market and the interactions between sub-markets. Class conflict within a sub-market is tempered by class differentials and class conflicts between sub-markets. And it is in such a structured situation that absolute rent is realized in the housing market in general.

A Concluding Comment

We accept the view that rent is a transfer payment out of a social rate of return on capital. We also accept the view that rent accrues to the inherent monopoly power of private property.[20] To understand how rent is in practice realized is therefore to understand all of those situations and conditions which permit transfer payments to occur and which affect the actual amounts transferred. The categories of differential, absolute and monopoly rent, to which Walker adds redistributive rent, provide generalized descriptions of the theoretical circumstances which contribute to the processes of transfer. The explanatory power of these categories depends, however, on our ability to specify in practice how actual transfer payments arise under the conditions theoretically specified in each category. In this paper we have shown that the category of absolute rent is meaningful in the contemporary urban scene. We have shown that the conditions for its realization are automatically generated by the way in which institutional arrangements are structured to integrate national and local aspects of housing market behaviour.

The absolute spaces created by institutional arrangements form a geographical framework within which absolute rent can be realized. Within this geographical framework we find different interest groups facing each other as classes. The relative power of these classes with re-

19. The concept of absolute space is further elaborated on in Harvey, D. (*op. cit.*)

20. This, of course, was Marx's main point—see Marx, K. (*op. cit.*) and *The Poverty of Philosophy* (International Publishers Edition, New York; 1963) pp. 154–66.

spect to each other, together with the possibilities open for substitution in other sub-markets, provides the social setting within which the realization of absolute rent becomes possible. The classes we identify here are not, of course, the classes relevant to understanding the production process. Rent is not, after all, inherent in production but arises only because the legal institution of private property is a necessary feature in the capitalist mode of production and because it proves difficult or impossible to restrict the legal right to production solely. The classes we are here concerned with are, when set against the broader class structure of society, perhaps best interpreted as sub-classes in conflict with each other over the transfer payment that rent represents. The rich, for example, may be forced to yield a relatively high transfer payment to other members of their own general social class (the company director may yield up absolute rent to the class monopoly power of the developer). A low-income tenant may likewise gain absolute rent by sub-letting. The general

pattern of transfer payments is, however, fairly obvious—poorer groups yield a net transfer payment to richer groups because the former have little power or possibility for substitution, while the latter have considerable class monopoly power and a greater range of choice.

We are not claiming that rent in an urban situation has to be totally understood in absolute terms. Differential, monopoly, absolute and redistributive rent all contribute to the formation of actual rent. But we believe we have shown, quite conclusively, that absolute rent can contribute substantially to actual rent in large urban areas. We have also shown that this contribution is made possible by the way in which social, institutional and geographical structures are created for the purpose of integrating local and national aspects of economies. We believe that we have also shown that a great deal can be learned if we are prepared to adopt a methodology appropriate for understanding society as a totality fashioned through a structured set of internal relations.

DENNIS E. GALE

Middle Class Resettlement in Older Urban Neighborhoods: The Evidence and the Implications

In recent years, a small but growing number of middle-class households have moved into declining, older central city neighborhoods in the United States. Though a few of these areas were the sites of Urban Renewal programs, most have undergone renovation and restoration through private investment activity. The significance of this movement, termed "neighborhood resettlement" here, lies in its stark contrast to the urban-to-suburban migration patterns which have predominated in metropolitan areas at least since the 1950s. Indeed, an elaborate body of residential location theory has developed since the 1920s, much of which assumes that households "filter up" through the housing supply as their family size and economic status grow. Housing and neighborhoods, on the other hand, filter downward as increasing age renders both architectural styles and technological features obsolete (Lowry 1960) and these areas became economic for progressively lower income groups (Grigsby 1963). One common result in older urban residential areas is invasion and succession, whereby households of lower socioeconomic status displace those of higher status (Duncan and Duncan 1957). Conversely, there is evidence that in the 1970s significant numbers of young households have filtered downward to an older housing stock and consequently, their neighborhoods have filtered upward through a myriad of individual rehabilitations. In effect, a reverse invasion and succession process is replacing households of lower socioeconomic circumstances with those of higher circumstances. To be sure, such patterns are not unprecedented. Theorists such as Firey (1947), Hoover and Vernon (1959), and Birch (1971) have identified isolated urban locations where deviations from these norms have occurred. Research on the 1960–1970 period has shown that a few older urban neighborhoods near central business districts experienced increases in median family income (Lipton 1977). Many of these however, appear to have resulted from redevelopment (e.g. Urban Renewal) rather than from private market investment in rehabilitation of the existing housing stock. But growing evidence suggests that in the 1970s the incidence of middle class inmigration to these types of areas has increased rather substantially.

In a survey of public officials and real

From the **Journal of the American Planning Association,** Vol. 45, No. 3, July 1979, pp. 293–304. Reprinted by permission of the **Journal** and D. E. Gale.

estate officials in 143 cities, Black found that 48 percent of communities over 50,000 population had some degree of private market, non-subsidized housing renovation underway in older deteriorated neighborhoods (1975). Another survey, of public officials and local citizen organizations in the thirty largest U.S. cities, discovered that resettlement was occurring in almost all of them. Fifty-three such neighborhoods were found (Clay 1978). In a study of forty-four cities, substantial private market rehabilitation was identified in almost 75 percent (National Urban Coalition 1978). Sixty-five resettlement neighborhoods were located.

One important key to understanding the reasons for this apparent departure from classical precepts of residential location theory is the development of broad-based data from opinion surveys of resttlement households. Unfortunately, such comprehensive statistics do not yet exist. Nevertheless, a number of individual, separately-conducted surveys have been performed recently in American resettlement neighborhoods and together their results provide some important indications as to the identity of the resettlers, their geographic origins, and the reasons for their residential location choice. These studies were conducted in Atlanta (McWilliams 1975), Boston and Cambridge (Pattison 1977), New Orleans (Ragas and Miestchovich 1977), New York (New York Landmarks Conservancy 1977), St. Paul (Urban Land Institute 1976), and Washington, D.C. (Gale 1977, 1976).

Other evidence indicates that negative externalities occur in the form of the displacement of many low and moderate income households by the renovation process. Together these data form a preliminary composite description of the extent and character of neighborhood resettlement. Though the condition of this evidence does not permit more sophisti-

cated analyses, the sheer paucity of published quantitative studies and the critical nature of the subject itself, warrant the present preliminary investigation.

Demographic Characteristics of Resettlers

Data sources are sufficient to permit observations on six demographic characteristics of resettler households: household size, racial composition, annual income, and the age, education, and occupation of the household head. (See Table 1.)

Household size. With comparatively few exceptions, resettler households tend to be small. At least one-half (48 percent) in one Boston neighborhood and as many as 97 percent in an Atlanta area are composed of one or two persons. Nationwide, about one-half of all households are composed of one or two persons (U.S. Bureau of the Census 1977, I). At least 60 percent in each neighborhood have no children present. Household size in the New York neighborhood tended to be larger, though this may be attributable to the fact that it underwent resettlement several years ago.

Racial composition. With pitifully few exceptions, the resettler households were composed of whites. In a few cases, mixed households (one black and one white) appeared. In three cities white households composed between 94 and 97 percent of all resettler households. One Washington neighborhood showed a black resettler proportion of 14 percent, though blacks make up 75 percent of the city's population. By contrast, the mean proportions of whites and blacks in metropolitan central cities in the United States in 1970 were 75 and 23 percent respectively (Advisory Commission on Intergovernmental Relations 1977).

Annual income. Neighborhoods in only four cities provided data on house-

Table 1. Demographic Characteristics of Recent In-migrants in Individual Resettlement Neighborhoods of Atlanta,[1] New Orleans,[2] New York,[3] St. Paul,[4] Washington,[5] Boston,[6] and Cambridge[6] (percentages of total sample in each study)

City in Which Resettlement Neighborhood Is Located	Household Size[b]				Age of Household Head[b]				Racial Makeup of Household			Household Annual Income[b]				Highest Education of Household Head			Occupation of Household Head		
	One-person	Two-person	Two or fewer	No children present	20–29	25–34	30–39	35–44	White	Black	Mixed	Under $15,000	$15,000 or more	Under $20,000	$20,000 or more	Less than 4-year college degree	4-year college degree	Graduate degree or graduate work	Professional & technical	Managerial	Other
Atlanta (1975)	27	70		66	41		39		99			39	56			38	38	24	57	12	31
New Orleans (1977)	45	27	72	75+			46[f]		97			4	88[g]								
New York (1977)	8			42		43		24							46	20	18	61	57/55	10/27	33/8
St. Paul (1975)				64		74[d]										80[e]					
Washington, D.C.[a] (1977/1976)	29/23	55/60		74/61		59/63		21/23	94/77	0/14	0/7			7/22	90/73	3/13	10/21	87/65			
Boston (1972–1975)		48[c]				63		21											60	5	35
Cambridge (1972–75)		80[c]				50		39											82	—	18

[a] Two neighborhoods reported.

[b] Categories are not mutually exclusive because each study was conducted independently of the others.

[c] Data for the period 1957–1975.

[d] Data for ages 21 through 39.

[e] Eight percent "have at least 4 years of college."

[f] Forty-six percent were between ages 25 and 44. None was under age 25. Fifty-four percent were over age 44.

[g] Twelve percent earned $15,000–$24,999. Forty-two percent earned $25,000–$49,999. Thirty-five percent earned $50,000 or more.

Sources: 1, McWilliams (1975); 2, Ragas and Miestchovich (1977); 3, New York Landmarks (1977); 4, Urban Land Institute (1976); 5, Gale (1976 and 1977); 6, Pattison (1977).

hold income and it is not apparent whether gross or net income figures were presented. Nonetheless, the evidence confirms suspicions that resettler households generally are comfortably middle income. More than one-half (56 percent) in the Atlanta neighborhood and 88 percent in the New York area had incomes of $15,000 or more. Almost one-half (46 percent) in New Orleans reported incomes of $20,000 or more while 73 percent and 90 percent in two Washington neighborhoods had such incomes. These figures compare closely to the 49.4 percent of families nationally earning $15,000 or more in 1975, when the median family income was almost $14,900 (U.S. Bureau of the Census 1977, I).

Age. Clearly, the largest group of household heads in resettlement families tends to range in age from the mid-twenties to the mid-thirties. No city reported less than 40 percent in this age group. Nationally, only 20 percent of household heads fell in this range in 1976 (U.S. Bureau of the Census 1977, I). Those resettlers in the age 35 to 44 interval represent the next largest group; at least 20 percent fell in this range while nationally 16 percent did so.

Education. No other indicators are as impressive as those on the level of education achieved by resettler household heads. Most had completed at least a four-year college degree program in Atlanta (62 percent), New York (79 percent), St. Paul (80 percent), and Washington (97/86 percent). By comparison, only 14.7 percent of the U.S. population age 25 and older held a four-year college degree in 1976 (U.S. Bureau of the Census 1977, II). In highly competitive employment markets such as New York and Washington, where specialized graduate education is often required, 61 percent and 87 percent had achieved graduate

degrees. But, even in Atlanta, a rapidly growing regional center, fully one-fourth (24 percent) of resettlers held graduate degrees.

Occupation. Closely correlated to education is the head-of-household's occupation. More than one-half of household heads in resettlement neighborhoods in Atlanta, New York, St. Paul, Boston, and Cambridge, Massachusetts were classified as professionals. Managerial and administrative occupations were much less in evidence in most neighborhoods, though in St. Paul 27 percent were found to fall in this category. Clerical, sales, and blue-collar employees constituted as much as 35 percent of the remaining portion. As a rough basis of comparison, 15.2 percent of U.S. employed persons were classified as professional or technical workers in 1976 and 10.6 percent were in managerial and administrative positions (U.S. Bureau of the Census 1977, II).

Collectively, these data lend considerable weight to popular characterizations of resettlers. The most typical such household is childless and composed of one or two white adults in their late twenties or thirties. College educated, often possessing graduate education, the household head is most likely a professional or (less commonly) a manager. The annual household income varies among metropolitan areas but is likely to range between $15,000 and $30,000, with several resettlers earning more than $40,000. Doubtless, many of those earning higher incomes are composed of two workers. For the most part, the above evidence seems to be supported by more descriptive accounts of resettlement in several American cities.

Geographic Origins of Resettlers

One of the most misunderstood notions about the inner city neighborhood resettlement phenomenon is the origin of its participants. Where are the resettlers moving from? The answer is important for obvious reasons. To the extent that the reinvestment process continues and grows, it could have a substantial effect on the future viability of central cities. The list of benefits which municipal governments derive from this process—improved housing stock, lower demands for social services, higher real estate taxes and other revenues, more affluent consumer participation in the central city economy—are considerable.

If the resettlers were migrating in from the surrounding suburbs in sufficient numbers, they would help to offset the well-documented suburban movement of city dwellers, the bane of large-city governments for many years. In order for public officials to stimulate private market investment in older urban neighborhoods, it is important for them to understand from where the current resettlers—and therefore, potential future resettlers—are coming.

Unfortunately, a popular wisdom has developed which refers to resettlement as the "Back-to-the-City Movement." Thus many observers have assumed, with little or no evidence, that most resettlers are dissatisfied, former suburbanites.

To the contrary, evidence indicates that a relatively small minority of households moved into resettlement neighborhoods from the city's encircling suburbs (see Table 2). Less than 20 percent of resettlers surveyed in Atlanta, Boston, Cambridge, and Washington said that they had done so. In fact, more appear to have located in some cities from outside the metropolitan area altogether (i.e., from communities in other parts of the United States). The data indicate that more than one-half (and in some cases as many as 90 percent) already were seasoned urbanites, having moved to the renovating area from somewhere within the city's municipal boundaries. Evidence

Table 2. Previous Location of Recent In-migrants to Resettlement Neighborhoods in Atlanta,[1] Boston,[2] Cambridge,[2] New Orleans,[3] and Washington[4] (percentages of total sample in each study)

City in Which Resettlement Neighborhood Is Located	Lived in the Central City	Lived in the Suburbs	Lived Outside the Metropolitan Area
Atlanta (1975)	57	8	35
Boston (1972–1975)	72	15[b]	—
Cambridge (1972–1975)	90	15[b]	—
New Orleans (1977)	—	—	26
Washington (1977/1976)[a]	71/67	15/18	14/16

[a] Two neighborhoods reported.
[b] The maximum proportion of households from the suburbs or elsewhere in Massachusetts was fifteen percent.

Sources: 1, McWilliams (1975); 2, Pattison (1977); 3, Ragas and Miestchovich (1977); 4, Gale (1976 and 1977).

on the previous housing type and tenure of resettling homebuyers is limited to studies of two Washington, D.C. neighborhoods. About one-half of the resettlers had moved to their current location from an apartment and two-thirds had been renters in their previous location.

If these figures are even roughly representative of resettlers in other cities, they suggest that most are first-home buyers. It is likely that they migrated to the city to attend college or graduate school or to take employment there. After working a few years, they accumulated enough capital to make a downpayment on a house and were encouraged to do so by their rising incomes and favorable federal tax policies.

Not only do few resettlers appear to be ex-suburbanites, there is evidence that most consciously embraced inner city living and/or rejected a suburban location when looking for a house to purchase. In other words, few appear to have "settled" for an inner city dwelling as a second-best alternative to a suburban home. On the contrary, other observers suggest that the life-style associated with suburban residence and/or the presumed ideology of its inhabitants is at odds with those of most resettlers.

. . . there is a very conscious rejection of suburbia, or rather a conscious rejection of the somewhat stereotyped "image" of suburbia . . . by residents in the area, and a correspondingly positive assertion of the values of "urban living." . . . From this perspective suburbia is seen as a retreat from the reality of major social problems facing American society; and residents who . . . move from the area are defined by others and to a degree, themselves as "selling out"—not simply a house—but an ideology and a movement (Hunter 1975).

Resettlers in Boston contrasted themselves to suburbanites as "more interesting" and "intellectual" and less concerned with traditional status symbols such as membership in a country club.

. . . there are very often feelings of superiority toward his or her suburban counterparts. In this sense, at least for the duration of their time in the core city, young professionals identify themselves as part of an elite within the middle-class elite (Parkman Center for Urban Affairs 1977).

Statistics from a survey of resettlers in an Atlanta neighborhood indicate that over two-thirds (69 percent) preferred a central city, rather than a suburban, residential setting. More than one-third looked only in the study neighborhood for a home. More than one-half of the remainder (51 percent) looked only in city neighborhoods, mostly renovation areas (McWilliams 1975).

The strongly urban-oriented predilections of resettlers, at least in transitional neighborhoods, contrast sharply with their earlier experiences, if the results of the Washington surveys are representative of most resettlers nationwide (Gale 1977, 1976). Slightly less than two-thirds (64 percent and 61 percent) in two such neighborhoods reported that they had spent all or most of their childhood years in a suburban, small town, or rural setting. In addition, at least three-fourths (77 percent and 88 percent) spent those years living in a single-family detached house, the style most associated with suburban and suburban-like living. This latter finding is significant because most Washington resettlers (indeed, it appears, most resettlers nationwide) live in rowhouses located in higher density areas, a dwelling type more commonly linked to inner-city living. Hence, their current locational choice, although a continuation of their adult urban locational preference, represents a decided departure from their childhood experiences.

Why Did They Move to the Neighborhood?

No factor related to the resettlement phenomenon so intrigues some researchers and public officials as the explanation of why it is happening at all. Though the varied sources of the data discussed here permit only loose comparisons, it is clear that four conditions most appealed to the respondents: an acceptable housing price, the investment potential of the property, accessibility to place of employment, and the architectural/historical character of the house and/or neighborhood (see Table 3). Of these four, the last showed the most consistently high ratings. From 72 to 85 percent of the respondents in Atlanta, New Orleans, and New York rated architectural/historical character highly,[1] and those in Washington valued it only slightly less so than their property's investment potential.

Generally, economic variables related to the price and the investment accessibility variable appear to be of approxi-

Table 3. Reasons Given by Resettlers for Their Residential Location Choice in Atlanta,[1] New Orleans,[2] New York[3] and Washington[4] (all figures given as percentages)

Cities in Which Resettlement Neighborhood Is Located	Acceptable Housing Price	Investment Potential of the Property	Accessibility to Place of Employment	Architectural-Historical Character of House and/or Neighborhood	Cultural, Social, and/or Shopping Opportunities Available in the City	Desire To Live in a Racially Integrated, Diverse Neighborhood	Desire To Live Near Friends Who Reside in or Near to Neighborhood	Proximity to a University
Atlanta (1975)[a]	70	—	66	72	73	—	27	29
New Orleans (1977)[a]	60	75	70	83	—	—	—	—
New York (1977)[a,b]	42	—	39	85	23	4	19	—
Washington (1977/1976)[c]	17/19	22/24	16/13	18/14	14/10	6/14	77	—

[a] Respondents could choose more than one highly favorable characteristic. Thus, percentages do not equal 100.
[b] Some figures represent responses from residents who moved into the neighborhood before historic designation and others from those who moved in afterward.
[c] Two neighborhoods reported. Figures represent the proportion of respondents identifying each factor as among the three most important in influencing their locational choice.

Sources: 1, McWilliams (1975); 2, Thayer and Waidhas (1977); 3, New York Landmarks (1977); 4, Gale (1976 and 1977).

mately equal importance overall. Though individual resettlers vary in the relative weight they ascribe to each characteristic, there are few who are likely not to cite one or more as critical in their locational choice. From 42 to 70 percent of resettlers in three cities rated an acceptable housing price as among their highest concerns in locational choice; in Washington, it was comparably rated. Though data are sparse, Table 3 hints that the resettler's concern over the investment potential of his property was an even more compelling consideration than its price. Because most resettlers are purchasing their first home, it is likely that they do so with an especially critical eye to the promise of a substantial, relatively rapid, capital gain in the future.

Easy access to place of employment was a salient matter also, ranging from 39 to 70 percent in the proportion of resettlers who rated it highly in three renovation neighborhoods. Again, in Washington, results were comparable.

Washington, D.C.: A Case Study

The preceding analysis, based on findings from studies of several reinvestment neighborhoods in the United States, is an attempt to characterize demographic and attitudinal traits of resettler households. The absence of standardized survey research among a representative sampling of such neighborhoods and households renders this exercise necessary. Nevertheless, though necessary, it is not sufficient.

Each study was conducted independently and therefore, the bases of comparison are limited to the topics discussed thus far. A second examination, an in-depth analysis of resettlers in the city of Washington, D.C., will yield further insights into their motivations and behavior. Of course, we cannot generalize nationwide on the basis of either approach; but together, the two investigations will provide a more comprehensive impression of the nature and character of neighborhood resettlement than the author has been able to discover anywhere in the literature.

Graduate students studying urban and regional planning conducted household surveys under the author's direction in the Mount Pleasant and Capitol Hill sections of Washington (Gale 1976, 1977). Both neighborhoods have been experiencing resettlement and reinvestment, though the process has been underway longer on Capitol Hill. Both are composed predominantly of masonry row dwellings built in the late nineteenth and early twentieth centuries and have significant populations of black, low- and moderate-income households. The close proximity of the Capitol Hill neighborhood to employment centers such as the U.S. Congress, Library of Congress, Supreme Court, Executive Branch agencies, and ancillary private organizations has made it a popular residential setting for those who work nearby. The Mount Pleasant area, located about two miles north of the White House, has a more varied work force among its resettler residents. The Capitol Hill neighborhood has no commonly accepted boundaries and thus, has spread to the northeast, east and southeast in a fanshaped pattern for at least one mile. Mount Pleasant, on the other hand, is tightly defined by an abutting linear park on the north and west and by wide, busily-travelled streets on the east and south. It is about one-quarter mile in width and length.

New homebuyers in these areas were randomly sampled and face-to-face interviews were completed. Data on their demographic properties (Table 1), their metropolitan geographical origins (Table 2), and their reasons for choosing to buy a dwelling in a reinvestment area (Table 3) are presented above. Generally, Washington resettler households tend to be composed of white, childless, singles and couples in their late twenties or thirties. Income and educational levels are somewhat higher than among resettlers in other cities but this is due to the overwhelmingly professional, managerial, and clerical nature of the employment market in the nation's capital. At least two-thirds of resettlers in each neighborhood had moved to their current location from within the city of Washington while 54 percent of Washington movers overall had done so (see Table 4) (Grier and Grier 1978). The proportion of resettlers moving in from outside the District of Columbia ranged from about one-fifth (Capitol Hill) to one-third (Mount

Table 4. Origins of Capitol Hill and Mount Pleasant Recent Movers Compared to All Households Who Move to or within Washington, D.C. (percent)

Previous Location	Capitol Hill Movers[a]	Mount Pleasant Movers[b]	All D.C. Movers[c]
Capitol Hill	52	—	—
Mount Pleasant	—	16	—
D.C.	71	67	57
Outside D.C.	22	34	35
D.C. SMSA	15	18	6
Outside D.C. SMSA	7	16	29
No answer	7	—	8

[a] All moves occurred in 1976.
[b] All moves occurred in 1974–1975.
[c] All moves occurred in 1970–1974.
Source: George and Eunice Grier, *Movers to the City*, Washington Center for Metropolitan Studies, Washington, D.C. (May 1977), p. 10.

Pleasant), though 15 percent and 18 percent, respectively, moved in from the city's suburbs.

The most consistently highly-rated reasons for choosing to locate in Mount Pleasant and Capitol Hill were the investment potential of the house purchased, the relatively affordable price, accessibility to place of employment, and the architectural/historical character of the house and/or neighborhood. Lesser, though not insignificant, concern was shown for the social and cultural attractions of city living (Table 3). The desire to live near friends who had preceded them into the resettlement area or to live in an integrated neighborhood were rarely cited reasons for the move.

Both neighborhood surveys sought insights on the reactions of resettlers to their new home and neighborhood. When asked to scale their sentiments about their dwelling unit and lot 71 percent of those in Capitol Hill rated their properties "most favorable" and 29 percent "favorable"; conversely, the Mount Pleasant sample rated theirs 37 percent "highly favorable" and 58 percent "favorable." Only negligible proportions showed neutral or unfavorable feelings. This divergence in enthusiam was evident also in the mover's reaction to the *neighborhood*. Forty-seven percent of those on Capitol Hill were highly favorable and 50 percent were favorable. The corresponding figures for Mount Pleasantites were 23 and 61 percent respectively. Clearly, the Mount Pleasant resettlers showed less extreme feelings for their living conditions than those shown for Capitol Hill.

Similarly, when queried about the length of time they expected to remain at their current address, 29 percent of Capitol Hill movers and 14 percent of their Mount Pleasant counterparts said "10 years or longer." Thirty-four percent of the latter expected to remain less than 10 years. Indeed, the proportion of Capitol Hill respondents who had lived in

that neighborhood prior to their current home purchase was three times as large as that of Mount Pleasantites who had lived previously in Mount Pleasant (52 percent vs. 16 percent). Finally, when queried as to the length of time each group had lived in its current neighborhood (both current and previous residences) 57 percent of Capitol Hill and 86 percent of Mount Pleasant residents said "less than four years." Almost five times as large a proportion of the first group had lived on Capitol Hill as had the proportion for Mount Pleasant (24 percent vs. 5 percent).

Another indicator of differences in level of commitment to each neighborhood was a question on future moving intentions. Forty-five percent of the Capitol Hill and 28 percent of the Mount Pleasant respondents would choose another dwelling in the same neighborhood if they decided to leave their current address. Nineteen percent of Capitol Hill and 32 percent of Mount Pleasant resettlers would move to a different neighborhood. Only five percent of each group would move to the suburbs, and the remainder were undecided or gave no response.

The differences in level of expressed enthusiasm between the two neighborhood resettler groups may be explained by the fact that Capitol Hill has been undergoing reinvestment for a considerably longer time than Mount Pleasant. To that extent, it is a more "mature" resettlement neighborhood. Therefore, those who choose to live there may be less interested in their homes as a stepping-stone to a more expensive dwelling in a more affluent area. Instead, they may have purchased homes on Capitol Hill with a commitment to remain several years. For them, living in that neighborhood appears to be an end in itself, not merely a way-station on the route to a better house and location. This could indicate that the Capitol Hill neighborhood has reached a more advanced level in the filtering-up process.

The significance of these data is their suggestion that reinvestment neighborhoods may experience gradual changes in the types of households who locate there. The reasons that they locate there, their reactions to the neighborhood and its residents, their participation and activity in citizen groups, and their willingness to exert time on behalf of efforts to improve neighborhood conditions and services may depend on the stage which the reinvestment neighborhood has reached demographically. This factor, in turn, would help to determine physical, economic, political, and social dynamics (Gale 1978).

Further evidence to support a stage theory about the resettlement process appears in a closer analysis of the Capitol Hill data. Even within a single reinvestment neighborhood, varying phases can be identified. The study area is composed of two census tracts. The western-most tract first experienced significant middle-class reinvestment in the late 1960s. This section is closest to the federal employment centers cited earlier. Because the reinvestment process is nearly complete and a large majority of the structures have been rehabilitated, it will be referred to here as the Mature Section. The other census tract, further to the east, has undergone reinvestment only since the early 1970s. It contains a substantial number of yet-unrenovated buildings and its population is more varied both racially and socioeconomically than the Mature Section's. This tract is identified here as the Transitional Section. Though these census tract sub-samples are too small to give statistically reliable distinctions, the consistency of their differences yields plausible support for the stage theory notion.

Generally speaking, among new home-buyers in the Transitional Section there were more single males, more childless households, more heads of households under age 35, and more households who had lived on Capitol Hill for less than three years. In addition, fewer respondents in the Transitional Section had "highly favorable" sentiments about their own property or their neighborhood. Too, fewer had moved to their current location from Washington's suburbs and more from other parts of Capitol Hill. However, about equal proportions of each group had been renters (two-thirds) just prior to purchasing their current dwelling. Finally, the Transitional Section respondents attached more importance to the sales price of their dwelling in making their locational choice; more felt it was less costly than other alternatives. For those in the Mature Section, sales price (even though generally higher) was less significant.

When asked how long they expected to live at their current address, resettlers in the Transitional Section clearly were less committed than those in the Mature Section to long-term residency. The latter group showed much less indecision about this matter and far more willingness to remain as much as ten years. Similarly, if Transitional Section respondents were to move in the future, they were less interested in remaining on Capitol Hill and more interested in moving to another area in the city than those in the Mature Section.

The comparisons between Mount Pleasant and Capitol Hill and those within Capitol Hill itself, suggest several tentative conclusions about the phases through which a resettlement neighborhood is likely to progress. In the earliest stage resettlers tend to be younger, single males purchasing their first dwelling. Prior to this, they are likely to have been renters and to have lived in the central city, though not usually in the resettlement neighborhood itself. Rarely, have they moved in from the suburbs.

They place great importance on the

affordability of their house's purchase price and on its potential for future appreciation in value. Being male, childless, and relatively young, they are able to take greater risks than other household types. Hence, they buy in deteriorated, predominantly moderate and lower income areas where crime rates and "aggravations" are higher than city-wide averages. In exchange, they receive high accessibility to various goods and services, quaint architectural and historical surroundings, and ultimately, sharp financial gains. These households, the most typical in Stage One of the resettlement process, are characterized most fully by their willingness to accept a substantial degree of risk (Clay 1978; Pattison 1977). In effect, most have "less to lose" than those resettlers who characterize Stage Two.

On the other hand, Stage Two households seem less willing to take these risks. More single and married women are likely to appear, and households with children are more common. Heads of households tend to be somewhat older and more are former suburban families. By the time these families arrive, significant physical and demographic changes have occurred and the resettlement neighborhood reveals a strong middle class influence. Consequently, they show greater enthusiasm for the area and more commitment to its future livability. They could afford to purchase a home in several parts of the metropolitan area and therefore, their house's price is not as important a locational constraint as is the price for Stage One resettlers.

Stage One resettlers are less committed to long-term residency in their current dwelling and show more indecision about the length of their stay than those in later stages. Also, fewer are likely to move to another dwelling in the same neighborhood in the future. They show more interest in relocating to another neighborhood in the city.

Thus far, the demographic characteristics of resettlers and their attitudes toward their neighborhood have been discussed. But, what about their reactions to specific conditions in their new location?

Respondents in both Capitol Hill and Mount Pleasant identified several disagreeable conditions which they had experienced in their neighborhoods. Inadequate public schools and public play space, and insufficient curbside parking space for automobiles were cited by some. Others mentioned excessive traffic in the neighborhood, high property taxes, and poor trash collection. However, "excessive crime problems" was the most commonly identified drawback in both neighborhoods. Similarly, when asked if any condition could cause them to move out of the neighborhood in the future, they mentioned excessive crime activities most frequently. More than half the respondents said that a member of their household had been the victim of at least one crime incident or threatening gesture occurring in the neighborhood. Several related two or more incidents. Most of these involved burglary or vandalism to property. Very few circumstances leading to assaults on the person occurred. However, incidents involving harsh words, harassment, or threatening gestures were not unusual. Most of these resulted between white resettlers and younger black residents. Most of the latter appeared to be passers-through in the neighborhood and not residents.

However, when interviewed on interracial behavior in the Capitol Hill neighborhood, 92 percent of the respondents said that conflict seldom occurred or happened only occasionally. Almost one-half (48 percent) of Capitol Hill interviewees said that they hoped that the neighborhood would stabilize in a racial composition that was 50 percent white and 50 percent black. About one-fourth hoped for a predominantly white population, with a minority of blacks. Almost none wanted an all-white, all-black, or largely-black residency. Not insignificantly, one-fifth gave no response, suggesting perhaps, the sensitive nature of this subject.

Implications for Theory

These data, though limited geographically, are important for the light they shed on the complexity of factors which enter into the resettler's locational decision. Unfortunately, the few published attempts at this subject have been confined to arguments based largely on economic assumptions. For example, one observer claims that rapidly rising suburban prices for new homes, due to inflation in labor, materials, and financing costs, and to restrictive growth controls, have "forced many homebuyers with limited economic means to stay in cities" (James 1978). As the evidence previously cited indicates though, most resettlers eschew suburban living, not for economic reasons, but due to matters of taste related to their life-styles. And, because few have children, most such households are not compelled to leave the cities to seek better public education. The absence of children and the high incidence of two-worker households increase family per capita income and, if anything, render many suburban housing opportunities quite affordable. Clearly, most resettlers' urban locational choices are their first preferences and not a "second-best" alternative to suburban living.

Another researcher presents an interesting theoretical "model" to explain resettler behavior and concludes that two variables predominate: the number of household workers and household size (Yezer 1977). He argues that in many resettler households both husband and wife are employed. Hence, commuting costs are considerably higher. Therefore,

it becomes economically rational to minimize commuting costs by living close to the central business district employment center. This argument, though plausible, ignores the fact that with two breadwinners, household income also rises. It is likely that this condition will overcome most increases in commuting costs and hence, two-worker resettler households will have flexibility of locational choice within the metropolitan area.

The second variable, household size, is somewhat more helpful in contributing to an explanation of the resettler's locational choice. It is claimed that because most such households are childless and therefore, need less dwelling and yard space, they act rationally in choosing the generally smaller properties available in older urban neighborhoods. Of course, it could be argued that many inner city homes in fact, are quite spacious when compared to new suburban dwellings. Built in the nineteenth century when larger numbers of children and extended families were *de rigueur,* many of these properties compete quite well with all but the most affluent suburban subdivision homes. It is true however, that inner city yard space is not likely to be as large. This argument aside, it is apparent that young singles and couples without children do have the option of reducing housing costs by purchasing less space. Therefore, the resettler's locational preference is economically rational (Gale 1977).

Residential location models based on economic rationale provide a critically important theoretical framework for understanding metropolitan development patterns. However, most such constructs have assumed that it is economically rational behavior for younger middle income households to move outward from the central business district to progressively more affluent neighborhoods as they pass through a conventional life cycle (Hoover and Vernon 1959). In doing so, they make a choice to trade off greater commuting distance (i.e., time and expense) for more living space, as well as a better "package" of public services. Generally, the models presuppose that these households will aspire to new housing and neighborhoods, leaving behind older areas as soon as economic circumstances permit (Birch 1971). Yet, as Firey demonstrated in the 1940s, many locational choices ignore these attractions (1947). Instead, they place an economic value on the cultural, historical, or architectural character of an area, as well as accessibility to the central business district. Consequently, small, centralized enclaves of older, well-maintained housing such as Boston's Beacon Hill or New York City's Gramercy Park have survived the "normal" deterioration process which accompanies architectural and technological obsolescence. The neighborhood resettlement phenomenon of the 1970s demonstrates a significant growth in this ethic. It is expressed in rising sales prices in neighborhoods where property values previously remained stagnant or declined. To the extent that this reinvestment process continues to burgeon, it will require planners and model-builders to reinterpret the filtering-up process, so as to include alternative economic choices based on architectural, historical, cultural, and accessibility values. The use of opinion survey data in conjunction with studies of economic indicators such as property value trends (Meadows and Call 1978) should help to explain the resettlement phenomenon and give insights as to its future.

The Displacement Dilemma

Neighborhood resettlement gives prima facie evidence of providing myriad benefits to local governments at very little cost. Improvement of the housing stock, increased real estate taxes and other revenues, reduced demand for social welfare services, lower serious crime rates, diminished neighborhood population densities, higher homeownership rates, and reduced enrollment pressures on neighborhood schools are all probable outcomes of middle class reinvestment in many older urban neighborhoods. Yet, it is apparent from mass media accounts and protests by neighborhood organizations that the rate at which disadvantaged households are being involuntarily displaced has increased significantly in recent years.

Typically, dislocation results when rapid reinvestment in formerly declining neighborhoods stimulates inflation in property values, causing rents and property taxes to rise and evictions for renovation to increase. Because most neighborhood resettlement is the result of private market investment activities and not a publicly controlled program such as Urban Renewal, the displacement impact is considerably more difficult to evaluate than it was when relocation programs were available to monitor and subsidize the process. The Uniform Relocation Assistance Act of 1970 does not provide for those uprooted by private rehabilitation efforts. Hence, the few dislocation relief programs which exist have been developed by local governments (Gale 1978).

Evidence on the magnitude and dimensions of displacement, especially by private market forces, is not yet in very precise form. One survey of realtors, public officials and civic leaders in the thirty largest cities has concluded that significant dislocation was occurring in 82 percent of the neighborhoods undergoing middle-class renovation (Clay 1978). An analysis of R. L. Polk Company data and other sources estimated that in no community were more than 100 to 200 households being displaced annually by private market forces except for a few cities such as Washington, D.C., and San

Francisco (Grier and Grier 1978). The U.S. Department of Housing and Urban Development studied unpublished tabulations of the 1974–1976 Annual Housing Surveys and estimated that the annual number of metropolitan households displaced by public and private actions ranged from 364,000 to 373,000. These households constituted slightly less than four percent of the total population of movers in each year. The highest proportion of those displaced among all movers occurred in the northeast region of the United States (4.3 percent) and the lowest, in the West (3.8 percent). Unfortunately, these data do not include moves due to rental increases, a major impetus in many household displacements (Cousar 1978).

The racial implications of resettlement were examined in a survey of local observers in forty-four cities by the National Urban Coalition (1979). About one-half of neighborhoods undergoing renovation were thought to have lost minority group members since resettlement began and about one-third experienced no change. Thirteen percent were thought to have had an increase. An analysis of a resettlement area in Alexandria, Virginia, projected an average decline in black housing occupancy of 85 households per year between 1975 and 1980. Many of these would be at or near retirement age (Hammer, Siler, George Associates 1976).

Other neighborhood surveys have touched upon the social effects of displacement but have been inconclusive about the costs of replacement housing for rental dislocatees. Estimates in a renovation neighborhood in St. Louis (Hu 1978) and in New Orleans (Ragas and Miestchovich 1977) concluded that about one-half of renovated homes in each had been vacant prior to renovation. Both implied that evictions for reinvestment purposes in these units do not appear to have occurred. Hu found that nearly all owner-households leaving the renovation area did so because of life cycle factors related to "old age, illness, and family problems." However, his study could not determine the reasons for which renters left the area. Ragas and Miestchovich discovered that most outmigrating households had little difficulty locating another nearby rental unit of comparable quality and size but may have had to pay a higher rent. They concluded that about 50 to 60 persons were displaced in the neighborhoods each year.

Collectively, these studies suggest that the involuntary movement of households, usually low or moderate income ones, in response to private market rehabilitation of neighborhoods has grown significantly in the 1970s. Blacks and other minorities, as well as the elderly, appear to be disproportionately affected. Yet, there is little evidence that, except for a few cities, dislocation directly affects a very large number of households per year. Where middle-class rehabilitation proceeds at a moderate pace and where the vacancy rate in the existing housing stock approximates national averages, the impact of resettlement is likely to be modest. Nonetheless, it will be important, on both political and humanitarian grounds, for local governments to carefully monitor the reinvestment process. Where the social costs become excessive, planners and public officials should be prepared to respond with effective measures to mitigate the rate and intensity of displacement.*

The Future of Neighborhood Resettlement

Thus far this discussion has been limited to the current extent and character of neighborhood resettlement in the United States. What is the likelihood that this phenomenon will continue at the same

* A section on implications for policy has not been reprinted here. (Ed. note)

rate or perhaps, increase in the future? As the previous data indicate, most resettler households are composed of one or two members. Very few have children present and recent national statistics indicate that the number and proportion of these types of households have increased and are likely to continue doing so. The number of one-person households grew 29 percent between 1970 and 1975 while two-person households rose 19 percent. These two groups now comprise almost one-half of all U.S. households (U.S. Bureau of the Census 1976, I). The incidences of other demographic conditions such as the postponement of marriage and of childbearing, divorce rates, and cohabitation of unmarried couples have increased significantly in the 1970s (Population Reference Bureau 1977). Many observers foresee a general continuation of these trends into the 1989s (Alonso 1977, Goetze 1976).

National demographic trends however, present only one dimension of the possible future of neighborhood resettlement. Decline or growth in white-collar employment in central cities, the impact of urban real estate taxes and other exactions, and the extent and character of criminal activity also will influence this recently emergent phenomenon. The extent to which it can reach beyond young singles and couples and attract families with children is related primarily to the future quality of inner city public education. At the present time though, it is clear that resettlement is limited largely to childless households whose life-styles embrace careerism and consumerism rather than "familism" (Johnston 1972). Because increasing numbers of these persons are postponing childbearing or are having smaller families, they have more income and time to devote to other pursuits. It is not apparent from the present analysis that neighborhood resettlement, *in vacuo,* can reverse the tide of net outmigration from central cities to suburbs which has continued since the post-war era. But, it is reasonable to suspect that this movement, an anomaly in metropolitan residential mobility patterns, will continue to grow in most central cities in the ensuing decade. To that extent then, it could help to mitigate some of the debilitating effects of suburban magnetism.

References

Advisory Commission on Intergovernmental Relations. 1977. *Trends in metropolitan America.* Washington, D.C.

Alonso, William. 1977. *The population factor and urban structure.* Cambridge, Massachusetts: Center for Population Studies, Harvard University, Working Paper Number 102.

Birch, David L. 1971. Toward a stage theory of urban growth. *Journal of the American Institute of Planners* 37, March: 78–87.

Black, J. Thomas. 1975. Private-market housing renovation in central cities: a ULI survey. *Urban Land* 34, November: 3–9.

Clay, Phillip L. 1978. *Neighborhood revitalization: issues, trends and strategies.* Cambridge, Massachusetts: Massachusetts Institute of Technology, Department of Urban Studies and Planning.

Cousar, Gloria. 1978. *Bulletin on HUD estimates of national displacement and pertinent program information.* Mimeographed. Washington, D.C.: U.S. Department of Housing and Urban Development.

Duncan, Otis D., and Duncan, Beverly. 1957. *The Negro population of Chicago.* Chicago: The University of Chicago Press.

Firey, Walter. 1947. *Land use in central Boston.* Cambridge: Harvard University Press.

Gale, Dennis E. 1976. *The back-to-the-city movement . . . or is it?* Occasional paper. Washington, D.C.: George Washington University, Department of Urban and Regional Planning.

Gale, Dennis E. 1977. *The back-to-the-city movement revisited.* Occasional paper. Washington, D.C.: George Washington University, Department of Urban and Regional Planning.

Gale, Dennis E. 1977. The unpredictable reasons for inner-city living, *The Washington Post,* August 6, 1977: A17.

Gale, Dennis E. 1978. Dislocation of residents, *Journal of Housing* 35, May: 232–235.

Gale, Dennis E. 1978. *Neighborhood resettlement and displacement: people and policies.* Occasional Paper. Washington, D.C.: George Washington University, Department of Urban and Regional Planning.

Goetze, Rolf. 1976. *Building neighborhood confidence.* Cambridge, Massachusetts: Ballinger Publishing Co.

Grier, George and Eunice. 1978. *Urban displacement: a reconnaissance.* Washington, D.C.: U.S. Department of Housing and Urban Development.

Grigsby, William G. 1963. *Housing markets and public policy.* Philadelphia: University of Pennsylvania Press.

Hammer, Siler, George Associates. 1976. *Final N.E.A. study report to the City of Alexandria, Virginia.* Mimeographed. Alexandria, Virginia: City of Alexandria.

Hoover, E. M., and Vernon, R. 1959. *Anatomy of a metropolis.* Cambridge, Massachusetts: Harvard University Press.

Houstoun, Lawrence O., Jr. 1976. Neighborhood change and city policy. *Urban Land* 35, July–August: 3–9.

Hu, Joseph. 1978. Who's moving in and who's moving out—and why. *Seller/Servicer* 5, May–June: 19–29.

Hunter, Albert. 1975. The loss of community: an empirical test through replication. *American Sociological Review* 40, October: 537–558.

James, Franklin. 1978. *The revitalization of older urban neighborhoods: trends, forces and the future of cities.* Washington, D.C.: The Urban Institute.

Johnston, Ronald J. 1972. *Urban residential patterns.* New York: Praeger Publishers.

Lipton, S. Gregory. 1977. Evidence of central city revival. *Journal of the American Institute of Planners* 43, April: 136–147.

Lowry, Ira. 1960. Filtering and housing standards: a conceptual analysis. *Land Economics* 36, November: 362–370.

McWilliams, Sybil W. 1975. *Recycling a declining community: middle class migration to Virginia-Highlands.* Unpublished Thesis. Georgia State University.

Meadows, George R., and Call, Steven T. 1978. Combining housing market trends and resident attitudes in planning urban revitalization. *Journal of the American Institute of Planners* 44, July: 297–305.

National Urban Coalition. 1978. *City neighborhoods in transition.* Washington, D.C.

New York Landmarks Conservancy. 1977. *Impacts of historic district designation.* New York.

Parkman Center for Urban Affairs. 1977. *Young professionals and city neighborhoods.* Boston: City of Boston.

Pattison, Tim. 1977. *The process of neighborhood upgrading and gentrification.* Unpublished Thesis. Cambridge, Massachusetts: Massachusetts Institute of Technology.

Population Reference Bureau. 1977. *Marrying, divorcing and living together.* Population Bulletin 32, October: 1–41.

Ragas, Wade R., and Miestchovich, Ivan. 1977. *Summary analysis of households in the Lower Garden District.* New Orleans: University of New Orleans, Urban Studies Institute.

Urban Land Institute. 1976. *Private market housing renovation: a case study of the Hill District of St. Paul.* Washington, D.C.

U.S. Bureau of the Census. 1977. I. *Household and family characteristics, March 1976.* Series P-20, #311. Washington, D.C.

U.S. Bureau of the Census. 1977. II. *Population characteristics, 1976.* Series P-20, #307. Washington, D.C.

Weiler, Conrad. 1978. *Handbook on reinvestment displacement.* Washington, D.C.: National Association of Neighborhoods.

Yezer, Anthony. 1977. Living patterns: why people move into the inner city. *The Washington Post* June 25: A17.

V

ACTIVITY SYSTEMS: Commerce, Industry, and Public Services

MARTYN J. BOWDEN

Downtown through Time: Delimitation, Expansion, and Internal Growth

The perplexing task of delimiting a study area consistently confronts the student engaged in comparative regional analysis. As a generic region commonly subjected to comparative analyses, the central business district of a city has "the normal qualities of a region. It has a core area in which the definitive qualities reach their greatest intensity; it has zonal boundaries, and these boundaries are, for the most part, impermanent" [33, p. 191].

Under these circumstances, some students of the city would prefer to identify the central business district simply as a "somewhat vague area with no definite boundaries" [3, p. 12]. Another concludes that "when it comes to drawing a firm boundary for the purposes of study, the extent of the central district must be determined arbitrarily" [39, p. 52]. However, as Vance has pointed out, "though the boundary itself may not exist in reality, the reasons behind the location of a line may be basically objective" [50, p. 280].

A case for drawing a boundary line to *approximate* the zonal edge of the central business district by the use of stan-dardized methods was made by Murphy and Vance some years ago [33]. Their delimitation method, adopted by many students of the city [5, 13, 15, 27, 43], clearly facilitated comparisons and contributed to a knowledge of the content and functioning of this critical urban region. But in all this work there have been two omissions. First, the central district of the *large* American city has been neglected. Second, no attempt has been published, using a consistent method of delimitation, to show how large central business districts have expanded and shifted in location through time.[1]

The first part of this article reviews the method used to delimit the central business district for historical analysis.[2] The second part deals with the application of the method to San Francisco in

1. A study of Boston used no clearly defined method of delimitation and relied on secondary sources [51]; and an unpublished study on Washington, D.C. traced the changing outline of the central district from 1888 to 1964, but was primarily concerned with land-use changes in selected blocks [27].
2. See the study by Bohnert and Mattingly for another attempt to delimit the CBD of past time periods [5].

From **Economic Geography,** Vol. 47, April 1971, pp. 121–35. Reprinted in revised form by permission of **Economic Geography** and M. J. Bowden.

1850, 1906, and 1931. The third part describes the phases and patterns of central district expansion and their relations to internal growth.

The main problem in this research is to identify the different activities that could be classified as central business uses (CBD-forming uses) since the urban-commercial revolution of the twelfth century. The key to the development of such a method of identification is the conception of the *CBD as a central place within the city* and the recognition of CBD-forming uses as those central functions that contributed to the *absolute centrality* of the CBD.

The Central Business District as a Central Place

Although central place theory has long been accepted by urban geographers as a descriptive scheme of interurban structure, it has only been recently applied to intraurban structure [*12*]. Christaller defined *centrality* as the central place's "relative importance" (relative centrality): the amount of central functions necessary to serve the complementary region, i.e., the population and activities outside the bounds of the central place [*14*, p. 22]. But centrality may also be defined in its absolute sense, as proposed by Carol [*12*, pp. 420–21, 438]. Absolute centrality is the amount of central functions necessary to serve the complementary region and the central place itself, i.e., the population and activities both inside and outside the central place. Now, in the delimitation of a central place such as the CBD, it seems essential to consider as CBD-forming uses the entire group of central functions that make up the central business district and contribute to its existence and growth as a central place. Consequently, all the central functions in the CBD, including those that serve only the population or activities of the CBD, or even a part or subdistrict of the CBD

should be classified as central business uses, for all of them contribute to the importance or absolute centrality of the CBD.

Central Business District-Forming Uses

Given this theoretical basis for identifying central business uses, what activities would be classified as central business in, say, American cities in the last century? It is clear, first, that all establishments that retail goods and services for a profit or that perform various office functions are central business in character. These are regarded by Murphy and Vance as central business uses [*33*, p. 203]. Also included are those central functions serving the CBD itself. Examples are the accountants and advertising firms with clients among the businesses located in the central area, and eating establishments serving the daytime population of the CBD. In addition, two types of land occupance considered by Murphy and Vance to be non-CBD in character—governmental and public, and organizational establishments (including charitable institutions)—clearly contribute to both the absolute and relative centrality of a central place [*33*, p. 204].

If all forms of residential use, vacancy, and commercial storage are regarded as noncentral business in character, then only the broad categories of wholesaling with stocks and manufacturing (except for newspapers) remain to be classified [*33*, p. 204]. Together, the latter constitute by far the most difficult problem in CBD delimitation, for at various times most types of wholesaling and manufacturing have been carried on in establishments that contributed to the centrality of the CBD. The question becomes: when, if at all, in the history of a particular CBD, did each of the functions under these two headings cease to be primarily central?

In the study of the contemporary CBD

Murphy and Vance considered it unnecessary to go into the "whole series of centrality judgments" that would be involved if they were to attempt differentiation of the wholesaling category [33, p. 204]. Making the exception of newspaper printing, therefore, they rejected outright both wholesaling and manufacturing. Carol rejected by omission most types of manufacturing and wholesaling with stocks, but implied that manufacturers with a strong tendency to locate as closely as possible to the center of the CBD should be considered potential CBD-forming establishments [12, p. 434]. Murphy and Vance made a somewhat similar judgment with regard to wholesaling [33, p. 203]. They wrote: "Wholesaling is not a central business function since it is localized more by the presence of railroads and other transportation media than by the pull of centrality.[3]

These two insights of Carol, and Murphy and Vance provide an answer to the difficult problem of classification: *any wholesaler and manufacturer localized more by the pull of centrality than by any other factor* (or sum of other factors) *is a potential central business use or CBD-forming establishment.* This principle may be taken as the theoretical basis for identifying central district uses of all types—retail, wholesaling, governmental, cultural, manufacturing—at any point in time and for any city.[4]

The following types of wholesaling and manufacturing activities were considered to be central business in character between 1850 and 1931 in San Francisco: (1) wholesalers of diamonds, jewelry, watches, and gold and silver products;

3. "Centrality" in their context refers to the gravitational attraction of the area of maximum accessibility (the core) upon all other establishments.

4. In practice it is difficult to weigh the relative attraction of the railroad, port, or other transportation medium against the pull of the area of maximum accessibility in the city and its region.

(2) manufacturing jewelers, diamond setters, watchmakers, gold and silversmiths; (3) wholesale fur dealers and manufacturing furriers; (4) wholesalers of women's apparel and specialty items in general (not including leather goods of a general type); (5) wholesalers of dry goods, fabrics, notions, dress patterns, embroideries, tailors' trimmings, supplies, and equipment; (6) manufacturing and wholesale tailors; and (7) wholesalers of men's clothing and footwear.

In the San Francisco study all other wholesaling and manufacturing establishments were considered to be noncentral business in character, except for the manufacturers of women's apparel and men's clothing. These were considered to be central business establishments up to 1906, not only because they appeared to benefit from their close proximity to the area of maximum accessibility, but also because it proved very difficult in this period to separate the garment manufacturers from the wholesale clothiers. Between 1906 and 1931, however, a clear separation of the two was apparent, such that by 1931 the garment manufacturers had begun to disperse throughout the city or to disappear from the city.

As against the noncentral business wholesalers and manufacturers, each CBD-forming establishment seemed to have some of the following characteristics: (1) it was accessible to an extremely large market for the particular good in the central business district itself: (2) it produced high value goods relative to volume; (3) it required rapid delivery to the large market of the CBD; (4) it depended on a large number of out-of-town buyers (mostly residing in the main hotel district); (5) it possessed a direct retailing function, and (6) in the case of manufacturers, it was closely tied to the wholesale-buying function. As Hoover and Vernon would have conceived it, the CBD-forming establishments were "selling-oriented wholesalers" (with some associated manufacturers) whereas the noncentral business establishments were the "seller-distributors" (or wholesalers acting primarily as distributors) and manufacturers [25, pp. 74–84].

Delimiting the CBD

Given a large number of potential CBD-forming establishments in the area of maximum accessibility, the problem of delimiting the central place is reduced to establishing a standard of contiguity, together with indexes of central business height and intensity, then deciding the size of the units for which CBD/non-CBD calculations will be made. Important contributions to this problem have been made by Murphy and Vance, and by Carol. The method suggested here for studies of the historical CBD follows their guidelines, but it introduces a finer mesh of "blocks," increasing slightly the Central Business Height Index and strengthening substantially the standard of contiguity.

INDEXES OF HEIGHT AND INTENSITY

Murphy and Vance [33, pp. 208–9] pointed out that:

A delimitation based on the Central Business Intensity Index (CBII) by itself has this fault: it takes no account of the gross amount of central business floor space. A block might have a Central Business Intensity Index of 50 percent (i.e., half the floor space devoted to central business uses), which would place it within the CBD, but this might be achieved by a one-story building, which though entirely devoted to central business uses occupied only half of an otherwise vacant block.

They concluded that an additional index, the Central Business Height Index (CBHI), was needed to eliminate this

situation.[5] But they could also have concluded that the adoption of a finer mesh of grid blocks would serve the same purpose. If a grid system is adopted which divides a low intensity city block into six parts, it is likely that at least two of the grid blocks will be classified as non-CBD. Furthermore, if the system of grid coordinates is aligned with the street system, particularly in a city with a rectangular pattern of streets, then the grid lines tend to follow building lines, and quite frequently the grid blocks consist solely of one building or of a vacant lot. As a result, when land use data are plotted on a fine mesh of grid blocks, a comparison of the CBD outlines derived from the CBII solely, and from the CBII and the CBHI combined are very similar (Figure 1).

Nevertheless, it was considered a necessary check to the CBII to set up a Central Business Index broadly comparable to that of Murphy and Vance (i.e., the equivalent of a one-story building devoted to central business uses and covering an entire city block). In this, one important difference was taken into account. Customer and commercial parking were regarded by Murphy and Vance as central business in character. This is wholly consistent with the conception of the CBD as a central place, for commercial parking lots clearly contribute to the absolute centrality of the central district. Unfortunately, one type of commercial parking—the ground-level commercial parking lot—was frequently found to cover many contiguous grid blocks on the edge of the central business district, and to have a CBII of 100 percent and a CBHI of 1.0. To ensure that large areas

5. The Central Business Height Index is the number of floors of central business uses if these are thought of as spread evenly over the block. It is obtained by dividing the total floor area of all central business uses by the total ground floor area of the block [33, p. 208]. In order to be included in the CBD, a block had to have a CBHI of 1.0 and a CBII of 50 percent.

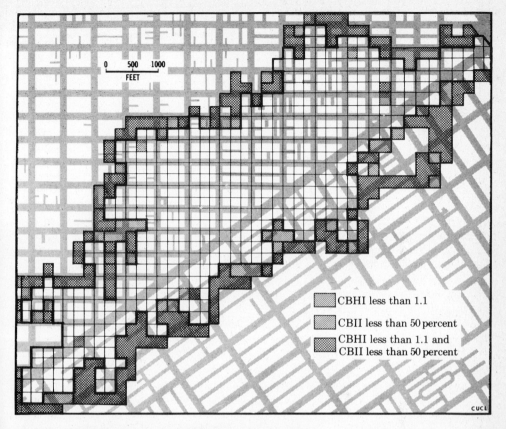

Figure 1. Delimitation of the Central Business District, 1931

of the city were not grafted onto a central district as a result of this loophole, it was necessary to increase the CBHI from 1.0 to at least 1.1.

STANDARD OF CONTIGUITY

Murphy and Vance considered separation of a potential CBD block from the main mass of the central business district as grounds for its exclusion. Therefore, a block only becomes part of the CBD if it satisfies the CBHI and CBII requirements *and* if it is contiguous with at least one other CBD block. The meaning of "contiguous" is interpreted quite liberally by Murphy and Vance, however. A block was considered contiguous with another if the two touched only at one corner [*33*, p. 219]. A stricter standard of contiguity is adopted here, primarily to balance less strict standards set for central-business uses:[6] *to be included in the central business district a potential CBD block had to be connected with the*

6. An attempt has been made throughout to maintain standards similar to those of Murphy and Vance. The CBHI and CBII were practically the same in both studies. The standard set for central-business uses by Murphy and Vance is higher than that set in this study. That is, more types of establishments were considered to be CBD uses in this study than in the study of Murphy and Vance. On the other hand, the standard set for contiguity by Murphy and Vance is lower than that set in this study.

core area (of contiguous CBD blocks) *on at least one of its four fronts.*[7] The one exception to this rule is the grid block that fails to reach the required CBHI standard, or the required CBII standard, or both, but which is surrounded on all sides by CBD blocks that have attained both standards; such grid blocks are considered part of the central business district.

In applying this modified version of the Central Business Index method to the delimitation of a particular CBD, it proves necessary to reconstruct (1) the morphology of the CBD (i.e., to determine the location, ground-floor-area, height and number of stories, and total floor space area of each building in the CBD), and (2) the functional structure (i.e., to apportion the establishments of the central district to buildings and floors).*

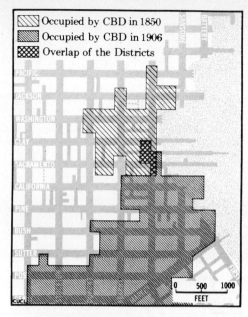

Figure 2. Locational Shift of the Central Business District, 1850–1906

A Shifting Center and a Growing Central District

The San Francisco central district emerged as a full-fledged CBD in the spring of 1850. By the summer of 1850 it consisted of the equivalent of seven blocks. Its geographical center was to the east-northeast of Portsmouth Plaza. The first center of San Francisco (or more properly Yerba Buena) had been left behind in the eastward migration of the central district, and was soon discarded by the central district in 1852, and occupied by Chinatown.

The rate of movement of the geographical center of the central district—15 yards per year in the first 17 years—was more than maintained up to the time of

7. This was consistent with Hartman's view of the theoretical shape of the central business district as a tilted square when developed on a gridiron [24]. It was also consistent with Murphy and Vance's empirically-based view of the central business district as a quadrate cross [34, pp. 326–330].
* The detailed discussion of data sources has not been reprinted here. (Ed. note)

the earthquake and fire of 1906. By that date the geographical center was more than one-half mile directly south of Portsmouth Plaza. There had been a five-fold areal expansion since 1850, accompanied by such marked peripheral discard in the north that the geographical center of the central district of 1850 was outside that of 1906. Of the original central district only the southeastern tip remained in 1906 as part of the new district (Figure 2).

After the catastrophe of 1906, central district growth took on a different form. Areal expansion continued unabated. The central district more than doubled in size between 1906 and 1931, the equivalent of 40 city blocks being added to the 35 occupied in 1906 (Figure 3). Even though this was by far the greatest period of CBD growth, in absolute terms, the geographical center shifted a bare 200 yards westward between 1906 and 1931— approximately eight yards per year.

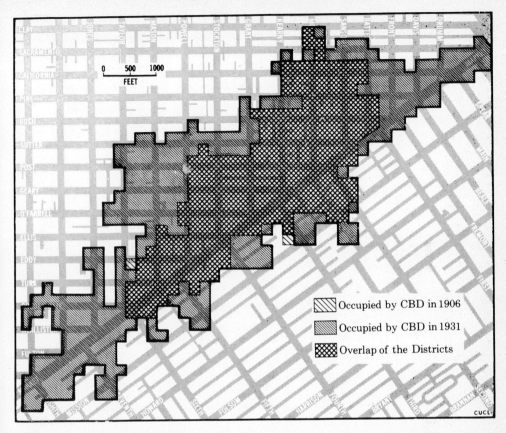

Figure 3. Central District, 1906–1931

In San Francisco, we have a central district whose geographical center shifted markedly in the early years, more slowly later, and a district that increased more than tenfold in size in eighty years. What were the characteristics of peripheral accretion—the pattern and phases of central district expansion—and how do these relate to internal growth?

Phases of Expansion and Internal Growth

Application of the delimitation method in one large city, San Francisco, and consideration of the growth of five others, Boston, New York City, Los Angeles, Washington, and London, have led this author to the conclusion that there are three quite distinct types of peripheral accretion to large central districts, each with attendant patterns of internal growth. One has been a steady, if somewhat irregular, small-scale accretion following localized lateral expansion of a district or two within the central district. A limited chain reaction of locational shifts of nuclei may develop as a contiguous district is displaced by its expanding neighbor. And a slight accretion takes place on a small section of the CBD boundary. Nuclei responsible for this type of accretion in San Francisco, 1850–1931, were the theater-entertainment, medical services, garment, hotel, furniture, and civic districts. During the greater part of San

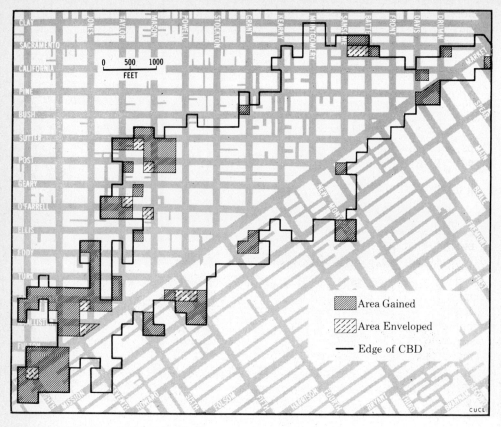

Figure 4. Pattern of Accretion to the Central District, 1921–1926

Francisco's history this was the only type of growth taking place, and when this was the case, the central district as a whole expanded little. During the extended phases of lull in peripheral accretion, a high proportion of the *transformation* (changeover of blocks from non-CBD to CBD uses) was concerned either with the *backfilling* of enclaves of formerly noncentral business activities surrounded during previous phases of marked accretion, or with *infilling* of the interstices between the predominantly axial extensions that were the legacies of former phases of rapid growth. Additions to the edges of the central district were shallow, and took place on a broad front.

The second type of growth and accre-

tion is the burst, in which the CBD expands rapidly in a very short time. There were five such periods in the history of San Francisco between 1850 and 1931, and most of the expansion of the central district took place in these short spells, as it appears to have done in London and New York City. In these phases of marked accretion, advances take place along the entire front of assimilation, and there is frequently an axial component to growth— an extended linear advance to a former exclave of blocks of central business activities (Figure 4). In such a phase, many blocks of noncentral business activities are enveloped by the rapidly advancing edge of the CBD and left inside the periphery as enclaves (the process of envelopment). These bursts on the edge are the external expression of major morphological and functional changes taking place throughout the central district. They are structural changes that take the form of a chain reaction of displacement and locational changes of most, if not all, of the constituent nuclei of the CBD. This *sequence of reaction,* gradually develops into a cumulative wave of displaced activities that surges to the advancing edge of the CBD some four to seven years after its inception in the core.

SEQUENCE OF REACTION AND A HIERARCHY

A full sequence of reaction only occurs when the financial district or the apparel shopping district, or both of these core districts, expand laterally at the expense of contiguous districts. In San Francisco, the sequence generally began in the banking nucleus of the financial district or in the women's apparel nucleus within the apparel shopping district, whence the movement spread to the other nuclei of the *two core districts.* Expansion takes place into the contiguous districts, each of which is in the process of, or on the verge of, expansion, and the displacement becomes compound. In the contiguous districts external pressures to expand are frequently as great as the internal growth pressures. And the contiguous districts expand laterally or sometimes leapfrog at the expense of the peripheral districts. The latter are subject to so much external pressure during the sequence of reaction that they are frequently forced to leapfrog beyond the former boundary of the central district and to expand at the expense of occasional CBD nuclei and districts of non-CBD type activities.[8]

8. For a discussion of the way districts grow within the central district, see Babcock [2, pp. 60–65] and Bowden [6, pp. 11–14, 266–269, 448–453, 708–711].

This sequence of reaction has led to a recognition of what Haig called an "order of precedence" among districts [21; 22, pp. 36–38; 28, pp. 81–85; 6 pp. 13–17], or what may be called here the hierarchy among nuclei: the ranking of the nuclei in the central district according to each one's ability to displace any or all other uses. At the top of the hierarchy is the financial nucleus, which is displaced by *no* other nucleus, and only moves as a result of its own internal expansion (Figure 5). The other core district, the apparel shopping district, has been broadly similar, although on occasion subject to external pressures from the financial district. It has tended to move farther than the latter and in a different way. Third in the ranking, and intermediate between the core and peripheral districts, has been the hotel district. While subject to external pressures from the financial district and, to a lesser extent, from the apparel shopping district, it has undergone locational changes mainly as a result of internal pressures, and has tended to move farther than the two districts above it in the hierarchy.

During bursts of expansion in the San Francisco central district as a whole, all the other districts—those on the periphery—have been subjected to at least as much external as internal pressure to relocate. External pressures[9] have been exerted by the higher order districts, but in some cases a peripheral district has forced another from its locale. In general, however, these districts have expanded at the expense of *both* the noncentral business activities that encircle much of the central district, and the central business type activities that are sometimes inside the CBD and sometimes outside, e.g., club-church-organizational, automo-

9. External pressures are those exerted on a district by other activities *within* the central district. There is no evidence of districts of non-CBD type activities expanding at the expense of (repelling) central district nuclei.

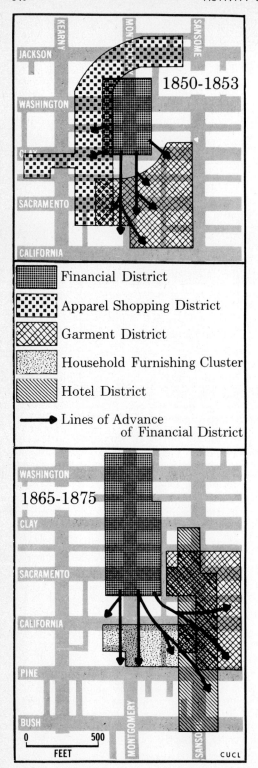

Financial District

Apparel Shopping District

Garment District

Household Furnishing Cluster

Hotel District

→ Lines of Advance
  of Financial District

bile service, public administration, and entertainment nuclei.

SEPARATION AND THE POLYNUCLEAR CENTRAL AREA

The third type of growth, *separation,* is a special case of the "burst," in which the central district breaks up into at least two discrete parts. It becomes in fact a polynuclear central area rather than a central district. In laissez-faire situations in the nineteenth century, this type of expansion seems to have occurred only in large cities. It occurred when the *set* was broken either by catastrophe, fire, or, more usually, by the leapfrogging of one or more of the core districts during and following very rapid growth of the metropolis.

Leapfrogging by the financial district is very rare, but is more frequent in the apparel shopping district, and when either or both jump to new and discrete locations, temporary separation is likely. This happened for a few years in San Francisco in the early 1870s. The financial district, formerly contiguous with the apparel shopping district, leapfrogged two blocks to the southeast, and the apparel shopping district jumped to a noncontiguous location five blocks south. These changes occurred between 1866 and 1869, and were followed by the leapfrogging of the theater, hotel, furniture, and garment nuclei to distinct locations between 1868 and 1873. For a short period, four central nuclei, including the two core districts, were separated from each other by bands of non-CBD activities. The leapfrogging was not extensive, and the interstices between the nuclei were quickly filled, so that by 1880 the central district was once more intact. But the circumstances that lay behind this unusual growth epitomize the conditions necessary to this type of growth else-

Figure 5. Expansion of the Financial District, 1850–1853, and 1865–1875

where. A tripling of San Francisco's population between 1855 and 1865 and an increase of similar proportions in the number of apparel shopping establishments in the Inner City (particularly medium-sized establishments) were sufficient to loosen the inertial burden and produce a polynuclear central area.

The extreme case of this type of central district expansion is the semipermanent separation of the core districts in the central area, characteristic of a metropolis that has undergone marked and rapid growth over a long period e.g., London and New York. The first polynuclear central area was probably London's, which followed upon the leapfrogging of the apparel shopping district westward between 1610 and 1630 [8, pp. 67–104, 502, 508; 47, pp. 127–29]. During this period, the population of London and the numbers of the gentry and aristocracy in the West End probably doubled [8, pp. 498–9; 17, pp. 318–19; 19, p. 181]. By the late nineteenth century the apparel shopping district had leapfrogged six times in moving almost three miles westwards from Cheapside, while the financial district has remained in the region of its original crystallization [8; 19, pp. 243–60; 45, pp. 530–37; 47; 48, pp. 24–26, 262–67; 40, pp. 284–308]. Separation has been the rule for more than 300 years in London where numerous districts have been isolated from other central nuclei by bands of non-CBD activities, although postwar development in these interstices may well reestablish a single and massive central district in the next two decades.

In New York City separation probably occurred between 1825 and 1835 as the apparel shopping district leapfrogged northward, soon to be followed by many other districts. During this period the population of the city more than doubled. By the 1950s the apparel shopping district had leapfrogged at least six times in moving four miles north of Wall Street [1; 9; 22, pp. 99–104; 25; 30; 32; 36; 37].

In sum, the type of growth prevalent in a central district at any given time under laissez-faire conditions would seem to depend in the main on the scale of demand for central district space by certain types of linked establishments that form nucleations; and this demand, in turn ultimately rests on the extent and rapidity of growth of the city and its hinterland. The lower and more steady the rate of a city's growth, the less the probability that central district growth will be affected in the short bursts of what may be called sequences of reaction, and the greater the probability that peripheral accretion will be of the shallow, piecemeal type. By contrast, the more rapid and marked the rate of a city's growth, the greater the chance that expansion of the central district will occur in bursts of peripheral accretion following sequences of reaction, particularly if the growth rate has been quite irregular, as in San Francisco. In those few metropolises where growth has been very extensive and the growth rate has been continuously high, separation and the emergence of a polynuclear central area are probable.

Conclusion

The central district boundary is a sensitive indicator of central district growth, and of growth in the city region. Detailed comparisons of the central district through time focus attention on critical periods and critical areas where chain reactions of locational changes are set in motion. They pinpoint growth processes in operation in the active sector of the interface between the central business district and the rest of the city. In this view, study and analysis of changing boundaries is an important aid to diagnosis of city and central district growth. When based on a consistent delimitation method and on the conception of the central district as a central place within a city, as proposed here, such study makes possible cross-cultural, interregional, and international comparisons, as well as the comparison of large and small downtowns throughout history.

Literature Cited

1. Albion, R. G. *The Rise of New York Port 1815–1860.* New York: Charles Scribner's Sons, 1939.

2. Babcock, F. M. *Valuation of Real Estate.* New York: McGraw-Hill Book Co., 1932.

3. Bartholomew, H. *Urban Land Uses.* Cambridge: Harvard University Press, 1932.

4. Barry, T. A. and B. A. Patten. *Men and Memories of San Francisco in the "Spring of '50."* San Francisco: A. L. Bancroft and Co., 1873.

5. Bohnert, J. E. and P. F. Mattingly. "Delimitation of the CBD Through Time," *Economic Geography,* 40 (1964), pp. 336–47.

6. Bowden, M. J. "The Dynamics of City Growth: An Historical Geography of the San Francisco Central District 1850–1931." Unpublished Ph.D. dissertation, University of California, Berkeley, 1967.

7. Bowden, M. J. "Reconstruction Following Catastrophe: The Laissez-Faire Rebuilding of Downtown San Francisco After the Earthquake and Fire of 1906," *Proceedings, Association of American Geographers,* 2 (1970).

8. Brett-James, N. G. *The Growth of Stuart London.* London: George Allen and Unwin Ltd., 1935.

9. Bridenbaugh, C. *Cities in Revolt: Urban Life in America 1743–1776.* New York: Capricorn Books, 1964.

10. Burgess, E. W. "The Growth of the City," *The City.* Edited by R. E. Park, *et al.* Chicago: University of Chicago Press, 1925, pp. 47–62.

11. Burgess, E. W. "The Growth of a City," *Proceedings of the American Sociological Society,* 18 (1923), pp. 85–89.

12. Carol, H. "The Hierarchy of Central Functions within the City," *Annals of the Association of American Geographers,* 50 (1960), pp. 419–38.

13. Carter, H. and G. Rowley. "The Morphology of the Central Business District of Cardiff," *Transactions, Institute of British Geographers,* 38 (1966), pp. 119–34.

14. Christaller, W. *Central Places in Southern Germany.* Translated by C. W. Baskin. Englewood Cliffs: Prentice-Hall, Inc., 1966.

15. Davies, D. H. "Boundary Study as a Tool in CBD Analysis: An Interpretation of Certain Aspects of the Boundary of Cape Town's Central Business District," *Economic Geography,* 35 (1959), pp. 322–45.

16. Dickinson, R. E. *City and Region: A Geographical Interpretation.* London: Routledge and Kegan Paul, 1964.

17. George, M. D. *London Life in the Eighteenth Century.* Harmondsworth: Penguin Books, 1965.

18. Glover, E. S. *The Illustrated Directory: A Magazine of American Cities.* Vol. 1 of *San Francisco.* San Francisco: The Illustrated Directory Co., 1894–1895.

19. Gras, N. S. B. *An Introduction to Economic History.* New York: Harper and Brothers, 1922.

20. Griffin, D. W. and R. E. Preston. "A Restatement of the 'Transition Zone' Concept," *Annals of the Association of American Geographers,* 56 (1966), pp. 339–50.

21. Haig, R. M. "The Assignment of Activities to Areas in Urban Regions," *Quarterly Journal of Economics,* 40 (1925–1926), pp. 402–34.

22. Haig, R. M. *Major Economic Factors in Metropolitan Growth and Arrangement,* Vol. 1. New York: Regional Plan of New York and its Environs, 1927.

23. *Handy Block Book of San Francisco.* 3rd ed. San Francisco: The Hicks-Judd Co., 1894.

24. Hartman, G. W. "The Central Business District — A Study in Urban Geography," *Economic Geography,* 26 (1950), pp. 237–44.

25. Hoover, E. M. and R. Vernon. *Anatomy of a Metropolis.* New York: Doubleday and Company, 1962.

26. Hoyt, H. and A. M. Weimer. *Principles of Urban Real Estate.* Rev. ed. New York: The Ronald Press Company, 1948.

27. Hughes, A. C. "The Delimitation of the Central Business District of Washington, D.C., Over Time." Unpublished M.A. thesis, University of Maryland, 1966.

28. Hurd, R. M. *Principles of City Land Values.* New York: The Record and Guide, 1903.

29. Kimball, C. P. *San Francisco City Direc-*

tory. San Francisco: Journal of Commerce Press, 1850.

30. King, M. *King's Handbook of New York City*. 2nd ed. Boston: Moses King, 1893.

31. Klein, H. J. "The Delimitation of the Town-Centre in the Image of its Citizens," *Urban Core and Inner City*. Leiden: E. J. Brill, 1967, pp. 286–306.

32. Kouwenhoven, J. A. *The Columbia Historical Portrait of New York: An Essay in Graphic History*. Garden City, Doubleday and Company, 1953.

33. Murphy, R. E. and J. E. Vance, Jr. "Delimiting the CBD," *Economic Geography*, 30 (1954), pp. 189–222.

34. Murphy, R. E. and J. E. Vance, Jr. "A Comparative Study of Nine Central Business Districts," *Economic Geography*, 30 (1954), pp. 301–36.

35. Murphy, R. E., J. E. Vance, Jr., and B. Epstein. "Internal Structure of the CBD," *Economic Geography*, 31 (1955), pp. 21–46.

36. Pomerantz, S. I. *New York: An American City 1783–1803*. 2nd ed. Port Washington: Ira J. Friedman, Inc., 1965.

37. Pred, A. "Manufacturing in the American Mercantile City: 1800–1840," *Annals of the Association of American Geographers*, 56 (1966), pp. 307–38.

38. Rannells, J. *The Core of the City*. New York: Columbia University Press, 1956.

39. Rasmussen, S. E. *London: The Unique City*. Harmondsworth: Penguin Books, 1960.

40. Reddaway, T. F. *The Rebuilding of Lon-don after the Great Fire*. London: Edward Arnold and Co., 1951.

41. *San Francisco Block Book*. 4th ed. San Francisco: The Hicks-Judd Co., 1906.

42. Schöller, P. "Centre-Shifting and Centre-Mobility in Japanese Cities," in *Proceedings of the I.G.U. Symposium in Urban Geography, Lund 1960*. Edited by K. Norborg. Lund: C. W. K. Gleerup, 1962, pp. 576–93.

43. Scott, P. "The Australian CBD," *Economic Geography*, 35 (1959), pp. 290–314.

44. Soule, F., *et al. The Annals of San Francisco*. New York: D. Appleton and Company, 1855.

45. Spate, O. H. K. "The Growth of London, A.D. 1660–1800," *An Historical Geography of England Before A.D. 1800*. Edited by H. C. Darby. Cambridge: The University Press, 1936, pp. 529–48.

46. Spear, D. N. *Bibliography of American Directories through 1860*. Worcester: American Antiquarian Society, 1961.

47. Stow, J. *A Survey of London, Written in the Year 1598*. Edited by W. J. Thoms. London: Chatto and Windus, 1876.

48. Summerson, J. *Georgian London*. Rev. ed. Harmondsworth: Penguin Books, 1962.

49. Vance, J. E., Jr. Review of *The Core of the City*, by John Rannells. *Economic Geography*, 33 (1957), pp. 278–80.

50. Ward, D. "The Industrial Revolution and the Emergence of Boston's Central Business District," *Economic Geography*, 42 (1966), pp. 152–71.

RONALD J. JOHNSTON AND
CHRISTOPHER C. KISSLING

Establishment Use Patterns within Central Places

Study of intra-urban central places has largely focused on inter-centre variations in the distribution of functions, functional units and establishments (for definitions, see Stafford, 1963), and in the patterns of facility usage (Berry, 1963, 1967). Few investigations have sought order at a smaller scale, within individual central places, and most of these have concerned themselves with only the largest such place in any one city, the Central Business District (Murphy, Vance and Epstein, 1955; Scott, 1959). Logically, however, any ordered pattern of facilities and their usage should not be peculiar to this one level of the intra-urban central place hierarchy, but should be common to all centres which contain more than a few establishments: the present analyses suggest a minimum of about 20.

As suggested above, order within a central place has two facets:

1. A patterned distribution of establishments in various functions.
2. A pattern of consumer behaviour among these various establishments.

These two patterns are causally interrelated: the distribution of establishments in part determines consumer behaviour (hence, for example, the considerable research by large stores on where to locate their various departments in order to maximize customer exposure and expenditure); on the other hand, consumer patterns, especially with regard to the least-cost principle in shopping and the minimization of distance travelled, influence entrepreneurial location decisions.

Such, in brief, are the generally accepted patterns of order within central places. Empirical studies, however, have been almost exclusively concerned with only one of the patterns, that of establishments, undoubtedly because of the ease of obtaining data on this relative to information on consumer movements. Thus the inferred patterns and interrelationships have not been fully validated. Clark and Rushton (1970, 487) have also pointed out that central place theory can only be confirmed or developed through studies of the locational behaviour of both entrepreneurs and

From **Australian Geographical Studies**, Vol. 9, 1971, pp. 116–32. Reprinted in modified form by permission of The Institute of Australian Geographers, R. J. Johnston and C. C. Kissling.

customers. The investigations reported here represent preliminary attempts to identify regularities in the patterns of consumer behaviour within central places.

The Internal Structure of Central Places

Knowledge of the internal structure of central places is necessary for studies of the contingent customer use of their facilities. According to Nystuen (1967, p. 55) "Stores vary in the degree to which they share customers on a scale ranging from independence to intense association," with the linked stores being found in spatial propinquity.

Two main studies have searched for such spatial affinities. In the first, Parker (1962) compared the percentage of establishments in suburban Liverpool with neighbours of a certain type against an expected percentage based on a random distribution of all establishments. He found tendencies towards two main groupings.

1. A daily shopping group, consisting of grocers, butchers, greengrocers and fishmongers, within which these establishments are basically complementary. Certain higher order establishments, such as chemists, hardware stores, bakers and dry cleaners, also tended to locate in such clusters.
2. An occasional shopping group, which had two sub-categories: (1) establishments oriented to a particular sector of the market, such as coffee bars and record shops; (2) establishments which compete with each other through consumer comparison of their goods (as with dress and shoe shops). In addition, certain uses were rarely found together (such as pet food and butcher shops), whereas others clustered because of benefits in similar trading hours (off-licences and fish-and-chip shops).

The second study, by Getis and Getis (1968), had a similar aim, but used only CBDs and employed a stronger statistical technique (Getis, 1967). Most of the groups which were isolated correspond to Parker's second type, though overall the results were not very promising.

A more detailed study, with a theoretical bias not particularly directed to the intense association existing between certain functions, was Garner's (1966) monograph on *The Internal Structure of Retail Nucleations*. He applied the intraurban model of relationships among accessibility, land values and retail location to the within-centre pattern, suggesting a zonal pattern of establishments reflecting their order within a continuum of thresholds (or required market sizes for economic viability). Accessibility to customers declines with distance from a central point in a retail nucleation, and the larger the market which an establishment needs, the closer it must be to this central point (hence the higher price which is offered for such locations): establishments requiring only a portion of the centre's market for economic success can obtain this in the outer portions of the retail nucleation (Figure 1). Garner's attempts to verify his model with Chicago data were disappointing, because of problems of threshold measurement (Garner, 1967) and "non-economic" store locations, but his formulation is logical and provides the basis for the ensuing model of within-centre consumer behaviour.

Consumer Behavior Within Central Places: A Formulation

A basic feature of the generally-held theory of establishment distributions within central places is thus that establishment types which are frequently linked on a multi-purpose shopping trip are found in spatial proximity within centres. As a

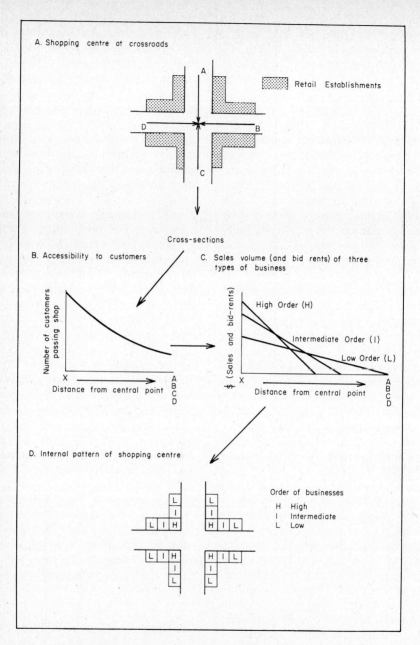

Figure 1. Model of the Internal Pattern of a Central Place, Showing the Relationships between Establishment Order and Location within the Centre (after Garner, 1966)

consequence, there should also be a clustering of establishments visited by individual customers. Instead of visiting various businesses throughout a centre, they should tend to patronize only a group located in one portion of it. (This of course assumes that competition between establishments selling the same goods is sufficiently perfect so that people will not travel considerable lengths *within* a centre to visit one.) Whether such clustering of visits exists could be tested in any central place which has more than one establishment in several functional types, but the present formulation—which draws heavily on the works of Garner and Parker—is concerned with relatively small centres only.

Our model concerns such a small central place, at a crossroad, which has its highest order establishments on the four corners and those of lower orders along the approaches (Figure 2). Along each of the latter four streets we might expect to find a cluster of complementary, daily shopping establishments (Parker's first

type): there might be such a cluster on each side of each street.

If customers are at least partly constrained by the distance factor when choosing which shops to partonize (and this barrier might be raised by the problems of crossing the street, especially at the crossroads), then the establishments which they visit should be clustered. Many trips to a high order centre are for lower order goods only, either because it is the closest to the customer's home or because it is more competitive in range and price of merchandise (Clark and Rushton, 1970; Campbell and Chisholm, 1970). Thus customer A in Figure 2 visits only the lower order establishments along the street of the hypothetical centre. Visits to both high and low order establishments could also involve a clustering of destinations (as with customer B in Figure 2): alternatively, the visits to higher order establishments might be widespread, as with customer C, but the low order choices are still clustered, perhaps because of stereotyped behaviour (Golledge, 1970; Pred, 1969). Finally, a customer visiting only high order establishments (D) is more likely to display a wide-spread pattern of choices, in shopping around.

The following specific hypotheses are therefore suggested.

1. There will be strong customer linkages among spatially proximal low order establishments.
2. High order establishments will be linked to a greater number of stores, though showing strongest ties with nearby lower order establishments.
3. Customers visiting a low order cluster within a centre will go to that one closest to their home.

The Study

Testing of these hypotheses requires data from shoppers on establishments visited

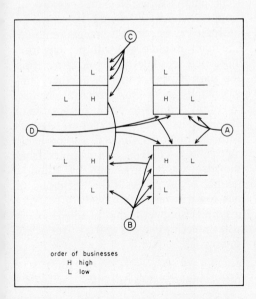

Figure 2. Hypothetical Patterns of Consumer Behaviour within a Small Central Place

during a typical trip, which are available from two surveys conducted in recent years.

FENDALTON SHOPPING CENTRE, CHRISTCHURCH, NEW ZEALAND

This centre was studied in April, 1967 as part of an investigation into its possible relocation consequent upon a road-widening scheme. At that time it contained 21 establishments, most of them among the most frequently occurring types within the Christchurch Urban Area (Clark, 1967). The centre rated in the third order of Christchurch's hierarchy. Within it, most of the highest order establishments were to the west of the crossroads (governed by traffic lights): the two main lower order functions—grocer and butcher—were represented on both sides of the road to the east, and there was also a grocer to the west (Figure 3).

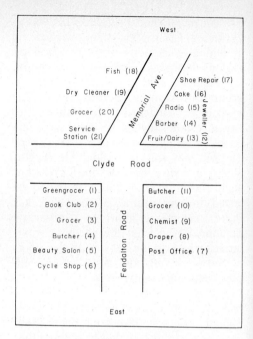

Figure 3. Schematic Diagram of the Location of Establishments in Fendalton Shopping Centre, Christchurch, New Zealand

GARDENVALE SHOPPING CENTRE, MELBOURNE, AUSTRALIA

This centre, also organised around a crossroads (again governed by traffic lights), is in the fourth order of Metropolitan Melbourne's central place hierarchy (Johnston, 1966). Unlike Fendalton, however, most of the shops were not facing the main highway converging on the crossroads. When surveyed, in August 1966, there were 93 different establishments (Figure 4). During the full day of interviewing, however (by ten interviewers), only 29 of the establishments were visited by at least 10 shoppers; 23 were not visited at all. Most of the ensuing discussion deals with the 29 frequently visited facilities, therefore, which are mainly of low order and grouped in clusters within the centre (Figure 4).

Data collection concerning establishment visits must be at the completion of a shopping trip, so interviewers were scattered throughout the centres—with especial emphasis on the main exits—asking shoppers who were leaving the centre for information on establishments entered. The main problem was with persons travelling by car, some of whom drove from one part of the centre to another (this was mainly so in the Gardenvale centre, and applied to a very small proportion of all shoppers). Truly random samples were not obtained (indeed it is probably impossible to obtain such samples from in-centre interviews), but by using a number of interviewers the likelihood of bias towards any one section of a centre or type of shopper is improbable. In each case, interviewing was spread over a full trading day.

Initial Analysis: Major Links

A data matrix was formed for each centre, with shoppers forming the rows and

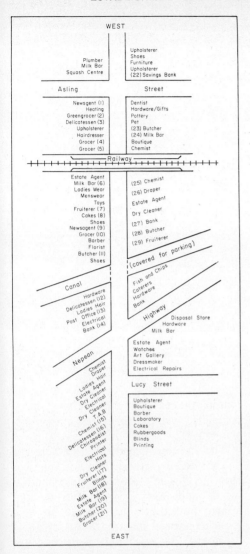

WEST

Plumber
Milk Bar
Squash Centre

Upholsterer
Shoes
Furniture
Upholsterer
(22) Savings Bank

Asling   Street

Newsgent (1)
Heating
Greengrocer (2)
Delicatessen (3)
Upholsterer
Hairdresser
Grocer (4)
Grocer (5)

Dentist
Hardware/Gifts
Pottery
Pet
(23) Butcher
(24) Milk Bar
Boutique
Chemist

Railway

Estate Agent
Milk Bar (6)
Ladies Wear
Menswear
Toys
Fruiterer (7)
Cakes (8)
Shoes
Newsagent (9)
Grocer (10)
Barber
Florist
Butcher (11)
Shoes

(25) Chemist
(26) Draper
Estate Agent
Dry Cleaner
(27) Bank
(28) Butcher
(29) Fruiterer

(covered for parking)

Canal

Hardware
Delicatessen (12)
Ladies Hair
Post Office (13)
Electrical
Bank (14)

Fish and Chips
Caterers
Hardware
Bank

Highway

Disposal Store
Hardware
Milk Bar

Estate Agent
Watches
Art Gallery
Dressmaker
Electrical Repairs

Nepean

Chemist
Draper
Ladies Hair
Estate Agent
Dry Cleaner
Electrical
Dry Cleaner
Dry T.A.B
Chemist (15)
Delicatessen (16)
Chiropodist
Printer
Electrical
Hats
Dry Cleaner
Fruiterer (17)
Blinds
Milk Bar (18)
Estate Agent
Milk Bar (19)
Butcher (20)
Grocer (21)

Lucy   Street

Upholsterer
Boutique
Barber
Laboratory
Cakes
Rubbergoods
Blinds
Printing

EAST

Figure 4. Schematic Diagram of the Location of Establishments in Gardenvale Shopping Centre, Melbourne, Australia

establishments the columns. An entry in any cell indicated that the shopper visited that establishment. Agreement matrices were then produced, with the establishments along both axes. Entries in these matrices showed the number of times pairs of establishments were both visited on one person's shopping trip; those along the major diagonal showed the total number of visits to each establishment.

Conversion of the values in each row of these matrices to a percentage of the largest value in it (that on the diagonal) showed the strength of links between the establishments: for example, 13.3 per cent of those shopping at establishment 1 in the Gardenvale centre (a newsagent) also visited the nearby greengrocers (establishment 2). Many of these percentages were very small: the larger ones, defined here as greater than 25 per cent, indicate the most intensely linked establishments. Two types of linkage have been identified: (1) the 25 per cent plus reciprocal links in which one-quarter of those visiting A also visited B, and vice versa; and (2) the 25 per cent plus one-way link.

In both centres, the 25 per cent plus reciprocal links indicate the role of proximity in consumer behaviour, and in particular the barrier effects of crossroads. Thus there were no links over the crossroads in Fendalton (Figure 5A). There were links across the main road to the east, however, mainly between the establishments located on both sides (grocer and butcher) and those on only one (greengrocer, chemist and post office). The pattern of one-way links was more complex (Figure 5B), but its main feature was of connections directed from the higher to the lower order establishments: from the beauty salon (establishment 5), for example, at least 25 per cent of the customers also visited one of the five establishments on the other side of the road (7–11). There were also links between some of the lower order establishments, showing, for example, variation in choice of butcher given choice of grocer. Relatively few links were between the two parts separated by the crossroads, however.

Similar linkage patterns based on propinquity were observed in the Gardenvale centre (Figure 6). Probably because of

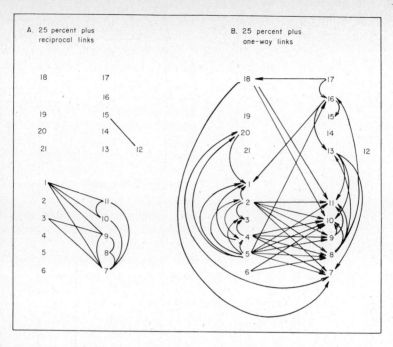

Figure 5. Major Linkages among Establishments. Fendalton Shopping Centre (for Key to Establishments see Figure 3)

the greater range of choice (four butchers and four grocers, for example), the number of 25 per cent reciprocal links was smaller than in Fendalton. Nevertheless, a clearer spatial pattern emerged (Figure 6A), polarised around the crossroads. The one-way links emphasised the two groups (Figure 6B), showing the functional affinities between less-frequently visited establishments and the nearby grocer-butcher-fruiterer clusters. Again, there were few links between the two parts of the centre.

A Functional Distance Analysis of the Patterns

Figures 5 and 6 suggest the validity of the hypothesis being tested, especially in the larger Gardenvale centre, for the most pronounced links were between nearby establishments. The mass of data makes full presentation and interpreta-

tion of the patterns difficult so a more complete, yet parsimonious, approach was sought.

The agreement matrices used here can be considered as transaction flow matrices showing "trade" between the establishments, and Berry (1966) has demonstrated how these might be factor analysed to unravel major patterns of nodal "regions." But such data matrices show only the direct links, omitting the ties between A and B which exist only because both are linked with C (Brown and Horton, 1970). Such indirect links are important in identification of the nodal "region," however: for example, a shoe and a dress shop may be part of the same functional cluster, not because many people visit both of them on a single trip but because most of the customers at each also visit a nearby cake shop. Brown (1970) has suggested that such functional groups can be identified by treating

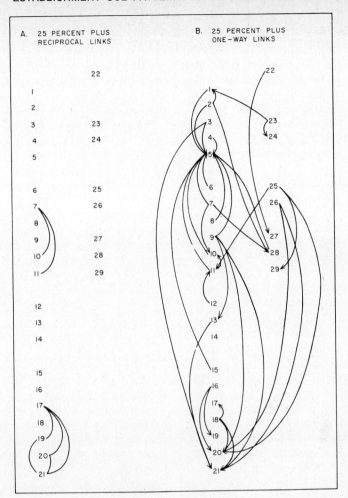

Figure 6. Major Linkages among Establishments: Gardenvale Shopping Centre (for Key to Establishments see Figure 4). Arrowheads show destinations in B

the agreement matrix as a Markov chain (with zeroes in the diagonal, Brown and Horton, 1970) and finding its associated Mean First Passage Time (MFPT) matrix in which each entry is a function of the number of direct and indirect links between the relevant states (establishments). Such matrices have been computed for the Fendalton and Gardenvale centres (Marble, 1967, provides a computer program) as bases for elucidating the underlying patterns. These have been analysed

(1) by isolating the major nodes in the system (see Brown, Odland and Golledge, 1970), and (2) by direct factor analysis to identify the "functional regions." Russett (1967) discusses the superiority of direct factor analysis over principal components analysis for transaction flow matrices (see also Brown and Holmes, 1971): direct factor analysis was preferred to the grouping techniques employed by Brown and his associates (Brown, Odland and Golledge, 1970;

Brown and Holmes, 1971), because they were interested in functional regions articulated around a single point but our concern was with multi-nodal functional groups. To facilitate interpretation of these factor analyses, the converse of each MFPT matrix was taken by subtracting each value from the largest in the matrix and adding one: in this way the strongest links were represented by the highest values.

Direct factor analysis of the MFPT matrices investigates whether all of the establishments in a centre are linked into one organizational network, or whether there are several separate groups. The latter situation was evident in the Gardenvale matrix, where 3 factors accounted for just 50 per cent of the variation. To interpret these, factor loadings of .5 or greater identify major destinations within the group, and factor scores greater than 1.0 identify major origins.

Figure 7A shows that the first Gardenvale factor was a bi-polar one emphasising two separate groups, one at the eastern end of the centre and the other at the western. The majority of the establishments in each group were both origins and destinations for major flows, suggesting that they were both clusters of low order establishments to which few higher order businesses were linked. A somewhat similar pattern emerges with the second factor (Figure 7B), which is again of a bi-polar nature, separating the eastern grouping this time from one organized around the middle part of the central place. Together, these factors suggest the existence of two virtually independent groups in the western part of the Gardenvale centre (establishment 5 is the only one to be a member of both): visitors to either of these groups are very unlikely to visit the eastern group (and vice versa). The positive component of the third factor (Figure 7C) links three of the higher order establishments in the western section, a newsagent (9), the

post office and the general draper, into a minor functional group: the negative loadings and scores link a widely scattered group of daily shopping establishments (a delicatessen, butcher and fruiterer), suggesting that some shoppers are not particularly constrained by distance.

Factor analysis of the Gardenvale centre's inter-establishment links thus provided strong evidence in support of the first hypothesis, concerning spatial clusters of linked businesses, but this was not repeated in the Fendalton analyses. Five factors were extracted in this case, accounting for just over half of the variation, but while some of the patterns of loadings and/or scores showed spatial grouping, they were extremely difficult to interpret.

Home-Shop Relationships

The third hypothesis presented for testing in this paper suggests that customers should visit the cluster of daily shopping establishments which is closest to their home. Since such clusters were clearly identified within the Gardenvale centre, these should also display the expected home-shop relationships. Since the Gardenvale centre is elongated east-west and the main clusters were located in the western, central and eastern parts, the home addresses of its customers were divided into those from west of the Nepean Highway, and those from the east (Figure 4). It was anticipated that the former group would tend to patronise shops in the western cluster, members of the latter group would patronize the eastern cluster, and that each group of respondents would use the central and cross-highway (members both east and west of the highway, Figure 7C) clusters in equal proportions. In addition a small group of respondents (39 of the 251) lived outside the general hinterland of the centre: these, termed the distant cus-

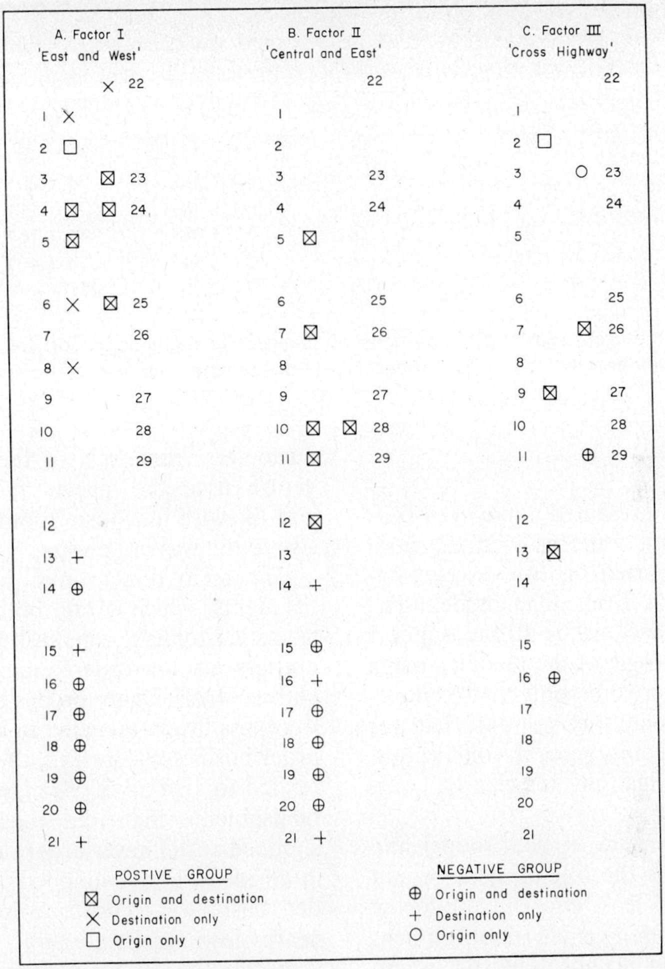

Figure 7. Major Factor Loadings and Scores from Direct Factor Analysis of Mean First Passage Time Matrix, Gardenvale Shopping Centre

tomers, should more likely visit the higher order establishments than any of the lower order clusters.

Any person who visited two or more of the establishments in any cluster was classified as a user of that group, which means that some respondents could have been classified more than once (in fact 51 of the 251 were) while others (100) used none of the clusters. Table 1 presents the results, and verifies the hypothesis (supported by one-sample tests of differences of proportions: Blalock, 1962). Residents living west of the centre mainly patronized the western and central clusters, those living to the east favoured the eastern cluster. Each used the cross-highway cluster to the same extent. Distant customers were much less likely to use one of the low-order clusters, as expected. As no separate clusters were identified in the Fendalton centre, the third hypothesis could not be tested there.

Table 1. Home-Shop Relationships: Gardenvale Centre[a]

Establishment Group Visited	Location of Respondent's Home			
	West of Centre	East of Centre	Distant	Total
Western	36 (.31)	13 (.13)	11 (.28)	60 (.24)
Central	43 (.37)	21 (.22)	10 (.26)	74 (.29)
Cross	13 (.11)	11 (.11)	3 (.08)	27 (.11)
Eastern	5 (.04)	33 (.34)	3 (.08)	41 (.16)
None	42 (.36)	37 (.38)	21 (.54)	100 (.40)
Total Persons	115	97	39	251

[a] Figures within brackets show the proportions of shoppers from the given origins visiting the relevant groups (that is, the proportions of the column totals).

Conclusion

This paper has presented a model of consumer behaviour patterns within central places and reported on two tests of hypotheses drawn from that model. The empirical evidence gives strong support to the internal logic of the model, though of course patterns in only two centres, one of them small, are not sufficient for the drawing of any general conclusions. Further investigation is clearly warranted, however.

A general feature of both model and empirical tests is the role of distance and the principle of least effort in producing patterns of within-centre establishment choice. Shoppers do not move all around a centre for their daily shopping requirements but tend to patronize a group of neighbouring establishments in that part of the centre closest to their home. This "friction of distance" is shown in Fendalton, for example, by the weak links between grocers and butchers on opposite sides of a road relative to those between similar establishments near to each other on the same side. In the Gardenvale centre it is even clearer. Occasional customers from east and west of the shops pass one set of intervening opportunities by proceeding to the central cluster of daily shopping establishments, but very few indeed by-pass two sets: hardly any

customers from west of the Gardenvale centre used the cluster at eastern end, and likewise for those from the east relative to the western cluster.

The main direct links, joining establishments which were both visited by many customers, emphasised the main clusters of low-order establishments in both centres. Higher order establishments were less firmly attached to certain lower order businesses: instead, their customers tended to visit a wider range of other establishments than did those who had shopped at the lower order shops (though in Gardenvale the shoppers at higher order businesses tended to patronize the nearby lower order cluster).

Within a shopping centre, establishments are linked not only directly (by customers visiting both of them on a single trip) but also indirectly (the establishments not sharing customers with each other, but with the same set of other establishments). Together, these links produce groups of establishments forming a "nodal region." Analysis of the Gardenvale centre suggested the existence of four such groups, three of which had a clear spatial identity, so to some extent it operated not as one central place but as an amalgam of four. The Fendalton centre, on the other hand, included 20 of its 21 establishments articulated into a single organizational structure, despite the duplication of three of the most frequently visited types of establishment. This suggests that there may be some critical threshold area of centre size below which there is no subdivision into separate groups of low order establishments, organized into a centre by the highest level businesses. Investigation of more centres may indicate that not only centre size but also internal layout combine to produce this threshold, and thereby suggest profitable methods for designing centres.

Finally, the two sample studies (especially that of Fendalton) suggested further lines of investigation. Berry (1959) has pointed out that classical central place theory does not apply to the distribution of all tertiary establishments within a city: some clusters obtain their trade from a local hinterland, others serve the whole city with specialized functions, and yet others depend on passing, often serendipitous trade. Thus different patterns of consumer behaviour should characterize these various types of central place and businesses (Boal and Johnson, 1965), and be influenced by different types of consumer (Stone, 1954). The Fendalton and Gardenvale centres contained a mixture of the three types of business; a feature which is probably common to many such nucleations. Consequently, consumer behaviour within them is an amalgam of three separate types, which must be unravelled for proper understanding of the functioning of central places.

References

Berry, B. J. L., 1959: Ribbon developments in the urban business pattern, *Ann. Ass. Amer. Geogrs.*, 49, 145–55.

Berry, B. J. L., 1963: *Commercial structure and commercial blight*, Univ. Chicago, Dept Geography, Res. Pap., 85.

Berry, B. J. L., 1966: *Essays on commodity flows and the spatial structure of the In-*
dian economy, Univ. Chicago, Dept Geography, Res. Pap., 111.

Berry, B. J. L., 1967: *Geography of market centres and retail distribution* (Englewood Cliffs, Prentice-Hall).

Blalock, H. M., 1962: *Social Statistics* (New York, McGraw-Hill).

Boal, F. W. and Johnson, D. B., 1965: The functions of retail and service establishments on commercial ribbons, *Canadian Geogr.* 9, 154–69.

Brown, L. A., 1970: On the use of Markov chains in movement research, *Econ. Geogr.*, 46, 393–403.

Brown, L. A. and Holmes, J., 1971: The delimitation of functional regions, nodal regions and hierarchies by functional distance approaches: an unconnected network example and overview, *J. Regional Sci.*

Brown, L. A. and Horton, F. E., 1970: Functional distance: an operational approach, *Geographical Analysis*, 2, 76–83.

Brown, L. A., Odland, J. and Golledge, R. G., 1970: Migration, functional distance, and the urban hierarchy, *Econ. Geogr.*, 46, 472–85.

Campbell, W. J. and Chisholm, M., 1970: Locational variation in retail grocery prices, *Urban Studies*, 7, 76–81.

Clark, W. A. V., 1967: The spatial structure of retail functions in a New Zealand city, *New Zealand Geogr.*, 23, 22–33.

Clark, W. A. V. and Rushton, G., 1970: Models of intra-urban consumer behaviour and their implications for central place theory, *Econ. Geogr.*, 46, 486–97.

Garner, B. J., 1966: *The internal structure of retail nucleations*, Northwestern University, Studies in Geography, 12.

Garner, B. J., 1967: Some reflections on the notion of threshold in central place studies, *Ann. Ass. Amer. Geogrs.*, 57, 788.

Getis, A., 1967: A method for the study of sequences in geography, *Trans. Inst. Brit. Geogrs.*, 42, 87–92.

Getis, A. and Getis, J. M., 1968: Retail store spatial affinities, *Urban Studies*, 5, 317–32.

Golledge, R. G., 1970: Some equilibrium models of consumer behaviour, *Econ. Geogr.*, 46, 417–24.

Johnston, R. J., 1966: The distribution of an intra-metropolitan central place hierarchy, *Austr. Geogr. Studies*, 4, 19–34.

Marble, D. F., 1967: *Some computer programs*

for geographic research (Evanston, North-western University).

Murphy, R. E., Vance, J. E. and Epstein, B. J., 1955: Internal structure of the CBD, *Econ. Geogr.,* 31, 21–46.

Nystuen, J. D., 1967: A theory and simulation of intraurban travel, in W. L. Garrison and D. F. Marble (eds.) *Quantitative geography.* Northwestern Studies in Geography, 13, 54–83.

Parker, H. R., 1962: Suburban shopping facilities in Liverpool, *Town Planning Review,* 33, 197–223.

Pred, A. R., 1969: *Behaviour and location, Part II* (Lund, C.W.K. Gleerup).

Russett, B. M., 1967: *International regions and the international systems* (Chicago, Rand McNally).

Scott, P., 1959: The Australian CBD, *Econ. Geogr.,* 35, 290–314.

Stafford, H. A., 1963: The functional bases of small towns, *Econ. Geogr.,* 39, 165–75.

Stone, G. P., 1954: City shoppers and urban identification: observations on the social psychology of city life, *Amer. Jour. Sociology,* 60, 36–45.

RAYMOND J. STRUYK

Empirical Foundations for Modeling Urban Industrial Location

While it is widely acknowledged that the intraurban location of jobs is one of the prime determinants of household location and urban spatial structure, comparatively little is known about the location decision process of firms in the *basic* industrial sector and, hence, the determinants of employment location. This ignorance is reflected in treatment of industry location within large-scale land use and transportation studies. Current studies are simply treating the location of primary jobs as exogenous rather than using mechanistic, nonbehavioral allocation models (Brown, 1972; Ingram *et al.,* 1972).

Two factors have contributed to the continued infancy of the within-city, industrial location decision modeling. First, until very recently little has been known about the process which produced net changes in the location of employment, i.e., were relocating firms relatively more important than the combination of new and defunct establishments? Second, little is known about the intrametropolitan location decision of firms themselves.

This article will review several studies of the process of net change in the intra-

urban location of manufacturing jobs, in order to provide a general overview of the findings and to draw the implications of these studies for modeling the intraurban location decision per se. This is a particularly fruitful time for such an assessment, because of the recently completed studies of the net change in manufacturing employment location; these employed establishment level data for a number of highly diverse metropolitan areas. The descriptive studies are in the tradition of research by the New York Regional Plan (Hoover and Vernon, 1962; Lichtenberg, 1961) and by Daniel Creamer (1936, 1969).

The emphasis, both in earlier and recent studies, has been on the disaggregation of the net change in employment by location into four components: employment changes associated with *new, defunct, relocating,* and *stationary* establishments. This particular emphasis reflects a strategy adopted to achieve an understanding of the *process* which produces the observed net changes. The strategy is to learn as much as possible about the individual components of net change and their interrelationships. Ulti-

From **Journal of the American Institute of Planners,** Vol. 42, No. 2, April 1976, pp. 165–73. Reprinted by permission of the **Journal** and R. Struyk.

mately this knowledge may lead to a statement of how the components in a behavioral (not definitional) sense determine net change.

While our understanding of the overall process is still too imperfect to provide clear guidance for the formulation of models of intrametropolitan industrial location, there are enough pieces of the total picture to furnish the basis for the first steps in development. This article describes some of these pieces and relates them to a general form which empirical models of the location decision must take in order to incorporate these lessons.

Recent Studies

The uniting element in the studies by Leone (1971), Struyk-James (1975), Schmenner (1972), and Kemper (1973) is the use of the establishment level Dun and Bradstreet data to analyze the process of net locational change in employment within metropolitan areas. Combined, these efforts have examined the components of the process in seven metropolitan areas for various time periods between 1965 and 1971.

The Dun and Bradstreet data have been available annually beginning in 1965. For each included establishment the data will generally include exact street address, four-digit standard industrial classification (SIC) codes, employment, date of establishment, relation to parent firm if the establishment is other than a single plant firm, and certain financial data (Leone 1972). The Dun and Bradstreet Corporation attempts to provide an exhaustive listing of establishments, representative data on employment, and extremely accurate information on locational and financial items. While there is no other data file to test the accuracy for individual establishments, the total establishment and employment counts have been compared

with data from the Census of Manufacturers with reassuring results.

The industrial and locational details of the D & B data, along with the availability over time, provide an especially rich data file. The typical procedure in these studies has employed the D & B files for a metropolitan area for two points in time. By matching the establishment entries for the different years, employment changes associated with new, defunct, relocating, and stationary establishments are determined. The metropolitan areas themselves were subdivided on several bases; in some instances jurisdictional boundaries were used while in others the subareas were defined by grouping postal zip code areas together. In general the geographical detail is not great, with each metropolitan area being disaggregated into some twenty to thirty analysis zones. These steps yield the most disaggregated and complete data of this type yet assembled. The various analyses of these data are the primary basis for the statements of this article.

Some Lessons Learned

Composition of net change. The first lesson is indeed a simple one: the composition of change in the location of manufacturing employment differs markedly between metropolitan areas. There are two aspects to this lesson: (1) the composition of aggregate change in manufacturing jobs in a metropolitan area (regardless of subarea location) and (2) shifts in jobs from one subarea to another within a metropolitan area.

The data in Table 1 show the composition of manufacturing employment change in three standard metropolitan statistical areas (SMSA) between 1965 and 1968, disaggregating industries into three equal-sized groups based on their employment growth rates. For each group of industries the table disaggregates the

Table 1. Composition of the Change in the Level of Employment in
Manufacturing Industries, 1965–1968

| SMSA and Industry Type | Net Change | Composition: | | 1965 Employment |
		New- Defunct	Change in Existing Establishments[a]	
Boston[b]				
Growing	18,768	−1,397	20,165	57,134
Stagnant	120	−5,502	5,622	75,722
Declining	−9,734	−11,472	1,738	159,633
Cleveland[c]				
Growing	2,950	−4,148	7,138	80,487
Stagnant	−297	−4,623	4,326	83,850
Declining	−19,887	−5,357	−14,530	127,165
Phoenix[d]				
Growing	15,116	4,054	11,062	33,552
Stagnant	286	−446	732	11,722
Declining	−1,164	−101	−1,063	6,822

[a] Existing establishments include those which changed location within the area as well as those which did not, plus a residual of 4–5 percent of establishments not explicitly identified in both 1965 and 1968. See Struyk-James (1975), appendix a for further explanation.
[b] Mean growth of manufacturing employment in Boston over the period was 3.4 percent; growing industries grew at a rate of 5 or more percentage points above average; and declining industries grew at 5 percentage points or more below average.
[c] Mean growth in Cleveland over the period was −4.7 percent; growing industries had a positive growth rate; and declining industries had a growth of less than −8.0 percent.
[d] Mean growth in Phoenix over the period was 27 percent; growing industries grew at a rate of 10 percent or more; and declining industries had a loss of over 5 percent of base-year employment.

Source: Tabulations of Dun and Bradstreet data used in Struyk-James (1975).

net change in employment between that resulting from firms starting and ceasing operations and that associated with existing firms, those present in 1965 and still somewhere in the area in 1968. The figures show a wide variance in the importance of existing establishments' employment relative to those of new and defunct (including out-migrating) establishments. For all industries combined in Cleveland, the absolute change in employment associated with new and defunct establishments dominates the net change of existing establishments, while in Boston and Phoenix the opposite is true. As might be expected during an upward swing of the national economy, the employment change of existing establishments in growing industries swamps all other change. For stagnant industries, on the other hand, the two sources of change are remarkably balanced; for de-

Table 2. Composition of the Change in the Location of Jobs in Manufacturing Industries, 1965–1968[a]

SMSA and Industry Type	Distribution of Relocation Activities by Activity Type[b]:				No. of Relocated Jobs[b]	Net Change in Jobs in Stationary Establishments
	Moving	New	Defunct	Total		
Boston						
Growing	45.9	12.6	41.4	100.0	4,839	20,020
Stagnant	21.4	10.8	67.8	100.0	9,666	6,505
Declining	30.3	9.2	60.7	100.0	22,315	2,238
Cleveland						
Growing	41.1	13.4	45.5	100.0	12,897	7,138
Stagnant	29.7	21.9	48.4	100.0	17,410	4,207
Declining	41.1	10.2	48.6	100.0	13,989	−14,666
Phoenix						
Growing	22.7	65.0	12.0	100.0	7,686	11,039
Stagnant	12.8	34.4	52.8	100.0	2,415	−633
Declining	18.8	36.9	44.2	100.0	1,374	−1,050

[a] See notes to Table 1.
[b] Employment of relocating establishments is counted only once, that is, the movement from one point in the area and arrival elsewhere are not counted separately.

clining industries no pattern is evident.[1]

At the second step, Table 2 demonstrates the importance of the components of within-SMSA change in job locations. In this accounting, each act, i.e., a firm closing or beginning operations at a location, is considered a locational change. Again a wide mix in the process of

1. The two studies by Creamer (1936, 1969) are the only ones not employing the Dun and Bradstreet data which contain information even indirectly comparable to that in Tables 1 and 2. The 1936 study used special compilations of Census of Manufacturers data to estimate the number of jobs associated with new and defunct firms only. The 1969 study for Pennsylvania SMSAs based on state employment security data contains all of the components of net change shown in Tables 1 and 2, although not in a form which permits direct comparisons. Overall, though, one pattern does stand out: the net employment change in metropolitan areas as a whole (our Table 1) produced by births and deaths is dwarfed by the net change in employment of existing establishments. See Creamer (1969), chapter 4 for details.

change is seen. Aggregating over all industries, in Phoenix the number of jobs produced by moving, new, and defunct establishments is roughly matched by the change in employment in stationary establishments; in Cleveland and Boston the three components clearly dominate.

Differences by the growth rate of the industry are also evident. For growing industries the net change in jobs in stationary firms exceeds those from moving, new, and defunct firms except in Cleveland. For stagnant industries job change associated with stationary firms is swamped in all cases. For declining industries the two sources of job relocation are about even, except in Boston where jobs associated with moving, new, and defunct firms are much more important.

Without belaboring these figures, two points can be made. First, according to these data, there is little commonality among the three cities in the relative importance of the various components of net employment change. Second, within each of the areas, only slight consistency in the relative importance of components of employment location change was found. On the other hand, a strong pattern did emerge, although not evident in the included tables. In the individual analysis zones, defined in these three metropolitan areas as clusters of spatially contiguous postal zip code areas with comparable levels of industrial employment, the largest single component of net change was the change in employment of stationary establishments. In fact, in about two-thirds of the zones the direction of overall net change was the same as the change in stationary establishments.

These same data can also be used to demonstrate the important processes which modeling net changes in employment can mask. The figures in Table 3 for two central-city Cleveland zones emphasizes this point. Both zones suffered a net employment loss over the 1965–68 period. Hough (the principal concentration of the poor in the Cleveland area),

on the one hand, suffered an out-migration of employment coupled with little new employment. The Cleveland central industrial district (CID), on the other hand, experienced a wave of closings but at the same time was the breeding ground for a number of new and initially small establishments. The composition of change clearly bodes much better for the CID than for Hough.

External economies. The second lesson learned from these studies is the apparent importance of external economies in the location decision of manufacturing establishments. The location of two-digit SIC industries which accounted for 5 percent or more of total 1965 manufacturing employment within each of the three separate SMSAs discussed above was examined by Struyk (1972). Each industry was found to be spatially clustered in at least two analysis zones within each SMSA. The consistency of these findings across cities and industries indicates spatial concentrations beyond those attributable to resource or transportation facilities or to simple agglomerative market effects. As such, this is a broader concept of external economies than that advanced by Hoover and Vernon in their seminal study.[2]

Struyk-James (1975) later used a multivariate analysis to determine if establishments within particular industries responded differently to economic factors, including external and internal economies, where the industry was concentrated and elsewhere. In the analysis of employment location across subareas, measures

Table 3. Components of Employment Change in Hough and the Cleveland Central Industrial District,[a] 1965–68

	Hough	Central Industrial District
Movers		
Origins	2,793	3,581
Destinations	1,767	2,714
Natural increase		
Births	296	2,262
Deaths	3,608	3,368
Change in stationary establishments	−3,948	992
Net change	−8,286	−981

[a] The CID includes but is not limited to the central business district. *Source:* Struyk-James (1975).

2. Hoover and Vernon saw externalities and centrality of location as highly correlated. The central location was valued as it provided a high degree of access to services provided by other industries or to customers. Although such factors undoubtedly play a role, the clustering of establishments and employment found at dispersed locations indicates other favorable externalities must be available from such groupings.

of the following phenomena were included as explanatory variables: external diseconomies due to congestion, internal economies available from large-scale operations, general externalities due to location (e.g., CBD) or history of location (e.g., traditional industrial area), and the general recent attractiveness of the zone as a site for industrial activity. The form of the analysis was such that the importance of economies from firms of the same industry locating together—localization economies—would be apparent indirectly from the estimated models.

The results indicated the significance of external economies, including localization economies. The effects were more evident in the analyses of the separate components of net change than in analysis of overall net change. This was especially the case for employment associated with new establishments. Also, those establishments located where their industry was concentrated placed a high value on production economies, as measured by average firm size. This finding and others are consistent with the hypothesis that establishments which are not located with other firms of the same industry are producing dominantly for local markets. The latter must be more responsive to local marketing criteria in selecting their location. Sites selected on the basis of these criteria would be expected to differ from those of the generally larger establishments producing for national or regional markets which emphasize production-associated economies in locating.[3]
Functional specialization. The third lesson, very closely related to the second, is that the functional specialization of establishments is clearly an important de-

terminant of location. The Dun and Bradstreet data code each establishment into one of the following categories: single-establishment firm, headquarters with manufacturing operations, branches with manufacturing operations, detached headquarters, and detached (office) branches. This coding corresponds to some degree with the distinction between market- and process-oriented establishments within the same industry. As our interest is in the location of primary employment, we will restrict our attention to results for those establishments involved in some production activity.

Leone (1971) classified establishments in the New York area by functional specialization; the data in Table 4 demonstrate that location varies systematically by function. For all of the disparate industries shown, the central-most area contains a lower proportion of branch plants than headquarters and single-establishment firms. Of course, functional specialization alone does not tell the story. There is, for example, a positive correlation between establishment size and decentralization for all three of the establishment types shown in Table 4. Any future modeling effort should take such specialization into account both when classifying establishments and when considering locational determinants.

Spatial incidence of components of net change. The fourth lesson is that the locational regularity of the components of net change, like the rate at which new firms locate in subareas, can be *explained* to a significant degree by characteristics of the establishments present in the zone and by the features of the zone itself. This lesson is of obvious importance for anyone attempting to forecast the future location of employment within an area as it indicates the presence of definable regularities. It is also important to those studying the economics of the locational process since the often crude characteristics of the

3. The trade-off between centralized market-dominated and suburban production-dominated sites has been analyzed theoretically and supported with data for Santa Clara County by M. Goldberg (1969). Additional insights on the space requirements and spatial groupings of individual industries in Pittsburgh are noted in Ira S. Lowry (1963).

Table 4. Geographic Distribution; Single establishment firms, headquarters with manufacturing activity present, and branch plants for selected industries in the New York SMSA, 1967

Industry	Percent Distribution:		
	Inner Core[a]	Outer Ring[b]	Ring[c]
Food and kindred products			
Headquarters with mfg.	83.2	14.1	2.7
Single-est. firms	78.3	14.1	7.6
Branch plants	76.9	14.9	8.2
Printing and publishing			
Headquarters with mfg.	85.6	11.9	2.5
Single-est. firms	85.9	9.9	4.2
Branch plants	70.9	16.0	14.0
Chemicals			
Headquarters with mfg.	82.9	11.9	5.2
Single-est. firms	73.8	21.1	5.1
Branch plants	72.3	21.4	6.3
Stone, clay, glass			
Headquarters with mfg.	76.5	19.2	4.3
Single-est. firms	69.8	16.8	13.4
Branch plants	45.2	30.6	24.2
Primary metals			
Headquarters with mfg.	74.0	22.0	4.0
Single-est. firms	72.8	22.0	5.2
Branch plants	54.0	27.0	19.0
Electric machinery			
Headquarters with mfg.	67.7	23.6	8.7
Single-est. firms	63.5	28.3	8.2
Branch plants	56.0	29.9	14.1

[a] The central city, less Staten Island.
[b] Richmond, Nassau, and Westchester Counties.
[c] Suffolk and Rockland Counties.

Source: Leone (1971), Tables 6.1 and 6.3.

zones employed in these analyses are undoubtedly summarizing the workings of more complicated economic processes.

Three analyses of this type are of particular relevance. First, the Struyk-James (1975) analysis explains the incidence of locational activity by a few characteristics of the firms at various locations and a couple of broad features of the location itself. Williamson (1969) employs explanatory variables that are detailed characteristics of the location or characteristics of the firm. Third, Kemper (1973) uses explanatory variables which are detailed characteristics of the industry to which the firm belongs, the size of the firm, and a few characteristics of the other firms at the location. Overall these studies demonstrate substantial systematic variation in the spatial incidence of locational activity with a wide variety of measures of characteristics of the location, the firms involved, and other firms present at the locations.

Struyk-James used the rate of each locational component in terms of employment in each analysis zone—defined, for example, as the number of employees in establishments ceasing operations between 1965 and 1968, as a fraction of total base year employment—as the dependent variable in a multiple regression analysis. The independent variables were (1) total manufacturing employment in the zone in the base year (1965); (2) a measure of the *shift* component of the change in manufacturing employment over the period (1965–1968);[4] (3) the average size of establishments in the zone in terms of employment; (4) dummy variables identifying the zone as a central industrial district, central city, and/or traditional manufacturing site; (5) dummy variables to control for variations between metropolitan areas in average rates. The cross-sectional analysis included zones from the Boston, Cleveland, Minneapolis-St. Paul, and Phoenix SMSAs.

The multiple correlation coefficients

---

4. While the dependent variable is the rate of a type of activity for concentrated or nonconcentrated industries *only,* this variable is for all industries, so that the identity problem is substantially mitigated for each subgroup. A complete description of these results is available in appendix g of Struyk-James (1975).

for the estimated models are movers' origins, .38; movers' destinations, .59; new establishments, .65; and defunct establishments, .51. (All are statistically significant at the 1 percent level.) For the movers' destinations and new firm models, total base-year employment, the shift-share measure, and average firm size as well as some location variables were significant. For firms ceasing operations and movers' origins there is no significant relation with the level of base-year employment, and movers' origins are unaffected by the relative prosperity (shift-share variable) of the zone. In brief, this analysis reinforced what other study of the data showed: the destination of movers and the locations of new firms demonstrated much more definite spatial patterns than other activities.

In his study of the origins and destinations of firms relocating in the Chicago area over a nine-year period, Williamson employed regression to analyze the number of origins or destinations per square mile. Origins were found to be roughly proportional to the number of firms present in the base year, so the study focused on explaining the distribution of destinations. Detailed land use data for the 576 Chicago area transportation zones provided uniquely rich information on the zones. The estimated model accounts for about 60 percent of the variance in the dependent variable. Of special note is the positive, significant effect of the percentage of land in the zone used for manufacturing, expressway access, and availability of blue-collar workers. Destinations were discouraged by high population density and the proximity of the zone to black residential areas.

Kemper analyzed the initial location of new establishments in the New York City area. The dependent variable in his regression analysis was the proportion of a four-digit SIC industry's new establishments locating in each of five zones into which he divided the SMSA. A separate model was estimated for each zone. The independent variables were detailed transportation, labor, and other requirements of the industry. Kemper also used discriminant analysis to classify births into the five zones, using firm employment and industry characteristics. The results of specific variables are too voluminous to summarize here. Note that, for the regression models, his correlation coefficients ranged from 0.65 for the central business district zone to 0.12 for his outer ring zone.

Association among components. The fifth lesson is that there is little obvious relationship among the spatial incidences of the four components of net employment change within individual metropolitan areas. For example, there is little relation between the zone of origin of relocating firms and the zones in which new firms choose to locate.

For present purposes it is sufficient to measure the degree of association simply by the correlation between the number of employees accounted for by each of the components of net change across analysis zones. Table 5 presents the simple correlation coefficients for four component pairs which might be of particular interest. The coefficients have been calculated on two bases: those in panel *a* are for employment levels of the components and those in panel *b* are for employment rates, i.e., the level of employment associated with a component of change in a zone divided by the zone's base-year employment. The interest in the correlations between new firms and destinations of movers and between movers' origins and defunct firms, shown in the first two columns, stems from the hypothesis that subareas doing well or badly will be doing so for all types of locational activity.

While this general idea was challenged earlier, the statistics in Table 5 further repudiate it. Although the correlations

Table 5. Simple Correlations of Relocation Activities for Employment in Selected Cities, 1965–1968

	A. Levels of employment			
	Birth/ Mover Destination	*Movers' Origins/ Deaths*	*Births/ Deaths*	*Births/ Movers' Origins*
Total[a] (75 zones)	.298[b]	.732[b]	.283[b]	.300[b]
Boston (20 zones)	.441	.460[b]	.476[b]	−.068
Minneapolis-St. Paul (24 zones)	−.066	−.159	.044	.316
Cleveland (18 zones)	−.075	−.087	−.024	−.024
	B. Employment rates[c]			
Total[a] (75 zones)	.077	−.007	.057	.038
Boston (20 zones)	.548[b]	.326	−.225	−.262
Minneapolis-St. Paul (24 zones)	.144	−.147	−.087	−.264
Cleveland (18 zones)	.227	−.050	−.121	.164

[a] Includes Boston, Minneapolis-St. Paul, Cleveland, and thirteen zones for Phoenix; Phoenix not reported separately due to fewness of observations. One Phoenix and one St. Paul zone with new establishment of several thousand employees excluded.
[b] Significant at 5 percent level.
[c] Location activity related to 1965 base.

Source: Compilation of Dun and Bradstreet data used by Struyk-James (1975).

computed with the level of employment provide support for this type of association, when the zones from the four metropolitan areas are pooled, the correlations are significant only for Boston of the individual SMSAs.

The correlations in the final two columns show the simple linear association between the location of employment of new firms and that of defunct establishments and between the employment of new firms and employment of relocating firms. The results are similar to the others. Across zones *and* across metropolitan areas, some association is evident, but within cities none appears. It should be stressed that the general insignificance of these simple relations does not mean that no association between activities exists: rather, such associations as do exist are subtle and only evident after disentangling them from other phenomena.

Individual industries. The sixth and final lesson concerns the consistency which an individual industry exhibits in its locational activity within and between urban areas. Two aspects are addressed in turn. The first is the extent to which a high (low) level of one locational component by an industry implies a similar level for the other locational components. Struyk (1972a) constructed a simple classification of two-digit SIC industries into the quartiles using the employment of a locational component relative to the industry's base year employment for each of the four components. His analysis for industries in the Boston, Cleveland, Minneapolis-St. Paul, and Phoenix metropolitan areas showed some regularity. In each SMSA several industries were in the upper or lower quartile for more than one of the components. Unfortunately, the way in which the data was assembled precluded a statistical test of this apparent consistency.[5]

The second aspect of the locational activity of individual industries of interest is whether some industries are generally more mobile and/or less stable than others within metropolitan areas. In this instance it was possible to test the significance of the observed patterns of high and low activity rates displayed by individual industries, with data pooled from the *four* SMSAs listed. These tests provided no support for the consistency of the mobility and/or stability of a given industry across urban areas.

Approaching a Formal Model

In the way of background, the implications of the lessons presented for modeling industrial location can be succinctly summarized in the following five points.

1. The composition of the net change in employment (both by industry and by component of change, i.e., expansion of existing firms, etc.) needs to be understood prior to attempting any formal modeling. Dividing industries on the basis of their local growth rates may prove effective in this task.
2. Differences among firms of the same industry in their market versus production orientation appear to have strong effects on the location decision.
3. The spatial incidence of the individual components of net change is significantly associated with the characteristics of the locations and the firms involved.

5. The comparison of the Dun's data at two points in time instead of continuous monitoring does not permit the computation of some conditional probabilities such as a new establishment relocating or going out of business. For this reason it was not possible to calculate the expected probability of an industry being in the upper or lower quartile for more than one activity.

volved. This association itself reflects various economic phenomena.
4. There is a lack of obvious spatial association among the components of net locational change, although more subtle associations appear to be significant.
5. While there is some evidence that rates of different locational activities vary systematically by industry within a metropolitan area, there is no support of an industry having consistently high (low) rates of locational activity across cities.

Two of the above points (1 and 5) indicate important differences among cities in the composition of growth and industry mix which must be accounted for to appreciate the locational behavior of firms. Additionally, the relative importance of the type of external economy, market versus production, is probably affected by the industry mix. Combined, these factors suggest difficulty in developing a behavioral model applicable to a number of urban areas. This is not to say that the structure of a model and its underlying causal relations would be invalid. The above factors and the enormous differences in the broad environment in which the location decisions are made will cause significant differences in the parameter values between cities or possibly groups of cities.

The systematic association of different types of external economies with the locations of firms of the same industry has several implications for behavioral modeling. In grouping establishments for analysis, separation along the traditional SIC lines will be of only limited value. Putman (1972) has pointed out the greater need to classify establishments on the basis of their market orientation (local, regional, national) and on the basis of their requirements for localization economies. While the SIC at higher levels of disaggregation effectively allows one to make these distinctions for some industries such as those used by Hoover and Vernon (1962) for communication-oriented industries, for many others this simply is not the case. A second implication is that since the location decision of establishments in the same industry is jointly determined (as are those of supplying and demanding industries), the modeling of any industry individually will miss the simultaneity of the entire locational process. This problem is likely more tractable than it may appear, thanks to the algorithms developed in simulation models of residential location, such as that by de Leeuw and Struyk (1975) in which neighborhood characteristics are dependent on those of the residents. However, the task of learning more of the nature of these interdependencies among establishments remains a prerequisite to such simulations.

Without brushing against the techniques one might employ in modeling the decision, some notion as to the degree of spatial disaggregation desirable in initial efforts can be advanced. Ideally, one would like to minimize the degree to which the environment of the decision (e.g., zoning regulations) controls the behavior being modeled, with the idea to abstract from secondary considerations. To accomplish this, a metropolitan area might be divided into a relatively small number of contiguous analysis zones, twenty-five or thirty as an upper limit, on the basis of several key factors such that zones are relatively homogeneous. Examples of such factors are the location of basic employment (possibly by specific industry) in the initial year being modeled as a measure of market and input availabilities, average residential rents weighted by density as a measure of the opportunity cost of sites, and, on a more sophisticated basis, the availability of industrial land, vacant land, and building

space. Again, studies of the residential location decision (Ingram et al., 1972, de Leeuw-Struyk, 1975) have used this method of delineation.

More germane to the actual model, several of the previously made points directly affect the broad form of a model which might be developed. A series of models may be required as is evident from two distinct observations. First, only slight correlation among the spatial incidence of the four components of net employment change was found. Thus, for example, models predicting which firms will be relocating may not accurately predict which will cease operations.

A second observation concerns the ratio of gross employment change to the net change in job location. This ratio on average is high—with a value of about three. Thus the dispersion (gross change) around the central tendency (net change) is great. This degree of departure from the central tendency underscores the difficulty of attempting to directly predict net change in employment location. Models of the individual components of net change, as advocated by Putnam, appear necessary.

In addition, two separate types of models are needed. The first are probabilistic models, that is, models with a dichotomous dependent variable taking on the values of one if the firm performs a certain act and zero otherwise. These models can be used to identify those establishments which will relocate within the area or cease operations, and those whose employment will change significantly while their location remains fixed. Clearly, such models must include as independent variables both the characteristics of the establishments and the characteristics of their locations. While the economic conditions for a firm to move or cease operations are evident, the task of inferring these conditions from available data will be extremely difficult.

The second class of models will be actual location decision models for new and relocating establishments, given that they are on the move.[6] Williamson's (1969) and Kemper's (1973) studies are pioneering efforts with this type of model. The apparent greater regularity of employment location change associated with new firms and movers' destinations, in comparison to the other components of net locational change in employment, also suggests that modeling of this type might be the most fruitful in the short term.

With respect to the development of formal models the foregoing discussion demonstrates two facts. First, the ignorance surrounding the process of locational change in manufacturing employment in metropolitan areas is being overcome. Second, this recently acquired knowledge impacts directly on the way in which any formal model of this process, either for predictive purposes or for hypothesis testing, should be formulated. These are obviously only the first steps in a formal modeling effort. Nevertheless, the possibilities for actual modeling work now appear particularly promising.

References

Brown, H. James et al. 1972. *Models of urban land use: a survey and critique*. New York: National Bureau of Economic Research.

Creamer, Daniel. 1936. The changing pattern of industrial location. In *Migration and economic opportunity,* ed. C. Goodrich. Philadelphia: University of Pennsylvania Press.

———. 1969. *Manufacturing employment by type of location*. New York: National Industrial Conference Board.

De Leeuw, Frank, and Struyk, Raymond. 1975. *The web of urban housing: policy analysis with a simulation model*. Washington, D.C.: The Urban Institute.

Goldberg, Michael. 1969. *Intrametropolitan industrial location: plant size and the theory of production*. Berkeley: University of California Center for Real Estate and Urban Economics.

Hoover, E. M., and Vernon, Raymond. 1962. *Anatomy of a metropolis*. New York: Anchor Books.

Ingram, G.; Kain, John; and Ginn, Royce. 1972. *The Detroit prototype of the NBER urban simulation model*. New York: National Bureau of Economic Research.

Kemper, Peter. 1973. The location decision of manufacturing firms within the New York metropolitan area. Ph.D. dissertation, Yale University.

Leone, Robert. 1971. The location of manufacturing activity in the New York metropolitan area. Ph.D. dissertation, Yale University.

Leone, Robert. 1972. The role of data availability in intrametropolitan workplace location studies. *Annals of Economic and Social Measurement* 1, no. 2: 171–82.

Lichtenberg, R. M. 1961. *One-tenth of a nation*. Cambridge: Harvard University Press.

Lowry, Ira S. 1963. *Portrait of a region*. Pittsburgh: Pittsburgh University Press.

Putman, Stephen H. 1972. Intraurban employment forecasting models: a review and a suggested new model construct. In *Journal of the American Institute of Planners* 38:216–30.

Schmenner, Roger. 1972. *City taxes and industrial location*. Ph.D. dissertation, Yale University.

Smith, David. 1971. *Industrial location*. New York: John Wiley.

Struyk, Raymond. 1972. Spatial concentration of manufacturing employment in metropolitan areas. In *Economic Geography* 48, no. 2: 189–92.

———. 1972a. Evidence on the locational ac-

6. This is not to imply that the decision to relocate and the destination decision are independent. The firm decides to relocate given that on at least one location the discounted present value of increased profits will more than compensate for moving costs. But because many firms apparently put off moving until they are substantially out of profit-maximizing equilibrium at their initial location, there will generally be a set of economically possible destination locations. The existence of such a set breaks the tight dependence between the relocation decision and some unique site. For a rigorous statement of the feasible set theory, see David Smith (1971).

tivity of manufacturing industries in metropolitan areas. In *Land Economics* 48, no. 4: 377–82.

Struyk, Raymond, and James, Franklin. 1975. *Intrametropolitan industrial location: the pattern and process of change in four* *metropolitan areas.* Lexington: Lexington Books.

Williamson, Harold F., Jr. 1969. *An empirical analysis of the movement of manufacturing firms in the Chicago metropolitan area.* Ph.D. dissertation, Yale University.

LAWRENCE A. BROWN, FORREST B. WILLIAMS,
CARL E. YOUNGMANN, JOHN HOLMES, AND
KAREN WALBY

The Location of Urban Population Service
Facilities: A Strategy and Its Application

Facilities related to population planning
and other services include such diverse
entities as planned parenthood offices,
health and social work clinics, employment agencies, day care centers, head
start centers, nursery schools, and adult
education or retraining centers. Despite
their varied nature, these facilities all involve the dissemination of either information or services (or both), largely
through personal contact with the target
population. Accordingly, the location of
the facility may bear directly on the success of the particular program or agency
it represents, and the locational question
is therefore important.

This paper proposes a four step strategy for locating population service facilities. Although developed with regard to a
specific problem, dealing with a system
of public day care centers, the strategy
has considerable generality and is applicable to a wide variety of situations and
scales. Since population service agencies
typically operate under budget, manpower, and other constraints that restrict
the number and size of facilities and preclude serving the entire population, par-

ticular attention is given to applying the
locational strategy to that situation. This
includes illustrating the procedure by examining the need for public day care service among the poor in Columbus, Ohio,
and locational options for a system of
public day care centers in its Model Cities
area.

A Locational Strategy for Population
Service Facilities and its Application

The general problem is to locate, within
an area, a given number of population
service facilities, that number being determined by resources available for construction, maintenance, and related costs.
Although there exist a multitude of possible locations, ideally those chosen will
maximize either service to the population
at large, profit to the locating agency, or
some similar criterion. The specific criterion depends upon the dominant motivation of the decision-making body.[1]

1. There is a good deal of work on location
problems to which this report is a contribution.
For a thorough review and synopsis including
an annotated bibliography of some 1400 items,

From **Social Science Quarterly**, Vol. 54, no. 4, March 1974, pp. 784–99. Reprinted by permission of the University of Texas Press, L. A. Brown, F. B. Williams, C. E. Youngmann,
J. Holmes, and K. Walby.

Presented here is a four step strategy for identifying locations for a given budget level or a given number of centers in accordance with a specified locational criterion. While we recognize that locations that are less than ideal (by the criterion specified) may be chosen as the result of factors such as political considerations or insufficient or inaccurate information about alternative locations, we believe that an optimization approach is advisable at the outset. At the very least it provides useful information for whatever other locational strategy is employed, a guide for designing alternative strategies, and a baseline for gauging their effectiveness.[2]

Step 1: Determine the Characteristics by Which the Target Population May Be Identified. Locations are evaluated in terms of their ability to serve the need or demand of the target population, the composition of which will vary from case to case. For this reason, it is important to determine those characteristics which will define the target population. If a system of day care centers for all families were being established, the target population might consist of families with children under five and an employable female. If a system of day care centers is being designed by private enterprise, an additional characteristic might be the ability to pay for the service. In the case of a day care

system for rural Appalachia important considerations are family attitudes toward day care and having the mother work, since they directly affect the likelihood of the facility being utilized.[3] For the public day care center problem reported here the target population was defined as families that receive ADC support and include children less than five years old and an employable (or trainable) mother.

In many cases determination of the pertinent characteristics of the target population is a simple procedure. ADC support, for example, is easily measured and data are available through welfare agencies. In other cases, however, the application of survey techniques to a sample population may be required. For example, in the case of the day care system for rural Appalachia one would want to know what family characteristics, in terms of readily available variables such as those from the U.S. Census, are related to a positive attitude towards day care, a variable that is not readily available. A private entrepreneur developing a day care system also might wish to utilize survey or other market research approaches.

Step 2: Determine the Spatial Distribution of the Target Population across Meaningful Areal Units. Funds for population service systems are allocated for areas such as Columbus or Model Cities, but these areas are generally too large to serve as meaningful targets for locating individual facilities. Units are needed with areal extents and target populations that do not exceed, and preferably are considerably less than, the service capacity of a facility. At the same time, to employ the proposed locational strategy the areal units must not be so small that their total number will result in exceeding the capacity of present-day computers and techniques of analysis. In our study, for example, block groups as designated for the

see A. C. Lea, *Location-Allocation Models: A Review,* M.A. Thesis (University of Toronto, Department of Geography, 1973); A. C. Lea, *Location-Allocation Systems: An Annotated Bibliography,* Discussion Paper Number 13 (University of Toronto, Department of Geography, 1973).

2. Our confidence in this statement is bolstered by the experience of congressional districting. In the mid-sixties several optimality models of redistricting were put forth, for example, B. C. Gearhart and J. M. Littschwager, "Legislative Districting by Computer," *Behavioral Science,* 14 (Sept., 1969), pp. 404–417; J. D. Thoreson and J. M. Littschwager, "Legislative Districting by Computer Simulation," *Behavioral Science,* 12 (May, 1967), pp. 237–247.

3. Information derived in the course of private conversation with W. Zink of the State of Ohio Bureau of Welfare Services.

1970 United States Census of Population were utilized. Census tracts were deemed too large; single blocks were considered too small to be effective as locational targets.

Frequently, one or more characteristics critical to defining the target population are gathered for areal units that are not meaningful locational targets. This was so in the day care center study, which thus necessitated designing a procedure by which the number of ADC cases could be estimated for block groups.[4] This was accomplished by deriving a regression equation employing socioeconomic variables tabulated at the census tract level to account for variation between tracts in the percentages of families that are ADC cases. The same variables for block groups were then substituted into the equation to estimate the number of ADC recipient families at the block group level.

At the time of analysis only the United States Census First Count Summary Tape was available. Although income, perhaps the best indicator of the number of ADC cases, was not included in the First Count, other socioeconomic variables proved sufficient. For our analysis, all variables were expressed as percentages in order to make the estimating equation independent of the size of the data collection units and applicable to areal units at different levels of spatial aggregation, the census tract and the block group. The variables were selected partly on the basis of an intuition that they would be important indicators of the level of ADC cases. The resulting model, estimated by stepwise regression procedures, explains 88 percent of the variance in ADC caseloads across the census tracts.[5]

$$Y_i = -0.0694 + 0.0043X_{1i} + 0.0248X_{2i} + 0.0092X_{3i}$$

where

Y_i is the predicted percentage of the families in areal unit i that are ADC cases.

X_{1i} is the percentage of persons in areal unit i that are less than 18 years old and living in housing units with greater than 1.51 persons per room.

X_{2i} is the percentage of families in areal unit i with a single male head and children less than 18 years old.

X_{3i} is the percentage of families in areal unit i with a single female head and children less than 18 years old.

Once Y, a percentage figure, is estimated for each block group, it is multiplied by both the number of families in the block group and the average number of children younger than five years of age per family. This figure, then, is an estimate of the actual number of children requiring day care services.[6]

---

variables were retained from the original 16 on the basis of total variance explained and the simplicity of the resulting model. Although there is no theoretical rationale for non-zero intercept, the model in which all parameters but the intercept were significant would have included 6 more variables with approximately the same level of explained variance. Therefore, the 3 variable model, which had an r^2 value of .88 and a standard error of estimate of .035 was deemed most appropriate for this study.

6. Not all ADC cases are considered trainable for work and thus eligible for day care services. However, our locational strategy employs intensity of an area's need relative to other areas, not its absolute need. Thus the use of number of ADC children as a surrogate for need assumes that "trainability" does not vary spatially, and skirts the problem of specifying the level of trainable ADC cases. The latter was a concern because estimates of the percent trainable were highly disparate, apparently depending upon the mission or bureaucratic role of the person making the estimate.

---

4. ADC caseload data aggregated at the census tract level were obtained from the Franklin County Welfare Department.

5. Since the model was designed only for estimation purposes, not for testing a theory, the analysis was not couched in a rigorous statistical framework. Using stepwise regression, 3

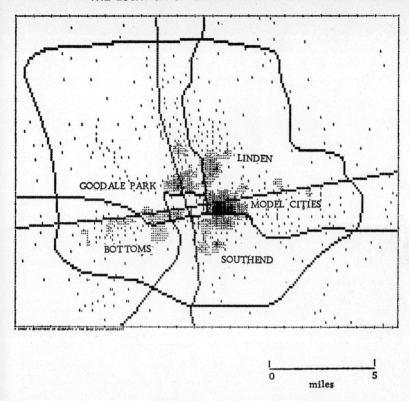

Figure 1. The Need for Public Day Care Service, Columbus, Ohio

The block group estimates of pre-school ADC children were mapped (Figure 1) to provide a visual representation of the spatial distribution of public day care service need.[7] A high concentration of public day care need occurs throughout the central area of the city, with the exception of those areas occupied by industrial and commercial land uses. This is expected, since central cities in general have a high proportion of low income residents. The highest peak of need occurs in the predominantly black Model Cities area. Secondary peaks occur in the Linden area, northeast of the central city, also predominantly black; in the Goodale

7. The map of the need for public day care service is presented in the form of a density surface which expresses the need *per unit area* for all locations within the city.

Park area, directly north of the central city; in the Bottoms area, west of the central city; and in the Southend area, southeast of the central city, all with considerable Appalachian white population.

Step 3: Determine Which Areal Units Should Receive the Population Service Facilities To Be Established, Using Rational Locational Criteria. One result of Step 2 was a map portraying the spatial distribution of the need or demand for day care. This indicates several neighborhoods that are possible candidates for receiving extensive day care assistance—Model Cities, Linden, Goodale Park, The Bottoms, or Southend. To illustrate a procedure for placing centers in these areas, attention is focused upon the highest and most extensive peak on the need surface (Figure 1) which is approximately

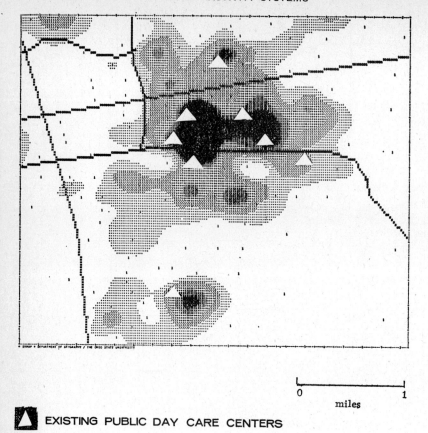

0   miles   1

▲ EXISTING PUBLIC DAY CARE CENTERS

Figure 2. The Need for Public Day Care Service, Columbus Model Cities Area and Vicinity

coincident with, but somewhat larger than, the Columbus Model Cities area (Figure 2). This area comprised 120 1970 Census block groups which are to serve as targets for locating the day care centers. Eight public centers already exist in the area, nearly half of the total presently in Columbus (Figure 2).

Within the Model Cities area, there are a considerable number of "good" locations for new day care centers. One approach to choosing among these is to depict the spatial distribution of need as a surface, the height of which at any given location corresponds to that location's level of demand or need. If n centers are to be established, one locational strategy,

then, is to choose the n highest peaks on the surface. Typically, however, the problem is more complicated. First, a center may be capable of serving an area larger than that represented by a given peak. Thus, the locational decision also should take into account the need in surrounding areas. A second complication is introduced by existing centers, since new centers should be located to serve populations other than those already served. Finally, accessibility of the population to the center is important.

But even considering these points, the appropriate locational criteria will vary from case to case. It is essential that these criteria be defined, and concomitantly, that there be designed a means of implementing them to produce alternative locational solutions under varying conditions. A reasonable set of criteria for the public day care center problem is to maximize the number of people served within the constraint of allowing no one to travel more than a specified distance for service and holding to a minimum the total distance travelled by all individuals served. The locational problem, then, becomes one of deciding which combinations of locations will best statisfy these criteria. This was accomplished by formulating the problem as a linear programming model. The strategy can be more generally described as follows.

First, the Model Cities area is divided into small areal units, the 120 block groups. Each block group's need for day care service is estimated by procedures discussed under Step 2, Then, a value is derived for each block group to indicate the level of service that might be provided if a day care center were situated there. The value for block group j is $\Sigma_i a_i (S-d_{ij})$, where a_i is the level of need (i.e. the size of the target population) in block group i, S is the maximum travel distance allowed, and d_{ij} is the distance from the center point of block group i to the center of j where the facility is assumed to be located. The value for block group j is computed only for block groups i for which $(S-d_{ij})$ is greater than zero. Thus, the weighting value for block group j reflects the need or the target population that would be served if a center were located there and the costs of serving that need, measured in terms of distance traveled. Once this value has been calculated, the block groups j can be ordered in terms of the need served by each, and locating n centers so as to maximize total service is in effect accomplished by choosing the n block group with the highest rankings.[8]

8. The actual task is more complicated because choosing one block group as a day care center location, serving itself and areas around it,

For a given maximum travel distance or threshold distance, the model was executed in two ways: first by locating centers without regard to the locations of existing centers; and second, by taking the existing centers into account.[9] The total number of centers located, including existing centers when taken into account, was varied from 8 (the number of existing centers), to 10, and then upward by steps of 5 to 45. This procedure reflects various budget constraints limiting the number of new centers. The maximum travel distance for day care was varied from one-quarter mile, to one-half mile, to one mile.[10] Thus, the model was executed 54 times.

To gain some insight into the utility of the model, it is useful to compare the locations of the 8 centers existing in the study area with the 8 locations suggested by the model (Table 1). For both the quarter-mile and one-mile maximum travel distance, there is agreement on only three centers; for the half-mile travel distance, there is agreement on four centers. However, this is somewhat misleading. Comparing the optimal locational scheme

changes the weighting values for other block groups. For discussion of technical aspects of the model and its specification in a mathematical programming format, see J. Holmes, F. B. Williams, and L. A. Brown, "Facility Location Under a Maximum Travel Restriction," *Geographical Analysis*, 4 (July, 1972), pp. 258–266.

9. In implementing the model, a_i was measured by density of day care need for a block group rather than by the actual number of children needing day care.

10. It is realized that any threshold distance selected would be arbitrary. Since questions of this nature are policy related the Franklin County Department of Welfare was consulted. On the basis of their experience the one-mile threshold was suggested. The authors included the one-quarter and one-half mile thresholds for comparative purposes and because they seemed more reasonable for a small and densely populated area such as Model Cities. This choice is supported by the results reported in Table 2.

Table 1. Comparison of Actual Locations with Recommended Locations, Eight Day Care Centers[a]

| | Recommended Locations | | |
Actual Locations	One-Quarter Mile Threshold Distance	One-Half Mile Threshold Distance	One Mile Threshold Distance
—	28–5	—	—
28–7	—	28–7	28–7
—	—	—	29–4
—	—	36–3	—
37–5	37–5	37–5	—
—	38–4	38–4	38–4
—	53–1	—	—
53–4	—	—	—
53–5	53–5	53–5	53–5
53–6	—	—	—
54.10–3	54.10–3	54.10–3	54.10–3
54.20–2	—	—	—
—	—	55–5	—
—	55–6	—	55–6
—	56.10–2	56.10–2	—
—	—	—	57–4
—	—	—	61–1
61–3	—	—	—

[a] Each of the block groups is identified by a code; the first number designates census tract; the second, the block group within that tract.

with the actual one on the basis of a measure of the total need served indicates only a slight disparity in service; for the one-quarter mile threshold distance, 5,207 versus 4,832; for the one-half mile threshold distance, 8,472 versus 7,931; for the one-mile threshold distance, 10,110 versus 9,063. This suggests that the locational procedures previously employed for day care centers are reasonably effective, but less so if applied to a day care system with one-mile service areas.

The recommended locations for public day care centers and the block groups assigned to be serviced by each are depicted in Figures 3, 4, and 5, respectively, for threshold distances of one-quarter, one-half, and one mile. These include only the results of the analysis in which existing centers were first taken into account, since the others are superfluous in terms of the real world problem.

One useful aspect of the outcome of these analyses is that recommended public day care center locations for a given budget level are generally contained within the recommendations for a higher budget level. For example, if 7 new centers can be added in 1972, the recommendation of the analysis for 15 centers can be followed (8 original centers plus 7 new ones), knowing that if 5 more centers can be added in 1973, the 15 centers in existence in 1972 will be a part of the recommendation for locating 20 centers.[11]

Prior expectations with regard to the locations recommended by the model were (1) that spacing of the centers would correspond with the population distribution, (2) that locating additional centers would result in serving a greater proportion of the total study area, and (3) that locating additional centers would result in serving a greater proportion of the total need for day care service. These expectations can be addressed in part by examining the maps of recommended day care center locations and their tributary areas, and by a measure of the total need served by each budget level for a given size tributary area (Table 2).

For all budget levels and threshold distances, the spacing of centers is fairly uniform and placing additional centers results in serving a larger proportion of the total study area. Furthermore, for all budget levels with a one-quarter mile tributary area, placing additional day care centers results in serving a great proportion of the total need or target population. However, if either a one-half or a

11. This clearly implies that critical variables entering into locational considerations are constant over the intervening time period. This is not likely to be the case, but the problem is inherent in any attempt to plan future decisions on present knowledge.

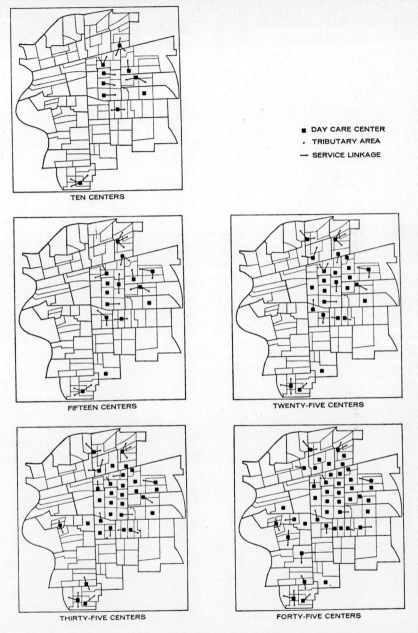

Figure 3. Columbus Model Cities Area and Vicinity: Day care centers and tributary areas recommended locations, maximum travel distance of one-quarter mile

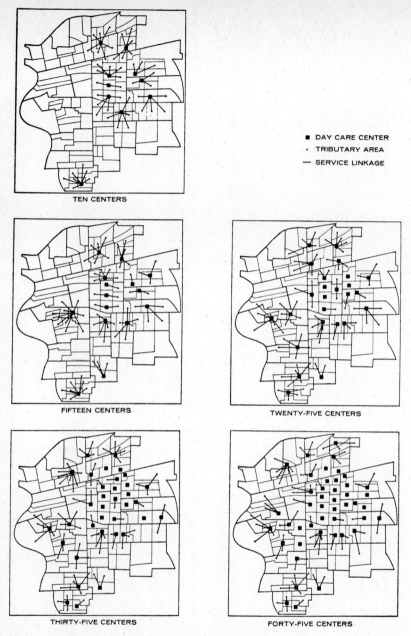

■ DAY CARE CENTER
· TRIBUTARY AREA
— SERVICE LINKAGE

TEN CENTERS

FIFTEEN CENTERS

TWENTY-FIVE CENTERS

THIRTY-FIVE CENTERS

FORTY-FIVE CENTERS

Figure 4. Columbus Model Cities Area and Vicinity: Day care centers and tributary areas recommended locations, maximum travel distance of one-half mile

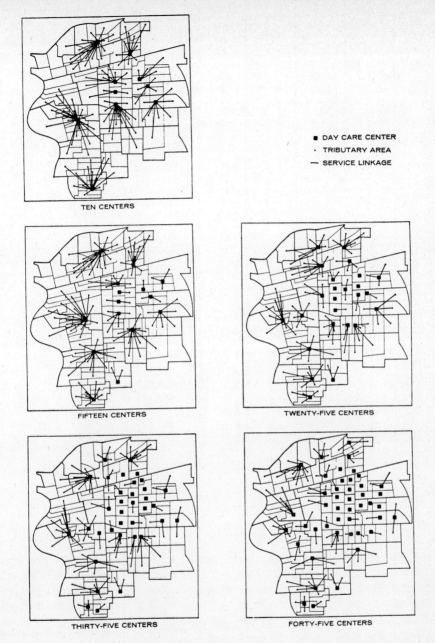

Figure 5. Columbus Model Cities Area and Vicinity: Day care centers and tributary areas recommended locations, maximum travel distance of one mile

Table 2. Measurements of Service Levels for Recommended Locations of Day Care Centers

Threshold Distance	Number of Centers	Need Served (density)[a]	Need Served (actual)[a]	Movement Cost (density)[b]	Movement Cost (actual)[b]
¼ mile	10	5405.31	1031.37	1209.84	253.86
	15	7065.52	1437.19	1465.87	323.13
	20	8014.18	1645.33	1538.55	338.94
	25	8237.02	1706.08	1393.07	322.59
	30	8536.41	1775.91	1346.11	313.02
	35	9014.62	1851.82	1388.60	312.30
	40	9355.11	1944.32	1432.45	330.44
	45	9603.80	2003.21	1392.04	323.30
½ mile	10	8660.87	1731.41	3187.04	680.97
	15	9568.73	2040.57	2969.43	680.44
	20	10229.79	2181.24	2824.08	661.38
	25	10300.70	2210.77	2512.32	615.15
	30	10245.05	2199.56	2272.13	555.07
	35	10304.50	2235.87	2081.77	520.22
	40	10285.77	2233.43	1909.29	476.09
	45	10337.85	2246.79	1805.09	447.99
1 mile	10	10345.24	2253.80	5221.39	1267.03
	15	10394.08	2268.27	3860.42	907.62
	20	10394.08	2268.27	3049.50	764.33
	25	10394.08	2268.27	2682.43	675.56
	30	10394.08	2268.27	2458.98	617.03
	35	10394.08	2268.27	2194.34	553.25
	40	10394.08	2268.27	2003.49	508.31
	45	10394.08	2268.27	1852.82	469.38

[a] $\sum_i \sum_j a_i x_{ij}$.

[b] $\sum_i \sum_j a_i d_{ij} x_{ij}$.

one-mile tributary area is employed, this is true only for budget allocations of up to approximately 20 day care centers. Otherwise, when new centers are added, they tend to be located in block groups that are tributary areas at the lesser budget level. For example, for a one-half mile threshold distance, increasing the number of centers from 25 to 35 results in placing new centers in block groups 35–5, 36–1, 37–7, 38–1, 38–2, 53–3, 54.20–1, 56.10–1, 57–3, and 61–3, all of which

are tributary areas at the 25 center level.[12]

Thus, the total need served is not markedly improved by increasing the number of centers if either a one-half or one-mile threshold distance is thought reasonable and 20 centers already exist. Put another way, the marginal return from building new centers under those conditions is

12. Each of the block groups is identified by a code, viz., 37–5. The first number designates census tract; the second the block group within that tract.

effectively zero in terms of total need served. However, another criterion is also relevant; the total movement cost for a given budget level and threshold distance, calculated by multiplying the need served by the distance to the day care center serving that need, for all day care centers (Table 2). Interestingly, for all one-half and one-mile tributary area solutions, the overall cost of service is decreased as more centers are placed since the average distance of a center from its clientele is decreased. In these terms, then, there is a continual marginal return from building additional day care centers. This return can be seen as a form of social welfare payoff, primarily reflecting the efficiency of service from the point of view of the client rather than the level of need served. It would be useful for planning purposes to calculate the ratio of this payoff to day care center construction costs, but data on which to base this calculation are not presently available.

Step 4: Determine the Exact Location of the Population Service Facility within Each Target Area Chosen To Receive a Facility. Population service facilities are placed on single land parcels, although the parcel generally is not practical as a locational target for technical reasons previously specified. Assuming that an existing building will be converted, choosing the parcel must involve considerations such as the accessibility of the parcel to main arteries and transportation, soundness of the building on the parcel and its conformance to public health and related regulations, costs of conversion, adaptability of the building to the particular population service use, and the proximity of related facilities and personnel. If a new building is to be constructed, availability of vacant land is important. Owing to time and data constraints, this step has not been considered in the day care center illustration. However, a strategy such as that discussed in Step 3 could be designed to take account of the aforementioned factors and choose among alternative locations. At the same time, in a real world setting it may be that there are so few locational alternatives within a given target area that design of a complex strategy is not required.

Summary and Concluding Remarks

This paper proposes a four step strategy for locating new population planning and service facilities. As an illustration, we considered the need for public day care in Columbus, Ohio, and the location of centers to meet this need in its Model Cities area. A series of recommended locations were derived for several budget levels and maximum travel distances. Implementing the locational strategy involved designing a regression and computer mapping procedure for Step 2 and a linear programming procedure for Step 3. One important aspect of this case study is the elucidation of the kinds of difficulties one encounters in applying academic dictates to a practical problem, and, for one problem, an illustration of solutions to those difficulties proposed by one group of social scientists.

The total costs of implementing the locational strategy described in this paper were substantial. Those related to estimating and mapping the demand or need surface for day care service, which in itself would provide valuable information for a service or planning agency, are relatively small. However, the cost of the computer time required for the solutions to the linear programming model could be prohibitive for an agency operating on limited financial resources, and wishing to allot as much money as possible to the actual provision of population planning or other services.

One of the reasons for the high computing costs for execution of the linear programming model was the consideration of a number of alternative budget levels and threshold distances. If an agency chose one threshold distance and knew the precise number of facilities it could afford to construct, the computing costs would not be substantial since only one run of the model would be required. Also, more efficient algorithms than the one we employed are available. Finally, an alternative more promising in terms of cost would be a heuristic solution that accomplished approximately the same tasks as the linear programming model.

However, other typical locational situations also exist. One is to locate a *given number* of facilities to serve the *entire* target population; a second is to locate facilities to serve the *entire* population with the stipulation that no individual is served by a facility more than a given distance (or cost) away, in which case the number of facilities needed as well as their location is determined.[13] If the locational situation being considered were one of these, the appropriate model would replace ours as Step 3 of the four step locational strategy. Thus, it seems apparent that a broad range of problems can be treated by the procedures presented here.

13. See C. S. ReVelle and R. W. Swain, "Central Facilities Location," *Geographical Analysis,* 2 (Jan., 1970), pp. 30–42; Rojeski and ReVelle, "Central Facilities Location Under An Investment Constraint"; C. Toregas, R. W. Swain, C. S. ReVelle, and L. Bergman, "The Location of Emergency Service Facilities," *Operations Research,* 19 (Oct., 1971), pp. 1363–1373.

KEVIN R. COX AND FRANK Z. NARTOWICZ

Jurisdictional Fragmentation in the American Metropolis: Alternative Perspectives

Fragmented local units and overlapping special districts have been the topic of much discussion in the literature on American urban politics. Earlier in this century, the literature was dominated by the "traditional reform" movement. This proposed that metropolitan consolidation was necessary in order to avoid the financial demise of the public service sector. Recently a critical body of literature has emerged indicating that fragmentation is not necessarily inefficient.

A dominant school of thought in this regard is that of public choice theory. Public choice theory, moreover, has moved beyond critique to advance its own theories of jurisdictional organization at the local level. As a result it has emerged as an important and, indeed, influential paradigm for the study of the local political economy. This is notwithstanding the fact that public choice has generated its own group of critics, particularly those approaching the problem of metropolitan fragmentation from a liberal direction.

However, both public choice theory and its critics share a common set of assumptions, and analyse jurisdictional or-ganization in much the same manner. Specifically, both approaches focus on individuals in the sphere of consumption. Notably absent is the role of production relations in the political organization of metropolitan areas. The objective of this paper is to rectify this imbalance and so arrive at an enhanced understanding of that spatial form. The approach adopted is an identification, review and critical evaluation of existing theories of jurisdictional fragmentation.

The Public Choice Paradigm

The public choice paradigm represents a neoclassical attempt to explain the public provision of certain goods and services which are broadly termed public goods (Tullock, 1970); and to rationalize and legitimate, in terms of the welfare criterion of efficiency, the spatially decentralized character of local government in American metropolitan areas (Bish, 1971). Thus, public goods are those which should be provided but for which there is no feasible method of charging the consumer. The concepts of collective con-

From **International Journal of Urban and Regional Research**, Vol. 4, No. 2, June 1980, pp. 196–209. Reprinted by permission of Edward Arnold (Publishers) Ltd., London, K. R. Cox, and F. Z. Nartowicz.

sumption and externalities are salient here. This is due to the publicness of the benefits provided: once a public good is purchased by a consumer non-purchasers cannot be excluded from its consumption. In such a situation, the rational consumer understates his true preference for the good and hopes to avoid payment for its provision. This results in a non-optimal level of output, and has been termed the free-rider problem.

The consequent problem of market failure provides the basis for a public choice theory of the state (Pejovich, 1972; Davis and Whinston, 1962). Goods characterized by substantial publicness in consumption can only be provided by an institution which has the authority to coerce consumers into payment for goods through taxation. In the public choice view, therefore, governments and public agencies with powers to provide goods and services and to levy taxes in payment are the public economy equivalent of the private sector firm producing goods and services for private exchange and consumption.

However, as in the case of the private economy the critical welfare criterion is that of efficiency. How can supply be so organized as to satisfy, at minimum cost, demand for those goods and services most intensely desired? In the private economy competition between consumers and between producers provides the necessary mechanism. Competitive bidding between consumers ensures that demand for those goods most intensely desired will be effective in terms of actual consuming power; i.e., effective demand for the most intensely desired goods and services will be maximized. Likewise, competition between producers ensures that those goods and services most intensely desired will be the ones produced and that they will be produced at minimum cost. Firms failing to observe consumer demand for a particular bundle of goods and services at minimum cost will go out of business.

The problem for the public choice theorist is that in the public economy the respective competitive relations between consumers and between suppliers are weak ones. Competitive bidding ensures demand revelation but we have seen that in the case of public goods the publicness of consumption provides incentives for concealing preferences; in other words, there are free-rider difficulties. Likewise, governments are monopoly suppliers of public goods and monopoly suppliers do not have to be responsive to the demands of those they cater to. It is true that party competition for legislative and executive authority provides some constraint on monopoly power and bureaucratic imperialism (Niskanen, 1971). But it is a weak constraint, particularly in the light of lengthy periods of office and the fact that the typical two-party relationship is more akin to oligopoly than to pure competition.

In this context jurisdictional fragmentation provides a necessary, if not sufficient, structure for efficiency; this is achieved by enhancing competition between government-suppliers and promoting preference revelation by consumers. Where jurisdictional fragmentation prevails government suppliers are forced into competition with each other through the residential preferences of consumers. Residents shift, for example, from those jurisdictions the governments of which are providing neither cheap public goods and services nor those which are in demand; to jurisdictions, the governments of which *are* so responsive. In this way individuals express their preferences for public goods: as Tiebout (1956) nicely expressed it, they "vote with their feet."

Mobility, moreover, has effects on respective tax bases and abilities to operate at the low point on the average cost curve and, consequently, upon the electoral prospects of respective governments, the ability of public service bureaucracies to obtain increased budget allocations, etc. Thus, competition can be fostered by simulating the private market via multiple suppliers: "If ample fragmentation of authority and overlapping jurisdictions exist, sufficient competition may be engendered to stimulate a more responsive and efficient public economy in metropolitan areas" (Bish and Ostrom, 1976, p. 116).

Thus, the public choice theorist is concerned with the *organizational form* of government in terms of efficiently meeting individual preferences for public goods. Metropolitan fragmentation, with each local unit providing different bundles of services at different costs, is seen to have the following consequences:

1. It presents an array of alternatives, thus maximizing the chances that heterogeneous individual preferences will be satisfied;
2. it fosters competition between governments, thus increasing the responsiveness of public officials to citizen demands while minimizing the cost of provision;
3. it forces the individual to reveal his preferences by selecting a residence thus eliminating the free rider problem.

The Liberal Critique

The liberal critique of public choice theory offers an alternative explanation of spatially decentralized local government in metropolitan areas, and situates public choice theory with respect to that explanation. In contrast to the deductive, efficiency maximizing approach of public choice theory, social scientists of liberal persuasion offer a theory which is more inductive and concerned with equity. And in place of taste variations and abstraction from income differences the liberal critique assumes an essentially homoge-neous utility function and income differentiation as central to jurisdictional fragmentation.

The point of departure for the liberal critique is an empirical observation: the marked correlation between jurisdictional boundaries within metropolitan areas and various indicators of social well-being (Newton, 1975, pp. 250–51; Danielson, 1972, p. 145; Cox, 1973, chapter 3). To some degree this is a matter of the central city-suburban fiscal disparities problem: relatively high tax rates in the central city jurisdiction and relatively modest expenditures on education. But the differences are confined neither to the central city-suburban dichotomy nor to fiscal issues. Differences between suburbs in tax rates and educational spending are greater than those between the central city and an "average" suburb. And coordinate with these are differences in public safety, school quality, property value appreciation, social homogeneity and the like.

This relation between metropolitan welfare geography and municipal boundaries can be traced, it is argued, to the spatially decentralized character of local government. Decentralization of powers of education provision and revenue raising provide incentives for the more affluent to club together in their own municipality so as to share out with each other the fiscal and behavioural externalities they have mutually to offer. At the same time decentralization of land-use planning, particularly the power to zone, facilitates exclusion of those poorer households who would erode tax bases, impose demands for poverty-linked services, and detract from local school quality (Downs, 1973; Wingo, 1973, pp. 14–16).

The spatial decentralization of local government, therefore, facilitates inequality in public provision, tax rates, public safety, etc. To some degree the institutional arrangements at issue may derive from considerations that have nothing to do with the achievement of inequalities in consumption and in individual life chances. Nevertheless they have been a necessary, if not sufficient reason for it, and their reproduction as inequality-creating mechanisms is now actively sought by those benefiting from them. The decentralization of zoning, and the possibilities of exclusion which it offers, create, therefore, incentives for municipal incorporation. The Black Jack case is a well-known instance but defensive incorporation is undoubtedly common and of substantially older vintage. And as one liberal advocate (Newton, 1975, p. 258) has written: ". . . the fact is that fragmentation *is* a solution to problems—the middle class solution which tries to ensure that other people's problems do not encroach on their suburbs. This is the intent of local zoning, house building and tax laws."[1]

Moreover to the extent that these institutional arrangements—decentralized land-use planning, fiscal home rule, local school districts, etc.—come under fire one can envisage struggles between distributional groupings according to the degree to which they gain from them; and that these struggles fortify the liberal explanation of metropolitan fragmentation is in no doubt. The struggle over educational finance, for example, has tended to be between wealthier school districts which gain from fiscal home rule and the poorer school districts which do not. It is the suburban municipalities which have sought refuge in the sanctity of *local* education in their attempts to resist the extension of busing for racial balance across school district lines. And the conflict over improving housing opportunities for the poor has, ostensibly at least, been between white middle-class suburbanites sheltering behind their municipal autonomy on the one hand, and central city blacks and low income groups on the other.[2]

These contrasting explanations of spatially decentralized local governments link up with broader streams of social thought. There are, for example, remarkable parallels between the economist's public choice theory and the political scientist's pluralism. The emphases upon decentralization of power, competition and individual rationality in the pursuit of self-interest are the same, as Newton has pointed out (1975, p. 245).

Not surprisingly pluralists have their own rationalization for metropolitan fragmentation coordinate with that of the public choice theorists. Thus, for Robert Dahl, fragmentation provides the possibility of choice in access to government; those who lose in a particular political contest can turn elsewhere either higher in the jurisdictional hierarchy or to a government at the same level (Dahl, 1972, pp. 211–39). As in public choice, therefore, pluralism facilitates satisfaction of diverse and incompatible policy preferences.

There are other points of similarity between pluralism and public choice. The economist's concern for monopoly finds

1. See also Danielson (1972, pp. 149–50): ". . . the underlying cause for the end of annexation and the political containment of the city was the almost universal desire of the periphery for political autonomy from the core, a goal rooted in class and ethnic conflict in the spatially differentiated city and the desire for community controls over their homogeneous neighborhoods."

2. "The American metropolis, thus, may also mirror the strivings of politically unequal persons (in the sense of having political influence) trying to maximize personal well-being. The spatial clustering of classes and races is not merely the consequence of personal choice and personal resources (although these are obviously important), but also the product of various classes of people who are relatively successful in using political power on their behalf or whose interests are served by public policies. This is frequently at the expense of those who are the political losers. The decentralized, spatially segregated aspects of metropolitan life may, then, reflect the relative political strength of either selected races or selected classes, or both" (Neiman, 1975, p. 70).

a mirror image in the political scientist's concern for the power of the state. Just as government fragmentation checks monopoly through competition, so the power of the state is bridled by the consequent decentralization of powers and responsibilities.

Further, while the counterpoint to public choice is a liberal theory of socially grounded power asymmetry, pluralism finds an antagonist in élite theories of community power. As Newton (1975, p. 246) has argued, "far from contributing to an open, pluralist and democratic system, fragmentation contributes towards a closed, élitist, and undemocratic one."[3]

Yet from another angle what strikes one is not so much the differences between public choice theorists and their liberal antagonists; or those between pluralists and those postulating an élitist power asymmetry. Rather it is the broad similarities of assumption that circumscribe their vision. Both public choice theory and liberal theory accept that consumption is the basic issue; both pluralists and élitists assume that the end of political activity is the achievement of policy preferences and political favours. Competition is between individuals or groups for consumptive advantage or for the political advantage that will yield benefits in the consumption sphere. Attribution of motivation revolves all too frequently around questions of greed or hunger for power. That political systems in general and metropolitan political systems in particular might be structured by deeper forces than consumption or power hunger, and flowing from the production relations of society, seems to have been ignored. It is this view that we will investigate in the remainder of this paper.

3. See also Newton (1975, p. 255): "Far from creating a whole set of political arenas with many different access points to them, as in the pluralist model, they create political arenas which are promptly sealed off to any form of potential political opposition."

A Radical Perspective

The liberal critique of the public choice perspective on metropolitan fragmentation, therefore, is an internal critique; its basic, albeit implicit, assumptions of consumption as the central dynamic of social change and of private property rights rest comfortably within the neoclassical paradigm. In contrast a radical perspective attempts to situate institutional forms, such as the decentralization of local government, with respect to modes of production and to the contradictions consequent to the reproduction and development of modes of production. Production rather than consumption becomes a focus and private property becomes a juridical relation subject to explanation rather than to mere assumption.

In the present instance the relevant mode of production at issue is, of course, the capitalist mode of production; and the critical contradictions are those between capitals on the one hand, and between capitals and labour on the other. Further, the class conflicts that we believe pertinent to an understanding of decentralized local governments are what Harvey has called elsewhere "displaced" (Harvey, 1978, p. 125). They are not conflicts over the extraction of surplus value in the workplace. Nor are they conflicts directly linked to this fundamental conflict. Rather their relationship is more indirect involving, for example, struggles in the consumption sphere over the realization of capital, or in the sphere of reproduction of labour power: health, social security, and education, for example. The critical consideration, however, is that they are struggles which find their ultimate origin in the separation of capital from labour which is, in turn, embedded in the commodity relation.

Capital, however, is not monolithic. Relevant to an understanding of jurisdictional fragmentation are industrial capital, merchant capital and property capital.

Industrial capital, for example, has imposed a distinctive stamp in the form of tax enclaves or preemptive incorporation in order to retain control of land-use regulation.[4] As far as merchant capital is concerned, incorporation has often been a means of securing control of the land-use regulation mechanism in order to restrict competition; also, as a result of their market interests, local Chambers of Commerce have frequently lent their weight to the attempts of property capitals to develop and this often necessitates incorporation. Indeed, it is to property capitals that we assign the critical role.

By property capital we understand those capitals centrally involved in, and accumulating on the basis of, the urban development process. They include, therefore, land companies, construction companies, property development companies, savings and loans, mortgage bankers and small land speculators. The objective of each property capital is to reproduce itself on an expanded basis by receiving in the form of rents, fees, mortgage interest, and/or revenue from sales, more than the money capital originally invested in the property, in holding it, etc. For each and every property capital, however, all other property capitals represent, through the competitive relation, an obstacle to self-reproduction. Decentralized local government is an expression, direct and indirect, of the attempts of property capitals, or of localized coalitions of property capitals, to suspend the barriers mutually imposed.

For in viewing the metropolitan area as an area of property development there

is no way in which individual property capitals can proceed independently of the state. As Roweis and Scott (1978, pp. 57–59) have emphasized urban land is not producible in the commodity form. Critical to its production are a variety of state, and particularly local state, interventions. Two major forms of intervention can be identified: physical infrastructure and a regulatory environment appropriate for development.

The first concerns the basic preconditions for development. Such things as water lines, sewer facilities, roads, etc. are fundamental and necessary inputs of land production, inputs which the developer may be unable, or unwilling, to provide himself. The public provision of these, socializing the costs of production while maintaining the private appropriation of profits, is highly desirable from the developer's point of view. Thus, the political unit becomes an arena of competition in terms of public policy decisions regarding the spatial allocation of these infrastructural supports.[5]

Conversely, if developers are unable to obtain access to needed services from existing municipalities special districts provide an alternative solution. Improvement districts, utility districts, special assessment districts are legal creations "for the worthy purpose of giving unincorporated areas the same power to tax and incur debts enjoyed by municipalities, in order to insure them of essential services" (Wolff, 1973, p. 209).

An example of such a case is Clear Lake City, located on the outskirts of Houston. A 15,000 acre site owned by Friendswood Development Corporation, a subsidiary of Humble Oil, was designated a special water authority district by

---

4. Crouch and Dinerman (1963, pp. 235–39) provide some interesting examples of this. The city of Dairy Valley, for instance, was created to forestall annexation by neighbouring residential communities concerned about flies and cattle odour. And "(T)he cities of Industry and Commerce were formed chiefly to protect industrial sites from encroachment by residential subdivisions and to prevent other cities from enhancing their property tax bases by annexing industrial sections piecemeal" (p. 239).

5. As Gaffney has stated, landowners "take a strong and steady interest in local government out of proportion to their numbers" (1973), p. 117). See also Molotch (1976) for a discussion of "growth coalitions" and competition over the spatial allocation of public resources.

the Texas legislature. The Development Corporation built six houses in the area, moved Humble employees in, held an election in a garage, and approved the sale of $24 million worth of bonds in order to finance water, sewer and drainage facilities for the developer, *at his request,* and at *no charge.* The burden, of course, falls on those who move in, and who pay more in taxes to the water authority to pay off the bonds than nearby incorporated areas pay in total property taxes. Nor should this be thought of as an isolated example. Speaking in terms of water districts only, the state of Texas allows for the creation of 16 different *types* of water districts; and Harris County, which contains Houston, has in excess of 200 such districts. Bonds can be, and have been, approved for sale by as few as two "residents" (Vetter, 1972).[6]

Property capitals, therefore, strive to reproduce by obtaining the publicly-provided physical infrastructure necessary to the development of their property. This may lead in the direction of annexation to an existing municipality; or, if this proves infeasible, to the creation of new local governments, even if only in the limited form of special districts. To some degree these strategies may be undertaken by single developers or alternatively by those property capitals with investments in a particular area acting in concert. For while property capitals compete one with another, an interest in localized infrastructure, be it in a sewage system, a waterworks expansion or a freeway interchange, has the capacity to create coalitions as a substantial assist to self-reproduction.

Regulatory considerations may lead property capitals in a similar direction.

If a publicly provided infrastructure is critical to self-reproduction so too is a propitious regulatory climate: zoning, subdivision regulations and subdivision exactions, for example. Maximizing rent depends upon appropriate land-use zoning, both for one's own property and for adjacent properties. Annexation may pose problems of negotiation with an existing local government with its entrenched special interests—property, labour, school boards, etc.—which creation of a new local government jurisdiction can effectively bypass.

The struggles of property capitals to reproduce themselves, therefore, contain the possibility of some decentralization of local government. At this stage of the analysis the creation of new jurisdictions in contradistinction to annexation would seem to be dependent upon the immediate political situation: links between developers and public officials in existing municipalities, for example.

This, however, would be to ignore the relation of property capital to labour in its communal living space (Cox, 1980). There are certain resources providing use values which labour consumes in common and access to which is contingent upon living in a particular neighbourhood or municipality. These include what commonly passes for residential amenity—quiet, aesthetics, public safety, local schools—as well as the fiscal resources of the municipality. In addition, to the extent that school quality, public safety, tax rates, etc., are capitalized into house values the communal living space may be a source of exchange values for labour; certainly the interest exhibited in property values and in value appreciation would seem to support this notion. It seems unreasonable, however, to regard these exchange values as anything other than consumption-oriented: i.e., an asset in moving to a "better" neighbourhood. Certainly we doubt that there are many homeowners who see their houses as

6. Nor is this type of situation peculiar to Texas. For examples of municipal improvement districts designed to promote property development in California, see Fellmeth (1973, pp. 315–20) and Scott and Corzine (1971).

financial assets to be parlayed into a cycle of reproduction on an expanded basis.

Not surprisingly the plans of property capitals are regarded with great suspicion by existing urban-fringe residents. Annexation is viewed as synonymous with water lines and sewer lines, and the latter with development. Annexation, therefore, is seen as a threat and the promises of developers to meet the legal costs of annexation (such as they are) and the prospect of improved services do little to allay residents' fears. Alternatively, in unincorporated areas residents may confront development plans without the concomitant of annexation, creation of special districts and the like. The ability to control development, however, may lie outside their hands at the level of, say, the county. In both instances labour finds strong incentives for obtaining some control over development through the creation of its own municipality. The result is that defensive incorporation of which students of suburban politics are well aware and which has been so central to the image of suburban exclusion.

It would seem therefore that pressures towards municipal fragmentation are set up whether or not property capitals secure their necessary infrastructure by the creation of new municipalities or special districts; or by attempted annexation to existing municipalities. For in both cases, residents have an interest in a preemptive incorporation, the structure and policies of which they can themselves dominate.

Nevertheless there is a certain weakness in this argument. Specifically the objectives of labour in the living place are given and lie outside the terms of the analysis. The fact that labour seeks certain use values and exchange values in the communal living space, values which it will seek to protect against the depredations of capital, is assumed rather than explained. A closer look at this assumption is both necessary and illuminating.

By refusing to challenge the assumption one is in danger of committing the same error as the liberal with his reified conception of consumer man. The liberal view is of households with unlimited demands for consumption, demands which they are willing to satisfy by forming coalitions with other households in order to take away from yet other coalitions of the similarly acquisitive. We have seen that one of the defects of this view is that it fails to recognize the significance of conflicts between property capitals and labour embedded in the urban development process. Yet equally it reifies human nature and confuses that which is specific to a mode of production with the eternal.

Needs are historical and social rather than natural: they have presuppositions in the relations of the individual to others at particular stages in the development of the conditions of production. The desire to protect and indeed enhance property values, for example, presupposes a society in which, among other things, there is all-round commodification so that money can buy everything, and needs are constantly being developed as a result of the development of the productive forces. Likewise it is impossible to understand the issue of suburban exclusion apart from the concept of externality and all that it presupposes: the splitting off of community from the individual in the form of publicly provided services—education, and public safety, for example; the concomitant decline of mechanisms of social control; the private property relation; the social definitions of externalities as goods or bads advanced, among others, by the real estate industry, etc.

Consequently, in its vision of metropolitan fragmentation as a product of conflict between competitive consumption groups the liberal perspective does have a certain element of validity. Coalitions of consumers *are* formed to some extent with respect to each other; it may not be so much development that is the issue, for example, but development for a particular distributive grouping. The liberal error is, however, twofold. First it fails to situate these conflicts over consumption within the capitalist mode of production as a whole. Second, in its allegiance to a social dynamic deriving from the motive to consume it overlooks the central role property capitals play. For property capitals not only live off that competition they also stimulate it. And they stimulate it as a necessary by-product of their attempts to reproduce themselves. New modes of housing consumption are a necessity to the survival of property capitals but also give an additional impetus to competitive consumption; and overcoming the barriers posed by labour in the communal living space is also an imperative but it is one which capital can achieve by setting one distributive grouping against another and putting itself on the side of the disadvantaged (Danielson, 1976, chapter 6).

A Concluding Comment

In this paper we have reviewed two major theories of the decentralization of local government in American metropolitan areas: public choice theory and what we defined as the liberal perspective. Both theories were unambiguously located within the bounds of conventional social science. For both of them the central dynamic of society is consumption; private property rights are assumed as the institutional substructure essential to achieving satisfaction in the consumption sphere. The disagreements between the two theories stem largely from their assumptions about the homogeneity of utility functions, income differentiation and the social welfare function. While public choice emphasizes efficiency and heterogeneity of utility functions and abstracts from income differences, the liberal perspective is more concerned with equity, assumes homogeneous utility functions and underlines the importance of quantitative rather than qualitative differences in material consumption. Within their own basic terms of reference both theories provide adequate ideologies for interest groups competing in the sphere of consumption. For the wealthy public choice theory provides a convenient rationalization for the advantages they enjoy under metropolitan fragmentation, as liberal theorists have been quick to point out. Equally the liberal perspective provides a banner behind which the disadvantaged can march.

Yet the fact that capital has often chosen to march behind the same liberal banner, as in the attempt to open up the suburbs, suggests that there is something more to life than consumption. This indeed was what we tried to explore, as it relates to jurisdictional fragmentation, in our radical critique of the orthodoxy.

Of course, we realize that our theory of jurisdictional fragmentation is vulnerable to the charge of limited applicability. In Britain, for example, jurisdictional fragmentation in metropolitan areas is substantially less than in the case of the United States; Canada seems to occupy an intermediate position relative to these two polar types. This type of contrast, moreover, underlines the so-called significance of institutional factors: the fact that in the United States state constitutional law tends to facilitate the creation of new municipalities whereas in Britain new incorporations are so difficult to engineer as to be virtually impossible. Nevertheless that in the American case these constitutional provisions have been exploited testifies to their significance to the reproduction of capital; and the fact that they are difficult to engineer in Britain points to the necessity for an historical analysis of the ways in which, in Britain, property capitals, in the absence of a congenial law of municipal incorporation, have reproduced themselves, as reproduce themselves they assuredly have.

References

Bish, R. L. 1971: *The public economy of metropolitan areas.* Chicago: Markham Publishing Company.

Bish, R. L. and Ostrom, V. 1976: Understanding urban government: metropolitan reform reconsidered. In Hochman, H., editor, *The urban economy,* New York: W. W. Norton, 95–117.

Buchanan, J. 1960: Individual choice in voting and the market. In *Fiscal theory and political economy,* Chapel Hill: University of North Carolina Press.

Cox, K. R. 1973: *Conflict, power and politics in the city: a geographic view.* New York: McGraw-Hill.

— 1980: Capitalism and conflict around the communal living space. In Dear, M. J. and Scott, A. J., editors, *Urbanization and planning in capitalist society,* New York: Methuen.

Crouch, W. W. and Dinerman, B. 1963: *Southern California metropolis.* Berkeley and Los Angeles: University of California Press.

Dahl, R. A. 1972: *Democracy in the United States: promises and performance.* Chicago: Rand McNally.

Danielson, M. N. 1972: Differentiation, segregation and political fragmentation in the American metropolis. In Nash, A. E. K., editor, *Governance and population: the governmental implications of population change,* Washington, DC: US Government Printing Office.

— 1976: *The politics of exclusion.* New York: Columbia University Press.

Davis, O. A. and Whinston, A. B. 1962: Economic problems in urban renewal. In Phelps, E. S., editor, *Private wants and public needs,* New York: W. W. Norton, 140–53.

Downs, A. 1973: *Opening up the suburbs.* New Haven: Yale University Press.

Fellmeth, R. 1973: *The politics of land.* New York: Grossman Publishers.

Gaffney, M. 1973: Tax reform to release land. In Clawson, M., editor, *Modernizing urban land policy,* Baltimore: The Johns Hopkins University Press for Resources for the Future.

Harvey, D. W. 1974: Class-monopoly rent, finance capital and the urban revolution. *Regional Studies* 8, 239–55.

— 1978: The urban process under capitalism: a framework for analysis. *International Journal of Urban and Regional Research* 2, 101–31.

Molotch, H. 1976: The city as a growth machine: toward a political economy of place. *American Journal of Sociology* 82, 309–32.

Neiman, M. 1975: From Plato's philosopher king to Bish's tough purchasing agent: the premature public choice paradigm. *Journal of the American Institute of Planners* 41, 55–73.

Newton, K. 1975: American urban politics: social class, political structure and public goods. *Urban Affairs Quarterly* 11, 241–64.

Nishkanen, W. A. 1971: *Bureaucracy and representative government.* Chicago and New York: Aldine and Atherton.

Ollman, B. 1976: *Alienation: Marx's conception of man in capitalist society.* Cambridge: Cambridge University Press.

Pejovich, S. 1972: Towards an economic theory of the creation and specification of property rights. *Review of Social Economy* 30, 309–25.

Roweis, S. T. and Scott, A. J. 1978: The urban land question. In Cox, K. R., editor, *Urbanization and conflict in market societies,* Chicago: Maaroufa Press, 38–75.

Scott, S. and Corzine, J. 1971: Special districts in the San Francisco Bay area. In Danielson, M., editor, *Metropolitan politics: a reader,* Boston: Little, Brown and Co., 201–14.

Stanford Environmental Law Society 1971: *San José: sprawling city.* Stanford: Stanford University Press.

Tiebout, C. 1956: A pure theory of local expenditures. *Journal of Political Economy* 64, 416–24.

Tullock, G. 1970: *Private wants, public means.* New York: Basic Books.

Vetter, C. E. 1972: Prepared statement on behalf of Clear Lake Council, Houston, Texas. In *Hearings before the Subcommittee on Intergovernmental Relations of the Committee on Government Operations of the United States Senate, ninety-second Congress, Second Session on the Impact and Administration of the Property Tax,* Washington, DC: US Government Printing Office, 79–83.

Wingo, L. 1973: The quality of life: toward a microeconomic definition. *Urban Studies* 10, 3–18.

Wolff, A. 1973: *Unreal estate.* San Francisco and New York: The Sierra Club.

VI

INTERACTION: Transportation, Communication, and Linkages

ROGER E. ALCALY

Transportation and Urban Land Values:
A Review of the Theoretical Literature

Transportation costs have long been recognized as a crucial determinant of both the formation of cities and of the spatial distribution of economic activities within urban areas. In fact, it is the traditionally neglected spatial dimension of economic organization, and the consequent emphasis on accessibility, which is the distinguishing feature of "regional" and "urban" economics. As Isard has noted, in conventional economic theory, "Transport costs and other costs involved in movement within a 'market' are assumed to be zero. In this sense the factor of space is repudiated, everything within the economy is in effect compressed to a point, and all spatial resistance disappears" [1956, p. 26]. In response to this failure Nourse has defined "regional economics" as "the study of the neglected spatial order of the economy" [1968, p. 1].[1]

The present paper is concerned primarily with the relationship between transportation costs and urban land

values. It begins, however, by placing that discussion within a general consideration of the role and importance of transport costs in the formation of cities. This is followed by an analysis and critique of the theoretical literature linking transport developments and urban land values.[2] The discussion proceeds from simpler to more complex models in an attempt to synthesize existing results, delineate the assumptions upon which the arguments are founded and, at the same time, indicate important omissions in the analyses and areas for much needed extension. The closing section summarizes the main findings and presents suggestions for additional research.

Transport Costs and the Formation of Cities

The relationship between transport costs and urban land values can best be ap-

1. The remarks of Isard and Nourse are also quoted by Heilbrun [1974, pp. 57 and 2, respectively]. Heilbrun's chapters 2–6 contain a useful summary of research on location theory and urbanization.

2. Most of the theoretical literature under consideration is oriented almost exclusively toward U.S. cities. A referee has suggested that this severely limits the generality of these writings, particularly "when viewed from a European (and even from a Canadian) perspective."

proached by first considering the role of transport costs in the formation of cities. In this context it is important to emphasize, as Vickrey and Mills have done recently, that while transport costs are necessary, they are not sufficient to produce agglomeration of economic activities on a large scale.[3] In the absence of transportation costs the distribution of economic activities in space would be essentially uniform. There would be no reason to locate near natural or produced resources, and transportation advantages of particular locations such as rivers, harbors and so on would be impossible or irrelevant by definition. In this case geographic concentration would depend entirely on the technological characteristics of production in the various activities. Economies of scale, which in a narrow sense govern the optimal size of economic activities, would also, therefore, be a major determinant of the spatial distribution of activities, although the precise location of even these large-scale units would be somewhat arbitrary. In short, in the absence of transportation costs geographic proximity is not necessary to preserve economic linkages.[4]

On the other hand, if we admit transportation costs but eliminate scale advantages in economic organization, the spatial distribution of economic activities would again be far more uniform than is actually the case. Small-scale groupings of activities, "hamlets" as opposed to cities, would minimize the costs of transporting goods and people from activity to activity. An unequal spatial distribution of natural resources would, of course, increase concentration, but it is doubtful whether geographical advantages can account for the size of cities actually observed. As Vickrey put it:

Cities are typically the result of substantial economies of scale in at least some of the activities carried on in the city, combined with costs of transportation. While some cities exist mainly because of natural resources or other geographical features such as mineral deposits, ports, or bridgeheads, in most large cities the influence of such features is largely historical and incidental. While it is possible to develop a model of a city in which there are no economies of scale within the industries, and in which activities related to the focusing feature of the city are located in a hierarchy of rings around this feature, the size of such cities would, in the absence of economies of scale, be far smaller than those actually observed [1969, p. 4].

Recognition of the role of economies of scale, together with transportation costs, in explaining the existence of cities, however, poses new problems for analysts of the process of urban growth and development. While significant economies of scale require abandonment of models based on perfect competition—economies of scale, after all, are one of the principal neoclassical explanations and justifications for the existence of monopolies and the consequent distortion of competitive optimality—analyses incorporating imperfect competition in an integral fashion are conspicuous primarily by their absence.[5]

Similarly, while transportation costs in

---

3. See Vickrey [1969, pp. 4–6], Mills [1969, pp. 234–237] and Mills [1972, chapter 1].

4. It is not entirely clear how externalities would be handled in this admittedly unrealistic conception. Vickrey [1969, pp. 3–4] distinguishes between effects which are transmitted through the market, such as those arising from economies of scale, and those effects which are transmitted by nonmarket mechanisms, generally some sort of physical interaction. He terms the latter "neighborhood effects." If neighborhood effects depend on proximity even in the absence of transportation costs then we have an additional source of agglomeration and geographical concentration in this case. But it might be maintained that the transmission of neighborhood effects is not geographically limited in the absence of transportation costs.

5. Cf. Vickrey [1969, p. 5].

conjunction with economies of scale and geographical heterogeneity are both necessary and sufficient for the existence of cities, they also tend to imply that there will not be complete centrality within urban areas. And although this proposition is consistent with the decentralizing tendency of American cities which has emerged since approximately 1920,[6] it can probably be ignored in much inter-urban analysis. For intra-urban investigations, concerned, as is the present study, with problems such as land values within a metropolitan region, the existence of multiple centers takes on far greater importance. In this case, Mills' more general observations about the effect of the centrality assumptions are even more poignant. "Simple models of centrality are," he wrote, "inadequate. . . . What is really needed are models that explain the attraction of population and economic activity to urban areas, but are not dependent for the explanation on complete centrality." Unfortunately, "we still await the first model with both characteristics" [1969, p. 236].[7]

As we shall see, the realities of less than perfect competition and less than perfect centrality are but two of the considerations which severely restrict the precision of theoretical assessments of the effect of transportation improvements on urban land values. As Vickrey observed, "In this area more than most, extreme models produce paradoxical results" [1963, p. 77].

Transport Costs and Urban Land Values

The work of Robert Murray Haig,[8] one of the first economists to consider explicitly the relationship between transportation and urban land values, amply illustrates Vickrey's proposition. For Haig,

Site rents and transportation costs are vitally connected through their relationship to the friction of space. Transportation is the means of reducing that friction, at the cost of time and money. Site rentals are charges which can be made for sites where accessibility may be had with comparatively low transportation costs. While transportation overcomes friction, site rentals plus transportation costs represent the social cost of what friction remains. Obviously an improvement in transportation, other things remaining the same, will mean a reduction in friction and, consequently, the diminution of the aggregate sum of site rentals. The two elements, transportation costs and site rentals, are thus seen to be complementary. Together they may be termed the "costs of friction" [1926, pp. 421–422].[9]

In Haig's model land is allocated, and site values determined, by a process of "competitive bidding, the relative size of the bids being determined fundamentally by the degree to which the various activities can profitably utilize sites" [1926b, p. 420]. The latter concept implies that the sum of site rents and transportation costs is not constant throughout the area. "On the contrary, it varies with the site. The theoretically perfect site for the activity is that which furnishes the desired

6. Mills calls "decentralization of metropolitan areas . . . one of the most intriguing issues in urban economics, as well as the key to many of the social problems found in urban areas" [1972, p. vii].
7. Mills' empirical work on land values, motivated by a mathematical model of land values which is "focused on a single center," but does not assume "that all workers are employed in the CBD or that all output is produced there," yields results which he terms "reasonably satisfactory." See Mills [1969, pp. 241–253].

8. See Haig [1926a and 1926b]. The latter article is particularly relevant for the problem at hand, while the former relates primarily to the earlier discussion. Elsewhere Haig acknowledges his intellectual debt to Johann von Thunen (*Der isolierte Staat,* 1826) who was primarily concerned with the configuration of agricultural land uses around a market town. See Haig [1927, p. 32] and Goldberg [1970, p. 153].
9. Also quoted in Goldberg [1970, p. 153].

degree of accessibility at the lowest costs of friction" [1926b, p. 423].

The site-rent gradient, that is, the relationship between site rents and distance from the center of the city, implied by the Haig model is negatively sloped and steeper at the center than at the fringes of the urban area, even if densities and building costs are everywhere the same. This result accords with empirically derived site-rent gradients and therefore lends greater credence to the Haig formulation. But it is only one of many factors that must be taken into consideration in evaluating the prediction that transportation improvements will decrease site values. The latter proposition, it will be argued, is crucially dependent on a host of assumptions which appear to be quite unrealistic.

In order to fully bring out the contingent nature of the relationship between changes in land values and changes in the transport system servicing the urban area—contingencies which derive from assumptions about the mononuclear nature of the city, the absence of monopoly power, the price elasticity of demand for land, the price elasticity of demand for trips, the exogenous character of transportation improvements themselves, and so on—we will examine in some detail the basic models which deal with this relationship. These formulations, which are closely related to that of Haig described above, are really just an application of von Thunen's conception to an urban setting.[10] The city is conceived of as a featureless plain with all production and distribution activity concentrated at the center or central business district (CBD). The population is uniform with respect to family size, demands for space, income, trips to the CBD, and so on. Finally, building costs are assumed to be uniform throughout the city and transportation

10. See Heilbrun [1974, pp. 106–109], Vickrey [1963, pp. 77–78], Mohring [1961, pp. 236–249] and n. 8 above.

costs are taken to be proportional to distance traveled.

In this model equilibrium requires that site values differ by the differences in transportation costs associated with living at the respective distances from the CBD. Thus, the sum of site values and transportation costs is constant throughout the city and is equal to the maximum annual outlay for transportation which occurs among those families living at the perimeter of the city where site rents vanish.[11]

If the city were only a line in space, the situation could be depicted in two dimensions, as shown in Figure 1.[12] Or if the city were thought to be a circular area, then the picture that emerges (physically, the transformation arises from rotating the linear city 360 degrees about its center) is one in which the "costs of friction"—land values plus transportation costs—are represented by the area of the cylinder which rises above the city to a height which is equal to the maximum annual expenditure on transportation. The site values alone appear as the area of the cone which can be embedded in the cylinder.[13]

11. This assumes that land has no alternative use save as residence sites for the city's population. Actually, site rents at the perimeter will be equal to the value of that land in its best alternative use. The conclusions are not really affected by assuming that this "opportunity cost" of urban land is zero. Cf. Mohring [1961, p. 238].

12. Figure 1 assumes that housing costs exclusive of site rent are zero, an assumption which is unrealistic but which does not affect the analysis. Recall that the model takes land development and building costs to be uniform throughout the city. If these building costs are constant but non-zero, Figure 1 is essentially unchanged; the rectangle representing the sum of the site rents and transport costs is merely shifted upward to the extent of the uniform building costs. Cf. Heilbrun [1974, p. 107].

13. The site-value and density (of both population and building improvements) gradients implied by this model—negatively sloped but linear in the former case and uniform in the latter—are clearly unrealistic. These features can be corrected by abandoning the assumption of

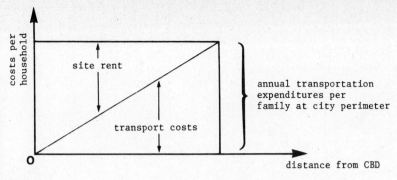

Figure 1

Now consider a uniform transportation improvement which is essentially cost-less, such as might result from retiming traffic lights.[14] If the demands for both transportation and land are independent of their cost, that is, if the price elasticities of demand for transport and land are zero, then land values will clearly fall. And it is important to recognize that this admittedly unrealistic assumption is contained in the model's conception of a population with uniform living conditions and travel propensities which are consequently independent of distance from the

CBD. If the relationship between land values and distance from the CBD were initially shown by *AB* in Figure 2, then after the transportation improvement the rent gradient will be something like *A'B*, indicating a decrease in land values proportional to the decrease in transportation costs.[15]

As has already been noted, the assumptions on which the foregoing analysis is based are severely biased toward a decrease in land values. Consequently, the basic model is useful only as a benchmark against which we can evaluate the effects of varying some of these unrealistic assumptions. For example, if some elasticity of demand for travel is introduced, then the decline in transport costs will increase the demand for trips and may at least partially offset reductions in land values stemming from the transportation improvements. Transportation expenditures, and hence land values, will fall, remain the same, or increase according to

uniform density of housing per acre and allowing for greater complexity of land use a la Haig and Alonso. See Heilbrun [1974, pp. 110–122], Alonso [1964], Lee and Averous [1973] and the preceding discussion of Haig's work.

14. To the extent that the transportation improvement requires that more land be devoted to transportation facilities, it tends to reduce the supply of land available for other uses. This factor will tend to increase the unit price of land; its effect on aggregate land values depends on the price elasticity of demand for land. The total effect on land values depends upon integrating this factor with those discussed above. Similarly, to the extent that the transportation improvement is costly, whether in land or otherwise, then its financing, and the effect of this financing on incomes and hence on the demand for land, trips, and so on, must also be taken into account. Lee and Averous [1973] consider explicitly the related problems of the optimal allocation of land to transport facilities and the optimal balance between modes given their differences in capital intensity.

15. Algebraically, *AB* may be expressed as $SR + TC = K = TC$ max, where SR denotes site rent, TC is transport cost and TC max is the transportation cost that obtains at the perimeter. Thus, $SR = TC$ max $- TC$, from which it follows that any reduction in transportation costs will reduce SR by the same proportion.

In the case of a nonlinear rent gradient which is the result of different land users competing for the land, the analysis is analogous to the case presented above. Cf. Edel and Sclar [1973, pp. 6–7].

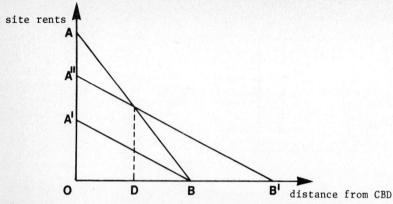

Figure 2

whether the elasticity of demand for trips is less than, equal to, or greater than unity.[16]

Similarly, if we admit a non-zero elasticity of demand for land, the initial fall in land values will induce the purchase of more land per family.[17] This requires an

expansion of the city's area. In terms of Figure 2, the new rent gradient, $A'B$, will shift upward in a parallel fashion to something like $A''B$. The site rents of land closer to the CBD than OD will fall and those beyond OD will rise. The net effect on land values depends on the elasticity of demand: aggregate land values will fall, remain the same, or rise (the case shown in Figure 2) as the elasticity of demand for land is less than, equal to, or greater than unity.[18]

This can also be seen in terms of the standard supply and demand diagram shown in Figure 3. SS and DD are the initial supply and demand curves for urban land. The transportation improvement induces an expansion in the size of the urban area, which is shown in the shift of the supply curve from SS to $S'S'$. Aggregate land values increase in the

16. Cf. Mohring [1961, pp. 242–243]. Notice too that the analysis is vastly simplified by the assumption that transportation costs vary linearly with distance and the related assumption that all evaluate their travel time equally. If that were not the case, and it would tend not to be true to the extent that we admit income variations among the population, then the precise relationship between transportation costs and distance would emerge simultaneously with the solution of the location problem.

Lee and Averous [1973] demonstrate that the elasticities of demand for the outputs of the city's various productive activities must also be taken into account in determining the effect of a decrease in transport costs on land values. Ceteris paribus, greater elasticities of demand tend to augment the tendency for land values to increase.

17. Thus, density will vary in response to changes in land values. But it still may be uniform throughout the area at any given time. Alternatively, and more realistically, we might relax the assumption of uniform density and admit that higher-priced land will develop more intensively than lower-priced land. As has been pointed out in n. 13 this is one of the factors which will tend to produce "exponential-type" rent gradients. For the problem under consideration non-uniform development means that

the tendency toward an expansion of city size in response to a transportation improvement is augmented. Lower prices per unit of land induce less-intensive site development which means that more land is required to house a given population. Cf. Mohring [1961, pp. 242–243]. In effect, this is a factor increasing the elasticity of demand for urban land.

18. On this point see Vickrey [1963, p. 78], Mohring [1961, pp. 242–243], Heilbrun [1974, pp. 124–125] and Goldberg [1970, pp. 156–158]. Goldberg employs a supply and demand diagram such as that shown in Figure 3.

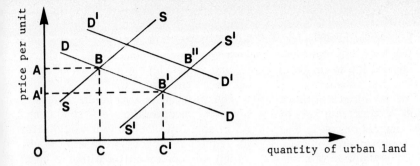

Figure 3

case of an elastic demand curve, as can be seen by comparing the areas $ABCO$ and $A'B'C'O$.[19]

Thus, even well within the context of the basic model, the relationship between land values and transportation costs depends crucially on at least two elasticities of demand which cannot be specified a priori and which can be combined in a variety of ways. About all we can say is that as long as the elasticity of demand for urban land is different from zero a transport improvement will, ceteris paribus, tend to produce an increase in the value of land at the periphery and a decrease in the value of land at the center, with the net effect depending on the precise value of the parameter.[20] And the

tendency for land values to increase in response to improved transportation is greater the greater the elasticity of demand for trips.

Vickrey [1963, p. 78] has noted that rents at the center will increase only if there is a sufficiently large increase in the demand for land at the center at the same time that the aggregate size of the city is increasing—behavior which he terms "perverse." Yet this might not be so unrealistic, even with an unchanging demand for trips, if we allow for a variety of users of a given city as well as hierarchy or specialization among cities. In such a conception certain activities such as corporate planning and finance will be highly concentrated at the center of a small group of cities. If this concentration is growing sufficiently rapidly at the same time that decentralization occurs, which indeed seems to be the case, then these major cities may well experience an increase in land values at both the center and periphery.[21]

19. As Goldberg [1970, p. 156] notes, if we define the urban area in terms of the maximum time people are willing to spend traveling to the CBD then a transportation improvement increases the effective city size. The increase in the supply of urban land causes the price per unit to fall, but the effect on aggregate land values depends on the elasticity of demand, as shown above.

20. Edel and Sclar [1973, pp. 5–6] use this result as one of the explanations for smaller capital gains on housing compared to other capital assets. Even this finding, however, may have to be further modified according to the type of transport improvement under consideration. Specifically, the rise of land values at the periphery will tend to be smaller the greater the extent to which the transport improvement adversely affects the environment. (For a discussion of capitalization of environmental costs see

Edel [1972], especially pp. 61–66.) Furthermore, the elasticities of demand for the goods and services produced in the urban area also affect the changes in land values resulting from a transport improvement. See Lee and Averous [1973] and n. 16 above.

21. Stephen Hymer has argued recently that urban growth and development exhibit a pattern of hierarchy which derives from the fact that the expansion of cities is both determined

Unfortunately for the predictability of the models in question, the latter discussion raises the general point that locational analysis of a given city must take into account its relationship to the entire network of cities within which it is embedded. A host of additional qualifications arise upon examination of the models' implicit assumption of a fixed population for the urban area in question and the related assumption of mononuclearity. Transport improvement in a given city, if not matched elsewhere, may attract both people and jobs. For example, Tiebout has argued that household location is determined essentially by preferences for local public goods and services in conjunction with their cost. And while the Tiebout analysis is marred by, among other things, its inadequate treatment of barriers to mobility due to restrictions on employment opportunities,[22] and while we have already noted the failure of the formulations under consideration to adequately integrate financing of the transportation improvements (see n. 14), migration certainly remains a real possibility.

To the extent that a redistribution of population occurs in response to the transportation improvement it will, of course, vastly complicate the analysis. An increase in population in the area which experienced the transportation improvement will shift the demand curve of Figure 3 outward, to something like $D'D'$, which will increase both the value of urban land and its quantity, as shown

by the new equilibrium at B''.[23] But land values will tend to fall in those areas losing population and the appropriate area over which to measure the net change in land values, let alone the net effect itself, is not entirely clear.

The problem is even more complex, however; incorporation of "competing" urban areas into the analysis would seem to require analogous treatment of the variety of foci or CBDs within a given urban area. And this not only further complicates the analysis along the lines indicated above, but it tends to highlight the artificiality of the assumption of a uniform transportation improvement.[24]

Finally, the analysis of the interdependence of transportation and land use must be carried at least one step further and this time in a manner potentially quite damaging to the entire framework of discussion. In a general sense what is required is explicit consideration of the question of causality in the relation between land values and transportation improvements: to what extent do transportation facilities follow the movement of capital, population and hence land values and to what extent do they determine the movement of these other variables? This is a largely unresolved issue in discussions of the role of the railroads in American economic development and has, un-

---

by, and a factor in, the development of the organization of production. In a world increasingly dominated by multinational corporations, the hierarchy of cities corresponds to the hierarchy of multinational corporate activities: top-management, coordination of the day-to-day operating decisions of the various branches of the corporation, management of the day-to-day operations, and so on.

22. See Tiebout [1961], Oates [1969] and Edel and Sclar [1974].

23. In the absence of transportation improvements, increased population will, ceteris paribus, cause increases in land values, density and the size of the urban area. See Heilbrun [1974, p. 125]. In the present case the effects on land values and density are uncertain since we are dealing with an increase in population in response to a transportation improvement.

24. Mohring [1961, pp. 239–242] offers a limited treatment of the case of a non-uniform transportation improvement, while Lee and Averous [1973] show that an "exponential-type" rent gradient, which results from incorporating diverse land use via a continuous intensity variable, is both necessary and sufficient for land value increases to be proportionately greater nearer a point of improved access.

fortunately, not received much more attention in the context of urban growth and development.[25]

On one level what is needed, at least in theory, is a model of the urban economy in which the provision of transportation services is explained rather than taken as a given datum. In other words, the supply of transportation services is endogenous rather than exogenous. As Mills has noted:

A major deficiency of many studies of urban land use and land value is that many explanatory variables in these studies are really endogenous to the urban economy. The basic problem is of course that whether a variable is endogenous or predetermined depends on the details of a simultaneous equation system, and few urban economists are accustomed to thinking in terms of simultaneous equation systems [1972, p. 38].

But even ignoring the unresolved question of whether such complex modeling efforts are worth the cost,[26] there are serious drawbacks to the approach in question. Primary among these obstacles is the absence of a theory of the state which is adequate to explain public ex-

penditure decisions. In some limited respects this observation takes us back to Vickrey's comment, cited at the outset of the paper, concerning the failure to incorporate imperfect competition into analyses of urban growth and structure. For, as has been widely observed in connection with the pattern of public transport expenditure which is so strongly biased toward the private automobile, large-scale concentrations of economic power must certainly occupy center stage in a realistic theory of state activity. And the "Watergate" revelations and the recent "energy crisis" have certainly underscored the inadequacies of the so-called "pluralistic" models of state activity which are incorporated in most economic analysis.[27]

Conclusions

The foregoing examination of much of the theoretical literature concerned with the relationship between transport improvements and urban land values has revealed shortcomings of essentially two types. On one hand, the inconclusive nature of the work in this area can be attributed to a myriad of significant problems concerning not only what factors to incorporate into the analysis but the precise way in which to do so. Questions related to the appropriate choice and combination of assumptions regarding elements ranging from price elasticities of demand for land, trips and the goods and services produced in the urban area, to population changes, the mononuclear na-

25. See Fishlow [1965], who rejects the hypothesis that railroad construction led demand in favor of an alternative explanation in which "the railroad construction of the late 1840's and early 1850's [led to] an on-going flow of westward migration that in turn led to continued railroad expansion. We have invoked a process of anticipatory settlement to explain both such a sequence and the vitality of private enterprise" [p. 204].

26. Even the so-called "basic theorem of urban economics that says in effect that if all cities were ideally organized, land rentals would in the aggregate be just sufficient and no more to supply the subsidies required to the various decreasing cost activities and industries within the city to enable them to price their output at levels conducive to their optimum utilization" [Vickrey 1974, p. 18] is derived from a complex analysis of a very simplified model of a long narrow city. See also Vickrey [1969, pp. 6–17] and Solow and Vickrey [1971, pp. 430–447].

27. For a detailed examination and critique of the pluralist conception see Miliband [1969], and cf. Friedman [1962], Rose [1967], and Buchanan and Tullock [1962]. Hymer [1972, pp. 122–125] discusses explicitly the relationship between the structure of business enterprise, the state, the provision of transport facilities and the location of economic activity, while O'Connor [1973] suggests a useful theoretical framework for analyzing state activity.

ture of cities and the relevant area over which to measure net changes in land values, emerged even in the relatively simple theoretical formulations discussed in some detail above.

Related to these considerations, on the other hand, are a variety of broader issues of overall conception. In a general sense what is lacking in most of the literature under review is adequate inquiry into the direction of causality in the relationship between transport improvements and urban land values. Analysis of this type would appear to require simultaneous equation modeling efforts which incorporate features of general equilibrium analysis as well as the political economy of public expenditure decisions. Unfortunately, these are areas in which the state of neoclassical economic theory is not particularly advanced, at least on a level which provides guidance to practical inquiries which go much beyond ad hoc empiricism. At the same time, however, these gaps in the discipline represent a research challenge which extends far beyond the immediate concerns of this paper.

References

Alonso, William. 1964. *Location and Land Use.* Cambridge, Mass.: Harvard University Press.

Buchanan, James M., and Tullock, Gordon. 1962. *The Calculus of Consent.* Ann Arbor, Michigan: University of Michigan Press.

Edel, Matthew, 1972. "Land Values and the Costs of Urban Congestion." In *Political Economy of Environment: Problems of Method,* Ecole Pratique des Haute Etudes, 6th Section. Paris: Mouton.

―――― and Sclar, Elliott. 1973. "The Distribution of Real Estate Value Changes: Measurement and Implications, Metropolitan Boston 1870–1970."

―――― and ――――. 1974. "Taxes, Spending and Property Values: Supply Adjustment

in a Tiebout-Oates Model." *Journal of Political Economy* 82 (Sept./Oct.): 941–954.

Fishlow, Albert. 1965. *American Railroads and the Transformation of the Ante-Bellum Economy.* Cambridge, Mass.: Harvard University Press.

Friedman, Milton. 1962. *Capitalism and Freedom.* Chicago: University of Chicago Press.

Goldberg, Michael A. 1970. "Transportation, Urban Land Values, and Rents: A Synthesis." *Land Economics* 46 (May): 153–162.

――――. 1972. "An Evaluation of the Interaction Between Urban Transport and Land Use Systems." *Land Economics* 48 (Nov.): 338–346.

Haig, Robert Murray. 1926a. "Toward an Understanding of the Metropolis: I. Some Speculations Regarding the Economic Basis of Urban Concentration." *Quarterly Journal of Economics* 40 (Feb.): 179–208.

――――. 1926b. "Toward an Understanding of the Metropolis: II. The Assignment of Activities to Areas in Urban Regions." *Quarterly Journal of Economics* 40 (May): 402–434.

――――. 1927. *Major Economic Factors in Metropolitan Growth and Arrangement.* New York: Regional Plan of New York and Its Environs.

Heilbrun, James. 1974. *Urban Economics and Public Policy.* New York: St. Martin's Press.

Hymer, Stephen. 1972. "The Multinational Corporation and the Law of Uneven Development." In *Economics and World Order,* ed. Jagdish Bhagwati. New York: The Macmillan Company.

Isard, Walter. 1956. *Location and Space Economy.* Cambridge, Mass.: MIT Press.

Lee, D. B., Jr., and Averous, C. P. 1973. "Land Use and Transportation: Basic Theory." *Environment and Planning* 5 (July–Aug.): 491–502.

Meyer, J. R.; Kain, J. F.; and Wohl, M. 1965. *The Urban Transportation Problem.* Cambridge, Mass.: Harvard University Press.

Miliband, Ralph. 1969. *The State in Capitalist Society.* New York: Basic Books, Inc.

Mills, Edwin S. 1969. "The Value of Urban Land." In *The Quality of the Urban Environment,* ed. Harvey S. Perloff. Washington, D.C.: Resources for the Future, Inc.

———. 1972. *Studies in the Structure of the Urban Economy*. Baltimore, Md.: Johns Hopkins Press for Resources for the Future, Inc.

Mohring, Herbert. 1961. "Land Values and the Measurement of Highway Benefits." *Journal of Political Economy* 69 (June): 236–249.

Nourse, Hugh D. 1968. *Regional Economics*. New York: McGraw-Hill Book Company.

Oates, Wallace E. 1969. "The Effects of Property Taxes and Local Public Spending on Property Values: An Empirical Study of Tax Capitalization and the Tiebout Hypothesis." *Journal of Political Economy* 77 (Nov./Dec.): 957–971.

O'Connor, James. 1973. *The Fiscal Crisis of the State*. New York: St. Martin's Press.

Putnam, Stephen P. 1974. "Preliminary Results from an Integrated Transportation and Land Use Models Package." *Transportation* 3 (Oct.): 193–224.

Rose, Arnold. 1967. *The Power Structure: Political Process in America*. New York: Oxford University Press.

Solow, Robert M., and Vickrey, William. 1971. "Land Use in a Long Narrow City." *Journal of Economic Theory* 3 (Dec.): 430–447.

Tiebout, Charles M. 1956. "A Pure Theory of Local Expenditures." *Journal of Political Economy* 64 (Oct.): 416–424.

Vickrey, William. 1963. "Pricing in Urban and Suburban Transport." *American Economic Review* 53 (May): 452–465.

———. 1969. "Externalities in Urban Development." *Proceedings of the American Real Estate and Urban Economics Association*.

———. 1974. "Improving New York's Transit Service—An Economist's View."

Warner, Sam B., Jr. 1972. *The Urban Wilderness: A History of the American City*. New York: Harper & Row.

———. 1973. *Streetcar Suburbs: The Process of Growth in Boston 1870–1900*. New York: Atheneum. (Originally published by Harvard University Press, 1962.)

KEVIN O'CONNOR AND CHRISTOPHER A. MAHER

Change in the Spatial Structure of a Metropolitan Region: Work–Residence Relationships in Melbourne

The process of growth and change in metropolitan areas is exceedingly complex. Growth involves not only accretion, but changing relationships between locational entities. Most research relating to the effects of the forces bringing about change has tended to rely on descriptions relating to the suburbanisation process (Hughes, 1974). However, more and more there is a dissatisfaction being expressed at the inability of a city–suburb dichotomy to account for recent trends (Masotti, 1973; Maher, 1980). Rather than seeing the suburbs as the product of growth accretion with the focus still turning inward to the central city, what is needed is a statement on the development of subcentres within the metropolitan region. Such a statement needs to account for the transition of parts of the outer city from a dependent urban fringe toward a self-contained "neo-city," nestled within a complex hierarchy of urban and suburban centres (Masotti, 1973).

The purpose of the present paper is to examine the structural evolution of the metropolitan area by paying specific attention not only to simple growth and redistribution of activities but also to the alterations in the relationships between locations that are undergoing change in their activity levels. We do not set out to explain why decentralisation is taking place, but rather what impact the process has on the subsequent spatial structure of the metropolitan region. Nowhere is the structural evolution of the metropolis more evident in a spatial sense than in the relationship of employment and resident location. Both of these have been previously studied in detail in isolation, but little effort has yet been devoted to their interrelationships. Using the metropolis of Melbourne as an example, changes in work–residence relationships are analysed for three census periods: 1961, 1966 and 1971.

The Evolution of Metropolitan Spatial Structure

The impact of growth and change on metropolitan spatial structure has occupied the attention of a number of recent works (Kain, 1975; Clawson and Hall, 1973; Hughes, 1974; Zimmer, 1975). The majority of works see the evolution of spatial structure in two parts:

From **Regional Studies,** Vol. 13, 1979, pp. 361–80. Reprinted in modified form by permission of the Regional Studies Association, K. O'Connor, and C. A. Maher.

the first is the suburbanisation of the population (Schnore, 1957); the second is the redistribution of economic activity outward from the central city to suburban locations (Moses and Williamson, 1967). While the two are seen jointly as elements in the "urban crisis," particularly in the U.S., their interrelationships have never really been fully explored. In most cases, spatial change is seen to be composed either of population change, or of change in economic activities, but seldom the mutually reinforcing impact of the two. Population shifts have been seen to precede employment change (Clawson and Hall, 1973, p. 101; Zimmer, 1975) reinforcing the notion that metropolitan areas have two components: a housing-extensive, job-deficient periphery, and a job-intensive, housing-deficient core.

The idea of a sprawling fringe around a tightly developed core is built into a typology of spatial development presented by Adams (1970) and discussed by Schaffer and Sclar (1973), which depicts a metropolitan region spreading along its major transport axes. This typology is especially useful to understand much of the research on urban sprawl (Gottmann and Harper, 1967; Chinitz, 1964) and relates directly to the theoretical analysis which sees land use intensity declining as distance from the central point increases (Alonso, 1964). Explanations of this part of the structural evolution of the metropolitan area have been sought in separate, although overlapping, criteria. Population redistribution on the one hand has been associated with changes in affluence, mobility and personal tastes. Accessibility in this framework has acted as an inferior good and has been traded-off for space and pleasant surroundings [although Stegman (1969) argues that suburban residents can have accessibility as well as space].

On the other hand, redistribution of economic activity, particularly manufacturing enterprise, has been seen as a function of changes in space requirements, transportation and communications technology, the location and availability of labour, and site costs. The overall redistribution of employment in fact is seen to be the net result of five separate elements of change: the central area can gain in jobs through either the immigration of new plants from elsewhere, or from the birth of new plants in the centre; the central area can lose employment through the out-migration of plants to elsewhere, or through losses through the death of plants; and the central area's employment numbers can also alter through changes in the capacity of plants that do not move (Harrison, 1974).

Therefore, while considerations such as cost, space and transportation are common to the explanation of both employment and resident change, the approaches have tended to overlook the fact that suburbanisation involves residences, jobs and the interlinkage between the two. For example, studies such as those of Schnore and Klaff (1972) on suburbanisation of the population are quite separate from the findings of Moses and Williamson (1967) and vice versa, even though labour availability is sometimes seen as a factor in manufacturing suburbanisation. The separation of these two strands of research has constrained the development of a new understanding of suburbia.

Urban analysts have always been aware that metropolitan regions have not been purely monocentric. Substantial secondary peaks in rental values, reflecting intra-metropolitan hierarchies have long been recognised (Berry et al., 1963; Johnston, 1968). What has been missing, though, is an understanding of the functional significance of the suburbs, and the recent evolution in the character of movement within them.

Recent studies have made a start toward expanding this new insight. Kasarda (1976) for example found the proportion of work trips originating and terminating in the suburbs has increased for both blue- and white-collar labour between 1960 and 1970; Guest (1976) in a study of 129 Los Angeles communities found 38% of workers lived and worked within the same community, and, taking a step further in this direction, Guest and Cluett (1976, p. 409) have shown that "workers can, in most cases, obtain a satisfactory residence within the range of housing offered in the vicinity of their suburban workplace." Ottensman (1975) concluding a study of travel patterns in Milwaukee, comments that future efforts directed toward modelling urban structure need to take into account multiple employment centres. Papageorgiou (1971) has shown a theoretical framework to handle multi-centred settlements.

Studies analysed by Castells (1968) show that even in a high-density region like Paris, the central core has lost its dominance and the suburbs are becoming relatively more important. Extrapolating trends into the future, Echenique (1976) illustrates that as travel costs rise due to increased energy charges, there will be a higher rate of dispersal in a city region, stimulating even more suburban activity. In short "core dominated concentration is on the move; the multi-node, multi-connection system is the rule, with the traditional multi-functional core simply a specialised one among many" (Berry and Kasarda, 1977, p. 267).

The Development of Suburban Centres in Metropolitan Regions

Accepting the premise that a new approach to the structural growth of a metropolitan region is needed, effort has been directed toward the identification, description and explanation of the development and importance of suburban centres in metropolitan regions. In simple terms, a suburban centre is the location of economic activity, whether of a manufacturing or service nature. This centre is functionally related to the surrounding section of the metropolitan region to a greater or lesser degree, where the relationship is expressed in part through the linkage between the job opportunities provided at the centre, and the home locations of the workers in the surrounding region.

Suburban centres evolve within a metropolitan fabric as the relationships between them and their surrounding regions change; this change could take at least two forms. First, a simple growth in the number of jobs will alter structural relationships which the subcentre has with the remainder of the metropolitan area, because it either draws on the additional workforce from further afield, or intensifies its contacts with the local resident workforce. Growth in jobs in a suburban centre, as outlined above, is the result of one or more of the following: the birth of new plants, in-migration of plants from elsewhere, or the increased capacity of existing plants, through the particular locational advantages of the area. The effect is an increased need for commuting into that centre which may be satisfied through the locally resident workforce changing their employment location from elsewhere in the metropolitan area to locally, or from the additional workforce coming from further afield.

The degree to which a node's labour requirements are supplied by the local region, as opposed to a wider region can be termed its self-containment. In the above situation where new jobs are increasingly taken up by local residents, self-containment will increase; where new jobs are taken up by residents outside the immediate "labour-shed," then self-containment will fall. While the degree of self-containment is very dependent on the definition of the "labour-shed" the utility of this concept lies in being able to gauge changes occurring in the labour-shed over time. The concept is described in more detail below.

A second factor which can influence the external relationships of a job-providing centre is a restructuring of job-type, such that even without any physical growth, the nature of the commuting field to the centre will change as the new type of employment draws on a different residential area. For example, if predominantly unskilled employment opportunities were to be replaced by those of a professional or technical nature, the centre's labour shed would expand to include the professional residential sector of the metropolitan area. An example of this type of replacement is the loss of small manufacturing establishments in areas adjacent to the central core with a compensating growth in business and professional services, whose employees are resident in quite a different area of the city.

The importance of a subcentre is, however, a function of more than sheer size. Other factors such as the nature and intensity of interactions between the particular node and the surrounding subregion are significant. These in turn depend on such things as the centrality, accessibility, and occupational diversity of each subregional node.

In terms of the nature and intensity of interactions, a suburban centre's importance is directly related to both the number of jobs it contains, and the proportion of the metropolitan region which provides it with labour. Under these conditions, the central core is practically always the most important centre because it contains the most jobs and because the labour for these jobs tends to come from the metropolitan region at large (Carroll, 1952). That is to say both the size, and interactional effects in terms of journey-to-work flows are at their greatest. Suburban centres are likely to be less important, first because they employ fewer workers, but second because their labour is drawn from a narrowly circumscribed sector within the metropolitan area.

Measures of interaction relate to the proportion of a centre's labour force which travels across its borders to work. By analysing interaction it should be possible to gauge relative importance through the nature of the labour shed for particular subcentres. In this context Smart's work, although at a more aggregate level, is of interest (Smart, 1974). His definition of labour market areas was based on two complementary concepts: first, the extent to which a given area is self-contained (as measured by the proportion of residents employed locally, and of employed population who live and work in the area); and second, the commuting relationships of the area to other areas (which is the inverse of the first). Clearly, the less self-contained a region is, the greater the interactions which that area has with others and hence in terms of the above discussion, the greater its significance in the metropolis as a whole. In these terms, self-containment is the inverse of importance: where there is complete self-containment there is no commuting across the defined boundary, and hence there is no connection between the employment location and the metropolis as a whole.

A centre's likely degree of self-containment also depends on its size or number of jobs. The greater the number of jobs, the more likely it is (other things equal) that the region will attract labour from a wider area of the metropolitan region. However, other things are seldom equal. It is necessary also to consider the role of centrality which influences the accessibility and occupational diversification of a centre. The ability of a centre to attract labour is partly a function of its centrality. Here the CBD has a natural advantage both through historical forces of the concentration of activities in it and through its position, representing the peak of accessibility. Accessibility is a more complex concept. Whilst centrality can be measured simply as distance from the CBD, accessibility represents the relationship of an observational unit to all other possible workplace zones.

Finally, a further consideration is the degree of occupational diversification. The greater the occupational specialisation of a subcentre, the greater is the likely area upon which it will exert influence because of the fact that a local residential area will not have the same degree of occupational specialisation. Conversely, when the range of job types is greater, the likelihood of these jobs being filled by local residents is also greater.

Thus the CBD is the least self-contained area because it is the most central, most accessible and most demanding in terms of specialised occupations. As one moves toward suburban centres, their degree of centrality and accessibility falls, and the occupational range becomes more limited. As a result, these areas are more highly self-contained, and draw on more narrowly circumscribed areas. A number of researchers have, for example, demonstrated that suburban employment centres tend to have a commuting field biased in directionality away from the CBD in a sectoral fashion (Taaffe, Garner and Yeates, 1963; Evans, 1973; Maher and O'Connor, 1976).

These ideas can be incorporated into the following hypotheses:

1. As suburban centres gain increasing shares of metropolitan employment their growing importance is reflected in greater interaction with their surrounding area (i.e. falling self-containment).

2. As the peripheral expansion of the metropolitan area proceeds, it widens the potential commuting field for existing suburban centres rather than for the CBD, and hence these suburban centres become less self-contained as time progresses.

The changes predicted in (1) and (2) above point to major structural change in the spatial evolution of a metropolitan area. Knowledge of the nature of change in structural and spatial relationships over time is important in an understanding of the future form of the city.

The following sections of the paper examine trends in the spatial structure of Melbourne as an example of the above process by studying the changing distribution of jobs and work-residence links for the 10-year period 1961–1971. Emphasis is given to the identification of major nodes of activity, and the assessment of relative importance within the whole system, together with changes in importance over the 10 years. The measure used is an index of self-containment which is derived by calculating the proportion of jobs in a subregional node filled by the resident workforce in the immediate subregion. This is expressed as

$$SC_i = \frac{WFR_i}{E_i}$$

where SC_i is the self-containment measure for area i; WFR_i is the workforce of i resident in i; and E_i is the total number of jobs in i.

Metropolitan Development in Melbourne

Melbourne, the second largest city in Australia (with a population of 2,604,000 in 1976) is a sprawling metropolis, reaching 80 miles around Port Phillip Bay, and northwards 25 miles from the bayside. The sprawl is attributable to plentiful land, little constraint by physical barriers, land speculation well in advance of demand (e.g. see Cannon, 1966), and a radial transport network which when first established in the 1890s extended well beyond the fringe of settlement (Johnston, 1968). Growth up until the 1950s was loosely contained within an extensive electrified suburban rail and streetcar network, which in 1950 reached out 20 miles

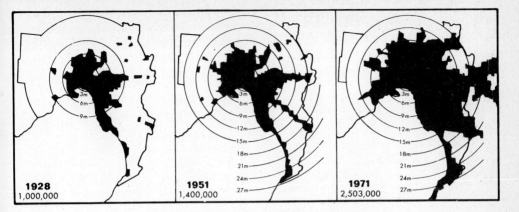

Figure 1. The Spatial Development of the Melbourne Metropolitan Area

to the south and east to provide commuter services. This transport network laid the basis for a distinctive finger-shaped pattern of development (Johnston, 1968) (see Figure 1).

Since the 1960s, with the growth of automobile ownership, housing developments less tied to the rail network have filled in the interstitial wedges; manufacturing industry now free of the constraints of a core location, has increasingly located in suburban areas (Rimmer, 1969); and retail activity has expanded into regional shopping centres in the suburbs (Johnston and Rimmer, 1968).

Because of the extensive outward nature of development in the city, the nature of accessibility has also undergone considerable change. Patton and Clark (1970) measured changes in the accessibility of each zone by summing all the jobs in the urban area, each job being weighted inversely according to travel time from that zone, and then comparing this for 1961 and 1966. They displayed the results on a map showing contours of accessibility, and it was apparent that the largest relative increases had occurred to the east, while the inner city, northern and western suburbs had actually fallen.

The physical extent of the growth can be shown by comparing the spatial pattern of jobs in Melbourne in 1961 and in 1971. One technique to illustrate the growth is to regress the number of jobs against centrality in terms of distance from the central area for 1961 and 1971 and compare the slope of the line (Figure 2). Although the fit of the relationship is not strong, the change in slope is interesting, and is indicative of the extent to which jobs have suburbanised over this period. Looking at the employment data it is clear that there has been substantial job growth between 10 and 12 miles from the CBD, and on the fringe. The central local-government area of the region (the City of Melbourne) is still overwhelmingly the main employer, largely due to high-density office development. By 1971, however, there were eight LGAs 10 or more miles from the CBD with 10,000 or more employees, whereas only two were in that category in 1961. With such a spatial spread of population and activity it is inevitable that subsidiary cores will emerge and thus that linkage patterns will change.

Work-Residence Relationships in Melbourne

The availability of data in the form of a detailed origin-destination matrix for jour-

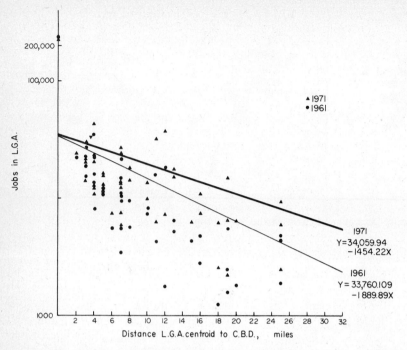

Figure 2. The Relationship between Jobs in Local Government Areas and Distance from the Central Business District, Melbourne 1961 and 1971

neys to work in Melbourne collected in three census periods, enables an investigation both of the changing relative concentrations of employment (physical growth), and of the relationships between employment location as destination and residence of worker as origin (structural evolution). The data are derived from census collected responses to questions relating to home location, work location, industry, occupation, and sex. The 1961 information is based on a 20% sample but both 1966 and 1971 data are derived from total enumerations. Within the data, because of a non-response factor and the inability of some occupations to state a definite workplace location, the total number of jobs will be underestimated, but this does little to affect the linkage patterns which are of primary interest.

The data are tabulated at a relatively fine spatial scale of origin and destination

zone. These can be aggregated to the basic administrative unit of local government area (LGA) of which there are 55 in the Melbourne Statistical Division (1971), and the majority of the present analysis is carried out at the LGA level. Initially, however, in order to deal with a description of structure and linkages, a larger spatial unit is employed. In 1973 the then Federal Department of Urban and Regional Development (it was disbanded after the 1975 election) delimited eight major regions in the Melbourne area, on the basis of demographic, social and economic homogeneity (Logan *et al.*, 1975). These are composed of groupings of LGAs, and while they do not have any functional identity in terms of work-residence flows, they do provide a convenient unit from which to begin an overview of structural change.

Matrices of the flows between region

of origin (residence) and region of destination (workplace) were constructed for the three periods. They can be viewed from two perspectives. First, by focusing on the column totals or the destinations, the total number of jobs in a region can be determined. When expressed as a proportion of the metropolitan wide employment, regional shifts in employment location can then be traced over the 10 years. Second, for each region the relative proportions of employees who travelled into the region each day can be derived. Changes in these latter figures over time represented the structural changes while change in the former index represents the physical growth component. From these two measures, changes in the size, and extent of influence of each employment subcentre can be found.

These patterns are shown in Tables 1 and 2. Table 1 reports on the percentage share of the total statistical division's employment in each region for the 3 years. It clearly demonstrates the lessening relative importance of the central core, and growing significance of suburban locations for job providing activities. In 1961 the Central region had 55% of the employment in the region, by 1971 this had dropped to 42%. The table shows that the suburban gains were distributed relatively evenly, with greater emphasis on the outer eastern regions where little economic activity was located in the earlier period.

Table 2 contains another perspective. It expresses the flows from origin region to destination region again in relative terms. The diagonal in this table represents that proportion of each region's employment which also resides within the region; that is, the degree to which it is self-contained. Clearly the Central region is the least self-contained; only 26% of the core's jobs were filled by core residents in 1971, a drop of over 4% from 1961. On the other hand, 81% of the Westernport region's workforce is drawn from within its boundaries in 1971, a 5% increase in 10 years. In terms of the extent of change over the period, the Inner Southern region shows out, dropping 10% in self-containment although still having almost 60% of its labour force resident in the region in 1971. Self-containment within the regions also fell for the North Western, Northern and Inner Eastern, while rising in the Western, Outer Eastern, and Westernport regions. The last two of these, Outer Eastern and Westernport, have both doubled their shares of the metropolitan labour force in the period under study (Table 1). Both regions are on the periphery of the metropolitan area where residential growth has been greatest, and this in itself has stimulated greater self-containment within the region.

In terms of flows to the Central region, Table 2 shows some interesting trends. Apart from the resident labour force in

Table 1. Changing Distribution of Workforce within the Melbourne Statistical Division by Region 1961, 1966 and 1971

| Region No. | 11 | 12 | 13 | 14 | 15 | 16 | 17 | 18 | |
| | | | North | | Inner | Outer | Inner | Western- | Total[a] |
Region	Central	Western	Western	North	East	East	South	port	Jobs
1961	55.0	12.2	5.4	5.6	5.4	3.3	10.0	3.1	692,145
1966	46.9	11.9	6.4	7.0	6.0	5.3	12.2	4.4	880,765
1971	41.8	11.4	6.8	7.7	6.0	7.3	12.8	6.3	907,060

[a] The total figure excludes jobs for which no destination was specified or which were filled by employees resident outside the metropolitan area.

Table 2. Origins of Regional Workforce 1961, 1966 and 1971[a]

			Destination Region							
			11	12	13	14	15	16	17	18
Origin Region		1961	30.0	7.8	7.8	6.4	6.0	2.4	6.6	2.9
	11	1966	27.8	6.5	6.8	5.5	5.1	1.9	6.5	2.2
		1971	25.9	5.2	5.7	4.1	4.4	1.4	5.4	1.4
		1961	9.1	71.7	6.1	1.9	1.3	0.6	1.0	0.5
	12	1966	9.9	72.7	7.5	1.8	1.1	0.5	0.9	0.5
		1971	10.1	76.3	9.5	1.9	1.3	0.4	0.7	0.3
		1961	8.7	8.1	65.8	7.4	1.2	0.6	0.9	0.5
	13	1966	8.5	8.8	62.9	8.1	1.6	0.6	0.8	0.7
		1971	7.8	7.8	60.7	7.3	1.2	0.5	0.6	0.2
		1961	11.2	3.1	12.1	75.0	4.0	1.1	1.1	0.5
	14	1966	11.1	3.2	13.4	73.2	4.5	1.3	1.2	0.7
		1971	11.1	3.0	14.7	74.0	4.9	1.5	1.1	0.5
		1961	13.1	3.0	3.5	5.1	62.9	11.6	5.3	2.1
	15	1966	13.0	2.8	4.1	6.3	58.6	10.6	5.2	2.1
		1971	13.2	2.5	4.2	7.3	56.0	9.3	5.1	1.6
		1961	6.7	1.5	1.3	1.3	16.4	74.9	5.6	4.6
	16	1966	8.7	1.8	1.8	2.4	20.5	73.3	8.3	6.7
		1971	10.6	1.8	2.1	2.9	23.2	75.5	10.8	6.7
		1961	18.9	4.4	3.1	2.5	7.3	6.9	69.9	13.2
	17	1966	17.9	3.7	2.9	2.3	7.2	8.2	63.9	11.7
		1971	17.4	2.8	2.5	2.0	7.2	6.4	59.6	8.3
		1961	2.4	0.5	0.4	0.4	0.9	1.8	9.5	75.7
	18	1966	3.1	0.6	0.5	0.5	1.3	3.7	13.2	75.3
		1971	3.9	0.6	0.6	0.6	1.8	4.9	16.7	80.9

[a] The origin of each region's workforce expressed as a percentage of total regional workforce.

the core, the most important origin of core workers is the Inner Southern region. While its contribution has fallen slightly over the time period, it was still providing 17.4% of the core's workforce in 1971.

The Northern and Inner Eastern regions, next in importance as the residence of core employees, have remained relatively stable, while the Outer Eastern region has shown a considerable rise (6.7%, 1961; 10.6%, 1971). The Western region has also displayed a rise in relative concentration of core employees (9.1–10.1%). In other words, even if the relative importance of the core as an employer is declining, the extent to which it draws from the remainder of the metro-

politan area for its labour force is not. More specifically, the change in the core's employment is quite selective of certain occupations (see Maher, 1978). Losses have been concentrated largely in the blue-collar occupations while in fact there has been an actual increase in white-collar jobs. It is well established that white-collar employment is drawn from a much wider range of locations than blue-collar employment (Carroll, 1952) and certainly that is the case here.

Insights can also be gained into changes which have occurred by examining the columns of Table 2. These show the proportion of a particular region's labour force originating from each of the other regions. For the largest suburban employer (Inner Southern region), large proportional increases of its workforce are provided by the two peripheral regions, Outer Eastern, and Westernport (e.g. 17% of the Inner Southern region's workforce originated in the Westernport region in 1971, compared with only 10% in 1961). This suggests that job growth in the Inner Southern region has had considerable effects beyond its border drawing the Westernport region into a greater degree of functional relationship. At the same time, reverse commuting to the Inner Southern region in terms of employees originating in the core has fallen, indicating the growing attraction of the suburban job location for growing numbers of outer urban residents.

In contrast, the Western region has become more self-contained, and has employed relatively fewer workers from adjoining regions. At the same time, as Table 1 demonstrated, its share of the metropolitan workforce has fallen. Hence, we have on the one hand, the Inner Southern region where job growth has influenced regions lying to the south and east, enabling an area of major residential expansion in the 1961–1971 period, such that the overall importance of this region is increasing. On the other hand there is the Western region, where less rapid job growth, combined with peripheral expansion within the region itself, has seen a weakening of linkages with surrounding regions.

A third important set of information relates to the column describing the Central region as a destination. Table 2 shows that all the regions other than the Inner Southern, and Northwestern contributed slightly more to Central region jobs in 1971 than in 1961. However, only for the Outer Eastern region is the change marked. The fact that this region is linked by two rail routes to the CBD, and in its western section houses a population of higher than average social status (Lo-

gan *et al.*, 1975), clearly helps explain its greater association with the Central region. Presumably the growth in linkages between this area and the core consists largely of workforce involved in white-collar professional, administrative, managerial, and clerical occupations in CBD offices. In contrast again, the Inner Southern and Northwestern regions contribute smaller shares to the Central workforce, becoming involved more in local exchanges.

To provide an additional perspective for the analysis of suburban centres, the flows were then looked at with each region as an origin as the focus of interest, and the flows of the resident workforce to all regions expressed as a proportion of total resident workforce (Table 3). The table shows firstly that in all but the Central region, the proportion of a region's workforce employed within its own region has increased. Some of these increases have been substantial. In the Outer Eastern region, for example, the proportion of its workforce employed locally increased from 30% in 1961 to 40% in 1971, while in the Northwestern region the increase was from 35–45%. Furthermore, the proportion working in the local region in 1971 was greater than the proportion travelling to the core in all regions other than the Inner Eastern where the white-collar workforce remains core oriented. In 1961 that situation existed only in the Western region, and the Westernport region. Again, the Central region is seen as a relatively less important destination for residents in most suburban regions, with falls up to 15% in the share of a region's workforce travelling to the Central region over the period of study. Finally, the Table shows how important flows to neighbouring subregions have become. In the Inner Eastern region for example, 60% of the 1971 workforce were employed either locally or in adjoining regions; in 1961 that figure was 48%.

Table 3. Destinations of Regional Workforce 1961, 1966 and 1971[a]

			Destination Region							
			11	12	13	14	15	16	17	18
Origin Region		1961	85.1	4.9	2.2	1.9	1.7	0.4	3.4	0.5
	11	1966	81.9	4.8	2.7	2.4	1.9	0.6	5.0	0.6
		1971	81.6	4.5	2.9	2.4	2.0	0.8	5.2	0.7
		1961	34.8	60.7	2.3	0.7	0.5	0.2	0.7	0.1
	12	1966	32.9	61.3	3.4	0.9	0.1	0.2	0.7	0.1
		1971	30.4	62.4	4.6	1.1	0.5	0.2	0.6	0.6
		1961	48.2	9.9	35.8	4.2	0.7	0.2	0.9	0.0
	13	1966	40.3	10.6	40.8	5.7	1.0	0.3	1.0	0.3
		1971	36.0	9.9	45.7	6.2	0.8	0.4	0.8	0.2
		1961	52.2	3.2	5.6	35.9	1.8	0.3	0.9	0.1
	14	1966	43.3	3.1	7.1	42.2	2.2	0.6	1.2	0.3
		1971	37.7	2.8	8.2	46.7	2.4	0.9	1.2	0.3
		1961	58.0	2.9	1.5	2.3	27.3	3.1	4.3	0.5
	15	1966	51.2	2.8	2.2	3.7	29.3	4.7	5.3	0.8
		1971	48.3	2.5	2.5	4.9	29.4	5.9	5.7	0.8
		1961	45.5	2.2	0.8	0.9	11.0	30.9	7.0	1.7
	16	1966	37.1	1.9	1.1	1.5	11.1	35.4	9.2	2.7
		1971	32.3	1.5	1.0	1.6	10.2	40.1	10.1	3.1
		1961	53.8	2.8	0.9	0.7	2.1	1.2	36.4	2.1
	17	1966	45.7	2.4	1.0	0.9	2.4	2.4	42.5	2.8
		1971	42.9	1.9	1.0	0.9	2.5	2.8	44.9	3.1
		1961	27.8	1.2	0.4	0.5	1.0	1.3	19.7	48.1
	18	1966	21.4	1.0	0.5	0.5	1.2	2.9	23.7	48.9
		1971	17.3	0.7	0.4	0.5	1.1	3.8	22.6	53.6

[a] The destination of each region's workforce expressed as a percentage of total regional workforce.

LABOUR-SHED IDENTIFICATION AND SMALL-SCALE ANALYSIS

The regions used earlier were a convenience and bore little resemblance to actual commuting fields. The next step in the analysis was to identify labour-sheds, particularly for the most significant employment concentrations, and to analyse the nature of changes occurring in these over time.

The labour-sheds were identified by an analysis of the 1971 work-residence flows on the basis of a 55 × 55 origin-destination matrix between the LGAs. Their identification is described in detail in a previous paper by the authors (Maher and O'Connor, 1976). Briefly, the flow data were used to obtain measures of linkages, or functional distance, between each pair of origins and destinations. The technique adopted was that developed by Brown and Horton (1970), Brown and Holmes (1971), and Brown, Odland and Gollege (1970), building on the work of Beshers and Laumann (1967). Functional distance "is a summary descriptive measure or index of the attentuation effect of nodal properties upon internodal interaction" (Brown and Horton, 1970). The actual measure entailed is the Mean First Passage Time (MFPT) derived from Markov Chain analysis of the original flow matrix. The result is a matrix of Mean First Passage Times representing the mean number of steps an observation beginning at state i (origin) would take to get to stage j (destination). Both direct, and indirect links are taken into account. The lower the MFPT between a pair of locations, the closer is their degree of functional linkage. By standardising the MFPTs by destination, and identifying those LGAs with MFPTs of less than −1 standard deviations from the mean it is possible to outline the labour-shed for a particular destination. The labour-shed then is defined as that group of LGAs most strongly linked to that destination by work-residence flows. As all origins and destinations have some degree of linkage in the intra-metropolitan case, selecting an arbitrary but standardised MFPT falling outside one standard deviation unit then represent those LGAs with the most marked degree of relatedness in terms of flows.

Once the labour-sheds were identified, interest lay in the degree of closure, or self-containment of each. Essentially, this stage of the research was concerned with two spatial units; on the one hand, the LGA as a destination or subregional centre, and on the other hand, the labour-shed which consisted of a group of LGAs with the greatest functional ties to that destination. Self-containment ratios were calculated for these units, and a study made of changes in these ratios between 1961 and 1971. Generally speaking, suburban job locations have labour-sheds that are far more self-contained than those in the Central area and the closer an LGA is to the periphery, the more self-contained is its labour-shed. However, those destinations away from the Central core which are significant employment locations, show lower levels of self-containment than many other suburban locations. Over time it is apparent that most outer-suburban areas have become more self-contained.

To take this analysis a stage further, effort was directed toward the identification of forces that influence the self-containment ratio. For example, if the number of jobs in an LGA were to increase but this change was matched by the number of workers originating in the defined labour-shed, the self-containment index would show no change. If, however, the number of jobs rose faster than the number of residents, of course the index would fall. Such a wide variety of processes cannot be revealed by a single index and no doubt the summary figure of the self-containment index masks many of these processes.

By plotting changes in the workforce against changes in residents in the labour-shed between 1961 and 1971, LGAs can be categorized into three broad groups on the basis of differential job and residence growth. First, areas where job growth has run ahead of resident workforce growth (the majority of LGAs, especially South Melbourne, Moorabbin and Oakleigh); second, those where job growth has been less than resident worker growth (e.g. Berwick, Caulfield) and finally those where there has been a net loss of jobs and population (e.g. Collingwood, Fitzroy).

The first group involves a large number of LGAs and can meaningfully be subdivided into two. On the one hand there are those where job growth has been in excess of 10,000 in the 10-year period, and on the other those with much less growth. This division is an important one as it isolates a few key areas for closer study. Suburban centres such as Moorabbin, Preston, Oakleigh, Waverley and Broadmeadows stand out as areas where substantial growth in employment has been associated with large changes in labour-shed numbers. These LGAs are component parts of the North Western, Inner Eastern and Inner Southern regions which were prominent in the preceding regional analysis. For all, jobs have grown faster than have the number living within their labour-sheds, meaning that they have all widened their sphere of influence over surrounding suburbs. Figure 3 shows the location of the LGAs and the

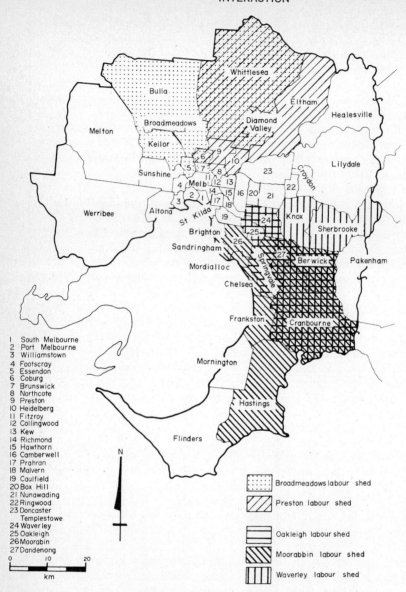

Figure 3. Labour-Sheds of Major Suburban Employment Locations, 1971

interwoven pattern of their labour-sheds. Clearly the growth of jobs in these suburban locations has stimulated worker residence growth in a wide arc of middle and outer suburbia.

A second group—those with change in employment of less than 10,000 jobs be-

tween 1961 and 1971, deserves comment. South Melbourne stands out as an area where job growth has been rapid but has not been matched by residence growth within its labour-shed. The job growth is no doubt related to the proximity of the area to the CBD. The result in terms of the labour-shed is that commuting is occurring from a much wider section of the metropolitan area. It is a good case of the effect of job growth in an inner area influencing resident patterns across much of the metropolis.

Conversely, job declines in Fitzroy, Williamstown, Collingwood and Melbourne are matched directly by resident declines within their labour-sheds; in the City of Melbourne, in fact, resident decline has been much greater than job decline. These cases reinforce the notion that the decline in inner-area job opportunities has had the effect of encouraging resident relocation and a part of growth in suburban areas is due to this force.

Conclusions

The data displayed above and their analysis assist in achieving a different view of the development and importance of suburban centres in a metropolitan region. The analysis has shown that there are three important and interrelated characteristics in the development of suburban centres: their size, as measured by the number of jobs; their degree of linkage with surrounding communities; and their location with respect to the periphery. The last is important as it controls a potential commuting field for a suburban centre. Taken a little further, this study has laid the basis for understanding the impact which the growth and development of suburban centres will have on metropolitan spatial structure. From the analysis it is apparent that the major suburban centres in a metropolitan region are those located centrally in a suburban sector, capable of drawing on a broad labour market on their periphery. Concomitantly, as the present periphery extends as part of a continued suburbanisation process, present peripheral suburban centres will increase in importance as the degree of relative accessibility changes.

Throughout this study, the evolution and development of suburban centres has been viewed solely in journey to work terms, involving analysis of the number of jobs and the spatial patterns of work residence links around a centre. Clearly the suburban centre involves more than that; in Muller's (1976) work, for example, it involves the study of retail, community service and administrative functions. It is as well to note, however, that these activities are sensitive to regional markets and distance from alternative supply points. For these reasons one would expect them to be better developed in suburban areas that are surrounded by population which will serve as a market.

The major thrust of this study has been to illustrate the increasing complexity in journey to work linkages in Melbourne, in particular to show the developing cross regional movements in the suburbs. The major suburbanisation of jobs that proceeded apace during the 1960s has had as a corollary the suburbanisation of residences. Throughout a band of middle- and outer-suburban areas, cross regional journey-to-work patterns are typical, and increasingly more important than the trip to the central city. This analysis shows that in journey to work terms Melbourne has shifted toward a fairly dispersed multinodal metropolis, though that needs to be qualified on two counts. First, the central city is still a major employer of labour and—probably more fundamentally—the suburban growth has been diffused among a large number of adjoining LGAs in a semi-continuous fashion which has constrained the development of major suburban centres. For example, three adjoining LGAs, Moorabbin, Waverley and Oakleigh, shared job growth of almost 50,000 employees between 1961 and 1971, but since these three units cover a north-south distance of 10 miles, it is difficult to identify nodes as such. Finally it is possible that the suburban work trip may involve particular occupations and industries.

In conclusion, the evolution of a metropolitan area along the lines indicated has important consequences. First, it has consequences for the map of job accessibility, increasing the accessibility of suburban residents to jobs. In the Melbourne context, this is particularly so in the south east. Second, because of the radial nature of many metropolitan public transport systems, it has underscored the inaccessibility of non-car-owners to jobs. These two dimensions taken together stress the important underlying feature in the study: increasingly work trips in many metropolitan areas are inter-suburban and probably largely oriented to the motor car. There are serious social, equity and energy considerations in that observation (Black and Conroy, 1977).

The present paper has shown that daily journey-to-work movement toward suburban centres has become more common, and that this strengthens the need to re-think the underlying structure of a metropolitan area. The implication is that in many metropolitan regions, planning for subcentre development and circumferential transport systems is long overdue, to accommodate the new character of the suburbs. More generally the paper has shown how the separate information on job dispersal and population spread can be integrated to show how metropolitan structures have evolved over time.

References

Adams, J. (1970) Residential structure of Midwestern cities, *Ann. Ass. Am. Geographers* 60, 37–62.

Alonso, W. (1964) *Location and Land Use,* Harvard University, Cambridge, Mass.

Berry, B. J. L., Garner, B., Simmons, J. W. and Tennant, R. J. (1963) Commercial structure and commercial blight, University of Chicago, Department of Geography Research Paper No. 85.

Berry, B. J. L. and Kasarda, J. D. (1977) *Contemporary Urban Ecology.* MacMillan, New York.

Beshers, J. M. and Laumann, E. (1967) Social distance: a network approach, *Am. Sociol. Rev.* 32, 225–236.

Birch, D. (1971) Toward a stage theory of urban growth, *J. Am. Inst. Planners* 78–87.

Black, J. and Conroy, M. (1977) Accessibility measures and the social evaluation of urban structure, *Envir. Plann. A* 9, 1013–1031.

Brown, L. A. and Holmes, J. (1971) The delimitation of functional regions, nodal regions and hierarchies by functional distance approaches, *J. Reg. Sci.* 11, 57–72.

Brown, L. A. and Horton, F. (1970) Functional distance: an operational approach, *Geogrl. Anal.* 2, 76–83.

Brown, L. A., Odland, J. and Golledge, R. (1970) Migration, functional distance and the urban hierarchy, *Econ. Geogr.* 46, 472–485.

Cannon, Michael (1966) *The Land Boomers,* Melbourne University Press, Carlton.

Carroll, J. D. (1952) The relation of homes to work and the spatial pattern of cities, *Social Forces* 30, 271–283.

Castells, M. (1968) Is there an urban sociology?, in Pickvance, C. G. (Ed.) *Urban Sociology.* Tavistock-Methuen, London.

Chinitz, B. (Ed.) (1964) *City and Suburb,* Prentice-Hall, Englewood Cliffs, N.J.

Clawson, M. and Hall, P. (1973) *Planning and Urban Growth,* R.F.F. Johns Hopkins Press, Baltimore.

Echenique, M. (1976) Function and form of the city region, in Hancock, T. (Ed.) *Growth and Change in the Future City Region.* Leonard Hill, London.

Evans, A. W. (1973) *The Economics of Residential Location,* MacMillan, London.

Gottmann, J. and Harper, R. A. (1967) *Metropolis on the Move,* John Wiley, New York.

Guest, A. M. (1976) Night-time and daytime populations of large American suburbs, *Urb. Aff. Q.* 12, 57–82.

Guest, A. M. and Cluett, C. (1976) Workplace and residential location: a push–pull model, *J. Reg. Sci.* 16, 399–410.

Harrison, B. (1974) Urban economic development: suburbanisation, minority opportunity and the condition of the central city, Urban Institute, Washington.

Hoover, E. M. and Vernon, R. (1959) *Anatomy of a Metropolis,* Harvard U.P.

Hughes, J. W. (1974) *Suburbanization Dynamics and the Future of the City,* Centre for Urban Policy Research, Rutgers, New Brunswick.

Johnston, R. J. (1968) Railways, urban growth and central place patterns, *Tijdschr. econo. soc. Geogr.* 59, 33–41.

Johnston, R. J. and Rimmer, P. (1968) *Retailing in Melbourne,* Research School of Pacific Studies, Dept. of Human Geography, Public. HG/3 A.N.U., Canberra.

Kain, J. F. (1975) *Essays on Urban Spatial Structure,* Ballinger, Cambridge, Mass.

Kasarda, J. D. (1976) The changing occupational structure of the American Metropolis: *apropos* the urban problem, in Schwartz, B. (Ed.) *The Changing Face of the Suburbs,* University of Chicago Press, Chicago.

Logan, M. I., Maher, C. A., Mckay, J. and Humphreys, J. S. (1975) *Urban and Regional Australia: Analysis and Policy Issues,* Sorrett Social Sciences, Melbourne.

Maher, C. A. (1978) The changing residential role of the inner city: the example of Melbourne, *Aust. Geogr.* 14 (2).

Maher, C. A. (1980) Suburban development and household mobility in Melbourne, in Burnley, I. H., Pryor, R. J. and Rowlands, D. T., *Mobility and Community Change in Australia.*

Maher, C. A. and O'Connor, K. B. (1976) Intra-regional labour movement in the Melbourne metropolitan area, *Papers of the First Australia–New Zealand Regional Science Conference,* Brisbane, Aug. 1976, 98–114.

Masotti, L. H. (1973) Prologue: suburbia reconsidered—myth and counter-myth, in Masotti, L. H. and Hadden, J. K. (Eds.) *The Urbanization of the Suburbs,* Vol. 7, Urban Affairs Annual Reviews, Sage.

Mills, E. S. (1972) *Studies in the Structure of the Urban Economy,* R.F.F. Johns Hopkins Press, Baltimore.

Moses, L. and Williamson, H. (1967) Location of economic activity in cities, *Am. Econ. Rev.* 57, 211–222.

Muller, P. (1976) *The Outer City: Geographical Consequences of the Urbanization of the Suburbs,* Commission on College Geography, Resource Paper No. 75-2 A.A.G.

Ottensman, J. R. (1975) *The Changing Spatial Structure of American Cities,* D. C. Heath, Lexington, Mass.

Papageorgiou, G. (1971) The population and rent distribution in a multicentred framework, *Envir. Plann.* 3, 267–282.

Patton, T. A. and Clark, N. (1970) Towards an accessibility model for residential development, Tewksbury Symposium, in Clark, N. (Ed.) *Analysis of Urban Development,* Melbourne, Dept. of Civil Engineering.

Rimmer, P. J. (1969) Manufacturing in Melbourne, Research School of Pacific Studies, Department of Human Geography, Publication H6/2. Australian National University, Canberra.

Schaffer, K. H. and Sclar, E. (1973) *Access for All: Transportation and Urban Growth,* Pelican, London.

Schnore, L. F. (1957) The growth of the metropolitan suburbs, *Am. Sociol. Rev.* 22, 165–173.

Schnore, L. F. and Klaff, V. (1972) Suburbanisation in the sixties: a preliminary analysis. *Land Econ.* 48 (1), 23–33.

Smart, M. W. (1974) Labour market areas: use and definitions, *Prog. Plann.* 2, 239–353.

South East Joint Planning Team (1976) Strategy for the South East: 1976 Review, Department of the Environment, H.M.S.O., London.

Stegman, M. (1969) Accessibility models and residential location, *J. Am. Inst. Plann.* 35, 22–29.

Taaffe, E., Garner, B. and Yeates, M. (1963) *The Peripheral Journey to Work: A Geographical Consideration,* Transportation Centre, Northwestern University.

Zimmer, B. (1975) The urban centrifugal drift, in Hawley, A. and Rock, V. (Eds.) *Metropolitan America in Contemporary Perspective,* John Wiley, London, pp. 23–91.

JOHN B. GODDARD

Movement Systems, Functional Linkages, and Office Location in the City Centre: A Study of Central London

The close connection between movement and the distribution of activities in spatial systems is a well-established geographical axiom. At the national level B. J. L. Berry has used multivariate statistical procedures to measure the relationships between the state of a system, expressed in terms of the distribution of productive activities, and the behaviour of that system, expressed in the form of commodity flows between various places.[1] He has structured these relationships within the framework of a general field theory of spatial behaviour, in which the pattern of flows, summarized as a set of functional regions, is held to be both a resultant and a determinant of the spatial distribution of activities, summarized as a set of uniform regions.[2] Berry's formulation is in some ways a more general state-

ment of A. K. Philbrick's principle of "areal functional organization."[3] Similarly, O. Wärneryd, in his conceptual model of the urban system, has stressed the importance of functional interdependencies in explaining changes in the state of the system.[4]

It would be reasonable to assume that the interdependence of flows and spatial structure also holds within urban areas, in particular within large metropolitan centres. However, at this level the measurement of the relationships involved creates numerous conceptual, empirical and technical problems, many of which are insuperable at the present time. While several studies of city centre structure have emphasized the role of "linkages" between highly specialized activities as a determinant of location, little progress has been made in measuring these linkages.[5] Most previous research has focused

1. B. J. L. Berry, "Interdependency of flows and spatial structure: a general field theory formulation" in "Essays on commodity flows and the spatial structure of the Indian economy," *Univ. of Chicago, Dept. of Geography Res. Pap.* 111 (1966).
2. B. J. L. Berry, "A synthesis of formal and functional regions using a general field theory of spatial behaviour" in *Spatial analysis* (Ed. B. J. L. Berry and D. F. Marble).

3. A. K. Philbrick, "Principles of areal functional organization in regional human geography," *Econ. Geogr.* 33 (1957), 299–336.
4. O. Wärneryd, *Interdependence in urban systems* (Gothenburg, 1968).
5. J. Rannells, *The core of the city* (New York, 1956).

From **Transactions,** Institute of British Geographers, Vol. 49, 1970, pp. 161–82. Reprinted in revised form by permission of The Institute and J. B. Goddard.

on the distribution of activities; linkages have then been inferred from locational associations among these activities.[6] For instance, within the financial core of the City of London, multivariate analysis of detailed employment data has highlighted the existence of distinctive spatial clusters of offices whose composition closely reflects the well-known functional organization of the City.[7] Within the broader compass of the London Central Area, floorspace data have suggested a number of sub-areas with distinctive land-use combinations.[8]

According to Berry's general field theory formulation, such pronounced spatial differentiation within city centres should simultaneously be determined by, and call forth, a correspondingly structured pattern of movement. Yet very few studies have been made of physical linkage patterns in the city centre, in relation to the activities that generate and attract these movements. In part this is because of data difficulties. While detailed information can be collected on the distribution of activities, a corresponding breakdown of movement patterns associated with each of these activities would require extensive surveys. More important, linkages frequently involve information flows that are extremely difficult to differentiate, that use a variety of communication channels and which often do not involve obvious physical movements.[9]

6. D. H. Davies, *Land use in central Capetown* (Capetown, 1965).
7. J. B. Goddard, "Multivariate analysis of office location patterns in the city centre: a London example," *Reg. Stud.* 2 (1968), 69–85.
8. J. B. Goddard, "The internal structure of London's Central Area" in *Urban core and inner city,* Proceedings of the International Studyweek, Amsterdam, September 1966 (Leiden, 1967).
9. G. Törnqvist, "Flows of information and the location of economic activities," *Geogr. Annlr.* 50 (1968), B, 99–107; B. Thorngren, "Regional economic interaction and flows of information," Paper presented to Regional Science Association seminar, Copenhagen (mimeo., 1967).

Some of these difficulties can be by-passed by considering only physical movements of a given type, as a single indicator of multi-faceted functional linkages. But even then, observed movement patterns are extremely complex. It is therefore the object of this paper to suggest a method for analysing the complex linkage structures that are represented by movement patterns in the city centre.

The Data and Study Area

For the purposes of this paper, the movements of taxis within Central London have been taken as the best available single indicator of functional linkages. Of the principal travel modes, the use of taxis is most characteristic of the Central Area; in fact, 55 per cent of all taxi trips in Greater London both begin and end in the centre.[10] However, taxis still represent only one type of communication and the subsequent analysis is therefore forced to ignore linkages maintained on foot, by private vehicles, public transport, telephone and post.

The Registrar General's definition of the Central Area for the 1961 census is taken as the limit for the study area, which for practical purposes has to be regarded as a closed system (Figure 1). This area was subjectively extracted from the existing administrative framework by aggregating enumeration districts to provide an additional unit for collecting future census and planning data. Defined in this way, the Central Area includes an area of 28 km^2, which is much larger than the Central Business District defined using R. E. Murphy and J. E. Vance's criteria.[11] In fact, the Central Area includes both CBD "core" and "frame" using E. M. Horwood and R. R. Boyce's terminology, thus containing the main-

10. *London County Council* (1964), *London traffic survey* 1, 154.
11. J. B. Goddard, op. cit. (1967), 120.

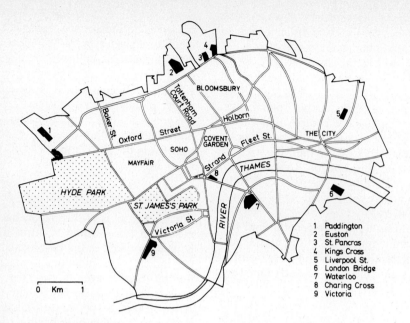

Figure 1. London Central Area

line rail termini, which are major generators of taxi traffic.[12]

The data were collected in 1962 as
part of the London Traffic Survey. They
are based on journey logs kept by an effective 10 per cent sample of all cabs registered in the Survey Area for one week
in July.[13] As the logs were completed by
taxi drivers, the data failed to differentiate trips according to passenger's journey
purpose. An additional shortcoming of
the data from the linkage standpoint is
that non-fare paying trips (that is, trips
made between setting down one passenger and picking up another) are not excluded. Because drivers tend to cruise
back into the areas where most trips are
generated, the major nodes in the system

could be over-emphasized. Both of these
limitations are overcome in a second survey of taxi usage conducted in July 1969
as part of a Home Office investigation
into the London taxicab trade.

Trip origins and destinations determined from the logs have been assigned
to seventy traffic zones in the Central
Area and averaged to give 24-hour weekday flows. All but eight of the zones consist of aggregations of enumeration districts delineated with due consideration
of land-use characteristics. The remaining eight zones comprise sections of major shopping streets, for example, Oxford
Street (three zones) and Piccadilly (two
zones).

The Pattern of Taxi Flows:
Cartographic Analysis

Figure 2 is an attempt to describe the
overall pattern of taxi flows between sixty-
nine traffic zones; for one zone no trips
are recorded. Flows of less than ten ve-

12. E. M. Horwood and R. R. Boyce, *Studies
of the C.B.D. and urban freeway development*
(Seattle, 1959).
13. *London traffic survey* 1, 41. Data on other
movement patterns were based on home interviews and are not reliable at the traffic-zone
level.

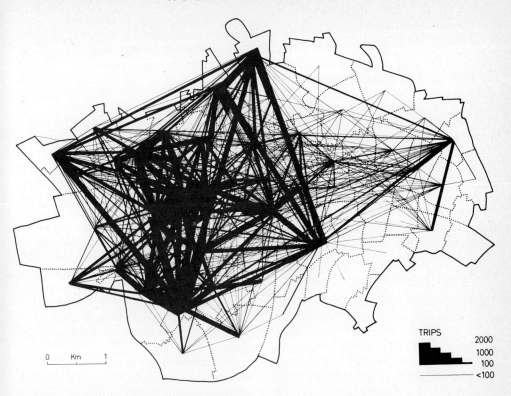

TRIPS

2000
1000
100
<100

Figure 2. Taxi Flows (24-hour average weekday)

hicles per day are excluded. This map at once illustrates the complexity of the linkage patterns and the limitations of cartographic analysis.[14] However, some points do emerge about the use of taxis in Central London. The most noticeable feature is that taxi flows reach a peak in the West End, particularly Mayfair and Victoria, while zones to the north and south of the City are only weakly connected, if at all, to the rest of the system. Apart from a mi-

nor node in the eastern part of the City, including the Bank, Liverpool Street and London Bridge stations, the level of taxi use is remarkably low in the financial centre. Because of the highly specialized nature of the City with its detailed clustering of linked activities, most commercial contacts are maintained on foot. In contrast, Mayfair, a recently colonized part of the commercial centre, while being characterized by broadly similar activities, does not show the same degree of clustering.[15] In addition to offices, the West End includes other major generators of taxi traffic, such as hotels, entertainments, shops and high-class residences. Such differences in the level of

14. Because of the difficulties of illustrating all zone-to-zone desires, the major urban transport studies have made use of a method of accumulating these movements on a "spider's web network" consisting only of links between adjacent zones. While this method helps in the cartographic display of flow patterns and is useful in traffic network analysis, it is of little value for a study of linkages which must be concerned with direct zone-to-zone connections.

15. J. B. Goddard, "Changing office location patterns within Central London," *Urban Stud.* 4 (1968), 276–85.

vehicular usage are one of the key characteristics distinguishing the "core" from the "frame" of the CBD.[16]

The diversity of the linkages and the limitations of cartographic methods indicate the need for some pattern-seeking technique that will eliminate the "noise" of minor flows and concentrate on the basic elements in the system. The analysis proceeds from the belief that the complex network of linkages represented by the taxi system contains some order in the form of sub-systems with strong internal linkages but with weaker connections to other subsystems elsewhere in the Central Area.

Correlation and Components Analysis

The flows shown in Figure 2 can be arrayed in a 69×69 origin/destination matrix, the leading diagonal representing intra-zonal flows. This matrix is not symmetrical since the outward movements from any one zone seldom correspond to the pattern of incoming trips. Several methods have been suggested for determining the basic structure of such flow matrices. In particular J. Nystuen and M. F. Dacey have suggested a method for defining nodal regions which considers flows as links in a directed graph.[17] However, this method is essentially hierarchical since it considers only largest flows; it is therefore unsuited to situations in which no theoretical hierarchy of regions can be assumed. Use is therefore made of correlation and factor analysis techniques first applied to binary connectivity matrices by W. L. Garrison, D. F. Marble and P. R. Gould but subsequently to matrices containing ratio data by Berry, S. Illeris and O. Pedersen.[18]

In the first stage of the analysis each column or destination vector in the matrix is correlated with every other, yielding a 69×69 matrix of coefficients.[19] Surprisingly many of these relationships were near-linear and no transformations of the data were required.

The next stage in the search for order in the taxi-flow system involved extracting characteristic values—latent roots or eigenvalues, together with their associated eigenvectors—from the correlation matrix.[20] Using the method of principal components, the sixty-nine correlated variables are transformed into sixty-nine uncorrelated variables or components in descending order of variability. Although as many components as variables can be extracted from the correlation matrix, this procedure is generally parsimonious as the leading components account for a substantial proportion of the total variance. In this instance the largest eigenvalue represents 26 per cent of the variance in the original data; together, the first five components account for 55 per cent of the variance and the first ten, 72 per cent. Geographical interpretation of the component loadings (the elements of the eigenvector scaled by the square root of their associated eigenvalue) indicates zones with common patterns of trip assembly.

Because each zone, no matter how

---

16. E. M. Horwood and R. R. Boyce, op. cit.
17. J. Nystuen and M. F. Dacey, "A graph theory interpretation of nodal regions," *Reg. Sci. Ass. Pap.* 7 (1961), 29–42.
18. W. L. Garrison and D. F. Marble, "A factor analytic study of the connectivity of a transport network," *Reg. Sci. Ass. Pap.* 12 (1964), 231–38; P. R. Gould, "On the geographical interpretation of eigenvalues," *Trans. Inst. Br. Geogr.* 42 (1967), 53–85; B. J. L. Berry, op. cit. (1966); S. Illeris and O. Pedersen, "Central places and functional regions in Denmark. Factor analysis of telephone traffic," *Lund Stud. Geogr.* (1968) Ser. B, 30.
19. A particular problem arises over the diagonal elements when correlating columns from a matrix containing flow information, since two unlike elements are compared, the flows within zone 1 being compared with the flows between zones 1 and 2. This source of error is very small, but cannot be eliminated.
20. For a discussion of the methods, see P. R. Gould op. cit.

Table 1. Explained Variance: Unrotated and Rotated Solutions[a]

Component	I	II	III	IV	V	VI	Total
Eigenvalue	17.96	7.23	4.83	4.44	3.86	2.92	
Percentage explanation	26.02	10.47	7.00	6.34	5.59	4.23	59.65
Rotated Factor	I	II	III	IV	V	VI	Total
Sum of squared factor loadings	10.84	8.29	6.85	6.02	5.43	3.83	
Percentage explanation	15.71	12.01	9.92	8.72	7.86	5.55	59.77

[a] The total percentage explanation for six components and six factors is approximately the same (59.7 per cent), although both totals do not exactly tally owing to different rounding levels in the computing.

weakly it is linked with the overall system, exerts an influence on the principal pattern of variation that is extracted and because of the absolute dominance of the West End, this stage in the analysis also failed to isolate meaningful subsystems. In fact every zone to the west of the City contributed strongly to the leading component, while subsequent components represented relatively minor patterns of variation.

The final step in the analysis, therefore, involved the application of factor analysis rotation procedures which concentrate on the significant patterns of variation or common factors and ignore all other influences. Examination of the eigenvalues showed that beyond the sixth, each additional component added little to the overall level of explanation. These six components, representing 60 per cent of the initial variance, were subjected to a normal varimax rotation to satisfy the criterion of simple structure, whereby each variable, as far as possible, is highly associated with only one factor. This method of principal components analysis on the complete correlation matrix, with unities in the diagonal, followed by analytic rotation of a specified number of leading components, contrasts with the classic methods of principal factor analysis whereby communality estimates of the amount of variance explained by the number of common factors specified are inserted in the diagonal before extracting

the latent roots of the matrix.[21] Table 1 compares components and rotated factors and indicates how the variance of the principal component has been redistributed among the factors.

The rotation succeeded in decomposing the dominant West End system, distinguishing between destinations and grouping them on the basis of their common origins. But what are the origins that are common to each set of destinations? The rotated factors are derived from the intercorrelations of the sixty-nine variables (destinations) which are measured over sixty-nine observations (origins). By computing each observation's score on each of the factors, it is possible to determine which zones are the principal origins for each group of destinations.[22]

The percentage communality, indicating the amount of variance of each variable explained by the common factors, ranges considerably, from 8.3 per cent to 89.9 per cent. The zones which are

21. For a full statement of the methods of these two approaches see H. H. Harman, *Modern factor analysis* (Chicago, 1966), 136 ff; Varimax rotation of principal component axes is also discussed, p. 304 ff. See also J. B. Goddard (1968) for an application and discussion of factor analysis in urban studies.

22. The use of an initial principal components solution means that the rotated factor scores can be computed without recourse to estimation procedures using multiple regression (H. H. Harman, op. cit., 348).

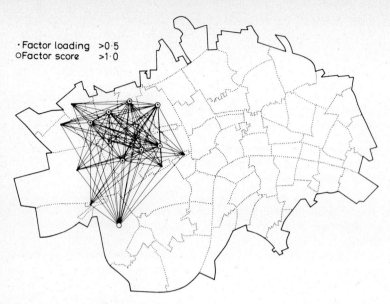

Figure 3. Factor One: The West End

poorly accounted for by the six factors are those with low levels of trip generation that are hardly linked to the rest of the system. These contrast with the zones containing the main-line termini, which mostly have high communalities because they load high on several of the factors. Having isolated the major sub-systems, it is possible to return to cartographic analysis and delineate each of these on the map. This is done in a series of maps by linking each group of destinations (factor loadings) to its respective set of common origins (factor scores).

Factor one (Figure 3) accounting for 15.7 per cent of the common variance, represents the dominant nodal sub-system centred in the heart of the West End, including Mayfair, Oxford Street and the area to the north. This is a region characterized by a unique combination of offices, shopping facilities and high-class residences. The core zones of this system are both major generators and attractors of trips, this being shown by high factor scores and high factor loadings. Periph-

eral to these are zones which are major destinations for trips generated in the core. These include other shopping areas along Piccadilly and Knightsbridge.

Factor two, explaining a further 12 per cent of the common variance, distinguished a second sub-system in the western part of the Central Area which was far from apparent in the cartographic analysis. As shown in Figure 4, this is centred in the administrative area of Westminster. The focal zones, with high scores and loadings, include the distinctive localities of Belgravia, Victoria, St. James's and Pimlico. Victoria Station, Paddington, King's Cross/St. Pancras and Waterloo stations are all major destinations for trips generated in the core of this system, while Charing Cross is a major origin. The importance of the stations in this pattern is in strong contrast to the West End system, which has no connections to the main line termini, only to the suburban services of Marylebone and Baker Street.

The failure of the initial unrotated solu-

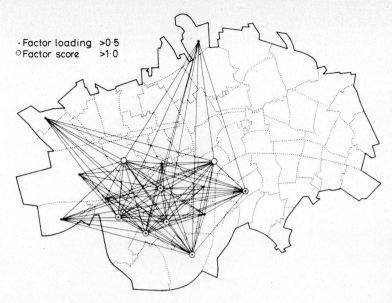

· Factor loading > 0·5
○ Factor score   > 1·0

Figure 4. Factor Two: Westminster

tion to separate these first two systems was mainly owing to a certain amount of overlap between them. The maps show that certain zones, including Piccadilly and Knightsbridge, are major destinations for trips generated in both systems. A plot of factor one against factor two, emphasizes this overlap. It shows a number of zones, loading high on both factors. The plot also shows the existence of independent sub-systems, indicated by zones that load highly on only one of the factors. The varimax rotation of the leading components has therefore resolved a simple structure, picking out two distinctive hyperplanes or groupings of variables. With non-independent systems, however, an oblique rotation might have achieved a better factor resolution, but the requirements of the grouping techniques applied later in the paper preclude this.[23]

The third sub-system focuses on the "mid-town" part of the Central Area and includes Soho, Covent Garden and the Strand (Figure 5). It accounts for a further 10 per cent of the variance. The core zones correspond to London's entertainment centre, including "clubland," St. James's and Leicester Square. High Holborn, the eastern end of Oxford Street and Fleet Street are peripheral destinations.

Factor four distinguishes a quite separate sub-system in the eastern part of the City that accounts for a further 9 per cent of variance (Figure 6). It is the only sub-system that could be easily isolated from the map of flows. There is little overlap with the other systems, apart from a weak link between the City and Mayfair.

Factor five (Figure 7), with 8 per cent of the variance, has been termed a

23. Oblique factors in geographical problems are discussed in J. Imbrie, "Factor and vector analysis programs for analysing geological data," *Office of Naval Research, Tech. Rep.* 6 (1963), Task No. 389–135, Contract 1228(26)

(Northwestern University, Ill.). The orthogonality requirement is discussed in E. Casetti, "Classificatory and regional analysis by discriminant iterations," *Office of Naval Research, Tech. Rep.* 12 (1963).

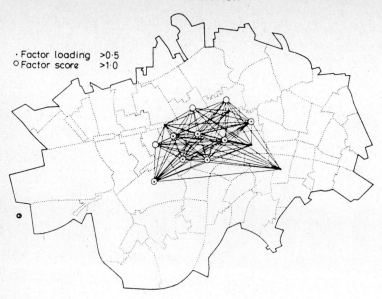

Figure 5. Factor Three: Covent Garden, Soho and Fleet Street

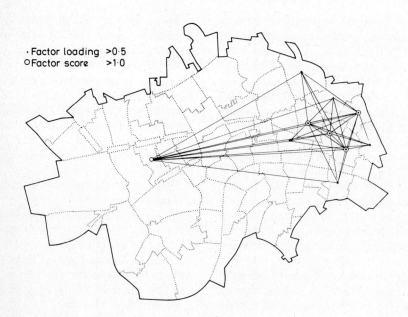

Figure 6. Factor Four: The City

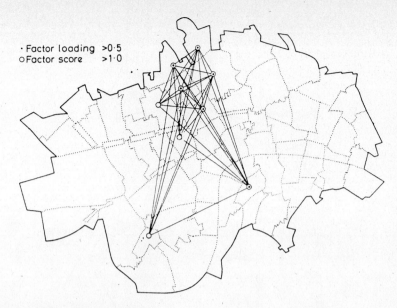

Figure 7. Factor Five: Bloomsbury

Bloomsbury system. The pattern is similar to that of the Westminster system (factor two) in that it includes a number of main-line termini as an integral part. These are Waterloo, Victoria, Euston, and King's Cross/St. Pancras. Again this area has a unique combination of activities. Besides the University, Bloomsbury has a large number of trade union offices whose London location is partly a reflection of their need for easy access from the rest of the country.

Factor six has a complex structure and has not been mapped. Experience has shown that it is necessary to rotate one more than the number of common factors identified by examination of the eigenvalues in order to obtain a meaningful composition in the last factor and this has not been done.

When combined, the various sub-systems represent a functional regionalization of Central London on the basis of a single measure of internal linkage. However, amalgamating all the maps would fail to satisfy the basic criterion of any regionalization or classification scheme, namely that each observation should fall into a separate group. This is because several zones belong to more than one sub-system. Furthermore, a certain degree of subjectivity has been introduced into the maps by specifying arbitrary limits for factor scores and loadings.

To obtain a more objective regionalization in which zones fall into discrete classes, grouping techniques may be applied to the similarities between zones according to their scores on the six factors; zones have therefore been combined on the basis of similarities in the way they distribute their taxi trips to give a regionalization with a specifiable level of efficiency.

Conclusion and Postscript (1974)

Subsequent research has revealed that the functional areas highlighted by this analysis of one type of physical movement do indeed correspond closely to various em-

TELEPHONE CONTACTS
SALIENT TRANSACTIONS

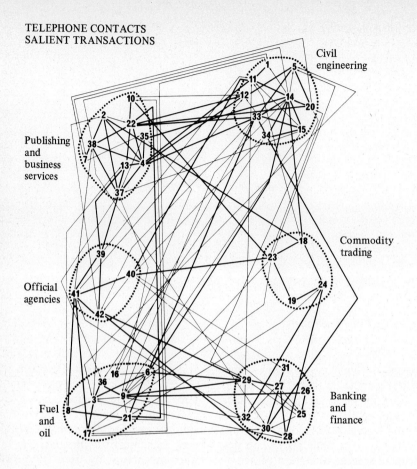

Key:

1. Primary industry
2. Food, drink and tobacco
3. Fuel and oil
4. Chemicals
5. Metals and metal goods
6. Mechanical engineering and machinery
7. Precision engineering
8. Electrical engineering
9. Transport equipment
10. Textiles, leather and clothing
11. Bricks, pottery, glass and cement
12. Other manufacturing
13. Paper, printing and publishing
14. General construction
15. Specialist contracting
16. Gas, electricity and water
17. Transport and communications
18. Transport services
19. Food wholesaling
20. Other specialist wholesaling
21. General wholesale merchants

22. Retailing
23. Export and import merchants
24. Commodity brokers
25. Insurance companies
26. Other insurance
27. Banking
28. Stockbroking and jobbing
29. Other finance
30. Property
31. Accounting
32. Legal services
33. Consulting engineers
34. Architects
35. Other specialist consultancy
36. Non-profit services
37. Advertising and public relations
38. Miscellaneous business services
39. Broadcasting
40. Public authorities
41. Central government
42. Local government

ployment areas in Central London which contain sets of spatially and functionally linked office activities.[24] The analysis of spatial linkages used a matrix of office employment categories measured over the same set of traffic zones; the analysis of functional linkages was based upon a matrix in which the entries represented not physical movements between geographical areas, but numbers of telephone and meeting contacts linking different office employment sectors. These data were derived from a diary survey of the external contacts of a sample of offices in different sectors. Correlation analysis of the employment data matrix indicated office activities with similar patterns of locational association within Central London while correlating the columns of the inter-sectoral contact flow matrix highlighted pairs of sectors linked by information flows to a similar set of other office activities. Components analysis followed by varimax rotation of the spatial structure matrix revealed sets of spatially linked sectors; the same analysis of the contact flow matrix revealed sets of functionally linked sectors.

Table 2 describes the groups of spatially linked employment categories in

24. J. B. Goddard (1973) *Office Linkages and Location: a study of communications and spatial patterns in Central London* Pergamon, Oxford.

terms of the loadings on five rotated components which together account for 51% of the variation in the distribution of office employment in Central London. Table 3 describes six sets of office sectors with similar patterns of functional linkage by way of telephone contacts; the groupings are identified by six rotated components which together account for 62% of the variation in the pattern of inter-sectoral contact flows. (The telephone and meeting contact networks are broadly similar, but as the telephone data contains more observations it gives a more complete definition of the contact network and is therefore used in preference to the meeting data.)

Comparison of Tables 2 and 3 suggests that many activities that have strong functional associations tend to locate in similar parts of Central London. Functional clusters composed of banking and finance, trading, civil engineering and publishing all have spatial equivalents. For example, component one derived from the analysis of the telephone contact data can be described as a civil engineering group, including architects, consulting engineers and brick and cement manufacturers. The group focuses on general construction companies as the activity generating most of the contacts in this sphere of business. It is well known that many aspects of a civil engineering project are sub-con-

---

Figure 8. Telephone Contacts: Salient Transactions. **Key:** 1, Primary industry. 2, Food, drink and tobacco. 3, Fuel and oil. 4, Chemicals. 5, Metals and metal goods. 6, Mechanical engineering and machinery. 7, Precision engineering. 8, Electrical engineering. 9, Transport equipment. 10, Textiles, leather and clothing. 11, Bricks, pottery, glass and cement. 12, Other manufacturing. 13, Paper, printing and publishing. 14, General construction. 15, Specialist contracting. 16, Gas, electricity and water. 17, Transport and communications. 18, Transport services. 19, Food wholesaling. 20, Other specialist wholesaling. 21, General wholesale merchants. 22, Retailing. 23, Export and import merchants. 24, Commodity brokers. 25, Insurance companies. 26, Other insurance. 27, Banking. 28, Stockbroking and jobbing. 29, Other finance. 30, Property. 31, Accounting. 32, Legal services. 33, Consulting engineers. 34, Architects. 35, Other specialist consultancy. 36, Non-profit services. 37, Advertising and public relations. 38, Miscellaneous business services. 39, Broadcasting. 40, Public authorities. 41, Central government. 42, Local government

Table 2. Factor Analysis of Three Digit Employment Categories (by traffic zone)

Factor One: Trading

Agriculture, forestry and fishing	—0.831
Food	—0.689
Transport	—0.667
Postal services and telecommunications	—0.920
Transport services	—0.932
Food wholesaling	—0.744
General wholesale merchants	—0.829
Export and import merchants	—0.666
Commodity brokers, merchants and dealers	—0.937
Other insurance	—0.938
(Explained variance = 18.54%)	

Factor Two: Clothing and Business Services

Vehicles	—0.573
Textiles	—0.689
Leather, leather goods and fur	—0.578
Clothing and footwear	—0.664
Miscellaneous manufacturing industries	—0.533
Clothing and footwear wholesaling	—0.737
Drugs, chemicals and other non-food goods wholesaling	—0.746
Property	—0.529
Management, production, marketing and costing consultants	—0.788
Advertising and public relations	—0.594
Drawing and photographic services	—0.571
(Explained variance = 12.72%)	

Factor Three: Civil Engineering

Bricks, pottery, glass, cement	—0.757
General construction and contracting	—0.600
Specialist contracting	—0.537
Consulting engineers	—0.781
Architects	—0.525
Other specialist consultants	—0.649
Employers' and trade associations	—0.824
Professional membership organisations	—0.593
Charitable organisations	—0.739
(Explained variance = 7.45%)	

Factor Four: Banking and Finance

Insurance companies	0.806
Central banking	0.855
Other banking	0.867
Stock brokering and jobbing	0.888
Other finance	0.755
Accounting, auditing and bookkeeping	0.943
Legal services	0.599
Office services	0.633
Head offices of offices operating abroad	0.601
(Explained variance = 6.84%)	

Factor Five: Publishing

Printing and publishing	—0.725
Paper, stationery and books wholesaling	—0.618
Drawing and photographic services	—0.508
(Explained variance = 5.27%)	

Table 3. Factor Analysis of Inter-sectoral Telephone Contacts[a]

Factor One: Civil Engineering

Chosen Sector	FL	Choosing Sector	FS
Architects	0.868	General construction	5.103
General construction	0.844	Consulting engineers	1.463
Consulting engineers	0.833	Bricks, pottery, glass and	
Specialist construction	0.763	cement	1.309
Metals and metal goods	0.689		
Primary industry	0.673		
Bricks, pottery, glass and cement	0.662		

(Explained variance = 12.54%)

Factor Two: Fuel and Oil

Chosen Sector	FL	Choosing Sector	FS
Fuel and oil	—0.904	Fuel and oil	—5.858
Non-profit services	—0.904		
Transport and communications	—0.876		

Table 3. (*Continued*)

Mechanical engineering and machinery	—0.797		
Central and local government	—0.648		
Office services	—0.516		

(Explained variance = 12.25%)

Factor Three: Banking and Finance

Chosen Sector	FL	Choosing Sector	FS
Stockbrokering	—0.885	Banking	—3.876
Property	—0.870	Property	—4.300
Banking	—0.862		
Legal services	—0.848		
Other finance	—0.658		
Accounting	—0.524		

(Explained variance = 10.95%)

Factor Four: Publishing and Business Services

Chosen Sector	FL	Choosing Sector	FS
Chemicals and pharmaceuticals	0.881	Chemicals and pharmaceuticals	4.518
Retailing	0.859	Advertising and public relations	2.696
Food, drink and tobacco	0.805	Paper, printing and publishing	2.100
Other special services	0.747		
Paper, printing and publishing	0.716		
Advertising and public relations	0.691		

(Explained variance = 10.56%)

Factor Five: Official Agencies

Chosen Sector	FL	Choosing Sector	FS
Electrical engineering	—0.906	Entertainment	—5.454
Entertainment	—0.901	Paper, printing and publishing	—1.663
Societies and Associations	—0.711		
Miscellaneous business services	—0.675	Miscellaneous business services	—1.191

(Explained variance = 9.05%)

Factor Six: Commodity Trading

Chosen Sector	FL	Choosing Sector	FS
Food wholesaling	—0.790	Export and import merchants	—4.980
Textiles, leather, and clothing	—0.772	Property	—1.438
Export and import merchants	—0.609	Commodity brokers	—1.426
Transport services	—0.600	Food wholesaling	—1.181
		Retailing	—1.064

(Explained variance = 6.70%. Total explained variance = 62.05%)

[a] FL = factor loading. FS = factor scores.
Note: Only factor loadings greater than ± 0.50 and factor scores greater than ± 1.00 are shown.

tracted out to different types of firms; inevitably this procedure will lead to a substantial volume of contact between the various contractors. This in turn encourages the linked firms to locate in close proximity within the city centre: this is reflected in the fact that many of these types of employment load high on spatial component four.

However, it will be noted that some spatial associations have no functional equivalent and vice versa. In part this discrepancy stems from data and analytic problems. For example, some sectors were over represented in the contact data and others under represented while the level of sectoral disaggregation is different. Nevertheless, the difference also reflects the very real fact that spatial association is *not* a necessary condition for functional linkage. This is perhaps increasingly the case as the physical constraints on contact are reduced through developments in communication technology. Many activities associated with traditional spatial complexes like civil engineering, banking and publishing are moving from these areas both to other locations within Central London and to places outside Central London altogether.[25] This is partly because the functional linkages that bind the activities into the complexes are maintained by a network of very routine contacts that can be satisfactorily performed by telecommunications over some distance.

Having said this the continuing interconnection between functional linkages, location and movement patterns within the city centre cannot be denied. This is principally because most business contacts are with nearby locations within Central London with the taxi being the most important mode of travel after walking.

25. See Goddard (1967) and Goddard and Morris (1974) *The Communications Factor in Office Decentralization* Location of Offices Bureau, London.

Thirty-eight per cent of all business contacts involving travelling to a meeting (including those outside Central London) require journeys of less than 10 minutes and 78% less than half an hour. Thirty-three per cent of these journeys are made on foot and 24% by taxi. So comparing the areas where the groups of spatially and functionally linked activities are located and the movement regions identified through the analysis of taxi flows (Figures 3–7) suggests that areas of functional specialization are sustained by strong patterns of internal circulation. Two employment clusters (trading and banking) are associated with the movement regions of the City. Civil engineering is associated with the Westminster movement subsystem, publishing with the Soho, Covent Garden, Fleet Street sub-system and business services with the West End subsystem.

However, the isomorphism between movement sub-systems and employment clusters is not perfect. Again this is partly due to data problems: the taxi movements include all trips not just those on business purposes. But it also reflects the fact that all contacts are not confined to a particular sub-system, be it spatial or functional. This again is clear from Figure 8 which displays the pattern of intra and intergroup functional linkages. In this diagram each sector is assigned to the functional group identified through the components analysis of telephone contacts. A heavy line indicates that both of the linked office sectors direct 50% more telephone contacts to each other than would be expected given their respective shares of all recorded contacts. A lighter line indicates a one-way relationship in the direction of the arrow. While there are indeed strong links binding offices into discernible business clusters, 46% of all telephone contacts are nevertheless between the clusters.

To conclude, this analysis has revealed that the centre of a large metropolitan city consists of a series of over-lapping spatial sub-systems that can be defined in terms of both movement and location patterns. Underpinning this interdependence between movement and spatial structure is a complex network of functional connections between central area business activities.

ROBERT L. KNIGHT AND LISA L. TRYGG

Evidence of Land Use Impacts of Rapid Transit Systems

In recent years studies have been conducted in a number of metropolitan areas in the United States to assess the feasibility of various public transit alternatives. More such studies can be expected in the future, partly because of continuing public concern over some of the externalized costs of automobile use such as energy waste and environmental degradation. Not unexpectedly, one result is that requests for capital grants to construct transit facilities already far exceed the available Federal funds. Particularly in such a competitive grant market, the heavy initial costs of proposed new transit systems must be offset by demonstration of massive public benefits.

In their search for evidence of such benefits, many of the local agencies involved in these studies have attempted to include consideration of land use impacts. The usual premise is that a new rapid transit system will stimulate, revitalize, order, compact and/or create infrastructure economies in urban development in contrast to what would have occurred without such a system. This is plausible and even appealing in some ways. However, a review of these studies shows that there are many more intriguing questions than convincing answers regarding the impact of transit on land use (Frye, 1971; Marcou and O'Leary, 1971; Libicki, 1975). Some of these include the following:

Will a transit system promote attraction of wealth or population from other regions?

Do different transit technologies (such as conventional rail, light rail, PRT, express bus) have different land use impacts?

What different physical and policy settings have significant bearing on these impacts?

Can a region's development be focused or its average density increased by transit?

Will declining CBD's be strengthened, or will suburbanization be speeded by a new transit system?

How quickly will any such impacts appear?

Unfortunately, most of these questions cannot be answered satisfactorily at present. In most cases the needed empirical research has not been done, often because

From **Transportation,** Vol. 6, 1977, pp. 231–47. Reprinted by permission of Elsevier Scientific Publishing Company, Amsterdam, Robert L. Knight, and Lisa L. Trygg.

methodologies or data for identifying such impacts are not available. Hopefully some current research, such as that of the Federal Department of Transportation's studies of the impacts of the Bay Area Rapid Transit (BART) system opened in 1972 in San Francisco and of empirical evidence of transit's land use impacts nationwide, will advance our understanding of these issues. However, in the interim there is a substantial need for a concise summary of available information to guide efforts in the transit feasibility studies now or soon to be in progress. This report seeks to provide such a summary.

Approach

From the outset our investigation was guided by an implicit, emerging theory. The conventional model is one of land use succession driven primarily by changes in access, in turn wrought by transportation improvements and only marginally influenced by other factors (usually modeled as "attractiveness" and "developable land area"). However, from experience in urban transit alternatives analyses we knew that modern urban transit systems rarely, if ever, provide a major effective increase in accessibility, because the areas served tend to be already more accessible by auto. Therefore, the conventional model seemed much less appropriate today than it was in earlier generations when transit and later highway innovations generated almost revolutionary increases in accessibility, overwhelming the influence of most other factors.

We felt, then, that the achievement of major land use "impacts" around transit stations today must require the concerted action of other powerful forces in addition to transit-induced accessibility increases. This led to a more general view of the land development process as one driven by a complex of forces each adding to or detracting from a site's development potential and timing. Some of these might be essential, but others were expected to be substitutable. In different situations, different factors might be dominant, and several might sometimes be much more critical than even the access afforded by transit. If true, this implies a need for a substantial broadening of the range of concerns which must be encompassed in the planning of transit systems.

Findings

Will a transit system promote interregional attraction of investment or population?

Here the oft-stated thesis is that a modern rapid transit system may increase the attractiveness of one region over others to such an extent that a healthy rate of local private investment and a steady supply of qualified labor can be more easily maintained. In certain economically declining cities in the northeastern United States, for example, this may be a major hope.

The only formal study found to address this issue was the BART Impact Program's analysis of that system's impacts on the regional economy (MacDonald and Grefe, 1976). No such interregional-transfer impacts were found by that study, despite its detailed reviews of the region's economic activity trends by sector and even including the effects of BART construction activity and the sale of BART bonds.

Some published material has asserted major increases in a city's assessed property valuation due to introduction of a transit system. In Toronto, for example, one observer has argued that of a $15 billion total increase over the ten-year period following construction of the rail transit system's first segment, $10 billion was directly attributable to the transit system and hence in effect paid for the system many times over (Heenan, 1968). However, this conclusion was based only on a simple comparison of the rates of tax assessment increases downtown near the transit system with those in the rest of the metropolitan area. No consideration was given to the effects of any other factors which encouraged downtown office development in Toronto, nor were any comparisons made with other Canadian cities. Many policymakers have been misled by this widely-publicized overstatement. Kovach (1974) did compare Toronto's growth with that of other Canadian cities. Her study revealed that while Toronto had a very large population growth during the 1960s, other large Canadian cities with no plans for transit systems exhibited similar or even larger growth rates.

Do different transit technologies have different land use impacts?

Since a common objective in transit feasibility studies is the identification of some optimal system, it would be useful to be able to differentiate among competing technologies such as rapid rail, light rail and express bus by their land use impacts. However, in this review no studies of land use impacts of urban transit technologies other than conventional rapid rail have yet been found. This is largely because there has been almost no use of technologies other than conventional rail and express bus in modern North American systems. Even express bus systems are typically limited in scale, and no case studies of the impacts of such bus transit systems have come to our attention.

Clearly more knowledge is needed, especially in view of the federal DOT trend toward emphasis on less capital-intensive transit solutions such as express buses. However, given the lack of effective research on this topic, the remainder of this paper must be limited to impacts of conventional rail rapid transit systems. Users of this information must be careful in attempting to apply it to any comparison of transit technologies, since there is no documented evidence to guide such ap-

plications. Surely other modes, particularly modern light rail, have similar if lesser potential effects; however, in the absence of empirical evidence, assessments of such effects must remain intuitive.

What different physical and policy settings have significant bearing on these impacts?

Given a conventional rail technology, what seem to be its land use impacts under various circumstances? Stated another way, where will a rapid transit system be most likely to generate such impacts? A scattered and uneven but substantial body of literature on this topic was found. Our observations and review of this literature suggested that several characteristics of the area served are significant in determining land use impact. A convenient grouping of the available evidence into factors influencing impact is the following: (1) local government land use policies; (2) regional development trends and forces; (3) availability of developable land; and (4) physical characteristics of the area.

LOCAL GOVERNMENT POLICIES

The issue here is whether local governmental bodies, through their land use policies, can or do exert a significant influence on the generation of land use impacts by transit. In Toronto, most observers agree that the rapid transit system appears to have significantly shaped and intensified development, particularly along the Yonge Street corridor (Heenan, 1968; Marcou and O'Leary, 1971; Kovach, 1974). However, the transit system alone did not cause these impacts. Introduction of the rapid transit system was soon followed by several pro-development public policies. These include: (1) aggressive marketing of air rights and available excess land parcels by the transit commission; (2) allowance of liberal floor area ratios (in some cases increased from 3 : 1 to 12 : 1) and density bonuses by the city in certain locations, especially around stations; (3) encouragement of coordinated station design efforts with developers desiring direct access from office, retail or apartment buildings; and (4) city zoning classification changes in certain districts, notably near metropolitan area transit stations, to permit much higher intensity development (City of Toronto, 1963, 1971). Toronto planners and developers interviewed in our check of these results agreed that these incentives were essential in inducing the extent and type of development which occurred.

Two other more general policy factors were also important in Toronto. One is the Canadian government's policy on income tax benefits of home ownership. In contrast to the United States, the Canadian homebuyer receives no special income deduction for mortgage interest, so this important encouragement to suburban living is absent. As a result, the postwar American exodus from urban apartments to suburban houses was never paralleled in intensity in the major Canadian cities, including Toronto. The second factor is in the Toronto governmental structure, which in 1954 was changed to a two-tiered regional form with a metropolitan authority responsible for regional functions and five municipal subunits (the City of Toronto plus four boroughs) to deal with primarily local concerns. Although the member municipalities retain zoning powers, Metro still exerts substantial influence on land development through its authority over regional transportation and the coordination of land uses among the boroughs. Such an empowered regional perspective is approached only in a few American cities, notably Nashville and Miami.

In addition, other observers (National League of Cities et al., 1973) note that the Toronto city government was actively involved in developing basic overall plans for the Eglinton Station, which later turned out to be the focus of one of the most heavily developed areas along the line. As an added boost, the city government constructed the first building in the complex near the Eglinton Station. Essentially, then, the local government, while encouraging intensive development, at the same time successfully attempted to direct and control it where it was most favorable.

The San Francisco BART experience is less dramatic but still somewhat similar to that of Toronto. For instance, density bonuses have been permitted for buildings providing direct access to downtown San Francisco BART stations. Smaller bonuses have been allowed for nearby development, based on proximity to stations up to a distance of 750 feet (Libicki, 1975). Development has been very heavy in this downtown area, with BART consistently acknowledged as one of the key forces involved (Lee and Wiech, 1972). However, as in Toronto, many other forces also acted to encourage and concentrate Bay Area office development in this location. Moreover, there is little evidence of any substantial land use impacts outside the CBD station areas (Gruen, 1977; Lee, 1973; Wells, 1973).

The observations of Boyce and his associates (Boyce et al., 1972) on the character of development along the Lindenwold rapid transit line in Philadelphia (opened in 1969) also illustrate the potential impact of specific local government policies. Two towns along the suburban line, Lindenwold and Voorhees, appear to have experienced different development patterns between 1960 and 1970 due to such policies. Boyce noted that while Lindenwold promoted multi-family development, Voorhees discouraged such development by not approving apartment projects and instead supporting single-family construction. This was further evidenced by the fact that developer willingness and available land were present in Voorhees but did not result in significant amounts of multi-family construction. Specifically, during the 1960's, Lindenwold doubled its housing stock, with apartments accounting for over 80 percent of the new construction. Voorhees, in contrast, saw a smaller increase (60 percent) in new housing with over 80 percent of the new construction in the form of single-family homes. Several other suburban Philadelphia communities not in the Lindenwold corridor matched or exceeded this level of growth.

This trend has only recently been changed when Voorhees Township approved construction of a regional shopping center which includes provisions for 3,700 apartments and town houses. Boyce reported that the project was approved and located there mainly because it was the only suitable place with a large amount of available land. This, only the second large-scale development project in Voorhees since 1960, was then scheduled for completion in 1975, six years after the opening of the Lindenwold Line.

In Washington, D.C. a study by the National League of Cities (1973) reported that station area development along the METRO transit system in that city has been influenced by government involvement. One example involves the Gallery station at 12th and "G" Streets in downtown Washington, D.C., which presently is not a highly desirable area in terms of character and development. Public capital was to be used to construct the city's nearby Convention Center, and consequently greatly enhance this presently declining area.

In contrast, a study by Marcou, O'Leary and associates (1971) concludes that the transit lines and extensions in Cleveland and Chicago provide very little evidence of transit-related development, partly due to the lack of demand in general but also because of the absence of pro-development public policies and incentives. The potential role of such policies and incentives was recognized later in Cleveland when air rights were leased above the station parking lot at the eastern terminal point of the transit system. However, the developer was never able to secure financing and nothing has been built. Similarly, air rights granted at sites along the seven-year-old airport extension have also spurred developer interest but no development has yet occurred, due largely to zoning delays.

The above evidence suggests that local government policies are important factors affecting development, with transit being an important but *not* sufficient condition for such development. For instance, policies such as allowance of liberal floor area ratios, density bonuses at designated locations, changes in zoning plans, marketing of air rights, sale of excess land parcels, and urban renewal—all implemented at strategic locations near a transit station or along the corridor—may have a very significant impact on development. Not only can intensive development be encouraged (or discouraged as has been the case with Chicago and Cleveland) through the use or lack of effective public policies, but there is strong evidence from these studies that it can be controlled to a significant extent both in terms of where it will occur and what type will occur. Thus the transit system can become the focus or catalyst around which the suggested policies are implemented, which in turn affect development in the area.

DEVELOPMENT TRENDS AND FORCES

Among North American examples, Toronto seems to have experienced the most spectacular rate of growth and development in parallel with construction of a major transit system during the post-World War II era. As noted in an earlier section, it seems unlikely that this regional growth is due to the transit system. However, the presence of such growth appears to have been a major force behind the development which subsequently occurred around the transit system.

Part of the high rate of economic growth which took place in Toronto during the transit system's early years may be attributable to a coincidental easing of credit and new availability of development capital. This resulted in freeing a large amount of pent-up demand for offices and apartments in the late 1950s. With this demand, capital, and the zoning incentives already noted, station areas on the Yonge Street Line became competitively attractive for investment with more expensive downtown sites. This explanation seems to be supported by the lack of an equal amount of construction associated with opening the Bloor-Danforth Line, the second phase of the subway system; once the supply and demand for offices and apartments achieved equilibrium and many more station areas were put on the market, the monopolistic position experienced by earlier station areas was destroyed and a much smaller scale of focused development took place.

Downtown San Francisco was experiencing an increasing amount of construction activity even before bonds were approved for financial backing of the BART transit system. Also, like Toronto, San Francisco has been considered as a regional financial and business capital. It has long been thought of as an attractive place to live and thus has experienced significant growth right up until as well as after BART. Thus, attempts to isolate BART's impacts from those due to the construction boom period have been difficult. Given the city's favorable attributes, much of the rapid rate of investment and construction in the downtown area, especially during the system's earlier planning and construction period, may be due to conditions completely independent from the presence of BART. For example, Lee and Wiech (1972) have estimated that much if not most of this new downtown development may be due to conditions completely independent from the presence of BART.

Downtown Philadelphia, in association with the Lindenwold Line, has not experienced the same development as downtown Toronto and San Francisco. It did not see a large amount of new office and business development after construction of the Lindenwold transit system. Looking at economic conditions of the city at this time, 1969 to 1971, Gannon and Dear (1972) noted that the general trend was not favorable (unlike Toronto and San Francisco) during the construction period of the transit system. Their data show that the City of Philadelphia experienced a decline in population between 1960 and 1970, and only a relatively small expansion in total employment. It appears, then, that the single Lindenwold Line was too small to have a substantial effect on the Philadelphia CBD.

Camden, just across the river from downtown Philadelphia and the first suburban stop on the Lindenwold Line, is an example of a declining older subcenter apparently not aided by the transit system. Gannon and Dear report that, if anything, the transit system initially triggered a spatial displacement of activity out of Camden rather than the generation of new activity there. Although evidence for such a conclusion was thin (a small survey of some 20 firms which relocated to Haddonfield), it is nonetheless clear from observation that Camden is not experiencing any significant redevelopment due to the transit line. Thus the Line may have been a factor in speeding the decline of Camden's aging CBD, and certainly contributed little or nothing to its revival.

In Toronto the trend toward middle-class suburbanization and resultant decline of central areas has never been so pronounced as in major cities of the United States. A strong middle-class element has tended to remain in the city's older, inner areas. This may have been reinforced by the provision of a modern downtown-oriented short-line transit system before expressways were built; the very heavy postwar immigration of Europeans accustomed to urban apartment life certainly aided as well. Finally, there is no significant racial problem in Toronto; there has been no discriminatory treatment of any racial group. This may contribute to the fact that crime is generally low and both urban and suburban areas are considered safe places to live.

When the general character of the area is favorable toward development, as in downtown San Francisco or Toronto, transit may further enhance such development. That is, transit-related growth seems more likely to occur in areas already ripe for development near a newly constructed transit station where some activity would probably have taken place even if the transit system had not been built. This suggests that the transit system can enhance and speed the already existing development process. Conversely, this conclusion also suggests that an area possessing deteriorating attributes, such as the City of Camden, may have that trend further accelerated rather than reversed by the introduction of transit. As a result, redevelopment may occur sooner in such areas than would otherwise be the case, but the transition from decline to renewal may be socially disruptive.

AVAILABILITY OF DEVELOPABLE LAND

Market forces—primarily the availability of land for development—may significantly affect the location and degree of development above and beyond other influences such as those already discussed. Land may become available through several means, some of which do not necessarily depend on the introduction of a transit system. These include new access to existing vacant or unused space, redevelopment of

occupied space to more intensive uses, and assemblage of privately-owned parcels to form a space large enough to accommodate significant development. In Toronto a significant amount of development has been attributed to introduction of the transit system. However, it has been pointed out that such development, particularly the apartment boom, was delayed in starting because of the scarcity of available land to build on. Over a period of time enough demand pressures were generated (perhaps by the transit system) to cause an increase in land value to a point where a change in land use intensity (acquisition and clearance of existing properties) proved to be economically justified. The point is that significant development was restrained until usable land was somehow made available (Wacher, 1970; Anderson et al., 1971).

Some studies have been made of impacts near specific BART stations. Lee reported, for example, that in downtown Hayward the anticipation and arrival of BART in the area had not (in 1972–3) appeared to have a significant impact on commercial property values within a half-mile of the BART station. Other market forces have acted to direct new commercial facilities to the newer outlying areas where inexpensive vacant land is much more available.

Wells (1973) argued that in the City of Fremont, which is BART's south-eastern terminus some 25 miles from the San Francisco CBD, availability of land seemed to have a potentially significant role in development associated with BART. It is one of the few areas along the system with large amounts of vacant land available for immediate use. However, development near this BART station has been occurring at a slow pace relative to that of Fremont as a whole. This suggests that mere accessibility and land availability are not enough.

Boyce (1972) points out that the

Township of Voorhees, which is on the Lindenwold Line, had no central business and residential area of consequence until the Echelon Mall was built one year after the opening of the line. The Mall, a large regional shopping center combined with a major apartment and townhouse development, has become a highly successful community center. The developer, in selecting a site for the Echelon Mall, needed to find a large parcel of available land (in this case an area which was previously a general aviation airport) and a location not near any existing regional center. The Voorhees site was virtually unique in meeting these basic requirements, neither of which had anything to do with transit. Thus, while the Lindenwold Line could be viewed as a positive factor in bringing customers to the area, it could not be considered as one of the most important determinants in the creation of the Mall.

In Toronto, at the intersection of Bloor and Yonge Streets where the two transit lines cross, no new development has yet occurred on two of the four abutting blocks, some 23 years after the first line segment opened. Private realty spokesmen attributed this to the difficulty and risk of land assembly, since many small parcel owners were involved. The two corners which have been developed into high-rise office buildings and department stores each involved assembly of five or fewer parcels; the other two (undeveloped) corners involved nearly 25 parcels each. Under such conditions development is likely to be delayed indefinitely.

PHYSICAL CHARACTERISTICS
OF THE AREA

The newer extensions of the Chicago rapid transit system are located in rights-of-way of the Dan Ryan, Eisenhower, Congress and Kennedy expressways. Thus, access to the surrounding developed area is difficult. In addition, these areas are themselves completely built up,

and many are not attractive locations for intensive new development. Such area characteristics have apparently made it difficult to encourage any substantial new growth (Department of Public Works, 1967; Marcou and O'Leary, 1971).

The first portion of the Cleveland transit system, which was opened in 1955, was built on an existing rail right-of-way. In one study it was pointed out that the line runs primarily through established or declining industrial areas (Marcou and O'Leary, 1971). Our own observations support this view. In addition, the line is removed from the direction of new downtown development. Such major constraints imposed by the surrounding area may have essentially neutralized any impetus for significant development generated from the transit system. Significant development interest did not come until the opening of the airport extension in 1968, which provided for an increased scope of service throughout the metropolitan area. This extension also introduced several new stations with transit system-owned parking lots potentially compatible with air rights development. However, only limited interest has been shown in the air rights and virtually no nearby development has occurred.

The experience of the Lindenwold Line in Philadelphia seems to support one of the conclusions reached by Spengler (1930) in his early study of New York's transit system: "It appears that a subway reflects the conditions of the section through which it passes, in any influences which it might exert upon land values." Along the Lindenwold Line, office development at the Haddonfield station has been associated with introduction of the transit system. But while the transit line may have served as an impetus for office development here, the Haddonfield Borough itself has been characterized by Gannon and Dear (1972) as a highly desirable location, irrespective of the presence of the transit system.

Can a region's development be focused or its density increased by transit? Can transit strengthen the CBD, or will it speed suburbanization?

It is often alleged or hoped that construction of a rapid transit system will promote orderly growth focused on its stations, in contrast to a previous pattern of urban sprawl or low density suburbanization. Such an effect is at least plausible both at a corridor level and on a smaller scale very near stations. The current interest in "activity centers" gives added impetus to this hope.

References cited earlier in this study support the view that some focusing of a region's development around rapid transit stations can be achieved, although favorable conditions of public policy, regional development trends, land availability and physical constraints seem to be essential. Most of such localized development impacts to date appear to have occurred around downtown stations, especially in Toronto and San Francisco. In Cleveland, conversely, CBD impacts appear to have been minimal due at least in part to lack of the favorable conditions just noted.

We found little documentation of the geographical extent of transit-related impacts. Gannon and Dear (1975) suggest from their Lindenwold study that most new transit-related office development occurs very close to a station. They noted that nearly all the new development in Haddonfield had taken place within a 5-minute walk (about 1,000 feet) of the station. The Marcou, O'Leary study (1971), which included some site visits and interviews as well as literature review, yielded an estimate of 1,200 to 1,800 feet from a station as the radius of the likely impact area. They cited planners' opinions and supporting incentive ordinances ranging from 500 feet (Washington) to 2,500 feet (London) in support of this contention. Some of this reasoning here may be somewhat circular, since such incentives would tend to create the impact area rather than respond to it.

Evidence on the occurrence of broader corridor-level development impacts includes several statistical studies. The continuing Lindenwold residential property value investigation, begun by Boyce and continued by a succession of his students, is the main source of information on this topic. Boyce's study yielded the conclusion that the transit line had tended to enhance property values, though only slightly, in its market area in contrast with values elsewhere in suburban Philadelphia. This finding was later supported in related but separate studies by Platt (1972), Mudge (1974), Slater (1974), Yang (1975) and Tang (1976). These later studies have tended to indicate a larger but still not massive impact on values.

Minimal evidence was found either to support or reject the hypothesis of reduced suburbanization (i.e., increased overall density) or its converse (more sprawl in transit corridors) due to transit. Gannon and Dear (1975) suggested that in the case of office development, transit may simultaneously strengthen the CBD and promote location of offices along the lines, apparently at the expense of other suburban locations. However, with systems which extend far into surrounding areas, such as Philadelphia's Lindenwold and San Francisco's Concord, the contention of increased residential as well as commercial suburbanization due to transit service merits further study. The BART Impact Program may provide some initial insights on this issue, although its early findings indicate that no such shaping of suburban development has yet occurred attributable to BART.

Conclusions

This review of available literature yields conclusions both with respect to future research directions and for application in current transit feasibility studies.

Interregional effects: There is no evidence that a new transit system will increase the overall level of development of a metropolitan area.

Transit technology: Only conventional rail transit appears in the literature. Study of differential land use impacts of competing technologies, especially light rail and advanced express bus systems, are difficult but need to be done in order to allow balanced evaluation of transit alternatives.

Influence of surroundings. Most of the available studies of transit impact dealt with this issue. Four general factors were identified as important determinants of the degree of land use impact of a new transit system:

1. Local government policies encouraging development
2. Regional development trends
3. Availability of developable land
4. Physical constraints of the site

For substantial land use impact to occur, it appears that nearly all of these factors must be favorable. For evaluation of impact potential for specific locations, then, these factors might be useful as the basis for composite rating of each site or corridor.

Focusing of development. Some concentration of development around transit stations can be achieved, given the conditions stated just above. This is most apparent in CBD locations, with little effect generally detected to date farther from downtown areas. Further study is needed, particularly on the growth-shifting effects from the central city and suburban areas not served by transit to suburban areas near the transit system.

Speed of impact. Most researchers have concluded that substantial land use impacts do not occur until several years after inauguration of transit service, although there is evidence of much earlier effects in the case of the Lindenwold Line. There is evidence that some commercial developers moved too quickly to build near suburban transit stations, with expected demand not materializing. However, timing of transit-related development may well be much more determined by the region's overall economic health and activity rather than by completion of the transit system itself.

These conclusions are only suggestive; much remains to be understood. It seems from the evidence available that rapid transit improvements can provide an impetus toward generation of new nearby development. However, transit alone seems no longer enough to insure such development, in this day of very high accessibility often only marginally improved by the transit system. If development is to be created, other factors such as those cited here must be effectively brought into play at the start of the transit planning process. This calls for a more coordinated land use/transit planning process than has often been evident in the past.

Unreasonable claims of transit's power to induce major land use change must be avoided. On the basis of the evidence reported here, claims of massive net increases in property value tax revenue because of a transit improvement seem hard to justify. The main effect, at best, seems to be a focusing of development rather than a net regional increase. It also seems the major potential of transit in encouraging development may be that of a catalyst in the local governmental process, providing the rationale needed to gain support for land development controls and incentives to focus growth. But these are still substantial benefits and an important role. Rapid transit will not automatically revitalize and reshape our cities, but it can do much—if we can learn to understand that role and the others which must accompany it.

References

Anderson, Warren *et al.* (1971), "The Impact of Rapid Transit on the Metro-Center," Baltimore: Department of Planning.

Boyce, David *et al.* (1972), "Impact of Rapid Transit on Suburban Residential Property Values and Land Development," for the U.S. Department of Transportation, Philadelphia: University of Pennsylvania.

City of Toronto Planning Board (1963), "Air Rights and Land Use Adjacent to the Bloor-Danforth Subway."

City of Toronto Planning Board (1971), "Report on a Proposal to Rezone Lands Along the East/West Route to Permit High Rise Apartments," (October 12).

Department of Public Works (1967), "Public/Private Development of Transit Stations," City of Chicago (December 14).

Frye, Frederick F. (1973), Alternative Multi-Modal Passenger Transportation Systems, NCHRP Report 146, Washington, D.C.: Highway Research Board.

Gannon, Colin A. and M. Dear (1972), "The Impact of Rail Rapid Transit Systems on Commercial Office Development: The Case of the Philadelphia-Lindenwold Speedline," for the U.S. Department of Transportation, Philadelphia: University of Pennsylvania.

Gannon, Colin A. and M. Dear (1975), "Rapid Transit and Office Development," *Traffic Quarterly* 29:2 (April), pp. 223–242.

Gruen Associates, Inc. (1977), "Indirect Environment Impacts," TM 24-4-77, BART Impact Program, Berkeley: Metropolitan Transportation Commission.

Heenan, G. Warren (1968), "The Economic Effect of Rapid Transit on Real Estate Development in Toronto," *The Appraisal Journal* (April), pp. 213–224.

Kovach, Carol (1974), "On Conducting an 'Impact' Study of a Rapid Transit Facility—The Case of Toronto," presented to Joint Transportation Engineering Meeting, Montreal, July 15–19; Meeting Preprint MTL–23.

Lee, Douglass B., Jr. (1973), "Impacts of BART on Prices of Single-Family Residences and Commercial Property," BART Impact Studies, Berkeley: Institute for Urban and Regional Development, University of California.

Lee, Douglass B. and D. F. Wiech (1972), "Market Street Study," BART Impact Studies, Berkeley: Institute of Urban and Regional Development, University of California.

Libicki, Martin C. (1975), "Land Use Impacts of Major Transit Improvements," Urban Analysis Program, Office of the Secretary of Transportation, Washington, D.C.

MacDonald, Angus N. and Grefe, Richard D. (1977), "Identification of Economic Sectors Influenced by Transportation Service," paper presented to Transportation Research Board, Annual Meeting, Washington, D.C. (January).

Marcou, O'Leary & Associates (1971), "Transit Impact on Land Development," Washington, D.C. (mimeographed).

Mudge, Richard R. (1974), *The Impact of Transportation Savings on Suburban Residential Property Values*, P-5259, New York City-Rand Institute.

National League of Cities, *et al.* (1973), "Transit Station Joint Development," prepared for USDOT and HUD, Washington, D.C.: U.S. Government Printing Office.

Platt, Jeffrey (1972), "Residential Property Value Gradients and Urban Transportation Impacts," Ph.D. dissertation, University of Pennsylvania.

Slater, Paul B. (1974), "Disaggregated Spatial—Temporal Analyses of Residential Sales Prices," *Journal of the American Statistical Association* 69:346 (June), pp. 358–363.

Spengler, E. H. (1930), "Land Values in New York in Relation to Transit Facilities," New York: Columbia University Press.

Tang, Foh-tsrang (1975), "Detection and Estimation of Transportation Impact with Models of Suburban Residential Property Sales Prices," Ph.D. dissertation, University of Pennsylvania.

Trygg, Lisa L. and Knight, Robert L. (1975), "Transit System Impacts on Urban Land Use," Denver: Regional Transportation District.

Urban Systems Research & Engineering, Inc. (1976), *The Growth Shapers: The Land Use Impacts of Infrastructure Investments,* prepared for the Council on Environmental Quality, Washington, D.C.: U.S. Government Printing Office.

Voorhees, Alan M. & Associates, Inc. (1974), *Baltimore Regional Environmental Impact Study,* for the Interstate Division for Baltimore City.

Wacher, T. R. (1970), "The Effects of Rapid Transit Systems on Urban Property Development," *Chartered Surveyor* (March).

Wells, William R. (1973), "Rapid Transit Impact on Suburban Planning and Development, Perspective and Case Study," Department of Industrial Engineering, Stanford, California: Stanford University.

Yang, Chin Ming (1976), "Impact of a Rapid Transit Line on Suburban Vacant Land Values," Ph.D. dissertation, University of Pennsylvania.

ITHIEL DE SOLA POOL

Communications Technology and Land Use

Communications technology, for the last 200 years, has been making operation at a distance increasingly easy. Such a steady trend, one might presume, should have engendered as one of its consequences a steady dispersal of population away from crowded city centers. But it is not so! Why did this trend of better long-distance communication, which has indeed promoted exurbia and sprawl recently, appear in an earlier era to have had the reverse effect of encouraging urbanization around superdense downtowns? And why is it different today?

When one finds a cause, at one time having one effect and at another time having another, one suspects that an interaction, with a third variable is at work. That is the case. We find intriguing interactions among urban topography and three technologies: production, transportation, and communications. Were we examining an earlier era, we would have to add one more variable, security, as a major factor in human agglomeration, but in the modern world the dominant needs served by common settlements rise from economic pursuits. The rise of the modern city came in part from the assemblage

of workers near factories and also from division of labor among producers who lived by exchange in markets.

Contributions of the Telephone and Modern Transportation

In the mid-nineteenth century, if one walked up to one of the big, red brick sheds that housed most American factories along the rivers of the Northeast or to one of the similar sheds in western Europe, one would have found the offices of the company and its president at the front of the same building with the production plant behind. By the 1920s, however, one would have found most corporate headquarters located in Manhattan, or London, or Paris, or sometimes in the downtowns of industrial cities like Pittsburgh, Chicago, Manchester, or Bremen. The factories were not there in the central cities to which the headquarters had moved, but were on the outskirts of the city or in smaller manufacturing towns.[1]

1. Cf. Jean Gottmann, Ronald Abler, and J. Alan Moyer in *The Social Impact of the Telephone*, ed. I. Pool (Cambridge, MA: MIT Press), 1976.

From **The Annals,** The American Academy of Political and Social Science, Vol. 451, September 1980, pp. 1–12. Reprinted by permission of The Academy and I. de Sola Pool.

This process of separation of the headquarters office from the plant and the congregation of offices all together is described by Peter Cowen in his book, *The Office*.[2] He notes that in New York "a cluster of central offices . . . began to accumulate in the late 1880's or early 1890's. . . . In London . . . the building of offices got under way during the first part of the century."[3] Cowen attributes the character of office activity to three inventions: the telegraph, the typewriter, and the telephone, especially the last two.[4] The company president located himself at the place where most of his most critical communications took place. Before the telephone, he had to be near the production line to give his instructions about the quantities, pace, and process of production. Once the telephone network existed, however, he could convey those authoritative commands to his employees at the plant and could locate himself at the place where the much more uncertain bargaining with customers, bankers, and suppliers took place.

Before the emergence of telecommunications and power-driven transportation, the limit to the number of people who could assemble in the city was set by the need for people to go on foot to see each other. J. Alan Moyer describes Boston in 1850 as a small city with residences, businesses, and factories intermingled. It was a tightly packed seaport where people normally walked to their jobs, to stores, and to visit frends and relatives. Face-to-face communication was dominant; it was a walking city whose densely settled area was within two miles of city hall.[5]

The combination of the streetcar and the telephone allowed this picture to change, with many more people coming to work in the downtown while living further out. Persons who were engaged in routine production work could be segregated to plants in the remote environs, but everyone who bargained and engaged in decisions found it important to work in the city.

The early telephones and the vehicles of the day were not habile enough devices to substitute for one's being located in person at the center during the day, in easy face-to-face contact with important others. The fidelity of the telephone was poor. It sometimes went out of order. Penetration was low; as a result, one could not count on being able to telephone anyone one wanted to reach. The phone provided a limited link to places where one had arranged for it to be in place; the streetcar served for a daily commute down and up its radial pattern. But for diverse important communications, face-to-face contact had to be available. The limited technologies of the day were neither a substitute for, nor an adequate aid to, personal interaction.

So business first used the new technologies of transportation and communication to assemble in an enlarged commercial center. While quantitatively the separation of corporate offices from manufacturing plants was the most important part of the process of creating a commercial downtown, the same sort of thing was happening in other enterprises besides industry. Before the telephone, doctors, for example, had to live near their offices to be readily available when needed; typically, in fact, the office was in the doctor's home. The telephone, however, allowed many doctors to separate home and office and to put the office where it was convenient for the patients to come.[6]

Before the telephone, businessmen, since they had to be in easy walking distance of their main contacts, located in clusters determined by occupation. The result was a mosaic city. Every city had a

2. New York: American Elsevier, 1969.
3. Ibid., p. 29.
4. Ibid., p. 30.
5. Pool, *Social Impact*, p. 344.

6. "Telephone and the Doctor," *Literary Digest* 44:1037 (May 18, 1912).

furrier's neighborhood, a hatter's neighborhood, a wool neighborhood, a fish market, an egg market, a financial district, a shipper's district, and many others. Businessmen would pay mightily for an office within the few blocks where their trade was centered; their way of doing business was to walk up and down the block and drop in to the places from which one might buy or to whom one might sell. For lunch or coffee, one might drop in to the corner restaurant or tavern where one's colleagues congregated.

Once the telephone was available, business could move to cheaper quarters and still keep in touch. A firm could move outward, as many businesses did, or move up to the tenth or twentieth story of one of the new tall buildings. Instead of an urban pattern of a checkerboard of different specialized neighborhoods, the new urban pattern created a large downtown containing a miscellany of commercial and marketing activities that needed to be accessible to a variety of clients and customers.[7]

The development of skyscrapers permitted more and more people to be packed into that downtown. Recognition of how the telephone contributed to a revolution in modern architecture, namely, by the creation of skyscrapers, appears as early as 1902 in an article in *Telephony*.[8] General Carty, the Chief Engineer of AT&T, used the same arguments in 1908.

It may sound ridiculous to say that Bell and his successors were the fathers of modern commercial architecture—of the skyscraper. But wait a minute. Take the Singer Building, the Flatiron, the Broad Exchange, the Trinity, or any of the giant office buildings. How many messages do you suppose go in and out of those buildings every day. Suppose there was no telephone and every message had to be carried by a personal messenger. How much room do you think

the necessary elevators would leave for offices? Such structures would be an economic impossibility.[9]

The prehistory of the skyscraper begins with the elevator in the 1850s; the first Otis elevator was installed in a New York City store in 1857, and with adaption to electric power in the 1880s, the device came into general use.[10] "The need to rebuild Chicago after the 1871 fire, rapid growth, and rising land values encouraged experimentation in construction." In 1884, Jenney erected a ten-story building with a steel skeleton as a frame; the fifty-seven-storied Woolworth Building was opened in 1913. "By 1929 American cities had 377 skyscrapers of more than twenty stories."[11]

There were several ways in which the telephone contributed to that development. We have already noted that human messengers would have required too many elevators at the core of the building to make it economic. Furthermore, telephones were useful in skyscraper construction; the superintendent on the ground had to keep in touch with the workers on the scaffolding, and phones were used for that. So in various ways the telephone made the skyscraper practical and thus allowed a burgeoning of city centers.

Another observation from the early days of suburban commuting was that husbands became more willing to leave their wives miles away in bedroom suburbs for the whole day, and grown children were more willing to leave their parents' neighborhood, once they had telephones and could be in instant touch

7. Cf. Pool, *Social Impact*.
8. "Application of the Modern Telephone," 4: (2):94–5.

9. John Kimberly Mumford, "This Land of Opportunity, The Nerve Center of Business," *Harper's Weekly* 52:23 (August 1, 1908). The point was first made in the trade journal *Telephony* 4:(2) (1902).
10. Charles N. Glaab and A. Theodore Brown, *A History of Urban America* (New York: Macmillan, 1967), pp. 144–5.
11. Ibid., p. 280.

in emergencies. That, too, facilitated the growth of a commuter-laden downtown.

A REVERSAL OF TRENDS

Side by side with the process of city growth that has just been described, a second trend was getting under way, first in a small way and then massively. That second trend was dispersion from the city to suburbia and exurbia. That movement had started in the decade before the invention of the telephone and long before the automobile; the street car initiated the process. Perceptive observers noted the new trend toward decentralization even in the 1890s. Frederic A. C. Perrine, one of the founders of the profession of electrical engineering in America, noted the beginnings of suburbanization in an article about how electricity would reverse the centralizing effects of the steam engine on society. He stressed the impact of the electric streetcar on the city.[12]

Eight years later, H. G. Wells, in his 1902 *Anticipations* of the twentieth century, forecast centrifugal forces on cities that might lead "to the complete reduction of all our present congestions."[13] A pedestrian city, he said, "is inexorably limited by a radius of about four miles, and a horse-using city may grow out to seven or eight." With street railways the modern city thrust "out arms along every available railway line."

Wells anticipated "that New York, Philadelphia, and Chicago will probably, and Hankow almost certainly, reach forty millions." The telephone was one factor Wells listed as fostering this development,[14] for he believed that there was no reason "why a telephone call from any point in such a small country as England to any other should cost more than a post-

card."[15] Yet Wells, like Jean Gottmann later, emphasized that urban sprawl did not mean uniformity of density.[16] Shopping and entertainment centers would continue to make for downtowns, even as people in some occupations would prefer to move out to the country or work by telephone from home.[17]

A *Scientific American* article of 1914, "Action at a Distance,"[18] has similar themes, but with special stress on the picturephone as likely to make dispersion possible. "It is evident," it starts out, "that something will soon have to be done to check the congestion" of the city. "The fundamental difficulty . . . seems to be that it is necessary for individuals to come into close proximity to each other if they are to transact business." The article argues that the telephone and picturephone will take care of that.

These anticipations of flight from the city came long before the fact. Even as late as 1940, an evaluation of the telephone's impact on the city stressed its centripetal rather than its contrifugal effect. Roger Burlingame concluded:

It is evident that the skyscraper and all the vertical congestion of city business centers would have been impossible without the telephone. Whether, in the future, with its new capacities, it will move to destroy the city it helped to build is a question for prophets rather than historians.[19]

He sensed that things were changing. The flight from downtown was perceptible

12. *Electrical Engineering* 3:(2):39 (1894).
13. H. G. Wells, *Anticipations* (New York: Harper Bros., 1902), pp. 51 ff.
14. Ibid., p. 65.

15. Ibid., p. 58.
16. *Megalopolis* (Cambridge, MA: MIT Press, 1961).
17. Wells, *Anticipations*, p. 66.
18. Suppl. no. 1985 77:39 (Jan. 17, 1914).
19. Roger Burlingame, *Engines of Democracy* (New York: Charles Scribner's Sons, 1940), p. 96; cf. also Arthur Page, "Social Aspects of Communication Development," *Modern Communication*, ed. Page (Boston: Houghton Mifflin, 1932). He notes the relation of the phone to both the skyscraper and suburb, and says it "allows us to congregate where we wish to" p. 20.

enough for him to note it, but as a quali-
fication to his description of a process of
concentration.

Today our attention is focused on the
dramatic movement outward and the resulting urban sprawl. We have tended to
lose sight of the duality of the movement.
The common effect of the telephone,
throughout, was to permit a freer choice
of residential and work location than in
the days of the walking city and the mosaic city. There were two options as
neighborhoods broke up, the economics
of location changed, and cities grew. One
was to move up into the new tall buildings, the other was to move out from the
center. Initially, the predominant choice
was to take advantage of this new freedom of location to get one's enterprise to
the center of the action. Skyscrapers
helped make this possible, with millions
of daytime workers piled high downtown,
but it was only possible thanks to the con-
current availability of mass transport and
telecommunications.

Later the pendulum swung, and the
predominant direction of movement was
outward. Even some headquarters of corporations moved from Manhattan to
Westchester or Connecticut. Small enterprises appeared in the fields around Route
128 or Silicon Valley rather than in lofts
in an urban ring between the downtown
and the slums, as 1930s sociological the-
tory of urban topography would have
predicted.

The ring theory of Park's and Burgess's
Chicago school of sociologists[20] was essentially American because that model
rested on assumptions of a rapidly growing city, with speculative land values
graduated downward from the center, and
of heavy taxes proportional to property
value. Under those circumstances, one

low-rental area in which to put a new and
possibly unstable productive plant was in
the ring just beyond the downtown, but
which was still too far out for high-rise
development and in which speculators
were holding properties at a loss in the
expectation of later appreciation when
the downtown spread out. In Europe, with
a different fiscal system, a ring of lofts
and empty lots at the edge of the downtown was not usual. So, in Europe, earlier
than in the United States, manufacturing
was extensively located in an outer ring,
like Paris's red ring of suburbs, but in
Europe the ring hugged tightly the city
in which the workers lived. Plant location
in scattered green sites well beyond the
built-up city was a later and also quite
American phenomenon.

The new mid-twentieth century pattern
of location was more diverse than that
which had preceded it. The typical city
that had emerged in the first part of the
century had a single hub. A ring theory
described it well. What has emerged since
the middle of the century is a proliferation of hubs, some of them within the old
city but away from the bull's eye, some of
them planted beyond the city in green
fields, some of them subsidiary downtowns, such as Neuilly or Shinjuku, and
some of them specialized single-purpose
developments like shoppers' malls or rural
industrial parks. The Los Angeles metropolitan area is prototypic of what is likely
to develop where there is cheap, good,
and universal motor transport and telecommunications. That type of city, as
Jean Gottmann emphasizes, is megalopolis and not antipolis.[21] It is not an undifferentiated sprawl of medium-density
settlement. It is a highly differentiated,
geographically dispersed structure of centers and subcenters with complex interrelations among them.

Homeseekers and businesses adopted
such a megalopolitan and in part even

20. Cf. Ernest W. Burgess, "The Growth of the
City," in *The City,* eds. Robert E. Park, Ernest
W. Burgess, and Roderick D. McKenzie (Chicago: Univ. of Chicago Press, 1967), first published in 1925.

21. *See* his chapter in Pool, *Social Impact.*

exurban location pattern partly because of improvements in telecommunications, and because they had automobiles. The role of the car in making it possible to both live and produce in very scattered locations is obvious. The millions of persons who live in suburbs well beyond the reach of public transport and without walkable neighborhood shopping streets, who carpool or bus their children to school, go to movies at a drive-in, and drive for shopping to a shopping mall could not exist without cars. And there are also many scattered plants where these people work and to which virtually everyone arrives by car. In the instance of Route 128, the very name of the development is the road which it straddles.

However, good and fast as it might be, transportation by car, with cheap gasoline, would not by itself have permitted such a topography of settlement to emerge. If every message, question, order, instruction, or change of instruction from and to such dispersed homes and plants required that someone jump into a car and drive for 20 to 45 minutes in order to communicate, no such dispersal of settlement would have taken place. The ability to pick up a telephone and get a message through without moving was just as essential as the car.

The improvements in telecommunications technology between about 1910, when the telephone was mainly found useful in pushing activities into the downtown, and about 1960, when it was more important in allowing activities to migrate out, were not very dramatic, but they were significant.

In the first place, in the United States telephones had become universal over that half century, and with that their use changed. It was all very well in 1910 for the remote office or plant to have a telephone, but its effective use depended on others whom one wanted to reach also having one. To avoid running an errand, to cancel an appointment, or to find out if something or someone was ready to be picked up required a telephone at both ends. One could not assume that a sick worker would telephone in or that a substitute could be telephoned in order to tell him to drive right out. One could not track down a deliveryman easily or always expect to be able to reach a customer with a question or with information. The universality of telephones made them more valuable to each subscriber.

In the second place, in the early years the quality of telephone service depended heavily on one's location. The gradually growing investment in telecommunications plants was concentrated where users in large numbers could share the cost. Rural subscribers had to be content with party lines and sometimes had to pay for running a line out to their location. Even when a business user was willing to pay for stringing lines to his premises, his rural exchange might not have capacity for added lines. In a rural area, with less redundancy of equipment to fall back on, when a line went out the outage was apt to be more protracted. Also the degradation of the signal with distance was a major problem in the early days and was more severe for scattered customers. That problem was only gradually fully overcome; only young people today fail to react with surprise when a caller from thousands of miles away sounds as though he were calling from next door. Automatic switching was introduced to urban exchanges first, and as direct distance dialing came in, that, too, was in the major commercial exchanges first. So in the early years, one reason for preferring a central location was its superior telecommunications facilities.

Third, the telephone facilities a business subscriber can have on his own premises have improved. Now he is likely to have a fully automatic PABX allowing calls to be made without waiting for a switchboard operator, and incoming calls may go directly to his Centrex line, also without operator intervention. Long-distance calls may be made over private lines or WATS lines at a marginal cost that the employee does not have to think about. For an employee who spends much of his day on the telephone, these are important efficiencies.

Fourth and finally, data communication in forms much faster and cheaper than telex has become available. For the past decade, in most large companies, employees from many locations have had access to the company's computers either in time-sharing or remote job entry mode. Orders and inventory information can pass to and from terminals.

Everything so far described is now history. We are describing changes in communications technology that were already pervasive enough in the 1960s and 1970s to help explain the numerous decisions made both by business firms and individuals to locate in noncentral and even remote and isolated places. These telecommunications developments were prerequisite to the viability of such new centers as Rosslyn, Bethesda, and McLean near Washington; or Shinjuku, Saitama, and Skuba around Tokyo; as well as to the much more modest sub-subcenters, such as a shopping plaza cut out of green fields or a housing development folded into woodlands.

Now, however, let us consider more advanced telecommunications developments that may become common over the next decades and which may serve to make remote locations even more attractive.

A Look to the Future

One particular development clouds our crystal ball. For the first time in the last two centuries, the trends in transportation do not parallel those in communications. In the late nineteenth century, both the streetcar and the telephone provided improved intercourse between selected pairs of points. The convenience this achieved, though considerable, was modest by modern standards, and the topography of both services were rigid. However, as we have already noted, by the mid-twentieth century, universalization of availability of cheap motor transport and of telecommunications was achieved, as was greater flexibility in the topography of both systems and in their uses. All these developments were common to both communications and transportation.

Now for the first time, the prospect in transportation is of rising prices and consequent restriction of liberal use, while the prospect in communications is of falling prices and abundance. How the balance between concentration and dispersion will work out in this new situation, time alone can tell. Without predicting the net balance, we can, nonetheless, analyze fairly well the direction that will come from communications technology. It is toward more diffusion.

Communications facilities in the past have tended to be organized in a hierarchical geographical structure. At the lowest level were local nodes, perhaps united under regional structures and united under a national one. There can be two, three, or more levels. The American press consists of a simple two-level system in which city newspapers are fed by national news services. American broadcasting is similar, with local stations fed by national networks. The most complex of the networks is the telephone system, sometimes described as the largest machine ever built. Subscriber premises are linked to local exchanges by wire pairs called "the local loop." The local exchanges are connected, ordinarily, by coaxial cable to nearby local exchanges and to a toll exchange on the long-distance network. That toll exchange is connected by microwave, or satellite, or cable to other toll exchanges and then on down in symmetrical fashion to the subscriber at the other end. Before satellites, the network structure reflected rather closely the volume of traffic, with much bandwidth installed, for example, between New York and Washington, but with little capacity installed on low-traffic routes.

The network of the year 2000 is likely to be quite different. The two technical developments underlying that difference are the coming availability of abundant, low-cost bandwidth from end to end and the low cost of digital switching.

Optical fibers are likely to carry great bandwidth capacity all the way to the customer's home or office allowing him to connect computers, videophones, or almost any communications device directly to the network. Wherever the optical fibers reach—and eventually that may be everywhere—the customer can have top-grade communications services. Also, insofar as the long-distance links are by satellite, the structure of a network with some heavy traffic routes and some thin routes gives way to random access. Every point at which an earth station is placed (within the satellite's beam) is reachable in the same way as every other. There is no difference in cost regardless of the distance traversed, and there is the same quality of service to every point. So the future broadband transmission system will equalize the service to all locations.

Low-cost switching has important effects, too. It is simply one aspect of the revolution in microelectronics. A digital switch is a digital computer that is being used for routing control. With the progress in microelectronics, such computing capability can be embodied on tiny chips all through the network. "Distributed intelligence," as it is called, means that there can be a computer operating as a switch—and also for other purposes—in the customer's telephone itself, elsewhere on his premises, on telephone poles outside his building, at any concentrator along the line, in telephone company exchanges, and elsewhere. One configuration which gets entirely away from having

exchanges is a packet network. For that kind of service, each terminal has a line to the network to which it is connected by a small interface switch which reads the address on the packet and forwards it, switch to switch, to the interface at the destination that is recorded on the header. There need be no hierarchy at all among the interface switches.

Another configuration which gets away from the historical hierarchy of exchanges is that of a switched satellite system. In such a system, the customer's telephone has a line to a concentrator and then on to the earth station. From there the signal, along with an address, is transmitted up to the satellite, and there, 22,300 miles above the equator, it is switched to a beam that will reach the particular earth station to which the receiver is connected.

Even a circuit-switched terrestrial system on a future all-digital network—what is called an "integrated services digital network" (ISDN)—may not have a geographic hierarchy of exchanges. On an ISDN, different functions, like billing, storing of messages when no one is home, and testing the availability of lines, may all be performed by specialized equipment at different places on the network. The distinction between local and long-distance calls may disappear. Some very local calls may never even enter an exchange, being switched at the local concentrator on a pole. Other local calls may be processed for some functions by special equipment hundreds of miles away.

The implication of all these technical facts is that the future telecommunications system is likely to eliminate the disparities in the quality of communications service now found in different locations. Until the energy crisis of 1973, it was a common fantasy in popular literature that advances in communications would engender reruralization. Exhibits at worlds' fairs and articles in popular magazines depicted the home/office of the twenty-first century, set in an idyllic countryside with its resident enclosed in a cocoon of a room, sitting at a console with a video screen, carrying on his business with anyone, to the ends of the earth, by telecommunciations. That fantasy in its fullness was always silly, but it captured a small element of reality, namely, that whatever expanded communications facilities the market will offer to customers two or three decades hence can be expected to be available just as well in a rural as in an urban environment. In all locations, be they metropolitan centers or remote hinterlands, the most sophisticated kinds of communications service should be available.

At a price, the customer of such a future communications system can be serviced with pictures of any fidelity he needs, with electronic mail, with word processing, and with voice processing, too. The barrier of price is an important one, but it is a very different kind of barrier from that of technical impossibility. In the past there were a limited number of things one could do with a telecommunications line. In the early days, one could use it for poor-quality, high-value voice conversations or for telegrams to limited destinations. Later, one could use it to almost anywhere, but still only for relatively standard voice output. For the future, a fairly accurate statement is that one will be able to have at any given terminal whatever quality of video, audio, or text representation one is willing to pay for and will be able to have these at any location without penalty for distance.

Given the rising cost of transportation, it will pay in many situations to substitute investment in sophisticated communications for the expense of travel. How far the energy crunch will lead to geographic reconcentration of activities in urban centers will depend on the cost of communications services good enough to be a satisfactory substitute.[22]

Much of the literature on the tradeoff between telecommunications and travel makes the naive assumption that if people have the means to communicate to a long distance, they will travel less. That is quite untrue. In the first place, traveling and communicating reinforce each other; people travel to see people with whom they have established a communicative relationship, and people communicate with people to whom or from whom they travel.[23] There is a significant positive correlation between long-distance telephone traffic and travel.

These comments, however, do not contradict what has just been said. We did not ask previously whether the improvement of communications facilities would in and of itself stop people from traveling. We asked what people would do in a situation in which an exogenous third variable, energy prices, forced them to curtail their travel. Under those circumstances, the geographically dispersed availability of very flexible communications devices could curb what otherwise might be a strong shift back into concentrated urban centers.

22. On the possibilities of telecommunications substituting for travel, *see* John Short, Ederyn Williams, and Bruce Christie, *The Social Psychology of Telecommunications* (London: John Wiley & Sons, 1976); Alex Reid, "Comparing Telephone With Face-to-Face Contact," in Pool, *Social Impact;* and Starr Hiltz and Murray R. Turoff, *Network Nation* (Reading, MA: Addison-Wesley, 1978).

23. Ithiel de Sola Pool, "The Communications/ Transportation Tradeoff," in *Current Issues in Transportation Policy,* ed. Alan Altshuler (Lexington, MA: D. C. Heath, 1979).

VII

PROBLEMS: Selected Issues in Planning and Public Policy

DAVID T. HERBERT

Urban Deprivation: Definition, Measurement, and Spatial Qualities

Deprivation as a Concept

Most attempts to define deprivation, or associated concepts such as poverty and substandardness, are imprecise and stress that any definitions must be couched in relative terms. "Deprivation" implies a standard of living or a quality of life below that of the majority in a particular society, to the extent that it involves hardship, in adequate access to resources, and underprivilege. Comparisons are made less to an average than to a threshold, and all writers upon the subject have emphasized the relative nature of these comparisons and standards. Living standards change in time so that houses built in the nineteenth century are no longer acceptable; Aneurin Bevan suggested that the causes of housing problems were higher social standards (Holman *et al.*, 1973). Standards also vary considerably from one part of the contemporary world to another and it has been reported (Cullingworth, 1973) that one-fifth of North Americans described as living in conditions of poverty in 1964, had objective standards of living which would have been classified as above average in many

countries of the world. These relative bases for deprivation have expressions other than contrasted absolute standards. Relative deprivation as a concept (Runciman, 1966) considers the reference groups which form the bases for individual self-assessment. Runciman identifies as deprived the individual who lacks a resource which he wants and sees with others, and research has suggested that most such comparisons are only made in limited terms. A discussion of levels of satisfaction in North American cities may be used as an illustration (Stagner, 1970). Stagner suggested that although the inhabitants of American ghettoes lived in luxury compared to a Pakistani peasant, the reference standard of the ghetto dweller is not the peasant but the wealthier families who are members of the same society.

The causes of deprivation are equally difficult to determine. It could be argued that deprivation is present at all levels of society—the boarding school child with insufficient family life, for example—but for the most part poverty is regarded as the basis from which much deprivation stems. The Social Science Research Coun-

From **The Geographical Journal,** Vol. 141, 1975, pp. 362–72. Reprinted by permission of the Royal Geographical Society and D. T. Herbert.

cil (1968) formed a classification of types of poverty which included crisis poverty, following events such as bereavement, illness, or unemployment; long-term dependencies, which occur when individuals prove unable to recover from these events; life cycle poverty, which affects families at particular times of life; and "downtown" poverty, which typifies the inner areas of cities and those housing classes (Rex, 1968) least privileged and least able to compete in the housing market. Within Britain, which has a more strongly developed system of welfare than most societies, the real poor are limited to small groups, such as the homeless, and to sections of the workless, the old, and the victims of broken homes.

Poverty leads to other expressions of deprivation and a cyclical or cumulative effect occurs. The idea of a cycle of poverty involves study of the disadvantages faced by children whose home circumstances militate against them. Children born into the cycle are faced with early developmental disadvantages, meet educational disadvantage at school, which prepares them for employment disadvantage and economic disadvantage (Williams, 1970). Similarly, a British government report (Department of Education and Science (DES), 1967) described the problems of children in situations where occupational skills are low, housing is poor, and a low premium is placed on educational attainment. "Thus the vicious circle may turn from generation to generation and the schools play a central part in the process, both causing and suffering cumulative deprivation" (Halsey, 1972). Poverty and deprivation may therefore be transmitted temporally and because the basic causes lead to more than one expression of deprivation, it may also be aggregative. Multiple deprivation describes a state in which individuals or groups are afflicted by several forms of underprivilege.

Spatial Qualities of Deprivation

The incidence of deprivation is not evenly distributed over society as a whole but is specific to sections of the population. Spatial segregation is an established fact of urban life, as demonstrated by the considerable literature of social geography which has been concerned with the study of residential differentiation (Herbert, 1972) and it is a corollary that there should be marked spatial concentrations of deprivation in those parts of the city in which the afflicted sections of society live. This "mirror image effect" of societal distributions in geographical space is one spatial quality; it is likely, particularly in the context of behavioural forms of deprivation, that other spatial qualities are involved. More recently, geographers have argued the existence of a "neighbourhood effect" (Johnston, 1974). This suggests that sets of values and associated forms of behaviour which exist within a given "territory" may be transmitted to individuals who live there; there is a contagion or contaminating effect. A corollary exists in those parts of the literature of criminology which suggest that values are transmitted over time from one generation to another (Sutherland and Cressey, 1960).

Within recent years a number of major government reports have recognized the fact that many forms of deprivation have spatial expression and have recommended policies and instituted courses of action which are area-specific. Area-based solutions were first applied in the housing field (Cullingworth, 1973) but a major impetus was given by the Plowden report on primary education (DES, 1967) and the Seebohm report on the social services (1968). Plowden recommended "positive discrimination" in the allocation of resources in favour of educational priority areas, Seebohm advocated that areas of special need should be designated within which extra resources should be provided. In 1968, the urban programme was launched (Batley and Edwards, 1975), one role of which was to fund neighbourhood-based action research in the community development projects. It is clear that governmental policies have actively adopted the concept of *areas* of multiple deprivation towards which priority action should be directed. In order to identify such areas, the indices of deprivation had to be defined.

Deprivation Indices

The social indicators movement dates from the mid-1960s and although it has received widespread acclaim, it is still at a fairly primitive stage and is characterized by a great deal of "peripheral verbosity" (Boal, Doherty and Pringle, 1974). Social indicators are usually referred to as measures of the quality of life, although this lacks precise definition, and most critics have stated the need to relate indicators to a social model and to define the issues before looking for empirical measures. P. L. Knox (1974) has argued that while "quality of life" is a recent and rather vague notion, the related concept of "level of living" has a longer history and a clearer definition. Level of living is basically a descriptive concept which refers to actual conditions and is defined in terms of a set of components representing distinct classes of human need. Basic items are nutrition, health, shelter and education but others may vary from one societal context to another, as would the thresholds which are set. Knox listed the components of a British model whilst D. M. Smith (1973) designated a similar set of criteria of social well-being for more general application.

Although studies of social indicators and levels of living have often tried to define their conceptual bases, the links between the "models" and the actual indices used are frequently tenuous. The range and diversity of indices is partly due to a lack of standardized practice but is more frequently the result of constraints which are imposed by the availability of data. Which information is available for which points in time, the form in which it is published, the kinds of classification which have been adopted, all these affect the forming of indices. An example of a recent attempt to develop indices derived from a more general model of deprivation was provided by the urban programme researchers (Edwards, 1973). They defined people living in deprivation as those least able to compete in the three major competitive markets of housing, employment and education: territorial concentrations of an inability to "compete" identify deprived areas. Seven variables were selected from available census statistics with at least one from each of the three subsets. Calculated for each enumeration district in England and Wales, the indices were to be used to identify those districts which qualified for urban aid.

Research projects concerned with particular cities have depicted intra-urban concentrations of deprivation and ways in which the inner city forms the main locale. In their study of social malaise in Belfast, F. W. Boal, P. Doherty and D. G. Pringle (1974) paid particular attention to the problems arising from the spatial units for which data were recorded. The form of the data-collecting grid strongly affects the pattern and their recommendation was that analysis should be carried out at more than one scale; a coarse net to produce a generalized pattern and a finer level to show detail.

In the discussion of indices, examples of attempts to classify deprivation into its various categories have already been given. S. Hatch and R. Sherrott (1973) distinguished between direct indicators, which could be seen as constituting deprivation in themselves, and indirect indicators, which infer that deprivation may be present. Similarly, J. Craig and

A. Driver (1972) spoke of sufficient and aggravating indicators. For geographers, however, a more useful typology might be made in terms of environmental contexts for deprivation. The *physical urban environment* describes the quality of buildings and spaces within which individuals live; its main components are housing quality, access to urban facilities and to recreational or play space. The *impersonal social environment* describes the main compositional characteristics of the territorial population group, its demographic structure, social class make-up and ethnic character; variables which can usually be derived from published statistics. The *personal social environment* is the product of less tangible, non-material qualities of life style in particular areas, and is made up of the prevalent value systems, attitudes, and forms of behaviour. In each part of this trilogy of environments, deprivation may occur. As the substandard dwelling is an index of deprivation in the first category and the unemployed head of household is an index in the second, so some forms of behaviour such as truancy and delinquency may be related to deprivations in the third. Data available for the city of Cardiff, which had a population in 1971 of 279,110, are used here to examine these environmental sources of deprivation.

Spatial Patterns of Deprivation in Cardiff

Measures of housing substandardness, the most commonly used index of a deprived physical urban environment, are diverse in detail but tend to identify broadly similar spatial patterns. Figure 1 shows the

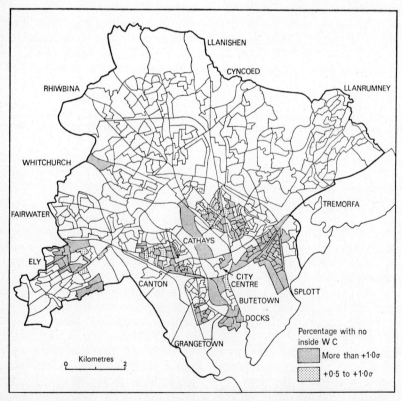

Figure 1. Cardiff: Distribution of substandard housing, 1971, based on 1966 enumeration districts (σ = standard deviation)

concentration of housing with no inside WC [toilet] within the inner city area. Other clusters occur where old, formerly separate, village nuclei are now engulfed in twentieth century urban growth or where terraces are dispersed along radial routes leading into the city centre, but in general it is clear that deprivation of the physical urban environment is a feature of the inner city. A latent problem is the low quality of much early local authority housing which may have a limited life span. As a measure of deprivation in the impersonal social environment, the distribution of low occupational skills has been widely used. Figure 2 shows a distribution no longer restricted to the inner city. As public sector policy has dispersed people to better housing it has been less successful in improving their access to improved economic opportunities. Inner

city problems remain, probably attenuated by a rehousing policy which leaves a residual population heavily over-represented in terms of the aged, the single, the recently arrived, and the jobless; but a socially disadvantaged group is now located in peripheral housing estates. Distribution of low educational attainment (Figure 3) shows a similar pattern.

These three measures show the spatial patterns of deprivation in housing, employment, and education, the fields which urban aid research has identified as the most critical competitive markets (Edwards, 1973). Whilst the individual indices have distinctive patterns they overlap to some extent and Figure 4 combines them to show areas of multiple deprivation and a pattern which contains both inner city and peripheral concentrations. These maps, based on census data, show

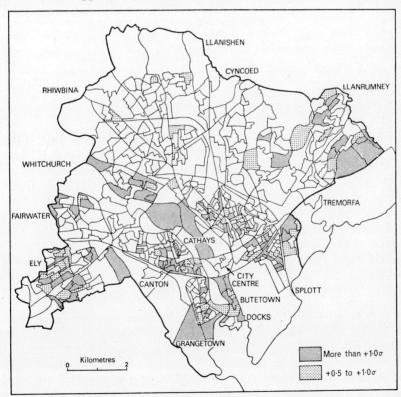

Figure 2. Cardiff: Low occupational skills, 1971. **Source:** socio-economic groups 7, 10, 11, 15. 1971 census

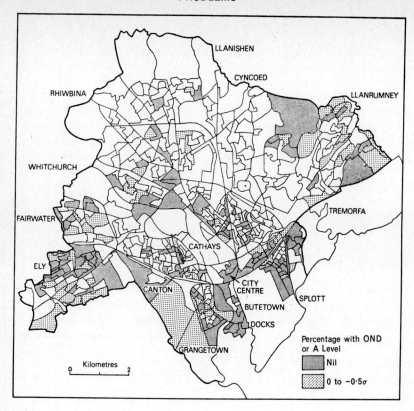

Figure 3. Cardiff: Educational attainment, 1971

deprivation in the physical urban environment and in the impersonal social environment. They do not include measures of the personal social environment and a study of juvenile delinquency allows this environment to be explored.

Many writers have recognized the place of delinquency in a scheme of indicators: Smith (1973) and R. Holman (*et al.,* 1973) suggested that a high incidence of delinquency was a feature of deprived areas. The causes of delinquency are multifarious and by no means fully understood. Although access to tangible qualities of life such as employment is important, delinquency may also be related to access to features of the personal social environment, the social values and life styles typical of the localities within which

individuals live (Wilson, 1962; Bernstein, 1965). Figure 5 shows the spatial distribution of standardized delinquency residence rates in Cardiff; there are concentrations in the inner city but also in peripheral areas. Comparison with Figures 1 to 4 shows that the concentrations often coincide, so that some areas are characterized by multiple deprivation. But the spatial distribution of delinquents also has some selective qualities; not all inner city terraced-row districts have high scores, nor do all peripheral local authority estates. From a detailed study of residential differentiation in Cardiff (Herbert and Evans, 1974) it was possible to control aspects of the physical urban and impersonal social environments with an area-sampling

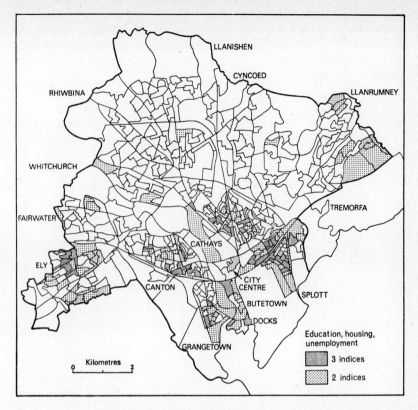

Figure 4. Cardiff: Areas of multiple deprivation (education, housing, unemployment), 1971

procedure and to select for detailed study two areas of the inner city which differed only in terms of the incidence of delinquency. Adamsdown had comparatively high, and Canton comparatively low delinquency residence. The research hypothesis was that area differences in qualities of the personal social environment—consistent with the difference in rates of delinquent behaviour—would exist between Adamsdown and Canton and, further, that these might be indicative of a neighbourhood effect. The three themes examined were parental attitudes towards education, parental sanctions on misbehaviour, and definition of delinquent acts.

Questions on parental hopes for their children in schooling revealed higher levels of aspiration in Adamsdown (Table 1). When data were collected on actual achievement, however, Canton had a far superior record. This apparent contradiction cannot be completely answered without further in-depth surveys but several possible explanations occur. The Adamsdown levels of aspiration may have been idealistic and overstated; or the aspiration level may have been real but was not translated into the kind of constructive help and guidance which would lead to better attainment. Further questions showed that Adamsdown parents had considerably less contact with schools, and much less interest in adult education; other research findings (Douglas, Ross and Simpson, 1968; Wilson and Herbert, 1974) suggest that these characteristics are significant. The results from Cardiff

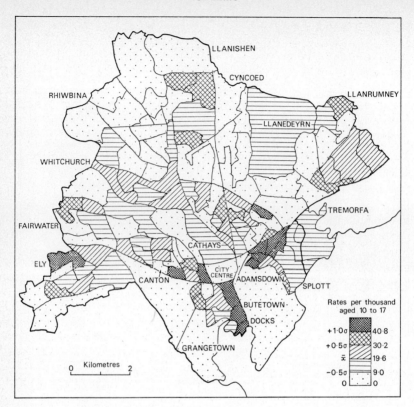

Figure 5. Cardiff: Distribution of delinquents by residence, 1971. Source: Cardiff Social Service Department data. Sample size, 650

Table 1. Educational Aspirations and Attainment

	Aspirations			Actual attainment		
	Canton	Adamsdown			Canton	Adamsdown
Level	(%)	(%)		Level	(%)	(%)
Up to CSE	9	12		None	45.0	72.9
Trade	5	2		CSE	3.3	4.2
GCE/OND	30	15		Trade	11.7	9.3
A Level/HND	15	0		GCE/OND	23.3	10.4
College or degree	41	71		A Level/HND	10.0	0.8
				College or degree	6.7	2.4

suggest that children in the delinquency area suffer greater deprivation in terms of access to educational attainment.

There are good reasons to suppose that relationships between parents and children are of great importance in understanding delinquent behaviour and that parental sanctions are a key part of that relationship (Andry, 1960). Parents in each area were asked how they would react to misbehaviour in a fourteen-year-old boy, the question being phrased in this way in order to standardize responses. As Table 2 shows, the difference between the two areas is that Canton parents favoured a verbal sanction whilst in Adamsdown physical punishment was much more commonly advocated—a difference strongly suggestive of better relationships in the non-delinquent area (see also Wilson, 1973).

Again with the model of a fourteen-year-old boy, parents in both areas were asked to examine a list of misbehaviours (Table 3) and to nominate those which they thought were wrong and should be reported. All the offences listed were illegal but ranged from the trivial to the serious. Over the less serious offences (the first four on the list) Adamsdown parents had significantly more tolerant attitudes; the differences were less marked with increasing seriousness of the offence. This difference, in the blurred area between right and wrong, was interpreted as direct evidence of a subcultural (Cohen, 1966), and possibly a neighbourhood, ef-

Table 3. Parental Definition of Serious Misbehaviour (serious enough to be reported)

	Canton (%)	Adamsdown (%)
Drinking under age	54	31
Taking money from child	56	21
Taking something from school	51	26
Travelling by bus without ticket	38	23
Damaging public property	74	67
Taking drugs	97	82
Stealing from unlocked cars	84	86
Breaking open meters	89	92
Breaking into shops	92	91
Group attack on strangers	97	93

fect within the delinquency area. A set of values is commonly held within the district which is at variance with that prescribed by society as a whole; for the individual youth the local set of values is likely to be the more accessible and relevant.

Results from this survey in Cardiff suggest that deprivation may exist not only in material terms but also in relation to the sets of values and codes of behaviour which exist on a neighbourhood basis. Children living in a delinquency area are deprived of access to a good quality of life in terms of its conduciveness to educational attainment, good child-parent relationships, and the existence of an adequate sense of what is right and wrong.

Conclusions

The inner city has a virtual monopoly of deprivation in the physical urban environment with its heritage of old, high density housing dating from the early stages of urban growth. Within the present century, however, it is this form of deprivation which has received the most attention and the polarities in housing standards have been considerably reduced.

Table 2. Parental Reaction to Misbehaviour; More than one response was allowed

Remedy Approved	Canton (%)	Adamsdown (%)
Physical punishment	17	38
Verbal sanction	64	48
Deprivation of privileges	48	12
Refer to institutional sanction	0	2

The inner city has heavy concentrations of social environmental deprivation and probably contains the worse problems. It has no monopoly over this kind of deprivation, however, and as inner city dwellers have been transferred to peripheral local authority estates, they have taken many forms of deprivation with them. E. Gittus (1969) suggested that there were two types of decaying area within the inner city which she labelled "residual" and "transitional"; R. N. Davidson (1975) added the "deprived council estate" to this typology within which disadvantage could be measured mainly in social terms. Measures of the impersonal social environment indicate that considerable variations remain and that the relative disadvantages of some sections of society are not being markedly reduced. The polarities remain and find clear spatial expressions.

The threefold classification of types of deprived area is useful but is not sufficient; for a real understanding of the qualities of the personal social environment which may contribute towards deprivation, it has an inadequate level of discrimination. Canton and Adamsdown are both "residual" terraced-row areas but their personal social environments have significant differences. Similar contrasts in the incidence of delinquency could be observed in otherwise similar local authority estates (Herbert and Evans, 1974). There is a source of deprivation, not easily measured, in the climates of opinion within which people live (Tyerman, 1968).

Government policies have recently moved strongly towards area bases for action against deprivation, though an interest in area-based welfare policy is not new. Area-based policies have been criticized. In education, for example, the positive discrimination policy and the identification of priority areas (Halsey, 1972) have their critics (Barnes and Lucas, 1974). Clearly the area-based policy in itself is not sufficient. There will be individuals in deprived areas who are not themselves deprived; there will be individuals outside deprived areas who are deprived. The area-base is useful at its prescribed scale; because many forms of deprivation have spatial expression and reflect spatial qualities, a disproportionate number of those affected can be identified within a comparatively small set of areas. This does not, of course, obviate the need for other approaches; an area-based policy complements those which are not set in a spatial framework and which seek to identify and treat individuals. A further quality of the area-based policy, which has been stressed by the educational priority area projects (Halsey, 1972) is that it allows deprivation to be seen in a more complete setting; the complex forces linking individual, institution, and community can be seen in clearer perspective.

Physical and urban planning policies have, of necessity, been territorially organized and their links with research in human geography have been considerable. As social planning gains momentum, it too has much to gain from established practices and methodologies in social geography. The concept of urban deprivation poses a range of questions, both academic and pragmatic, but the social geographical research tradition is never far removed from these.

References

Andry, R. 1960 *Delinquency and parental pathology*. Methuen.

Barnes, J. H., and Lucas, H. 1974 Positive discrimination in education: individuals, groups, and institutions. In Leggatt, T. (ed.) *Social theory and survey research*. Sage.

Batley, R., and Edwards, J. 1975 *The notion of deprivation in community development projects and the urban programme*. Unpublished discussion paper.

Bernstein, B. 1965 A socio-linguistic approach to social learning. In Gould, J. (ed.) *Penguin survey of social science*. Penguin Books.

Boal, F. W., Doherty, P., and Pringle, D. G. 1974 *The spatial distribution of some social problems in the Belfast urban area*. Northern Ireland Community Relations Commission.

Cohen, A. 1966 *Deviance and control*. New Jersey: Prentice Hall.

Craig, J., and Driver, A. 1972 The identification and comparison of small areas of adverse social conditions: a study of social indicators and social indices. *Jl. R. statist. Soc.* Series C (Applied Statistics), 21, 1:25–35.

Cullingworth, J. B. 1973 *Problems of an urban society: the social content of planning*. Allen and Unwin.

Davidson, R. N. 1975 *Social deprivation: an analysis of intercensal change*. Unpublished paper presented to the Institute of British Geographers at Oxford.

Department of Education and Science, Central Advisory Council for Education 1967 *Children and their primary schools*. [Plowden Report] HMSO.

Douglas, J. W. B., Ross, J. M., and Simpson, H. R. 1968 *All our future*. Davies.

Edwards, J. 1973 *Social indicators, urban deprivation, and positive discrimination*. Unpublished paper read to the Census Research Group at Chester.

Gittus, E. 1969 Sociological aspects of urban decay. In Medhurst, F., and Lewis, J. P. *Urban decay*. Macmillan.

Halsey, A. 1972 *Educational priority: Vol. I. EPA problems and policies*. HMSO.

Hatch, S., and Sherrott, R. 1973 Positive discrimination and the distribution of deprivations. *Policy and Politics* 1, 3:223–40.

Herbert, D. T. 1972 *Urban geography: a social perspective*. David and Charles.

———, and Evans, D. J. 1974 Urban sub-areas as sampling frameworks for social survey. *Tn Plann. Rev.* 45, 2:171–88.

Holman, R., Lafitte, F., Spencer, K., and Wilson, H. 1973 *Socially deprived families in Britain*. Bedford Square Press.

Johnston, R. J. 1974 Local effects in voting at a local election. *Anns Ass. Am. Geogr.* 64, 3:418–29.

Knox, P. L. 1974 Social indicators and the concept of level of living. *Soc. Rev.* 22, 2: 249–57.

Rex, J. A. 1968 The sociology of a zone in transition. In Pahl, R. E. (ed.) *Readings in urban sociology*. Pergamon Press.

Runciman, W. G. 1966 *Relative deprivation and social justice*. Routledge and Kegan Paul.

Seebohm Report 1968 Report of the committee on local authority and allied personal social services, HMSO.

Smith, D. M. 1973 *The geography of social well being in the United States*. McGraw-Hill.

Social Science Research Council 1968 *Research on poverty*. Heinemann.

Stagner, R. 1970 Perceptions, aspirations, frustrations, and satisfactions: an approach to urban indicators. *Am. Amer. Acad. Political Social Science*. 388:59–68.

Sutherland, E. H., and Cressey, D. 1960 *Principles of criminology*. New York: J. P. Lipincott.

Tyerman, N. 1968 *Truancy*. University of London Press.

Williams, F. (ed.) 1970 *Language and poverty*. New York: Markham.

Wilson, H. 1972 *Delinquency and child neglect*. Allen and Unwin.

———, 1973 The socialisation of children. In Holman, R. *et al.* (eds.) *Socially deprived families in Britain*. Bedford Square Press.

———, and Herbert, G. W. 1974 Social deprivation and performance at school. *Policy and Politics* 3:55–69.

GEORGE STERNLIEB, ROBERT W. BURCHELL,
JAMES W. HUGHES, AND FRANKLIN J. JAMES

Housing Abandonment in the Urban Core

Residential abandonment is the final symbol of all the urban ills of our society. Although it may have become an urban commonplace, it is little known or understood. The very definition of abandonment is far from precise. It has been defined as a condition in which buildings are vacant of tenants; commonly this is coupled with the virtual disappearance of the owner either *de jure* or *de facto*. But this definition fails to recognize that abandonment appears to be a process, a reflection of a much more deeply-seated and extensive phenomenon—the disinvestment of private capital in core cities (Sternlieb and Burchell, 1973).[1]

An abandoned structure has been perceived as a positive token of housing betterment. Through the filtering-down process, the development of new and better housing has precipitated the successive

1. A report recently completed for the U.S. Department of Housing and Urban Development summarizes the literature as a prelude to discussing the various stages of neighborhood evolution. These stages correspond almost exactly with Hoover and Vernon's except for the last stage. In this report abandonment is recognized as a legitimate end for urban core realty (Public Affairs Counseling, 1973).

shifting of families into increasingly better accommodations; the vacant buildings they have left behind are no longer competitive within the market. But the obvious anomaly is that abandonment occurs amidst substantial housing shortages. In a growing number of cities, abandonment has swept away both good housing and substantial shells which are much needed. There is no reason to believe that abandonment will not spread within the areas already experiencing it, or that it will not appear in several other metropolitan areas. The current abandonment process, then, may not be explained simply in terms of the "normal market" forces.

The Uneven Fit of the Theoretical Base

The reality of abandonment is challenging the theoretician's capacity to explain the phenomenon or predict its growth. Analysts have brought their entire theoretical arsenal to bear on the subject but the dynamics are elusive. Intrametropolitan job dispersal; shifting transportation facilities; changes in the level and distribution of income and consequent change in housing and neighborhood demand;

From **Journal of the American Institute of Planners**, Vol. 40. No. 5, September 1974, pp. 321–32. Reprinted by permission of the **Journal** and the authors.

demographic and racial turnover; local government fiscal systems; housing obsolescence; and numerous other factors are inextricably interrelated.

The urban ecologists Park and Burgess (1925) saw neighborhood change in terms of population *invasions* of a neighborhood by lower-status *racial and ethnic groups* and by *nonresidential uses.* As such groups immigrated into the center of the metropolis and as the central business district (CBD) expanded, the city grew radially from its center, forming a series of concentric zones or annules. Each of the zones, five in total, represents a type of area differentiated in the growth process. The driving force of this concentric zone model is the expansion of the CBD—continual pulses of growth pushing out from the center. The inner rings of the model, already aging and obsolete, are not only invaded by business and industry, but also by newly arriving racial and ethnic groups to the city. The owners of inlying properties were assumed to be only interested in the long-term profits to be made from the expansion of the CBD and the short-term profits obtainable from subdivided residential units.

Thus, external causes of central city instability were seen as occasioned by growth—both of the commercial heart and of new immigrations to the city. While these forces caused decay of neighborhoods, they also created an economic rationale for the continued usage of inlying areas. With the decline of immigration and the decline of the CBD, the inner zones (the processing places for new migrants to the city) lose a portion of their justification for being. With need diminished the ultimate fate of the worst structures is abandonment.

The Sector Theory

Land economist Homer Hoyt (1939) recognized the existence of these forces of neighborhood evolution, but he also gave emphasis to their differential effects on different *sectors* of the metropolis, and to the existence of *pull* as well as *push* forces of change. His sector theory described how high-rent residential neighborhoods move slowly but predictably across the urban landscape, exerting a gravitational pull on the middle-class, leaving behind the structure by which slums are made. Added to the obsolescence and invasion-succession dynamics, a cluster of forces is thus isolated.

The effects of these changes vary according to the type of neighborhood or sectors of different types of housing. The deterioration of low-rent sectors leads to great change. Because the buildings in these sectors are occupied by the poorest unskilled or unemployed persons, collection losses and vacancies are highest. The worst structures are demolished. Unless subsequent waves of poor immigrants enter the city to create a demand, many obsolete structures are removed from the supply.

Supply and Demand Approach

Yet despite this early theory, the dynamics of neighborhood evolution continue to be poorly understood. Conventional economic concepts of supply and demand lose much of their defining power at this level. Nevertheless, some researchers have successfully used a *supply-demand* framework to illuminate the abandonment decision of individual landlords (Kain and Ingram, 1972; James, Burchell and Hughes, 1972). In these analyses, *supply* embraces those factors that affect the landlord's expenditures in servicing his property. Some examples of such factors are: (1) "problem tenants," often accused of wearing out housing faster than do normal tenants; problem tenants are usually assumed to be poor and unwilling or unable to recompense landlords sufficiently to allow adequate maintenance; (2) problem neighborhoods, where high rates of crime and vandalism increase both operating and maintenance costs; and (3) the widely disparate kinds of housing stock that prevail in different neighborhoods; this is perhaps the most important example of supply side variation in the cost of providing housing. Although some versions of this third argument are almost indistinguishable from demand factors, on the simplest level it is apparent that maintenance and operating costs differ with structure and unit design, that is to say, older structures typically require greater maintenance outlays.

Demand factors are those that affect the landlord's gross revenues. Examples are neighborhood quality, the level of public services, and the race of neighborhood residents. Some empirical evidence has been developed indicating that the segregation of black households in urban ghettos maintains these often obsolete neighborhoods beyond their normal limits. Another important demand factor is the location of housing within urban areas, especially as it affects accessibility to jobs and various services; accessibility patterns have been markedly changed as a result of secular decentralization of metropolitan areas (James, Burchell, and Hughes, 1972).

Although this supply-demand approach to the analysis of abandonment offers potentially important insight, it is fundamentally limited by its omission of the factors producing neighborhood change. Such change is largely the result of individual landlord decisions producing further changes. Because this pattern can be quite complex and difficult to predict or understand, some analysts have chosen to make inductive generalizations about neighborhood evolution patterns.

Stage Theories

Edgar Hoover and Raymond Vernon offered a more explicit five-stage model of neighborhood evolution in the classic New York Metropolitan Region Study. Five evolutionary stages were hypothesized (Hoover and Vernon, 1959):

Stage 1: transforms undeveloped rural land to residential use. The building boom of the 1920s defined this stage for many northeastern cities—frame multidwelling units responsive to the needs of that era.

Stage 2: comprises a time of apartment construction. Many of the development sites are either patches of open space, bypassed in the first building wave for various reasons, or obtained through the demolition of the oldest single-family homes. This stage is most evident in the inner rings of metropolitan areas.

Stage 3: can occur several years later, and is a period of housing downgrading and conversion. Population and density increase through the crowding of existing structures by the newest immigrants to the region. The growth of young families generates additional strains on an aging infrastructure. This downgrading stage is often associated with the "slum invasions" by segregated ethnic and minority groups.

Stage 4: occurs after the immigrants have settled down. This "thinning out" stage, characteristic of long-established slum areas, is mainly a phenomenon of household size shrinkage as children and boarders move out. Large portions of Newark appear to be at this development stage.

Stage 5: is the renewal stage, where the obsolete areas of housing arriving at Stage 4 are replaced by new multifamily units. Most often this has either been subsidized moderate- or low-income housing, or luxury apartments. In almost every case, this stage is initiated through public intervention.

Hoover and Vernon optimistically assumed that some kind of renewal would follow the neighborhood collapse represented by stages three and four. But they suggested few specifics about the nature and implementation of these new land uses beyond their assumption that public intervention would probably take the form of community renewal programs. The role of private housing abandonment in their scheme is unclear. It has been suggested that so long as public and private demolition programs are adequate, abandonment may act as a sort of piecemeal land clearance program. On a sufficient scale, abandonment might facilitate the private renewal of slum neighborhoods. Moreover, it might supplement existing public renewal programs, and substitute for inadequacies in their scale.

Anthony Downs, in a preliminary report to the U.S. Department of Housing and Urban Development, was one of the few early researchers to acknowledge the stages of neighborhood decline and to recommend the introduction of counteractive measures at various points along the way. His description of neighborhood evolution includes five basic steps along with subsequent variations and repetitions (Public Affairs Counseling, 1973):

1. Racial transition—from white to black
2. Decline in average income of residents as a result of the "filtering" process
3. Declining levels of security accompanying increase in number of low-income households
4. Increasing difficulty with tenants involving rent payment, maintenance of the parcel, and turnover

5. Inability of landlords to obtain loans through normal mortgage channels

The remaining steps in the process are essentially repetitions or combinations of 2 through 5 as they interact with each other to produce steadily worsening conditions:

6. Physical deterioration
7. Declining tenant quality
8. Psychological abandonment by the landlord
9. Final tenancy decline and evacuation— the actual physical abandonment of the structure

Downs regards abandonment as resulting from a dual process that involves both neighborhood and landlord. Decaying *neighborhoods* are unable to attract households with steady incomes and to reduce significantly the level of local insecurity. And the *landlord* contributes to the process through his inability to secure financing, his slackening off of property maintenance, and his worsening relationship with his tenants.

The Newark Data

In our detailed analysis of residential abandonment in Newark, New Jersey, we have attempted to cull existing theory on abandonment and to document the resulting hypotheses empirically. Our approach, which is largely exploratory, employs only a limited model of landlord behavior and housing demand. It is our hope that our research will serve as a guide to more precise hypothesis testing and to the ultimate isolation of early indicators of residential abandonment.

We have chosen to approach abandonment from two directions—*environmental* and *behavioral*. First, we used gross patterns of residential abandonment to examine the relationships of neighborhoods and abandonment within the city of Newark. Second, we examined the abandonment decisions of a sample of Newark landlords, with special emphasis on the behavioral aspects of abandonment.

The environmental data have been selected according to the traditions of Social Area Analysis (Shevky and Bell, 1955), which seeks to define types of residential areas within cities in terms meaningful to scholars interested in social differentiation. The theoretical basis of the approach seeks to relate the areal differentiation of American cities to basic societal changes. The empirical tests of Social Area Analysis have shown the variables we selected to be most important in defining urban social structures (Murdie, 1969). The measurements of abandonment associated with these data were not obtained by sample but rather for the city as a whole—from fire and planning department records. They contain only the address of the structure and the fact that it has been abandoned. Although these measures of abandonment are limited in depth, when combined with the previously mentioned census tract variables they provide a broad framework for viewing both characteristics of neighborhoods that were the scene of heavy abandonment and the changes in characteristics of these neighborhoods.

The behavioral data are those characteristics of owner and tenant and those specific features of residential structures and their operation which comprise the rental relationship in the low-end real estate sector. Whites renting to blacks in aging frame structures, collecting their rents weekly while shunning taxes are behavioral situations peculiar to the environment of abandonment (Sternlieb, 1966; Stegman, 1970). The abandonment variable here is made up of a sample of formerly responsible landlords who have currently abandoned their property or who have chosen to retain it but are neglectful of their maintenance duties. The sample contains extensive information including, for example, type of structure, condition of structure, whether or not it is owner occupied, landlord's management techniques, and so on. Our analysis of these data is particularly significant given the focus of recent policy on changes in ownership and management practices.

Before delving any further into the abandonment phenomenon it is necessary first to elaborate our definition of an abandoned building and second, to gauge the scope of the problem both locally and nationally.

Abandonment Defined

In the first of two major surveys of the magnitude of abandonment as a national problem, the following definition was suggested:

When a landlord no longer provides services to an occupied building and allows taxes and mortgages to go unpaid, it is clear that the building is uninhabitable by all but desperation standards. We consider such buildings to be finally abandoned. On the other hand, when a building is temporarily unoccupied or to be demolished for another socially or economically useful purpose, it cannot be considered finally abandoned.

In 1971, the Center for Community Change and the National Urban League, using this definition, investigated the nature, extent, and causes of abandonment in seven cities—New York, Hoboken, Cleveland, St. Louis, Atlanta, Chicago, and Detroit. Housing abandonment was found to be a serious problem in all except Detroit and Atlanta, although the former was found to have an incipient problem. (At present, the Federal Housing Administration holds some 7,000 Detroit parcels, most of which are slated for demolition.) It was estimated that in New York City as a whole, approximately 2 percent of its residential structures had been abandoned; in the East New York section of Brooklyn, abandonment rates ranged from 6 percent to 10 percent. In the most afflicted section of St. Louis, approximately 16 percent of structures were abandoned. And the abandonment rates in the Woodlawn and Lawndale sections of Chicago approached 20 percent.

The second major national survey (Linton, Mields, and Coston, 1971) employed a somewhat different definition of abandonment. In this study, structures were considered abandoned if they were *unoccupied* and vandalized; boarded up; deteriorated or dilapidated; or had unmaintained grounds.

This study surveyed the extent of housing abandonment in neighborhoods of four metropolitan areas. In January, 1971, the city of St. Louis had 3,500 vacant and derelict buildings containing approximately 10,000 housing units—or approximately 4 percent of its housing stock. Moreover, 1,444 of these 3,500 structures had been abandoned in the seven-month period between July 1970 and January 1971. Although it was concluded that abandonment was concentrated in the poorest neighborhoods (abandonment rates exceeded 20 percent in one such neighborhood), abandoned structures were found throughout the city. In Chicago's North Lawndale area, fully 2.6 percent of the housing units were abandoned during a two-month period between September and November 1970. In the city as a whole, over the same short period, 0.4 percent of the housing stock was abandoned, with concentration in seven inner-city neighborhoods. Despite current municipal demolition rates of 30 units a week, the backlog of abandoned buildings in Chicago is increasing.

These two studies offer dramatic evidence that abandonment is devastating neighborhoods in several metropolitan areas. They also suggest that it is a phenomenon concentrated in neighborhoods dominated by poor, principally black,

households. Although they document the proportions of the abandonment crisis, they provide only fragmentary evidence on the reasons for the process. Nor do they afford the insights necessary for the design of ameliorative policy.

Our study defines an abandoned building as a residential structure which the owner, through active or passive action, has removed from the housing stock for no apparent alternative profitable reason and for which no succeeding land use occurs. Our definition, which is broader than its predecessors, includes not only standing, vacant residential buildings which serve no shelter function, but also those buildings whose physical traces have been demolished with the owner's consent. Our definition excludes private demolitions for purposes of commercial gain as well as housing removal dictated by either proposed urban renewal or other government development. A building is considered abandoned, however, if it is either vacant and standing or has been removed for reasons of public hazard, with no replacement forthcoming.[2] Abandonment, then, measures the housing loss resulting from a failing local housing market.

In our view, abandonment occurs after the cessation of housing services by the owner; it can either be the cause or the result of housing vacancy. It may occur before or after local municipal records show a significant tax delinquency problem. And further, it may occur before or after the owner, via paper sale, has ab-

2. The definition of abandoned structures does not include vacant structures as defined by the U.S. Census. A vacant structure, according to Census definition, is one which is unoccupied at the time of survey but physically *capable* of being occupied. According to this study's definition, an abandoned structure, if still standing, usually *cannot* be occupied due to structural deficiencies and/or housing services and the absence of interior fixturing. The reciprocal of occupancy, that is, vacancy, is thus *not* a surrogate for abandonment although the two may frequently occur in similar neighborhoods.

solved himself from complete responsibility for the building.

The Environmental Aspects of Residential Abandonment

We shall first attempt to establish the relationship between the probability of structure abandonment and both the initial characteristics of its surrounding neighborhood and the changes in those characteristics. This will be accomplished in two steps: first, using factor analysis, we shall distill data on initial 1960 and 1960 to 1970 change in census tract population and housing characteristics.[3] The large array of social and economic indicators from the census will be reassembled into a few clusters of intercorrelated variables, which are used as a set of quantitative indices differentiating census tracts. In other words, we shall delineate the "factorial ecology" of the city of Newark, both at a single point in time (static) and over time (dynamic).

Our next step will be to enter both the static and dynamic descriptions of neighborhoods into regression equations as a means of explaining variation in abandonment levels. Abandonment will be presented first as a function of the basic characteristics of neighborhoods, and second, as a function of neighborhood changes.

The first question to be answered is, "What were the dominant characteristics of neighborhoods in 1960 in which residential abandonment was rampant in 1970?" We shall then try to determine whether certain neighborhood changes might have further lessened the neighbor-

3. Thirty population and housing characteristics of census tracts were utilized in factor analyses of both the static and dynamic situations. Those factors with eigenvalues greater than one were then subjected to orthogonal rotation. The emerging factor srtuctures interpreted approximately 70 to 80 percent of the variance in the thirty census variables.

hood's desirability, stimulated housing obsolescence, and also contributed to subsequent housing abandonment.

NEIGHBORHOOD PRECURSORS OF ABANDONMENT (THE STATIC CASE)

The factor structure of Newark's residential patterns in 1960 is similar to those found in older core areas (Hughes, 1973).* Four principal factors appear: (1) a *Race and Resources* factor measuring the presence of nonwhite population, housing crowding, and low income; (2) a *Social Status* factor, correlated with the percentage of professional and managerial employment, income levels, educational attainment, rental payments and housing value, and residential crowding. This factor thus serves as a socioeconomic index of census tracts; (3) a *Stage in the Life Cycle* factor, delineating family-raising areas of the city, that is to say, areas with relatively large families and numerous school-age children; and (4) a *Puerto Rican Segregation* factor, correlated with low income, female labor force participation and number of rooms per housing unit. When census tracts with high negative factor scores on this dimension are examined closely, one finds the dominant Puerto Rican concentrations in the City of Newark. The Race and Resources factor and the Puerto Rican Segregation factor thus serve to measure the concentration of each of the two minority groups within census tracts.

Also resulting from the analysis are the following two factors of less importance: (1) a *Housing Stability* factor, gauging housing vacancy rates, the proportion of housing units lacking a private bathroom, rental levels, and degree of owner occupancy; (2) a *Male Unemployment* factor, peculiarily related both to high male un-

* The detailed factor analysis results for 1960 are not reprinted here (Ed. note).

Table 1. Static Environmental Precursors of Residential Abandonment

Dependent Variable: Percent Structures Abandoned per Census Tract

Factor	Name	Cumulative R^2	Coefficient	F Statistic[a]
X_1	Race and Resources	.29	−5.49	32.93
X_4	Puerto Rican Segregation	.34	−2.15	4.39
X_2	Social Status	.36	−1.21	2.13
X_5	Housing Stability	.38	−1.44	1.68
X_3	Stage in Life Cycle	.38	+0.59	0.22
X_6	Male Unemployment[b]			
$R^2 = 0.38$	Intercept = 8.40			

[a] $F(0.05) = 3.99$.
[b] Did not attain statistical significance necessary to enter equation.

Source: Center for Urban Policy Research, Rutgers University, Newark Area Resurvey—Spring 1972.

employment rates and concentrations of elderly white women.

The factor scores on each of the census tracts were entered into the regression equation as independent variables. The dependent variable is the rate of residential abandonment in tracts between 1967 and 1971. The results of this analysis, presented in Table 1, show that only two factors proved to be significantly related to abandonment—Race and Resources and Puerto Rican Segregation. In each case, the regression coefficient displays the expected sign. Of these, by far the most significant is the Race and Resources factor. The coefficient suggests that abandonment is positively related to a tract's concentration of nonwhite population, crowded housing, and poverty. Abandonment is also highly associated with the concentration of the Puerto Rican population in a census tract—those tracts scoring highly on the Puerto Rican Segregation dimension tend to have high abandonment rates as well.

Although not statistically significant, the sign of the regression coefficient shows abandonment to be inversely correlated with a tract's socioeconomic character, that is, Social Status. Not surprisingly, areas with high rent and high value housing and with upper-middle-class populations tend to experience little housing abandonment. Abandonment is also insignificantly related to the so-called Housing Stability factor. As pointed out above, this factor gauged housing occupancy rates, rental levels, owner occupancy, and the proportion of units in a tract lacking a private bathroom. Of course, several of these constituent characteristics did correlate significantly with other factors which in turn were related to abandonment. Nevertheless, the insignificance of the Housing Stability factor underlines the importance of social characteristics of neighborhoods for understanding abandonment. The basic physical features of housing may be of secondary importance.

The basic and unsurprising finding of our environmental analysis is simply that *residential abandonment occurs more frequently in areas of general neighborhood instability,* that is, areas socially and economically substandard in terms of a variety of criteria.

NEIGHBORHOOD PRECURSORS OF
ABANDONMENT (THE DYNAMIC CASE)

In examining the dynamics of neighborhood change in Newark, we had a choice of two possible analytical approaches. The first is the analysis of interrelations of changes in individual variables over time—changes in race, income, or age composition, for example. It attempts to identify the *structure of neighborhood change*. The second approach attempts to isolate *change in neighborhod structure* by analyzing changes in the structure of interrelations among variables over time. It involves, for example, examining the relationships of race, income, and age in 1960; and again in 1970.

We shall employ the first approach, using principal components factor analysis to estimate the *structure of neighborhood change* in Newark between 1960 and 1970. A matrix of relative change quotients gauges the degree of change in each descriptive variable during the intercensal period.[4] The factors of change are interpreted in the light of both short-run local processes and major societal changes occurring during the 1960s.

The factoring of the relative change quotient matrix resulted in eight factors or variables accounting for 72.2 percent of the total matrix variance (see Table 2). The great complexity of the change phenomenon and the degree of random noise in the system are attested to by the high number of factors emerging in the analysis (only those factors with eigenvalues greater than one were included) as well as the number of minor loadings.

The most significant dimension of change summarizes a number of variables relating to the age succession dynamic that is currently prevalent in Newark. This *Age Succession* factor differentiates census tracts according to how rapidly an

4. This quotient is defined as the ratio of the 1970 percentage to the 1960 percentage for each variable characteristic (Murdie, 1969).

aging population is giving way to younger and larger families. It therefore measures the degree of change in the age and family structure characteristics of neighborhood residents. At the same time, areas of the city are also experiencing changing levels of *Socioeconomic Status,* the second dimension. Of vital importance in identifying neighborhood status change is the rate of housing occupancy; it appears that areas of declining socioeconomic condition are also characterized by declining occupancy rates.

Longitudinal change also has important and complex racial components. Change in black population is not a singular phenomenon, but appears as two distinct, independent elements. Factor 3, *Young Black Families,* differentiates census tracts according to the increase or decrease of young black families, crowded housing, and holders of manufacturing jobs. A second element of racial change gauges the penetration of impoverished blacks into the city's neighborhoods. This process is isolated by the fourth factor: *Black Poverty.*

There is definite evidence of the social segregation of black households during the process of neighborhood change. This lends validity to the hypothesis that the more successful black households constantly attempt to segregate themselves from those who are less successful (exactly as do white households), but that such segregation is too unstable to persist within the geographic confines of the ghetto.

Housing characteristics are important in factors 5 and 6. The fifth factor relates positively to home ownership, families with young children, stable or increasing home values, and increasing proportions of immigrants from foreign countries. There are also important inverse correlations with increases in both median education and female labor force participation in clerical occupations. This factor, which appears to group lower-middle

Table 2. Factor Analysis of Socioeconomic Change Variables (1960–1970) Employing Newark Census Tracts as a Data Base

	Factor							
Variables	Age Succession	Social Status	Young Blacks	Black Poverty	Ethnic Neighbor- hoods	Multi-Unit Female Employment	Poverty	Young Puerto Ricans
Percent white population: > 65 years of age	(.90)	−.01	.19	.07	.12	.11	−.07	−.06
Percent population: > 65 years of age	(.86)	.04	.26	.00	−.21	.02	−.01	−.16
Median age female	(.84)	−.04	.41	−.15	.10	.04	.03	−.14
Population per households	(−.76)	.23	−.23	−.04	.13	−.35	.10	.06
Percent population: elementary school enrollment	(−.69)	.10	.06	.18	−.23	.10	.24	.04
Percent population: foreign-born	(.65)	−.11	.16	−.25	(.50)	.07	−.01	.18
Median rooms/unit	(−.59)	−.10	.15	−.19	.14	.11	−.09	.15
Percent housing units: occupied	.01	(−.87)	−.03	−.03	−.03	−.11	.08	−.05
Percent labor force: professional, managerial	.15	(−.82)	.11	−.11	−.30	−.18	−.12	.04
Percent population: college graduate	.14	(−.82)	.10	−.13	.09	.11	−.13	.13
Median contract rent	−.28	(−.79)	.13	−.15	.24	.08	−.01	.09
Median education	−.42	(−.63)	.07	.04	(−.48)	.10	−.12	−.09
Percent population: high school graduate	.38	(−.63)	.11	.04	−.06	−.11	.01	−.12
Percent housing units: > 1.01 persons/rm	−.30	.11	(−.87)	.10	.08	−.05	−.01	−.14
Percent labor force: manufacturing	.02	.17	(−.81)	−.19	−.11	−.02	.13	.13
Percent population: < 5 years of age	(−.47)	.08	(−.79)	.11	−.01	−.01	.06	.08
Percent population: Negro	−.07	.03	(−.68)	(.52)	.11	.13	.03	−.08
Percent population: income < $3,000–$4,000	−.04	.14	.11	(.75)	−.11	.03	−.03	.03
Percent population: income > $10,000–$12,000	.11	−.42	.10	(−.50)	−.17	.30	−.15	.22
Percent housing units: no bath or share	.03	.12	−.21	(.62)	.15	.08	.07	.19
Percent housing units: owner occupied	.03	.12	−.02	−.09	(.84)	−.05	−.02	−.02
Percent labor force: female clerical	.07	.03	.12	−.35	(.70)	.10	.03	.10
Percent population: married	(.58)	−.07	.04	−.17	(.62)	.15	−.01	.10
Median house value	−.05	.08	.11	.13	(.60)	.41	−.13	−.07
Percent housing units: single-family	.10	.01	.09	−.12	−.20	.18	.18	−.36
Percent labor force: female	.12	.12	−.14	−.07	−.12	(.68)	.29	−.19
Median family income	.00	−.04	.06	.02	.11	.09	(−.76)	.04
Percent labor force: male unemployed	−.24	.13	−.11	.15	.08	.35	(.60)	.16
Percent population: Puerto Rican parentage	−.12	−.07	−.01	.29	.10	.08	.23	(.74)
Median age white female	.43	−.02	.02	.14	.08	.03	.22	(−.68)
Sum of Square Loadings	5.46	3.87	3.03	2.91	2.04	1.65	1.50	1.35
Variance explained by factor (percent)	18.2	12.9	10.1	9.7	6.8	5.5	5.0	4.5

Source: U.S. Census of Population 1960, 1970.

class, family-raising neighborhoods with a pronounced ethnic flavor, has therefore been labeled *Ethnic Neighborhoods.*

The sixth factor differentiates areas with increasing numbers of multifamily units, increasing labor force participation by female residents, and, at the same time, increasing home value. It is termed *Multi-Unit Female Employment.*

Factors 7 and 8, which indicated change in regard to poverty and Puerto Rican segregation, were omitted from our final equation since they were not significant at the 0.05 level.

Using regression analysis we employed these several dimensions of neighborhood change between 1960 and 1970 to analyze residential abandonment between 1967 and 1971. We found that the dimensions accounting for the greatest explanation of variance in residential abandonment are respectively: the Ethnic Neighborhood Factor (x_5), Age Succession (x_1), Black Poverty (x_4), the Multi-Unit Female Employment Factor (x_6), and finally, the Young Black Factor (x_3). Together, these five variables comprise 65 percent of the variance of census tract abandonment rates (Table 3).

These results must be interpreted with some care. It must be kept in mind that our factors describe *change* rather than level. For instance, census tracts scoring highly on the Black Poverty factor are neighborhoods where poor black households are becoming more prevalent. However, the tracts need not be predominantly poor or black; in fact, just the opposite might be true. Furthermore, one must avoid inferring causality from these correlations.

Our regression results tended to complement our foregoing analysis of the static neighborhood structure. For example, both analyses showed that the ethnic neighborhood dimension of neighborhood change is most importantly related to abandonment. The sign of the coefficient (-7.8) and of the factor loadings suggest that the evacuation of ethnic families from neighborhoods has marked destabilizing effects on the city's housing market. Abandonments occur least often in those areas of the city that have retained the

Table 3. Dynamic Environmental Precursors of Residential Abandonment

Dependent Variable: Percent of Structures Abandoned per Census Tract

Factor	Name	Cumulative R^2	Coefficient	F Statistic[a]
X_5	Ethnic Neighborhoods	.42	−7.79	69.18
X_1	Age Succession	.52	−2.94	18.22
X_4	Black Poverty	.58	−2.56	13.99
X_6	Female Employment	.62	−2.02	3.99
X_3	Young Blacks	.64	1.41	5.29
X_2	Social Status	.65	−1.02	2.36
X_8	Young Puerto Rican	.65	0.88	1.19
X_7	Poverty[b]			
$R^2 = 0.65$	Intercept $= 8.52$			

[a] $F(0.05) = 3.99$.

[b] Did not attain statistical significance necessary to enter equation.

Source: Center for Urban Policy Research, Rutgers University, Newark Area Resurvey—Spring 1972.

strong ethnic and family character of their neighborhoods.

The causal relationships operating here are difficult to specify, because each of these dimensions of neighborhood change constitutes a complex network of cause, effect, and coincidence. The Ethnic Neighborhood factor, for example, loads heavily on homeownership. Homeowners' attitudes and behavior with respect to a property may differ sharply from those of absentee landlords. A homeowner's upkeep of his property, although motivated largely by profit considerations, is also a response to his own enjoyment and consumption needs. Homeowners may therefore retain unprofitable housing in active use. As a result, the institution of homeownership may have important effects on abandonment.

Several elements of the Ethnic Neighborhood factor reflect powerful stabilizing forces. Homeownership, the presence of children, and ethnic ties all tend to militate against neighborhood change. Homeowners tend to be far less mobile than tenants and to have a much greater stake in their homes than tenants have. The presence of children may strengthen community ties. Similarly, ethnicity offers a shared culture which provides a potentially strong bond among residents against newcomers.[5]

Neighborhood change can significantly affect property values both directly and indirectly. Given the durability of real estate, its value is also affected by the prevailing climate of expectation—the hopes and fears of future change. In Newark, where hopes are few, the resultant stability mitigates against adverse change, and thus tends to retain property values

and retard abandonment. Whatever the exact causal links, there is a considerable relationship between the Ethnic Neighborhood factor and abandonment.

The rate of housing abandonment is also significantly related to the Age Succession factor. This factor indicates increases in the relative importance of older, smaller households, and diminishing number of children. It also loads heavily on increases in the foreign-born population. Tract scores on this dimension of neighborhood change are inversely related to the incidence of abandonment. It appears that, in part, this factor identifies the same sort of stabilizing change mapped by the Ethnic Neighborhood factor.

Aging ethnic households appear to be a positive force for the preservation of Newark's housing. The factor breaks new ground by introducing the effects of household age and size. Abandonment accelerates when younger and larger households predominate in a neighborhood. Housing serving these larger and more active households must be subjected to a great deal of wear and tear. The factor offers no evidence that this increased wear is matched by increased maintenance costs or higher rentals. Therefore, housing serving these households must deteriorate relatively rapidly, with abandonment being the apparent end product.

Our earlier analysis showed that abandonment tended to be higher in predominantly black neighborhoods. It is also significantly related to the dimensions of neighborhood racial change. The abandonment of housing appears to occur at higher rates in neighborhoods experiencing an influx of black households, as measured by both the Black Poverty and Young Black factors.

In addition to race and poverty, the Black Poverty factor loads heavily on changes in the percent of housing units lacking a private bathroom—one of the principal defining qualities of substandard housing. The landlords of such units,

5. The explosive furor over the Kawaida Towers housing development in Newark is founded upon these ties that bind neighborhood residents together. Gerald Suttles has generalized the ties into the concept of the "defended neighborhood" and examined the defense motives and mechanisms (Suttles, 1972).

which are prime targets of urban renewal demolition, are offered little incentive to maintain them. Thus "low-end" housing not retired via public programs tends ultimately to experience a similar fate through housing abandonment.

Our regression analysis shows quite similar results for the Young Black factor (x_3), which appears to represent an influx of blue-collar black families and an increase in housing crowding. From the regression coefficient, we infer that the influx of such households is associated with higher rates of abandonment, although the relationship appears not to be as strong as that between abandonment and black poverty. A previous analysis suggests that the presence of low-income and impoverished households depresses housing values in Newark's neighborhoods (James Burchell, and Hughes, 1972). Thus it is not surprising that the Black Poverty factor is more closely related to abandonment than is the Young Black factor.

The only other factor significantly related to abandonment is the Multi-Unit Female Employment factor. This factor loads most heavily on changes in the tract's percent of single-family housing units; secondary loadings occur on changes in female labor force participation and home value. In Newark, changes in the importance of single-family units result largely from housing demolition and from the limited construction of multifamily structures. The factor appears to identify areas in the city's periphery, where home values have been relatively stable, and where new construction has been concentrated.

The relationship of neighborhood change and abandonment is quite complex. This is particularly true with respect to racial and ethnic change. Analysis of both the Ethnic Neighborhood and Age Succession factors suggests that Newark's white immigrant population exerts a popular stabilizing force while increases in a neighborhood's black residents are associated with a higher incidence of abandonment. The picture that seems to emerge is a complex social process of initial neighborhood solidity and subsequent dissolution. The process of neighborhood arbitrage is clearly of vital importance for the understanding of abandonment.

Behavioral Aspects

Our analysis of abandonments in Newark is based on comparative data spanning seven years. It employs considerable information gathered by George Sternlieb in 1964 on the physical and financial characteristics of 567 structures and on the attitudes and characteristics of 391 landlords; these same structures, and where possible their current landlords, were resurveyed in 1971. Between the first and second interviews, 84 (almost 16 percent) of the 567 structures had been abandoned, and an additional 141 (25 percent) had been withdrawn from the housing market and demolished for some alternative use. Of the 391 original landlord interviews, we were able to use 286 in analyzing the behavioral precursors of abandonment. We chose to eliminate from our study those buildings removed from the housing stock for some useful alternative purpose in order to focus exclusively on those structures ·actually abandoned and those still producing housing services.

We employed 28 variables relating to characteristics of structure, tenant, landlord, and financing in our analysis of abandonment probability; one-way analysis of variance was used to test the significance of variations in the probability (Nie, Bent, and Hull, 1970). Table 4 presents the results of these tests.

Our most surprising finding was that the parcel's physical condition is rela-

tively unimportant in contributing to the abandonment decision. The size of the parcel (variable 1), its construction (variable 2), the extent of commercial occupancy (variable 5), the prevalence of adjacent nuisances (variable 6), and its specific location within urban renewal zones (variable 8) are not related to its probability of abandonment. This finding is especially striking because a structure's physical condition has traditionally been considered as vital to the level of housing services it provides, and thus its value.

Only three physical features significantly relate to abandonment probability: the quality of its maintenance (variable 3), the level of neighborhood vacancy (variable 7), and the condition of neighboring housing units (variable 9). The quality of maintenance of these structures is in large part determined both by the demand for the housing services and the costs of meeting those demands. It is not in itself an independent variable affecting the abandonment decision. Its significance here undoubtedly reflects the number of structure and neighborhood characteristics impacting both on structure value and the costs of adequate maintenance. This is certainly true of neighborhood housing condition.

The second variable indicative of physical condition and significantly related to abandonment is neighborhood vacancy rate. Again we may have here something more of symptom than cause. Vacancy, like tax delinquency, may well be a way station enroute to ultimate structure loss, considerably after social and economic forces have rendered local neighborhoods no longer viable (see footnote 2).

The third significant physical variable— the deterioration of neighborhood housing—is highly correlated with poverty, crime and vandalism, housing crowding, and a number of other pathologies affecting the housing market. As in our first analysis, social events appear to be crucial to the understanding of housing abandonment.

The landlord's abandonment decision appears, then, to hinge upon his relationship with his tenants and the strength of his commitment to his property. Landlord dissatisfaction with tenants bears a particularly important relationship to abandonment;[6] those who consider their tenants to be serious problems are much more likely to abandon. Landlords told interviewers of case after case of tenant vandalism and destruction. Although some of their complaints appeared well-founded, in other cases their unhappiness seemed to mirror their own social and racial prejudice.

Race and Abandonment

The significance of landlord-tenant conflict is highlighted by the relationship of race and abandonment. Structures inhabited by black and Puerto Rican tenants were much more likely to be abandoned than those inhabited by whites alone; furthermore, white landlords (in most cases the popularized "slumlord") were more likely to abandon than were black, minority landlords.[7] It appears, then, that the interaction of white landlords with nonwhite tenants may significantly affect the decision to abandon.

Undoubtedly, racial tensions are translated into both tenant vandalism and the erosion of the landlord's commitment to his property and to his abdication of responsibility. In many cases, landlords reported that they were afraid to visit their own structures. When fear and prejudice pervade the relationship between landlord and tenant, effective mangement is impossible.

6. The statistical significance of this relationship exceeded 0.01 (F Test).
7. The statistical significance of each of these relationships exceeded 0.01 (F Test).

Table 4. Behavioral Precursors of Abandonment—Analysis of Variance

Variable Number	Variable Name and Definition	Significance (.05 level)	Finding
A. Structure Physical Characteristics			
1.	Number of rental units in structure	No	
2.	Type of construction (masonry versus frame structures)	No	
3.	Absolute quality of structure maintenance	Yes	Better maintained structures are abandoned less frequently
4.	Comparative quality of structure maintenance (relative to neighboring structures)	No	
5.	Number of commercial occupants in structure	No	
6.	Nuisance land users adjacent to structure	No	
7.	Neighborhood vacancy rate	Yes	Abandonment is more frequent in areas of high neighborhood vacancy
8.	Location of structure in urban renewal area	No	
9.	Census measures of deterioration of neighborhood housing	Yes	Abandonment is less frequent in areas characterized by low rates of housing unit deterioration and dilapidation
B. Structure Tenant Characteristics			
10.	Racial composition of tenants	Yes	Abandonment is more frequent in structures inhabited by blacks and Puerto Ricans
11.	Tenants considered by landlord to be "problems"	Yes	Landlords who consider tenants troublesome were most likely to abandon
C. Structure Financial Characteristics			
12.	Purchase price of structure	No	
13.	Mortgage outstanding on property	Yes	Mortgaged properties are less likely to be abandoned
14.	Multiple mortgages oustanding on property	No	
15.	Structure in property tax arrears	Yes	Structure in tax arrears are more likely to be abandoned
D. Landlord Characteristics			
16.	Form of ownership	Yes	Structures held through institutions (example, corporations), are more likely to be abandoned
17.	Size of owner's real estate holdings	Yes	Structures held by large-scale owners are more likely to be abandoned
18.	Owner's race	Yes	White owners are more likely to abandon
19.	Owner's age	No	
20.	Length of ownership	No	
21.	Owner's place of residence	Yes	Landlords residing in or near their structures are less likely to abandon
22.	Owner's employment professional manager	Yes	Structures with professional managers are more likely to be abandoned

Table 4. (*Continued*)

Variable Number	Variable Name and Definition	Significance (.05 level)	Finding
23.	Owner's income	Yes	Higher-income owners are more likely to abandon
24.	Owner's experience in real estate	No	
25.	Portion of owner's income derived from real estate activities	No	
26.	Owner's labor force participation	No	
27.	Owner's reasons for initial purchase of structure	Yes	Owners inheriting structures or purchasing them for rental income are more likely to abandon
28.	Owner's desire to sell structure	Yes	Owners who initially desired to sell their structures were more likely to abandon

Source: Center for Urban Policy Research, Rutgers University, Newark Area Resurvey—Spring 1972.

Management as a Variable

The management techniques themselves are strongly related to abandonment. The probability of structure abandonment apparently increases with institutional ownership (variable 16); ownership by a large-scale landlord (variable 17); the owner's use of professional managers or rent collectors (variable 22); and absentee ownership (variable 21). All these techniques imply management at arms' length; they remove the landlord from personal involvement in decisions about tenant choice, eviction, repairs, and frequently even rent collection. Because hired managers, superintendents, and rent collectors have less at stake than the owner, they tend to be less rigorous in fulling their duties.

Despite the welcome demise of the large-scale slumlord, it has been generally agreed that large-scale ownership offers distinct competitive advantages. For example, it provides economies in maintenance expense, by allowing for the hiring of plumbers, electricians, and so forth, on a reasonably continuous basis. It facilitates access to both internal and external financing, and the exploitation of tax shelters.

The disadvantages of large-scale ownership—lack of personal supervision and servicing, ineffective screening and control of tenants—can be irreversible, and in the case of the Newark housing market, apparently lethal.

The decision to manage his property from a distance may result from a landlord's justifiable fear for his health and safety. The crime and violence rampant in some neighborhoods often create dangerous situations for rent collectors, for instance. But landlord withdrawal is not an independent variable because it usually results from the demands imposed by an already deteriorating or pernicious situation.

Mortgage Status

The presence of a mortgage binding the landlord to the structure (variable 13) significantly *reduces* the probability of abandonment. This finding contradicts the traditionally held notion that abandoned structures are usually those with top-heavy financing. We found that in most instances of abandonment, the parcel was owned free and clear; those that were heavily mortgaged appeared to have secured their indentures *after* the decision to abandon had been made. This is suggested by the fact that many structures later to be abandoned were sold for only purchase money mortgages; no cash actually changed hands. If there is a later public taking of the parcel, the holder of these mortgages may be able to cash them in. If not, he can claim a bad debt loss.

Both these scenarios suggest that abandonment and mortgages should be directly related. That they bear an inverse relationship to one another may be attributable to the impact of "red-lining" by banks and other financial institutions. Abandoned structures with no mortgages may be structures for which mortgages were unavailable from lending institutions. Lending institutions in Newark, rapidly withdrawing financing from all but a few stable ethnic neighborhoods on the city's fringe, issue virtually no credit to city properties, except through some purchases at sub-par prices of insured mortgages (Sternlieb and Burchell, 1973). This withdrawal appears to have significantly increased housing abandonment in Newark.

In summary, then, abandonment is affected by a combination of neighborhood degradation, absentee ownership, racial antagonism, tenant vandalism, landlord abdication, and credit shortages.

Conclusions

Residential abandonment appears to be more a function of owner-tenant interplay and neighborhood change than of the physical characteristics of the building itself.

Where the landlord sees tenant behavior as obstructive to his operation, there exists a potentially volatile abandonment situation. Abandonment may be imminent if the situation is exacerbated by racial differences generating mistrust or noncooperation.

Locational factors suggest that abandonment is a function of poor areas, principally black and Puerto Rican. Yet, this finding, based on a one-shot appraisal in 1960 may be too outdated or too limited to afford an adequate explanation.

Residential abandonment appears not only to be a function of poor areas but also of changes occurring within these areas. The last remnants of European ethnic neighborhoods seems to resist abandonment. On the other hand, black penetration into neighborhoods seems to increase housing abandonment.

Black home ownership appears to promise stability for inner-city neighborhoods. The trend in Newark toward resident, minority ownership provided a brief ray of hope for the city. However, our subsequent interviews with these new owners tended to diminish the mood of optimism even though they were indeed providing better maintained structures than equivalent nonresident owners. Many minority owners, expressing doubts about their properties' future, cited the weakness of financing mechanisms and the decline in the municipal services, such as schools, sanitation, and the like.

Are the various stage/sector theories helpful in attempting to explain abandonment within this associational arena? The answer must be yes. Abandonment is largely a Park/Burgess inner ring phenomenon impacted by the push-pull forces detailed by Hoyt. The resulting obsolescence neighborhoods appear as Stage 4 in Vernon and Hoover's urban evolutionary process.

Yet, viability of these neighborhoods may have been preserved and their dysfunctional end state halted were it not for a variety of social factors. The fear of reduced public safety, the decline of public services, the emergence of a dominant new core population, and the change of the city's pace from vibrance to mere sustenance all impact upon an owner's decision to abandon.

This study has only attempted to deal with a narrow aspect of the abandonment process—its findings are neither startling nor revolutionary. Much more research needs to be performed in this area. Probably the most important thrush for future endeavors is the abandonment contagion phenomenon. Does the abandonment of one structure lead to a similar disposition of others? To date this frontier is virtually unresearched.

We have paid a high price for our overoptimism about the central city's future. Public policy directed toward merely cosmetic once-over-lightly efforts has failed to restore the city to its earlier preeminence.

The precursors of abandonment which have been isolated here are at work in most of the older industrial cities of the Northeast and Midwest. A glance at the 1970 Census indicates the prevalence of the advance indicators which were at work ten years earlier in the Newark experience.

References

Allihan, M. (1939) *Social Ecology*. New York: Columbia University Press.

Anderson, M. (1964) *The Federal Bulldozer*. Cambridge, Mass.: The M.I.T. Press.

Birch, D. L. (1970) *The Economic Future of City and Suburb*. New York: Committee for Economic Development.

Federal Home Loan Bank Board (1939) *Waverly: A Study in Neighborhood Conservatism*. Washington, D.C.: Federal Home Loan Bank Board.

Frieden, B. J. (1964) *The Future of Old Neighborhoods*. Cambridge, Mass.: The M.I.T. Press.

Greenberg, M. R. and T. D. Bosewell (1972) "Neighborhood Deterioration as a Factor in Intraurban Migration: A Case Study in New York City," *The Professional Geographer* 24 (February) 11–16.

Grigsby, W. G., et al. (1973) *Housing and Poverty*. Philadelphia, Pa.: University of Pennsylvania, Institute of Environmental Studies.

Hoover, E. M. and R. Vernon (1962) *Anatomy of a Metropolis*. New York: Doubleday Anchor.

Hoyt, H. (1939) *The Structure and Growth of Residential Neighborhoods in American Cities*. Washington, D.C.: Federal Housing Administration.

Hughes, J. W. (1973) *Urban Indicators: Metropolitan Evolution and Public Policy*. New Brunswick, N.J.: Rutgers University, Center for Urban Policy Research.

Ingram, G. K. and J. F. Kain (1972) "A Simple Model of Housing Production and the Abandonment Problem." Paper presented at the Annual Meeting of the Allied Social Science Association, Toronto, Canada. Mimeographed.

James, F. J., R. W. Burchell and J. W. Hughes (1972) "Race, Profit, and Housing Abandonment in Newark." Paper presented at the Annual Meeting of the Allied Social Science Association, Toronto, Canada. Mimeographed.

Linton, Mields and Coston (1971) *A Case Study of the Problems of Abandoned Housing and Recommendation for Action by the Federal Government and Localities*. Washington, D.C.: Linton, Mields and Coston.

Murdie, R. (1969) *The Factorial Ecology of Metropolitan Toronto*. Chicago: Department of Geography, University of Chicago.

Nachbaur, W. T. (1971) "Empty Houses: Abandoned Residential Buildings in the Inner City (Factors Causing Vacant Housing in Inner Cities Experiencing Shortages in Housing Stock)," *Howard Law Journal* 17 (1):3–68.

National Urban League (1971) *The National Survey of Housing Abandonment*. New York: The Center for Community Changes.

Nie, N. H., D. H. Bent, and C. H. Hall (1970) *Statistical Package for the Social Sciences*. New York, N.Y.: McGraw-Hill.

Nourse, H. O. (1972) *Urban Decay in St. Louis*. St. Louis, Mo.: Washington University, The Institute for Urban and Regional Studies.

Park, R. E., E. W. Burgess and R. D. McKenzie (1925) *The City*. Chicago: University of Chicago Press.

Phares, Donald (1971) "Racial Change and Housing Values: Transition in an Inner

Suburb," *Social Science Quarterly* 52 (December): 560–573.

Public Affairs Counseling (1973) *HUD Experimental Program for Preserving Declining Neighborhoods: An Analysis of the Abandonment Process*. San Francisco, Calif.: Public Affairs Counseling.

Rapkin, C. and W. G. Grigsby (1960) *Residential Renewal in the Urban Core*. Philadelphia: University of Pennsylvania Press.

Shevky, E. and W. Bell (1955) *Social Area Analysis: Theory, Illustrative Application and Computational Procedures*. Stanford, Calif.: Stanford University Press.

Smith, W. F. (1963) "Forecasting Neighborhood Change," *Land Economics* (August).

Stegman, M. (1970) "The Myth of the Slumlord," *American Institute of Architects Journal* 53 (March): 45–49.

Sternlieb, G. (1966) *The Tenement Landlord*. New Brunswick, N.J.: Rutgers University Press.

——— (1971a) *Some Aspects of the Abandoned House Problem*. New Brunswick, N.J.: Rutgers University, Center for Urban Policy Research.

——— (1971b) *Abandonment and Rehabilitation: What is to be Done*. New Brunswick,

N.J.: Rutgers University, Center for Urban Policy Research.

——— and R. W. Burchell (1973) *Residential Abandonment: The Tenement Landlord Revisited*. New Brunswick, N.J.: Rutgers University, Center for Urban Policy Research.

Suttles, G. (1968) *The Social Order of the Slum: Ethnicity and Territory in the Inner City*. Chicago: University of Chicago Press.

——— (1972) *The Social Construction of Communities*. Chicago: University of Chicago Press.

Timms, D. W. G. (1971) *The Urban Mosaic*. Cambridge, England: Cambridge University Press.

U. S. Commission on Civil Rights (1970) *Home Ownership for Lower Income Families: A Report on the Racial and Ethnic Impact of the Section 235 Program*. Washington, D.C.: U. S. Government Printing Office.

U. S. Congress, House of Representatives, Committee on Banking and Currency (1971) *Housing and the Urban Environment*. Washington, D.C.: U. S. Government Printing Office.

DOREEN B. MASSEY AND RICHARD A. MEEGAN

Industrial Restructuring versus the Cities

Introduction and Methodology

The decline of manufacturing in the cities has been the subject of much recent research. One unfortunate side-effect of this concern, however, has been the tendency for the problem to be defined in spatial terms, and, consequently, for the causes of the problem to be sought within the same spatial area. This tendency to study the working of the city in economic and spatial isolation from the rest of the national economy has often seen emphasis being placed, for example, on assessment of the influence of such factors as the built-environment of the inner-city areas (congestion, dereliction, site availability, etc.) or the personal characteristics of their residents (relating unemployment, say, to age, race, or skill). The outcome of such research is often to blur and confuse the issue of causality.

The present decline in manufacturing in the cities is occurring at a time when fundamental structural changes are taking place at the level of the economy as a whole (Chisholm, 1976; Treasury, 1976). It is part of the wider phenomenon of contraction and change in the manufac-

turing base of the UK economy. The argument of this paper is that it is only in this wider context that the specific problems of manufacturing in city areas can be properly understood. The aim is therefore to demonstrate the link between locational change and developments at the level of the national and international economy.

The paper draws on research the broad purpose of which was to examine the locational implications of financial restructuring in British manufacturing since the mid-1960s (Massey and Meegan, 1978). This interest was focused down in the research project into a study of the spatial repercussions of the intervention of the Industrial Reorganisation Corporation into the electrical, electronics, and aerospace equipment sectors. The Industrial Reorganisation Corporation (IRC) was established by the Labour government in 1966 ". . . for the purpose of promoting industrial efficiency and profitability and assisting the economy of the United Kingdom or any part of the United Kingdom" (HMSO, 1966). Its intervention, before it was abolished in 1971, took the form of encouraging mergers, intra-sectoral re-

From **Urban Studies**, Vol. 15, 1978, pp. 273–86. Reprinted by permission of **Urban Studies**, the University of Glasgow and the authors.

organisation, and investment.[1] It should be stressed, however, that the fundamental concern of the research was with the processes of restructuring themselves rather than with their specific attribution to intervention by the IRC. The purpose of this paper is to draw out the implications of the results of this research for the major cities which were significantly represented in the survey.

The survey examined the interests of 25 firms in the following Minimum List Headings of the 1968 Standard Industrial Classification:

Order VIII: Instrument Engineering
MLH 354: Scientific and industrial instruments and systems

Order IX: Electrical Engineering
MLH 361: Electrical machinery
MLH 362: Insulated wires and cables
MLH 363: Telegraph and telephone apparatus and equipment
MLH 364: Radio and electronic components
MLH 365: Broadcast receiving and sound reproducing equipment
MLH 366: Electronic computers
MLH 367: Radio, radar and electronic capital goods
MLH 368: Electrical appliances primarily for domestic use.
MLH 369: Other electrical goods

Order XI: Vehicles
MLH 383: Aerospace equipment manufacturing and repairing

The sector produces both consumer goods and capital goods, includes major suppliers to the public sector and encompasses some of the country's major exporters. The sector is important not just for the stage that it has reached in its own technological development (with, for example, the transition from electrical to electronic components) but also for its potential contribution to technological changes in other manufacturing sectors.

1. These various forms of intervention will be referred to collectively under the general heading of "financial restructuring."

Although still predominantly based in the South East, some of its industries, especially in electronics, are exhibiting an increased degree of mobility and are accordingly important in terms of regional policy. In 1966, there were 1,911,000 people employed in the sector, representing about 14 per cent of the total workforce in all manufacturing industries (Department of Employment, 1975b). According to the Census of Production, the sector accounted in 1968 for 10 per cent of the net output of all manufacturing industries. At the time of IRC intervention, the survey firms employed 226,000 people in the sector, approximately 19 per cent of total employment in these industries.[2]

The restructuring processes which were analysed resulted in an overall net employment loss, in the survey firms, of 36,016 jobs: a decline of 16 per cent.[3] In terms of its geographical distribution, this overall change was dominated by three regions (the South East, the North West and the West Midlands) which experienced major declines in employment in both absolute and percentage terms (Massey and Meegan, 1978). Together they accounted for 94 per cent of the net overall loss (34,016 out of 36,016). Further disaggregation of the data, however, showed that 89 per cent of the losses suffered by these regions could be explained by the significant declines which occurred

2. The total figure does not relate to a single point in time since the individual cases of intervention took place over a period of four years. The percentage is therefore a 'rule of thumb' measure derived by comparing the survey total with total national employment in the sector at the beginning of the period (1966).
3. Between 1966 and 1972. Although the IRC was most active in the sector in 1968 and 1969 and was abolished early in 1971, evidence was found of post-merger rationalisation, following its intervention, as late as 1972. Indeed there was one case identified which involved the opening of a new plant in 1976 as a direct result of the production reorganisation following an IRC-sponsored merger six years before.

in the four major cities located within them, namely Greater London, Liverpool, Manchester and Birmingham.[4] These four cities together lost 30,315 jobs in the sector, or 84 per cent of the overall net decline in the survey firms' employment. The seriousness of this decline for the cities was emphasised by the fact that at the beginning of the period they had only accounted for some 32 per cent of survey employment in the sector.

The problem addressed by this paper is therefore that of the explanation of this net loss of 30,315 jobs by direct reference to the economy-level pressures that were operating on the sector at the time. The approach will therefore be to suggest ways in which these various pressures moulded the form taken by inter- and intra-sectoral restructuring and helped to shape its differential spatial impact—and hence its specific consequences for the cities. Before this, however, it is necessary to describe briefly the classification of employment change that will be used in the analysis.

A TYPOLOGY OF EMPLOYMENT CHANGES

The employment changes can be divided into four categories: absolute loss, locational loss, absolute gain and locational gain. An *absolute* change is one which occurs at the level of the economy as a whole, where new jobs were created, or where they disappeared altogether. A *locational* change is one resulting from the locational transfer of production, the loss or gain thus being specific to a particular geographical area within the nation. The point of this categorisation is to enable a distinction between those employment changes due to mobility of jobs and those due to differential growth and

4. The geographical areas used were as follows: Birmingham: Birmingham CB; Liverpool: Liverpool CB (inc. Netherton); London: Greater London Council Area; Manchester: Manchester CB.

decline. This distinction is of obvious importance in any consideration of the potential effects of spatial policies.

Locational change needs to be more precisely defined, however. At any given level of spatial disaggregation, the total number of jobs lost through locational shift will equal the number gained. Such figures refer to jobs which were neither gained nor lost to the economy as a whole, but which changed location. Locational shifts, however, are rarely symmetrical. The figures given here under "locational shift" represent the employment which actually arrived at the recipient location. This number is far smaller than the loss recorded at the original factories. Job movement, in other words, has frequently been either part of a process of overall cutbacks or has been the occasion for cutback. In the first case, overall cuts in capacity often entail concentrating the work of smaller factories on a reduced number of larger ones. Such moves are frequently announced as transfers, and indeed some production may well be moved. They do not, however, represent a transfer of all jobs at the previous location. In the second case, locational shift may be the occasion for major changes in production technology, again leading to a reduced workforce in the recipient region. The locational shift may be brought about because the nature of the technological change demands either new fixed capital or a new workforce. In the first case it may be necessary, in the second prudent, to move, thus reducing conflict with the Trade Unions. The figures for the number of jobs lost in the origin region, but never recreated in the recipient region, are included under the category of "absolute loss." Such jobs were lost to the economy as a whole. They are separately accounted for in the tables, however, by a disaggregation of absolute loss into *in situ* and *in transit* losses. *In situ* losses are straightforward losses in which no locational transfer of employment or production was involved. *In transit* losses are just as absolute, but they took place in the context of a locational change. The classification of *in transit* losses as part of absolute losses is important since, while a particular area may appear to be losing considerable numbers of jobs through locational shifts, only a small proportion of this employment loss may subsequently benefit another locality.

The Forms of Restructuring and their Employment Implications for the Cities

Three different groups of stimuli for the financial restructuring were identified[5]:

Group 1: Restructuring in the face of over-capacity and high costs;
Group 2: Restructuring to achieve scale advantages; and,
Group 3: Restructuring for reasons of market standing.

The inclusion of major multi-divisional firms (e.g., AEI, English Electric and GEC) made the analysis more complex, however, in that it necessitated a differentiation between those divisions which acted as stimuli to the subsequent reorganisation and those which did not. The fact that certain divisions were not important stimuli for restructuring, however, does not mean that they can be assumed to be unaffected by it. The merger of multi-divisional firms including both stimulant and non-stimulant sectors alters the situation of the latter, which can be affected both by the indirect impact of the reorganisation of the stimulant sectors (with, say, a shifting of emphasis within the newly merged firm) and by their own

5. The group titles relate specifically to the forms of restructuring identified in the survey and do not constitute absolute types which can be expected to occur in every instance of restructuring. Thus "restructuring in the face of over-capacity and high costs" will not always produce the particular forms discussed in this paper.

independent organisational integration. Moreover, such sectors are also subject to economy-level pressures (albeit not requiring financial restructuring). Non-stimulant sectors can therefore be regarded as responding to the *fact* of the merger rather than, as in the case of the stimulant sectors, to the reasons for it. To accommodate them in the analysis a separate "secondary" classification was therefore required.

The detailed impact of the three forms of restructuring on stimulant sectors are best examined by taking each Group in turn.

GROUP 1: RESTRUCTURING IN THE FACE OF OVER-CAPACITY AND HIGH COSTS

This group included product groups within the following industries: heavy electrical machinery: particularly turbine-generators, switchgear and transformers (part MLH 361); supertension cables (part MLH 362); aerospace equipment (part MLH 383).

The circumstances of the individual product groups were different; but they all shared the same problems of excess capacity and the need to cut costs, and were all suffering from a pronounced deterioration in their competitive position. The power engineering industry, in its domestic market, had to contend with a major downward revision of demand from its main customer (the Central Electricity Generating Board).[6] The potential for raising exports to counteract this shift was heavily constrained by increasing competition in overseas markets, particularly as a result of the end of Commonwealth Preference. The industry had therefore lost hitherto secure markets at

6. This was not an *ad hoc* phenomenon. It occurred in the context of a general decline in the rate of growth of demand for electrical energy, a situation exacerbated by the onset of recession in industrial activity.

home and abroad and faced increasingly severe competition in those that remained.

There were thus two particularly dominant pressures for financial restructuring at work in Group 1: (1) there was a problem of over-capacity; and (2) there was a need to cut production costs in the context of increasing international competition and a general slackening of the rate of growth of markets. Financial restructuring was needed in this situation to enable co-ordinated capacity cutting and to facilitate the reallocation of capital into other more profitable areas of production. The financial restructuring itself allowed a number of responses in terms of actual production reorganisation. The reaction to the problem of excess capacity involved straight cutbacks in production, characterised by factory closures and major redundancies. The need to cut production costs and increase relative profitability resulted in an attempt by the firms concerned to increase individual labour productivity and to reduce aggregate labour costs. This was attempted in a number of ways:

1. The selection for closure of the most labour-intensive plants;
2. intensification—the reduction of the labour force in any given production process (without any change in output or production techniques);
3. partial-standardisation (which in turn allowed some automated methods in production, and cuts in labour costs with the ensuing requirement overall for less-skilled labour);
4. the introduction of numerically-controlled machine tools in production processes where full automation was not possible (usually small-batch processes). This allowed an overall reduction in the labour required and a dichotomisation of skills of the remaining labour force;
5. finally, in some cases a shift to mass-production techniques was possible,

Table 1. Employment Change in Group 1: The Four Cities

Category of Employment Change	Number
Absolute loss	
in situ	(15,528)
in transit[a]	(4,980)
Locational loss[b]	(606)
Total loss	(21,114)
Employment gain	
Absolute gain	0
Locational gain[b]	30
Total gain	30
Net gain/(loss)	(21,084)

[a] Figure includes 1750 jobs which were linked to transfers of production within or between cities.
[b] Figure excludes 330 jobs which were transferred within or between cities.

enabling large reductions in the workforce and a change in the type of labour from craft to semi-skilled.

These measures all featured in the reorganisation of production in the industries in Group 1. How did they make themselves felt in the cities? Table 1 shows the overall employment changes in Group 1 in the four conurbations. It is clear from the table that the restructuring in Group 1 had a particularly severe impact on the four cities. Together they lost some 21,084 jobs as a result of the processes at work in this group. This amounted to 70 per cent of the cities' total net loss of survey employment during the period under study.

The "typology" of this overall employment change is particularly revealing. Nearly three-quarters of the jobs lost to the cities in this Group were not linked in any way to the transfer elsewhere of either capital equipment or jobs (15,528 in situ absolute loss). This is not surprising however, for, as argued above, the pressures for capacity-cutting and cost reduction, and the nature of technological change in this group of industries, meant that employment change was dominated by absolute cutbacks in employment— losses both to individual locations and to the economy as a whole. Furthermore, of those jobs actually linked to some locational transfer, the vast majority (89 per cent) disappeared *in transit*.[7] Even in such cases of transfer, then, the loss to the cities was not matched by corresponding gains elsewhere, potential job mobility being constrained by the overriding need for absolute cutbacks in both capacity and employment. Thirdly, the cities themselves did not experience any significant gains from the locational shifts of jobs that were occurring in the country as a whole. In return for their locational loss of some 606 jobs, the cities received 30. Finally, there were no new jobs created in the cities as a result of the restructuring in Group 1 (absolute gains were zero). The consequences for the cities of restructuring in the Group 1 industries were therefore especially traumatic. There are three major threads in the explanation for this:

1. The Group 1 industries were heavily represented in the cities. At the time of IRC intervention, the survey plants located in the cities accounted for approximately 44 per cent of employment in the dominant Group 1 industries (MLHs 361, 369 and 383)[8] yet

their share of total employment in the survey only amounted to 32 per cent. Therefore, even had the impact of the production reorganisation in Group 1 been in proportion to employment, the cities could be expected to have been significantly affected.

2. The plants in Group 1 industries located in the cities were particularly susceptible to the processes of restructuring. In fact, however, the cities experienced higher than proportionate employment losses as a result of the restructuring in Group 1—approximately 88 per cent of the total net national employment loss in Group 1 occurred there (21,084 out of a total net national decline in Group 1 of 24,013). This was largely explained by the fact that the choice of plants for closure (the first of the five measures listed above) was based primarily on considerations of labour productivity. The overriding pressure in the production reorganisation in Group 1 was the need to cut labour costs. The plants chosen for closure therefore had to be those which were relatively labour-intensive and these factories were predominantly located in the older industrial areas of the cities.

3. The cities did not gain from the locational shifts of production that occurred in the restructuring in Group 1. The cities were the origin of the bulk of the jobs which actually shifted location in the restructuring in Group 1. Nationally, there was a locational shift of some 966 jobs in Group 1 and, of these, 936 had their origins in the conurbations. 330 of these 936 jobs were transferred either within or between individual cities whilst the remaining 606 jobs shifted to locations outside them. At first sight, this locational shift appears relatively small but it must be remembered that it in fact represents only one (and the smaller) component of the process of

7. That is, *in transit* absolute loss expressed as a percentage of total *in transit* and locational loss (4980 out of 5586).

8. These industries do not correspond exactly to Group 1. Indeed it is important to stress again that the Group classification was based on examination of national economic pressures for restructuring. These did not follow any precise sectoral breakdown. In particular, parts of MLH 361 fall into Group 3, and parts of MLH 354 could be included here under Group 1. It was not possible to tabulate the initial distribution of the survey firms' employment by group.

job movement. In forms of restructuring in which retrenchment is the dominant feature, job relocation is inevitably linked to high *in transit* absolute loss. In Group 1 locational loss and *in transit* absolute loss accounted for approximately 26 per cent of total employment decline in the cities (5586 out of 21,114).

Even in those cases where the cities retained some employment in the geographical reorganisation of production, employment losses far outweighed any gain. Part of the restructuring in Group 1, for example, involved the redistribution of 150 jobs previously carried on in London, between factories in Birmingham, Manchester and Newcastle. The gain to these locations, however, has to be balanced against the disappearance of 1850 jobs at the original sites in London. The same phenomenon also occurred at an intra-city level. Economies of scale were frequently achieved by the closure of small and outlying factories with the "drawing-in" on major locations thus allowing savings primarily on service-labour costs.

Locational transfer was also linked to the changes in production techniques. One important case of production transfer in this group followed the introduction of product standardisation which allowed the use of mass production methods (involving an *in transit* absolute loss of 300 jobs and a locational transfer of 100 jobs). This change not only meant that new plant and equipment were needed but also, and perhaps more importantly, that the production process in question was effectively freed from its existing ties to the cities as a result of the changed skill requirements of the labour force. The location which benefitted from this particular transfer was in a Development Area—a site which now combined the attraction of government assistance with a newly suitable and readily available labour-

force (predominantly unskilled workers). Such developments clearly have serious portents for the inner cities.

GROUP 2: RESTRUCTURING TO ACHIEVE
SCALE ADVANTAGES

The cases in Group 2 were primarily in the following sectors: industrial systems, process control, etc. (MLH 354); electronic computers (MLH 366); radio, radar and electronic capital goods (MLH 367).

Pressures for restructuring in this group operated at two distinct levels: at the level of the economy as a whole, and at the level of the individual firms involved. In the first case, government intervention was designed to facilitate the increased *application* of the products of these capital goods industries to improve the productivity of *other* manufacturing sectors. There was, therefore, general pressure at the level of the economy for both an increase in, and a cheapening of, the output of the Group 2 industries. At the same time there was growing pressure at the level of the individual electronics firms for increased scale of resources to keep up with the rapid rate of technological innovation which was, for them, the dominant aspect of international competition. An integral feature of the financial restructuring in Group 2 was thus the need to increase the absolute amount of financial resources at the disposal of individual firms. This was necessary to enable a reduction in the proportion of funds devoted to research and development, the financing of high absolute costs of development of new products and the self-financing of large investment programmes (to overcome the problem of raising capital for long-term, high-risk projects).

The pressures for restructuring in Group 2 were therefore: (1) to increase the output of these industries; (2) to cheapen the production of that output; and (3) to keep up with the rapid rate of technological innovation. The subsequent reorganisation of production responded to these pressures in a number of ways:

1. The need to cheapen output led to increased efforts to reduce the labour content of the products with the introduction, where possible, of numerically-controlled machine tools and mass-production techniques. This is a long-term process and not one produced just as a result of restructuring.[9] Moreover, the potential for the introduction of automated techniques varies between and within industries and product groups. Mass production, for example, is not feasible in the manufacture of industrial and scientific instruments, which is still heavily dependent on small batch production processes. In those cases where automated techniques were introduced, however, there was a significant reduction in the overall size of the labour force.

2. This enabled a reduction in the level of skill required of the production workforce, and produced a growing dichotomisation of skills in the labourforce between production (predominantly semi-skilled assembly work) on the one hand and R & D control functions on the other.

3. The need for increased output meant that major new capital investment was required.

4. The consolidation of research and development facilities into a smaller number of larger groupings was generally necessary if the rate of technological innovation was to be maintained.

How did the reorganisation in Group 2 affect the cities? Table 2 shows the over-

9. With each new generation of computer, for example, it is estimated that the direct labour content is reduced by one-tenth (interview with survey firm).

Table 2. Employment Change in Group 2: The Four Cities

Category of Employment Change	Number
Absolute loss	
in situ	(1350)
in transit[a]	(136)
Locational loss[b]	0
Total loss	(1486)
Employment gain	
Absolute gain	0
Locational gain	20
Total gain	20
Net gain/(loss)	(1466)

[a] Figure includes 130 jobs which were linked to a transfer of production between two cities.
[b] Figure does not include a transfer of production between cities of 13 jobs.

all employment changes that occurred in this group. Together the cities lost some 1466 jobs as a result of the restructuring in this group—5 per cent of the cities' total net loss of employment during the period. This small proportion nevertheless represented 42 per cent of the total national employment decline in Group 2. The significance of this loss is emphasised even more by the fact that, at the time of IRC intervention, the cities only accounted for 18 per cent of total national employment in MLHs 354, 364, 366 and 367 in the survey.

The explanation for this performance, as in Group 1, is to be found in the economic pressures which created the need for restructuring. The overall process of output cheapening including the impact of long-term technological change was particularly important for the cities. The 1486 absolute loss of jobs in Group 2 occurred in MLH 366 and the factories affected were relatively labour-intensive, mainly producing electro-mechanical equipment. The increasing pressure for savings in labour costs within the industry and the concomitant move towards more automated production techniques rendered such plants obsolete. This orientation meant that the plants were particularly susceptible to the increasing pressure for labour cuts in the production workforce.

This is only part of the explanation for the effects of Group 2 restructuring on the cities, however. Nationally, Group 2 was responsible for 90 per cent of the absolute gains in the survey (1750 out of 1970). The cities did not benefit from any of these developments. This is partly explained, of course, by the fact that the initial distribution of employment in the Group 2 industries was biased against the cities. As already stated, the cities only accounted for about 18 per cent of this employment. Any "incremental growth" (i.e. additions to existing facilities on site) in these industries was unlikely therefore significantly to benefit the cities. Yet even where major new developments occurred they were not sited in the conurbations. In the cases examined in the survey, these new investments took the form of "greenfield developments" in locations outside the cities, and particularly in the Development Areas.

GROUP 3: RESTRUCTURING FOR REASONS OF MARKET STANDING

This Group can be quickly dealt with. The mergers which it covered came from a range of product groupings, as follows: military manpacks and nucleonics (part MLH 354); medium-sized electrical machines (part MLH 361); computer software (part MLH 366).

The financial restructuring in this group was aimed essentially at increasing the market standing of the firms involved through sheer size, and, for example, market share. The achievement of this did not require any major reorganisation of production and there were therefore no major effects on the spatial distribu-

tion of employment. Some changes in production did occur, however, usually as a result of organisational integration after the mergers (with, say, the elimination of duplicated research facilities). Moves of this type accounted for a net loss of 200 jobs from the cities.

Employment Change in the Cities

This section will attempt to draw together the employment implications of the forms of restructuring discussed above to show how they shaped the overall performance of the cities in the survey. This perspective is best provided by a breakdown of the overall employment change into its different components.

The complete breakdown of *employment loss* in the four cities is given by the figures quoted in Table 3. It is immediately clear from this table that the majority of jobs lost to the inner cities (58 per cent) resulted from either closures or capacity cuts *in which no locational change was involved*. This is an important finding, for it contradicts the widely-held view that the inner cities are losing employment predominantly because of job relocation—usually, so the argument proceeds, to the Assisted Areas, and as a result of the various government incentives. The great majority of the employment lost in the inner cities in our survey

Table 3. Employment Losses in the Four Cities

Job Loss	No.	Per Cent
Absolute loss	27,113	89
in situ	17,478	58
in transit	9,635	31
Locational loss[a]	3,252	11
Total	30,365	100

[a] Excluding 373 jobs transferred within or between cities.

Table 4. Net Change in Employment: The Four Cities

City	Total Employment at Time of IRC Intervention	Absolute Loss	Locational Loss	Locational Gain	Absolute Gain	Result	Difference	% Change
Birmingham	11,950	− 3,020	− 0	+40	+0	= 8,970	(2,980)	(25)
Greater London	26,473	10,228	2,563[a]	20[a]	0	13,702	(12,771)	(48)
Liverpool	11,350	4,910	250	0	0	6,190	(5,160)	(45)
Manchester	22,740	8,955	542[b]	93[b]	0	13,336	(9,404)	(41)
Total	75,513	−27,113	−3,252[c]	+50[c]	+0	=42,198	(30,315)	(42)

[a] Excludes 30 jobs transferred within London but includes 103 jobs transferred to other cities.
[b] Excludes 240 jobs transferred within Manchester.
[c] Total column does not add as it excludes all jobs transferred within and between cities.

(89 per cent) comprised jobs lost to the economy as a whole, and such losses are in no sense locationally divertible by regional policy measures. Locational losses (in other words, that employment which was actually lost to the inner cities and gained by another location[10]) formed a relatively insignificant component of decline in the cities. Excluding those jobs which were transferred either within or between the four cities in the survey, this category comprised only 3,252 jobs or 11 per cent of total job loss.

It is nevertheless the case that of the jobs which did shift location, 62 per cent (2012) went to the Development Areas. The argument is not therefore that the cities do not lose employment to locations in Assisted Areas but rather that the numerical significance of this loss can be much exaggerated. Moreover the policy-significance even of the employment which was relocated to Assisted Areas is further reduced by the fact that only 3 per cent (60) of these gains to such areas were in city locations.[11] In other words, it

is entirely possible that restructuring could have led to a city/non-city move even in the absence of regional policy. The argument is further strengthened when Liverpool's performance in the survey is examined. As Table 4 demonstrates, that city's status as a Development Area certainly did not accord it any immunity. The processes examined in this paper would have resulted in serious employment losses in the inner cities with or without the existence elsewhere of Development Areas.[12]

The *employment gains* to the cities as a result of locational shifts of production were negligible. In the survey as a whole, there were 4495 jobs identified as locational transfers. Of these, 3625 had their origins in plants in the four conurbations whilst the remainder (870) were initially located in other parts of the country. The cities only retained 373 of the former and only received 30 of the latter. Moreover, there were *no new jobs* created in the cities as a direct result of the processes examined in this paper (absolute gains were zero). The lack of employment

10. We are only concerned here with numbers of jobs—the type of employment may also change *in transit*—see later.
11. These gains were all in Newcastle.

12. Of course, it could be argued that the processes themselves were enabled by the very existence of regional policy.

Table 5. The Components of Employment Change

Components of Employment Change	All Survey Firms		Cities	
	No.	No. as % Initial Employment	No.	No. as % Initial Employment
Absolute loss	(37,986)	17	(27,113)	37
	—	—	—	—
in situ	(26,741)	12	(17,478)	24
in transit	(11,245)	5	(9,635)	13
Locational loss	—	—	(3,252)	4
Absolute gain	(1,970)	1	0	0
Locational gain	—	—	50	0
Net change	(36,016)	16	(30,315)	42

gains (both locational and absolute) could, of course, again be argued to be a result of the diversionary impact of regional policy. But, once again, it should be pointed out not only that Liverpool (which is in a Development Area) performed in the same manner as the cities in the non-assisted parts of the country, but also that, conversely, of the mobile employment identified in the survey only 10 per cent (433/4495)[13] went to cities at all.

Table 5 illustrates the impact of the employment changes on the four cities. The proportionate change, expressed as a percentage of initial employment, was significantly greater for the cities than it was for the aggregate national total in every component of employment loss. The gains were negligible.

The discussion of the employment changes has so far been conducted solely in terms of the numbers of jobs gained or lost. The restructuring, however, also had profound implications for the *type of labour* demanded, both in the sector as a whole and in the cities in particular.

The first point to be noted is that, in absolute terms, the bulk of the losses in the cities was of relatively skilled jobs.* In

13. Figure includes results for Newcastle.
* The detailed discussion of occupational structure has not been reprinted here (Ed. note).

Group 1 the reorganization had a particularly significant impact on male, skilled labor. Many of these workers, when new employment is found, face a decline in the skills used and a fall in income.

The employment losses occurring in the conurbations as a result of the restructuring in Group 2 also had implications for the skill levels of the workforce involved. The losses in this Group took place in the older electro-mechanical factories which employed more traditional engineering craft skills. Moreover, the restructuring was itself part of an overall trend towards a further dichotomisation of skills within the Group 2 industries and this too has its implications for the cities. The workforce in these industries is increasingly coming to be divided between highly qualified scientific and technical staff and semi-skilled (predominantly female) assembly workers. This dichotomisation of skills within the labour force has some tendency to be reflected within the spatial pattern of the industry. On the one hand there is a growing concentration of skilled and qualified workers predominantly in the outer South East; on the other hand semi-skilled production increasingly favours non-urban locations within the Development Areas.

The general conclusion must therefore

be that, as far as the processes we are studying are concerned, the bulk of the losses are of relatively skilled jobs. Moreover, most of these losses are absolute (see Table 3).

The implications of the categories used in the present paper bear on the nature of the macro-economic process which "produced" the change at the level of the city. The present classification is also concerned with categories of employment change *in general,* rather than with specific jobs. Thus, in our terms, the number of jobs relocated out of the inner cities may indicate, *as a category,* the degree of possibility of changed policies of industrial location enabling the retention of such employment for the inner city.

The second major conclusion from our examination of skill categories concerns the nature of the change in the demand for skills brought about by technological change and increasing capital intensity. There appears to be some division of opinion on this matter. Thus Falk and Martinos (1975) write that "rising levels of mechanisation do away with the need for unskilled labour" (p. 4), and, talking of the kind of large firms that should be retained in cities, recommend "labour intensive . . . industries that would create high unemployment for unskilled and semi-skilled workers if they moved out of the inner city areas" (p. 16). Although, evidently, the process will vary both with different industries and with the level of automation being considered, our evidence indicates that increased mechanisation, standardisation, and technological advance lead to a *relative* decline in demand for skilled labour. Some distinctions can be made, for instance, between trends towards standardisation and mass-production of specified commodities and major technological shifts such as that from electrical to electronic; but the overall movement in each case is in the same direction.

Conclusions

A major aim of this paper has been to reformulate the "problem of the city" in such a way that it can be related to an analysis of the changing structure of the national economy.[14] It is clear that the repercussions of the processes of restructuring outlined in this paper have had considerable implications for the cities, and, further, that it is only at this level of analysis that the employment changes identified could have been adequately accounted for. It is also clear that such a form of analysis may lead to rather distinctive policy conclusions.

First, while the focus of *interest* in the present paper remained at the level of the city, the nature of the definition of the problem meant that its causes did not also have to be located within the same confines. One result of this is that, to a considerable extent, such an approach shifts the locus of "blame" away from local authorities. This is not to deny that the processes of planning and of development control have any negative impact at all; it is rather to stress that that impact operates within the context of circumstances determined at, for instance, the level of the economy as a whole.

In another way, too, the results of this research lead us to argue that it is incorrect to interpret the present problems of the cities as in some way the "fault" of State policies. In this case we refer to regional policy. It is a common proposition that the existence of regional policies has been significantly responsible for the decline of manufacturing employment in major cities. A number of points on this have already been made in the preceding section. The major consideration is of course that a large part of the decline

14. It should be emphasised that this is a study of only one branch (though a major one) of that economy. In particular, we have not considered the possibility of employment growth in the service industries.

identified consisted of *absolute* loss. Such job losses are in no way divertible by spatial policies, nor are the reasons for the cutbacks likely to be influenced by such policies. These reasons were discussed in the second section; it should be noted here, however, that the losses did *not* result from company failure, a possibility which might, in turn, be attributable at least in part to detrimental locational conditions. On the contrary, it must be stressed that the closures, the redundancies, and the cutbacks which occurred indicate not failure but the only possibility for "success." Such action was necessary in order to increase the firms' profitability and international competitiveness.

The remaining loss (11 per cent gross) did, however, as recorded previously, occur through, or as part of, a locational change. Two questions arise here: the first is whether regional policies form part of the stimulus to, or critically enable, the processes involved in the locational change; the second is, given that some locational change may occur, whether the existence of regional policies influences the "destination" of these changes.* Falk and Martinos (1975), who discuss the importance of factors such as those considered here, argue that the system of regional incentives has not merely influenced subsequent locational choices, but has made possible the processes themselves: regional assistance "has made mergers and the subsequent rationalisation of plants easier, and has encouraged concentration and the substitution of capital for labour" (p. 14). One of the implications of this argument is that regional policy is, at least to some extent, part and parcel of overall national economic policy. It is part, in other words, of the same strategy as the IRC. This is an important point, and one for

which there is considerable evidence. However, if regional policy is not simply regional policy, but is part of the attempt to increase the productivity of industry, and if it is thereby reinforcing employment problems in inner cities, that does not mean that one can simply abandon regional policy. Alternative and at least equally effective means have to be found, which increase competitiveness without producing such problematical spatial repercussions.

References

Chisholm, M. (1976). Regional policies in an era of slow population growth and higher unemployment. *Regional Studies,* Vol. 10: 201–213.

Department of Employment (1975a). *The Changing Structure of the Labour force.* London: Project Report by the Unit for Manpower Studies.

Department of Employment (1975b). New estimates of employment on a continuous basis: United Kingdom, *Department of Employment Gazette.*

Eversley, D. (1975). *Employment in the Inner City: An Introduction.* EIC WP. 1.

Falk, N. and Martinos, H. (1975). *Inner City.* Fabian Research Series 320.

Firn, J. (1975). External control and regional policy. In *Red Paper on Scotland.* Edinburgh: E.U.S.P.B.

Harris, D. F. and Taylor, F. J. (1976). *The Service Sector: Its Changing Role as a Source of Employment.* Department of Environment, Leeds Regional Office.

HMSO (1966). *The Industrial Reorganisation Corporation Act.* London: HMSO.

Keeble, D. (1971). Employment mobility in Britain. In M. Chisholm and G. Manners (eds.) *Spatial Problems of the British Economy.* Cambridge: Cambridge University Press.

Lomas, G. (1974). *The Inner City.* London: London Council of Social Service.

Massey, D. (1977). A review of D. Keeble, "Industrial location and Planning in the United Kingdom" (Methuen, London,

---

* The initial paper included an extended discussion of regional policy (Ed. note).

1976), *Town Planning Review,* 48, 454–456.

Massey, D. and Meegan, R. A. (1978). The geography of industrial reorganisation: the spatial effects of the restructuring of the electrical engineering sector under the Industrial Reorganisation Corporation. *Progress in Planning,* Pergamon.

Treasury (1976). Economic Progress Report (February).

HAROLD M. ROSE AND DONALD R. DESKINS, JR.

Felony Murder: The Case of Detroit

The level of homicide victimization in large American cities has increased sharply since the mid-1960s. While the causes of this increase have been variously explained, ranging from an increase in the availability of handguns to a lack of toughness on the part of the American judicial system, no consensus has yet emerged. What is clear is that homicide victimization has a target population and a modal environment of occurrence. Black Americans tend disproportionately to be represented, both as victims and offenders, in interactions leading to homicidal death. Likewise the territorial configuration of modal black residence is the zone within the central city in which such interactions most often occur. Hostile outbursts leading one person to take the life of another are frequently attributed to the practice of life-styles in which the outcomes are normative. Such acts tend to attract little attention as long as this normative behavior does not spill over and subsequently lead to the victimization of persons not thought to belong to a subculture of violence. Traditionally, homicide deaths have occurred as an expression of anger, provoked by denials of self-esteem or a challenge to one's integrity. Such interactions are most likely to occur among friends, acquaintances, and relatives, with whom strong social bonds are likely to exist. Homicides of this type have been defined as conflict motivated by Wilt and Bannon (1974).

Of growing importance, and even greater concern, is the issue of instrumental behavior as a contributor to homicidal death. Instrumental acts leading to death are seldom an outgrowth of interaction among intimates. These are acts which are most often provoked by the desire to acquire material resources, and most often take place between strangers or at least persons with whom the strength of the social bond is weak. The central focus of this study is on the growing incidence of instrumental acts ultimately leading to death. Instrumental deaths are operationally defined here as those deaths which, on the basis of the FBI Monthly Homicide Reports, were thought to be committed by strangers or under unknown circumstances.

In a growing number of American

From **Urban Geography,** Vol. 1, No. 1, 1980, pp. 1–14, 20, 21. © V. H. Winston & Sons, Silver Spring, Md. Reprinted by permission of V. H. Winston & Sons, H. R. Rose and D. R. Deskins, Jr.

cities, nonconflict motivated homicides are increasing in importance, both relatively and absolutely. Block and Zimring (1973) reported a 290% increase in homicide among strangers in Chicago between 1965 and 1970, while Rushforth et al. (1977) reported a sharp increase in stranger homicide in Cleveland between 1969 and 1974. Stranger homicides are most often felony related, i.e., they are committed in conjunction with another crime. These and other felony murders, at least in terms of the current magnitude, represent an emerging homicide pattern that is beginning to attract scholarly attention. One of the goals of the present research is to bring the issue of felony murder into sharper focus, through an investigation of recent changes in its incidence and spatial character in the city of Detroit.

The Growing Importance of Felony Murder in Detroit

The city of Detroit was selected for this investigation because of its sharp increase in instrumentally motivated acts of lethal violence since 1965. In that year only, approximately 12% of all homicides were estimated to be instrumental; by 1975, approximately 50% could be attributed to instrumental action. Not only has there been a sharp alteration in the relationship between the victim and offender, there has also been a precipitous increase in the frequency of annual homicide totals (Table 1). There was more than a 300% increase in the frequency of victimization between 1965 and 1975. The primary time frame for this study, however, will be the period 1970 to 1975, for by 1970 the role of instrumental behavior leading to homicide death had become more commonplace.

Most homicide victims in Detroit, regardless of victim-offender relationships, are black. This pattern can be observed in most large American cities where blacks

Table 1. The Incidence of Homicide Death in Detroit: 1965–1975[a]

Year	Level of Victimization
1965	211
1966	239
1967	346
1968	440
1969	485
1970	565
1971	699
1972	685
1973	731
1974	691
1975	584

[a] There exists a minor discrepancy in the annual reporting of homicide victimization between the Health Department and the FBI. The Health Department data includes all resident Detroit homicide victims, regardless of place of death. The FBI data includes all persons killed in the city of Detroit, regardless of place of residence.

Source: Detroit Health Department.

constitute at least one-third of the population. The prevalence of homicide death in large urban environments has resulted in its becoming the fifth ranking killer of black males in the United States (Dennis, 1977). Although intraracial violence has a long history in this country, its sharp intensity is a rather recent phenomenon. Of the more current explanations for this increase are those which attribute this phenomenon to a shift in values and the subsequent expansion of potential targets of victimization, e.g., the inclusion of felony targets. Handgun availability also continues to receive much attention as a primary contributor to this increase. Both Zimring (1979) and Fisher (1976) are proponents of the increased contribution of handgun availability. Analyzing Detroit data for the years 1963 to 1971, Fisher concludes, "only the handgun murder rate exhibits a significant upward trend." The value shift thesis has received less general emphasis, but is one which should not be overlooked as a causative variable.

Value Shifts and Cultural Explanations

Value shifts reflect adjustments which are taking place in the American core culture and are thought to impact differentially upon subpopulations. The value shift thesis might best be treated within the context of a set of existing cultural explanations of homicide propensities. Cultural orientations have not, to date, been very productive as explanations of the differential propensity to violence on the part of individuals or groups in American society. The primary cultural schemas, developed in association with the commission of lethal acts of violence, are those associated with the work of Wolfgang and Ferracuti (1967) and Gastil (1971). These works, while widely cited, have come under severe criticism from a host of authors. Wolfgang and Ferracuti's concept of a subculture of violence and Gastil's concept of a regional culture of violence imply a propensity for groups to engage in violent acts on the basis of socially learned or provoking stimuli.

A distillation of the essential differences between the subculture of violence and the regional culture of violence leads to the conclusion that the former concept is characterized by offensive acts of violence, whereas the latter is more often associated with defensive acts of violence. The latter acts are usually committed as a means of preserving or protecting valued resources. The applicability of these concepts to the differential propensity for blacks to engage in acts of lethal violence seems to revolve initially around region of socialization and urban vs. rural or small-town residence. Blacks who were socialized in the rural or small-town South, prior to 1950, might be found to engage more frequently in defensive acts of violence. On the other hand, blacks who were socialized in the urban North,

since 1950, are likely to exhibit a greater affinity for engaging in offensive acts of violence. Social status, life cycle stage, personality characteristics, and context are each likely to impact on the decision to commit a violent act, but culture is likely to define the appropriate stimuli which provoke a violent response.

Acts of expressive violence more often fall in the category of defensive violent responses. Instrumental violence, on the other hand, is usually of the offensive type. The motivations for many acts, however, are not clear-cut and tend to defy attempts at a simple dichotomous categorization. Hostile outbursts of anger are more commonplace responses to the loss or threatened loss of a valued resource, e.g., honor, respect. Instrumental acts are oriented toward the acquisition, rather than the preservation, of resources. The latter acts seldom involve feelings of anger and are often committed against persons with whom there does not exist a social bond.

Instrumental acts of violence are more likely to occur in large urban environments with only very weak links to a system of agrarian values. The regional culture of violence is often associated with a rural value system. Both white and black southerners during an earlier period were thought to be carriers of the inclination for defensive violence. The urbanization of the South and northern migration of blacks have led to shifts in values as a function of both altered status and changed environmental context. Value shifts have occurred more slowly among black migrants than among the children of migrants, whose contact with the South is ephemeral at best. The South, while only recently entering the industrial development stage, continues to cling more strongly to rural values than does the post-industrial North. Thus a general set of value shifts growing out of regional differences in stage of economic development is thought to impact on the validity of the cultural schemata forged to explain the differential propensity of groups to commit acts of violence.

A regional lag in stage of economic development is likely to influence the speed with which value shifts occur. It was recently concluded that the moral orientation associated with transition from an industrial to a post-industrial society is one which fosters the struggle for luxuries. In a pre-industrial setting, the struggle was for necessities (Lesse, 1977): "Economic slavery in a world in which luxuries have become equated with necessities is psychosocially traumatic and is a major source of psychological decompensation." The struggle for luxuries on the part of black youth, who lack the requisite attributes favoring the legitimate pursuit of these goals, often leads to the legitimization of violence as a tool to be employed in their pursuit. This condition is intensified by the images projected by a hedonistically oriented, visual media, according to Jefferson (1976). He has linked the content of the media-provided images which appear in the form of graffiti to the increase in homicides in the Los Angeles black community. Jefferson (1976), in addressing this issue, states specifically:

Clearly then, black graffiti offers us a unique clue and parameter by which to judge the effects of conditioned mentacide. A preoccupation with beating the system like a film hero without effort; an identification with the power of a screen character whose life-style has been distorted and exaggerated beyond any reason of reality, and the taking on of the characteristics of a white-created black image is tested against the reality of the society—the results are disastrous.

The changes taking place in American society, which are associated with the transition from one stage of economic development to another, require cultural adjustments, some of which impact negatively upon those who are affected by these changes. The contention here is that the subculture of violence is a product of

an urban industrial society, and it is undergoing further modification in response to post-industrial economic development. Thus, the mix of persons with a propensity for expressive violence vs. instrumental violence is a function of the mix of persons socialized under a system of agrarian values and those who have been socialized in an industrial or post-industrial context, as well as the age structure of the population. A cultural orientation provides one means of approaching the question of urban violence, but like most loosely structured approaches it is not without its weaknesses.

Lethal Violence in Detroit and Other Manufacturing Belt Cities

A number of American manufacturing belt cities have shown a sharp increase in the incidence of homicide victimization during the last decade (Table 2). Like Detroit, felony related victimizations have increased most rapidly. A similar pattern of victim-offender relations also existed during an earlier period. Boudouris (1971) reported a similarity in the risk of family homicide between Detroit and Chicago during the period 1948 to 1952 and again

Table 2. The Change in Risk of Homicide Victimization in Selected American Manufacturing Belt Cities Between 1963–65 and 1971–72

Place	Per 100,000 Population: 1963 and 1965 rate	1971–1972 rate
Chicago	10.83	22.78
Philadelphia	8.11	21.74
Detroit	9.64	38.93
Baltimore	14.77	36.08
Cleveland	11.99	38.47
St. Louis	17.01	34.16

Source: Barnett, Arnold; Kleitman, Daniel J.; and Larson, Richard C. (1975).

in 1965, although by the latter year it appeared that instrumental behavior leading to death was more common in Chicago than in Detroit. In most of these cities the risk of victimization has more than doubled since the early 1960s, while that of Detroit and Cleveland has more than tripled. It has been demonstrated by Block (1976) and by Rushforth *et al.* (1977) that the sharpest increase in incidence of victimization in Chicago and Cleveland has occurred in the area of felony related homicides. Block (1976), in describing changes in the homicide pattern in Chicago between 1965 and 1973, indicated that in 1965 non-robbery homicides were 12 times as frequent as the robbery homicides, but by 1973 they were only approximately 4.2 times more frequent. The changing pattern of homicide victimization appears to be occurring in a number of manufacturing belt cities, and although Detroit is often singled out as representing an extremely violent environment it does not appear to differ significantly from its regional neighbors with whom it possesses much in common.

The Character of Place and Potential for Violence

The contextual dimension of urban violence is one which should not be overlooked. Detroit, a 20th century industrial center where violent confrontations between unions and management were the order of the day during its early years of development, is characterized by a historical tradition of violence. It is believed by some that this tradition provided the context for the several riots which have occurred in the city, including the 1967 riot. Support by blacks for the use of both collective and individual violence was noted as early as 1960. The level of support, however, appeared to differ in selected east and west side neighborhoods (Leggett, 1968). The violent acts engaged in by a segment of Detroit's blue-collar labor force were designed to secure valued gains, particularly from the "Big Three" automakers. These actions were essentially instrumental in intent. Thus, instrumental violence evolved as a normative tactic in the struggle between labor and management during an earlier period. Likewise, it was clear in the late 1960s that the militant tradition associated with unionism was being carried on by segments of the black work force in specific automotive production plants. A tradition of employing acts of instrumental violence to secure valued gains seems to have grown up with the city. It now appears that the sons of some blue-collar workers are carrying on the tradition under a very different set of circumstances.

By the early 1970s, Detroit acquired the title of murder capital, U.S.A. The continued upward spiral in the incidence of homicide seemed to provide some support for this unflattering designation. Why was this occurring in a city that housed one of the better paid, if not the best paid, blue-collar labor force in the nation? Green (1977) notes, however, that in 1973 "one in three of the production workers employed by the large auto corporations were out of work" (p. 48). He goes on to indicate that conditions worsened by 1975 as unemployment benefits had run out, such that conditions resembling the great depression of 1930 were in effect. Blacks, as a group, were the most severely disadvantaged by this turn of events. Young blacks who had not yet gained a foothold in a faltering economy were even more severely disadvantaged. This, coupled with the previously noted value shifts, paved the way for an escalation in acts of lethal violence. By 1975, Detroit, like other American manufacturing cities, was suffering from the impact of the transition from an industrial economy to a post-industrial economy, and there seems to be only limited opportunity for unskilled entrants to enter the labor force in a changing economy.

Post-War Changes in the Demographic Characteristics of the City

In the period between 1940 and 1970, Detroit's black population had grown from slightly fewer than 150,000 to 670,000, with 100,000 black migrants settling in the city during the 1960s. By 1970, only New York and Chicago's black population exceeded that of Detroit. The rapid growth of the black population was accompanied by large-scale white abandonment of the city in both the 1950s and 1960s. This, according to Long (1975), has been primarily responsible for the changing racial composition of the city. Blacks constituted approximately 16% of the population in 1950, but by 1970 were almost 45% of the population.

In the wake of black population growth and white abandonment of the city, the physical scale of the black community has changed enormously since 1940. Prior to 1950, the core of the black community was confined to a rectangular zone east of Woodward Avenue. During the 1950s, rapid physical expansion of the black community was in evidence as a sizable zone of west side housing became available for black occupancy. Although blacks have moved to the edge of the city in the southeastern quadrant in Detroit, this movement has been far less dramatic than the large-scale expansion which occurred on Detroit's northwest side during the 1960s, and which has continued into the 1970s. Today, the city's projected population of more than 800,000 blacks is distributed over a broad area of the city, but the housing market which serves most blacks is racially segmented. A recent study by Farley provides little support for the notion that major changes in this pattern are likely to be forthcoming. The Farley, Bianchi, and Colosanto (1979) "Detroit study" generally indicates little in the way of compatible pref-

erence, in terms of black and white responses to a comfortable racial mix.

The spatial sorting out of the population, especially since 1960, has led to the emergence of spatial segmentation within the black community by social status. During the 1960s a sizable middle-income community emerged in the northwest sector of the city. The rapid abandonment of the city by the white population, and the subsequent emergence of an excess housing supply, have probably had the effect of weakening spatial segmentation within the black community, on the basis of status attainment. Block (1979) found in Chicago that the residential proximity of the poor and middle class was strongly correlated with crime rates in general and homicide rates in particular. It is apparent that the poor show little reluctance to engaging in outbursts of violence against one another, but it is evident that the poor perpetrate property crimes against each other as well. Nevertheless, the non-poor provide a potentially more productive felony related target. The juxtaposition of poor and non-poor neighborhoods within the black community provides the access necessary to facilitate a heightened incidence of felony related acts.

Neighborhood Stress Levels as a Measure of Internal Variation in Detroit's Black Community

While most acts of homicide take place within the city's black community, one would expect the distribution of those acts to be more highly concentrated in zones of lesser affluence. Heterogeneity, in terms of status attainment, is more characteristic of the black community as a result of housing dynamics and shared experiences. Because of this heterogeneity, a simple measure of the internal variations in socioeconomic status probably fails to illustrate the complexity of the population mix at the neighborhood

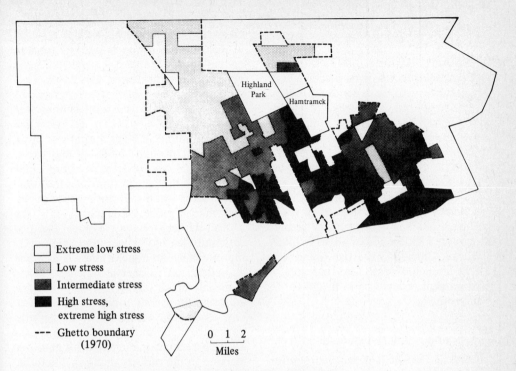

Figure 1. Neighborhood Stress Levels in Detroit's Black Community

scale. It might be shown that a more sensitive indicator of the prevailing quality of life at this scale is an index of neighborhood stress. Territorial stress levels are employed to illustrate the level of disaffinity between residents and their external environments. Only recently, Harburg *et al.* (1973) devised an approach that would permit the measurement of stress levels at the neighborhood scale. Their stress model was designed to allow them to identify high and low stress neighborhoods in black and white residential areas in the city of Detroit. Employing a variation of their technique, stress levels were derived for each neighborhood in Detroit's black community in 1970 (Figure 1). Unlike Harburg *et al.* (1973), the stress levels derived in this instance did not include crime variables. But the variables do reflect the other ele-ments of economic deprivation, residential instability, and family instability.

Because of the large number of neighborhoods involved and the difficulty in interpreting the actual values measuring neighborhood stress, a nominal value scale was established. Neighborhoods were classified as extreme high stress, high stress, intermediate stress, low stress, and extreme low stress. It was thought that as neighborhood stress levels increased so would the risk of homicide victimization. There was only a moderate association between stress levels and homicide rates, as stress levels explained only 7% of the variance in Detroit in 1970. Only in high stress and poverty neighborhoods was the stress model successful in providing a satisfactory explanation in terms of risk of victimization. Much of the risk of victimization in high stress neighborhoods is the result of hostile outbursts and has only limited association with felony related acts. Nevertheless, Kasl and Harburg (1972) indicated that black Detroit residents perceive residential robbery to be a serious problem in both high and low stress neighborhoods. This finding, however, may stem from the fact that only neighborhoods representing polar cases were employed in the Kasl and Harburg citizen survey. The 1975 pattern of felony related homicides occurred more frequently in neighborhoods of intermediate stress. In intermediate stress neighborhoods, a greater diversity in socioeconomic status is likely to prevail. Block (1979) has found that robbery-homicide tends to represent a more frequent occurrence in this environmental context.

Robbery and Robbery-Homicide

Robbery in Detroit had reached serious levels in 1970. An increase in robbery usually increases the risk of physical harm as violence frequently accompanies robbery (Wilson and Boland, 1976). The highest risk of robbery victimization among 26 large American cities is said to exist in Detroit; also, it has been shown that "the risk of being robbed is greater for blacks than for whites, for the young than for the old, for males than for females, and for the poor man than for the rich" (Wilson and Boland, 1976). Police reported that robberies in Detroit increased steadily from fewer than 6,000 in 1965 to more than 23,000 in 1970. Between 1970 and 1975, there was a pattern of fluctuation in the annual number of robberies reported to the police. But during the latter 2 years of this interval, the movement was upward.

The increase in the incidence of robbery has led to an increase in robbery-related deaths, but Zimring (1979) points out that fewer than half of the robbery deaths can be explained by the increase in robberies. He attributes the sharp increase in robbery deaths to the changes in the kinds of weapons employed in the commission of robberies. In 1965, guns were employed in fewer than 21% of all Detroit robberies. In that year, guns and knives were employed with similar frequency. By 1974, 43% of all robberies were committed with guns, whereas knives were used in only 12.5% of the cases. The switch from less lethal to more lethal weapons is thought to represent the principal factor leading to an increase in the incidence of robbery-homicide.

Non-robbery related felonies also occasionally lead to violent interaction ending in death, but none of these is as commonplace as robbery-homicide. More than half of all felony related homicides are associated with robbery. Thus, in a city where the incidence of robbery is unusually high, and the vast majority of all robberies are committed with guns, an increase in the robbery death rate is to be expected. Burglary, which is a much more frequent offense, seldom brings victim and offender into direct confrontation, and thereby reduces the probability of the occurrence of violence. In Detroit, however, death associated with breaking and entering ranks second to robbery in frequency of occurrence. It is said by some that burglars, as a rule, are less violence oriented than are robbers. But this statement no doubt refers to professional burglars rather than street criminals. Yet, according to Silberman (1978), young street criminals do not engage exclusively in a single type of criminal behavior. The same writer also concludes that some robberies are not economically motivated, but instead tend to be a reflection of expressive behavior rather than instrumental behavior. He specifically states "it would be more accurate to say that younger criminals' motivation is expressive rather than instrumental" (Silberman, 1978, p. 60). The latter statement is of questionable validity, even though it is apparent that some evidence of expressive behavior is sometimes associated with street crime.

Since robbery-homicide is the most frequently occurring form of felony murder in Detroit, an assessment of robbery trends within city subareas might prove instructive in shedding light on one aspect of the violence syndrome. The incidence of robbery varies greatly from one district to another within the city. By and large, robbery is a frequently occurring event in low-income black districts, and, while present, is a far less frequently occurring event in more affluent white districts. During the period 1970 through 1975, there were fewer than 4,000 reported robberies in one of the largest remaining white districts in the city. In two core ghetto areas, more than 13,000 robberies were recorded in each. The actual number of robberies occurring in the two predominantly black districts was likely even higher, but it is well known that blacks exhibit a reluctance to report offenses to the authorities. Thus, white districts that are primarily residential appear to be only one-third as likely as black districts to represent zones of extremely high risk of victimization.

The Spatial Pattern of Robbery Victimization

The risk of robbery victimization can be more clearly delineated in terms of place of occurrence by viewing variations in both risk and incidence within the city's police districts. The city has been divided into 13 districts by the Police Administration. Five of these districts served ghetto core neighborhoods in 1970, whereas three others were the sites of ghetto fringe neighborhoods. Districts 5, 7, 13, and 10 were the places of occurrence of approximately 43% of all robberies during the 1970–75 interval. These were also the districts where the risk of victimization was generally greatest (Figure 2). Only

the downtown district with its small residential population, and an adjacent district, which also had a relatively small population, were areas in which robbery rates were higher.

Variations in the annual frequency of robbery within the above five districts reflect evidence of ongoing internal variations in the composition of the population at risk. But in each district the number of robberies had declined by 1975. The greatest declines occurred in districts 5 and 10, which reported levels of 59 and 55%, respectively, of the 1970 level. Districts 7 and 13, which are located closer to the center of the city, reported 76 and 93% of their 1970 robbery levels. The latter two districts experienced a smaller decrease in the incidence of robbery throughout this interval. District 13 showed the smallest decrease of any district and by the end of the period showed a decrease of the same order of magnitude of that for the total city. While robbery was generally decreasing in inner districts, it had become a more severe problem in outlying police districts than it had been in the past.

Explanations for the shift in spatial pattern of robbery victimization are associated with the changing pattern of residence of those choosing to engage in robbery; the increased mobility of robbery offenders, made easy by an expanded freeway system; and the juxtaposition of potential predator and prey, resulting from an anchoring in place of a less mobile, elderly population. An expanded robbery target zone has accompanied the physical expansion of the black territorial community since 1970, an indication that both robbers and victims continue to be predominantly black. The decline in the total population of the city from 1970 to 1975 has no doubt impacted on the total number of robberies. The result has been a reduction in the total number of robberies with an apparent reduction in the risk of victimization.

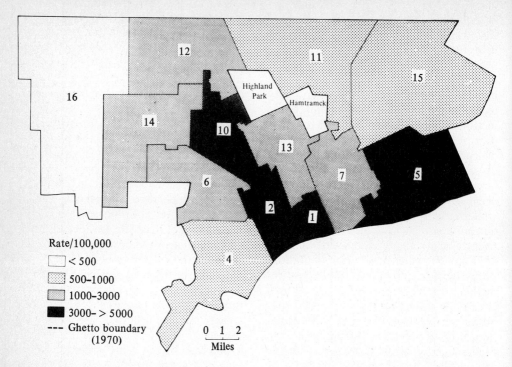

Figure 2. Robbery Rate by Police District

Detroit Homicide Patterns: A Place Perspective

Homicide in Detroit, unlike robbery, increased steadily until 1974, and then showed a small decrease in 1975. That decrease has continued through 1978. The police districts in which most of the robberies occurred during this period also accounted for 46% of all homicides. The two west side districts (13 and 10) were slower to experience a downturn in homicide occurrence than were their east side counterparts (7 and 5). Like the spatial pattern of robbery victimization, all outlying districts recorded an increase in number of homicides between 1970 and 1975.

Most homicides in Detroit, as elsewhere, are conflict motivated. As indicated previously, conflict motivated homicides are likely to occur more frequently in high stress districts than elsewhere. The neighborhood effect of conflict motivated homicide is thought to differ from nonconflict homicide. Wilt and Bannon (1974), using 1972 Detroit Police records, indicated that conflict motivated homicide occurred with greater frequency in police districts 5, 7, and 10. District 13 was the site of the occurrence of a disproportionate share of nonconflict motivated homicides. Nonconflict motivated homicides, while occurring frequently in the same districts that account for the majority of all homicides, also tend to favor specific environmental settings. These are settings with a greater number of commercial targets, more vulnerable populations, and the presence of a threshold population committed to a subculture of violence.

Internal Changes in the Pattern of Homicide Victimization within the Black Community

The spatial organization employed earlier to evaluate trends in robbery and robbery homicide in Detroit was police administrative units. Within that organizational framework, spatial differences in the incidence of violent behavior can readily be detected. But these administrative units are usually spread over large areas and therefore fail to identify those spatial pockets in which persons are at greatest risk of victimization. In order to correct for this shortcoming, high incidence clusters will be identified employing data describing the place of residence of victims in both 1970 and 1975. While place of residence and place of occurrence usually represent separate locations, the distance separating the two is generally short. Police district data refer to place of occurrence, but when moving to a neighborhood scale analysis one shifts to an alternate data source, the city health department. Data provided by the latter unit refers to place of victim residence. High incidence clusters embrace a set of contiguous census tracts in which three or more homicide victims resided in both years. It is assumed that these clusters identify life-style zones in which specific behavior leading to violent conflict is thought to represent frequent occurrences.

High incidence clusters may embrace as many as 15 or more contiguous neighborhoods or no more than 2. Most clusters, however, include five to six neighborhoods. For the purpose of generalization, clusters will be referred to as east or west side clusters. This division of the black community into east and west side components is done in order to pursue the notion that subcultural differences may possibly be associated with this division. Going back to the earlier argument regarding value shifts and subcultural differences in motivations to violence, this general compartmentalization of the black community will allow us to specify a modal orientation to violence on the basis of social origins of the population. It is believed that east side residents are more likely to be supporters of a behavior pattern associated with the regional culture of violence, whereas west side Detroiters will show a greater inclination to support aspects of behavior associated with the subculture of violence. These assumptions are based on the belief that east side Detroiters will more likely represent persons of southern origin, while west side Detroiters are more likely to represent persons who are natives. The west side represents a zone of more recent settlement by segments of the black population. Blacks, in large numbers, have only been present in this zone for slightly more than a single generation. East side Detroiters represent more than two generations of residence. If these assumptions are valid, a somewhat different pattern of victim-offender relationships should prevail in east and west side clusters.

Instrumentally motivated homicides are thought to have a stronger association with the subculture of violence, as interpreted here, than the regional culture of violence. West side clusters, then, should contain a larger proportion of instrumentally motivated acts than those occurring in east side clusters. Thus, some differences in the frequency of expressive vs. instrumental acts should emerge within the context of our east side-west side dichotomy.

The number of high incidence clusters multiplied between 1970 and 1975. But the principal clusters continued to embrace a set of common neighborhoods. The new clusters emerged in zones which were not intensely settled by blacks in the initial year (Figure 3). The ratio of acts of expressive violence to instrumental violence in these outlying neighbor-

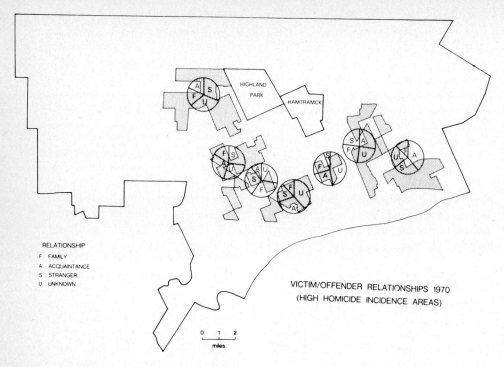

RELATIONSHIP
F   FAMILY
A   ACQUAINTANCE
S   STRANGER
U   UNKNOWN

VICTIM/OFFENDER RELATIONSHIPS 1970
(HIGH HOMICIDE INCIDENCE AREAS)

0   1   2
miles

Figure 3. Victim/Offender Relationships, 1970

hoods tended to favor expressive violence. Expressive violence was also dominant in each of the four major east side clusters. In these neighborhoods, violent interactions among acquaintances and members of the family were most commonplace. West side clusters were characterized by greater instrumental violence in the latter year, whereas in 1970 four clusters were dominated by violence between strangers and unknowns. The single largest number of robbery-homicide victims in the city in 1975 were residents of that west side cluster (Figure 4). By 1975, instrumental homicides had become more dispersed and less concentrated, giving the appearance that instrumental acts had declined in relative importance. But, even so, robbery-homicides were apparently more common on the west than on the east side of the city.

It was previously shown that the inci-

dence of robbery was high on both the east and west side of the city. A major difference among these zones was the extent to which armed robbery was a more frequently occurring west side phenomenon. During the 3 years for which robbery data were reviewed, armed robbery accounted for approximately two-thirds of all robberies in west side districts. Clearly, the higher percentage of armed robberies on the west side led to the higher incidence of robbery-homicide. The west side appears to be the site of a larger number of narcotics outlets which are frequent robbery targets. Operators of "narcotics pads" seldom passively allow themselves to be robbed. In situations such as this, both the offender and the robbery target are armed, thereby increasing the risk of death. Block (1977) has indicated that the presence of a gun and victim resistance are the most important determi-

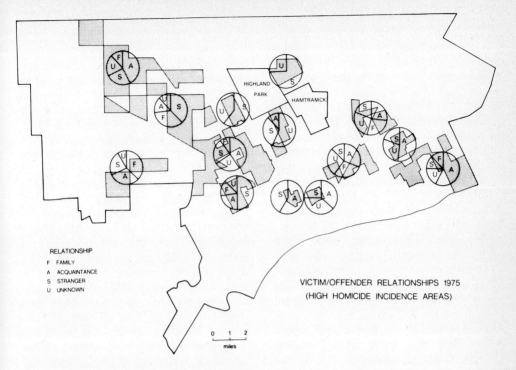

RELATIONSHIP

F   FAMILY
A   ACQUAINTANCE
S   STRANGER
U   UNKNOWN

VICTIM/OFFENDER RELATIONSHIPS 1975
(HIGH HOMICIDE INCIDENCE AREAS)

0   1   2
miles

Figure 4. Victim/Offender Relationships, 1975

nants of outcome. Armed confrontations motivated by the desire for material gain tend to occur more often among selected west side than east side residents. Thus we partially attribute this pattern to a difference in cultural orientation among segments of east and west side populations.

Age Structure of Victimization

The epidemic quality of the changing level of homicide victimization is basically related to the increase in the risk of victimization of black males 15 to 29 years of age. The changing and unsettled life-styles of this segment of the population place them at greater risk of victimization. This increase is most often reflected in the changing level of victimization in both acquaintance and stranger categories. The young adult group accounts for only approximately 25% of the black male population, but frequently as many as half of the male victims. This group is an even greater contributor to the incidence of offenses. Nationally, the modal age of black male victimization shifted downward from 35 to 44 during 1958 to 1962, to 25 to 34 years during the interval from 1969 to 1974 (Rushforth *et al.,* 1977). So serious has this problem become that it represented the leading cause of death among black males 20 to 24, and 25 to 29 in 1972 (Dennis, 1977). The downward shift in the modal age range of victimization is basically related to the chosen targets of violence of youthful perpetrators.

It is evident that the young adult black population has made a break with the past in terms of its willingness to adopt values and engage in life-styles which increase the potential for violence. These life-styles are abetted by the increased secularization of society in general, and the heightened emphasis on the macho image in particular. Jefferson (1976) provides some support for this finding in his analysis of graffiti content. He points out that the following elements are most often contained in the graffiti that is found on physical structures in one black community: sexual preoccupation, elements of control, identity, and violence as a way of life. It should be noted, however, the graffiti content including these elements was found in a city with one of the lower black homicide rates among the nation's largest cities. The risk of young adult male victimization is partially associated with involvement in nonconflict motivated acts of violence. In Detroit, where nonconflict motivated acts are widespread, one-half of the risk of male victimization is concentrated in the young adult population. But, in Atlanta, where conflict-motivated acts are common, the risk of victimization is less concentrated in this age segment.

Young male offenders who engage in instrumental violence are more likely to choose persons much older than themselves as targets, although it is also clear that their peers are not immune from attack. The increase in incidence of victimization in Chicago during the period 1964 to 1974 resulted in older black males accounting for almost 40% of the excess increase, whereas young black males accounted for only 25% of the excess increase (Block, 1976). The increased participation of young adults in felony related activities has also increased the risk of the offender becoming a victim. Among black male robbery-homicide victims under 30 in Detroit, the risk of the robber being victim was approximately one in three during the study period. But it should also be noted that young adult victims of robbery-homicide constituted 41% of the total during this interval.

The Changing Importance of Interracial Homicide

Interracial homicide is not a frequently occurring event in the United States; however, an increase in acts of instrumental violence has resulted in an increase in the percentage of homicides which are interracial. Among interracial crimes in general, robbery is the most frequently occurring. While the principal focus of this study centers on black victimization, it would be illogical to ignore white victimization in a study emphasizing felony related acts, for it is only in the area of felony related acts that a serious risk of interracial victimization exists. In 1975, white robbery-homicide victims in Detroit accounted for 37% of the total in that category. At the same time, whites comprised only 25% of all homicide victims in the city. The risk of white victimization is strongly influenced by the increase in frequency of instrumental violence.

Most interracial homicides are an outgrowth of a robbery involving a black offender and a white victim. In those instances where the victim of a robbery-homicide is black and the offender is white, the latter generally involves public or private police or the operator of a commercial establishment. A review of 34 of the 48 robbery-homicides involving white victims in Detroit in 1975 reveals 44% were street robberies, one-third commercial robberies, and only approximately 6% were residential robberies. In 87% of the cases, the offender was black and in 94% of the cases the offender was under 30. Fifty-five percent of the offenders were between 15 and 19 years of age, while only 30% were in the 20 to 24 age group. Multiple assailant victimizations represented the modal pattern, a characteristic which others have found to be commonplace in robbery-homicides where the offenders are youthful. The age structure of victimization, however, places more than half of the victims in the over-50 age group.

Robbery-homicide cases involving black victims reveal both similarities and differences to the pattern observed in white victims. The most striking similarity is the pattern of multiple assailants, most of whom were under 25 years of age, with the largest concentration in the 15 to 19 age category. Differences exist in the age structure of victimization, with more than half of the victims similar to the offenders in age, although a secondary concentration was detected in the over-50 group. The most notable difference, however, distinguishing black from white victims, was the site of victimization.

The modal site of victimization in this instance was residential units, a departure from the street robbings which were more commonplace when white victims were involved. Street sites involving black victims occurred in fewer than 20% of the homicide victimizations. Commercial targets represented approximately one-third of the sites in both white and black victimizations. Generalizing from a small number of cases confined to a single year, it appears that the most significant attribute in robbery-homicide victimizations is the behavior of black youth, rather than the racial identity of the victims. The differences which appear possibly reflect the perceived greater vulnerability of older victims and the ambiguous character of sites in terms of function, i.e., a number of residential sites in which black victimizations occur are in fact functionally commercial sites. It is not uncommon for residential robberies to take place in structures that are known outlets for the sale of narcotics. Thus, it appears that in an atmosphere where the acquisition of material objects is an overriding concern, and legitimate outlets for acquiring valued goods are restricted, a modified subcul-

ture of violence will attract a growing number of adherents. The availability of handguns is the modal weapon of choice in Detroit robbery-homicides, a critical element promoting active rather passive participation in the subculture.

A Centrographic Analysis of the Spatial Pattern of Robbery-Homicide

The general description of the spatial pattern of robbery-homicide has been improved by providing point data which describe the location of the place where the act occurred, the place of residence of the victim, and the place of residence of the offender. This level of descriptive analysis utilizes centrographic techniques to illustrate the pattern of dispersion of the location of all three sites.*

The data employed in this analysis include most white and black robbery-homicide victimizations occurring in the city of Detroit in 1975. Unfortunately, data describing the entire universe were not secured, but missing data are minimal in the case of white victimizations and slightly larger in the case of black victimizations. A slightly smaller number of victimizations than that which represents the universe was thought superior to the use of sample data points to illustrate the spatial dimensions of robbery-homicide, where the racial identity of the victim was to represent the central focus.

When the distribution of white homicides sites is compared with the residential location of the victims, the victim residences are more dispersed, with 18% of the white victims residing in the city's suburbs. A similar relationship holds when the pattern of black homicide locations are compared to the residential locations of the victim.

Naturally, since the white victim residences are widely dispersed, including

* The detailed centrographic maps are not reprinted here (Ed. note).

Table 3. Age of Felony-Murder Victims and Defendants

Race	Number of Observations	Years: Mini-mum	Maxi-mum	Mean	Standard Deviation	Median
White victims	50	17	89	42.6	18.8	39
White victims defendants	64	15	48	24.2	8.3	21
Black victims	59	12	75	29.4	14.1	24
Black victims defendants	74	16	72	29.0	13.1	25

the suburbs, this group travels the longest average distance, 2.9 miles to the homicide site. The site of white victimizations is the high-risk, retail-commercial establishment, where they usually work. Most of the offenders in these cases are residents of the black community, who travel shorter distances to commit robbery that may result in homicides, averaging 2.2 miles per trip. There is little difference in the distances that black victims travel to the site of the crime and the distance that the offenders travel, since both of these groups (victims and offenders) reside in Detroit's black community. The centrographic statistics describing these two distributions verify this finding.

Black participation in felony-robbery is high whether the victims are black or white. The age data in Table 3 clearly reveal that when looking at the range of ages, nearly every age group is at risk when robberies are committed. However, the median age data allow some further generalizations to be made. These data show that the white homicide victims are the oldest, with a median age of 39 years. The offenders of white victims, who are black in 80% of the cases, have a median age of 21, suggesting that older white victims who participate in retail-commercial activities which are prime robbery targets are often victimized by young blacks.

When the age data of the victims and offenders in cases of black homicides are compared, both the victims and offenders are young, with median ages of 24 and 25 years, respectively. Although 10% of the offenders in cases of black homicide are white, they tend to be older and often include store owners and police officers. Young blacks, while frequently guilty of victimizing older whites, are inclined to victimize younger blacks as well. The median age of black victims and offenders who participate in intraracial robbery-homicide is the same (29 years).

The spatial components of black robbery-homicide are characterized by smaller standard distances and generally a different orientation of ellipses than characterizes white victimizations. None of the distributions, however, represents a normal spatial distribution in terms of the expected distribution of these attributes around the mean center of the distribution.

The dispersed pattern of both black and white distributions of the site occurrence is obviously related to the choice of target of victimization. The principal role played by commercial targets in white victimization should result in a more dispersed pattern of homicide locations than that which characterizes black victimization. But an even greater dispersal of place of residence of white victims is evident. Assailants are drawn from a smaller zone in instances of both black and white victimization.

Summary and Conclusions

Felony-murder began its path of rapid growth in the city of Detroit during the late 1960s and continued into the mid-1970s. A similar pattern has been observed in other cities in the industrial North. The motivations for felony-murder are primarily thought to be associated with value shifts and with the increase in the availability of more lethal weapons, i.e., handguns. These two variables, however, are often set in motion by an economic downturn which limits opportunities for participation in the regular economy.

The spatial pattern of victimization within the city of Detroit is associated with the evolution the city's black territorial community. Pockets of high incidence victimization appear throughout the black community, but robbery-homicide is seldom the prevailing form of violence in these pockets. In Detroit, west side clusters show a greater propensity for nonconflict motivated homicide than is true of their east side counterparts. This has been conjectured to represent the influence of regional differences in socialization, where greater emphasis on offensive violence is thought to characterize recent northern socialized populations than is true of those of southern origin. The kind of data available, however, does not permit one to easily validate this notion.

The sharp upturn in acts of instrumental violence during the 1970 to 1975 period has led to an increase in the incidence of interracial homicide. Black youth bent on acquiring wealth and/or other material goods seem insensitive to the racial identity of the victim. The circumstances which bring the victim and offender together seem much more important than race in terms of outcome. It cannot be said, however, that blacks killing whites and whites killing blacks does not have some influence on the perception of one group by the other. The motivations and circumstances surrounding these acts impact most severely on segments of the black community. The presence of commercial wastelands through this community, in both high and low stress neighborhoods, attests in part to the prevalence of the violence syndrome in the city. But this visual manifestation obscures the more complex issues which energize the whole process of violence provocation and the future status of segments of the black community.

Literature Cited

Barnett, Arnold, Kleitman, Daniel J. and Larson, Richard C., 1975, On urban homicide: a statistical analysis. *Journal of Criminal Justice,* Vol. 3, 90.

Block, Richard, 1976, Homicide in Chicago: a nine-year study (1965–1973). *The Journal of Criminal Law & Criminology,* Vol. 66, 496–510.

———, 1977, *Violent Crime.* Lexington, Mass.: Lexington Books.

———, 1979, Community, environment, and violent crime. *Criminology,* Vol. 17, 46–57.

Block, Richard and Zimring, Frank E., 1973, Homicide in Chicago, 1965–1970. *Journal of Research in Crime and Delinquency,* Vol. 10, 1–12.

Boudouris, James, 1971, Homicide and the family. *Journal of Marriage and the Family,* Vol. 33, 667–676.

Dennis, Ruth E., 1977, Social stress and mortality among non-white males. *Phylon,* Vol. 38, 315–328.

Farley, Reynolds, Suzanne Bianchi and Diane Colasanto, 1979, Barriers to the racial integration of neighborhoods: the Detroit case. *Annals,* Vol. 441, 97–113.

Fischer, Claude S., 1976. Toward a subcultural theory of urbanism. *American Journal of Sociology,* Vol. 80, 1319–1339.

Gastil, Raymond D., 1971, Homicide and a regional culture of violence. *American Sociological Review,* Vol. 36, 412–427.

Green, Robert L., 1977, *The Urban Challenge-*

Poverty and Race. Chicago: Follett Publishing Co.

Harburg, Ernest et al., 1973, Socioecological stressor areas and black-white blood pressure: Detroit. *Journal of Chronic Disease,* Vol. 26, 595–611.

Jefferson, Roland S., 1976, Black graffiti: image and implication. *Black Scholar,* Vol. 7, 11–19.

Kasl, Stanislav, V. and Harburg, Ernest, 1972, Perceptions of the neighborhood and the desire to move out. *Journal of the American Institute of Planners,* Vol. 38, 318–324.

Leggett, John C., 1968, *Class, Race and Labor.* New York: Oxford University Press.

Lesse, Stanley, 1977, Moral codes and the post-industrial era. *American Journal of Psychotherapy,* Vol. 31, 1–5.

Long, Larry H., 1975, How the racial composition of cities changes. *Land Economics,* Vol. 51, 258–267.

Rushforth, Norman B. et al., 1977, Violent death in a metropolitan country, changing patterns in homicide (1958–1974). *New England Journal of Medicine,* Vol. 297, 531–538.

Silberman, Charles E., 1978, *Criminal Violence, Criminal Justice.* New York: Random House.

Wilson, James Q. and Boland, Barbara, 1976, Crime. In William Gorham and Nathan Glazer, editors, *The Urban Predicament.* Washington, D.C.: The Urban Institute, 179–230.

Wilt, G. Marie and Bannon, James, 1974, A Comprehensive Analysis of Conflict-Motivated Homicides and Assaults—Detroit, 1972–1973. Final report, unpublished.

Wolfgang, Marvin and Ferracuti, Franco, 1967, *The Subculture of Violence.* 179–230. London: Tavistock Publications.

Zimring, Franklin E., 1979, Determinants of the death rate from robbery: a Detroit time study. In Harold M. Rose, editor, *Lethal Aspects of Urban Violence.* Lexington, Mass.: Lexington Books, pp. 31–50.

JULIAN WOLPERT, ANTHONY MUMPHREY,
AND JOHN SELEY

Community Discretion over Neighborhood Change

The neighborhoods that constitute our metropolitan areas have inherited a substantial residual from the past, and only modest incremental changes are possible (Natoli, 1971). Yet the changes that are taking place are significant, because they may reveal shifts in the complex resolution of forces from those that have shaped present neighborhood patterns.

The neighborhood is part of the package that an individual acquires when renting or purchasing a home or any other establishment within a metropolitan area. The price of rental or purchase includes neighborhood effects. Because this implies that market value will be affected by neighborhood changes, it is reasonable to assume that residents would prefer at least to maintain, and possibly improve, the external environment that lies beyond their own immediate territory or property rights. In observing the variety of neighborhood development, however, we find that highly differential patterns are clearly visible. Some neighborhoods, according to the point of view of their residents, are actively deteriorating, others remain sta-

ble, and others are improving. The most significant determinants of this process are probably external to the neighborhood, such as national economic forces or social and economic stratification and its associated syndromes at the lower level: unemployment, poor health, crime, and family instability. Control of the physical neighborhood and its land-use functions and activities is thus only a localized symptom of stratification and the institutions through which it is maintained and cycled. The neighborhood unit is a localized vantage point from which to observe not only the consequences of stratification but also the innovating exceptions in community activities that are to become even more prominent in the future.

The neighborhood has a population, a set of land-use types, architectural styles, and a set of functional and nonfunctional activities that link the people with each other and with the physical setting. The population can be stable or highly fluid as can the land use. Population change and land-use change can result in variations of neighborhood satisfaction.

From **Geographical Perspectives and Urban Problems**, 1973. Reprinted by permission of the National Academy of Sciences, Washington, D.C., and the authors.

The physical artifacts of a neighborhood are parallel to its population. Some new activities, functions, and artifacts enter periodically; others are restructured or adapted *in situ* to contemporary influences; and still others depart permanently or shift to other neighborhoods. Three categories of activities are available for the neighborhood or community to function as a collectivity: inducement, maintenance, and prevention. The community can induce entry into the neighborhood of people, activities, functions, institutions, and artifacts that will have beneficial neighborhood effects. The community can promote the maintenance of the present stock through minimizing negative neighborhood effects. The community can act to prevent the entry of activities that will have net negative neighborhood effects. Elimination of unwanted facilities is a fourth possible community activity.

Who has control over such changes? How is such discretion distributed? What are the legitimate and *ad hoc* institutions that determine such discretion and its relevant sanctions? What are the limits of such control when considering the mammoth social and economic problems that swamp some neighborhoods?

The community as a constituency is only one of the relevant actors with a right to exercise such discretion. Individual residents, property owners, and entrepreneurs from within and without the neighborhood may exercise their own discretion. The political unit within which the neighborhood is located may also participate on the basis of its own set of aggregate objectives and goals. Government at the county, state, and federal levels may also have established the right to participate. The objectives of these participants are likely to be in severe conflict, and the outcome of such contention is neither easily predictable nor so patterned through precedent as to enforce its tradition through any simplified causal analysis.

Our objectives here are to attempt to structure the resolution of discretion at neighborhood or community levels. We begin with several scenarios of the present, followed by a discussion of what is meant by noxious facilities, with taverns as an example. In addition, a set of suburban strategies, both formal and informal, is outlined for its relevance to inner-city neighborhoods. A number of activities that have been suggested or tried in ghetto neighborhoods of Philadelphia, such as community planning efforts, technical services, and remapping, are then discussed briefly.* A number of scenarios are presented to abstract a range of community experiences with land-use change. In conclusion, we offer some policy recommendations that are suggested by the processes we have observed.

Present Scenarios

Land-use changes in a community are the result of at least four contributing factors: individual resident action, individual nonresident action, community attitude and action, and city policy. These factors interact in such a way that any community may seem to be upgraded, downgraded, or remain the same according to the perspective used by the observer. A community may thus define its own utility differently from the way the city or an individual defines it. Any community, in turn, may have a definition of utility that differs from that of other communities. The process of community land-use change, with the available options, can thus be represented in diagrammatic form as in Figure 1. At each stage, a community has several options open to it. (Three has been arbitrarily chosen as the number of options here.) Depending on the discretion of the community, these options are more or less constrained by individual and city actions or failures to

---

* The detailed Philadelphia example has not been reprinted here (Ed. note).

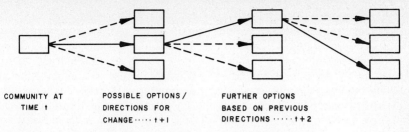

COMMUNITY AT
TIME t

POSSIBLE OPTIONS /
DIRECTIONS FOR
CHANGE ····· t + I

FURTHER OPTIONS
BASED ON PREVIOUS
DIRECTIONS ····· t + 2

Figure 1. Process of Community Land-Use Change, with Available Options

act. Each step in the life cycle of the community leads to further possibilities for change, either upgrading or downgrading.

The interactions of the forces listed as affecting a community's life cycle can be represented in a series of scenarios of existing conditions. The scenarios indicate the importance of active community groups, which effectively promote their own discretionary powers at the cost of the short-run profits of insiders and outsiders and which can compete with more affluent communities in the larger urban arena to attract positive facilities and to bar negative ones. Such community efforts can benefit from a number of specific activities while participating in them. The first three scenarios represent more or less current short-run processes of neighborhood threat and response.

are posted in the area, they are generally ignored and subsequently torn down. The residents don't really become aware of the impending installation of the restaurant until construction begins. By questioning construction workers, they are able to find out the proposed use of the site. They become concerned over the traffic problems (several of the adjacent families have small children) and the late hours. Representatives go to the local ward politicians and eventually to their councilman. He informs them that the change in zoning to allow construction of the restaurant is handled by the City Zoning Board of Adjustment, which approved a variance for the site well in advance of the planned construction. Hadn't they seen the notices of a public hearing? The residents are urged to give up the fight.

SCENARIO 1

Community A is a low-income black community with a number of empty lots and vacant houses. There is little community mobilization and no resident organization. Almost all residents rent their homes. A private developer decides that an abandoned commercial strip in the area would be a good location for a hamburger take-out and short-order restaurant. The restaurant would need adequate parking as well as entrance and exit driveways. The developer anticipates good business from maintaining late hours (until 2 A.M.) for the restaurant.

Although the required zoning notices

SCENARIO 2

Community B is also a low-income community. Although there are several vacant lots and empty houses, the residents have developed a certain amount of community pride. Several of them have been able to purchase their own homes and have begun to renovate them. A neighborhood civic association has conducted a campaign to clean up the empty lots to make areas suitable for play, and they have petitioned the city to do something about the empty houses.

The same developer wishes to install his restaurant in the area. This time, however, the public-hearing notice for a zoning change is not ignored. The residents organize a busload of people to attend the hearing and to register their sentiments. They inform their councilman of their intentions and their strength. They also notify the City Planning Commission and ask for assistance in understanding and fighting the zoning change. They go into the public hearing armed with numbers, facts, and alternative proposals for development.

At the public hearing the Board of Adjustment is overwhelmed by the community presentation. The developer decides that it is not worthwhile to fight, and he withdraws his petition for a variance. The community has won, and it is now in a position to develop and rezone as it wishes.

SCENARIO 3

Community C is a low-middle-income ethnic community situated close to center city. The location is ideal for a residential area with access to an expanding downtown, but the neighborhood has traditionally avoided encroachment because of its high stability. An enterprising young architect decides that he likes the character and location of the neighborhood and decides to purchase an old shell to renovate. Other young professionals learn of his successful renovation, and he forms a company to repair and sell old empty houses. Still others, encouraged by the upgrading, the location, and the relatively low price of the houses, start buying homes. The residents are quick to grab what seem to them to be immediate and substantial profits from selling their homes. As more young affluents move in and long-time residents move out, the character of the neighborhood changes. Pockets of ethnicity remain, but the community can no longer be classified as ethnic. Although only a few minor zoning changes were made, the community has been transformed.

NOXIOUS FACILITIES

Tavern location may be a good predictor of community discretion or its absence; where taverns are highly concentrated, community discretion is generally low. By examining the locational clusterings of such services and facilities, we may be able to find indicators of community discretion.

Within the city limits of Philadelphia, 2,961 establishments have liquor licenses (one for every 600 residents), whereas a 1951 Pennsylvania State law permits only one license for every 1,500 persons, which would mean 1,285 establishments. Because new licenses may not be issued, and there have been none since 1939, new tavern locations can be based only on transfers from existing sites, and liquor licenses are bought and sold. As a result of the transfers, taverns have a tendency to shift in their concentration and to form clusters in areas in which there is little community discretion. In one section of the city, a ninth bar is being added to a two-block zone in the immediate vicinity of an elementary school and other public facilities. In one fourth of Philadelphia's wards, one license exists for every 360 residents; in some of the newer sections of the city, there is only one tavern for more than 8,000 residents.

The neighborhood bar may serve as a beneficial social focus for a community; it may provide employment for community residents and an economic base for the local businessmen with only modest spillover effects on surrounding properties. As the market price of such licenses rises, however, ownership is becoming increasingly controlled by outsiders, and tavern clusters in low-income neighborhoods are beginning to replace the neighborhood bar. Such clusters are becoming more frequently the scene of drug traffic, prostitution, and violent crime in the city. They escalate the downgrading of neighboring land use and promote out-migration of those who can afford to leave.

The Liquor Control Board may refuse a location transfer if the proposed site is within 200 ft of another tavern; within 300 ft of a restrictive institution, such as a school or church; or can be proved to be harmful to the health, welfare, peace, and morals of the residents living within a 500 ft radius.

Use of the site as a tavern may be prevented only by the actions of well-organized indigenous community groups who can act quickly to investigate the proposal, assemble evidence and petitions, voice their objections to the city solicitor and the police, and produce a mass showing at the public hearing. Recent tavern sitings can be explained by an insufficient community awareness or response.

Taverns are not the only kind of establishment that can have negative neighborhood effects. Other examples are gas stations, used-furniture stores, pawnshops, and public housing. Facilities such as these are overwhelmingly concentrated in the older and poorer sections of the metropolitan area where their clustered existence exceeds the local demand.

On the basis of data derived from two disparate population groups, we have attempted to determine preferences with respect to a set of 50 facilities that might be located in residential neighborhoods. The control group consisted of university students whose responses indicated preference for two alternative patterns: a suburban neighborhood consisting only of housing within a narrow price category and with convenient stores collected into a shopping center, or a center-city location of housing intermixed with high-amenity facilities and with other needed facilities, such as hospitals or repair shops, confined to neighboring communities.

The other population group that was sampled consisted of residents of a low-income blue-collar white area of Philadel-phia. The residents in this area were mainly homeowners of two-story row houses with a value of $7,000–$9,000. They seemed proud to own their homes, often given to them by their parents, and had positive feelings toward their community, even though most recognized that it was a poor or a tough neighborhood. Often they were resigned to annoying problems in their immediate neighborhood and thought they were incapable of changing things themselves. There were strong feelings about the threat from outsiders (especially the "colored"), but no sense of strategy about responding to such threats.

Many noxious facilities were in the neighborhood, but these posed little threat in comparison to such invasions as an expressway, public housing for blacks, or other facilities that might be used by black children. The overriding factor was wariness of any change, because they were sure that it would bring about downgrading; the city (the outsiders) would not help the area, and they would be powerless to prevent the intrusion. Residents wanted more police stations, libraries, day-care centers, and schools, but no other facilities, because these would attract black residents.

Suburban Strategies

Why are suburban areas not subject to this kind of problem in land use? Perhaps they have been able to develop better ways to control their communities.

The strategies employed by suburbs to control land use within their areas seem to fall into two general categories: formal strategies, or those that utilize existing codes to justify exclusionary policies; and informal strategies, or those that fall outside the realm of existing codes and regulations. Both sets are aided by existing laws that are either too loosely defined or too loosely enforced, or some combina-

tion of both. The informal strategies are
aided, specifically, by a decision-making
process that allows for traditional political pressures. In reality, the strategies
work well enough for the suburban resident to maintain and perpetuate his homogeneous community with very little
effort. We shall examine here some of the
formal and informal strategies used by
suburban communities to control land use
and discuss the value of these strategies to
the city dweller for control of his community.

FORMAL STRATEGIES

Formal strategies of exclusionary zoning
are used to determine the supply, desirability, mix, and specific nature of housing permitted in an area (U.S. Commission on Civil Rights, 1970; Trubeck,
1970). Following is a list of the most
commonly used strategies, employed generally in conjunction with each other to
standardize and enforce the exclusion involved. This exclusion is justified for
vague reasons of health, safety, public
services, finance, land values, and aesthetics (Sager, 1969).

Large-lot zoning (U.S. National Commission on Urban Problems, 1968) spec-
   ifies a minimum area per dwelling
   unit. Its effect is to reduce the total
   amount of housing available for an
   area.
Exclusion of multiple dwellings effectively
   excludes apartment houses. This is now
   successful, except in some token areas
   (National Commission on Urban Problems, 1968).
Establishment of minimum floor areas for
   houses was meant originally to ward off
   overcrowding and density problems.
High subdivision requirements determine
   minimum house size and cost, the costs
   of improvements of land, and the
   amount of land within each subdivision

that can be specifically devoted to housing. This requirement is used to maintain the rural character of suburban
communities.

INFORMAL STRATEGIES

Informal strategies are possible under
zoning regulations because those regulations are set up in a manner conducive to
community pressure (Williams and Norman, c. 1970; Weiner, 1971). As Allen
Muglia (1961) points out, a board of
adjustment for a suburban community
generally equates the spirit of the community with the spirit of the law. In the
absence of clear definitions of the public
interest, local boards of adjustment rely
on vocal pressures to determine the community attitude.

In other ways, too, the nature of suburban communities allows for more direct
citizen control over zoning. The small size
of the community generally makes control easier, and size and homogeneity imply that problems of suburbs are not as
complex as for cities. This in turn, means
that citizens can more easily comprehend
town problems and politics and can devote more energy to problems, such as
zoning, that are considered to be important. Citizens don't have to apply much
pressure because of the self-perpetuating
nature of the political process in suburban
communities and because of more direct
control over that process. The citizens of
a suburban community elect commissioners who are generally known to them.
These commissioners then appoint the
zoning board of adjustment for that community. The commissioners reappoint the
board of adjustment members only if they
maintain the "community spirit" (as interpreted by the commissioners). In addition, the zoning board members are subject to pressures (informal strategies)
from local neighborhood and civic associations. The circular, ingrown nature of

the process (community elects commissioners, who appoint zoning board, which is pressured by the community, which elects commissioners, and so forth) creates "tight little exclusionary islands" (Sager, 1969) that perpetuate their homogeneity by utilizing the loose enforcement of zoning codes on a regional level and strict enforcement on a local level.

Thus, informal strategies are related not so much to a specific political system as to the general makeup of suburban communities, including their politics (Babcock, 1966). In a very homogeneous suburb, the resident may have to do little or nothing to maintain and perpetuate his suburb. In a less homogeneous suburb, a resident may join a civic association to lobby for his zoning rights, but this seems more of a preventive safeguard than a necessary offensive. Unless his community is subject to a major change of form, the suburban resident can rest assured that the homogeneity of his area will, almost without aid, perpetuate itself.

The informal strategies noted above are those common to many activist groups. Sometimes a controversy splits a suburb; for instance, when businessmen propose expansion of the commercial district and are opposed by residents. In this case, strategies are aimed more at responding indirectly to specific opponents and less at directly influencing the formal decision makers. The deliberate mix of strategies, important though it may be to the ultimate outcome, does not generally affect the kinds of strategy available to suburban groups. A tentative list of informal strategies includes public hearing—speakers, petition, letters of support; picket; boycott; national advocate group support; legal threats or lawsuit; sit-in; local neighborhood groups referenda; general influence.

Zoning, as it is used in the suburbs, is a middle-class phenomenon. It is used to protect exclusively, which is the backbone of homogeneity or compatibility. In low-income urban neighborhoods, homogeneity is not at such a premium, because restrictions on land use mean restraints on possibilities for change. If a resident wants to add a store or apartments to his dwelling or a store or a factory wishes to expand, it is more convenient not to have to fight strict zoning ordinances that prohibit such changes. The opportunity to enhance property for monetary advantage may be much more important in the low-income neighborhood than maintaining a homogeneous community. Middle- and upper-class communities see neighborhood value as crucial to house value; the pure value of a house is supplemented by a neighborhood value to make up the market value. In the ghetto, neighborhood value is less crucial to property value, and it is possible to alter the pure value of a property by simply changing its use. Conversion of individual properties becomes the road to optimal market value.

One can only ignore neighborhood value for a limited time when attempting to raise the market value of a property, which makes a certain amount of stability desirable in the long run. The short-run individualistic approach demands flexibility, but the long-run neighborhood approach demands stability. In the short run the low-income property owner can raise market value by adding to his property directly; in the long run, his property can only be enhanced by a general upgrading of his neighborhood (Fagin, 1955).

POLICY IMPLICATIONS

Flexibility, permitted by loose zoning restrictions, is more of a fringe benefit and is gained at the expense of discretion over the kinds of land use in a neighborhood. This becomes evident when the low-income resident tries to make the transition from flexibility to stability, or from individual property enhancement to neighborhood upgrading. At that point, he finds that he has no control over neighborhood change and that more often than not he cannot change the flexible character of zoning for his community.

What seems to happen is that the low-income resident finds that not only is he unable to affect neighborhood value, but his neighborhood is subject to an influx of outsiders who take advantage of the short-run flexibility and profit to build whatever they want. In a community striving for some kind of long-term stability, this creates a negative effect. In an efficient situation, the benefits that an outsider receives from installing a noxious land use in a neighborhood (such as a take-out hamburger house) are transferred as loss to the neighborhood. With no discretionary powers, the low-income community remains in the short-run position of flexibility. Middle-class communities, on the other hand, have developed discretionary powers, so that noxious facilities are placed in low-income communities both for traditional (i.e., economic) and practical (i.e., political) reasons. The ratio of pure and total or market (i.e., pure plus neighborhood enhancement) value (P_v/T_v) of property to discretion is defined as in Figure 2, with middle-class and low-income communities in the indicated places.

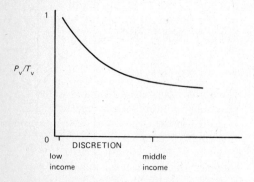

Figure 2. Ratio of Pure and Total Value of Property to Discretion

In some sense, too, the forced flexibility in low-income communities forms part of a vicious circle. Because of existing flexibility, the property owner finds that he can control his own property use and expects that others can control theirs. Mainly because of naïveté and existing practices, he does not try to control neighborhood value as a whole by an orderly pattern of land uses. This lack of neighborhood control is emphasized by outsiders, who take advantage of the flexibility not to upgrade but to ensure continued short-run advantages. The resident, perhaps later desirous of the advantages of increasing neighborhood value, must now face a great number and variety of land uses. His naïveté turns into defeatism when he tries to challenge outside forces that are better organized and have more political clout than himself. Whereas, initially, flexibility meant that he could easily enhance his own property, its exploitation soon indicates that it is a mixed blessing. The cycle is complete.*

Conclusions and Recommendations

For low-income communities to exercise a greater degree of discretion over the neighborhood environment implies greater control over four major functions: maintenance of existing properties, elimination of undesired land-use activities, prevention of noxious facilities from entering, and inducement of desired services and other land use. The strategies that have been described, including remapping, Community Technical Services, Community Alerting Service, and community organizing principles, all deal with some aspects of these community functions. (For another example of alternative strategy see Twentieth Century Fund Task Force on Community Development Corporations, 1971.) These strategies do not

---

* A section on future scenarios has not been reprinted (Ed. note).

ensure greater community discretion or neighborhood satisfaction, either alone or in combination. In practice, as has been demonstrated, the strategies do not always mesh with the political system as it exists and operates.

To make metropolitan policy making more responsive to the needs of communities requiring the most attention, the demands of such communities must be felt. Community mobilization in low-income neighborhoods must first overcome the self-fulfilling defeatism and self-perceived marginalism that breed defeat. The community that does not mobilize is subject to severe costs because of the wedge left open for outsider opportunism and the city's expediency. Sometimes a community must run just to stay in place.

There is another relatively minor danger. Imitating suburban strategies can also lead to dysfunctional aspects. Just as many suburban areas are locked into the bind of having produced a sterile form of homogeneity (compatibility) at a severe cost to the overall metropolitan area, low-income neighborhoods might find as well that too much success can yield dissatisfaction. This is not a danger as yet, but mindless admiration for the middle-class mode may lead to ever-increasing metropolitan sterility.

References

Altschuler, Alan A., 1970. Community Control: The Black Demand for Participation in Large American Cities. New York: Western Publishing Company.

Babcock, Richard, 1966. The Zoning Game. Madison: University of Wisconsin Press.

Boyce, David, Chris McDonald, and André Farhi, 1971. An interim report on procedures for continuing metropolitan planning. Philadelphia: Regional Science Research Institute.

Fagin, Henry, 1955. Regulating the timing of urban development. Law and Contemporary Problems, 20 (1955).

Malko, Barry, 1970. Notes on the development of a community opposition group. Research on conflict in locational decisions. University of Pennsylvania Regional Science Department Discussion Paper No. VI.

Michael, Donald, 1968. On coping with complexity: Planning and politics. Daedalus, 97 (4), 1179–1193.

Muglia, Allen, 1961. An inquiry into the philosophy and practice of zoning. M.A. thesis, University of Pennsylvania.

Natoli, Salvatore, 1971. Zoning and the development of urban land-use patterns. Economic Geography, 47 (1971).

Reiner, Thomas, 1967. The planner as value technician: Two classes of utopian constructs and their impacts on planning. In H. Wentworth Eldredge, Ed., Taming Megalopolis, Vol. I, pp. 232–247. Garden City, N.Y.: Doubleday (Anchor Books).

Reiner, Thomas, John Seley, and Robert Sugarman, 1971. The Crosstown controversy: A case study. Research on conflict in locational decisions. University of Pennsylvania Regional Science Department Discussion Paper XII.

Sager, Lawrence Gene, 1969. Tight little islands: Exclusionary zoning, equal protection, and the indigent. Stanford Law Review (April).

Trubeck, David, 1970. Exclusionary zoning: Cases, statutes, materials. New Haven, Connecticut: Yale Law School.

Twentieth Century Fund Task Force on Community Development Corporations, 1971. CDCs: New Hope for the Inner City. New York: Twentieth Century Fund.

U.S. Commission on Civil Rights, 1970. Land use control in relation to racial and economic integration. Washington, D.C.: U.S. Commission on Civil Rights. Staff Report.

U.S. National Commission on Urban Problems (Douglas Commission), 1968. Building the American city. 91st Congress, 1st Session. House Document No. 91-34.

Weiner, Peter, 1971. Report: Fifth Conference on Exclusionary Land Use Problems. Report prepared for the National Urban Coalition.

Williams, Norman, and Thomas Norman, undated (c. 1970). Exclusionary land-use controls. The case of north-eastern New Jersey. (Mimeo)

THE URBAN INSTITUTE

Fiscal Woes Multiply for Large Central Cities

Are New York City's fiscal traumas a special case, or do they represent a fore-shadowing of what lies ahead for many large American cities? While there is still considerable disagreement about the primary factors contributing to New York City's difficulties, a study by Thomas Muller of The Urban Institute's Land Use Center identifies paramount components of that city's, and other cities', financial conditions.

Muller's work, *Growing and Declining Urban Areas: A Fiscal Comparison,* examines many factors affecting the financial health of cities—migration, income changes of city inhabitants, municipal costs and revenues, among others. Distinct patterns emerge for the nation's large cities of half a million people or more: about half of these cities have expanding population and adequate financial resources; the others have declining population and insufficient or severely strained financial resources.

Where Are the Declining and Expanding Cities?

During the first half of the 1970s there has been a considerable net outmigration

of households from the large urban areas of the East North Central states and the Middle Atlantic states. And there has been substantial net inmigration into the South Atlantic, South Central, West, and Mountain states. These shifts appear to occur for various reasons.

Areas losing population tend to have *high energy costs* compared to growing areas. Consumers in the New York region paid 170 percent more than Houston area consumers for the same amount of electricity in 1974. Manufacturing in declining areas tends to be characterized by a high proportion of *aging capital stock* and *high labor costs.* The relatively newer industrial plants and lower wages in the expanding areas attract further industrialization, resulting in more job opportunities. *Federal government expenditures* for both military and civilian programs are concentrated in the states that are attracting inmigrants. For example, during 1969, total federal payrolls accounted for 12 percent of all personal income in the ten most rapidly growing states, but for only 3 percent in the five states with the largest absolute outmigration. *Military contracts* were also allocated in ways that favor growing over declining areas—

From **Search**, Vol. 5, No. 5–6, Winter 1975, pp. 3–9. Reprinted by permission of the Urban Institute, Washington, D.C.

$134 per capita in the Northeastern and North Central states as against $196 in the rest of the nation in 1972.

Contrary to the common notion that *public transfer payments*—welfare, social security, and so forth—are concentrated in the declining areas, such payments constituted a higher percentage of total personal income in the growing states in 1969. Also, their rate of increase between 1969 and 1973 was substantially more rapid in these same states. For example, transfer payments increased by 68 percent in New York State and 71 percent in Massachusetts in the four-year period; they more than doubled in Arizona, Florida, Nevada and Hawaii.

Another factor is the *cost of living,* especially housing costs and local-state taxes. Also, the *warmer, sunnier regions* are attracting many older people at or near retirement and many young people, too.

Why Are Population Changes Important?

Migrants are not representative of the population generally. Interregional migrants tend to have higher family incomes, more job skills, lower age levels, and higher educational attainment than nonmigrants. These attributes benefit the areas which attract them; the cities and regions they leave behind are disadvantaged.

The important *family income* impact of migration may be illustrated by comparing the Houston area, which gained population, and the Pittsburgh area, which lost population. Houston in 1970 had 14 percent more families with annual incomes of $15,000 and up than it would have had in the absence of its new inmigrants of the previous five years. The Pittsburgh SMSA (Standard Metropolitan Statistical Area) had the opposite experience: it had 14 percent fewer families in the $15,000-and-up category in 1970

than it would have had if its outmigrants of the previous five years had not moved away.

The largest metropolitan areas still enjoy the highest levels of personal income, but their *rate of income growth* has been below average. The two largest urban areas, New York City and Los Angeles, had annual income increases of 5.8 percent and 6.5 percent, respectively, between 1969 and 1973. At the same time, all other SMSAs enjoyed a per capita income growth rate of 8.7 percent.

Wealth is also shifting to southern and western states. In 1961, taxable assessed property in SMSAs of the Northeast and North Central states averaged about $2,330 per capita as compared to $1,700 in the South and West. By 1971 that gap had narrowed substantially: per capita property wealth in the Northeast and North Central states had increased to $3,640, while the other states doubled their property value to $3,400.

Private job growth also accompanies population growth, and the SMSAs losing population register a drop in private jobs, in part because of the migrants' characteristics which were cited earlier. (See Figure 1.) *Public employment* has been expanding in both growing and declining areas. However, these gains in declining areas did not offset private job losses.

Population Size and Costs of Urban Services

Economies of scale come about when unit costs drop as the volume of production increases. Unhappily, economies of scale are rare in the production of local government services. On the contrary, providing municipal services becomes more costly on a per capita basis for the more heavily populated areas. This is evident in Table 1. The SMSA size categories shown are all quite large so this is not a rural-urban comparison. Per capita outlays for local public services in 1973 for the smallest of

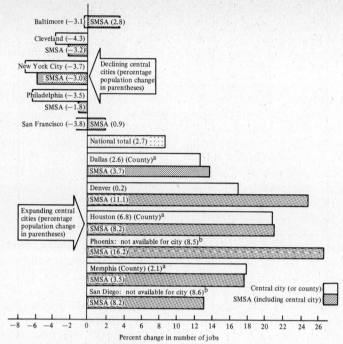

a. Only county employment data available in these cases, but these data are dominated by the central city job market.
b. The county in these cases constitutes the SMSA boundary.

Figure 1. Changes in Private Employment, 1970-1973: Selected declining and growing cities (or counties) and their SMSAs

Table 1. Relations of SMSA Population Sizes with Local Government Costs, Public Employees, and Wage Rates, Fiscal 1973

SMSA Size (Population)	Public Service Outlays per Capita	Outlays as Percent of Aggregate Personal Income	Local Government Employees per 1,000 Residents	Average Monthly $ Wage of All Local Government Employees
400,000 to 700,000	$362	7.1	27.2	729
700,000 to 1 million	372	7.4	28.1	750
1 to 2 million	422	8.0	31.1	749
2 to 4 million	465	8.3	31.8	819
4 to 9 million	493	8.3	31.9	974
9 million and over	748	12.0	42.5	1,014

Table 2. Growth and Decline among All U.S. Cities with Population of Half a Million or More, 1960–73

Growing	% Population Gain	Declining[c]	% Population Loss	New York City
Jacksonville[a]	172.6	St. Louis	−25.6	
Indianapolis[a]	66.3	Cleveland	−22.5	%
Phoenix	45.1	Pittsburgh	−20.7	Population
Houston	40.9	Buffalo	−20.2	Gain,
Honolulu	37.2	Detroit	−16.9	1960–70:
Memphis[b]	32.3	Cincinnati	−15.3	1.5
San Diego	32.1	Boston	−11.3	
San Antonio	28.6	Chicago	−10.6	%
Dallas[b]	20.0	Seattle	−9.7	Population
Columbus, Ohio	14.9	New Orleans	−8.8	Loss,
Los Angeles[b]	10.8	San Francisco	−7.2	1970–73:
Kansas City[b]	8.4	Philadelphia	−7.0	−1.8
Denver	4.5	Milwaukee	−6.9	
		Baltimore	−6.5	

[a] City-county consolidations.
[b] Since 1970, population has begun to decline.
[c] Excluding Washington, D.C.

these categories were less than half the outlays for the largest. People in the larger urban areas pay a larger share of income for local services.

A substantial portion of these higher costs stem from two personnel factors— the number of public service employees and wage levels. Table 2 shows there were 27.2 public employees per thousand residents in the 400,000 to 700,000 class SMSA in 1973, but 56 percent more in the largest class. Average monthly wages also showed a fairly steady increase with SMSA size.

If one turns from absolute size to *direction* of growth, however, the picture changes. Large growing areas enjoy advantages over large declining areas in terms of public service outlays. Partly this is because the declining areas cannot easily cut back on many established services and facility operations, and partly because the growing areas acquire extensive land areas with residents who do not require a high concentration of public services. Also, growing cities tend to be in states with lower municipal wages.

With this background, the remainder of the discussion focuses on the nation's cities of half a million or more population, except for Washington, D.C., which is a kind of city-state plus federal territory with revenue and service patterns that are not readily comparable. These largest cities—13 growing, 14 declining, and New York City in a class of its own—are shown in Table 2.

Costs of Municipal Government (Table 3)

Personnel Costs. Total wages for municipal workers account for a dominant share of outlays for local government services. In 1972–73, the declining cities spent 71 percent more than growing cities for personnel costs—$240 and $141 per capita, respectively. New York City spent $637 per capita. More specifically, to provide the same set of common municipal ser-

Table 3. Costs and Revenues of Municipal Government

	Growing Cities	Declining Cities	New York City
Municipal personnel costs per capita, fiscal 1973	$140	$240	$637
Number city workers (common functions) per 1,000 residents, 1972	8.9	12.5	12.2
Average municipal wage levels (common functions), 1972	$795	$899	$1,190
Municipal retirement payments (pensions per capita), fiscal 1974	$17	$29	$60
Capital improvement outlays per capita, fiscal 1974	$61	$73	$195
Interest on long-term debt per capita, fiscal 1974	$16	$21	$66
Total outstanding general obligation debt per capita as of fiscal 1974	$221	$351	$1,031
Per capita income, 1972	$4,011	$3,760	$4,309
Effective residential property tax rates, 1971	1.73%	2.52%	1.80%
Residential property tax rate change, 1966–1971	−4%	+22%	−10%
Revenue sharing distribution per capita, 1974	$18	$28	$35
Income and payroll taxes per capita, fiscal 1973	$7	$43	$104

vices, declining cities employed 40 percent *more workers per thousand residents* than did growing cities in 1972. Also, *average wages* of city employees performing these basic services in the declining cities were 13 percent higher in the growing cities—$899 per month versus $796. In New York City the average monthly wage was $1,190. Further, declining cities were increasing wages at a much steeper rate.

Higher costs of living account for part of the wage differentials. Rent and state-local tax differentials, in turn, are the major explanation for differences in living costs. Strong municipal employee associations that are concentrated in older cities with large unionized industrial bases also have an impact. Finally, some believe that adverse conditions such as crime and congestion require extra compensation.

Muller emphasizes that fiscal comparisons do not take account of quality differences. Cities with more employees and higher wages may be offering citizens a greater variety and better quality of service. But that is little comfort when the budget does not balance.

Benefit Packages. Retirement plans are a major non-wage benefit. Ignoring variations in the features of retirement plans, the costs are higher in declining cities because of the relatively higher numbers of city workers. Declining cities in fiscal 1974 allocated $29 per capita to city-administered retirement payments (excluding those connected with public school systems), whereas growing cities contributed $17. New York City paid $60 per capita, surpassed by San Francisco ($72) and Detroit ($81). Because of their somewhat older work forces and substantial underfunding, declining cities will have to expand their pension fund allocations even more in the coming years to keep the funds solvent.

Capital Outlays. One might expect that growing cities, with their influx of new residents, would have higher public works expenditures. Not so. In 1973–74, declining cities spent $73 per capita for capital improvements; growing cities, $61; New York City, $195.

Long-Term Debt. Many local governments use short-term borrowing, for example, to tide them over in the weeks or months before property tax receipts begin flowing into the treasury. Long-term debt, to pay for present and past capital improvements, is the serious debt item. In 1973–74, interest payments on long-term general obligation debt amounted to $16 per capita in the growing cities, $21 in the declining cities, and $66 in New York City. In addition to annual interest payments, one should also consider total outstanding indebtedness, which averaged $351 per capita in declining cities, 59 percent more than the $221 in growing cities. New York City's outstanding debt amounted to $1,031 per capita. (This discussion concerns only general obligation debts repaid from tax revenues, not revenue bonds such as those repaid from bridge tolls.)

Revenues to Pay for Municipal Services

Large declining cities do not enjoy the same ability to pay for services as do the large growing cities, according to four criteria:

Incomes. Per capita income in growing cities averaged $4,011 in 1972, about 7 percent higher than the $3,760 in declining cities. New York City had a higher level—$4,309.

Cost of Living. Data are given for SMSAs rather than central cities. In SMSAs of growing cities, the intermediate budget for a family of four in 1972 was $11,160. It was $11,808 in SMSAs of declining cities. It was $13,179 in New York City's SMSA.

Property Wealth. One might expect that cities with a greater share of commercial and industrial properties would have the advantage—but at least under the present tax structures and service requirements the opposite appears to be the case. The growing cities have 27 percent of their property base in nonresidential properties, declining cities about 40 percent. On a per capita basis, market value of *all* taxable property per capita in 1971 was $9,284 for growing cities, $9,206 for declining cities, and $13,660 for New York City.

Property Tax Rates. Effective residential property tax rates (dollar amounts paid as a percentage of market value of the property) in 1971 averaged 1.73 percent in growing cities, 2.52 percent in declining cities, and 1.80 percent in New York City, which taxes nonresidential property at higher rates. The actual per capita tax bill on residential properties averaged only $52 in growing cities, $75 in declining cities, and $151 in New York City.

Turning from ability to pay to actual revenue, the declining cities had to raise more money to meet their higher spending levels. Between fiscal 1965 and fiscal 1973, declining cities increased their total local revenues by 113 percent per capita, compared with a 95 percent increase among growing cities.

Property Taxes. Per capita property tax payments in 1973 were 44 percent higher in declining cities than in growing cities: $71 per capita in growing cities, $127 in declining cities, and $309 in New York City. These data are not entirely comparable, however, because New York City and three of the fourteen declining cities—Buffalo, Baltimore, and Boston—provide public education from these taxes, whereas separate school districts provide this service and levy separate property taxes in all of the growing cities except Memphis.

Income and Payroll Taxes. Income or payroll taxes (paid by both nonresidents and residents) accounted for 21 percent of the locally raised revenues of declining cities in 1973, but only 5 percent of the revenues of growing cities. New York City derived 19 percent of its local revenues from this source. On a per capita basis, growing cities received $7, declining cities $43, and New York City, $104 from these taxes. Since commuters pay part of these taxes, burdens to local residents are reduced.

Sales Taxes. Growing cities receive more revenue from sales taxes on the average than declining cities—$35 and $29 per capita, respectively, in 1973. New York City's sales tax amounted to $115 per capita.

Local Tax Effort. Adding property taxes, sales taxes, income and payroll taxes, and other taxes, for a sum of all locally-raised taxes (but excluding local funds for public schools in five of the cities), growing cities in 1973 collected $120 per capita, declining cities, $196 per capita, and New York City, $539 per capita.

Intergovernmental Transfers. Other revenues to cities from state and federal agencies also play a role in local finance. However, the formulas are so varied from state to state and from program to program that it is difficult to make valid comparisons. Some cities, notably New York City, fund a substantial share of welfare services while many others do not; in Texas, for example, welfare is totally a state responsibility.

Annexation—A Crucial Factor in Growth

Growth of cities, as opposed to metropolitan areas, is not explained merely by the large migratory shifts discussed earlier. Perhaps the most important element is annexation or consolidation. By taking on new territory, the central city typically gains a much higher proportion of middle-income residents who are generally homeowners. This means a reduction in the proportion of inner-city low-income households who require greater expenditures for social services. If one considered growing cities only in terms of their old boundaries, their population composition and fiscal problems would be more nearly comparable with the declining cities.

If central cities could annex or consolidate with their suburbs, this clearly would be a major fiscal gain for most declining cities. Yet cities that most need this remedy may find it most difficult to obtain under present laws and in the absence of state mandates for territorial changes. The older cities tend to be completely hemmed in by incorporated jurisdictions which can refuse to be absorbed. The metropolitan movement which was gaining steam during the 1960s has been considerably slowed by two racial factors—the acquisition of major political control by blacks in the central cities, and the resistance of suburban whites to school busing.

Options for Avoiding Disaster

In recent years, declining cities were often able to overcome revenue gaps or impending deficits through higher local taxes and increased funding from federal and state governments. The reasons for the gaps are continuing, but the revenue growth is not keeping pace.

Cities may meet their fiscal difficulties by further *raising taxes and fees.* However, where taxes are already relatively high, this could be self-defeating by driving away more higher-income residents and businesses. Income potential from service charges and fees appears limited.

Reduction of the municipal work force is a major option already being exercised by about half of the declining cities. Pittsburgh and Cincinnati have taken this route without apparent adverse effects or citizen disfavor. Yet potential problems are cited: (1) efficiency may be impaired if dismissals according to seniority remove the younger, most fit workers, leaving older persons to carry out the more physically demanding jobs of firefighting, policing, and so forth; (2) if workers are encouraged to take early retirement, this may strain pension funds; (3) some federal matching funds would be withdrawn as local programs are pared; and (4) a disproportionate share of minority workers may be hurt.

Redirecting federal employment and federal contracts is needed to reverse the higher flow of federal funds and jobs into growing areas. Declining areas deserve an equal—or somewhat larger—share, Muller suggests.

There is now a ceiling on the cities' portion of *federal revenue sharing funds,* tied to a statewide average, which in some instances results in less revenue than the allocation formula would provide. Thus, lifting this ceiling would enable these funds to favor some declining cities to a greater degree than they now do.

Muller contends that extensive outmigration—especially of a magnitude of 10 percent or more during a five-year period—is a fiscal danger signal for any city of over half a million residents. The prospects are grim for large aging cities that are losing population—their municipal costs are rising, their taxpayers face relatively higher tax levels, and employment conditions in the private sector are worsening. Tighter budgeting and more involvement by state governments, not on a crisis basis but as an ongoing venture, are needed to control the pressures leading to fiscal failure.

WILLIAM ALONSO

The Population Factor and Urban Structure

There has been much speculation in recent years as to how our urban areas may be reshaped by shortages of energy or of capital, by technological changes, by changes in moral sentiment or "new ethics," by environmental limits, and even by sociopolitical revolution. While these may have their role, to my mind greater changes may be expected from factors which are not usually so much in the public consciousness. These include the increase and nationalization of transfer payments (such as welfare), the accounting procedures and tax deductibility allowed to business and people, the evolution of the Serrano and Brown decisions, growth-control legislation and its legal interpretation, and the possible deregulation of the transportation and communication industries. But in this paper I want to call attention to the effects on urban structure of what I shall call the "population factor."

By the "population factor" I mean the number of people as a whole and its age composition, the ways these people arrange themselves into families and households, and how and how often they rearrange themselves; the population factor

also involves their participation in the labor force, how they run their households, and how they raise their children if they have them. And the population factor must include consideration of the social, economic, cultural, and attitudinal components and shifts that accompany behavioral changes.

The recent and prospective changes in the population factor are remarkable and will mold the evolution of urban areas in years to come. These effects are already being felt and the popular press begins to report on singles in the suburbs, the "gentrification" of parts of central cities, the pains of school consolidation in the suburbs, the absolute decline in population in whole metropolitan areas (not just their central cities), and most recently on the rapid increase in the cost of single-family homes and the fact that a diminishing proportion of American "families" can afford them. The quotation marks in the last sentence are meant to alert the reader to the ambiguousness of what a family is.

The recent and impending changes in the population factor are so strong that their influence has not gone unperceived

From Arthur Solomon, **The Prospective City,** Chapter 2 by W. Alonso, The MIT Press, 1980. Reprinted by permission of The MIT Press and W. Alonso.

in urban matters. Some extrapolations have been made of the coming patterns of age composition and the formation of households, but these are highly aggregated and try to estimate future housing demand or need, without distinguishing between these two very different matters. Moreover, whatever their accuracy, they do not tell us enough about the changing social and economic characteristics of the units which go to make up the aggregate. These changes in the units not only affect the total number of households, they importantly shape the internal structure of the housing market and its manifestation in urban geography.

The three most visible changes in the population factor in the mid-1970's are (1) the increasing prevalence of population decline in entire metropolitan areas, (2) the seismic waves passing through the age composition of the population as a result of the baby boom which followed World War II and the more recent drop in fertility, and (3) the radical changes in life-styles which are reflected in the shifting composition of households and their economics.

The Increasing Prevalence of Metropolitan Population Decline

In the past almost all metropolitan areas grew in population, except for some of the smaller ones (and very rarely a large one, such as Pittsburgh in the 1960's) which encountered severe economic deterioration. But in recent years it has become commonplace for metropolitan areas to decline in population. In the early 1970's ten out of the largest twenty-five metropolitan areas were losing population in absolute terms. In the period from 1970 to 1974 one sixth of all metropolitan areas were losing population; in the last year of that period more than one fourth of all areas were doing it, so that the trend is accelerating. Because the phenomenon of decline is stronger among the larger met-

ropolitan areas, the proportion of the metropolitan population living in declining areas is even larger, and stands now at about one half of all metropolitan residents.

Much has been made of another startling change in the population factor in relation to this decline. Ever since the Industrial Revolution in the XVIII century people have migrated in the net from rural to urban areas; but since 1970 net migration has proceeded from metropolitan to nonmetropolitan areas. A reversal in a trend with more than two centuries standing is indeed important and interesting. The net flow out of metropolitan areas amounted to nearly 400,000 people in the single year 1975–76, and this is a large number indeed, and a strong contributor to the decline of metropolitan populations. But it is not the principal factor.

The factors behind the prevalence of metropolitan population decline are three: changes in the rate of natural increase, changes in the net migration of metropolitan areas, and migratory exchanges among metropolitan areas. Of these, the strongest is the decline in the rate of natural increase which has resulted from the drop in the birthrate. Whereas in the 1960's the natural increase of metropolitan areas stood at 1.1% per year, in the 1970–74 period it amounted to 0.7% and under 0.6% in recent years. This amounts to a drop of 0.5% in the rate of population growth from the last decade to the present. The net migration rate from metropolitan to nonmetropolitan areas was under 0.3% in 1975–76; it had been between 0.1 and 0.2% in the other direction in the 1960's, for a change of about 0.4% per year. While these numbers are comparable, the drop in the natural increase is larger and more important than the reversal in metropolitan migration. At the same time, net migration from abroad has continued at a substantial rate (about 0.2% for net legal migration, and perhaps at least as much for illegal immigration), so that metropolitan areas have had a net immigration in spite of their losses to nonmetropolitan areas.

About one half of the non-metropolitan growth results from the overspill of metropolitan functions beyond censal definitions. These are not people who have gone back to the land, but people who work in the suburban ring or in economic activities which can thrive at a modest distance from metropolitan centers, with access to major airports, business services, and other facilities. The remainder of nonmetropolitan growth is attributable to shifts in the location of labor-intensive industry to small cities and rural areas, to the growth of the recreation industry, to the increased number of retired people whose income is not tied down geographically, to increase rates of investment in energy, resources, and environmental projects, and, in the recession of the past few years, to the return of earlier migrants to metropolitan areas for whom it is easier to endure the hard times back home. A number of these factors, but not all, may be expected to continue to operate in the coming years and a net migration toward nonmetropolitan areas will probably be a frequent if not a continuing condition.

The decline in the birthrate together with outmigration will result in very low but still positive rates (about 0.6% per year) of population growth for the set of metropolitan areas for the foreseeable future. But because many metropolitan areas will be net winners in their population exchanges with other metropolitan and with nonmetropolitan areas, the simple arithmetic of differences in the rates of growth means that many metropolitan areas will have declining populations.

While I know of no reason why slight rates of decline need to be especially problematic, the fact remains that up to now our experience has been one of population growth in our metropolitan areas.

We are therefore ill prepared for the phenomenon of decline. We have neither well-developed theories of how it works nor practical experience for how to deal with it.

Consider for instance two conceptual work horses of our perception of how urban areas are put together. One is our concentric view of the geography of metropolitan areas which has evolved in many variants from Ernest Burgess's original formulation in the 1920's. The other is the conception of housing markets that work by the filtering process. Both of these, which are really two forms of the same idea, are premised on continued growth. As new housing is added at the geographic margin of the urban area, the older housing nearer to the center is taken up by those of lesser income. But note that unless there were a high rate of demolition, this requires that there be an expanding population to inhabit the expanding housing stock. Or, perhaps more accurately, it presumes that there is a certain interplay in the rates of population growth, of increases in income for various groups, of physical obsolescence, of additions to stock, and so forth.

How then does the geography of the urban area evolve and the housing market function if there is a decline in the total population? Will the rate of new construction be reduced sharply? Will there result a growing hole in the center in the form of abandonment? What will happen to the linked chains of prices, quality, and location?

Our existing models, both formal and informal, have been based on an arrow of time which has always pointed upward for population. It is unlikely that these models will serve without major modifications in situations of population decline. They cannot merely be run backward because growing and shrinking are not symmetric. Disinvestment is not the mirror image of investment, and cutting down the size of an operation is not the same as expanding it, only in reverse. This can already be seen vividly in many areas where school enrollments are sharply down.

The Effects of Population Composition

It will be seen, however, that the decline in population is no simple matter of the arithmetic of total numbers. It is strongly influenced in its effects by changes in the composition of the population. Note, for instance, that the average size of households has been declining steadily and rapidly. Average household size was 3.67 persons in 1940, 3.33 in 1960, 3.14 in 1970, and 2.89 in 1976. The drop from 1970 to 1976 alone amounted to 8%, and no metropolitan area has approached this rate of population decline. Therefore decline is accompanied by increased numbers of households.

And since even households consisting of one or two people require a bathroom, cooking facilities, corridors, and the like, the amount of space per capita is higher for smaller households. Thus, the total amount of space in terms of square meters of housing increases faster than the number of households, and total demand for housing space can increase quite briskly in a metropolitan area of declining population.

One might then say that, thank goodness, as luck would have it, smaller household sizes come along just at the time of population decline and we need not worry about reversals in the filtering process and other complications. Things are to go on as usual. But it is the thesis of this paper that neither is it coincidence that the decline in household size accompanies population decline, nor it is possible for things to go on as usual.

The decline of household size stems from changes in our society that encourage more adults to set up their own households, so that for every sex and age category of the population the proportion of

people heading their own households (headship rate) has been increasing. At the same time, these same social changes have resulted in lower birthrates, and hence in even smaller households. And it is, of course, the same drop in the birthrate which is the principal factor in the phenomenon of metropolitan population decline.

Neither can things go on as before. The decline in household size must end sooner or later. Moreover, smaller households are not shrunken versions of larger ones. As we shall see, they represent changes in attitudes, behavior, and economics. And most clearly, we will continue to be buffeted by the waves of changing age composition.

The Waves in the Age Composition

Everyone knows that the birthrate was quite low during the Great Depression, that it rose dramatically during the "baby boom" which followed World War II, and that it has been plummeting in recent years in what has been termed the "baby bust."

But there is a simpler way of looking at this. The birthrate has been declining steadily from the turn of the century in this country as in the rest of the developed nations. The baby boom, whatever its causes, was a very large and unusual departure from this long term trend. It produced very large cohorts of people at a particular time, far larger than those who preceded them or those who followed them. Much of our recent and future history consists of this "giant" generation passing through infancy into youth, the middle years and, eventually, old age.

The effects of this giant generation are part of our common experience. As children in the late 1950's they produced, not unnaturally, a high degree of child-orientation, and it was not uncommon for half of the population of a suburb to be

Table 1. Five-Year Changes in the U.S. Population by Age Class: Population 20 years and older, 1970–1990, in thousands

| Period | Age Class | | | | | |
	20–25	25–35	35–45	45–55	55–65	65+
1970–75	2,208	5,902	−375	334	1,131	1,433
1975–80	1,640	5,720	2,706	−1,153	1,284	2,114
1980–85	−751	3,819	5,807	−319	328	1,814
1985–90	−2,514	885	5,624	2,638	−990	1,993

Source: Computed from Bureau of the Census, *Statistical Abstract* projections.

enrolled in its public schools. In the late 1960's, when this giant arrived on college campuses, its very size contributed significantly to unrest and to youth culture. And now the peak of the wave is coming to young adulthood, joining the labor force, making in its diversity their choices of housing and way of life. It is because this giant is so large that the choices it makes will be decisive to our urban future in the coming years.

The magnitudes of these changes in the age composition may be seen in Table 1. Note the increase in the population aged 25 to 35 years old through 1985. It amounts to 14,553,000 people from 1970 to 1985 (a 58% increase), and to 9,539,000 from 1975 to 1985. Thereafter the increase in this age group will slow down markedly, and after 1990 it will begin to decline in absolute numbers.

The 25- to 35-year-old group is of particular importance because that is the age at which most people have in the past settled down to family life and moved to single family housing in the suburbs. After 1980, when their increase is combined with the decline in the numbers under 25 years of age, who tend to live in apartments, and with the sharp growth in the 35- to 45-year-old group, the following picture emerges as a possible one:

A large demand for multifamily units and mobile homes will continue into the early 1980's. . . . However, overcapacity in apartments may occur by the late 1980's as the number of households under 25 greatly declines.

By the late 1970's and 1980's a great increase in demand for one-unit structures should occur. This demand will at first be greatest for some type of moderately priced housing unit. Later, the demand for more expensive homes should build up as the households begin to update their housing units.[1]

In spatial terms this picture amounts to a tremendous wave of suburbanization, for this is what single family housing amounts to. In areas of declining population the phenomenon may be even stronger in relative terms because it is the young who migrate, and thereby increase the proportion of older people.

One may wonder what this picture implies for energy and transportation, for central cities, and for metropolitan governance as the wave of suburbanization (which has been quiescent recently because of the age composition of the population and the economic recession) meets the rising dams of local growth-control in the suburbs. But even if this scenario of massive suburbanization comes true, one must consider that the suburbs would be very different from those of the 1950's and 1960's in at least one respect: the relative scarcity of children. With all that

1. Thomas Marcin, "The Effects of Declining Population Growth on the Demand for Housing," U.S. Department of Agriculture, General Technical Report NC-11, 1974, p. 11.

this means for their fiscal situation and the manner of their daily life, one must conclude that these suburbs would be different.

Changes in Lives

The picture just presented must be considerably modified if we consider that the last years have seen strong changes in the ways Americans live their lives. If these changes are not transitory fashions, as I believe they are not, then coming waves of changes in age composition may result in different outcomes. This is because the picture just presented rests on the children of the baby boom behaving as their parents did in matters of housing and residential location. If substantial portions of them behave differently, that picture changes.

We have noted the steady decline in the size of households, and the rise in the proportion of individuals who head their own households, together with the drop in the birthrate. These are, to my mind, signals of a deep and abiding social change which is mirrored in statistics but which is rooted in the evolution of a modern society. Since talk about ongoing social change often sounds excitable and utopian, in the next pages I will present a statistical picture of some aspects of this change to nail down that something is indeed going on, whatever interpretation one may place upon it.

From 1970 to 1976 the U.S. population grew by slightly over 5%.[2] Total households grew by 15%. The number of households consisting of primary families grew by 9%, and of these, husband-wife families grew only by 6%, while single-parent families headed by a male grew by 16% and those headed by a female grew by 33%. Meanwhile, the

2. In this section I rely heavily for recent data on U.S. Bureau of the Census, *Current Population Reports,* Series P-20, No. 307, "Population Profiles of the United States: 1976," 1977.

number of households consisting of primary individuals increased by 41%; the number of individuals living alone increased by 38%, and the number of households consisting of nonrelatives by 67%. The number of two person households consisting of unrelated persons of the opposite sex more than doubled, and increased more than fivefold for younger people. Obviously the population is distributing itself more finely into households, and the traditional husband-wife mode is growing least.

Consider child-bearing. The current fertility rate of 14.7 births per thousand population is at a historic low, at less than three-fifths the rate of the late 1950's. Moreover this rate is in a sense inflated, because at this time we have such a large proportion of young women in their prime childbearing ages. The total fertility rate is the lifetime number of births which a young woman would have if she followed during the course of her life the current fertility pattern of women of various ages today. A rate of 2.1 births per woman represents the replacement level of the population in the long run. While the fertility rate was as high as 3.7 in the late 1950's, it is now below 1.8.

Note in Table 2 the steady increase in the proportion of single young women, the proportion of married women who remain childless, and the consequent drop in married women who have borne children. When asked in 1976 how many children they expect ever to bear, young women aged 18 to 24 answered 2.031 on the average, a remarkably low figure.

One may go on citing statistics that relate this basic change in the family and household composition of our society. It is not only that there has been a diminution of the proportion of the population in the traditional family of husband–wife–children; there has been a marked increase in the fluidity of family and household arrangements, so that individuals change their circumstances far more

Table 2. Women Aged 20–24 and 25–29 by Marital Status, and
Childlessness, 1960, 1970, and 1976

	Aged 20–24			Aged 25–29		
	1976	1970	1960	1976	1970	1960
Single	42.6	35.8	28.4	14.8	10.5	10.5
Married, childless	23.9	23.0	17.3	18.5	14.1	11.3
Married having borne children	33.5	41.2	54.3	66.7	75.4	78.2
Total	100.0	100.0	100.0	100.0	100.0	100.0

Source: Computed from U.S. Bureau of the Census, *Current Population Reports,*
Series P-20, No. 307, "Population Profile of the United States: 1976," 1977.

often. Indeed, since the current number of divorces is half as large as the number of marriages and the median duration of marriages has been dropping steadily (it is now 6.5 years) while remarriages have recently decreased, the image of marriage for life at an early age as the dominant mode must now come into question.

In the light of these changes, it is difficult to believe that the choice of housing type and location can remain unaffected. It is unlikely that the same mix of housing units can accommodate this bubbling social soup that held the calmer broth of some years ago, although no one to my knowledge is in a position to make firm predictions. Yet as the vast numbers of the children of the baby boom set on their life paths, their changing mix of housing and location choices will play a determining role on the evolution of urban form.

Working Women

I have up to this point avoided giving my interpretation of the causes and meanings of these rapid social changes and have limited myself to trying to show from data that they are real and strong, not mere rhetorical fashion. But I will now suggest that they are manifestations of a long-run social and economic evolution. The principal causes for these changes

seem to me to be the result of the greater emphasis placed upon the individual and the greater legitimacy accorded to a variety of life choices, including that of changing choices. This is in contrast to the earlier emphasis on the nuclear family and its stability as the dominant mode. The reasons for the change in emphasis lie in the increasing education of the population, which has revealed the variety of choices open to individuals and broadened the range of choices acceptable under evolving social norms.

But rather than essaying an extended discussion of overall social change, I will focus on the changes which have been occurring in female employment because this seems to me one of the root causes, because decent statistics are available, and because of its importance for the evolution of urban structure.

Anyone living in this country is aware of the increasing labor force participation of women, but the numbers are so startling that they bear some recapitulation.[3] The rate of labor force participation for women has risen steadily from 33.9% in 1950 to 46.7% in 1976. But it is among married women that the increase has been strongest. In 1900 less than 6% of

3. Data for this section are drawn largely from Howard Hayghe, "Families and the Rise of Working Wives—An Overview," *Monthly Labor Review,* May 1976.

wives worked outside the home. The share had risen to 9% by 1920 and to 24% by 1950. The growth has continued steadily to 30% in 1960, 41% in 1970, and 44% in 1975.

After World War II, the increased participation in the labor force began with older married women, but in recent years it has been fueled primarily by the increased participation of younger wives, who had traditionally been more housebound by their children. In 1950 only 12% of mothers with children under six years of age worked, but in the mid-1970's 35% of such mothers were working. This is a greater share than the 34% rate of participation for *all* women, married and single, in 1950. It should also be kept in mind that a far smaller proportion of women are now mothers of young children.

By 1975 the number of married couples in which both husband and wife worked was greater than those in which only the husband worked (41% versus 34%), and four out of every ten children were in families in which both parents were working.

Nor must it be thought that most wives were working casually or for pin money. At the time of the latest survey (March, 1975), in spite of the recession, 72% of working wives were on full-time jobs, and nearly two thirds of working mothers of preschool children worked full time. About two out of five working wives were employed full-time all year. In 1974, where only the husband worked, the median family income was $12,360, whereas where both worked the median income was $14,895.

Not surprisingly, the total number of employed women grew by 17% from 1970 to 1976, while the number of employed men grew by only 6%. Women accounted for nearly two thirds of the increase in the employed labor force during the period. While this is not the place to explore the effects of working women on the overall economy, it is useful to keep in mind that what we are examining in the small (families and households) has important ramifications in the large. It is also useful to remember the link between the rise in working women and the rise of the service economy, since 63% of women work at white collar jobs while only 41% of men do so.

Are These Enduring Changes?

All of these statistics indicate that there are radical changes going on in the ways in which Americans live their lives. It is impossible for me, whatever interpretation one places on these statistics, to think that they will not affect the decisions and behavior of millions of people in ways which will determine how our urban areas are to evolve. But there is a substantial segment of opinion that says that these are momentary aberrations, that soon traditional life-styles will be resumed, that the foolishness of women's liberation will be outgrown, and that the missing babies have only been postponed and will soon be had.

Social forecasting is a chancy thing, but I think that these changes are permanent indications of a new social reality for three reasons. First, because they represent a consistent story that has been evolving for many decades, with only the temporary anomalies of the baby-boom era. Secondly, because comparable changes are being experienced in every developed country so that it is unlikely that temporary local peculiarities are at work. And thirdly, because these changes are deeply anchored and mutually reinforcing.

Consider, for instance, the fact that women are now working and doing so under increasingly fair conditions and levels of pay. This makes having children more expensive both in direct costs, because children are a labor-intensive commodity and labor costs are rising, and in opportunity costs because women can more easily work outside the home for better wages so that earnings foregone in having and rearing children are also increasing. The simple economics of the matter stand against any increase in fertility, and to my mind the current claims that this is the calm before the storm, that babies are only being postponed, is merely a conditioned reflex by people who were trained during the scare of the population explosion and who are loath to give up on this source of worry.

To my mind the ongoing changes will be of long standing. This is because women can think of other lives for themselves beyond those of wives and mothers, because sexual drives can be satisfied outside of conventional modes, because labor in the home has become expensive relative to labor outside of it, because the economy provides the economic means for a reduction in the economic dependency of women, and thereby opens alternatives to wives and husbands. Recall only how exotic divorce seemed twenty years ago, or the decision of a couple to have no children. Divorce today is more common because it is more feasible, and it is more feasible because it is more acceptable, because there are fewer children, and because the wife is more able to earn a living. Having no children is more common because there are other things to do.

I cannot believe, given the coherence of these interrelated strands, that a traditionalist time-bomb awaits us. For instance, for there to be a rise in the birthrate there would have to be reversals in the other factors, such as the participation of women in the labor force. Indeed it seems reasonable to expect that in the 1980's when the proportion of women in the most fertile ages begins to thin out, voices will be raised in favor of pronatalist policies. This is already the case in much of Europe.

The Effects of the Population Factor on Urban Form

In the light of these societal changes, the view that the coming of age of the giant generation will result in a suburban explosion requires considerable modification. As in any other guess at the future, there must be a mixture of extrapolation and of intuition. In this case the task is all the more difficult because we do not even have a good statistical basis as to current patterns. Our statistics on employment, on households and families, on housing type, and on urban location are not coordinated, and the essential cross-tabulations are not available. But I will make some suggestions nonetheless.

Since many will continue to live more or less in the traditional patterns and the giant generation is so large, there will be continued growth in the suburbs. But since many will behave in different ways, there will not be the suburban explosion which would be implied if there were no change in behavior. At the same time, many millions will lead lives substantially different from those of their parents and my speculations will focus on these.

It seems reasonable that there will be a shift away from the free-standing, owner-occupied single family house. Table 3 already shows some of this shift occurring from 1960 to 1970 for young and old people. This is because, first, smaller households require less space. Second, because the fluidity of households and the looser legal links among their members is contrary to the rigidity of tenure associated with ownership. Third, because the maintenance of such a house is expensive and time consuming and with most people working, time for domestic work becomes scarce and costly. One may therefore expect a greater prevalence of apartments, row or town houses, and innovative forms of design. Similarly one may expect more

Table 3. Housing Occupancy Rates in the United States by Type of Structure and Age of Household Head for 1960 and 1970

		Age of Household Head							
Year	Housing Type	15–19	20–24	25–29	30–34	35–44	45–54	55–64	65+
1960	One-unit structure	47	55	68	75	79	78	75	73
	Multi-unit structure	47	41	30	23	20	21	24	26
	Mobile units	6	4	2	2	1	1	1	1
	Total	100	100	100	100	100	100	100	100
1970	One-unit structure		33[a]	57	72	79	77	74	67
	Multi-unit structure		59	38	25	19	21	23	30
	Mobile units		8	5	3	2	2	3	3
	Total		100	100	100	100	100	100	100

[a] This estimate is for all households under 25 years.

Source: Adapted from Thomas C. Marcin, "The Effects of Declining Population Growth on the Demand for Housing" U.S. Department of Agriculture, General Technical Report NC-11, 1974, p. 5.

experimentation in forms of tenure, such as condominiums and cooperatives, which preserve some of the tax advantages of ownership but which provide greater liquidity. One may also expect increases and new forms of contracting arrangements for the operation and maintenance of housing.* Since many of these features are already available when renting or leasing, it would be reasonable to expect that these traditional forms of tenure will prosper.

The fact that most adults will be working points to other consequences. First and simplest, to there being more money per member of the household. A household in which the husband is the sole earner, making $25,000, living with his wife and three children has a per capita income of $5,000. A household of two

* These trends no doubt have been accelerated by the recent escalation of financing costs (Ed. note).

where one makes $11,000 and the other $9,000, has a per capita income of $10,000. The second effect, as mentioned above, is that time for domestic work is scarce and therefore valuable. Especially if there is more money available, the economic response is to substitute money for time. This can be done by investing in capital goods such as household equipment, by purchasing food that embodies more prior preparation (including eating out), by shopping less often and buying larger quantities (in effect transferring inventories from the retailer to the household), by contracting for services in the house or sending work to be done outside. All of these carry fairly obvious implications for the geographic relation between households and services and for the design of dwellings.

Travel to work may also have important consequences when there are several commuters rather than only one per household, and when non-working time is more valuable. It suggests to me that locational factors may play a stronger role, and that this factor may result in more concentrated development to reduce travel time. The most convenient point to two distant suburban work places may in many cases be a location more near the center. Nonetheless, the geometry of the relations between houses and workplaces may hold surprises, especially since the location of services and industry will in turn respond to the location of workers and customers.

This is reinforced by an interesting consideration raised in the sociological literature on women. They point out that in most households the role of the woman, even if she works, retains responsibility for such tasks as shopping, dropping the children off to school or to the doctor, stopping at the laundry, and many other errands. Therefore the woman's travel is more complex than the man's, who takes a straightforward route from home to work. Since the working woman typically retains in addition much of the domestic work in the home, as shown in time-budget studies, her time is particularly at a premium. Therefore working wives place great stress on access to work jointly with access to services. They also place high value on flexible working hours. It must be remembered, too, that when women work they gain in economic power and independence and that their wishes gain weight in family decisions.

These factors of housing type, journey to work, and access to services seem to point quite clearly to more clustered development than that which has prevailed in the expansion of urban areas for the past quarter century. This would apply whether the development is central or suburban.

Further, these various factors also point to the possibility of increasing locational attractiveness of more central locations, in the core city and the older suburbs, where there is an appropriate stock of housing and access to services and probably in many cases locational convenience for the journey to work. Moreover, since many of these households have no children, the racial factors of school integration would not act as they have in the white flight to the suburbs. In addition, surveys of residential preferences over the years have indicated that people thought the suburbs were good places in which to raise children. Obviously this plays no part in the location preferences of those without children.

It seems to me that this phenomenon is already taking place at a considerable rate, from the Mission District in San Francisco to the South End in Boston, but no statistics are available as to its rate. Yet it remains an important one to watch and one which is easy to misunderstand. For instance, some are interpreting it as a return of the upper classes and the term "gentrification" has been coined for it. Georgetown in Washington, D.C. is a well-known older instance. Undoubtedly some of this has happened and may continue to happen, but the numbers can never be large. The large numbers would come from households of few dependents if any and multiple workers, none of whom necessarily has a large income or a high social status. Such households may have very considerable income and they are increasingly numerous.

Some may view this as a very good development, the often proclaimed and long-delayed "rebirth of the cities." It would indeed have many virtues, such as strengthening the fiscal base, increasing the life and animation of many districts and supporting city businesses, reversing the disinvestment in many urban properties and, not least, increasing the amount of racial and social integration among adults on a reasonably voluntary basis. But there is a strong danger that it may be regressive in certain consequences and that these may be aggravated by the increasing anti-redlining legislation.

Much of this process appears to be taking place in neighborhoods which are poor and run down but not desperate. These are typically inhabited by lower working class blacks or white ethnics who rent rather than own. Because of rising taxes, fuel costs, and sometimes rent control, these properties have become poor investments for their owners, as is amply attested by the prevalence of abandonment. The owners are very happy to sell. The new laws regulating the issuance of mortgages in these areas in effect give greater weight to the earning capacity of the household over the consideration of the credit-worthiness of the property as security.[4] Therefore they make it possible for the new households to borrow, buy the property, and displace the former occupants.

Over the past twenty years the housing of the poor and the working poor has improved primarily because they have fallen heir to what used to be called "the grey areas." The softening of middle class demand for this housing stock lowered its relative price and permitted a sharp decline in overcrowding for low income people. Whatever the troubles of the cities, this has been a fortunate outcome. But the danger appears imminent that the housing stock available to working and welfare poor will now be sharply diminished, squeezed between abandonment at

one end and the childless multiworker household at the other. The consequence would be higher prices and more crowding for those of lower incomes. Yet another reform may benefit the middle class rather than those to whom it was ostensibly aimed.

In Conclusion

Earlier in this paper I said that, whatever happens, the population factor insures that things cannot stay the same. In a nutshell, if people behave as they always have, we will have an explosive suburbanization. If behavior changes, we will have clustering and re-urbanization, or perhaps some other effect that has not occurred to me. But over the next ten years things will not stay the same and it becomes important that we act intelligently and with foresight about these changes.

I am quite aware that there are many changes occurring concurrently with those in the population factor. Some reinforce my inferences. For instance, the higher costs of energy would push toward clustered development for savings both in space-heating and in transportation. No doubt others pull in other directions. And perhaps, since the world is full of surprises, women will return to domesticity, the birthrate will rise, economic activity will return to the production of goods rather than services, and energy will become relatively cheap.

4. It should be noted that legislation forbidding discrimination on sex complements this by forcing the lender to consider the income of females rather than only that of the male.

VIII

OPTIONS: Emerging Policy Questions and Alternative Strategies

BRIAN J. L. BERRY

Inner City Futures:
An American Dilemma Revisited

Gunnar Myrdal posed two interrelated dilemmas, the first of race relations and the second of differential regional growth caused by what he called a process of circular and cumulative causation. He saw the play of forces in the market as tending to increase rather than decrease the inequalities between regions. This, he said, was the consequence of the clustering of activities in areas that promote increasing returns through both the internal and the external economies that are present in centres of agglomeration. He believed that the agglomeration advantages of the major north-eastern urban industrial complexes so swamped the cheaper factor prices of the periphery that they produced a continuous stream of disequilibrating flows of labour, capital, goods and services from poor to rich regions. He concluded that free trade in an interregional system will always work to the disadvantage of poor regions, inhibiting their growth prospects and distorting their pattern of production. This led him to strong advocacy of governmental intervention to correct what he perceived to be the 'normal tendencies' in a capitalist system to sustain and increase inequality.

The kind of direct governmental intervention sought by Myrdal never came. Instead, the key premise underlying policy development in the United States has always been and remains today the belief that solutions to the nation's needs and problems must be found, for the most part, in the private sector. Market processes are relied upon to allocate resources efficiently and to provide new jobs, rising incomes, and better housing. An essential prerequisite is believed to be the necessary mobility of capital and labour to realize differential market opportunities. The principal roles of government are thus those of regulator, facilitator, and occasionally social engineer in preserving, supporting, and enhancing mainstream objectives: providing information if it is lacking on the part of buyers or sellers; preventing emergence of undue concentrations of economic power which results in higher prices and fewer services than if competition prevailed; reducing market fluctuations; and facilitating mobility—in other words, promoting the mainstream values of democratic pluralism. Other forms of governmental intervention are believed to be justified only

From **Transactions,** Institute of British Geographers, Vol. 5, No. 1, 1980, pp. 1–27. Reprinted in modified form by permission of The Institute and B. J. L. Berry.

if public welfare is endangered by change and if adequate remedies are not available in the market-place. There are several cases:

1. If market prices do not reflect the full social costs or benefits of development because of congestion or external costs such as pollution, noise, and other man-made hazards, so that too much or too little of a commodity or service will be provided unless the competing interests of those who benefit and those who pay are arbitrated.
2. If there is an inability to determine or collect a proper price, as in the case of a public commodity whose consumption by one individual does not reduce the consumption of it by others.
3. If there are demonstrable advantages to society from maintaining minimum levels of service to population groups or communities which otherwise would be unable to obtain it—frequently such minimum levels of service are characterized as basic "rights."
4. If market fluctuations give rise to periodic problems of unemployed resources.
5. If rapid changes in the market produce short-term hardships—both adjustments to growth and the need to rationalize in the face of decline.

As late as 1970, U.S. urban policy was being formulated in the belief that the circular and cumulative causation described by Myrdal would continue, and that increasing urbanization did in fact endanger the public welfare in a variety of ways, demanding reactions that would both redirect mainstream growth in the future and correct the problems resulting from cumulative growth in the past. Thus, Title VII of the *Housing and Urban Development Act of 1970* (Public Law 91–609, 84 Stat. 1791; 42 U.S.C. 4501) stated in Section 702 that

the rapid growth of urban population and uneven expansion of urban development in the United States, together with a decline in farm population, slower growth in rural areas, and migration to the cities, has created an imbalance between the Nation's needs and resources and seriously threatens our physical environment . . . the economic and social development of the Nation, the proper conservation of our natural resources, and the achievement of satisfactory living standards depend upon the sound, orderly, and more balanced development of all areas of the Nation. . . . The Congress . . . declares that the national urban growth policy should (1) favor patterns of urbanization and economic development and stabilization which offer a range of alternative locations . . . (3) help reverse trends of migration and physical growth (4) treat comprehensively the problems of poverty and employment associated with disorderly urbanization and rural decline.

To those who drafted the 1970 Housing Act, Myrdal's American Dilemma was a continuing reality.

Barely a decade later, beliefs about the nature of change appear to have reversed, however, and along with them the opinions on apparent growth directions to be promoted and the corrective reactions to be taken. Thus, President Carter's Urban and Regional Policy Group's March 1978 report *A new partnership to conserve America's communities: a national urban policy* declared as follows:

Three major patterns of population change can be traced in the Nation today: migration from the north-eastern and north central regions of the country to the south and west; the slower growth of metropolitan areas and the movement from them to small towns and rural areas; and movement from central cities to suburbs. . . . Today's widespread population loss in the Nation's central cities is unprecedented . . . the thinning out process has left many people and places with severe economic and social problems, and without the resources to deal with them. . . . Our policies must reflect a balanced concern for people and places . . . to achieve several broad goals: (to) preserve the heritage and value of our older cities; maintain the investment in our older cities and their neighborhoods; assist newer cities in confronting the challenge of growth and pockets of poverty . . . and provide improved housing, job opportunities and community services to the urban poor, minorities, and women. . . . If the Administration is to help cities revitalize neighborhoods, eliminate sprawl, support the return of the middle class to central cities, and improve the housing conditions of the urban poor it must increase the production of new housing and rehabilitation of existing housing for middle class groups in cities . . . We should favor proposals supporting: (1) compact community development over scattered, fragmented development; and (2) revitalization over new development.

The New American Dilemma, at least in the eyes of those who would remake U.S. urban and regional policy, is apparently the reverse of Myrdal's. The issue has become that of the older inner cities, the former leaders in the nation's growth, now believed to be suffering from employment declines, population losses, "ghettoization" of the poor, physical deterioration, and fiscal distress.

Background: Regional Shifts and Demographic Changes

That major changes have taken place, and that many of these changes involve a reversal of Myrdal's theory is without question. Contrary to Myrdal's expectations, regional incomes have converged since 1929, not diverged. Nominal income convergence is only part of the story, however. Some of the nation's most affluent urban-industrial regions of half a century ago, New England in particular, have slipped to the bottom of the ranking in real income terms (Table 1).

These regional shifts are in large measure a result of the changing location of American industry with the breakdown

Table 1. Regional per Capita Incomes, 1977 (Indexed): Nominal and adjusted for cost of living

Region	Nominal	Adjusted
New England	102	88
Mid East	107	98
Great Lakes	105	103
Plains	97	98
South East	86	93
South West	95	101
Rocky Mountain	94	98
Far West	111	106

Source: Bureau of Economic Analysis, U.S. Department of Commerce (1978). Cost of living adjustment based on Grasberger (1978). Comparison adapted from Peterson and Muller (1978).

of the traditional heartland–hinterland organization of the U.S. economy in which leadership in technological innovation and industrial growth was exercised by the major urban centres of the North-eastern Manufacturing Belt. For the first half of the twentieth century, the Manufacturing Belt accounted for some 70 per cent of the nation's industrial employment. Between 1950 and the mid-1960s, manufacturing jobs continued to grow in the North East, but the growth was more rapid in other regions of the country and the Manufacturing Belt's relative share fell to 56 per cent. By 1970 relative decline had been replaced by absolute losses. From 1969 to 1977 the Manufacturing Belt lost 1.7 million industrial jobs, almost exactly the job growth of the former periphery. Relative growth of the service industries has paralleled these industrial shifts, multiplying the effects of the changes.

Traditionally, the Manufacturing Belt was the centre of innovation. It was able to introduce new industries to offset losses of standardized industries to areas of cheap labour elsewhere. But now this role has reversed. The economy's rapid growth industries (electronics, aerospace, scientific instruments, etc.) are dispersed throughout the former periphery; it is the older slow-growth industries that remain in the former core. These remaining industries are the most cyclical, which compounds the distress of north-eastern cities when the economy is in recession. But what is even more critical is that the Manufacturing Belt appears to have lost its traditional seedbed function. The locus of innovation and growth has shifted elsewhere.

Job shifts have been accompanied by population shifts. Following the bulge in the population pyramid formed by the post-Second World War baby boom, there has been a rapid decline in fertility rates to less than replacement levels. As natural increase has diminished, migration has become an increasingly important source of population change. This growing importance of migration as a factor of growth has been intensified by the movement of the baby boom cohort into its

most mobile years. In all urban-industrial countries, a certain minimum amount of geographical mobility is a structured part of the life-cycle stage associated with leaving the parental home and the establishment of an independent household shortly after formal schooling is completed (Figure 1). In the United States, with its emphasis upon achievement through mobility, the structuring effect of the life-cycle combined with the baby boom cohort has served to emphasize already high mobility rates at all age levels.

In a market economy, spatial differences in real wage rates and in employment opportunities provide signals to workers that encourage, in addition, migration related to social mobility. This migration not only increases the well-being of the movers themselves, but also results in improved resource allocation. Thus, job shifts in a period of maximum potential mobility have resulted in massive reversals of the migration streams

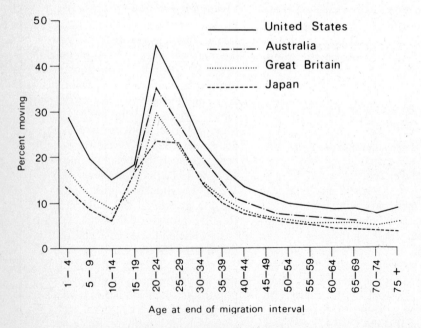

Figure 1. Percentage of Population Residentially Mobile in One Year: Australia, Great Britain, Japan and the United States, by age, around 1970. Source: Long and Boertlein (1976)

Table 2. U.S. Interregional Migration, 1970–75ª (in thousands)

	Non-minority			Net as Percentage of 1970 Regional Population by Race	Minority			Net as Percentage of 1970 Regional Population by Race
	Contrib.	Rc'd.	Net		Contrib.	Rc'd.	Net	
North East	2160	919	−1241	−2.8	240	138	−102	−2.1
North Central	2714	1568	−1146	−2.2	214	163	−51	−0.1
South	1939	2739	1790	3.6	314	354	40	0.3
West	1561	2155	594	1.9	79	193	114	3.4

ª Excludes foreign immigration.

Source: U.S. Bureau of the Census (1976a and b).

described by Myrdal. Net migration has increased from Manufacturing Belt to periphery, for both majority and minority members of the U.S. population (Table 2). The South has experienced a dramatic and accelerating migration reversal. Within regions net migration reveals moves from central cities to suburbs and exurbs and from metropolitan to nonmetropolitan areas (Table 3). Throughout the nation, migrating workers have left jobs located in major metropolitan cores for workplaces in smaller urban areas, suburbs, and non-metropolitan America (Table 4).

As noted, the migration reversal has affected all groups. Take, for example, black men born in the South. As with all other groups, migration rates are higher for the young and for the better educated. Between 1955 and 1960 there was net migration of these black men out of the South; by 1965–70 the out-migration had fallen and the return migration rate had

Table 3. Migration Streams 1970–75 and Net Migration by Type of Residence and Race, 1970–77, Excluding Net Immigration from Abroad

	Migration streams 1970–75 (in millions)		
Residential Category in 1970	Residential Category in 1975:		
	Central City	Suburb	Non-metropolitan Area
Central City	[17.11]	9.8	3.2
Suburb	3.8	[18.2]	3.5
Nonmetropolitan Area	2.1	3.0	[19.0]

Figures in brackets are movers who remained in same residential category during relocation

	Net Migration 1970–77 (in thousands)		
Type of Residence	All Races	White	Black
Metropolitan areas	−2260	−2411	145
Central cities	−10451	−9533	−653
Suburban areas	8190	7122	798
Nonmetropolitan areas	2260	2411	−145

Source: U.S. Bureau of the Census (1975a and 1978).

Table 4. Place-to-Place Net Migration of Work Force for Metropolitan and Nonmetropolitan Counties, 1960–63 and 1970–73 (in thousands)[a]

| | Central Counties with Populations of: | | | | | | | |
| | 2 million or more | | Less than 2 million | | Suburban | | Non-metropolitan | |
Type of County	1960–63	1970–73	1960–63	1970–73	1960–63	1970–73	1960–63	1970–73
Central, with population of:								
2 million or more	—	—	−13.4	141.5	65.1	75.8	−24.6	53.5
Less than 2 million	13.4	−141.5	—	—	−35.1	−14.7	−109.5	−30.9
Suburban	−65.1	−75.8	35.1	14.7	—	—	−25.4	−3.3
Nonmetropolitan	24.6	−53.5	109.5	30.9	25.4	3.3	—	—

[a] Positive numbers indicate net in-migration, and negative numbers indicate net out-migration.

Source: Regional Economic Analysis Division (1976).

gone up, and most of the net flows favoured the South.

Since 1970, the North East as a whole has lost population as a result of declining natural increase and of the net migration reversal; in the South continued high levels of growth have occurred, despite declining natural increase, because of increasing in-migration.

As a result of these shifts, non-metropolitan areas are now growing more rapidly than metropolitan areas and central cities are declining, especially within the largest metropolitan regions (Table 5). Thirty of the nation's fifty largest cities have lost population since 1970; one in five registered a loss of at least 10 per cent between 1970 and 1975. Because the incomes of out-migrants were greater than those of immigrants, the income loss of metropolitan areas (gain for non-metropolitan areas) was over $17 billion between 1975 and 1977 alone.

The Shaping Effect of Housing Market Dynamics

To understand why an inner city problem should have emerged—why the nation's leading central cities should now be the places where population declines are concentrated—demands that one understand salient features of U.S. housing market dynamics. First, urban growth has been strongly cyclical in both the long and the short term. American cities have not grown in a smooth or continuous manner, but in a series of major bursts, each of which has added a new ring of structures dominated by a particular building style. Nationwide, the magnitude of housing investment probably has done more than any other factor to shape urban growth. The historical record of urban expansion in this century closely follows the peaks and troughs in the rate of capital formation in the housing sector.* From 1910 to 1914 and again from 1921 to 1929, when real estate investment boomed, metropolitan boundaries surged outward; later, when housing investment nearly came to a halt during the Depression and the Second World War, urban expansion slowed to a virtual standstill; then, in the 1950s, an unprecedented volume of housing investment was accompanied by a record pace of suburbanization.

* See Adams' paper in Section III.

Table 5. Population by type of residence: 1977 and 1970 (numbers in thousands, 1970 metropolitan area definition)

Type of Residence	1977	1970	Numerical Change 1970–77	Percentage Change 1970–77	Percentage Distribution 1977	Percentage Distribution 1970
United States	212,566	199,819	12,747	6.4	100.0	100.0
Metropolitan areas	143,107	137,058	6049	4.4	67.3	68.6
Central cities	59,993	62,876	−2883	−4.6	28.2	31.5
Suburban areas	83,114	74,182	8932	12.0	39.1	37.1
Metropolitan areas of 1 million or more	82,367	79,489	2878	3.6	38.7	39.8
Central cities	31,898	34,322	−2424	−7.1	15.0	17.2
Suburban areas	50,469	45,166	5303	11.7	23.7	22.6
Metropolitan areas of less than 1 million	60,739	57,570	3169	5.5	28.6	28.8
Central cities	28,095	28,554	−459	−1.6	13.2	14.3
Suburban areas	32,644	29,016	3628	12.5	15.4	14.5
Nonmetropolitan areas	69,459	62,761	6698	10.7	32.7	31.4
Counties designated metropolitan since 1970	9980	8373	1607	19.2	4.7	4.2
Other nonmetropolitan counties	59,479	54,388	5091	9.4	28.0	27.2

Source: U.S. Bureau of the Census (1978).

Regionally, the expression of these cycles is to be seen in the different size of successive housing stock increments. Cities in older growth regions, especially those in the North East, have several growth rings with substantially differentiated housing stocks; indeed, a good working definition of the "inner city" is that area substantially constructed before the Great Depression. Cities located in newer growth regions, especially those of the South and West, are dominated by housing built since the Second World War.

Until the Second World War less than half of the nation's population owned their own homes, and less than half of the housing stock was in single family units. The great surge in home ownership came in scarcely more than a decade between 1948 and 1960. This boom in home ownership followed hard on the heels of the effective introduction of tax subsidies for owner occupancy, a by-product of the mass income tax first adopted during the Second World War, and the formulation in the early 1930s of a national housing policy which sought to promote home ownership as a stabilizing social force, relying very heavily on new construction as the tool to upgrade national housing standards and to provide for needed geographic mobility of urban households seeking better neighborhoods.

In the United States, tax incentives are perhaps the chief instrument the government possesses for allocating investment resources among competing sectors of the economy. Housing investment reached its height during the years 1948 to 1960, partly because of the many new tax laws passed during or after the Second World War which singled out housing for favourable tax treatment. Historically, perhaps the most consistent bias in the federal tax code has been the preferential treatment given to investment in new structures over investment in the improvement and repair of existing structures, which accelerates the rate at which buildings are replaced. Although this speeding up of the replacement cycle for structures does not in itself give a locational bias to development, it compresses the period during which urban regions adjust to changed private market prices or new transportation technologies. When favouritism towards new construction is combined with other tax policies that favour home ownership, important locational effects do result, however.

It is a peculiarity of the tax subsidy method of investment stimulation that the value of the tax advantage granted to home ownership is proportional to an investor's marginal tax bracket, for those who claim the home ownership deduction. This deduction took on an allocative significance for the first time during the Second World War when the marginal federal tax paid by most Americans was raised from 4 per cent to 25 per cent, making the deductibility of home owner expenses far more valuable than they previously had been. Today, the value of the tax benefit jumps sharply by household income level. The relative favour granted by the tax code to home ownership at different income levels is the net difference between the value of the home ownership subsidy, which increases with household income, and the value of the tax subsidy for rental housing, which is approximately uniform across income levels. At very low household incomes there is no net tax inducement to owner occupancy; in fact, the balance of tax incentives tips slightly toward rental tenure. At upper middle income levels, the tax system creates an annual cost advantage for owner occupancy of about 14 to 15 per cent.

The growth in home ownership rates since 1900, and especially since 1940, cannot be attributed solely to federal tax policy, of course. A number of other national policies—such as the introduction of F.H.A. financing in the 1930s, V.A. financing after the Second World War, and the opening up of the suburbs through highway construction in the 1950s—lent force to the home ownership boom. Household income growth also contributed to higher rates of owner occupancy because home ownership rates are a function of income level. Together, both directly and indirectly, these forces encouraged low-density single-family living patterns, with generous amounts of land consumption on the urban fringe, since large-scale single-family subdivisions require extensive land parcels that can be assembled most easily at the urban periphery. On average over the period 1950–70, each newly constructed single-family home added approximately six-tenths of an acre to the nation's urbanized area, as defined by the Bureau of the Census. This is far more than the immediate lot space occupied by new housing. Although records on land usage in new construction are incomplete, data assembled by the National Association of Homebuilders indicate that the average lot size for new single-family homes in metropolitan areas was about 0.35 acre in the mid- to late-1960s. The effect has been that single-family construction has tended to stretch metropolitan boundaries, whereas most multi-family development has occurred as infill within the older inner city.

The link between new housing construction and inner city depopulation is straightforward. Since the early 1960s new housing construction has far exceeded household growth. Between 1963 and 1976 household expansion was some 17 millions, but 27 million new housing units were constructed. The crucial role of housing construction in excess of household growth, which can be termed *replacement housing construction,* in determining the value and maintenance of older housing is not surprising. It is part and parcel of one of the basic theories of how urban housing markets work to provide housing for lower-income families, the so-called filtering theory. This theory states that when new housing is built and occupied, more often than not by relatively well-to-do families, the older housing vacated by these families "filters" or trickles down to provide good-quality homes for lower-income families. Following this theory, the worst, least desirable housing left vacant after this housing game of musical chairs comes to an end is either abandoned or demolished and redeveloped. More often than not this housing is the oldest and the most outmoded—the remaining products of the earliest housing cycles.

Housing retirement is not a surgical operation. No invisible hand neatly excises substandard units from the housing stock. Rather, substandard units are retired only when they are judged substandard in the market-place, i.e. when they are not worth anything in cash terms, and are abandoned by their owners. Thus, large-scale retirement means the devaluation of an entire stock of existing housing concentrated in the innermost of the historical growth rings. Before abandonment, housing maintenance falls with housing values, and the end result is deterioration, both of older houses and of older neighbourhoods. Put quite simply, periods of abundant housing investment are years of vigorous new housing construction, and in the United States most new housing always has been built near the urban periphery. But since 1960 more than one-third of all new housing construction has replaced older stock rather than adding to the total supply of housing. As a consequence, the high rate of housing production not only pushed the urban boundary outward, but also produced faster abandonment of older housing located in the inner city.

Seen in this light, the nation's housing policy has been, *de facto,* the only explicit national policy for urban development that we have had. This policy has been direct and successful, promoting household wealth through home ownership, improved living conditions through new construction, and increased efficiency by means of mobility. Its very success as a facilitating force has contributed both to the emergence of a new scale of low-slung, far-flung metropolitan regions and to a new force of *counter-urbanization:* the transfer of the locus of new growth to some of the most remote and least urbanized parts of the country. The settings where this growth is now occurring are exceedingly diverse. They include regions oriented to recreation in northern New England, the Rocky Mountains, and the Upper Great Lakes; energy supply areas in the Northern Great Plains and Southern Appalachian Coal Fields; retirement communities in the Ozark-Ouachita Uplands; small manufacturing towns throughout much of the South; and non-metropolitan cities in every region whose economic fortunes are intertwined with state government or higher education.

Factors contributing to these shifts appear to be: (1) changes in transportation and communications that have removed many of the problems of access that previously served to constrain the growth prospects of the periphery, permitting decentralization of manufacturing on the inexpensive land and benefiting from the low wage rates of non-metropolitan areas; (2) the revival or expansion of energy extraction and highly localized large-scale energy-related industrial development; (3) the trend toward earlier retirement and semi-retirement, which has multiplied the ranks of retired people and lengthened the interval during later life when a person is no longer tied to a specific place by a job; (4) new sources of income, such as pensions and other payments which were either earned elsewhere in younger years or are a transfer of public funds from taxes paid elsewhere, which have expanded pensioners' roles as consumers whose presence in an increasingly service-oriented society creates jobs wherever they go; and (5) an increased orientation at all ages toward leisure activities, caused in part by rising *per capita* income and centred on amenity-rich areas outside the daily range of metropolitan commuting. A common feature of these several changes is that they have laid the foundation for the expansion of non-metropolitan employment. Servicing the arriving migrants and temporary residents provides opportunities which induce existing residents to stay and which also entice newcomers. But there are even more profound forces at work.

As I said in an earlier paper in the *Transactions,* the concentrated industrial metropolis only developed because proximity meant lower transportation and communication costs for those interdependent specialists who had to interact with each other frequently or intensively. One of the most important forces contributing to counter-urbanization is thus the erosion of centrality by time-space convergence. Virtually all technological developments of industrial times have had the effect of reducing the constraints of geographical space. Developments in transportation and communications have made it possible for each generation to live further from activity centres, for these activity centres to disperse, and for information users to rely upon information sources that are spatially more distant (yet temporally more immediate). In other words, large, dense urban concentrations are no longer necessary for external economies to be present. Contemporary developments in communications are supplying better channels for transmitting information and improving the capacities of partners in social intercourse to transact their business at great distances at great speed. The time-eliminating properties of long-distance communication and the space-spanning capacities of the

new communication technologies are combining to concoct a solvent that has dissolved the agglomeration advantages of the industrial metropolis, creating what some now refer to as an urban civilization without cities. The edges of many of the nation's urban systems have now pushed one hundred miles and more from declining central cities. Today's urban systems appear to be multi-nodal, multi-connected social systems sharing in national growth and offering a variety of life-styles in a variety of environments. And what are being abandoned are those environments that were crucial in the traditional metropolis-driven growth process: the high-density, congested, face-to-face city-centre settings that are now perceived as ageing, polluted, and crime-ridden, with declining services and employment bases, and escalating taxes. Such is the New American Dilemma.

What Price the Inner City?

Seen in this light, abandonment may be viewed as a measure of the success we have achieved in our housing policy and in responding to new growth opportunities. Yet the inner city cannot and should not be so lightly written off. There is clearly a national interest in the problems of the central city that derives from three distinguishable premises:

1. That it is socially wasteful to under-utilize, abandon, or destroy capital investments made by preceding generations in urban infrastructure, housing, places of business, and public buildings. The national product is diminished by our present course of reproducing these facilities elsewhere rather than using what already exists.

2. That although their populations are decreasing, central cities still hold a very large number of people whose lives and fortunes are unfavourably affected by their physical and social

environments. Even assuming that suburbanites and exurbanites entirely escape these adversities, over one-fourth of the nation's people live in central cities and contend daily with their stresses. The welfare of these people is surely a matter of national interest.

3. That although central cities, as large, dense concentrations of people and jobs, have become technologically obsolete, the shift to a new spatial organization can perhaps be made less painful to those who must adapt to it. Orderly change would be less costly to society as a whole than allowing stresses to accumulate within a system trying desperately to maintain itself until the system as a whole fails.

National concern about these problems has been evident in a series of federal programmes designed to reverse or at least to slow down the decay. Over time, these programmes have reflected a widening perception of the interplay of forces that cause inner city deterioration, have tested a variety of remedies, and have spent many billions of dollars, all to little avail.

The sequence of federal programmes begins in the 1930s with emergency public works and public housing construction, supplemented in 1949 by a large commitment of federal funds to slum clearance and redevelopment. Beginning in 1954, the emphasis shifted to less capital-intensive programmes of housing rehabilitation and neighbourhood preservation. Along with this changed emphasis came a growing array of capital grants to improve the urban infrastructure and increasing support for the common functions of city government.

The urban riots and racial strife of the early 1960s testified that the urban poor did not believe in the efficacy of these remedies. President Johnson declared "war" on poverty and his new programmes stressed both neighbourhood political mobilization and integrated planning to improve the physical, social, and economic circumstances of the urban poor and racial minorities. Unpersuaded of the effectiveness of these programmes, the Nixon administration withdrew the federal presence from the cities, turning urban problems back to city hall. Instead of advice and supervision, Washington would dispense only money.

In each of these episodes, the Congress and the Administration were responding partly to new circumstances, but mostly to the perception that the programmes confidently offered a few years earlier were ineffective or even perverse in their consequences. It may be that the mistakes they recognized retrospectively form a larger pattern that we can at this greater distance perceive, for the post-1970 evidence indicates, as we have seen, that deterioration is spreading to more cities and accelerating in those where it has long been evident.

First, the majority of these urban programmes failed because they were targeted towards areas left behind by the forces of change, forces that in turn were reinforced by the more effective *de facto* urban policy embodied in the nation's housing programmes.

Turning the housing equation around, investment in new housing construction is to some extent a substitute for investment in the preservation, repair, and upgrading of old housing. High interest rates and high labour and material costs tend to discourage housing investment of all kinds, but the same price changes enhance the value of the existing housing stock by making it more expensive to reproduce. It then becomes more economical to preserve and improve buildings rather than to allow them to deteriorate. New housing construction increased rapidly during the building boom of the early 1970s, and the numbers of building permits taken out in central cities for residential alterations and additions slumped.

After 1974, as the housing industry entered a period of combined inflation and recession, new housing construction lagged and private market revitalization of the inner city began to take hold. The fixed interest rate mortgage system in use in the United States provides a financial motive for this kind of upgrading of existing housing during periods of capital market tightness. Many home-owners would have to surrender their old, low-interest mortgages if they acquired new homes; such households often find it more profitable to satisfy their demand for more housing by making additions, replacements, or alterations to their present homes, while retaining their old mortgages. Considerations like these have made the home repair industry one of the strongest counter-cyclical sectors in the American economy. When total housing investment is high, rehabilitation and repair expenditures tend to lag; when total housing investment declines, capital expenditures on the standing stock actually intensify.

Unfortunately, both cheap, plentiful new housing and vibrant older neighbourhoods in central cities are desirable goals. But if no choice is made between conservation and the encouragement of new housing production on a broad scale and both goals are pursued simultaneously, the results are likely to be extremely wasteful. The national housing experience during the early 1970s illustrates the costly waste resulting from uncoordinated attempts to combine large-scale new housing production with large-scale conservation of older housing. As the 1960s drew to a close, the nation undertook major new initiatives to achieve the goal of a decent home in a decent neighbourhood for everybody, the poor as well as the rich. Major new federal programmes set up in the Housing Act of 1968 produced a massive upsurge in both federally subsidized new housing construction and in federally subsidized housing rehabilitation. By 1970, over 425,000 new units

were receiving direct federal subsidies. This amounted to more than one in five new units being built within the nation. Federally subsidized housing rehabilitation also grew apace. In 1972, 51,000 units were rehabilitated using federal subsidies. Federal rehabilitation programmes were focused largely on central city home-owners and landlords. It appears that the federal government subsidized between 8 and 11 per cent of the total dollar volume of reinvestment in owner-occupied housing in central cities during the early 1970s.

The enormous levels of new housing production encouraged by federal subsidies during these years cut deeply into private demand for the existing stock of owner-occupied housing in cities. Private unsubsidized reinvestment by central city home-owners fell more rapidly than federally subsidized reinvestment increased. Between 1969 and 1970, federally subsidized expenditures for the rehabilitation of owner-occupied homes in cities are estimated to have doubled, increasing by $150 million (measured in constant 1973 dollars). In the same years, private unsubsidized reinvestment by central city home-owners fell by $250 millions, or 10 per cent.

Thus, the attempt to combine massive new housing production with large-scale rehabilitation of the existing housing stock cut into housing values in central cities, encouraging mortgage defaults and abandonment, and thus contributed to the crisis in federal housing policy which brought President Nixon's moratorium, putting an end to many of the housing programmes which underlay the federal housing initiatives.

Private-Market Inner City Rehabilitation: Prospects and Limits

Since the early 1970s, however, there have been signs of private-market renovation of some neighbourhoods in some inner cities, a function of both a slow-down of new housing construction and of life-style shifts in the baby boom generation. During the 1960s, privately renovated neighbourhoods such as Georgetown in Washington, D.C., Greenwich Village in New York, or Boston's South End were dismissed as unique. But more recently home-owners have begun to renovate old neighbourhoods all across the country.

Capitol Hill in Washington is one noteworthy example of revitalization. Restoration on the Hill now covers 100 blocks of downtown Washington. Once a middle-class neighbourhood of Victorian terraced houses, Capitol Hill fell into disrepair in the 1930s and 1940s. By 1950, when the first tentative signs of renovation appeared, the neighbourhood contained some of Washington's worst slums. Renovation caught on in the neighbourhood during the early 1960s. In areas of the Hill overtaken by restoration during the 1960s, housing rents and values rose more than twice as rapidly as in the District as a whole. A recent small-scale survey of new home-buyers on Capitol Hill found that 80 per cent of home-buyers are white. The average age of buyers was 35 years. Ninety per cent received annual incomes of more than $20,000 and eight out of ten were buying their first home. This general profile is typical of home-buyers in neighbourhoods being renovated around the country. By contrast, families leaving these renovated neighbourhoods are very different, tending to be poor, tenants, and blacks or other minorities, or elderly.

Part of the reason for revitalization is certainly the decline in new housing construction since 1974. There are regional differences. The metropolitan areas with the lowest rates of replacement supply have been those experiencing the most rapid inflation of housing prices and the most substantial neighbourhood revitalization. It should be borne in mind that replacement supply is the difference between new household creation and new housing construction. Since 1970 there have been many changes affecting the number and nature of new households entering the housing market, and it is these changes that appear to be the causes of the regional differences. An increase in owner-occupancy rates from 69 to 75 per cent between 1970 and 1975 has been accompanied by rapid change in the nature of households created by the baby boom generation.

The increase in home ownership, occurring most rapidly among one-person or single-parent households (Table 6), occurred at a time of massive inflation of housing costs, and surely represents an investment rather than a consumption decision: an inflation hedge against being priced out of the market in the future. The inflation, in turn, has been both cause and effect of the slower pace of new housing construction, which of itself should have made inner city reinvestment more attractive.

But superimposed on this have been the housing preferences of new higher-income young home-owners not pressed by child-rearing, with two workers, one or both of whom may be a professional, seeking neighbourhoods in the inner city with:

1. Geographic clusters of housing structures capable of yielding high-quality services.
2. A variety of public-good amenities within safe walking distance of these areas, such as a scenic waterfront, parks, museums, or art galleries, universities, distinguished architecture, and historic landmarks or neighbourhoods.
3. A range of high-quality retail facilities and services, including restaurants, theatres, and entertainment.

These preferences follow directly from life-style and compositional shifts. First, the continued development of American

Table 6. Household Characteristics and Home Ownership in Metropolitan Areas, 1970–75

| Household Composition | Metropolitan Households by Type | | | | Rates of Home Ownership (percentage) | | |
| | Number (000s) | | Change 1970–75 | | | | |
	1970	1975	Number (000s)	Per- centage	1970	1975	Change 1970–75
Two or more person households	35,925	39,539	3614	10.1	64.8	67.5	2.7
Husband-wife families	29,597	31,200	1603	5.4	69.0	73.8	4.8
Under 25 years	2070	2115	45	2.2	22.1	26.2	4.1
25–34 years	6366	7338	972	15.3	55.3	61.3	6.0
35–44 years	6472	6398	−74	−1.1	76.6	80.7	4.1
45–64 years	11,164	11,464	300	2.7	79.5	85.1	5.6
65 or more years	3624	3885	261	7.2	74.7	78.8	4.1
Other male heads	1711	2304	593	34.7	48.4	46.3	−2.1
Under 65 years	1424	2008	584	41.0	44.8	42.8	−2.0
65 or more years	287	295	8	2.8	66.2	69.8	3.6
Other female heads	4616	6035	1419	30.7	44.0	42.8	−1.2
Under 65 years	3810	5125	1315	34.5	39.3	38.1	−1.2
65 or more years	806	910	104	12.9	66.0	69.3	3.3
One person households	7933	10,125	2192	27.6	35.5	36.5	1.0
Under 65 years	4728	6138	1410	29.8	27.9	27.5	−0.4
65 or more years	3205	3988	783	24.4	46.6	50.3	3.7
Total all households	43,858	49,666	5808	13.2	59.5	61.2	1.7

Source: James (1977) and U.S. Bureau of the Census (1970 and 1975b).

society has resulted in increased economic parity for women; this enables them to have the option of other roles than that of housewife and mother. In consequence, men and women lead more independent lives, and are able to exercise more options in life-course transitions. Increasing numbers of couples live together without the formal ties of marriage. The direct and opportunity cost of child rearing is rising, birth control technology has improved and abortion laws have been liberalized, and hence the birth rate is dropping. There are increasing numbers of families with two or more workers and more working wives than ever before.

Revitalization, then, has been taking hold first in superior neighbourhoods in those metropolitan areas which have the lowest rates of replacement supply. These, in turn, are those areas in which there is a sufficient cluster of professional jobs to support the youthful college-educated labour force most likely to evidence supportive life-style shifts. An implication is that significant revitalization may be limited to the metropolitan centres with clusters of post-industrial management, control, and information processing activities.

Alonso (1977)* highlights the relationship of type of housing unit occupied to stage in life-cycle, showing a shift away from the free-standing owner-occupied

* See Alonso's paper in Section VII for an elaboration (Ed. note).

single-family house between 1960 and 1970 for younger households.

Increasing locational attractiveness of more central locations in the core city and the older suburbs follows, for it is there that there is an appropriate stock of housing and access to services as well as locational convenience for the journey to work. Since many of these households have no children, the racial factors of school integration do not act as they have in the White flight to the suburbs.

But there are polarizing effects here as well. Over the past 20 years the housing of the poor and the working poor has improved primarily because they have fallen heir to what used to be called "the grey areas." The softening of middle-class demand for this housing stock lowered its relative price and permitted a sharp decline in overcrowding for low-income people. Whatever the troubles of the cities, this has been a fortunate outcome. But the danger appears imminent that the housing stock available to the working and welfare poor will now be sharply diminished, squeezed between reduced rates of filtering at one end and the childless multiworker household at the other. There is, in this, an incipient class conflict between the new young well-educated professional class, actively pursuing alternative living arrangements and life-styles, and'the majority of the children of working-class Americans for whom marriage and the home in the suburbs remain a desirable goal: Harris polls continue to report that of the 35 per cent of American dwellers who plan to move in a 2- to 3-year period, 53 per cent of them plan to move to a suburb or a rural area. Indeed, one may argue that the main value struggle in the United States today is between an upper-middle-class intelligentsia and a newly middle-class proletariat, which rejects both "alternative" life-styles and the left wing's egalitarian arguments. For the intelligentsia, material goals have been succeeded by those of the quality of life and of self-actualization; for the middle-class workers, however, material welfare remains a dominant concern.

Is it possible, then, for private market revitalization to be sustained? A variety of factors suggest otherwise. First, the baby boom generation will age, and is followed by much smaller age cohorts (Alonso, Sec. VII). The population bulge, as it ages, will continue to disrupt one national institution after another. In the 1950s and 1960s it created problems of expansion for the public schools and universities—institutions which more recently have had to cope with the ordeal of shrinkage as their user populations have subsided. When the population crest reached the 18–24 bracket, it multiplied crime rates and redirected national job creation efforts to the alleviation of youth unemployment. Perhaps the greatest adjustments for public policy of all kinds lie ahead, when the babies of 1950 become the aged of the year 2015. Among those adjustments, as before, will be those in housing preferences. Movement of the baby cohort along the scale of housing preferences will undoubtedly cause the demand for inner city living in revitalized neighbourhoods to subside rather than increase, at least until the early twenty-first century. Additions to the supporting job base may not be there either. There appears little likelihood that new post-industrial employment clusters will develop in inner city locations in the near future as they did in the 1960s; headquarters decentralization now appears the stronger force. Further, as the cohort ages, mobility will decrease. For all of these reasons, the prospect for wider inner city revitalization appears to be bleak, unless a deep continuing recession cuts deeply into the new housing industry, and if that comes to pass there will still be an inner city problem of the displaced and the disadvantaged.

There are other reasons, too, why we might expect the dilemma of the inner city to continue, and even to deepen. The regional income convergence discussed earlier was a product of the extraordinary factor mobility that enabled new growth opportunities to be exploited and growing regions, in turn, to become increasingly autonomous through import substitution. The branch plant movement, for example, has been one of the most potent sources of manufacturing job decentralization from the North East since 1950. Declining mobility suggests the likelihood of progressive regional income *divergence* in the future. Already the signs are there, for nominal income convergence in fact does imply real income divergence to the disadvantage of the major cities and the traditional heartland. Costs of living and the burden of negative externalities appear to be higher in the inner cities of the urban-industrial regions, whereas real or perceived environmental amenities are greater in the Sunbelt and in the inter-metropolitan peripheries. Lessening factor mobility would imply a decrease in autonomy and a commensurate increase in commodity trade. The Heckscher–Ohlin theorem postulates that when factor endowments and prices vary, the response is regional specialization and commodity trade. The Siebert corollary states that if factor prices are equalized by factor mobility, the result is regional income convergence and autonomy through import substitution. Myrdal's dilemma was one of deepening factor endowment differentials and of progressively more profound heartland dominance of poverty-stricken hinterland economies. Mobility produced the equalization of Siebert's corollary. Overshoot and increasing immobility can only then lead to hinterland dominance of increasingly poverty-stricken heartland economies. Indeed the balance of political power in the Congress has already shifted in this direction.

There is no reason to believe that ageing industrial cities will be, able to revitalize unless they are able to develop a post-industrial high technology or service activity base. Neither is there any reason to believe that those metropolitan regions developing such a base will do so in a manner which re-creates the inner cities of the past. Unless there is a prolonged recession, there is little basis for believing that private market revitalization of inner city neighbourhoods will diffuse much further. There is every reason to believe that settlement patterns that have emerged in the past decade will continue to diffuse and differentiate.

The continuing public policy problem will then be that of ameliorating the heavy social costs incurred by the concentrations of captive individuals without access to the real economy, concentrations which continue to be characterized by high unemployment rates, especially among minorities (Table 7), and by low educational achievement, drug addiction, crime, and a sense of hopelessness and alienation from society. Attention to causes rather than symptoms demands that factors which exclude individuals from the mainstream of society and from meaningful work opportunities be of prime concern, for work is a measure of worth in the United States. Such factors include poor skills, cultural gaps, language barriers, and race, and may have to be addressed by both law and remediation. Programmes aimed at creating work situations, intensifying quality educational assistance, and improving health and nutrition so that children will be able to learn, are essential.

More basically, a restructuring of incentives played a critical role in the increase in home ownership and the attendant transformation of urban form after the Second World War. There is no reason to believe that another restructuring could not be designed to lead in other directions, for in a highly mobile market

Table 7. Labour Force Status of Persons 16 Years Old and Over, by Sex and Type of Residence: March 1977 and April 1970 (numbers in thousands. 1970 metropolitan area definition)

Race, Sex, and Labour Force Status	March 1977			April 1970		
	Central Cities	Suburban Areas	Nonmetropolitan Areas	Central Cities	Suburban Areas	Nonmetropolitan Areas
All Races						
Male						
In civilian labour force	15,363	23,181	17,848	15,395	18,908	14,756
Percentage of total 16 years old and over	73.5	78.9	73.6	75.1	79.4	72.3
Employed	13,967	21,648	16,572	14,702	18,269	14,168
Unemployed	1397	1534	1275	693	639	588
Unemployment rate	9.1	6.6	7.1	4.5	3.4	4.0
Not in civilian labour force	5526	6214	6408	5106	4915	5651
Female						
In civilian labour force	11,688	15,732	11,955	10,796	10,944	8645
Percentage of total 16 years old and over	48.2	50.0	45.4	44.7	41.8	38.6
Employed	10,627	14,440	10,967	10,241	10,432	8148
Unemployed	1061	1291	988	555	513	497
Unemployment rate	9.1	8.2	8.3	5.1	4.7	5.7
Not in civilian labour force	12,578	15,738	14,369	13,365	15,237	13,757
Black as Percentage of Total						
Male						
In civilian labour force	17.9	4.5	7.0	16.7	3.5	6.7
Employed	16.5	4.2	6.7	16.3	3.4	6.5
Unemployed	32.1	8.7	10.7	25.4	6.6	10.5
Not in civilian labour force	23.8	5.9	9.8	19.2	5.6	9.8
Female						
In civilian labour force	20.9	5.7	8.7	20.1	5.2	9.0
Employed	19.6	5.5	8.2	19.7	5.0	8.6
Unemployed	33.9	9.0	14.8	28.6	8.0	15.5
Not in civilian labour force	20.5	4.3	8.8	17.1	3.7	7.7

Source: U.S. Bureau of the Census (1978).

system nothing is as effective in producing change as a shift in relative prices. There is, then, a way. Whether there is a will is another matter, for under conditions of democratic pluralism, interest group politics prevail, and the normal state of such politics is "business as usual." The bold changes that followed the Great Depression and the Second World War were responses to major crises, for it is only in a crisis atmosphere that enlightened leadership can prevail over the normal business of politics in which there is an unerring aim for the lowest common denominator. Nothing less than an equivalent crisis will, I suggest, enable the necessary substantial inner city revitalization to take place. Until that crisis occurs, dispersion and differentiation will prevail. Some limited private market revitalization will continue, to be sure, but within a widening environment of disinvestment manifested geographically in the abandonment of the housing stock put into place by earlier building cycles.

References

Alonso, W. (1977) 'The population factor and urban structure', Joint Centre for Urban Studies.

Garnick, D. H. (1978) 'A reappraisal of the outlook for northern states and cities in the context of U.S. economic history', Joint Centre for Urban Studies (based on data from U.S. Department of Commerce, Bureau of Economic Analysis).

Grasberger, F. J. (1978) 'Developing tools to improve Federal grant-in-aid formulas', *Formula Evaluation Project Prelim. Rep.* No. 3, Centre for Governmental Research, Rochester, N.Y.

Homenuck, H. P. M. and Morgenstern, J. P. (1977) 'A study of high rise', *Urban Land* 36, 17–19.

James, F. J. (1977) 'Private reinvestment in older housing and older neighborhoods', Committee on Banking, Housing and Urban Affairs, U.S. Senate.

Long, L. H. (1978) 'Interregional migration of the poor', *Current Population Reports, Special Studies* Ser. P-23, No. 73, p. 4, U.S. Bureau of the Census.

Long, L. H. and Boertlein, C. G. (1976) 'The geographical mobility of Americans', *Current Population Reports, Special Studies* Ser. P-23, No. 64, p. 11, U.S. Bureau of the Census.

Long, L. H. and Hansen, K. (1977) 'Selectivity of black return migration to the South', *Rural Sociol.* 62, 317–31.

Marcin, T. C. (1974) 'The effects of declining population growth on the demand for housing', *Gen. Tech. Rep.* NC-11, p. 5, U.S. Dept. of Agriculture.

Peterson, G. E. (1977) 'Federal tax policy and the shaping of the urban environment', National Bureau of Economic Research.

Peterson, G. E. and Muller, T. (1978) *Income growth differential study* (Washington D.C.) Advisory Commission on Intergovernmental Relations, Urban Institute.

Regional Economic Analysis Division (1976) 'Work force/migration patterns 1970–73', *Survey of Current Business* pp. 23–6.

U.S. Bureau of the Census (1970) *Census of housing: metropolitan housing characteristics, United States and regions,* HC(2)–1.

U.S. Bureau of the Census (1975a) 'Mobility of the population of the United States: March 1970 to March 1975', *Current Population Reports* Ser. P-26, No. 285.

U.S. Bureau of the Census (1975b) 'Financial characteristics of the housing inventory', *Annual Housing Survey* Part C.

U.S. Bureau of the Census (1976a) *Population characteristics,* p. 20 (Table 30).

U.S. Bureau of the Census (1976b) *Statistical Abstract of the U.S.* (Table 37).

U.S. Bureau of the Census (1977) *Current Population Reports,* Ser. P-25, No. 709.

U.S. Bureau of the Census (1978) 'Social and economic characteristics of the metropolitan and non-metropolitan population, 1977 and 1970', *Current Population Reports* Ser. P-23, No. 75.

U.S. Department of Commerce, Bureau of Economic Analysis (1978) *Survey of Current Business.*

MANUEL CASTELLS

The Wild City

Beyond the Myths of the Urban Crisis

"There was an urban crisis at one time," said William Dilley 3d, Deputy Assistant Secretary of Policy Development at the Department of Housing and Urban Development.[1] But now, according to President Ford's aides, "the urban crisis of the 60's is over." What the officials wanted to express was that the black ghettoes were under control in spite of the recession. As right-wing ideologist Daniel Moynihan declared in the Congress, there is not an urban problem but a Negro problem.[2]

Is that really true? Is the urban crisis just the ideological expression used by the ruling class to "naturalize" (through an implicit ecological causation) the current social contradictions[3]?

This is the most current understanding of the political elite. So, Senator Ribicoff,

opening the famous Congressional "Ribicoff hearings" on urban problems in 1966 put it in unambiguous terms[4]:

To say that the city is the central problem of American life is simply to know that increasingly the cities are American life; just as urban living is becoming the condition of man across the world. . . . The city is not just housing and stores. It is not just education and employment, parks and theaters, banks and shops. It is a place where men should be able to live in dignity and security and harmony, where the great achievements of modern civilization and the ageless pleasures afforded by natural beauty should be available to all.

The popular mood is similar. A survey conducted by Wilson and Banfield on a sample of homeowners in Boston in 1967 in order to identify what the "urban problems" were for the people, concluded that[5]:

The conventional urban problems—housing, transportation, pollution, urban renewal and

1. Quoted by Ernest Holsendolph, "Urban Crisis of the 1960's is Over, Ford Aides Say," *The New York Times*, March 23, 1975.
2. Quoted in Charles O. Jones and Layne D. Hoppe, *The Urban Crisis in America*, Washington National Press, Washington, 1969.
3. See, for example, M. Castells, "Urban Sociology and Urban Politics," *Comparative Urban Research*, 6, 1975.

4. *The Ribicoff Hearings*, U.S. Congress, 1966, p. 25.
5. See James Q. Wilson, "The Urban Unease," *The Public Interest*, Summer 1968, pp. 26–27.

From **Kapitalstate**, Vol. 4–5, 1976, pp. 2–9, 21–30. An extended version of this paper appeared in M. Castells, **The Urban Question**, Edward Arnold, London, 1977, Chs. 15, 18. Reprinted in modified form by permission of the author.

the like—were a major concern of only eighteen percent of those questioned and these were expressed disproportionately by the wealthier, better educated respondents. . . . The issue which concerned more respondents than any other was variously stated—crime, violence, rebellious youth, racial tension, public immortality, delinquency. However stated, the common theme seemed to be a concern for improper behavior in public places.

Nevertheless, while the urban crisis of the 60's remained largely associated with poverty and racial discrimination and with the social programs designed to control blacks and unemployed, the urban crisis of the 1970's has progressively developed rather different connotations:

The urban crisis has been used to speak of *the crisis of some key urban services,* like housing, transportation, welfare, health, education, etc., characterized by an advanced degree of socialized management and a decisive role of the state intervention.[6]

The urban crisis is also *the fiscal crisis of the cities,* the inability of the local governments to provide enough resources to cover the required public facilities because of the increasing gap between the fiscal resources and the public needs and demands.[7]

The urban crisis is, at another level, the development of *urban movements and conflicts* rising up from the grass-roots community organizations and directed towards urban stakes, that is towards the delivery and management of particular means of socialized consumption.[8]

And, currently, the urban crisis is also the impact of the *structural and economic crisis* on the organization of the cities and on the evolution of social services.[9]

Is the multiplicity of meanings of the urban crisis an ideological effect? It is, if by this we would mean that the roots of the different levels of crisis that we have cited are produced by a particular form of spatial organization. But if the crude use of the term "urban crisis" is an ideological artifact, the association between the different connotative levels is not an arbitrary one. It is a biased reading of actual connections experienced in social practice.

In fact, *our hypothesis is that the U.S. urban crisis is the crisis of a particular form of urban structure that plays a major role in the U.S. process of capitalist accumulation, in the organization of socialized consumption and in the reproduction of the social order.* Since the urban role is performed at multiple levels, so is the crisis, its connections and its effects. This is the unifying perspective that will underlie our exploration of the multi-dimensionality of the urban crisis.

6. See: Alan Gartner and Frank Riessman, *The Service Society and the Consumer Vanguard,* Harper and Row, New York, 1974. And also: Paul Jacobs, *Prelude to Riot. A view of urban America from the bottom,* Vintage Books, New York, 1966.

7. See: Daniel R. Fusfeld, "The Basic Economics of the Urban and Racial Crisis," Conference Papers of the Union for Radical Political Economics, December 1968. And also Barbara Bergeman, "The Urban Crisis," *American Economic Review,* Sept. 1969.

8. See: John Mollenkopf, *Growth Defied: Community Organization and the Struggle Over Urban Development in America,* forthcoming book on the base of a 1973 Harvard Ph.D. dissertation, the best research that we know on urban movements in the U.S. Also, the useful reader: Robert H. Connery (ed.), *Urban Riots: Violence and Social Change,* Vintage Books, New York, 1969. And the now classic article by Michael Lipsky, "Protest as a Political Resource," *American Political Science Review,* LXII, N.4, December 1968.

9. City Bureau of the San Francisco Socialist Coalition, "Cities in Crisis," Package on the Economic Crisis of the Union of Radical Political Economists, 1975.

THE U.S. MODEL OF CAPITALIST ACCUMULATION AND THE U.S. PATTERN OF URBAN STRUCTURE: ECONOMIC DUALISM, CLASS DOMINATION, AND SPATIAL SEGREGATION

The specificity of the U.S. urban structure since World War II—underlying the crisis of American cities—results from the historical articulation of the processes of *metropolitanization, suburbanization,* and *social-political fragmentation.*[10]

Metropolitanization. Concentration of the population and activities in some major areas at an accelerated rate. Such population concentration follows from the process of uneven development and from the concentration of capital (means of production and labor) in the monopolistic stage of capitalism. At the periphery, regional economies and agriculture are devastated/re-structured by the penetration of their markets and the transformations in productivity under the hegemony of financial capital. Mass migration follows. In the dominant urban centers, the combined effect of externalities, transportation networks, urban markets and concentration of the management units and of the institutions of circulation of capital concentrate workers, means of production, means of consumption and organizations. These major cities are soon called metropolitan areas as an expression of their dominance over the "hinterland," that is, over the entire society.

Suburbanization.[11] The process of selective decentralization and spatial sprawl of population and activities within the metropolitan areas, starting at a large scale after World War II, accelerating during the 50's and maintaining its trend in the 60's. This is a selective process in that the new suburban population has a higher social status. There is a double differentiation of economic activity. On the one hand, business activities and major administrative services remain in the urban core while manufacturing and retail trade tend to decentralize their location. On the other hand, within the industrial and commercial sectors large-scale monopolistic plants and shopping centers go to the suburbs, leaving in the central cities two very different types of firms: a small number of technologically advanced activities and luxury shops; the mainstream of industrial and service activities of the so-called "competitive sector" (backward) as well as the marginal activities known as the components of the "irregular economy."

In the U.S. urban structure[12], this pro-

10. For some data concerning the basic information on the characteristic functions and transformation of the process of metropolitan growth and urban structure in the United States, see Leo Schnore, *The Urban Scene,* The Free Press, Glencoe, Ill., 1965; Beverly Duncan and Stanley Lieberson, *Metropolis and Region in Transition,* Sage Publications, Beverly Hills, Ca., 1970; Sylvia F. Fava and Noel P. Gist, *Urban Society,* Thomas Y. Crowell, New York, 1975; Leonard E. Goodall, *The American Metropolis,* Charles E. Merrill, Columbus, Ohio, 1968; Amos H. Hawley and Basil G. Zimmer, *The Metropolitan Community,* Sage Publications, Beverly Hills, Ca., 1970; Jeffrey K. Hadden and Edgar F. Borgatta, *American Cities: Their Social Characteristics,* Rand McNally Co., Chicago, 1965, etc. For a well informed presentation of the historical evolution on American cities, see: Charles N. Glaab, *The American City.* A documentary history, The Dorsey Press, Homewood, Ill., 1963.

11. The best source of data, bibliography and interpretations on the suburbanization process is the reader edited by Louis H. Masotti and Jeffrey K. Hadden, *The Urbanization of the Suburbs, Urban Affairs Annual Reviews,* Sage, Beverly Hills, Ca., 1973. Elliott Sclar (Brandeis Univ.) is finishing an important book on the subject: we have benefitted from one discussion on the topic as well as of a chapter ("Levels of Entrapment").

12. See: Bennett Harrison, *Urban Economic Development: Suburbanization, Minority Opportunity and the Condition of Central City,* The Urban Institute, Washington, D.C., 1974.

cess is a self-reinforcing one. The immigration of poor blacks expelled from the agricultural south has been concentrated in the inner cities.[13] The exodus of the upper and middle income groups attracts trade and service activities to the suburbs. "Competitive sector" jobs locate in geographical proximity to the low-income workers residing in central cities. Service and industrial employment locate in terms of the transportation system for suburban workers. The ecological patterns of residence will be increasingly differentiated[14]: yard-surrounded suburban single family houses versus increasingly obsolete inner city apartment dwellings. The cultural style, rooted mostly in social class and family practices, will be symbolically reinforced by the social-spatial distance and by the environmental imagery. The two worlds will increasingly ignore each other until they will develop reciprocal fears, myths, and prejudices, often articulated to racial and class barriers.[15] The segregated school will become a major instrument of self-definition and perpetuation of the two separate and hierarchically organized universes.[16]

The suburbanization process has been facilitated by major technological changes in transportation, in the mass production

of housing and in the increasing spatial freedom of the plants and services in terms of the functional requirements for their location. Suburbanization is not a consequence of the automobile. On the contrary, the massive auto-highway transportation system and the new locational patterns of residence and employment express the new stage of capitalist accumulation and have been made possible primarily by the policies of the state designed to serve this purpose.[17] Let us summarize briefly the specific connections between capital accumulation, state policies, and suburbanization.

The recovery of U.S. capitalism after the Great Depression of the thirties was made possible by the war and three major post-war economic trends[18]: (1) The internalization of capital and the increase of the rate of exploitation on a world scale under U.S. hegemony, as a direct consequence of the economic and political situation of each country after World War II; (2) the rapid expansion of new profitable outlets through the development of mass consumption; (3) the decisive structural intervention of the state in the process of accumulation, in the creation of general conditions for capitalist production and in the socialization of costs of social investment and the reproduction of labor power. As a simultaneous cause and consequence of this accelerated capitalist growth, the stability of the social relationships of exploitation was achieved through the combined use of economic integration and political re-

13. See: Ira Katznelson, *Black Men, White Cities, Race, Politics and Migration in the United States, 1900–30 and Britain 1948–68,* Oxford University Press, London, 1973, for an explanation of the mechanisms although the period studied is not exactly the same.
14. See: Leo Schnore, *Class and Race in Cities and Suburbs,* Markham, Chicago, 1972.
15. Reminder: Herbert J. Gans, *The Urban Villagers: Group and Class in the Life of Italian Americans,* Free Press of Glencoe, New York, 1962; *The Levittowners, Ways of Life and Politics in a New Suburban Community,* Pantheon Books, NY, 1967; "Urbanism and Suburbanism as Ways of Life," in Arnold M. Rose (ed.), *Human Behavior and Social Processes,* Houghton Mifflin, Boston, 1962.
16. See: Reynolds Farley and Alma F. Taeuber, *Racial Segregation in the Public Schools,* Institute for Research on Poverty, University of Wisconsin, Madison, May 1972, mimeo.

17. See the different analyses contained in Robert H. Haveman and Robert D. Hamrin (editors), *The Political Economy of Federal Policy,* Harper & Row, New York, 1973. And for the specific and crucial point on transportation: George M. Smerk, *Urban Transportation. The Federal Role,* Indiana University Press, Bloomington, 1965.
18. See my draft paper *The Graying of America. The World Economic Crisis and the U.S. Society,* University of Wisconsin, Madison, August 1975.

pression of the mainstream of the working class.

How do these trends relate themselves to the process of suburbanization? On the one hand, the increasing profits of monopoly capital allowed the expansion of material production and of the investment in new technology and transportation facilities that led to the decentralization of larger plants. On the other hand, the economic growth allowed a less than proportional rise of the workers' wages and gave some of them a prospective job stability, increasing their purchasing power and their financial reliability. The requirement for immediate and massive new outlets was met just in time by the sudden expansion of mass production of new housing, highway-auto transportation and all complementary public facilities. In twenty years, America practically built up a new set of cities, contiguous to the preexisting metropolises. The reason that improved housing conditions were realized through new suburban settlements was that land was much cheaper in the urban fringe, that mass production of housing with light building materials required new construction and that the whole impact on the economy was considerably higher, particularly if we consider the implied necessity of a decentralized individual transportation system.[19] Under these conditions of production and relying on a system of easy installment credit, the construction and auto industry could draw into their market a substantial proportion of the middle-class American families, later including in this new world a sector of the working class.

Nevertheless, the decisive element in

the feasibility of this economic, social, and spatial strategy was the role of the state, particularly of the Federal government, introducing key mechanisms for the production of housing and highways, in a form subordinated to the interests of monopoly capital. In the case of housing, the provision of a mortgage system that provided risk-free credit for financial capital, the state overcame the major obstacle to the profitable mass production of housing within capitalism: the absence of a reliable home ownership market.[20] Once the government undertook the risk of mortgage foreclosures, middle-class families could afford to enter the market, starting the process that allowed the relative modernization of the building industry and the lowering of costs which further enlarged the suburban market. In addition, the government issued (during the past forty years) a number of fiscal measures to protect real estate investors and to favor home ownership.[21]

Concerning the development of the *highway-auto transportation system,* three elements have to be considered: (1) The deliberate destruction by the auto corporations (under the tolerance of the state and federal authorities) of alternative means of transportation, namely by acquiring the streetcar and railway companies and dismantling them . . .[22]; (2) the government paid ninety percent of highway construction and it has spent, in 1973, sixty times more in this category

19. For an outline of the interaction between these three levels (the process of capital accumulation, the process of urbanization and the State) see the fundamental paper by David Harvey, "The Political Economy of Urbanization in Advanced Capitalist Societies. The Case of the United States," *Urban Affairs Annual Review,* Sage Publications, 1975.

20. The most important source of data on housing for the U.S.: *Housing in the Seventies,* Hearings on Housing and Community Development Legislation, 1973, Part 3, House of Representatives Subcommittee on Banking and Currency, 93rd Congress, First Session, Government Printing Office, Washington, D.C., 1973. 21. A clear description of the financial mechanisms of the housing market is: Roger Starr, *Housing and the Money Market,* Basic Books, New York, 1975. 22. Glenn Yago, "How Did We Get to the Way We Are Going?, General Motors and Public Transportation," University of Wisconsin, Sociology Department, Madison, 1974, mimeo.

than in urban collective transportation for the whole country[23]; (3) the residential and industrial sprawl was necessarily connected to the highway-auto transportation, and in that sense the capitalist interests and the state policies created a set of mutually reinforcing trends. The auto, and therefore the highway, *became a need*.

The role of the suburbs in the process of capitalist accumulation was not limited only to providing outlets for the capital directly invested in their production. The whole suburban social form became an extremely effective *apparatus of individualized commodity consumption*.

Shopping centers and supermarkets were made possible by suburban sprawl. A new set of leisure activities (from the drive-in to the private swimming pool) was linked to suburbanization. But even more important was the role of the suburban single-family house as the perfect design for maximizing capitalist consumption. Every household had to be self-sufficient, from the refrigerator to the TV, including the garden machinery, the do-it-yourself instruments, the electro-domestic equipment, etc.

At the same time, the suburban model of consumption had a very clear impact on the *reproduction of the dominant social relationships*. Because the (legally owned) domestic world, was in fact borrowed, it could be kept only on the assumption of a permanent pre-programmed job situation. Any major deviation or failure could be sanctioned by the threats to (job-dependent) financial reliability. The mass consumption was also mass dependency upon the economic *and cultural* rules of the financial institutions.

The social relationships in the suburban neighborhood also expressed the values of individualism, conformism and social integration, reducing the world to the nuclear family and the social desires to the maximization of individual consumption.

Without discussing here the alternative hypotheses about the suburbs being produced by the combination of technological possibilities and of subjective values towards suburbanism, three remarks must suffice: (1) Peoples' consciousness and values are produced by their practice, a practice determined by their place in the social relationships of production and consumption[24]; (2) it is true that there is a "return to nature" dream linked to the myth of recovering, at least in the evening, the autonomy of the petty commodity and peasant production from which salaried labor power was historically drawn; (3) this myth is as strong in Europe as in the United States and nevertheless the suburban pattern *has not been the same*. In this sense the United States is *unique* in the world. Obviously the suburbs have grown everywhere with the expansion of the metropolitan areas, but the pattern of social segregation is not the same (with the non-U.S. central cities having frequently a higher social status on the average). Suburban owner-occupied housing is much less diffused outside the United States and the automobile is not the major mode of urban transportation. Indeed, this is not a matter of "inferior level of development": the "suburban-like-U.S. pattern" is being reversed in Paris in the last ten years after having increased to some extent in the early sixties.[25] This is not to claim the irreducible

23. See George M. Smerk, *op. cit.*, 1965: and especially the readings included in the chapter on "The Politics of Transportation" in Stephen M. David and Paul E. Peterson (editors), *Urban Politics and Public Policy: The City in Crisis,* Praeger Publishers, New York, 1973.

24. See: Francis Godard, "De la notion de besoin au concept de pratique de classe," La Pensee (Paris), n. 166, December 1972: and also: Edmond Preteceille, "Besoins sociaux et socialisation de la consommation," La Pensee, n. 180, March–April, 1975.
25. See: M. Freyssinet and T. Regazzola, Segregation urbaine et deplacement sociaux, Centre de Sociologies Urbaine, Paris, 1970; and Chris-

specificity of each society but to show how the process of U.S. suburbanization was determined and shaped by a particular pattern of capitalist development at a particular critical stage characterized by the decisive intervention of the state.[26]

The other face of the process of suburbanization was the new role played by the central cities in the process of accumulation and in the reproduction of the labor power. There is a major differentiation between the Central Business District (CBD) and the central cities at large.[27] The CBD kept the major directional and organizational economic functions, as well as a number of luxurious commercial activities and several major cultural and symbolic institutions, while losing a large proportion of the retail trade and many residents. The central cities lost jobs especially in large-size manufacturing plants and a significant residential proportion of the middle-class as well as monopoly workers. On the other hand, central cities received increasing numbers of black and poor white immigrants, mostly from the southern depressed areas, as a consequence of the mechanization of agriculture and of the destruction of the backward regional economies.[28] The central

cities became the location, at the same time, of the "competitive sector" activities, of the corresponding low skilled and low-paid segment of the labor market, of the surplus population (unemployed and underemployed), and of the discriminated ethnic minorities. Therefore, the central cities organized consumption on an entirely different basis than the suburbs.

The housing market, in particular, was supposed to work according to a "filtering down" theory. Namely, the upper strata of central city residents (excluding from our analysis the top elite, mostly concentrated in self-defended high-society ghettoes) left their urban dwellings for their new suburban homes. This allowed the middle-strata to occupy the vacated houses, freeing their standard housing for the bottom level that could leave their slums to the newcomers. In fact, such a theory never corresponded to reality, since its basic assumption was the extension of upward income mobility to the whole population.[29] Given a process of uneven development, the low and middle strata of the inner city were not able to afford the level of rents or interest payments necessary to jump to the following housing level. In addition, the racial discrimination operated against any actual access of the minorities to an equivalent standard of living, imposing a "race overprice."[30] The result for inner city housing was that to maintain profit levels, the landlords combined lower rents with overcrowding and lack of maintenance. Some neighborhoods were *nevertheless* well-maintained on the base of ownership through savings and loan asso-

tian Topalov, "Politique Monopoliste et propriete du logement," *Economie-et-Politique*, March, 1974.

26. Leo Schnore has insisted several times on the dependency of the social patterns of the cities upon the specificity of the historical processes and stages. For a re-assessment of this perspective, see: Leo F. Schnore (editor), *The New Urban History*, John Wiley, New York, 1975.

27. The best available source of data and references on the problem of the central city in the U.S. is the study prepared by the Congressional Research Service for the Subcommittee on Housing and Urban Affairs, United States Senate: The Central City Problem and Urban Renewal Policy, 93rd Congress, Government Printing Office, Washington, D.C., 1973. See also for a detailed analysis of the functioning of the irregular economy, William Tabb, *The Economy of the Black Ghetto*, NY, 1970.

28. See: Karl E. Taeuber and Alma F. Taeu-

ber, *Negroes in Cities: Residential Segregation and Neighborhood Change,* Aldine Publishing Co., Chicago, 1965.

29. See: "The Central City Problem," *op. cit.,* 1973, p. 103.

30. See: Stanley H. Masters, "The Effect of Housing Segregation on Black-White Income Differentials," Institute for Research on Poverty, Univ. of Wisconsin, Madison, 1972, mimeo.

ciations linked to non-monopolistic financial markets, mostly ethnically (white)-based.[31]

The fixed assets of the inner-city residents were reduced in value[32]; what was occasion of profit for capital in the suburbs was cause of impoverishment for the inner-city white working class, of indebtedness for the suburban middle class and of deterioration of living conditions for the slum dwellers. The reduction of the economic base of the central city revenues also reduced the public services needed by the social groups that could not afford commodified consumption. Thus, the process of suburban expansion was, at the same time, the process of the central city decay. Both were produced by the dominant capitalist interests which differentially affected the different social class segments.[33]

The specific model of the post-war U.S. urban structure is completed by the functioning of a third major trend. The political fragmentation of autonomous local governments, and their role in the maintenance of the social residential segregation and the corresponding organization of consumption.[34]

"Separate and unequal," the communities of the metropolitan areas have transformed the Jeffersonian ideal of grass-roots local democracy into a barbed-wire wall of municipal regulation which prevents redistribution of income through the public delivery of goods and ser-

vices.[35] An interesting analysis by Richard Child Hill on a large number of metropolitan areas shows a close relationship between the level of metropolitan income inequality and social status, and local government resource inequality.[36] This reflects both the major cleavage between central cities and their suburbs, and intra-suburban stratification. So, the more low income residents are dependent on socialized consumption, the less the local government, the major agency of provision of public facilities, has the resources to meet those needs and demands. Thus, not only are exploited people trapped in the labor market, but, in addition, public institutions are *structurally regressive* concerning the mechanisms of redistribution. Furthermore, fragmentation becomes a social and racial barrier that connects cultural prejudices to real estate interests. The school system plays a major role in channeling expectations of generational social mobility within each particular stratum and reproducing the whole system, economically and ideologically.[37] The wage-earning population is split so that each social position is crystallized in physical and social space, in consumption of services, in organizational networks and in local government institutions. Future conflicts are channeled towards intra-city competition among equally exploited resi-

31. See David Harvey, *op. cit.,* 1975.
32. Elliott Sclar, *op. cit.,* 1975.
33. See: "Exploitative Transfers in the Metropolis," Part I, of the interesting reader edited by Kenneth E. Boulding, Martin Pfaff and Anita Pfaff, *Transfers in an Urbanized Economy, The Grants Economics of Income Distribution,* Wadsworth Publishing Co., Belmont, Ca., 1973.
34. I have borrowed several interesting ideas from a paper by Ann Markussen (Economics Department, University of Colorado). Since she does not want to be quoted, I do not quote the paper.

35. See the now classic analysis on the subject by Norton E. Long, "Political Science and the City," in Leo F. Schnore and Henry Fagin (editors), *Urban Research and Policy Planning, Urban Affairs Annual Review,* Vol. 1, Sage, Beverly Hills, Ca., 1967.
36. Richard Child Hill, "Separate and Unequal: Governmental Inequality in the Metropolis," *American Political Science Review,* Dec. 1974.
37. See: Alan K. Campbell and Philip Meranto, "The Metropolitan Education Dilemma: Matching Resources to Needs," in Marilyn Gittell (ed.) *Educating an Urban Population,* Sage Publications, Beverly Hills, Ca., 1967; and also, James S. Coleman et al., *Equality and Educational Opportunity,* U.S. Government Printing Office, Washington, D.C., 1966.

dents for a structurally limited pie. The suburban local governments enforce this situation through all kinds of discriminatory land-use regulations: large-lot zoning, minimum house size requirements, exclusion of multiple dwellings, obstacles to non-reliable building permits, etc.

Thus, class-based metropolitan inequality is derived from uneven capitalist development. Expressed in the unequal social composition of the urban structure, it is ultimately preserved and reinforced by the state through the institutional arrangement of local governments and the class-determined fragmentation of the metropolitan areas.

The U.S. urban development pattern individualizes and commodifies profitable consumption, while simultaneously deteriorating non-profitable socialized consumption. At the same time the institutional mechanisms for the preservation of the social order are structurally provided.

The coherence and the elegance of this model appeared as neat, well ordered, and impeccable as the uniforms of the guards who stand behind the smiling facade of the advertising society.

The new metropolitan world seemed able to go on and on. . . .

POLICIES FOR THE URBAN CRISIS,
GRASS-ROOTS MOVEMENTS AND
THE POLITICAL PROCESS

There is no alternative model to the crumbling pattern of urban-suburban development within the parameters of the unrestrained dominance of corporate capitalist interests. The almost perfect functionality of this urban form, at the same time, for the accumulation of capital, the organization of centralized management, the stimulation of commodity consumption, the differential reproduction of labor power and the maintenance of social order, explains why the dominant capitalist interests will tend, in all circumstances, to respond to the multi-level crisis by

mechanisms that, ultimately, will reestablish the already-proven model with slight modifications. There has been some speculation about the lack of interest of corporate capital in maintaining the central cities, but this is pure science fiction. As Roger Friedland says:

Such a scenario is highly unlikely, given the importance of the big city vote for national elections, the continued concentration of corporate and financial headquarters in the major central cities, and the economic imperative of maintaining the value of public infrastructure and private construction in the central cities. . . . The value of central city properties is the bedrock upon which the residential, commercial, and municipal loans are based. Thus the viability of the financial institutions of this country and ultimately the nation's capital market itself are dependent on maintaining the value of central city properties.[38]

But then, how are corporate interests to handle the growing contradictions shown by our analysis? The virtue and shortcoming of U.S. capitalism is its pragmatism. Instead of launching big national projects—"a la francaise"—urban policy makers tried specific successive solutions to the specific problems following the moment and intensity of their appearance. The "trouble" with this piecemeal approach is that eventually it triggers new contradictions and conflicts less and less susceptible to control.

In the United States, local authorities are more socially conservative than the federal government, since they are embedded in the network of socially dominant interests in each city, rarely representative of grass-roots needs and demands. The analysis of the first two years of the revenue-sharing program shows that in half of the cases the money was not spent but used to reduce local taxes. Concerning the funds actually used, the two more important areas were law enforcement (police) and education, which

38. Roger Friedland, *op. cit.*, 1975.

are the usual responsibility of local authorities. Less than three percent was spent on welfare or some kind of special social program. In most larger cities there was no expenditure at all in activities that could replace the cancelled federal programs.[39]

Using repression more than integration in handling the central-city problem, the next step was to reorganize the productivity of services in the public sector and to coordinate more effectively at the technical and economic level the socially and politically fragmented metropolis. But in order to improve productivity and to mobilize resources to increase the functionality of the metropolis without affecting either the major privileges of corporations or the established political network, it necessitated cutting off social services, reducing wages, and increasing fares. This was to deny the sixties, to reorganize the model of metropolitan accumulation with tougher policies and tightened controls.

The implementation of this hard line in urban policies is not going to be easy since the heritage of the sixties is not only more services and higher public wages but also more experience of struggle and organization at the grass-roots level. In fact, the evolution of urban structure and of urban services in the U.S. will depend upon the contradictory interaction between the capitalist-oriented hardline urban policies and the mass response that could emerge from city dwellers.

In that sense, more recent information seems to point towards a surpassing of the shortcomings of community movements during the sixties.[40] These were stalled by two major problems, almost in-

evitable in the early period of their development: (1) their localism, defining themselves more in terms of their neighborhood and/or ethnicity than in regard to some specific issues; (2) partly as a consequence of the latter trend, their *social* and *political isolation,* at the same time with respect to other groups and in relation to the political system.

Making alliances (and then winning allies) and penetrating the political system (and then winning positions in the network of power) seem to be the major requirements for the shift from grass-roots pressure to grass-roots power in the shaping of the urban policies. Contrary to Cloward and Piven's insightful analysis, the problem with the 1960's protest movements was not their integration by the system and the loss of their spontaneity, but, on the contrary, their insufficient level of organization and their role as political outsiders. Thus, the results were the absence of any cumulative mass movement, the inability to ensure the advantages obtained in urban services, and their political isolation, opening the way to their repression and dismantlement.[41]

The lessons were well learned to a large extent. The 1970's urban movement grew up mostly around particular issues, organizing a large sector of people not on the grounds of their spatial togetherness, but on the base of their common interests and in a long-run perspective: tenants' unions, mass-transit riders' committees, schools' parents and teachers, public utilities users, etc., spread all over the country in the process of creation, step by step, of a huge decentralized network of protest-oriented mass organizations and activities.

This movement is extremely diversi-

---

39. See: M. Aiken and M. Castells, *op. cit.,* 1975.
40. See: Ira Katznelson, "Community Conflict and Capitalist Development," Paper delivered at the Annual Meeting of the American Political Science Association, San Francisco, Sept. 1975.

41. I have trusted (and perhaps misunderstood) information provided personally by John Mollenkopf, Roger Friedland, Janice Perlman, Ira Katznelson, Marvin Surkin, and Ron Lawson. Also, I have done in some cases, a bit of "tourist participant observation."

fied. On the one hand, there is a proliferation of self-help activities at the level of the community: co-ops, health centers, independent schools, community radio stations, local construction, local agricultural and industrial production (obviously on a very small scale), and even black cooperative capitalism in some ghettos.

At a second level, defensive movements of resistance against the consequences of the urban policy for people (i.e., to stop urban renewal) or to fight back the attack on the quality or level of services (i.e., protests against the reduction of hospital facilities in San Francisco, unrest in the New York subway to oppose the rise of subway fares, etc.) are general to all large metropolitan areas.

At a third level, some of these movements are trying to recover the initiative along two major lines of development:

1. The transformation of a reaction into a specific demand capable of being translated into a progressive measure potentially implying a new social content for urban policy. Perhaps the best example is the evolution of the tenants movement facing the process of residential abandonment in New York. After having realized that most attempts to launch a rent strike led to abandonment by the landlord, many tenants' committees stopped their action. But after verifying that some abandoned houses were rehabilitated by the city and sold at a low price to another landlord, groups implemented a new tactic. They triggered a process of rent strikes forcing abandonment and then applied to the city for a rehabilitation grant that transformed them into cooperative owners, eventually using the rents saved through the strike for paying for the repairs. The logic of urban decay was reversed, not by urban planners but by urban movements.

2. The other developing line is the emergence of real "public facilities consumers unions" that try to respond to the deterioration of social services and to their growing weight in the family budgets by sustained economic action concerning the production, distribution, and management of collective goods and services. An example is the nation-wide campaign launched in 1975 against the rise in electricity rates by a movement of several thousand members significantly called "Just Economics."

The exploitative and increasingly contradictory model of urban-suburban expansion that dominated metropolitan America in the last thirty years will be transformed only if the peoples forces win decisive gains in upcoming battles. But such a result would be an almost intolerable setback to the corporate interests. This explains why the Establishment has been so violent in repressing New York City and also why the dominant emphasis in current local policies is given to the development of the repressive apparatus. The aftermath of the sixties has provided an incredible mass of sophisticated weaponry for repressing mass protests in the large cities. Since it has become clear now that the costly desperate riots have been replaced by long-run oriented, permanent mass movements, the FBI has reconverted hundreds of special agents and sent them to infiltrate the grass-roots organizations. Emergency procedures and day-to-day repression have now been articulated to pave the way for a new edition of the monopoly capital pattern of urban development. The stake is important, so "they" are ready to pay a high price, even in terms of political legitimacy.

So, unless the progressive forces of the United States are able to develop a major movement, with enough social and political support, to rectify the dominant trend in forthcoming urban policies, what could emerge from the current urban crisis is a simplified and sharpened version of the exploitative metropolitan model with the addition of mass police repression and control and in a largely deteriorated economic setting. The suburbs will remain fragmented and isolated, the single-family homes closed over themselves, the shopping centers a bit more expensive and a lot more surveyed, the highways less maintained and more crowded, the central districts still crowded during office hours and more deserted and curfewed at night, city services increasingly crumbling, public facilities less and less public, the surplus population more and more visible, the drug culture and individual violence necessarily expanding, gang society and high society ruling the bottom and the top in order to keep a "top and bottom" social order, the urban movements repressed and discouraged and the urban planners eventually attending more international conferences in the outer, safer world. What could emerge from a failure of urban movements to undertake their present tasks is a new and sinister urban form: The Wild City.

CHARLES L. LEVEN

Growth and Nongrowth in Metropolitan Areas and the Emergence of Polycentric Metropolitan Form

The Emergence of Maturity in the "Traditional" Metropolis

In 1958, a volume entitled *Exploding Metropolis* [4] attracted widespread attention. It reflected the apparent emergence of large, continuous "megalopolitan conurbations" like "Bos-Wash" and "Chi-Pitts." On the one hand, private gains available to people willing to move there were seen as almost limitless, stemming mainly from the comparative advantage of the large metropolis in production; on the other hand, the attendant growth in scale and density was seen as imposing substantial increases in unit costs of public services. Less than twenty years later a number of authors began to deal with the onset of apparent malfunction in large-scale metropolises; for recent examples see Pettengill and Uppal [10] and Sternlieb and Hughes [11]. Instead of a crisis of agglomeration, we find a crisis of disappearing industrial jobs; instead of a crisis of shortages in public service capacity, we find an inability to finance local government; instead of a crisis of bottlenecks in subdividing suburbia, we find a crisis of physical decay in central cities.

While many forces have led to metropolitan maturity, perhaps the most basic and most easily understood are economic. They are directly related to the emergence of the modern metropolis in the nineteenth century, when the driving economic phenomenon was the rise of the factory system with its attendant economies of scale, related both to production in larger scale individual units and economies related to the congregating together of a large number of complementary activities.

Other forces followed, first intensifying the trend toward concentration, but later leading to maturity, with the declines now emerging. In the nineteenth and into the twentieth century, the steam engine and the intercity railroad made it both possible and profitable to initiate large-scale manufacturing efficiently located at or between raw materials and markets. But compared to the present, industry used a vast bulk of raw material. Coupled with the fact that intracity movement of goods was very expensive compared to the cost

From **Papers,** Regional Science Association, Vol. 41, 1978, pp. 101–12. Reprinted by permission of the Regional Science Association, McMaster University, and C. Leven.

of moving people and coupled with the relatively high cost of utilizing steam, or even electric power, very far from its source, the early industrial metropolis contained pressures for compactness as well as for scale.

As the twentieth century progressed, a variety of technological developments produced sprawl and what we came eventually to recognize as stagnation. The private passenger car was one of these developments; but perhaps even more important was the motor truck. It vastly reduced the cost of internal movement of goods compared with the horse-drawn wagon it replaced, permitting work places to spread out from central terminal areas. With the passenger car, it allowed both residences and work places to be free of locations proximate to fixed rights-of-way, permitting still more spread which, in turn, permitted even greater scale. These technological forces were enhanced by two kinds of government action in the early post-World War II period; the building of high-speed expressways wherever projected traffic demand seemed to be in prospect, and the ready availability of mortgage credit at preferential terms for new single-family detached suburban housing.

Locating economic activities near the core of an urban area or within a metropolitan area at all is much less important today due to more recent technological developments. Most significant has been the steady reduction in the bulk of raw materials associated with many occupations. At least two-thirds of American workers are not involved with any raw materials, due to expansion of the service sector. For the remainder, there has been a fairly steady drop in bulk-to-value ratios for most commodities. At the same time, the need for large individual production units has been reduced, since the extent of economies to scale at the establishment level is much more limited for services than for goods. Finally, closely

related activities need not be located near each other, owing to technological developments in information storage, retrieval, and transmission.

All of these factors add up to a substantial reduction in the holding power of the central city or the SMSA on economic activities. Other contributing factors also can be identified. The more widespread use of air-conditioning has led to more dispersal of economic activities regionally, though not necessarily away from metro areas within a region. On the other hand, the increase of television, of nationally standardized eating places, and of discount stores has reduced substantially the cultural isolation of smaller cities and towns, adding to the ease with which a growing variety of economic activities elude the higher costs of public service and congestion found in metropolis. What kinds of economic activities, then, will find a congenial location in the large metropolis?

The manufacturing prospects for a metropolis in decline translate into a necessarily conservative view, though some counter forces will emerge: ". . . one factory or warehouse in five within twenty miles of Marble Arch [the center of London] is now vacant; at some point this trend should produce some cost advantage"; Macrae [8]. The likely development of general-purpose jigs—what are loosely referred to as "industrial robots"—will brighten prospects for the kind of small-scale industrial establishment that historically has been attracted to central city locations. And the degree of trade unionization may be *less* for new industries in the declining cities than it may become in outer areas.

What Is "New" about Recent Trends?

The demographic trends associated with contemporary metropolitan change show clearly that the kind of economic changes indicated above are neither as abrupt nor as recent as is popularly supposed. Since the early 1960's the number of people moving away from SMSAs has been greater than the number moving to them. Net outmigration dates from even earlier for larger, older SMSAs. Until recently, however, this trend was not generally noticed. To 1970 the excess of births over deaths exceeded net outmigration; SMSAs continued to show absolute growth for all SMSAs combined, and, with few exceptions, for individual SMSAs as well. The high rates of natural increase were partly due to high, if dwindling, birth rates, and partly due to the heavy representation of the child-bearing cohort in metropolitan areas. With the precipitous decline in the birth rate since 1970, the long-term trend directing activities away from metropolis was dramatically revealed.

As Alonso [1] points out: "The principal reason for the decline in metropolitan population is simple: the rate of natural increase has plummeted." More than any other factor, the fall in the birth rate has produced the unprecedented phenomenon of absolute declines in metropolitan population since 1970. Prior to 1960 no large SMSA had ever lost population; between 1960 and 1970, only Pittsburgh showed an absolute loss: Between 1970 and 1975, ten areas showed absolute declines and several more showed only nominal rates of population increase.

The apparent population losses in metropolis also reflect the sprawl of population beyond the official boundaries of SMSAs, with some time lag to be expected before the boundaries are adjusted outward. This does not mean that nothing of real consequence has happened!

First, most counties well beyond metropolitan hinterlands are growing in significant numbers in almost all sections of the country for the first time in this century. Second, the more recent patterns of spread are producing an organization of metropolitan life which may be as different in kind as it is in degree, as will be discussed in the next section.

Basic to the spread of SMSAs is the progressive outward shift of job locations, permitting residential locations to bound one more commutation jump outward, and so on. Now we find that job growth is not following a course of continuous suburbanization, but one of leap-frogging development to outlying ex-urban sites. Thus, any attempt to draw metropolitan boundaries that would include this outward development also would catch large amounts of nonmetropolitan activity in its boundaries, and might come close to exhausting space. It is not so much that metropolitan life is being forsaken for a return to a small town or rural existence, but rather that metropolis itself actually is moving to the countryside. Increasingly, individuals and families can be participants in economic, informational, and even cultural and social aspects of metropolitan life without actually having to live in metropolis in the sense that we know it.

Since sometime around 1950, however, it has been less necessary to go to metropolis to find work in nonrural pursuits and the communications revolution has lowered the cultural and informational advantage of metropolis. At the same time, it appears that the "safety" advantage of distance from metropolis may have increased substantially until, as Coleman asserts, ". . . the much lower crime outside the city may allow the nonmetropolitan resident *greater* participation in cultural life and entertainment outside the home than the city resident." And just as there may be conflict for individual families as to whether to live in metropolis or not, there may be conflicts for the larger society as to whether population growth trends in metropolis should be maintained or other ends should be fostered. Four examples of this kind of conflict can be cited.

First, believing that a massive housing shortage loomed, we erected a home finance system calculated to spur the effective demand for new suburban units, but paid little attention to the system's technical characteristics that made residential investment in central cities unattractive.

Second, maintaining a large and growing output of passenger automobiles was seen as very important in the postwar period. Stimulating and maintaining this demand took the form of heavy underwriting of urban expressways (which also lowered the access value of central city locations), incidental to the larger social goal of putting America on wheels; but intended or not, it certainly stimulated the escape from the central city and reduced the comparative advantage of metropolis as a whole.

Third, in metropolitan areas increase in crime has been substantial. Perhaps more important is the growing belief that "no one" is determined to do anything about it. Although the crime rate had more than doubled in conjunction with a larger population, the number of persons in prisons had actually decreased between 1960 and 1970; from six per 100 imprisoned to two per 100 (FBI-indexed crimes) in this decade. At this point in time the strengthening of civil rights in the service of another of society's needs also served to increase the value of distance from metropolis.

Fourth, policies were set in motion to end racial discrimination, with specific goals for achieving integration, particularly in public schools. We cannot escape the observation that school integration attempts and outmigration rates are related.

In large metropolitan areas, the number of commuters from the suburbs to the central city has grown slowly in recent years, while the number commuting from the city out to the suburbs, though still smaller, has grown at a much more rapid rate. We see a sharp rise in the number of workers with both home and work place in the suburbs, and a drop in those with both home and work place in the central city. Overlaying this pattern is a very rapid increase in the number of workers commuting from residences inside to working places outside the SMSA, underscoring the blurring of the distinction between metropolitan *area* and metropolitan *activity;* see Anas and Moses [2].

Does all of this mean that the regional allocation process has undergone some fundamental shift? The next section will argue that this is not the case, though traditional ways of looking at the process turn out to be less "general" than might have been supposed.

The Polycentric Metropolitan Region

In an earlier paper [6], the present author once had occasion to point out that the Loschian framework was not quite as general as ordinarily supposed. Specifically, the size of individual farms and the distance between them—Losch's initial conditions—were exogenous to the theory. What this meant was that if the initial conditions were specified as a single settlement, or as indefinitely small distances between individual settlements, however small, there was nothing in the theory itself that would motivate dispersion or deconcentration. In terms of its formal statement, a single metropolis containing all of the world's population would be a stable locational equilibrium solution.

The areal extent of that single area would depend on the density of deposits (or fertility of the soil) of the ubiquitous resources, if any, on which the production of goods was based. Note that since an indefinitely large number of people can live on a pinhead in theory, diseconomies of building height would not produce an areally extended settlement.

Actually, however, the special assumptions of the Loschian system are even more extensive than indicated above. Specifically, in the world of Losch, no one ever goes to a concert! Put more particularly, for all practical purposes the world of Losch has only goods, not services, and even though the hierarchy of settlements is generated by economies of scale, no one has to commute to work. To a certain extent, of course, service production could be allowed for. Let a farmer develop a comparative advantage in haircutting and offer haircuts for sale, in exchange for, say, wheat. In this case, haircuts would be produced at the producer's location, as would, say, beer, but unlike the case with beer, consumers would have to journey to the farm to have their hair cut (or the barber could visit them). Thus, in this sense haircuts are really no different than beer, except that their transport cost relative to their value is very high. But this means only that at least these kinds of services will be produced at a very low-order central place, but otherwise will fit nicely into the ordinary Loschian world.

But a concert is not quite like a haircut! Most particularly, over substantial ranges of consumption, its consumption by the $(n + 1)$st consumer entails no marginal cost. The interesting thing about Samuelson goods in a spatial framework is that generally, though not necessarily always, all of the consumers of the good would have to come to a single point-location to engage in consumption, and in many cases they might have to assemble at the same time. This then gives us four cases of commodity production to consider, rather than what is really a single major case covered in Losch. These are:

Examples of these four kinds of commodities are beer, haircuts, a heart-transplant facility, and concerts, for types I, II, III, and IV, respectively. As indicated above, the Losch world is really about Type I commodities, though Type II could fit into the lowest order of central place in the equilibrium network, whatever its extent.

The extreme in a non-Losch world would be one with only Type IV commodities. Obviously, if there are economies of scale (discontinuities) in consumption, technically there would have to be economies of scale in production *within* a consumption module, say a concert season. By "no economies of scale in production" here, we mean no economies of scale measured in units appropriate to the scale of consumption.

In the extreme case of a Type IV world with only a single commodity, starting from Loschian initial conditions we would get a network of settlements all of identical size, and at a distance from each other that was a function of the extent of economies of scale in consumption of the good. These would generally not be limitless (if they were, of course, we would get a single settlement point no matter what the initial conditions). For example, enjoyment of a concert is not reduced by an additional listener for some number of listeners, but at some point it is just too hard to see, too much trouble to get into or out of the hall, and/or it would be necessary to switch from natural sound to electronic amplification.

Thus, we would get a network of

	Consumption	
	No economies of scale	Economies of scale
Production Economies of scale	Type I (Losch)	Type III (non-Losch)
No economies of scale	Type II (semi-Losch)	Type IV (contra-Losch)

equally spaced settlements that would be smaller as the limits of crowding was smaller, and larger as the cost of producing a concert (say, number of required musicians) was larger; they would be farther apart as the cost of establishing new settlement points other than those in the original network fell, and closer as the cost of transporting musicians rose. This kind of uniform distribution of about equal-sized, equally spaced settlements probably is much like the pre-Columbus settlement pattern of the forest Indians of northeast United States. It may also be something like the settlement pattern of Heaven if the afterlife really consists only of eating manna (ubiquitous) and listening to bands of angels singing. It should be noted that to get a multiple settlement equilibrium, we had to start with dispersal as an initial condition, but then so did Losch.

Even a purely contra-Losch world is hardly as simple as indicated above, since a hierarchy of consumption economies would be expected to exist, much as there is a hierarchy of economies of scale in production in a normal Losch system. It easily could be demonstrated that these would lead to a hierarchy of hexagonal networks of different size orders, which when rotated would produce a frequency distribution of central places by order, as in Losch or Christaller; see Isard [5, ch. 3]. But two important differences should be expected in terms of their empirical nature. First, so far as Type IV goods are concerned, we should expect the size of the largest region to be much smaller than for Type I goods, given that over long distances goods generally are cheaper to ship than are people (and becoming more so). Second, congestion effects are likely to be more pronounced in consumption than in production.

Adding Type III goods to the contra-Losch world does cause more of a problem than adding Type II goods to the Type I goods of the pure Losch world.

Type II goods, as it were, could fit into the lowest order of central place network in the Losch solution, whatever it was; given the constant returns to scale in Type II goods, by definition the smallest hexagons would be small enough. In the contra-Losch world, on the other hand, Type III goods would, as it were, have to be fit into regions of the highest order central places and, clearly, depending on the economies of scale involved, the largest regions might not be large enough. This is so even though the transport costs involved might be very high, since the largest of Type IV regions, it was argued above, would not be very large. Thus, the addition of Type III goods would give us a hierarchy, but probably not a very articulated one. Casual empiricism indicates that networks of not more than two or three size orders would probably do, defined on something like an elementary school district or neighborhood shopping area; territory served by a junior college or medical center; and for some metro regions, the territory served by a major attraction like a world-famous zoo or symphony orchestra.

Second, goods production still does and certainly will continue to exist in significant volume, although the fraction of labor involved in goods (as opposed to service production) has been declining steadily for the past few decades, at least in the United States. In addition, many of those employed in manufacturing, even those classified as production workers, are information rather than materials processors, whose proximity to the materials handlers may or may not involve some external economies. In any event, manufacturing will still be an important sector, even with competition from abroad. Central cities are much more likely to be losing manufacturing jobs to Asia than they are to their own suburbs. On the other hand, the economy of locating in the very large-scale metropolis for much of manufacturing clearly is diminishing for a variety of reasons. Partly this is due to changes in materials-processing itself (more versatile machine tools, i.e., industrial robots), but even more it may be due to the increasing separability and footlooseness of the information and control aspects of the manufacturing process, together with a fall in the cost of shipping information. But we will continue to have significant amounts of "giant" industry for some time to come—automobile assembly, petrochemical complexes, and so on—that will preserve a somewhat higher order of regional network than might be the case, hopefully easing the transition of the older core-dominated SMSAs.

Third, we must recognize that resources are not really ubiquitous, forcing an obvious "greater concentration" bias on the equilibrium regional hierarchy than might otherwise exist. This means that significant transport collection points for materials such as grain, sulfur, and petroleum will be required and will add to scale at the points selected; sizable cities are likely to continue at break-in-transit points.

Despite the qualifications listed above, it becomes difficult to think up advantages—production or consumption—to be had in the great metropolis. The activities of church and neighborhood never required living in much of a town, and while having a kosher meat supply available for an American Jew probably still means living in a large city, it surely does not require living in a great one, especially if one's beliefs permit the freezing of flesh. Similarly, a large-scale population within a distance such that they can be readily assembled does seem necessary to support professional athletics, symphony orchestras, zoos, and medical centers. But once a rather modest metropolitan scale has been achieved, additional market potential seems to make little difference in quality; next time around the Royals are as likely as not to beat the Yankees. And nothing would stop us from scheduling

baseball games, some of which were, and some of which were not, "telecast before a live audience."

Why, it might be asked, could not these lower orders of central places compact themselves in space forming a community of small towns cheek-by-jowl; the kind of place most of us have learned to call "Los Angeles"? The simple answer in terms of the argument above is that there is nothing to impel its occurrence given the initial conditions of evenly dispersed population on a uniform transport plane. That this is no more than a simple Loschian trick is no excuse, either; at least dispersal was pretty much the case historically, prior to the rise of the Loschian industrial world, while for us the prior condition to the postindustrial world has been a concentration of people in great metropolises. Actually, the spread becomes obvious if we add only the existence of congestion diseconomies in pure or partly pure Samuelson goods, and a positive preference of households for more rather than less social distance from those who are "different." After all, at least up until World War I, the flocking of people to the cities was seen largely as a cultural misfortune made necessary by their economic redundancy in primary activities in the much more wholesome rural sector, or the small town serving the rural sector. And while the segregated (not necessarily racially, but certainly class-segregated) neighborhood or suburb is a way of achieving social distance, it only imperfectly permits escape from congestion. Substantial costs of maintaining "distance" may also be involved, and may be increasing, given the change in legal philosophy about exclusivity, Petaluma notwithstanding.

In this sense then, the separate suburb in the contiguous metropolis may always have been a second-best solution dictated by the need to travel to work, and the need for the work destination to be near other employment activities. Neither of these needs is predominant today. The life-style we always wanted is now available—friendly, nonthreatening neighbors next door; the New York Mets or the Metropolitan Opera on TV; good hunting, fishing, or hiking a mere ten or fifteen minutes away; and work, if not right at home on the old terminal, not more than a fast, cheap (even at very high fuel prices) automobile or bike ride away. *The urban world of 2010 may resemble the world of 1910 more than the world of 1960.* People will still want to go to ballgames, the zoo, and the opera; occasionally they will need organ transplants, seek consultation of an expert on Egyptology, or have a desire to purchase Peruvian antiques. Thus they will organize themselves into a regional system, probably with a dominant community, probably somewhere near the transport center of gravity of the system. The size of a regional system would converge on the size of a second-order hexagon in the contra-Losch world, and would include as many nodes as there were settlements in a hexagon at that level.

In this sense the distinction between metropolitan and nonmetropolitan—or even between urban and rural—may lose finally, any real definition. The spaces "in between" the employment-work-service centers in a given metropolitan region will be taken up by farms, mines, open-space, and in some cases just plain wilderness. If we still define SMSAs in 2010, I would think that the state of Ohio, for example, would see present SMSAs combining until there were only about four such areas in the entire state, but every county in the state would be in one of them.

The SMSA of the twenty-first century will look rather like Massachusetts without Boston, or at least with a much smaller Boston than today. Oddly enough, people will probably live at higher net residential densities than in the suburbia of today, and density gradients in individual nodes are likely to be steeper than now, particularly if the nodes are connected by a mass transit system. Most personal travel trips, including journeys-to-work, are likely to be by private passenger car, though in smaller, lighter, and more fuel-efficient cars. As noted, even with very high fuel cost, private cars would continue to be cheapest (and probably most energy conserving) since the length of the typical trip would be much shorter, with rather modest traffic volume over any single route segment.

Internodal travel within a single region might be by bus or by mass transit, depending on the population size and spatial extent of the metropolitan region-system itself. In very large (perhaps over 8 or 10 million) or very extensive (perhaps more than 200 miles across) metro regions, a spine system of mass transit is likely with most internode travel on it. In the case of metro regions centered on old, large SMSAs (like Chicago), the mass transit system is likely to be star-shaped. In newer, emerging metro regions (like the Piedmont Crescent), the system is more likely to be linear, with any single central city less dominant. Where metro regional-systems are neither very big or very extensive, private cars or radio-dispatched minibuses are likely to dominate internode travel.

Travel between metro regions is likely to be almost exclusively on mass transit, either airbus or fixed-rail ground mode, depending on density of travel, distance, and technological development.

Probably the most important institutional organizing principal for individual communities within a metro region is the size, or range of sizes, at which the provision of public goods is most efficient—at present technology from about 50 to maybe 500 thousand. The time for metro government, as we thought about it in the '50s and '60s, may have passed, with existing state and municipal governments coming tolerably close to the two-tier system which still seems needed. Except for some fairly rigid rules on whether development can or cannot take place in any zone, the need for conventional detailed zoning probably will become weaker.

Admittedly, these prognoses are highly speculative and the theorizing employed to reach the conclusions is casual. Nonetheless, it does reflect the kinds of rather spectacular shifts in spatial organization which do seem underway and hopefully it relates these shifts to what we have in the way of a theory of regional organization without tearing down inherited frameworks for thought, but in a way that could lead to a more careful study of location theory and development of the modifications in it that seem called for.

References

1. Alonso, W. "The Current Halt in the Metropolitan Phenomenon," in C. L. Leven, ed., *The Mature Metropolis.* Lexington, Mass.: D. C. Heath, 1978.
2. Anas, A., and L. Moses. "Transportation and Land Use in the Mature Metropolis," in [1].
3. Coleman, J. "Social Processes and Social Policy in the Stable Metropolis," in [1].
4. *Exploding Metropolis.* New York: Fortune Magazine, 1958.
5. Isard, W. *Location and Space Economy.* Cambridge: M.I.T. Press, 1956.
6. Leven, C. L. "Determinants of the Size and Spatial Form of Urban Areas," *Papers of the Regional Science Association,* Vol. 22 (1968).
7. ————. "Regional Variations in Metropolitan Growth and Development," 1977 LBJ Symposium on Regional Confrontation, University of Texas, publication forthcoming.
8. Macrae, N. "Tomorrow's Agglomeration Economies," in [1].
9. Morrison, P. "Emerging Public Concerns over U.S. Population Movements in an Era of Slowing Growth," Rand Paper Series, October 1977.
10. Pettengill, R., and J. Uppal. *Can Cities Survive? The Fiscal Plight of American Cities.* New York: St. Martin's Press, 1974.
11. Sternlieb, G., and J. Hughes, eds. *Postindustrial America: Metropolitan Decline and Interregional Job Shifts.* New Brunswick, N.J.: Center for Urban Policy Research, Rutgers, 1975.

JANET L. ABU-LUGHOD

Designing a City for All

This workshop on city planning and the changing roles of American women is long overdue. Its rationale is *not* that females and their welfare should have priority in the design of our cities. I do not believe that the welfare of any group should be achieved at the expense of another, nor do I feel that, as a class, women constitute the group most shortchanged by our cities as they are currently designed. Other characteristics, such as age, race, and income, determine more than does sex, per se, the kind of life we lead in cities. Holding a workshop on women, then, in no way absolves us from our legitimate concerns with other urban problems; but, on the other hand, our other concerns should not keep us from demanding from urban design a city pattern adapted to our special needs. We have been, perhaps, too diffident and modest. And, while we have been reluctant to complain, the sexism of many of our male colleagues, in and out of city planning, has gone unchallenged.

Do not think I exaggerate the level of unconscious bias from which male planners need to be shaken! Last spring I was invited to participate in a conference which drew together some of the coun-

try's best known and respected city planners and some of the world's most renowned urban archaeologists and historians. The illness of another participant left me the sole representative of the female sex. In one of the closed-to-the-public sessions we considered the relevance of earlier urban models for the city of the future. Discussion moved to the issue of increased leisure and its implications for projected alterations in the workday and workweek and, hence, for anticipated changes in the physical arrangement of the metropolis. Great interest and indeed excitement began to generate, revolving around the prospect of the four-day week. This, one after another concurred, would be an absolutely marvellous design for living. It would permit even *more complete* separation of work from residence! "A *man* could go into the city to work, spend three nights there, and then *return to his family* out in the country for the other four nights."

The more excited they became, the more appalled and angry I became. The vision of the future city they were so enthusiastic about was one which maximized the interests of a very small class, the rul-

From Karen Hapgood and Judith Getzels, **Planning, Women, and Change,** 1974, the American Planning Association, Chicago. Reprinted by permission of the Association and J. L. Abu-Lughod.

ing class of our society, if I may be so blunt. It was designed for the upper-middle and upper class, since it presumed ability to maintain two dwellings, albeit perhaps only a hotel room in the city. It was designed for men only. Married females with children presumably were to remain on rural "breeding farms." The status of single women was indeterminate; perhaps they were to be kept in the city for those other three nights? Sex roles were to be totally differentiated for, obviously, both women with children *and* their husbands could hardly expect to desert the children in the exurbs for four days and three nights, even given the existence of TV dinners!

I sputtered an agitated response to this "for upper-class males only" utopia. My outburst was followed by a deafening silence, some shuffling of papers and feet, and finally, someone recovered with an embarrassed joke. No woman I have told this story to has felt that it was a matter to joke about. We are frightened by this handwriting on the wall.

City design will not solve the "woman problem," just as it cannot solve most social problems. But city design, and the life design it adjusts to and indeed intensifies, can often be quite effective in preventing solutions. The issue of the workweek is tightly linked to past urban design decisions. The four-day week, for example, will encourage additional changes in our cities which will place women in an increasingly difficult bind. It is possible to envisage a different set of solutions which will require a different physical design and which will make it easier, not more difficult, for women to become full participants in society. Let us look at two alternative schemes—social and physical—either of which could accommodate to increased leisure time, reduced demand for labor, and the somewhat slower rate of economic growth that will be associated with the achievement of zero population growth.

In Solution I, the society adjusts to increased leisure by an even more rigid division of labor, in which a reduced proportion of the population is harnessed to the money economy, thus enabling the society to support a very large class specializing in nonremunerative, "leisurely," though perhaps not less necessary, activities. Worker "ants" are highly differentiated in their activities from breeders, nurses, resters, and keepers of the "consumption nest," which is designed to maintain and enhance the environment within which worker ants spend what small leisure is granted to them. Whole classes, based upon sex (female) or upon age (abnormally prolonged youth and sharply delineated and perhaps prematurely defined oldsters), constitute, if not leisure classes, at least classes considered supernumerary by the economic system.

Given this rigid division of labor, there is much to be gained by segregating places of work from places of leisure and nest-keeping, except insofar as those work places are directly engaged in providing the consumption needs of these so-called leisure classes. Separating place of work from home, of course, has its cost: the period of daily commuting for the worker ants. The period is more or less fixed by distance and means of transportation; in large cities it may be up to two hours per work day. Since this friction of space is a given and a clear waste, efficiency is maximized by reducing the number of times per week that it is required.

Let me illustrate. A person who works 40 hours a week over a five-day week and spends two hours per workday in commuting wastes ten hours a week, the equivalent of one-fourth of the time worked or one-fifth of the gross work-related day. If the 40 hours are worked in four 10-hour days, time wasted in commuting is reduced to eight hours per week, only one-fifth of the hours worked or one-sixth of the gross work-related day. Clearly this is both economically advantageous and personally liberating for the worker. Further advantages can be gained by reducing the workweek to three days of about 13 hours each, but fatigue is assumed to counterbalance this gain by a decline in worker efficiency. Even lower ratios of waste to work time can, of course, be achieved by eliminating the daily periodicity altogether, as proposed by the male planner at the conference I attended. If a worker slept near or at his place of work three nights and worked four consecutive days, commuting time could be reduced to only one-twentieth of the workweek. This appears, however, to have some other costs, namely, the human cost involved in being or having an absentee father or husband. Additional housing needs would be a further cost, even though for the unmarried or childless, dual housing would more likely take the form of a near-job flat and a vacation place in leisure-land.

For some time now this is the situation toward which we have been heading. We have been increasing the distance between home and work and increasing (or at least not decreasing) the time required to move between them. Concentration of the labor force within a more narrowly defined age band has certainly occurred, as youth delays its entrance into the labor market or is increasingly "unemployable" (witness the very high rates of teen-age unemployment), and as pressures build for forced or encouraged "early retirement." Women, on the other hand, have not been willing to accept exclusion and have bucked the trends by joining the labor force in increasing numbers. But they have often constituted a potential pool from which are drawn workers of lowest pay and least security; they have been marginal workers with no bargaining power. Their lack of bargaining power has to some extent been due to the fact that they cannot afford the costs which regular workers must pay for their power,

i.e., mobility, full workdays, commuting time, and so forth.

Solution I strikes me as not particularly good in itself and especially inauspicious for women. The four-day week is a logical and economically attractive next step in the trend which Solution I entails, and it will make women even more marginal and weaker in bargaining power, since it will exact even higher costs because of the inherent conflict between traditional housewife roles and the roles required of "workers." Let me then propose a perhaps utopian alternative.

In Solution II the society adjusts to increased leisure by dividing the jobs. A large—in fact, an overwhelming—majority of the population participates equitably in bearing the burdens and deriving the satisfactions associated with the wage-for-labor economy. All participate equitably in the nonremunerative, but no less necessary, activities of nurturing-nesting and leisure. In this instance, rigid division of labor is eschewed in favor of shorter average workweeks and workdays, coupled with higher labor force participation rates. Teen-agers are absorbed into employment, albeit for hours which are not too taxing. Older persons taper off gradually, instead of undergoing the often traumatic experience of abrupt retirement, with or without gold watch. The traditional division of labor along sex lines is substantially reduced, due both to declining family size and the more egalitarian training and expectations of males and females, an egalitarianism no longer counteracted by job discrimination or confused by socially generated home-job role conflicts.

What are the urban requirements of this social system? First, with increased participation in the labor force it should be possible to reduce the average workday to a norm of six hours, although some might choose to work more and some less. This in itself would not solve any problems, for if everyone worked the same six hours, no improvement over the present situation would be attained. Nurturant-nesting-consumption tasks, now assigned to the housewife, would still conflict with business hours. Conflicts between working hours and personal business (dentist appointments, shopping) would persist. Furthermore, if travel time to jobs remained constant, in all but the smallest cities and towns the time required for commuting would grow to an outrageous proportion of the working day. If an individual commuted two hours daily for a six-hour work day, the time wasted in traveling would become equivalent to one-third of the time on the job and one-fourth of the gross time connected with work. The scheme, it is clear, is only economically feasible and socially desirable if travel time can be reduced. There remains the residual problem of synchronizing the economy so that the shorter work hours do not make work and life mutually exclusive.

I suggest that the solutions to both of these problems are one and the same. Given the high rates of labor force participation and the relatively low differentiation between social roles (i.e., between "workers" and "unpaid workers"), the wide separation between place of work and place of residence becomes totally indefensible. Efficiency requires a smaller-grained land-use mix than sufficed under the older system, which separated the money economy (or males) from the household economy (for females). Furthermore, with shortened workdays there are now compelling economic reasons to reduce travel time.

Let me now draw an explicit picture of Utopia II. Imagine a society in which the usual workday is six hours and most adults are in the labor force. Businesses and industries operate on two to three shifts per day, which overlap for a total potential operating period of about 12 hours. (This is already beginning to oc-

cur. Many grocery chains and other commercial establishments near homes actually remain open this long just because of the conflict between work hours and the need to conduct personal business during working hours.) Not only will such conflicts be minimized in our scheme, but all physical plants will be more efficiently used. Doctors and dentists, for example, could share office equipment by arranging dovetailed shifts. Commercial and industrial establishments might prefer three overlapping shifts.

The first shift in this hypothetical society might begin at 8:00 or 9:00 and end at 2:00 or 3:00. The second shift might begin at noon and end about 6:00. A third shift might begin at 2:00 or 3:00 in the afternoon and end about 9:00. Options would be available to students, to mothers of young children, and to older persons to work only three-hour shifts. Let's consider the advantages. If they don't appear to be worth it, all right.

One of the advantages would be regular, spread-out demands upon the transportation system. This is an old saw. If cars remain the mainstay of communication, more even distribution of work-related traffic will cut a substantial portion of time from commuting, even in the absence of greater land-use mix and improved roads. Construction of more efficient mini-mass transit also becomes more feasible, for the capital wasted in peak-load rolling stock on restricted lines could then be deflected to moving a smaller stock more regularly, more efficiently, and along more reticulated lines.

The physical and economic gains, however, are only a small part of the story. The primary gains are social. Think of the options such a social organization of work could offer. First, we know that individuals differ radically in their diurnal energy cycles. Some function best during the day, while others reach their stride toward night. The two or three work shifts would permit the society to benefit from these differences, particularly during those portions of the family cycle when there are no young children present.

Second, think of the possibilities this system could offer during the decades in a family's life when care and nurturance of the next generation is a critical responsibility. Males and females could combine these responsibilities with an active work life if only that work life were more flexible! I suggest that day care centers, as necessary as they are to American society at present, are not the perfect solution. One of the virtues of taking care of children in one's home is, in addition to the enjoyment and intimacy it allows, that one can also get a lot of the mechanics of nest-care and consumption done at the same time. One can wash or clean or cook with children around; women have been doing it for thousands of years. Why not men and women, perhaps dividing some of the responsibilities?

During the years when preschoolers are in the home, husbands and wives could work different shifts, utilizing day care centers or part-time help from adolescents or older persons for the three- to four-hour overlap, or sacrificing a bit of time together for a few years by working dovetailed shifts. But in any case, in place of the fixed and inflexible binds young parents often find themselves in today, the options are liberating.

Even greater flexibility is introduced when children are all of school age. In those instances, the obvious best shift is 9:00 to 3:00, i.e., the shift which conforms most closely to school hours. Women with children of school age might, in fact, be given priority for this shift, at least until women no longer bear the ultimate responsibility for childrearing.

One of the social benefits of such sharing of paid and unpaid employment by men and women will be simultaneous solution of the not unrelated problems of the absentee father, the trapped mother,

and the unparented or overmothered child. That might not be a bad set of gains against which the complications of the proposed system might be weighed. Employers once thought the eight-hour day was a pain in the neck and too much trouble to administer, too.

I have strong feelings that Solution II is the one which women must work toward. Not only would it allow women to escape the forced choices and/or hidden costs which today's organization of work requires, but it would yield, indeed would require, a city which more humanely meets the needs of all its inhabitants. It would require less separation between home and job, which in turn might prevent the work-leisure mental split and permit the maintenance of work-associated friendships in the leisure hours. Furthermore, it would demand less rigid economic segregation in residential areas, for work places employ a range of status levels. In addition, it would reduce the time wasted in the limbo of commuting and would permit a more equitable division of labor between the sexes.

At this point we may be accused of lack of realism. This utopia may sound nice, but it will be argued that women are not interested in working or work because they have to. The point is that, increasingly, women are working, and all the trends seem to indicate that their participation rates in the labor force will continue to rise. In that sense, Solution II is much more realistic than the atavism of Solution I.

The problem is that, given the fact that women are in the labor force despite the conflicts which present-day work organization and city design create or intensify, women are unfairly penalized for these socially engendered conflicts. They are penalized because part time is all they often can manage. They are viewed as marginal workers and are punished for their failure to overcome the hurdles which society has set up to make their

Table 1. Labor Force Participation Rates for Women[a] in the United States, 1890–1970

Year	Per Cent of Women in Labor Force
1890	18.2
1900	20.0
1920	22.7
1930	23.6
1940	27.4
1950	31.5
1955	33.5
1960	34.8
1965	36.7
1970	42.6

* Fourteen years and older until 1966; 16 years and older after 1966.

work difficult. They are victims of an urban design which has helped to reduce them to a marginal role in the labor force—available as a noncompetitive, and hence cheap and often sadly underutilized, pool for local and part-time jobs. It is viewing this dilemma as "natural" which seems to be unrealistic.

Let us look at some of the impressive facts about female labor force participation. Only a generation ago, one in four women worked; by 1955 this proportion had risen to over a third; in 1970 the comparable figure was 43 per cent (see Table 1). It is now rising so rapidly that one can safely predict that by the end of the decade the majority of women will be in the labor force. (These figures are averaged from unmarried and married, with or without children, and therefore are less revealing than more specific rates.)

As one might expect, by now there is scarcely any difference at all between the labor force participation rates of unmarried males and females. For example, in 1971, at ages 20 to 24, some 73 per cent of the unmarried men were working, as were 72 per cent of unmarried women. Eighty-six per cent of the unmarried men

between 25 and 44 worked, as did 80 per cent of the unmarried women. At ages 45 to 64, 75 per cent of the unmarried males and 73 per cent of the unmarried females worked. (See Table 2.)

Marriage, of course, still tends to remove women from the labor force, but nowhere near the extent to which this was true even a decade ago. As recently as 1960, the labor force participation rate for married women was only a third as high (33 per cent for ages 20 to 44 and 39 per cent for ages 45 to 64) as that for married men. But by 1971 it was up close to one-half of the male participation rate (ages 20–24, 50 per cent; ages 25–44, 44 per cent; ages 45–65, 48 per cent). In 1960 as many single women as men worked in the 45–64 age bracket; 96 per cent as many in the 20–24 age bracket; and 92 per cent as many in the 25–44 age bracket. By 1971, there were 99 per cent as many women as men working in the 20–24 age bracket, 93 per cent at ages 25–44, and 97 per cent at ages 45–64.

As recently as 1959, the typical white husband and wife family, with or without children, was one in which the hus-

Table 2. Labor Force Participation Rates by Marital Status, Age, and Sex, U.S. Civilian Population, 1960 and 1971

Selected Age Groups	Marital Status and Year					
	Single		Married		Other	
	1960	1971	1960	1971	1960	1971
Ages 20–24						
Males	80%	73%	97%	95%	97%	88%
Females	77	72	32	48	58	59
Ages 25–44						
Males	90	86	99	97	95	92
Females	83	80	33	43	67	66
Ages 45–64						
Males	80	75	93	91	93	77
Females	80	73	36	44	60	62

Source: Adapted from Table 343, Statistical Abstract of the United States 1972 (Washington, D.C.: U.S. Bureau of the Census, 1972).

Table 3. Husband-Wife Families: Work
Experience by Race, 1959 and 1970

Race and Year	Number of Husband-Wife Households	Per Cent in Which Only Husband Worked	Per Cent in Which Husband and Wife Worked
White households			
1959	29,371,000	58%	42%
1970	32,402,000	43	57
Non-white or Negro households			
1959	2,288,000	44	56
1970	2,654,000	29	71

Source: Recomputed from Table 347, *Statistical Abstract of the United States 1972.* Families with other combinations of workers have been excluded from the total number of households. Percentages were recomputed for households with husband the only worker or husband and wife combinations the only combination. The direction of change is in no way altered by this computation and the true significance of the work status of wives is brought out more clearly.

band was the only one of the pair who "worked," i.e., got paid for his work. By 1970, the typical family was one in which both the husband and the wife brought home paychecks, a situation which had always been true for non-white husband and wife families. (See Table 3.)

It is the presence of children, much more than marital status per se, which has had the most marked effect in moving women from the money to the domestic economy. But even here there have been dramatic inroads on the stereotype of the full-time mother and the exclusively bread-winning father. Only 20 years ago, jobs were held by a scant 30 per cent of the married women with spouses present and no children under 17. Today, 42 per cent of these women are holding jobs

in addition to house care. In 1950, only 12 per cent of the married women with spouse present and children under six held a paid job. By 1971, almost 30 per cent of the women with children this young were in the labor force. Today the rates of labor force participation for the group whose conflicts between home and job are most severe are as high as the labor force participation rates of women with the least conflict only two decades ago. The very highest and fastest-growing rates of labor force participation, however, are found today among married women with spouse present whose children are of school age, i.e., over six but still under 17. One out of every two of these women is now working, as contrasted with only 28 per cent some 20 years ago. These rates, however, do not reach the highs recorded by divorced women, two-thirds of whom are in the labor force.

It is time for planners to divest themselves once and for all of the glossy magazine-ad family image, a stereotype for which they have blithely been planning. That image is dead, if indeed it ever lived, and it is likely to become even deader, if we can push a ridiculous metaphor to absurdity. The goal of planners and urban designers should be to work toward a city which facilitates, rather than hinders, the type of joint work-home-children family which already has made its appearance in American life and which will become increasingly common.

Thus far, in that type of family women have borne most of the pains and derived too few of the benefits. Statistics tend to exaggerate the role women now play in the remunerated sector of the economy. Yes, high proportions of women are in the labor force—but mostly as part-time or part-year workers. In 1967, for example, 58 per cent of the women workers fell into this category, as contrasted with only 30 per cent of the male workers.

Most likely to be part-time or part-year workers were women with spouses present and with dependent children, i.e., those with maximal conflict between home and work. Lack of either children or spouse yields a higher tendency to be a full-time, year-round worker. The subgroups with the greatest tendency to assume the male-specific work load are women between 45 and 64 and women whose marriages have been terminated by widowhood, divorce, or separation. But the planner seems to ignore the needs of all these groups in his preoccupation with building cities for male worker ants and female breeders.

Trends in labor force participation indicate clearly that the roles of women are moving in the direction of Solution II, even though the structure of our cities and the organization of work are still designed to fit, and indeed reinforce, Solution I. Changing demographic patterns in the United States also demonstrate that the groups of women who have thus far shown the greatest proclivities for change are exactly those groups which within the next generation will constitute the overwhelming majority of American women. Evidence from this quarter strengthens the argument that, in fact, less and less specialization between "breeding" and "working" ants is foreordained.

First is the much discussed issue of zero population growth (ZPG). As everyone knows, the U.S. crude birth rate has been dropping precipitously since about 1959 and appears not yet to have reached bottom, despite the significant fact that, had *ceteris* remained *paribus,* the rate should have risen substantially as girls born in the postwar baby boom reached childbearing ages. Our population replacement rate has, indeed, fallen slightly below the intrinsic rate required to reproduce the parental generation. This does not mean that our population growth has stopped; it simply means that if we sustained this

rate for many decades our actual numbers would eventually stop increasing. That is ZPG.

The U.S. Census Bureau in 1972 published a series of projections of the total population and its age composition under a variety of assumptions. I would say that their "W" projection (one of five) seems most likely. According to this projection, we can expect a total population of about 250 million by the year 2000. By that time more than half of the females will be in the older age groups which already have the highest rates of labor force participation. By the year 2000, Americans will be older on the average. Median age of the population will have risen from the 29 of today to about 35 or 36. A declining minority (20 per cent) will be in the early childbearing-childrearing ages between 20 and 34, and they will be responsible for far fewer children on the average than their counterparts today, since less than 30 per cent of the population will be under 20 by then, in contrast to the present 35 per cent.

In short, if we are preparing cities for future populations, we can safely assume the following: (1) that the number of children per family will be significantly lower than at present, thus reducing the conflicts which a woman will face between work and home, and, if child spacing does not change, also reducing the real and proportionate period of her life when conflicts tend to be most intense, namely, when there is a child of preschool age; (2) that the proportion of women who will be fully engaged in child and home care will be substantially less than at the present time, due not only to the smaller average number of children but also to the age distribution of females, most of whom will be beyond the period of greatest conflict; and (3) that the age and marital status groups which have traditionally demonstrated the highest labor force participation rates are exactly those groups which can be expected to grow fastest in the coming decades.

Putting all these things together, I find the conclusion inescapable. If women are not to be shortchanged in the future, they will need to work not just for liberation on the job but for liberation of the job—and that means working for social reorganization as well as the significantly linked reorganization of the city. The two are not independent, and I doubt whether we can get either one without the other.

STEPHEN M. GOLANT

Residential Concentrations of the Future Elderly

The elderly are not today and are not likely in the future to be distributed evenly throughout the United States. This fact both simplifies and complicates the planning process. On the one hand, the very way in which members of a population locate themselves reflects the diversity of their needs. For example, while the needs of the rural elderly are hardly uniform, they nevertheless contrast with the needs of the elderly in inner cities. On the other hand, legislative programs and funding resources must be administered in a manner that equitably takes into account these varying concentrations and consequently the varying housing and service needs.

A failure to consider how the residential distribution of the elderly will change in the future may result in a less efficient allocation of available resources to this group. The success of any program will depend largely on whether it is correctly designed for the elderly consumer group it is intended to serve. The dynamics of regional and metropolitan growth, however, result in continuous change in the demography, economic and political structures, and physical environments of

potential service areas. Except for very short-run planning, adequate concern must be given to how these dynamics will result in changes in the size and characteristics of the elderly population. In replying to this need, this paper considers the past locational trends of the elderly and speculates on how these patterns are likely to change by the year 2000.

Population and Spatial Dynamics of the 1950s and 1960s

In the last two decades the population over age 65 in the United States grew at almost twice the rate of the total population. Of equal importance, but less well documented, is the increasing propensity of older persons to form their own households rather than to live in the household of their children or other family member. In 1950, for example, 16% of the 65$^+$ population lived in the household of a child; but the proportion had dropped to 9% by 1970. Since 1950 there has also been a decline in the proportion of elderly persons living in households headed by other relatives. Between 1950 and 1970 the elderly household rate (i.e., the

From **The Gerontologist**, Vol. 15, No. 1, February 1975, pp. 16–23. Reprinted by permission of **The Gerontologist** and S. Golant.

percentage of 65^+ population who headed their own households) increased from 52% to 61%. These trends are reflected in the changing size of elderly households. The proportion of elderly persons living alone has almost doubled since 1950, and in 1970 represented 40% of all houeholds in the United States headed by persons 65^+.

While there is no simple explanation for this trend, it reflects a greater preference and capability of recent generations of elderly to live independently. Clearly many factors are responsible: greater economic security, improved housing opportunities, and the ability to maintain close family ties without living under the same roof (due to improved transportation and communication technologies). Thus not only has the elderly population grown rapidly in size, but an increasing proportion of its members are independently making decisions of where to live.

During the last two decades, metropolitanization in the United States has been reflected by major changes in the spatial organization of people and activities in urban and rural areas. Transportation and communication technologies—the automobile, the large scale truck, superhighways, refrigerated cars, truck-train piggyback, electronic communications—released the producer from the locational restraints of the central city. In conjunction with rising taxes, the declining quality of public services, higher land costs, and the increasing congestion of the central city, contrasted with suburbia's relatively inexpensive land costs, little congestion, lower taxes, and increasingly larger supply of accessible labor, industry had strong incentives to decentralize and move to outlying suburban locations. Rising consumer incomes and a reinforcing federal housing policy contributed to a rapid decentralization of primarily white persons who were contemplating or engaged in childrearing and who were attracted to the suburbs by homeownership, open space, and perceived improvement in public services and facilities. In response to this growing auto-oriented suburban market, retail establishments grew rapidly in suburban areas, with regional shopping centers assuming the role of central business districts and offering a complete range of high and low order goods and services (Cohen, 1972).

This growth of the large multi-nodal metropolitan center and of nonmetropolitan areas within its commuting field (Berry, 1970; Fuguitt, 1972) was accompanied by population and economic declines of other nonmetropolitan counties, particularly those with a high proportion of farm population. Many of these latter areas experienced declining tax bases, substandard housing, poor social, health, and medical services, and high outmigration rates of younger age groups who were seeking improved employment opportunities. Left behind were the older and less skilled population. About 44% of all United States' counties declined in population between 1960–1970, particularly in the Great Plains, southern Appalachia, the Mississippi delta, and the Alabama blackbelt (Beale, 1972).

Very recent census statistics reveal a possible reversal or shift in the dominant metropolitan growth patterns of the 1950s and 1960s. During the 1960s metropolitan counties grew by 17% while nonmetropolitan counties grew by only 7% (Beale, 1972). Between 1970 and 1972, however, nonmetropolitan counties grew by 3% while the metropolitan counties grew by only 2% (Beale, 1974).

These and other interrelated population and spatial dynamics have had a continuing impact on the locational patterns and on the quality of life of the older population in United States. They have resulted in an elderly population that is at the same time both residentially concentrated and residentially dispersed.

Concentrations of Elderly in Metropolitan Agglomerations

The past trend. Like the total United States population, the aged have increasingly become metropolitanized, located in centers that are both structurally and functionally parts of larger metropolitan agglomerations. This is reflected in the declining growth rate between 1960 and 1970 of elderly persons in small urban and rural places. By 1970, only 45% of elderly persons were located outside Urbanized Areas in contrast with 56% in 1950 (Figure 1).

The areal pattern of growth of the elderly population is largely due to younger cohorts aging "in place" and to residential relocations made earlier in the lifespan (Golant, 1972) rather than to migrations made after retirement. For example, close to 40% of elderly persons who head their own households in small

urban (under 50,000 population) and rural places have lived in their same residences for over 25 years. Mobility statistics do indicate, however, that of the small group of elderly who relocated from *nonmetropolitan* areas during the 5-year period from 1965–1970 (about 3% of total elderly population), about 41% moved into a metropolitan area and the remainder into another nonmetropolitan area. There is also a small but significant movement of elderly persons who relocated from *metropolitan* areas (about 4% of total elderly). Of this latter group, about 39% moved into nonmetropolitan areas (in the 1965–1970 period) and the remainder into another metropolitan area. (There has been little study of these small but important groups of elderly migrants.)

The future. Despite recent trends of nonmetropolitan area growth, it is expected that by the year 2000 a larger proportion of the total USA elderly will be located within metropolitan agglomerations than at present. Even if a greater rate of nonmetropolitan growth continues, its impact on the distribution of the elderly will not be felt until well after the year 2000. The migration of older persons into nonmetropolitan areas probably will not increase greatly, either in an absolute or relative sense—except into those nonmetropolitan places that contain recreation oriented activities, or planned retirement communities.

Several factors will contribute to the increasing size of elderly concentrations within metropolitan areas. (1) Because of past outmigrations of younger persons, there will be a smaller proportion of persons growing old in peripheral areas. (2) Older persons moving into nonmetropolitan areas will be counterbalanced by older persons moving into metropolitan areas. (3) In particular the "old-old" (age 75$^+$), who will represent an increas-

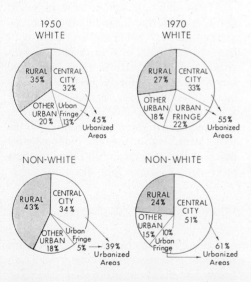

Figure 1. Location of White and Nonwhite Elderly in the United States, 1950 and 1970. Sources: U.S. Population Census, 1950, Vol. 4, Part 5A. U.S. Population Census, 1960, Vol. 1, Part 1. U.S. Population Census, 1970, Vol. 1, Part 1

ing proportion of the total elderly, will have strong motivation to move to the larger agglomerations because of varied housing and service opportunities that provide physical and psychological security. (4) Government subsidies covering all or part of the costs of relocating, plus providing for "social work" information and referral services, will probably be available for older persons who wish to relocate into metropolitan areas.[1] (5) Subsequent generations of older persons living in nonmetropolitan areas will have greater capability of moving as a consequence of their better education and more accurate information about the increased housing opportunities in metropolitan areas (Golant, 1974). (6) The importance of part-time employment to future generations of "retired" persons may increase. The greater employment opportunities found in the metropolitan agglomeration will therefore be attractive.

Concentrations of Elderly in "Retirement States"

The past trend. Between 1960 and 1970 the states of Florida, Arizona, and California together had net gains of well over one-half million migrating older persons. The attractiveness of these and other states with warm or moderate year-round climates is well-documented, particularly for the wealthier older person who can afford to relocate and to live in a planned retirement community (Wilner, Sherman, Walkley, & Dodds, 1968).

Because the total elderly population has grown rapidly within the last two decades and because only a few "warm" states are the major recipients of older migrants, these net migration gains are not surprising and, if anything, are low. In fact a comparison of elderly migration

1. Beyer and Nierstrasz (1967) have emphasized the importance and success of advice and casework for preparing older persons who needed new housing in England.

in the periods 1955–1960 and 1965–1970 shows no significant change in the propensity of older persons to make long distance moves. In both periods, about 3% of all older persons and about 9% of all those older persons who moved at all made noncontiguous interstate moves.

The future. Between now and the year 2000, states with warm or temperate climates will probably experience significant economic growth in both their metropolitan and nonmetropolitan areas. A high proportion of those elderly persons who will live in nonmetropolitan centers will probably live in these states. Improved communication and transportation will continue to facilitate the location of "footloose" industries in these areas. Thus the economic prosperity of these areas will contribute to the development of new planned retirement centers as well as age-integrated communities with a wide range of services, facilities, and leisure-type activities that will serve older persons.

At the same time, the percentage of the total elderly attracted to these climate-attractive communities will continue to be small. In regions with less favorable climates, settings much "closer to home" for most elderly, both in or near metropolitan agglomerations, are likely also to provide a wide range of services and facilities. These will represent far more attractive settings for older persons living in these regions, thus reducing their motivation to make long-distance moves.

Intrametropolitan Population Dispersion

The past trend. In 1970, over 34% of the elderly in the United States were still concentrated in central cities of Urbanized Areas. However, this static picture fails to catch the implications of the changing dynamics of metropolitan growth. During the last two decades suburbanization proceeded at a rapid rate. The greatest growth of metropolitan areas occurred in their fringe or suburban areas, while many central cities lost population.

More specifically, the greatest amount of growth in an urban area is at the edges of its built-up area. Suburbs which initially represented the outer perimeter of growth are eventually encompassed by new suburbs. As these suburban neighborhoods age, so too do the persons occupying them, so that over time increasingly larger numbers of older persons are found further from the city center. A high proportion of these persons own their homes. Since older persons tend to move relatively infrequently, particularly homeowners, the replacement of older populations by younger age groups proceeds very slowly. Moreover, even when older persons relocate, many move only very short distances. Metropolitan areas which have historically experienced more rapid spatial expansion are more likely, therefore, to have higher proportions of old dwelling units within their fringe or suburban areas; and these dwelling units in turn are more likely to be occupied by higher proportions of older families.

In 1950, 12% of the age 65$^+$ population was located in suburban areas of Urbanized Areas in contrast to 21% in 1970. In these 20 years, the growth rate of older persons in these fringe areas was over three times the national growth rate of older persons. Moreover, intrametropolitan residential moves by elderly tend to reinforce this pattern. In the period 1965–1970, for example, only 6% of the elderly making intrametropolitan moves made "reverse" migrations—from suburb to central city—while 14% moved from central city to suburban areas. The remaining 80% relocated either *within* the central city or *within* the suburban area. As a result, central cities during this 5-year period had net migration losses of about 275,000 older persons.

The future. The geometrics of suburban growth will probably result in an older population that is spatially dispersed over an increasingly larger geographic area. At the same time, however, technological advances in transportation and electronic communications are likely to reduce the "friction of space" such that geographical distance will become a less accurate predictor of either the frequency or intensity of interpersonal or interneighborhood interactions. The smaller concentration of older persons in the central city will represent merely another population node among several such nodes that will be widely scattered throughout the metropolitan area.

This changing intrametropolitan spatial pattern will probably be accompanied (albeit only after considerable time lag) by new technologies and new administrative strategies that will be designed to cope with a less concentrated population of elderly consumer-clients.

Central City Concentrations of Black Elderly

The past trend. A more accurate picture of central city population changes emerges from a separate examination of black and white populations. Population increase in central cities was mostly a function of large natural increases of blacks in all regions of the country and of large black net migration gains in the Northeast, North Central, and West. The major losses in central cities, primarily in the Northeast and North Central regions, were due to large net migration losses of whites, particularly in the largest metropolitan areas.[2] By 1970, 58% of the total black population in the United States

2. In the South and West, this trend was true only in the largest metropolitan areas, while the central cities of their smaller metropolitan areas actually experienced increases in the numbers of white persons. These latter growth rates, however, were generally less than half the population growth rates of black persons (Taeuber, 1972).

lived in central cities in contrast with only 43% in 1950.

The changing distribution of the elderly black population was no less dramatic than the locational shifts of the total black population. In 1950, 43% of the nonwhite 65$^+$ population lived in rural areas in contrast to only 24% in 1970. Similarly by 1970, 51% lived in central cities of Urbanized Areas in contrast with only 34% in 1950.

The future. The growth of the black elderly in central cities (as a result of natural increases) will continue. In combination with out-migrations of white population, by the year 2000 an increasing proportion of the elderly in central cities will be black. Thus the white elderly will become increasingly dispersed throughout suburban areas and the black elderly increasingly concentrated in central cities.

It is not expected that the attractiveness of redeveloped residential areas of central cities will motivate a significant number of white elderly to relocate from their suburban locations. On the contrary, such central city development will have the effect of increasing the costs for shelter, so that accommodation will be beyond the financial means of all but the affluent elderly. Moreover, it is likely that these central areas will be increasingly occupied by a growing group of relatively affluent young and middle-aged black families.

The outward migration of more affluent black residents into suburban or fringe areas probably will proceed at a faster rate (Connolly, 1973). At the same time, higher proportions of blacks will also grow old in suburban neighborhoods that they have occupied since they were younger. Accordingly, an increasing number of black communities with relatively high concentrations of elderly will probably be found, by the year 2000, in distinctive pockets and wedges outside the central city.

Elderly Concentrations in Neighborhoods and Housing Structures

The past trend. The natural increase in numbers of older persons in metropolitan areas, combined with their lower propensity to move, has resulted in an increase in the number of *neighborhoods* with relatively high concentrations of elderly. While there has been little study of these environments, piecemeal evidence suggests that the greater visibility of older persons found in some of these older communities has made public agencies more cognizant of their problems and has consequently led to the greater availability of special services.

During the last decade there has been a significant increase in the percentage of the old who either own or rent *mobile homes*. The proportion in owned mobile homes increased from 1% in 1960 to 4% in 1970; the proportion in rented mobile homes increased from 0.4% to 1%. These units were located equally inside and outside metropolitan areas. The extent to which mobile home communities occupied by elderly are age-segregated is not clear. They represent, however, relatively inexpensive and increasingly popular forms of residential accommodation capable of housing new and larger concentrations of elderly.

It appears also that the incidence of *condominium* and cooperative ownership by the elderly is increasing. While statistics were not available for 1960, in 1970, 2% of elderly homeowners were in condominiums or cooperatives, compared with 1% of households headed by persons under age 65. Elderly persons living alone had the highest rate of condominium ownership. Condominiums and cooperatives were predominantly located (over 90%) in metropolitan areas, with a slightly higher proportion in central cities (47%) than in urban fringes or suburbs (44%).

There has been an increase in the incidence of planned *retirement communities* located *in the fringe areas* of metropolitan areas in midwestern and eastern regions of United States. Like their Arizona and California counterparts, these are age-segregated communities that offer a complete range of life-enriching services and facilities. While not located in all year-round warm climates, they have two other important attributes: (1) they are very accessible to the social, medical, commercial, and recreational facilities of multi-functional regional "shopping" centers; and (2) their occupants are accessible to members of their families and friends who live in the metropolitan area. Thus, while segregated *in situ* space, these elderly persons are integrated over *extended* space.

A critical latent function provided by the retirement community—far more effectively than by the natural community setting—is the predictability of its future status. Neighborhoods in major urban centers have changed rapidly with respect to their demographic and racial characteristics and the quality and variety of their services. The recently retired person has little guarantee that the neighborhood which in the past may have possessed attractive attributes will continue to have these attributes in the future. The retirement village, on the other hand, gives considerable assurance to its occupants that the social environment and the facilities that presently exist will not significantly change in the near future. It represents, therefore, an example of a stable, planned community whose future is predictable. This suggests that as the physical and social stability of "natural" urban neighborhoods decline, the growth and the attractiveness of the retirement community will increase.

While *low rent public housing* designed for the elderly is at present insufficient to meet the existing demand, over the last 15 years this form of accommodation has experienced a remarkable growth (Figure 2). In 1960 there were just over 18,000 elderly designed dwelling units developed by local housing authorities in contrast to almost 350,000 in 1972. In the same period Section 202 (nonprofit sponsored) elderly housing increased from 200 units to over 46,000 units. The number of elderly housing concentrations has grown proportionately. At the end of 1972, 66% of all "low rent public housing" dwelling units specially designed for older persons (age 62^+) were in projects that were age-segregated (U.S. HUD, 1972).

Like the retirement village, the public housing project is increasingly providing more than merely "shelter." It has gone

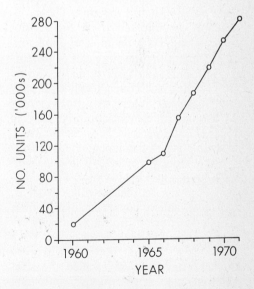

Figure 2. Cumulative Low Rent Public Housing Units—Elderly Designed, 1960–1971 (under annual contributions contract). Source: Dept. of Housing & Urban Development. 1971 HUD Statistical Yearbook. USGPO, Washington, 1972

far beyond its income subsidy function and it has assumed four additional roles: (1) the special design features providing increased physical and emotional security; (2) on-site congregate facilities such as central dining room and food services; (3) age-segregated social environments providing sympathetic and responsive support systems (Rosow, 1967); and (4) as elderly concentrations have become more visible to state and local agencies, they facilitate the assessment of need and make it economically more feasible to supply a particular service (like transportation).

The future. The number of neighborhoods and housing structures with relatively high concentrations of elderly will increase by the year 2000 if only because of their natural increases in numbers. Elderly persons in an increasing number of these neighborhoods will develop, through volunteer groups of nonprofit agencies, their own self-help programs. These will probably be initiated by a better educated, young-old population who are concerned about the development of supportive and enriching services and facilities. Over time, such neighborhoods may develop strong images as attractive residential environments supportive of the needs of older persons. As a consequence, they may act as catchment areas for relocating elderly persons. These natural communities may evolve into a form comparable to the retirement village, that is, with an all-elderly population living within an infrastructure of housing and services that is oriented to their needs.

These communities, however, will probably be exceptions rather than the rule. Age-integrated neighborhoods containing persons in all stages of the life cycle are likely to increase. This will be the result of an increase in the availability of a diverse range of dwelling unit types and sizes located within the same neighborhood. Older populations, therefore, will

be at the same time both age-segregated and age-integrated, depending on breadth of the areal perspective. Apartments, for example, containing concentrations of older persons will probably be increasingly dispersed among single family (detached or attached) dwelling units occupied by younger persons.

The growth of multifamily public housing projects designed for elderly persons will continue, and these residents are likely to assume an increasingly more complex set of roles. In addition to congregate eating facilities, a varied array of social, homemaker, and medical facilities will serve not only the occupants of the project, but also elderly persons living in the immediate neighborhood. These housing complexes will help all but the most frail elderly person to remain in the community. They may, therefore, represent a major alternative to institutionalization.

Planned retirement communities or towns for the elderly can be expected to increase, particularly in the midwest and eastern regions of the United States. These too will evolve into more complex forms. Increasingly, they will offer a more complete range of housing types—from owned to rented units, from single detached to highrise structures. These planned centers will become more readily accessible to both white and nonwhite low income persons through some system of direct or indirect income subsidies. Like the public housing project, the retirement village will benefit from economies of scale enabling it to provide a more diverse housing environment appealing to elderly with various life styles and levels of competence.

Summary

In describing the past and speculating on the future locational patterns of the elderly, the following predictions seem reasonable (see Figure 3):

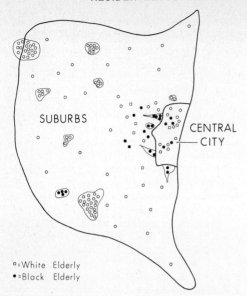

° = White Elderly
• = Black Elderly

Figure 3. Elderly Residential Concentrations in the Future Metropolitan Agglomeration: Increasing proportion of U.S. elderly in metropolitan agglomerations; lower proportion of central city elderly who are white; higher proportion of central city elderly who are black; more black communities with relatively high proportions of elderly in margins of central city and older suburbs; more white elderly persons dispersed throughout suburbs; more elderly concentrations in natural communities, planned retirement communities, and multi-purpose housing complexes

1. A higher proportion of the elderly population will be concentrated in metropolitan agglomerations, primarily as a function of natural increases in numbers.

2. "Retirement states" with warm or temperate year-round climates will experience significant economic growth in both their metropolitan and non-metropolitan centers. This will facilitate the growth of new planned retirement centers and new age-integrated communities, both with housing and services catering to the needs of older persons. However, the percentage of American elderly population occupying these communities will continue to be small.

3. The older population living in metropolitan areas will be spatially dispersed over an increasingly large suburban area. Technological advances in transportation and electronic communications will result in geographical distance becoming a less accurate predictor of the frequency or intensity of interpersonal or interneighborhood interactions. The concentration of elderly persons in the central city will represent merely another population node among many such nodes scattered throughout the metropolitan area.

4. An increasing proportion of the elderly in central cities will be black. Thus the white elderly population will become increasingly dispersed throughout the suburban areas and the black elderly, increasingly concentrated in central cities. At the same time, an increasing number of black communities with relatively high concentrations of elderly will occupy suburban locations outside the central city.

5. The number of neighborhoods and housing structures with relatively high concentrations of elderly persons will increase by the year 2000. A small number of these natural communities will contain an almost all-elderly population living within an infrastructure of housing and services primarily oriented to their needs. In the main, however, age-integrated neighborhoods containing persons in all stages of the life cycle, occupying a diverse array of housing structures, are likely to predominate.

6. The growth of multifamily "public housing" projects designed for age-segregated elderly persons will continue. These will assume an increasingly more complex set of roles enabling all but the most physically

and mentally frail older person to remain in the community, and thus delay institutionalization.

7. Planned retirement communities or towns for the elderly will increase, particularly in the midwest and eastern regions of the United States. These will be accessible to both white and nonwhite low income elderly persons appealing to elderly with various life styles and levels of competence.

References

Beale, C. L. Rural and nonmetropolitan trends of significance to national population policy. In S. M. Mazie (Ed.), U.S. Commission on Population Growth in the American Future, Vol. 5, Population distribution and policy. USGPO, Washington, 1972.

Beale, C. L. Rural development: population and settlement prospects. Journal of Soil & Water Conservation, 1974, 29, 23–27.

Berry, B. J. L. The geography of the United States in the year 2000. Transactions, Institute of British Geographers, 1970, 51, 21–53.

Beyer, G., & Nierstrasz, F. H. S. Housing the aged in western countries. Elsevier, Amsterdam, 1967.

Cohen, Y. S. Diffusion of an innovation in an urban system: The spread of planned regional shopping centers in the United States, 1949–1968. Univ. of Chicago, Dept. of Geography, Research Paper #140, Chicago, 1972.

Connolly, H. X. Black movement into the suburbs. Urban Affairs Quarterly, 1973, 9, 91–111.

Fuguitt, G. V. Population trends of nonmetropolitan cities and villages in United States. In S. M. Mazie (Ed.), U.S. Commission on Population Growth in the American Future, Vol. 5, Population distribution and policy. USGPO, Washington, 1972.

Golant, S. The residential location and spatial behavior of the elderly. Univ. of Chicago, Dept. of Geography, Research Paper #143, Chicago, 1972.

Golant, S. Behavioral components underlying intraurban residential mobility: A clarification and a potential model. In E. Moore (Ed.), Models of residential location and relocation in the city. Northwestern Studies in Geography, No. 2. Evanston, IL, 1974.

Rosow, I. Social integration of the aged. Free Press, New York, 1967.

Taeuber, I. B. The changing distribution of the population in the United States in the twentieth century. In S. M. Mazie (Ed.), U.S. Commission on Population Growth in the American Future, Vol. 5, Population distribution and policy. USGPO, Washington, 1972.

U.S. Dept. of Housing & Urban Development. Low rent project directory for elderly families, Report S-101 (Elderly). HUD Housing Production & Mortgage Credit—FHA, Division of Research & Statistics, Statistics Branch, Washington, 1972.

Wilner, D. M., Sherman, S. R., Walkley, R. P., & Dodds, S. Demographic characteristics of residents of planned retirement housing sites. Gerontologist, 1968, 8, 164.

JON VAN TIL

A New Type of City for an Energy-Short World*

The spectre of a permanent oil shortage has loomed ever larger in the United States in recent years. At the same time, the future of nuclear energy is very much in doubt and solar and other renewable energy sources are still in the early stages of development. Conservation measures, it is said, could allow us to maintain much of our high standard of living in the face of worsening energy shortages—perhaps even achieving as much as 50% savings in energy use—but these savings cannot be accomplished overnight and would require massive changes in life-styles.

Even with substantial conservation, a permanent energy shortfall would have a tremendous impact on the American way of life—not just on the way people live but also on where they live. For this reason, it is imperative that we do some serious thinking—and, hopefully, careful planning—about future energy supplies.

How Much Energy?

To stimulate systematic thinking about the influence of energy on our lives, I

* See also Jon van Til, *"Living with Energy Shortfall: A Future for American Cities and Towns,"* Westview Press, 1981.

have developed five scenarios, the first three of which are based on those developed by the Energy Policy Project of the Ford Foundation in 1974. The last two are based on more recent research suggesting that no-growth or even declining-supply scenarios are distinctly possible visions of the future.

It is, of course, impossible to determine which of these scenarios will prove to be the most accurate in the years ahead. However, each is possible, and increasingly it is beginning to appear that the least energy-rich visions are at least as likely to emerge as the more bountiful ones. In any case, it is wise to be prepared to deal with a wide range of alternative energy futures. Thus, for better or worse, I offer the following five scenarios:

1. Pre-1973 trends projected. An orderly transition takes place from oil and coal to eventual exploitation of breeder technology. Energy use continues to grow at a 3.5% annual rate.
2. Modest growth. Energy use continues to grow, but at a slower rate (1.9% per year). The trend is toward a viable multi-based energy future, including nuclear energy. An orderly transi-

From **The Futurist**, Vol. 14, no. 3, 1980, pp. 64–70. Reprinted by permission of **The Futurist**, published by the Work-Future Society, Washington, D.C., and J. van Til.

tion from oil to coal to nuclear power as the primary energy source takes place—along with increased development of renewable energy sources. The successful implementation of a number of conservation measures permits continued economic expansion with largely unchanged patterns of energy usage.

3. Steady-state of energy availability after 1990. The energy supply grows slowly until 1990 and then levels off. As oil is exhausted, it is replaced by coal and renewable energy sources. Increasing demands for energy for industrial and household uses are accompanied by intensified conservation efforts, since the energy supply is no longer growing.

4. Steady-state of 1973 level of energy usage through the year 2000 and beyond. The energy supply stabilizes at the 1973 level, with the development of renewable sources begun in the late 1970s continuing to permit an orderly transition as oil becomes increasingly scarce. A heavy emphasis is placed on conservation, and a dramatic decline in per capita citizen and household use of energy takes place.

5. Decline to 75% of 1973 level of supply by year 2000, with even grimmer future prospects. Renewable energy sources are not developed, and frequent crises occur as the traditional non-renewable energy sources are exhausted and nuclear power continues to be plagued with difficulties.

These scenarios contain variations not only in the *amount* of energy available, but also in the *forms* that energy will take.

Energy comes in a variety of forms—each having different properties. Some forms of energy are permanently depleted upon use, and others are perpetually renewed. Some forms are relatively easy to transport, while other forms, because they require continuous transmission or are relatively unconcentrated, are not economical for purposes such as fueling motor cars. Energy sources also differ in the amount of pollutants resulting from their use. Finally, we may distinguish between sources that require central generation and refinement and those that permit local generation.

When these characteristics are considered in relation to principal energy sources available, four different patterns of energy form and structure emerge. (See Table 1.) First, there is a group of energy sources that are non-renewable, difficult to transport, highly-polluting, and centrally generated. This group includes coal and nuclear fission (in its present forms), applied to the generation of electrical power. A second category of energy sources includes those that are non-renewable, transportable, highly-polluting, and centrally-refined. This category includes oil and its derivative, gasoline. Third is a group of sources that are renewable, difficult to transport, potentially highly-polluting, and centrally-generated. This category includes the two nuclear forms yet to be commercially developed—breeder and fusion sources. Finally, there is a group of sources that are renewable, generally non-transportable (but not entirely so), low-polluting, and potentially decentrally-generated. This category includes the various forms of solar energy, including hydroelectric, methane, and wind power—the soft energy paths.

How Much Energy for Transportation?

Today's spread-out residential patterns—featuring urban sprawl and heavy commuter traffic from remote areas into urban centers—were built on the assumption that cheap and abundant gasoline would always be available for transportation. However, there is wide agreement among experts that, in the event of a severe energy shortfall, the amount of energy available for transportation would be deeply

Table 1. Characteristics of Major Energy Forms: Energy comes in a variety of forms, each having different combinations of properties. The mix of energy forms can have a major impact on the shape of cities.

Major Energy Forms	Degree of Renewability	Transportability	Pollution	Typical Pattern of Power Generation
Oil	None	High	High (carbon monoxide)	Central refinement
Coal	None	Low	High (thermal, particulates, oxides)	Central
Nuclear fission	None to possibly high	Low	High (thermal, radioactivity)	Central
Nuclear fusion	Possibly high	Low	High (thermal, radioactivity)	Central
Hydroelectric	High	Low	Low	Central
Solar	High	Low—but some high	Low	Decentral

cut. My own most pessimistic scenario envisions a loss in transportation energy of 52% by the year 2000. And such a drastic shortfall in energy for transportation will have a major impact on future residential patterns.

Pursuing further the implications of the 52% decline scenario, it quickly becomes apparent that an even greater decline will ensue in energy available for automobiles. Energy for transportation must be shared among seven major categories of use, according to the Ford Foundation study. The Ford planners see the demand for three of these uses—automobiles, buses, and airplanes—as being highly elastic, while energy use for rail, farm machinery, and ships is viewed as highly inelastic. Truck use is seen as moderately elastic. Transportation energy, after all, is used both for passenger transit and the shipping of freight, and the latter purpose is more inelastic in the event of energy shortfall.

The energy trade-offs required in the most pessimistic scenarios (steady-state and declining-growth) would be among the most difficult decisions made in American history—and would surely require a rationing system for users.

The impact of an energy shortfall on individual mobility is likely to be substantial. If a mix of transit options aimed toward maximum feasible mileage is chosen, the 1973 constant level (scenario four) will produce almost as many miles of transit per capita as the steady-state after 1990 scenario (scenario three), and the 75% level scenario (scenario five) will produce just two-thirds the miles of the two preceding scenarios, or five-sixths the level of present travel. On the other hand, continued reliance on the automobile as the primary conveyance will yield far less mileage per capita.

What Form Might Our Cities and Suburbs Take?

Now, what impact will these energy patterns have on the way in which we will choose, or be compelled, to organize our cities and suburbs in the years ahead? To answer this question, it will help to have in mind the major patterns that human settlements might assume. One highly useful way of viewing these possibilities was suggested by Catherine Bauer Wurster some 15 years ago. Combining two dimensions in her analysis—degree of concentration or dispersion, and degree of region-wide specialization or subregional integration—Wurster derived four models of the future of American urbanization: "present trends projected," "general dispersion," "concentrated supercity," and "constellation of relatively diversified and integrated cities."

The first type, "present trends projected," involves a continuing trend toward suburban expansion, with a lesser degree of urban concentration, all within a regional pattern of economic specialization. This type closely resembles the shape of the contemporary Northeastern metropolitan centers. The second type, "general dispersion," is the vision of metropolitan sprawl that characterizes so many of America's newer Sun Belt cities. The third type, the "concentrated supercity," is the one envisaged by visionary architects like Soleri and Small, in which a population density much greater than that of present-day Manhattan is accommodated in an urban megastructure. The fourth type, "constellation of relatively diversified and integrated cities," involves more concentration than the present form,

but also provides a high degree of subregional integration, allowing particularly for people to live near their places of employment. Its closest embodiment is in the commercial cities of the eighteenth century.

How Will Energy Patterns Affect Residential Patterns?

Examining Wurster's typology, in combination with the constraints implied by the five energy scenarios, suggests the set of interrelations depicted in Table 2. The table presents my estimation of the viability of each urbanization model in each energy scenario, and suggests that the options will decrease dramatically as energy prospects diminish.

Thus the first model, "present trends projected," is well-suited to energy-rich scenarios, but becomes increasingly unviable as we move toward energy-poor conditions; this model involves more dispersion than concentration, and implies an increasing dependence upon automobile transit. Such dependence is unlikely to be sustained in energy scenarios 3, 4, and 5, which provide fewer auto miles per person in the year 2000 than at present. Nor is such dispersion consistent with a large increase in dependence upon bus

Table 2. Viability of Urbanization Models in the Year 2000

Urbanization Models	Scenario 1 Pre-1973 Projected	Scenario 2 Modest Growth	Scenario 3 Steady-state after 1990	Scenario 4 1973 ZEG	Scenario 5 75% Decline from 1973
Present projected	Yes	Yes	Questionable	Probably No	No
General dispersion	Yes	No	No	No	No
Concentrated super-city	Yes	Questionable	No (too expensive to build)	No	No
Diversified-integrated	Yes	Yes	Yes	Yes	Yes

Source: Van Til, 1979.

and rail transit, which themselves require a greater concentration of population in residential clusters than can be anticipated in the projection of present trends. In sum, it is unlikely that the projection of present trends can accommodate a decline in energy available for transit, or a decline in automobile miles per person. Therefore, the first Wurster model can be sustained only in the two most plentiful energy scenarios.

Obviously, the general dispersion model is even less viable, barring a return to agrarian economic patterns and life-styles. It can be sustained under current economic expectations only by an increase in energy available for transit, and by a substantial increase in miles per person available by automobile. Only the most plentiful energy scenario, pre-1973 projected, meets these criteria clearly. Under the three least bountiful energy scenarios, general dispersion is simply an unworkable form.

The concentrated supercity model is energy-efficient *once built,* but too expensive to construct save under energy-rich conditions—a cruel paradox. It might well have been built earlier, but it is not a present option for salvation from energy shortfall.

Thus we are left with the diversified-integrated model, the form of the old commercial city, as the one most congenial to an energy-short future. Only this form provides clear energy savings, without extensive ruralization, for its social organization could be maintained even in the face of very tight energy supplies:

What fuel there is available for transportation could be allocated on the highest priority to the transport of resources and the delivery of goods.

Workers could be strongly motivated to reside within walking or bicycling distances of their jobs, supplemented by increased bus availability and use of precious automobile mileage (where winter climate or physical limitation require). This approach would require the development of "motel-type" housing permitting the maximum of worker mobility with the minimum of moving costs.

Personal transportation by fuel-powered vehicle could be substantially curtailed; wherever possible, communication could be conducted by telecommunications (including telephone). Pleasure travel would be drastically limited (particularly air travel, which would be largely limited to national defense and the use of top elites' business travel) and would be greatly reduced from present levels.

The distribution of goods and services could be provided within subregional centers, as would, insofar as feasible, the production of goods and services.

As for capital construction in a time of constraint, it is clear that insufficient energy will be available for the sort of crash building program of more energy-efficient dwellings envisaged in recent years by Paolo Soleri, Glen Small, and other architects. Policy-makers will seek to maximize the usage of existing shells, and will approve construction of new ones only on a modest basis. There simply will not be sufficient resources for a policy of reconstruction. In the case of energy shortfall, we shall have to rely on the stock of shells we have in existence for our basic residential, commercial, and industrial needs.

Therefore, in an energy-short future, American settlement patterns might take the following form:

Residential and economic patterns emerge around a number of regional nodes, within which most transportation, except that used for production, is confined.

The most desirable housing within these subregional centers is located within two kilometers of the node, with other housing concentrated within a kilometer radius of the node.

The locations of these nodes emerge on the basis of current land use, and they occupy, in large part, existing shells. Node development occurs where there is a high density of building space (residential, commercial, industrial) and where there is proximity to the circulation system of an energy-poor society (rail lines for goods transport; interstate highways for goods transport; limited transport of persons by buses and automobiles).

Land outside the 10-kilometer radius of subregional nodes is available for settlement only by farmers, self-sufficient nomads, and workers in the long-term vacation business. Included in this category is a large portion of current suburban land, most existing towns with populations under 10,000, and almost all land in mountainous and rural areas.

Such a settlement pattern would obviously differ greatly from that of the present. Least changed from the present pattern would be the middle-sized cities of the Northeast, already concentrated in land-use. They would diversify in production, but would largely rely on existing shells. Larger cities, and smaller more spread-out cities, would see the development of multiple nodes within their present limits, each of which would take on an increasing autonomy. And most different would be the spread-out cities, and most present suburbs and small towns, much area within which would become largely depopulated as it falls outside the radius of the subregional nodes that would develop around present malls, apartment centers, suburban town centers, and other areas of potential concentration.

Almost all new construction would be contained within the nodes; house and land prices would skyrocket within the central ring in particular; and resettlement compensation would be required to assist those suburbanites whose real estate investments would be almost totally lost by the shifting residential patterns. Cultural experience would continue to be most accessible in those nodes that were formerly the central cities of great metropolises; and these would become the most highly valued places of residence in the new immobile urban world.

It is probably unlikely, given the traditional American resistance to long-range planning, that any foresightful effort to reshape settlement patterns to accommodate energy shortfall will be undertaken. Rather, we shall more likely be left to muddle through with the guidance provided by a market economy and reactive political leadership. These market and political forces will surely cushion the impact of energy shortfall, bringing sharply increased prices for land and houses that are centrally located. Such a policy will be justified by many as a prudent course, given the uncertainties of future restrictions on energy.

However, without a strong planned commitment to guide this process of concentration, it is likely that, under conditions of shortfall, inequalities between citizens will be exacerbated, elites will monopolize access to energy for their own personal use, and levels of social tension and disruption will rise as real living standards for most Americans plummet to intolerable levels. In such a future, neither democracy nor social order will be assured.

Major References and Further Reading

Abler, R. ed. 1976. *A Comparative Atlas of America's Great Cities*. Minneapolis: University of Minnesota Press.

Abu-Lughod, J. and Hay R. Jr. eds. 1980. *Third World Urbanization*. London: Methuen.

Adams, J. G. U. 1972. "Life in a Global Village," *Environment and Planning*, 4 (4): 381–394.

Adams, J. S. 1972. "The Geography of Riots and Civil Disorders in the 1960s," *Economic Geography*, 48 (1): 24–42.

Adams, J. S. ed. 1976. *Urban Policy Making and Metropolitan Dynamics: A Comparative Geographical Analysis*. Cambridge, Mass.: Ballinger Publishing Co.

Alao, N. 1974. "An Approach to Intraurban Location Theory," *Economic Geography*, 50:59–69.

Alcaly, R. and Mermelstein, D. eds. 1977. *The Fiscal Crisis of American Cities*. New York: Vintage Books.

Alonso, W. 1964. *Location and Land Use*, Cambridge, Mass.: Harvard University Press.

Alonso, W. 1978. "Metropolis without Growth," *The Public Interest*, 53:68–86.

Ambrose, P. and Colenutt, R. 1975. *The Property Machine*. London: Penguin.

Andrews, F. M. and Withey, S. B. 1976. *Social Indicators of Well-Being: The Development and Measurement of Perceptual Indicators*. New York: Plenum.

Annals, American Academy of Political and Social Science. 1980. *Changing Cities: A Challenge to Planning*, Vol. 451, Sept.

Arnott R. 1981. *Urbanization and Urban Structure*. Toronto: Butterworths.

Ball, M. and Kirwan, R. 1977. "Accessibility and Supply Constraints in the Urban Housing Market," *Urban Studies*, 14, 11–32.

Ball, M. 1979. "A Critique of Urban Economics," *International Journal of Urban and Regional Research*, 3(3):309–332.

Banfield, E. C. 1974. *The Unheavenly City Revisited*. Boston: Little, Brown & Co.

Bastié, J. and Dézert, B. 1980. *L'Espace Urbain*. Paris: Masson.

Bassett, K. and Short, J. 1980. *Housing and Residential Structure. Alternative Approaches*. London: Routledge and Keagan Paul.

Bater, J. H. 1980. *The Soviet City: Ideal and Reality*. Beverly Hills: Sage Publications.

Batty, M. 1976. *Urban Modelling*. London: MacMillan.

Batty, M. 1979. "Progress, Success and Failure in Urban Modelling," *Environment and Planning A*, 11(8):863–878.

Bennett, R. J. and Chorley, R. J. 1978. *Environment Systems: Philosophy Analysis and Control*. London: Methuen.

Bentham, G. and Moseley, M. J. 1980. Socioeconomic Change and Disparities within the Paris Agglomeration: Does Paris Have an 'Inner-City Problem'." *Regional Studies*, 14(1):55–70.

Berry, B. J. L. 1964. "Cities as Systems within Systems of Cities," *Papers and Proceedings* of the Regional Science Association, 13: 147–163.

Berry, B. J. L. 1970. "The Geography of the USA in the Year 2000," Transactions, Institute of British Geographers, 51:21–53.

Berry, B. J. L. ed. 1971. "Comparative Factorial Ecology," Economic Geography, 47:2.

Berry, B. J. L. 1973. The Human Consequences of Urbanization. London: MacMillan.

Berry, B. J. L. 1974. "The Economics of Land Use Intensities in Melbourne, Australia," Geographical Review, 64:483–497.

Berry, B. J. L. 1975. "The Decline of the Aging Metropolis: Cultural Bases and Social Process," in G. Sternlieb and J. Hughes, eds. Post-Industrial America: Metropolitan Decline and Inter-Regional Job Shifts. New Brunswick, N.J.: Rutgers University, pp. 175–185.

Berry, B. J. L. 1979. The Open Housing Question: Race and Housing in Chicago 1966–1976. Cambridge, Mass.: Ballinger.

Berry, B. J. L. 1980a. "Creating Future Geographies," Annals Association of American Geographers, 70(4):449–458.

Berry, B. J. L. 1980b. "Urbanization and Counterurbanization in the U.S." Annals, American Academy of Political and Social Science, Sept., 13–20.

Berry, B. J. L. et al. 1974. Land Use, Urban Form and Environmental Quality. Research Paper 155, Department of Geography, University of Chicago.

Berry, B. J. L. and Horton, F. eds. 1974. Urban Environment Management: Planning for Pollution Control. Englewood Cliffs, N.J.: Prentice-Hall.

Berry, B. J. L. and Kasarda, J. 1977. Contemporary Urban Ecology. New York: MacMillan.

Betz, D. M. 1972. "The City as a System Generating Income Inequality," Social Forces, 51:192–198.

Birch, D. et al. 1975. Patterns of Urban Change: The New Haven Experience. Lexington, Mass.: Lexington Books.

Black, J. 1980. Urban Transport Planning: Theory and Practice. London: Croom Helm.

Black, J. and Conroy, M. 1977. "Accessibility Measures and the Social Evaluation of Urban Structure," Environment and Planning A, 9:1013–1031.

Blowers, A. et al. eds. 1974. The Future of Cities. London: Hutchinson.

Blowers, A. 1980. The Limits of Power: The Politics of Local Planning Policy. London: Pergamon.

Blumenfeld, H. 1979. Edited by P. Spreiregen. Metropolis . . . and Beyond. New York: J. Wiley.

Boal, F. 1971. "Territoriality and Class: A Study of Two Residential Areas in Belfast," Irish Geography, 6:239–248.

Boddy, M. 1976. "The Structure of Mortgage Finance, Building Societies and the British Social Formation," Transactions, Institute of British Geographers, New Series, 1: 58–71.

Boddy, M. 1979. The Building Societies. London: MacMillan.

Boots, B. N. 1979. "Population Density, Crowding and Human Behaviour," Progress in Human Geography, 3(1):13–63.

Boulding, K. 1953. "Toward a General Theory of Growth," Canadian Journal of Economics and Political Science, 19:326–340.

Bourne, L. S. ed. 1971. Internal Structure of the City. New York: Oxford University Press.

Bourne, L. S. 1974. "A Descriptive Typology of Urban Land Use Structure and Change," Land Economics, L(3):271–280.

Bourne, L. S. and Simmons, J. W. eds. 1978. Systems of Cities: Readings on Structure Growth and Policy. New York: Oxford University Press.

Bourne, L. S. and Hitchcock, J. eds. 1979. Urban Housing Markets. Toronto: University of Toronto Press.

Bourne, L. S. 1981. The Geography of Housing. London and Washington: E. Arnold, V. Winston.

Bradbury, K., Downs, A., and Small, K. 1980. "Some Dynamics of Central City-Suburban Interactions," American Economic Review, 70, 2:410–414.

Bradford, C. P. and Rubinowitz, L. S. 1975. "The Urban-Suburban Investment-Disinvestment Process: Consequences for Older Neighborhoods," Annals of the American Academy of Political and Social Science, 422:77–86.

Broadbent, A. 1977. Planning and Profit in the Urban Economy. London: Methuen.

Brooks, M. E. 1976. Housing Equity and En-

vironmental Protection: The Needless Conflict. Chicago: Planners Press.

Brown, D. M. 1979. "The Location Decision of the Firm: An Overview of Theory and Evidence," *Papers of the Regional Science Association,* 43:23–39.

Brown, L. and Moore, E. eds. 1971. "Perspectives on Urban Spatial Structure," *Economic Geography,* Special Issue.

Brown, L. 1981. *Diffusion of Innovations: A New Perspective.* London: Methuen.

Brown, M. A. 1980. "Do Central Cities and Suburbs have Similar Dimensions of Need?," *The Professional Geographer,* 32 (4):400–411.

Brunn, S. O. and Wheeler, J. O. eds. 1980. *The American Metropolitan System: Present and Future.* London: E. Arnold.

Bunge, W. and Bordessa, R. 1975. *The Canadian Alternative. Survival, Expeditions and Urban Change.* Geographical Monographs No. 2. Downsview, Ont.: York University.

Burchell, R. W. and Listokin, D. 1975. *Future Land Use: Energy Environmental and Legal Constraints.* New Brunswick, N.J.: Center for Urban Policy Research, Rutgers University.

Burchell, R. and Listokin, D. eds. 1976. *Energy and Land Use.* New Brunswick, N.J.: Center for Urban Policy Research, Rutgers University.

Burchell, R. and Sternlieb, G. eds. 1979. *Planning Theory in the 1980s. A Search for Future Directions.* New Brunswick, N.J.: Rutgers University.

Cameron, G. 1973. "Intraurban Location and the New Plant," *Papers of the Regional Science Association,* 31:125–144.

Cameron, G. 1980. *The Future of the British Conurbations.* London: Longmans.

Campbell, A. *et al.* 1976. *The Quality of American Life. Perceptions, Evaluations and Satisfactions.* New York: Russell Sage Foundation.

Carey, G. W. 1976. "Land Tenure, Speculation and the State of the Aging Metropolis," *The Geographical Review,* 66(3):253–265.

Carlstein, T., Parkes, D. and Thrift, N. eds. 1978. *Timing Space and Spacing Time. Volume 2: Human Activity and Time Geography.* London: E. Arnold.

Carter, H. 1977. "Urban Origins: A Review,"

Progress in Human Geography, 1(1): 12–33.

Carter, H. 1981. *The Study of Urban Geography.* London: E. Arnold.

Castells, M. 1977. *The Urban Question.* London: E. Arnold (original ed. 1972).

Castells, M. 1978. *City, Class and Power.* London: MacMillan.

Castells, M. 1980. *The Economic Crisis and American Society.* Princeton: Princeton University Press.

Chapin, F. S. Jr. 1974. *Human Activity Patterns in the City: Things People Do in Space and Time.* New York: J. Wiley.

Chapin, F. S. Jr. and Kaiser, E. J. 1979. *Urban Land Use Planning.* 3rd Ed. Urbana, Ill.: University of Illinois Press.

Chinitz, B. ed. 1979. *Central City Economic Development.* Cambridge, Mass.: Abt Books.

Clark, W. A. V. 1980. "Residential Mobility and Neighborhood Change: Some Implications for Racial Residential Segregation," *Urban Geography,* 1(2):95–117.

Clark, W. A. V. and Moore, E. M. eds. 1978. *Population Mobility and Residential Change.* Studies in Geography No. 25. Evanston: Northwestern University.

Clark, W. A. V. and Moore, E. eds. 1980. *Residential Mobility and Public Policy* Vol. 19, Urban Affairs Annual Reviews. Beverly Hills: Sage Publications.

Clay, Phillip L. 1979. *Neighborhood Renewal. Middle-class Resettlement and Incumbent Upgrading in American Neighborhoods.* Lexington, Mass.: Lexington Books.

Clavel, P., Forester, J. and Goldsmith W. eds. 1980. *Urban and Regional Planning in an Age of Austerity.* Oxford: Pergamon.

Cliff, A. D., Haggett, P., Ord, J. K., Bassett, K. and Davies, R. 1975. *Elements of Spatial Structure: A Quantitative Approach.* London: Cambridge University Press.

Colenutt, R. J. 1972. "Building Models of Urban Growth and Spatial Structure," *Progress in Geography,* 2:109–151.

Colenutt, R. J. 1976. "The Political Economy of the Property Market," *Antipode,* 8(2): 24–29.

Conzen, M. and Conzen, K. 1979. "Geographical Structure in Nineteenth Century Urban Retailing: Milwaukee, 1836–90," *Journal of Historical Geography,* 5(1):45–66.

Cooper, Sandra. 1980. "Growth Control Evolves in Boulder," *Urban Land,* 39(3): 13–17.

Corsi, T. M. and Harvey, M. E. 1977. "Travel Behavior under Increases in Gasoline Prices," *Traffic Quarterly,* 31:605–624.

Cox, K. 1973. *Conflict, Power and Politics in the City.* New York: McGraw-Hill.

Cox, K. ed. 1978. *Urbanization and Conflict in Market Economies.* Chicago: Maaroufa.

Cox, K. 1979. *Location and Public Problems.* Chicago: Maaroufa.

Cox, K., McCarthy, J. J. and Nartowicz, F. 1979. "The Cognitive Organization of the North American City: Empirical Evidence," *Environment and Planning A,* 11(3):327–334.

Cox, K. and McCarthy, J. J. 1980. "Neighborhood Activism in the American City: Behavioral Relationships and Evaluation," *Urban Geography,* 1(1):22–38.

Craven, P. and Wellman, B. 1973. "The Network City," *Sociological Enquiry,* 43: 57–88.

Cybriwsky, R. A. 1978. "Social Aspects of Neighborhood Change," *Annals, Association of American Geographers,* 68:17–33.

Daniels, P. 1979. *Spatial Patterns of Office Growth and Location.* London: J. Wiley.

Daniels, P. W. and Warne, A. M. 1980. *Movement in Cities: Spatial Perspectives on Urban Travel and Transport.* New York: Methuen.

Danielson, M. N. 1976. *The Politics of Exclusion.* New York: Columbia University Press.

Davies, R. L. 1972. "Structural Models of Retail Distribution," *Transactions, Institute of British Geographers,* 57:59–82.

Davies, R. 1979. *Marketing Geography.* London: Methuen.

Davies, R. and Hall, P. 1978. *Issues in Urban Society.* London: Penguin.

Dawson, J. ed. 1980. *Retail Geography.* London: Croom Helm.

Dear, M. and Scott, A. J. eds. 1981. *Urbanization and Planning in Capitalist Societies.* New York: Methuen.

de Leeuw, F. and Struyk, R. 1975. *The Web of Urban Housing.* Washington, D.C.: The Urban Institute.

Deskins, D. R. Jr. 1978. "An Index of City Structure Based on Empirical Observation" in G. Enyedi, ed. *Urban Development in*

the U.S.A. and Hungary. Budapest: Akademiai Kiado, pp. 155–168.

Detwyler, T. and Marcus, M. eds. 1972. *Urbanization and Environment.* Belmont, Calif.: Duxbury Press.

Dicken, P. and Lloyd, P. 1978. "Inner Metropolitan Industrial Change: Enterprise Structures and Policy Issues: Case Studies of Manchester and Merseyside," *Regional Studies,* 12:181–197.

Dingemans, D. 1979. "Redlining and Mortgage Lending in Sacramento," *Annals, Association of American Geographers,* 69:225–239.

Donnison, D. 1980. *The Good City: A Study of Urban Development and Policy in Britain.* London: Heinemann.

Downing, P. B. ed. 1977. *Local Service Pricing Policies and their Effect on Urban Spatial Structure.* Vancouver: U.B.C. Press.

Downs, A. 1975. *Urban Problems and Prospects.* Chicago: Rand McNally.

Downs, A. 1979. "Key Relationships between Urban Development and Neighborhood Change," *Journal, American Planning Association,* 45(4):462–472.

Duncan, G. J. and Morgan, J. N. eds. 1975. *Five Thousand American Families: Patterns of Economic Progress.* Ann Arbor: University of Michigan.

Edel, M. and Rothenberg, J. eds. 1972. *Readings in Urban Economics.* New York: MacMillan.

Edel, M. 1976. "Marx's Theory of Rent: Urban Applications," *Kapitalistate,* 4–5:100–124.

Emery, F. and Trist, E. 1973. *Towards a Social Ecology: Contextual Appreciations of the Future in the Present.* New York: Plenum Press.

Evans, A. and Eversley, D. eds. 1980. *The Inner City: Employment and Industry.* London: Heinemann.

Feldman, M. 1977. "A Contribution to the Critique of Urban Political Economy: The Journey to Work," *Antipode,* 9(2):30–50.

Frazier, J. and Epstein, B. eds. 1979. *Applied Geography Conferences.* Binghamton, N.Y.: SUNY.

Forrester, J. 1969. *Urban Dynamics.* Cambridge: MIT Press.

French, R. A. and Hamilton, F. E. Ian, eds. 1979. *The Socialist City: Spatial Structure and Urban Policy.* Chichester, U.K.: J. Wiley.

Frey, W. H. 1979. "Central City White Flight: Racial and Nonracial Causes," *American Sociological Review*, 44(3):425–449.

Friedmann, John. 1978. "On the Contradictions Between City and Countryside," *Comparative Urban Research*, VI(1):5–41.

Gaffney, M. 1972. "The Sources, Nature and Functions of Urban Land Rent," *American Journal of Economics and Sociology*, 42: 241–57.

Gale, S. and Moore, E. G. eds. 1975. *The Manipulated City*. Chicago: Maaroufa Press.

Gilbert, G. and Dajani, J. A. 1974. Energy, Urban Form and Transportation Policy," *Transportation Research*, 8(4/5):267–275.

Glickman, N. J. and White, M. J. 1979. "Urban Land Use Patterns: An International Comparison," *Environment and Planning A*, 11:35–49.

Glickman, N. J. ed. 1980. *The Urban Impacts of Federal Policies*. Baltimore: Johns Hopkins.

Godschalk, D. R. ed. 1974. *Planning in America: Learning from Turbulence*. Washington, D.C.: American Institute of Planners.

Goheen, P. G. 1974. "Interpreting the American City: Some Historical Perspectives," *Geographical Review*, 64:362–384.

Golant, S. ed. 1979. *Location and Environment of the Elderly Population*. Washington, D.C.: V. H. Winston.

Gold, J. R. 1980. *An Introduction to Behavioral Geography*. London: Oxford University Press.

Goldberg, M. A. and Mercer, J. 1980. "Canadian and U.S. Cities: Basic Differences, Possible Explanations and Their Meaning for Public Policy," *Papers, Regional Science Association*, XLV:159–183.

Goldstein, B. and Davis R. eds. 1977. *Neighborhoods in the Urban Economy. The Dynamics of Decline and Revitalization*. Lexington, Mass.: Lexington Books.

Golledge, R. and Cox, K. eds. 1980. *Behavioral Geography Revisited*. London: Methuen.

Goodman, J. L. Jr. 1979. "Reasons for Moves Out and Into Large Cities," *Journal of the American Planning Association*, 45:407–416.

Gordon, D. A. 1977. *Problems in Political Economy: An Urban Perspective*. 2nd Ed. Lexington: D. C. Heath.

Greene, David L. 1980. "Urban Subcentres:

Recent Trends in Urban Spatial Structure," *Growth and Change*, 11(1):29–40.

Gregory, D. 1978. *Ideology, Science and Human Geography*. London: Hutchinson.

Guest, A. 1972. "Urban History, Population Densities, and Higher Status Residential Location," *Economic Geography*, 48(4): 375–387.

Hägerstrand, T. *et al*. 1974. *The Biography of a People: Past and Future Population Changes in Sweden*. Stockholm: Royal Ministry for Foreign Affairs.

Hall, P. 1977. *The World Cities*. London: Weidenfeld and Nicolson.

Hall, P. 1980. *Great Planning Disasters*. London: Weidenfeld and Nicolson.

Hall, P. and Diamond, D. 1980. *The Inner City in Context: Summary Report*. London: Heinemann.

Harries, K. D. 1980. *Crime and the Urban Environment*. Springfield, Ill.: C. Thomas.

Harloe, M. ed. 1977. *Captive Cities*. New York: J. Wiley.

Harrison, B. 1974. *Urban Economic Development*. Washington, D.C.: The Urban Institute.

Harrison, D. and Kain, J. F. 1974. Cumulative Urban Growth and Urban Density Functions," *Journal of Urban Economics*, 1: 61–98.

Hartshorn, T. A. 1980. *Interpreting the City: An Introduction to Urban Geography*. New York: Wiley.

Hartwick, J. M. 1973. "Spatially Organizing Human Environments," *Papers of the Regional Science Association*, 31:15–30.

Harvey, D. 1973. *Social Justice in the City*. London: E. Arnold.

Harvey, D. 1974. "Class Monopoly Rent, Finance Capital and the Urban Revolution," *Regional Studies*, 8:239–255.

Harvey, D. 1975. "Class Structure in a Capitalist Society and the Theory of Residential Differentiation," in *Progress in Physical and Human Geography*, R. Peel, P. Haggett eds. London: Heinemann, 354–369.

Harvey, D. 1978. "The Urban Process under Capitalism: A Framework for Analysis," *International Journal of Urban and Regional Research*, 2(1):101–131.

Heilbrun, J. 1979. "On the Theory and Policy of Neighborhood Consolidation," *Journal of the American Planning Association*, 45(4):417–427.

Henderson, J. 1977. *Economic Theory and the Cities.* New York: Academic Press.

Herbert, D. 1972. *Urban Geography: A Social Approach.* London: David and Charles.

Herbert, D. and Johnston, R. J. eds. 1976. *Social Areas in Cities,* Vol. 1. Chichester, U.K.: J. Wiley.

Herbert, D. and Johnston, R. J. eds. 1978–80. *Geography and the Urban Environment: Progress in Research and Applications,* Vols. 1, 2, and 3. London: J. Wiley.

Herbert, D. and Smith, D. eds. 1979. *Social Problems and the City: Geographical Perspectives.* London: Oxford University Press.

Hill, R. C. 1977. "Capital Accumulation and Urbanization in the U.S.," *Comparative Urban Research,* IV (2):3:39–60.

Hockman, O., Fishelson, G. and Pines, D. 1975. "Intraurban Spatial Association Between Places of Work and Places of Residence," *Environment and Planning A,* 7:273–278.

Hunter, A. 1979. "The Urban Neighborhood: Its Analytical and Social Contexts," *Urban Affairs Quarterly,* 14(3):267–288.

Ingram, G. K. ed. 1977. *Residential Location and Urban Housing Markets.* New York: National Bureau of Economic Research.

Janson, C. G. 1974. "The Spatial Structure of Newark, New Jersey," *Environment and Planning A,* 6:273–290.

Johnson, J. H. ed. 1974. *Suburban Growth.* London: J. Wiley.

Johnson, S. and Kau, J. 1980. "Urban Spatial Structure: An Analysis with a Varying Coefficient Model." *Journal of Urban Economics,* 7(2):141–154.

Johnston, R. J. 1971. *Urban Residential Patterns.* London: G. Bell.

Johnston, R. J. 1978/1979. "Urban Geography: City Structures," *Progress in Human Geography,* 2/3:148–152/133–138.

Johnston, R. J. 1979. *Political, Electoral and Spatial Systems.* London: Oxford University Press.

Johnston, R. J. 1980. *City and Society: An Outline for Urban Geography.* London: Penguin (forthcoming).

Johnston, R. J. 1982. *City and Society in the United States.* New York: St. Martins Press.

Jones, C. 1979. *Urban Deprivation and the Inner City.* London: Croom Helm.

Jones, E. and Eyles, J. 1977. *An Introduction to Social Geography.* London: Oxford University Press.

Kain, J. F. 1975. *Essays on Urban Spatial Structure.* Cambridge: Ballinger.

Karlqvist, A., Lundqvist, L., and Snickers, F. 1975. *Dynamic Allocation of Urban Space.* Lexington, Mass.: D. C. Heath.

Kasperson, R. and Breitbart, M. 1974. *Participation, Decentralization and Advocacy Planning.* A.A.G. Resource Paper No. 25, Washington, D.C.: Association of American Geographers.

Keeble, D. 1979. "Industrial Geography," *Progress in Human Geography,* 3(3):425–432.

Kendig, H. 1979. *New Life for Old Suburbs.* London: Allen & Unwin.

Kennedy, D. and M. 1974. *The Inner City.* New York: J. Wiley.

King, L. and Golledge, R. 1978. *Cities, Space and Behavior.* Englewood Cliffs, N.J.: Prentice Hall.

King, T. A. 1973. *Property Taxes, Amenities and Residential Land Values.* Cambridge, Mass.: Ballinger.

Kirwan, R. 1980. *The Inner City in the U.S.* London: Social Science Research Council.

Knowles, R. 1978. *Energy and Form: An Ecological Approach to Urban Growth.* Cambridge, Mass.: MIT Press.

Knox, P. 1975. *Social Well-being: A Spatial Perspective.* New York: Oxford University Press.

Knox, P. 1978. "The Intraurban Ecology of Primary Medical Care: Patterns of Accessibility and Their Policy Implications." *Environment and Planning A.* 10:415–435.

Larson, R. C. and Odoni, A. R. 1981. *Urban Operations Research.* Englewood Cliffs, N.J.: Prentice-Hall.

Laska, S. and Spain, D. eds. 1980. *Back to the City: Issues in Neighborhood Renovation.* New York: Pergamon Press.

Leven, C. et al. 1977. *Neighborhood Change: Lessons in the Dynamics of Urban Decay.* London: Martin Robertson & Co.

Leven, C. ed. 1978. *The Mature Metropolis.* Lexington, Mass.: Lexington Books.

Ley, D. 1974. *The Inner City Ghetto as Frontier Outpost.* Washington, D.C.: Association of American Geographers.

Ley, D. 1980. "Liberal Ideology and the Post-Industrial City." *Annals Association of American Geographers,* 70(2):238–258.

Ley, D. 1982. *Social Geography of the City*. New York: Harper & Row (forthcoming).

Ley, D. and Mercer, J. 1980. "Locational Conflict and the Politics of Consumption," *Economic Geography*, 56(2):89–109.

Ley, D. and Samuels, M. eds. 1979. *Humanistic Geography*. Chicago: Maaroufa Press.

Lineberry, R. 1977. *Equality and Urban Policy*. Beverly Hills: Sage Publications.

Long, L. 1975. "How the Racial Composition of Cities Changes," *Land Economics*, L1(3):258–267.

Long, L. and Dahmann, D. C. 1980. "The City-Suburb Income Gap: Is it Being Narrowed by a Back to the City Movement," CDS-80-1, U.S. Department of Commerce, Bureau of the Census, Washington, D.C., March 1980.

Lorimer, J. 1972. *The Real World of City Politics*. Toronto: J. Lorimer.

Lynch, K. 1960. *The Image of the City*. Cambridge, Mass.: MIT Press.

Lynch, K. 1981. *A Theory of Good City Form*. Cambridge, Mass.: M.I.T. Press.

Manners, G. 1974. "The Office in Metropolis: An Opportunity for Shaping Metropolitan America," *Economic Geography*, 50(2): 93–102.

Marsh, W. M. 1978. *Environmental Analysis for Land Use and Site Planning*. New York: McGraw-Hill.

Martin, L. and March, L. 1972. *Urban Space and Structures*. Cambridge: Cambridge University Press.

Masotti, L. H. and Hadden, J. K. eds. 1973. *The Urbanization of the Suburbs*. Beverly Hills: Sage Publications.

Massey, D. and Meegan, R. A. 1979. *The Geography of Industry Reorganization: Spatial Effects of Restructuring of Electrical Engineering Sector under Industrial Reorganization Corporation*. London: Centre for Environmental Studies.

Mayer, H. 1979. "Changing Railroad Patterns in Major Gateway Cities," in J. Frazier and B. Epstein (eds.), *Applied Geography Conferences*, 2:106–122.

Meadows, P. and Mizruchi, E. eds. 1976. *Urbanism, Urbanization and Change: Comparative Perspectives*. Reading, Mass.: Addison-Wesley.

Mercer, C. 1976. *Living in Cities*. London: Penguin Books.

Mercer, J. 1979. "On Continentalism, Distinctiveness and Comparative Geography: Canadian and American Cities," *Canadian Geographer*, XXIII(2):119–139.

McDonald, J. F. and Bowman, H. W. 1979. "Land Value Functions: A Re-evaluation," *Journal of Urban Economics*, 6:25–41.

Michelson, W. 1977. *Environmental Choice, Human Behavior and Residential Satisfaction*. New York: Oxford University Press.

Mieszkowski, P. and Straszheim, M. eds. 1979. *Current Issues in Urban Economics*. Baltimore: Johns Hopkins.

Mills, E. 1980. *Urban Economics* 2nd Ed. Glenview, Ill.: Scott, Foresman.

Molotch, H. 1978. "The City as a Growth Machine: Toward a Political Economy of Place," *American Journal of Sociology*, 82(2):309–332.

Molotch, H. 1979. "Capital and Neighborhood in the U.S.: Some Conceptual Links," *Urban Affairs Quarterly*, 14(3):289–312.

Moore, G. and Golledge, R. eds. 1976. *Environmental Knowing*. Stroudsburg, Penn.: Hutchinson and Ross.

Morgan, B. S. 1980. "Occupational Segregation in Metropolitan Areas in the U.S., 1970," *Urban Studies*, 17:63–69.

Morley, D. *et al*. eds. 1980. *Making Cities Work*. London: Croom Helm.

Morrill, R. L. 1979. "Stages in Patterns of Population Concentration and Dispersal," *Professional Geographer*, 31(1):55–65.

Morris, A. E. J. 1979. *History of Urban Forms Before the Industrial Revolution*. 2nd Ed. London: G. Godwin Ltd.

Mudden, J. F. and White, M. J. 1980. "Spatial Implications of Increases in the Female Labor Force: A Theoretical and Empirical Analysis," *Land Economics*, 56(4):432–446.

Muller, P. 1976. *The Outer City: Geographical Consequences of the Urbanization of the Suburbs*. A.A.G. Resource Paper 75–2. Washington, D.C.: Association of American Geographers.

Muller, T. 1975. *Growing and Declining Areas: A Fiscal Comparison*. Washington, D.C.: Urban Institute.

Muraco, W. 1972. "Intraurban Accessibility," *Economic Geography*, 48:388–405.

Muth, R. 1977. "Recent Developments in the Theory of Urban Spatial Structure," in M. Intriligator, ed. *Frontiers of Quantita-*

tive Economics, Vol. III-B. Amsterdam: North Holland, pp. 387–397.

Norton, R. D. 1979. *City Life Cycles and American Urban Policy.* New York: Academic Press.

Olsen, S. 1979. *Baltimore.* Baltimore: John Hopkins University Press.

Ostro, B. and Naroff, J. 1979. "Urban Structure, Trip Generation and Pollution: A Review," *Journal of Environmental Systems,* 9(1):17–28.

Ottensmann, J. R. 1975. *The Changing Spatial Structure of American Cities.* Lexington, Mass.: D. C. Heath.

Pack, H. and J. R. 1977. "Metropolitan Fragmentation and Suburban Homogeneity," *Urban Studies,* 14:191–201.

Pahl, R. 1975. *Whose City?* 2nd Ed. London: Penguin.

Palm, R. 1976. *Urban Social Geography from the Perspective of the Real Estate Salesman.* Berkeley: Center for Real Estate and Urban Economics.

Palm, R. 1978. "Spatial Segmentation of the Urban Housing Market," *Economic Geography,* 54–3:210–221.

Palm, R. 1979. "Financial and Real Estate Institutions in the Housing Market," in D. Herbert and R. Johnston eds., *Geography and the Urban Environment,* Vol. 2. New York: J. Wiley, pp. 83–123.

Palm, R. 1981. *The Geography of American Cities.* New York: Oxford University Press.

Papageorgiou, G. ed. 1976. *Mathematical Land Use Theory.* Lexington, Mass.: Lexington Books.

Parkes, D. and Thrift, N. 1980. *Times, Spaces and Plans. A Chronological Perspective.* New York: J. Wiley.

Peach, C. 1975. *Urban Social Segregation.* London: Longmans.

Peet, R. ed. 1977. *Radical Geography: Alternative Viewpoints on Contemporary Social Issues.* Chicago: Maaroufa Press.

Perin, Constance, 1978. *Everything in Its Place: Social Order and Land Use in America.* Princeton, N.J.: Princeton University Press.

Pickvance, C. 1976. *Urban Sociology: Critical Essays.* London: Tavistock Publications.

Porteous, J. 1977. *Environment and Behaviour: Planning and Everyday Urban Life.* Reading, Mass.: Addison-Wesley.

Pred, A. 1977. "The Choreography of Ex-

istence: Comments on Hägerstrand's Time –Geography and its Usefulness," *Economic Geography,* 53(2):207–221.

Preston, R. and Russwurm, L. eds. 1980. *Essays on Canadian Urban Process and Form.* Department of Geography Publication Series No. 15, University of Waterloo, Waterloo, Ontario.

Proudfoot, S. 1979. "Private Gains and Public Losses: The Distributive Impact of Urban Zoning," *Policy Sciences,* 11:203–226.

Putnam, S. 1979. *Urban Residential Location Models.* Boston: Nijhoff.

Pyle, G. F. 1979. *Applied Medical Geography.* New York: Halsted Press.

Quigley, J. M. and Weinberg, D. H. 1977. "Intra-Urban Residential Mobility: A Review and Synthesis," *International Regional Science Review,* 2:41–66.

Radford, J. P. 1976. "Race, Residence and Ideology: Charleston, S.C. in the mid-nineteenth Century, *Journal of Historical Geography,* 2(4):329–346.

Rand Corporation, 1977. *The Urban Impacts of Federal Policies: Vol. 2. Economic Development.* R-2028 KF/RC. Santa Monica: Rand Corporation.

Richardson, H. W. *et al.* 1975. *Housing and Urban Structure: A Case Study.* London: Saxon House.

Richardson, H. W. 1977. *The New Urban Economics: And Alternatives.* London: Pion.

Ridgeway, J. 1979. *Energy Efficient Community Planning.* Washington, D.C.: J. G. Press.

Rittel, H. W. J. and Webber, M. 1973. "Dilemmas in a General Theory of Planning," *Policy Sciences,* 4(2):155–169.

Roberts, B. 1979. *Cities of Peasants: The Political Economy of Urbanization in the Third World.* Beverly Hills: Sage Publications.

Robson, B. 1975. *Urban Social Areas.* London: Oxford University Press.

Romanos, M. C. 1976. *Residential Spatial Structure.* Lexington, Mass.: D. C. Heath.

Romanos, M. C. 1978. "Energy Price Effects on Metropolitan Spatial Structure and Form," *Environment and Planning A,* 10:93–104.

Romanos, M. C. ed. 1979. *Western European Cities in Crisis.* Lexington, Mass.: Lexington Books.

Rose, H. M. 1972. "The Spatial Development of Black Residential Subsystems," *Economic Geography,* 48(1):44–65.

Rose, H. M. ed. 1972. *Geography of the Ghetto: Perceptions, Problems and Alternatives.* De Kalb: Northern Illinois University Press.

Rose, H. M. 1976. *Black Suburbanization.* Cambridge, Mass.: Ballinger.

Rose, H. M. and Gappert, G. 1975. *The Social Economy of Cities.* Beverly Hills: Sage Publications.

Rose-Ackerman, S. 1974. "Location, Space and Urban Structure: The Wingo Model Reconsidered," *Land Economics,* 50:281–284.

Rosenthal, D. B. ed. 1980. *Urban Revitalization.* Urban Affairs Annual Review Vol. 18, Beverly Hills: Sage Publications.

Rossi, P. H. 1980. *Why Families Move.* 2nd ed. Beverly Hills: Sage Publications.

Rothblatt, D. N. *et al.* 1979. *The Suburban Environment and Women.* New York: Praeger.

Schwirian, K. P. ed. 1974. *Comparative Urban Structure: Studies in the Ecology of Cities.* Lexington, Mass.: D. C. Heath.

Scott, A. J. 1980a. "Locational Patterns and Dynamics of Industrial Activity in the Modern Metropolis: A Review Essay." *Discussion Paper No. 27,* Dept. of Geography, University of Toronto.

Scott, A. J. 1980b. *The Urban Land Nexus and the State.* London: Pion.

Scott, R. W. ed. 1974. *Management and Control of Growth.* Washington, D.C.: Urban Land Institute.

Segal, D. ed. 1979. *The Economics of Neighborhood.* New York: Academic Press.

Shannon, G. W. and Spurlock, C. W. 1976. "Urban Ecological Containers, Environmental Risk Cells and the Use of Medical Services," *Economic Geography,* 52(2): 171-180.

Sharpe, R. 1978. "The Effect of Urban Form on Transport Energy Patterns," *Urban Ecology* 3:125–135.

Short, J. F. ed. 1971. *The Social Fabric of the Metropolis.* Chicago: University of Chicago Press.

Smith, D. 1979. *Where the Grass is Greener.* London: Croom Helm.

Smith, G. C. 1976. "The Spatial Information Fields of Urban Consumers," *Transactions IBG* (New Series), 1:175–189.

Smith, M. P. 1979. *The City and Social Theory.* New York: St. Martins.

Smith, N. 1979. "Toward a Theory of Gentrification: A Back to the City Movement by Capital, not People," *Journal of the American Planning Association,* 45(4):538–547.

Smith, P. F. 1977. *The Syntax of Cities.* London: Hutchinson.

Smith, P. and Morrison, W. I. 1975. *Simulating the Urban Economy: Experiments with Input-Output Techniques.* New York: Academic Press.

Smith, W. 1975. *Urban Development: The Process and the Problems.* Berkeley: University of California Press.

Solomon, A. P. ed. 1980. *The Prospective City.* Cambridge, Mass.: MIT Press.

Speare, A., Goldstein, S. and Frey, W. 1975. *Residential Mobility, Migration and Metropolitan Change.* Cambridge, Mass.: Ballinger.

Stapleton, Clare, 1980. "Reformulation of the Family Life-Cycle Concept: Implications for Residential Mobility," *Environment and Planning A,* 12:1103–1118.

Steiss, A. W. 1975. *Models for the Analysis and Planning of Urban Systems.* Lexington, Mass.: Lexington Books.

Sternlieb, G. and Hughes, J. 1975. *Post-Industrial America: Metropolitan Decline and Inter-regional Job Shifts.* New Brunswick, N.J.: Rutgers University.

Sternlieb, G. and Hughes, J. 1977. New Regional and Metropolitan Realities of America," *Journal of the American Institute of Planners,* 43(3):227–240.

Sternlieb, G. and Hughes, J. eds. 1979. *Shopping Centers: U.S.A.* New Brunswick, N.J.: Center for Urban Policy Research, Rutgers University.

Strauss, A. L. 1976. *Images of the American City.* New Brunswick, N.J.: Transaction Books.

Sweet, D. C. ed. 1972. *Models of Urban Structure.* Lexington, Mass.: D. C. Heath.

Taab, W. and Sawers, L. eds. 1978. *Marxism and the Metropolis.* New York: Oxford University Press.

Taaffe, E. J., Gauthier, H. L. and Maraffa, T. A. 1980. "Extended Commuting and the Inter-metropolitan Periphery," *Annals, Association of American Geographers,* 70(3): 313–329.

Taebel, D. and Cornehls, J. 1979. *The Political Economy of Urban Transportation.* Port Washington, N.Y.: National University Press.

Taylor, P. J. and Johnston, R. J. 1979. *Geography of Elections*. Harmondsworth: Penguin.

Thrall, G. 1979. "States of Urban Spatial Structure," *Environment and Planning A*, 11:23–34.

Thrall, G. 1980. "Property, Sales, Income Taxes and Urban Spatial Structure," *Environment and Planning A*, 12:1287–1296.

Tilly, C. ed. 1974. *An Urban World*. Boston: Little, Brown.

Timms, D. 1971. *The Urban Mosaic*. Cambridge: The University Press.

Tobin, G. A. ed. 1979. *The Changing Structure of the City*. Urban Affairs Annual Review Vol. 16, Beverly Hills: Sage Publications.

U.S. Advisory Commission on Intergovernmental Relations, 1977. *Trends in Metropolitan America*. Washington, D.C.: A.C.I.R.

U.S., Council on Environmental Quality, 1979. *Environmental Quality, 1979*. Tenth Annual Report. Washington, D.C. U.S. G.P.O.

U.S. House of Representatives, 1977. *How Cities Can Grow Old Gracefully*. Report to the Subcommittee on the City of the Committee on Banking, Finance and Urban Affairs. Washington, D.C.: U.S. G.P.O.

Vance, J. Jr. 1971. "Land Assignment in the Precapitalist, Capitalist and Post Capitalist City," *Land Economics*, 47(2):101–120.

Vance, J. Jr. 1976. "Cities in the Shaping of the American Nation," *Journal of Geography*, 76:41–52.

Vance, J. Jr. 1977. *This Scene of Man: The Role and Structure of the City in the Geography of Western Civilization*. New York: Harper's College Press.

Vance, J. Jr. 1978. "Institutional Forces that Shape the City," Chap. 3 in D. Herbert and R. Johnston eds. *Social Areas in Cities*, New York: J. Wiley, pp. 97–126.

Van Til, Jon. 1979. "Spatial Form and Structure in a Possible Future: Some Implications of Energy for Urban Planning." *Journal of the American Planning Association*, 45(3):318–329.

Walker, R. A. 1978. "The Transformation of Urban Structure in the Nineteenth Century and the Beginnings of Surburbanization," in K. Cox, ed. *Urbanization and Conflict in Market Societies*. Chicago: Maaroufa Press, pp. 165–213.

Walker, G. 1977. "Social Networks and Territory in a Commuter Village, Bond Head, Ontario," *Canadian Geographer*, XXI(4): 329–350.

Walton, John. 1979. "Urban Political Economy: A New Paradigm," *Comparative Urban Research*, 7:5–17.

Ward, D. 1971. *Cities and Immigrants*. New York: Oxford University Press.

Ward, D. 1975. "Victorian Cities: How Modern?" *Journal of Historical Geography*, 1(2):135–151.

Warnes, A. M. and Daniels, P. W. 1979. "Spatial Aspects of an Intrametropolitan Central Place Hierarchy," *Progress in Human Geography*, 3(3):384–406.

Webber, M. J. 1980. *Information Theory and Urban Spatial Structure*. London: Croom Helm.

Webber, M. M. *et al.* eds. 1970. *Explorations into Urban Structure*. Philadelphia: University of Pennsylvania Press.

Wellman, B. 1979. "The Community Question: The Intimate Networks of East Yorkers," *American Journal of Sociology*, 84(5): 1201–1231.

Wheaton, W. 1974. "A Comparative Static Analysis of Urban Spatial Structure," *Journal of Economic Theory*, 9:223–237.

Wheaton, W. 1977. "Income and Urban Residence: An Analysis of Consumer Demand for Location," *American Economic Review*, 67:620–631.

Wheeler, J. O. 1974. *The Urban Circulation Noose*. North Scituate, Mass.: Duxbury.

Whitehand, J. W. R. 1977. "The Basis for an Historical-Geographical Theory of Urban Form," *Transactions, Institute of British Geographers*, New Series, 2:400–416.

Williams, P. 1976. "The Role of Institutions in the Inner London Housing Market: The Case of Islington," *Transactions, Institute of British Geographers*, New Series, 1: 72–81.

Wilson, A. 1974. *Urban and Regional Models in Geography and Planning*. Chichester: J. Wiley.

Wilson, A. and Kirby, M. 1975. *Mathematical Models for Geographers and Planners*. London: Oxford University Press.

Wingo, L. and Evans, A. eds. 1977. *Public Economics and the Quality of Life*. Baltimore: Johns Hopkins.

Wiseman, R. F. 1978. *Spatial Aspects of Aging*.

AAG Resource Paper 78–4, Washington, D.C.: AAG.

Wolch, J. R. "Residential Location of the Service-Dependent Poor," *Annals, Association of American Geographers,* 70(3): 330–341.

Wolpert, J., Mumphrey, A. and Seley, J. 1972. *Metropolitan Neighborhoods: Participation and Conflict over Change.* AAG Resource Paper No. 16. Washington, D.C. AAG.

Yeates, M. 1980. *North American Urban Patterns.* London: E. Arnold.

Yeates, M. and Garner, B. 1980. 3rd Ed. *The North American City.* New York: Harper & Row.